G000071156

How to Use the CD-ROM

Watch and listen to over 40 on-screen movies for your computer.

Please review the Appendix in the back of this book for more information on what is included on and how to use the companion CD-ROM.

Suggested System Requirements

- Computer: Pentium IBM PC-compatible

- Memory: 16MB of RAM

- Software: Windows 95 or NT

- Hardware: 4X CD-ROM Drive

Windows Sources Microsoft Word 97 for Windows SuperGuide

PLEASE NOTE—USE OF THE DISK(S) AND THE PROGRAMS INCLUDED ON THE DISK(S) PACKAGED WITH THIS BOOK AND THE
PROGRAM LISTINGS INCLUDED IN THIS BOOK IS SUBJECT TO AN END-USER LICENSE AGREEMENT (THE "AGREEMENT")
FOUND AT THE BACK OF THE BOOK. PLEASE READ THE AGREEMENT CAREFULLY BEFORE MAKING YOUR PURCHASE
DECISION. PURCHASE OF THE BOOK AND USE OF THE DISKS, PROGRAMS, AND PROGRAM LISTINGS WILL CONSTITUTE
ACCEPTANCE OF THE AGREEMENT.

Windows Sources Microsoft Word 97 for Windows SuperGuide

Bill Camarda

Ziff-Davis Press
An imprint of Macmillan Computer Publishing USA
Emeryville, California

Publisher	Stacy Hiquet
Acquisitions Editor	Lysa Lewallen
Development Editor	Karen Lamoreux
Copy Editors	Margo Hill, K.D. Sullivan, and Candice Crane
Technical Reviewers	Leigh Yafa, Maxine Wyman
Project Editors	Edith Rex, Ami Knox
Proofreaders	Jeff Barash, Beth Grundvig, and Kayla Sussell
Cover Illustration and Design	Megan Gandt
Book Design	Paper Crane Graphics, Berkeley
Page Layout	Janet Piercy
Indexer	Christine Spina

Ziff-Davis Press, ZD Press, and the Ziff-Davis Press logo are trademarks or registered trademarks of, and are licensed to Macmillan Computer Publishing USA by Ziff-Davis Publishing Company, New York, New York.

"Windows" and "Windows Sources" are trademarks of Microsoft Corporation and "Windows Sources" is used by Ziff-Davis Press under license from Ziff-Davis Publishing and by Ziff-Davis Publishing under license from the owner. *Windows Sources™ Word 97 for Windows SuperGuide* is an independent publication not affiliated with Microsoft Corporation. Microsoft Corporation is not responsible in any way for the editorial policy or other contents of the publication.

Ziff-Davis Press imprint books are produced on a Macintosh computer system with the following applications: FrameMaker®, Microsoft® Word, QuarkXPress®, Adobe Illustrator®, Adobe Photoshop®, Adobe Streamline™, MacLink®*Plus*, Aldus® FreeHand™, Collage Plus™.

Ziff-Davis Press, an imprint of
Macmillan Computer Publishing USA
5903 Christie Avenue
Emeryville, CA 94608

Copyright © 1996 by Macmillan Computer Publishing USA. All rights reserved.
PART OF A CONTINUING SERIES

All other product names and services identified throughout this book are trademarks or registered trademarks of their respective companies. They are used throughout this book in editorial fashion only and for the benefit of such companies. No such uses, or the use of any trade name, is intended to convey endorsement or other affiliation with the book.

No part of this publication may be reproduced in any form, or stored in a database or retrieval system, or transmitted or distributed in any form by any means, electronic, mechanical photocopying, recording, or otherwise, without the prior written permission of Macmillan Computer Publishing USA, except as permitted by the Copyright Act of 1976, and the End-User License Agreement at the back of this book, and except that program listings may be entered, stored, and executed in a computer system.

EXCEPT FOR THE LIMITED WARRANTY COVERING THE PHYSICAL DISK(S) PACKAGED WITH THIS BOOK AS PROVIDED IN THE END-USER LICENSE AGREEMENT AT THE BACK OF THIS BOOK, THE INFORMATION AND MATERIAL CONTAINED IN THIS BOOK ARE PROVIDED "AS IS," WITHOUT WARRANTY OF ANY KIND, EXPRESS OR IMPLIED, INCLUDING WITHOUT LIMITATION ANY WARRANTY CONCERNING THE ACCURACY, ADEQUACY, OR COMPLETENESS OF SUCH INFORMATION OR MATERIAL OR THE RESULTS TO BE OBTAINED FROM USING SUCH INFORMATION OR MATERIAL. NEITHER MACMILLAN COMPUTER PUBLISHING USA NOR THE AUTHOR SHALL BE RESPONSIBLE FOR ANY CLAIMS ATTRIBUTABLE TO ERRORS, OMISSIONS, OR OTHER INACCURACIES IN THE INFORMATION OR MATERIAL CONTAINED IN THIS BOOK, AND IN NO EVENT SHALL MACMILLAN COMPUTER PUBLISHING USA OR THE AUTHOR BE LIABLE FOR DIRECT, INDIRECT, SPECIAL, INCIDENTAL, OR CONSEQUENTIAL DAMAGES ARISING OUT OF THE USE OF SUCH INFORMATION OR MATERIAL.

ISBN 1-56276-506-X
Manufactured in the United States of America
10 9 8 7 6 5 4 3 2 1

To my wife Barbara, and my son Matthew. You bring me joy beyond words.

■ Contents at a Glance

■ Table of Contents

Chapter 4:   Printing and Faxing: The Complete Guide

Chapter 13: Master Documents: Manage Even the Longest Documents   393

■ Acknowledgments

To all the talented people at Ziff-Davis Press who labored long, hard, and well to bring you this book, including Lysa Lewallen, Valerie Perry, Margo Hill, Edith Rex, Ami Knox, Janet Piercy, Carol Burbo, and lots of other folks I haven't met. To Karen Lamoreaux, my development editor, and Leigh Yafa, my technical editor, who made my life difficult in the interest of improving yours. They were virtually always right. And thanks to Bruce Hallberg, whose idea this was.

■ About the Authors

Bill Camarda is a professional computer consultant and author who uses Word for Windows to create documents ranging from business reports to booklength manuscripts. He is the author of *Inside Word for Windows 95, Inside Lotus 1-2-3 Release 5,* and *OS/2 in the Fast Lane,* among other books.

Greg Perry, an internationally best-selling author, is known for effectively teaching programming topics on all user levels. He has been a programmer, instructor, and author for the past 16 years. He is the author of more than 25 computer books, including international bestsellers such as the *Absolute Beginner's Guide to Programming.*

Trudi Reisner is a computer technical writer specializing in software technical writing and course development. Trudi has written numerous books including Que's *10 Minute Guide to Excel 5, 10 Minute Guide to Windows 95, Easy Excel 5 for Windows, Easy Microsoft Office 97,* and *Easy Word for Windows 95.* Trudi has also written user guides and software documentation manuals on manufacturing, clinical and financial, and font creation software, as well as courseware on Lotus 1-2-3 and Lotus Notes Web Navigator.

Victor Wright is a popular lecturer for the School of Engineering and Computers Science at California State University, Fullerton. For the past seven years he has taught PC courses for the University's Department of Extended Education. Also employed with Hughes Aircraft Company, Wright serves as training coordinator for the Systems and Software Engineering Council. He is the author of *How to Use Microsoft Works for Windows 95,* published by Ziff-Davis Press.

Leigh Yafa is a software consultant, writer, courseware developer, and teacher. She owns a consulting and training company in San Anselmo, California.

I'd like to pass along my appreciation to the very talented writers and Word experts who have made significant contributions to this book—often on terrifyingly short notice. Many thanks to all of you.

—Bill Camarda

■ Introduction

This book is about getting more done in less time.

Word is a truly remarkable word processing program. It can follow you around, if you want, fixing your most common spelling mistakes before you know you made them. It can number lists, manage cross-references, automatically number your headings, format your documents for you—even shrink them, if they're too long.

It can create business forms, manage revisions from multiple reviewers, automate the creation of indexes and tables of contents, and send e-mail. For your more creative side, it can produce drawings, graphs, and even twist your characters into any shape or form you desire. Word can help you publish virtually anything you can imagine on the Internet's World Wide Web, for the whole world to see.

But you still have to know how to command Word to do these things for you, and that's what this book is for.

■ Finding the Best Way to Do the Job

There's a hard way and an easy way to do everything. Take for example, writing business letters. It's a good bet that 95 percent of business letters written today are written from scratch. But you could have Word automatically place your name, address, today's date, writer's and typist's initials, and closing in every letter you write from here on. How long would it take to get Word to do that? About five minutes.

You could start with one of Word's built-in letter templates—and, when the time comes, use corresponding Word templates for memos, reports, and other kinds of documents. Suddenly, you've got a complete, unified set of well-designed corporate documents—without paying a designer thousands of dollars to establish your graphic design standards.

And there really are scores of examples like this. Often, you can save literally 90 percent of the time and keystrokes involved in a specific Word task if you know the best way to perform that task.

Which would you rather do? Spend all that time keystroking, formatting, and compiling your documents—or learn how to have Word do it for you? That's what we thought. So *Windows Sources Microsoft Word 97 for Windows Superguide* doesn't just tell you how to get things done, but how to get them done most efficiently.

There's a lot to tell. Word 97 might just be the most powerful word processor ever created. We're out to help you grab as much of that power as you possibly can—as painlessly as possible.

■ Who Should Read This Book

This book assumes you've at least installed Word and created some basic documents with it, and you're now ready to go a lot further. But among the millions of people who fit that description, there are several types of users for whom this book offers specific assistance.

If you're moderately experienced with Word, skim Chapters 1 through 6 for a quick overview of the latest in Word, and for shortcuts and concepts you may have missed. Then dive headfirst into the following chapters.

If you're very experienced with Word, use this book as a comprehensive reference, offering in-depth discussions of all features, including those you only use occasionally.

If you're responsible for managing Word at your office, note the extensive coverage of many features that make Word work especially well in a business environment, such as templates (Chapter 8), forms (Chapter 20), and techniques for customizing Word (Chapter 22), which can help you create a word processor that meets the precise needs of your organization.

If you're planning to use Word to publish documents on the Internet, look for the all-new, detailed coverage of Word's World Wide Web, HTML, browser, and FTP features in Chapter 14. You'll learn everything you need to know to create great Web pages with Word—and how to use Word to retrieve and work with pages that already exist.

If you're planning to use Word for desktop publishing applications, like publishing a newsletter, pay special attention to Chapters 17 through 19, which cover Word 97's desktop publishing features, including its powerful new text boxes and drawing capabilities, as well as the latest version of Microsoft Graph, which allows you to create graphs of virtually every kind.

If you're planning heavy-duty office work and correspondence, pay special attention to Chapters 6 through 9; Chapter 15, which reviews Word's extensive features for sharing and reviewing documents with colleagues, and Chapter 16, which presents detailed, step-by-step coverage for getting the most out of Word's Mail Merge feature.

If you're planning to write a book, study Chapters 6 and 15 to learn how to manage and track all your files and drafts; and especially 10 through 13, which specifically target features that will help you create long documents more easily.

■ How This Book Is Organized

Here's a quick look at how we've structured *Windows Sources Microsoft Word 97 for Windows Superguide:*

Chapters 1 through 6 take a close look at the fundamentals of working with Word, including headers and footers, tables, printing, file management, and using Word's four built-in literacy aids: spell check, thesaurus, grammar check, and AutoCorrect.

Chapters 7 through 9 focus on the essential Word tools that can dramatically reduce the amount of time it takes to create, format, and compile a document: styles and AutoFormat, templates and wizards, AutoText, fields, and macros.

Chapters 10 through 13 focus on Word's features for creating long documents, managing revisions, and generating mass mailings.

Chapters 14 through 16 shows how you can take full advantage of Word's comprehensive features for electronic publishing, including its ability to create sophisticated HTML pages for publishing on the World Wide Web; how to make the most of Word's mail merge feature, and how to use Word's extensive capabilities for helping you work with others in real-world business environments.

Chapters 17 through 25 focus on Word's capabilities to go way beyond traditional word processing, into desktop publishing, graphing, calculating, and forms production. You'll also learn how to take advantage of the rest of Microsoft Office, and how to customize Word to your own work style.

Chapter 26 presents a detailed introduction to Word's new Visual Basic for Applications macro language and development environment, which allows you to extend Word in virtually any way imaginable. You'll start with simple macros that you can record without any knowledge of programming; then build on that knowledge, and finally, walk through the development of two sample real-world VBA applications.

■ About the Windows Sources Microsoft Word 97 for Windows Superguide CD-ROM

You've read the book, now see the movie! The *Windows Sources Microsoft Word 97 for Windows Superguide* CD-ROM contains movies that walk you through dozens of the most important procedures covered in the book, complete with audio commentary. You'll find everything from creating Web pages to running a Word mail merge here—all on video, all right on screen.

■ Let's Get Started

When you think about it, Microsoft Word 97 is an awesome intellectual achievement. Think of what software *is*: pure thought, crystallized into electrons. Now think about the decade-plus of pure thought that has gone into Word 97's dozens of megabytes—by some of the world's smartest programmers (not to mention the marketers). All with one goal: to get you to buy this program and make the most of it.

It doesn't matter who you are, Word is packed with goodies you don't know about yet. Let's go dig 'em up.

- *Features Shared with the Rest of Microsoft Office*
- *Extensive Integration with the Internet and World Wide Web*
- *A New Macro Language: Visual Basic for Applications*
- *Better Support for Workgroups*
- *Better Tools for Creating Graphical Documents*
- *More Automation—in Ways Big and Small*
- *Interface Changes Galore*

- *Little Things You Might Never Notice*
- *Getting the Most Out of Word 97*

1

What's New in Word 97?

W HAT'S NEW IN WORD 97? A LOT. AND MOST OF IT CAN MAKE YOU A whole lot more productive—*right out of the box.*

That's our goal for this chapter: to quickly flag the most important new Word 97 features, especially the ones you might not notice right away, so you can get productive with those features *fast*. In particular, we'll show you ways in which Word 97:

- Provides more automation and built-in intelligence than ever before

- Integrates tightly with the World Wide Web—for authoring, browsing, and retrieving resources

- Makes it easier to share and review documents within your workgroup

- Supports a new macro development language, Visual Basic for Applications, which is shared throughout the Office family of applications

- Makes it easier to create highly visual documents, for both print and on-line viewing

■ Features Shared with the Rest of Microsoft Office

More than half of the code in Office 97 is shared across applications. That's a significant achievement, if for no other reason than that it restrains the extraordinary growth in hard disk requirements that seems to inevitably accompany new versions of Office.

The Office Assistant

One way all this shared code manifests itself to the user is through several shared applets and applications that work within all or most Office programs. The one you'll probably encounter first is Office Assistant, an animated paper clip that has elbowed aside Word 95's Answer Wizard.

The idea is simple: click the Question Mark button on Word's standard toolbar (see Figure 1.1), and the Office Assistant appears; then enter your question in English, and "he" displays a list of Help windows that might possibly answer your question. Does the Office Assistant work? Well, in my experience, it works roughly half the time—and when it doesn't work, it at least *starts* you on the way to manually finding the information you need to excavate from Word's labyrinthine help files.

You'll also find updated versions of several vintage Word applets, including:

- *Microsoft WordArt* for creating text effects (see Chapter 17)

- *Microsoft Clip Art Gallery* for managing clip art (see Chapter 17)

- *Microsoft Equation 3.0* for inserting and formatting equations (see Chapter 23)

Figure 1.1

The Office Assistant

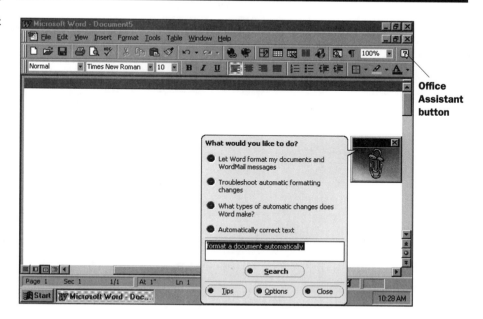

Office Assistant button

- *Microsoft Organization Chart* for creating and inserting organizational charts (see Chapter 23)

In particular, WordArt and ClipArt Gallery have been dramatically improved.

If you've purchased Word as part of Microsoft Office Professional, you'll also find bonuses such as:

- *Microsoft Photo Editor*, a basic photo effects program that can also capture images from your scanner (see Figure 1.2 and additional coverage in Chapter 23); and

- *Microsoft Camcorder*, a utility that can record your screen with accompanying audio, so you can make movies that walk people through procedures they need to learn (see Figure 1.3).

Microsoft Camcorder is similar to Lotus ScreenCam. Both programs have been used to capture the movies on this book's accompanying CD-ROM. See Chapter 24 for more coverage of Camcorder.

Figure 1.2

Microsoft Photo Editor

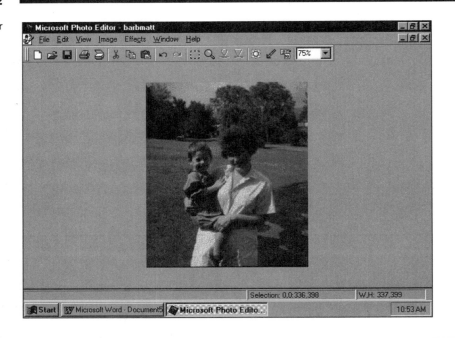

Figure 1.3

Microsoft Camcorder

■ Extensive Integration with the Internet and World Wide Web

One morning not long ago, Bill Gates woke up and discovered that Microsoft was mortally threatened by the explosive growth of the Internet, which could conceivably make Windows obsolete—to be replaced by browsers like Netscape Navigator. He then proceeded to turn his multi-billion-dollar company around on a dime, committing to integrate Internet and Web functionality into virtually every Microsoft product. The fruits of this investment are to be found virtually everywhere in Word 97.

For example, you can use Word 97's Web toolbar to search the Web (see Figure 1.4), using the free copy of Internet Explorer 3.01 that's included with Microsoft Office Professional (and available for download from Microsoft's Web site). Figure 1.5 shows Microsoft Explorer 3.01 at work.

Figure 1.4

The Word 97 Web Toolbar

Figure 1.5

Internet Explorer
3.01 at work

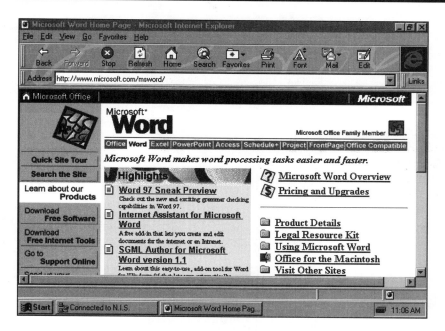

You can download new templates and clipart—and get online support—directly from Microsoft's Web site by choosing Help, Microsoft on the Web.

You can automatically add hyperlinks to Web and FTP sites in your Word documents—and click on those hyperlinks to connect to those sites (see Figure 1.6 and more detailed coverage in Chapter 12).

Word 97 now contains fairly extensive Web page creation features. You can easily create HTML documents for display on the Web, or load HTML documents from the Web into Word. Word makes it easy to see how your documents will appear on the Web with its new Online Layout View. There's even a Web Page Wizard that helps automate the creation of Web pages (see Figure 1.7).

If you have Microsoft Office Professional, you'll also find a Netscape plug-in that makes it possible to open Office documents within Netscape; a personal Web server you can use on your Windows 95 or Windows NT system; and WebPost, a wizard that walks you through posting your documents to the Web.

Figure 1.6

Hyperlinks that connect
directly to the Web

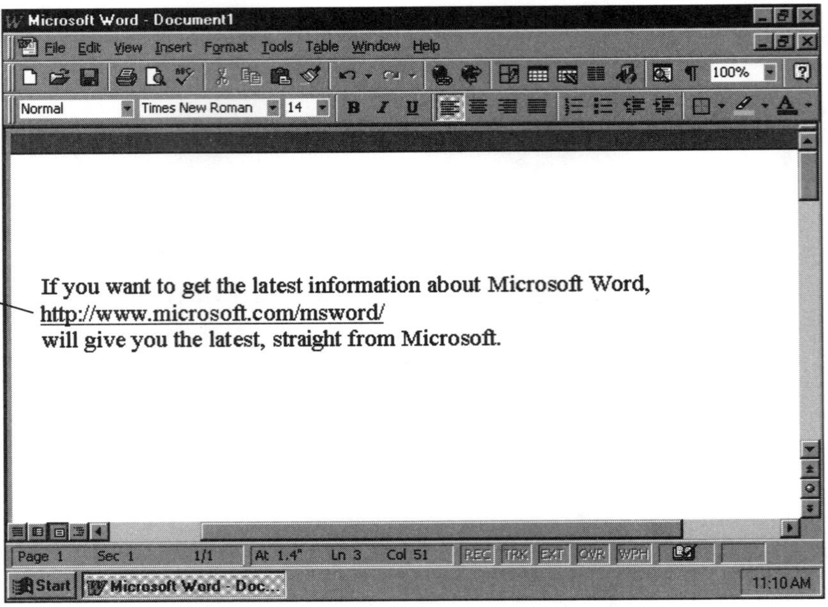

Hyperlink

Figure 1.7

The new Web Page Wizard

Finally, if you download Word documents from the Web, you may be familiar with the Concept virus, which can infect Word macros. Word 97 can't detect this virus, but it *can* detect whether a downloaded document contains macros—so you can decide whether you trust the document's source *before* you open the document and risk infection.

■ A New Macro Language: Visual Basic for Applications

For years, Microsoft has promised to deliver a unified macro language that would work across all Microsoft Office applications. With Word 97 and Office 97, Microsoft has delivered. WordBasic has been replaced by Visual Basic for Applications (VBA), and along with VBA comes a complete development environment (see Figure 1.8 and more detailed coverage in Chapters 25 and 26).

Figure 1.8

The Visual Basic development environment

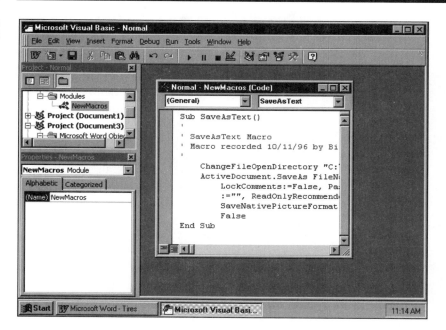

If you're a casual macro writer accustomed to WordBasic, VBA adds some complexity and will require you to learn a new way of doing things. But once you overcome those hurdles, you can accomplish much more with VBA, a modern language closely patterned on the enormously successful Microsoft Visual Basic. And the VBA techniques you learn with Word will help you automate Excel, PowerPoint, Access, and Outlook as well.

If you're a professional developer, you'll appreciate not only VBA's more complete development environment, but also its full support for the Word Object Model, which allows you to access Microsoft's entire feature set from within VBA—giving you more flexibility and control in responding to user input. You'll also appreciate VBA's ability to easily embed ActiveX controls in Microsoft Word templates—which will allow you to create more sophisticated, interactive custom applications.

With the move to VBA comes a new Word document format, which (among other things) allows macros and templates to be stored in documents. This means you can distribute files to colleagues without worrying about whether they have the appropriate templates to run the macros you've written.

Word 97 can automatically update most WordBasic macros to VBA code, though a few WordBasic features won't convert properly, and macros using those features will have to be edited. (Once the WordBasic macros are converted to VBA, you can't convert them back.)

You don't have to do anything special to open Word 95 or Word 6 documents in Word 97—and when you save those files, they're automatically stored in the new Word 97 format unless you specify otherwise.

■ Better Support for Workgroups

In Word 97, Microsoft provides an extensive set of features to help you share and review documents with your colleagues. You can store multiple versions of the same document in a single file, making it easier to track changes. You can make a document accessible to specific reviewers, providing specific levels of access (such as read-only or full editing rights). When revisions arrive, you can automatically merge them into your existing document. And you can use the new Reviewing Toolbar (Figure 1.9) to make comments more easily, or to quickly walk through comments made by others.

■ Better Tools for Creating Graphical Documents

Web documents are graphical documents—or they should be. So along with making it easier to develop documents for online viewing, Word 97 provides extensive new features for developing highly visual documents. Of course you can use these features whether you're creating online or printed documents. In Word 97, you can:

- Insert pictures from a Clip Art library that includes more than 3,000 images (if you have Microsoft Office Professional), as covered in Chapter 17; or directly from a scanner; or from the Web.

- Create slicker text effects with the completely revamped WordArt 3.0 (see Chapter 17).

- Use new gradients, textures and backgrounds, including backgrounds that can cover your entire page (see Chapter 17).

- Create page borders, including borders consisting of images—which can be ideal for newspaper advertising (see Chapter 17).

Figure 1.9

Word 97
Reviewing Toolbar

**Reviewing
Toolbar**

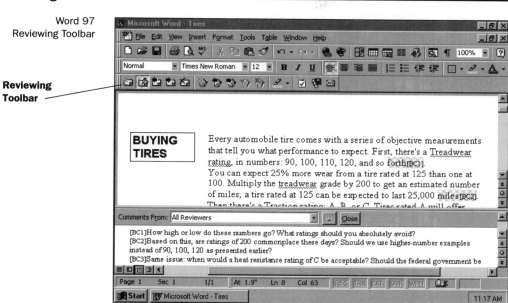

- Edit photographs in the new Microsoft Photo Editor application (see Chapter 23).

- Create effects like embossing, engraving, and animated text using the updated Format, Font command (see Chapter 2).

- Design tables more easily, using the new Draw Table feature, which lets you draw tables on screen freehand (see Chapter 3).

- Create much more sophisticated charts and graphs using the extensive new chart and formatting options built into Microsoft Graph 97 (see Chapter 19).

- Use a new set of built-in drawing tools that include over 100 AutoShapes which make it easy to draw the shapes you'll need most. (AutoShapes, however, can't be used in Web documents.)

New Text Box Features

Word 97 almost entirely replaces the confusing Frames feature that bedeviled users of previous versions. The replacement *text boxes* are much more flexible, and make it much easier to combine and precisely position text, graphics and other document elements.

One of the most important advantages of text boxes is they can be *linked:* copy that overflows beyond the borders of one text box can automatically appear in the next text box, as shown in Figure 1.10. If you put out newsletters or other publications that contain story "jumps" between one page and another, you'll find this feature absolutely invaluable. It may be the one improvement that convinces you to create your publication in Word, rather than a dedicated desktop publishing program.

Figure 1.10

Linked text boxes in Word 97

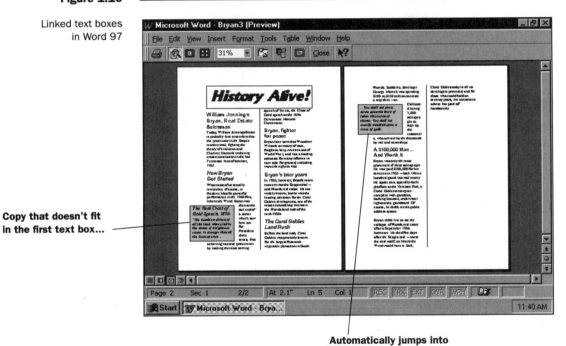

Copy that doesn't fit in the first text box...

Automatically jumps into the second text box.

■ More Automation—in Ways Big and Small

Word 97 continues along a path begun in Word 6, adding more automation and built-in intelligence. As a result, the program can function as your assistant—handling many of the basics for you automatically, so that you can focus on creating more effective documents. In Word 97, some existing automation features have been enhanced and some new features have been added. The enhancements include:

- A more useful AutoCorrect feature that now includes roughly 500 entries, including incorrect phrases and a much wider variety of common errors and typos, and is available from all major Office programs.

- The ability to AutoFormat network and Web addresses, and even add hyperlinks to those locations automatically, if you want.

- A completely revamped AutoText feature that is easier to access and includes a wide variety of built-in entries for letters, headers, footers, and other business uses (see Figure 1.11).

Figure 1.11

Choosing from Word's built-in list of AutoText entries

- The ability to automatically complete words or blocks of text when Word recognizes them as dates, times, or AutoText entries (see Figure 1.12).

- The ability to automatically create styles based on your manual formatting, and to automatically update a style globally when you manually reformat it in *one* location.

- Revamped Wizards that automate the process of creating letters, newsletters, faxes, memos, resumes, Web pages and legal pleadings (see Figure 1.13 and coverage in Chapter 8).

Automatic, Integrated Grammar Checking

Word 97 also includes automatic, integrated grammar checking based on new grammar software. As you work, potential grammar errors are displayed with a green underline—accompanying the red underline that appears under potential spelling errors in both Word 95 and Word 97. In addition, you can now proof grammar and spelling together, using the new Spelling and Grammar dialog box (see Figure 1.14).

Figure 1.12

Using Word's AutoComplete feature: just press Enter to include the entire AutoText entry.

AutoComplete Screen Tip

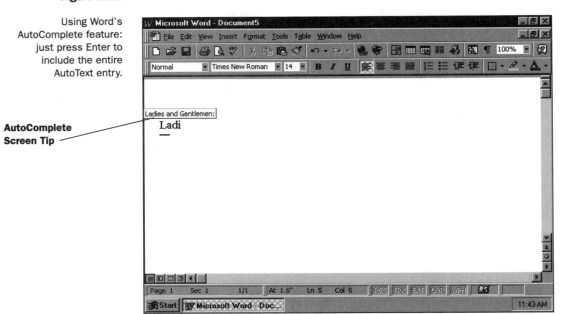

Figure 1.13

The revamped Word 97 Memo Wizard

Figure 1.14

The new Spelling and Grammar dialog box

Spelling and Grammar: English (United States)
Possessive Use:
Please check your customers order to make sure it is correct.
Ignore
Ignore All
Next Sentence
Suggestions:
customer's
OR
customers'
Change
Check grammar
Options...
Undo
Cancel

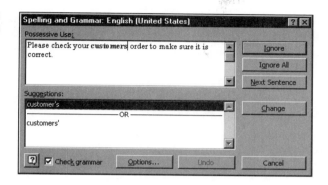

AutoSummarize Creates Automatic Document Summaries

Word can now automatically summarize your document, highlight key points, or build an executive summary or an abstract (see Figure 1.15 and the more detailed coverage in Chapter 9). Word can place the summary at the beginning of your document, or in another new document. This feature, which works best on highly structured documents such as reports, can even be used on Web pages and other online documents.

Figure 1.15

Word 97's new AutoSummarize feature

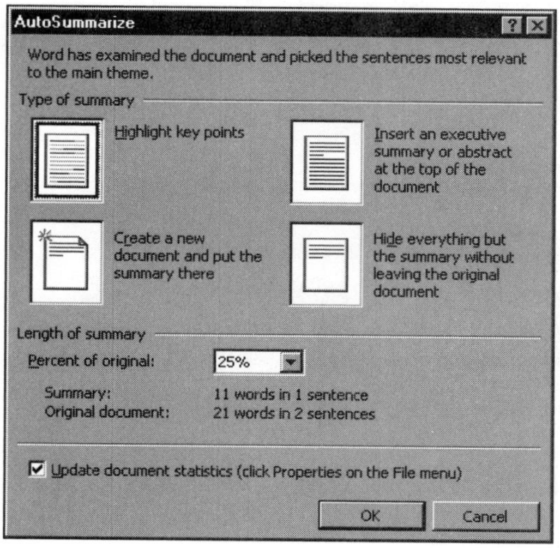

AutoSummarize
Word has examined the document and picked the sentences most relevant to the main theme.
Type of summary
Highlight key points
Insert an executive summary or abstract at the top of the document
Create a new document and put the summary there
Hide everything but the summary without leaving the original document
Length of summary
Percent of original:
25%
Summary:
11 words in 1 sentence
Original document:
21 words in 2 sentences
Update document statistics (click Properties on the File menu)
OK
Cancel

■ Interface Changes Galore

Word 97 looks and feels different—perhaps a bit more different than you might expect (see Figure 1.16). In some ways, the changes are minor: for example, there are no longer borders between every toolbar button. Also, as we've already mentioned, there's a new Online Layout View—and a new Online Layout View button at the bottom of the horizontal scroll bar. The vertical scroll bar now contains double-arrows that allow you to scroll through a document one page at a time; there are also new Select Browse Object (see Figure 1.17) and Document Map (Figure 1.18) features designed to make it easier to navigate throughout your document.

Figure 1.16

The Word 97 interface

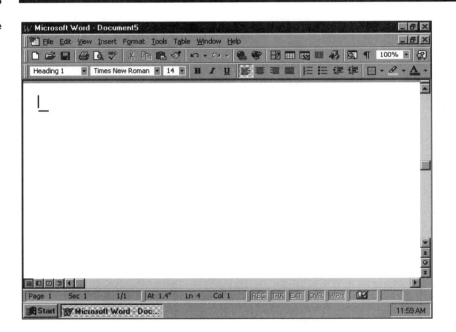

Figure 1.17

Select Browse Object makes it easy to find footnotes, tables, comments, graphics and other elements.

Figure 1.18

Document Map lets you
quickly move to a
specific section.

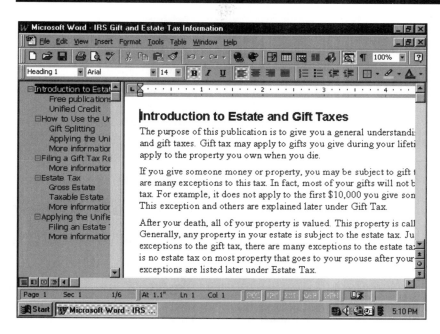

You'll find some menu options in unexpected locations. For example,
File, Templates is now Tools, Templates and Add-Ins; Bookmark has moved
from the Edit to the Insert menu. You'll also find revamped toolbars—and
lots more of them, including new Web, Reviewing, AutoText, Tables and Borders, and WordArt toolbars.

■ Little Things You Might Never Notice

One of Microsoft's strong points is creating new features that can be effectively marketed—slick features like direct access to the Web, automatic
corrections, and document Wizards. But Microsoft has done quite a bit
of "infrastructure" work in Word 97, as well, adding improvements you
might never notice unless you suddenly need to take advantage of them.
These include:

- The Portable Document feature, which means that documents look the
  same on screen regardless of where they will ultimately be printed—so
  you no longer have to worry about reformatting documents when you
  switch printers.

- Automatic compression of graphics, so your file sizes won't increase as much when you insert graphics into your documents.

- Better encryption of documents you password-protect, using the 40-bit standard (while not state of the art, this is the strongest encryption the United States will currently allow to be exported).

- Support for Unicode, making it easier to create and display documents which contain text in a wide variety of Pan-European languages. The English version of Word 97 also supports viewing of documents created in Far East language versions of Word.

■ Getting the Most Out of Word 97

There's a lot to learn in Word 97, and a lot to like. How do you get the most out of it? Start by poking around. Click some new buttons; see what they do. Open a document with some WordBasic macros (make a backup copy of them first); see what they look like in VBA. Make sure Internet Explorer 3.01 is installed, and use Word to connect to the Web.

Spend a few minutes in the Tools, Options dialog box, check out Word's default settings and see if you'd like to make changes. At minimum, make sure your name, initials, and mailing address are correct in the User Information tab—Word can use that information to help automate a wide variety of tasks.

Especially if you purchased Word as part of Microsoft Office Professional, browse the CD-ROM: there are many goodies there which don't automatically install as part of Word. In particular, look for:

- More than 3,000 clip art images that must be installed separately by running the Setup program stored in the \Clipart folder

- Some very useful macros stored in \Office\Macros

- An up-to-date copy of Internet Explorer that can be installed by double-clicking \Valupack\Iexplore\Msie30.exe and then running the setup program

- The new Microsoft Camcorder applet, installable by double-clicking \Valupack\Mscam\Camcordr.exe and running the setup program

- A library of additional textures such as cotton candy and liquid metal, stored in \Valupack\Textures

- A supplemental library of more than 100 fonts, in \Valupack\Msfonts

- The Word Viewer program that Word 6 and Word 95 users can use to view documents in Word 97 format; double-click \Valupack\Wordview\Wd95vw71.exe and run the install program

Finally, take a look at the Word 97 movies we've included on the CD-ROM, which walk you through many of these new features, showing you how to use them—complete with audio annotation. To learn how to run these movies, see the Appendix.

■ Summary

If you've used previous versions of Word, Word 97 can help you create documents that look a whole lot better—whether those documents will be printed or posted online. Word 97 is more customizable: you can do virtually anything with its new Visual Basic for Applications language. Best of all, Word can help you get the job done faster and more conveniently—with more automation features than ever before.

In Chapter 2, we'll start taking a closer look at this remarkable piece of software—beginning with the essentials that virtually every writer will use regularly.

- *The Word Interface*
- *Creating a New Document*
- *Font and Paragraph Formatting*
- *Using Section Breaks*
- *Page Setup Basics*
- *Using Headers and Footers*
- *Time-Stamping a Document*

- *Adding Page Numbers to Your Document*
- *Using Bullets and Numbered Lists*

2

Document Essentials:
Build More Effective Documents

THIS CHAPTER STARTS WITH A VERY QUICK REFRESHER ON THE basics of using Word, with some pointers on important new Word 97 features and how they can help you get the job done more quickly and effectively. Next, the chapter moves on to covering Word's fundamental document creation tools—the ones you're likely to use most often. You'll take a closer look at Word's selection and editing tools; basic font and paragraph formatting; headers and footers; time-stamping a document and adding page numbers; and using Word's bulleted and numbered lists. But first, a quick look at the Word 97 interface.

■ The Word Interface

Word's interface was carefully designed to resemble the other Microsoft Office programs as closely as possible. For example, many toolbar buttons are identical, and only one menu name varies among Word, Excel and Power-Point—the Table menu. (It becomes the Data menu in Excel and the Slide Show menu in PowerPoint.)

Figure 2.1 shows the Word 97 interface. If you've used Word before, most of this will look familiar. In this section, we'll point out a few things you may not have noticed before, or are new to Word 97.

Figure 2.1

The Word 97 interface

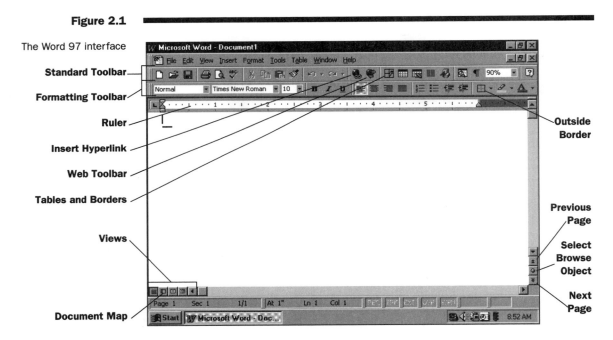

Standard Toolbar
Formatting Toolbar
Ruler
Insert Hyperlink
Web Toolbar
Tables and Borders
Views
Document Map

Outside Border
Previous Page
Select Browse Object
Next Page

Word 97's Toolbars

As you examine the Word 97 interface in Figure 2.1 above, you'll notice the standard toolbar and the formatting toolbar, in their usual places. The standard toolbar contains basic commands, and the formatting toolbar contains commonly used formatting commands, such as boldface, italics, underline, paragraph alignment, indents, bullets, and numbering. In particular, notice the Insert Hyperlink, Web Toolbar, and Document Map buttons on the Standard toolbar, and the Font Color button on the Formatting toolbar.

As you work with Word 97, you'll come across many new toolbars, some of which you're likely to use extensively. For example, the Web toolbar allows you to connect with and move around the World Wide Web. You can always display or hide a toolbar by choosing View, Toolbars and picking from the list of toolbars that appears.

New Scroll Bar Gizmos

The usual Windows scroll bars are here—though keep in mind that if you've purchased Microsoft Office 97 Professional, you may have a new Intellimouse that can replace the scroll bars with a scrolling wheel between its left and right buttons.

At the bottom of the on screen vertical scroll bar, you'll notice Word has made a few design changes to make it easier to navigate through Word documents. The Previous Page and Next Page buttons, which used to be available only in Page Layout view, are now available in Normal view as well. They allow you to scroll through a Word document one page at a time, use the double-up-arrows and double-down-arrows. Or, click the Select Browse Object "ball" icon between the Previous Page and Next Page buttons to immediately move to the next section, footnote, heading, table, drawing, or a variety of other document elements.

The Split Box

You know the old joke about pork factories: They use everything but the squeal. Microsoft is similarly economical when it comes to the Word screen. Just above the vertical scroll bar, there's a useful Word feature that's so inconspicuous you'd never know it was there unless you tripped over it—and then you'd never know how to get rid of it. It's called the split box (see Figure 2.2).

Suppose you want to view two parts of a long document at once. Position your mouse pointer on the tiny rectangle indicated in Figure 2.2 above, click, and drag the mouse pointer down to where you want the document to split. A bar appears, splitting your document in two. You now have two views on the same document, and two vertical scroll bars. You can use either scroll bar to find the parts of the document you want to view. The split bar is covered in more detail in Chapter 6.

Switching Views

To the left of the horizontal scroll bar, notice the Document View icons that represent each available Word view, as indicated in Figure 2.1 above. These icons have been around since Word 6, but many Word users don't realize they provide a one-click way of switching quickly among Word's view of a document.

Figure 2.2

The Split box

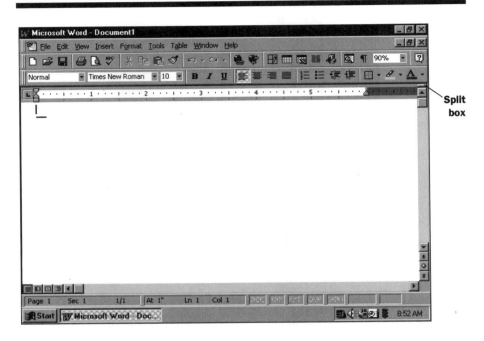

Split box

In this row of icons, you'll find Word's default Normal view of a document (left button), Page Layout view (third button), and Outline view (right button), plus Word 97's new Document Map view (second button) which gives you a quick look at the organization of your document and an easy way to navigate through it. Document Map is also covered in more detail in Chapter 6.

Here's one more part of the Word interface that's been around awhile, but you may not have used to full advantage: the status bar. You'll notice five grayed-out options on the status bar:

- REC, which records a macro

- TRK, which tracks revisions as you make them in a document

- EXT, which makes it easier to extend a selection of text or graphics

- OVR, which places you in Overtype mode, so the type you enter replaces the type that was previously there; and

- WPH, which provides special help for WordPerfect users

You can turn these feature on or off by double-clicking on its box.

Another attractive feature of the Word 97 interface is ScreenTips, which display when you hover the mouse pointer over a comment (annotation), footnote, endnote, or change (revision). For example, if you are reviewing changes to a document that have been recommended by several colleagues, you can see who suggested a change by positioning the mouse pointer over the change (see Figure 2.3). For more information about tracking revisions, see Chapter 15.

Figure 2.3

A ScreenTip displaying the name of a document's reviewer

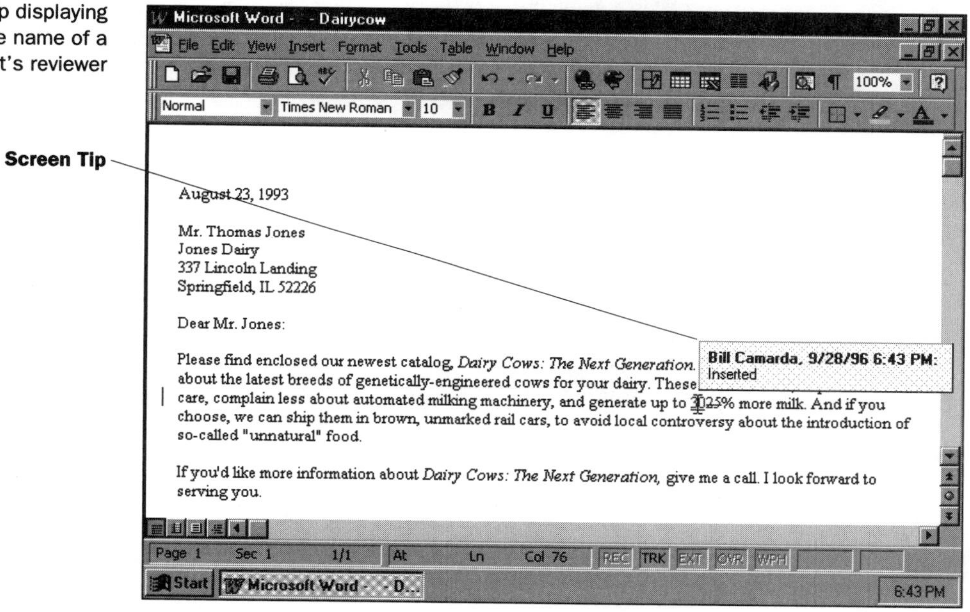

Screen Tip

Keyboard Shortcuts

If you're a dyed-in-the-wool keyboard user who still hates to take your fingers off the home keys, even in the Age of the Mouse, you'll appreciate knowing that Word has some 250 keyboard shortcuts built in. You'll never remember them all; nobody can. But you can get a little help from Word 97.

You can tell Word to display the keyboard shortcut for any toolbar button (if there is one) whenever you hover your mouse pointer over it. That way you're likely to start memorizing the shortcuts you use most. To tell Word to display these keyboard shortcuts, choose View, Toolbars, Customize, Options, and check the Show shortcut keys in ScreenTips button.

I'll help you a little, too. Table 2.1 lists Bill Camarda's Top 20 Great Word Keyboard Shortcuts—the ones you'll use all the time, once you know about them.

Table 2.1

TASK	KEYBOARD SHORTCUT
All Caps	Shift+Ctrl+A
Change case	Shift+F3
Clear all font formatting	Ctrl+Spacebar
Clear all paragraph formatting	Ctrl+Q
Close document	Ctrl+F4
Find again	Shift+F4
Go back where you were last	Shift+F5
Go to beginning of document	Ctrl+Home
Go to end of document	Ctrl+End
Hanging indent	Ctrl+T
Insert an AutoText entry	F3
Next window	Ctrl+F6
Quit Word	Alt+F4
Repeat last command	F4
Run thesaurus	Shift+F7
Select the whole document	Ctrl+A
Start selecting text	F8
Undo last command	Ctrl+Z
View all formatting	Shift+F1
View Office Assistant to get help	F1

The Office Assistant

One last element of the Word 97 interface that's worth mentioning is the Office Assistant, who appears whenever you click the question mark button on the standard toolbar. To get help, click on the Office Assistant and ask a question, as shown in Figure 2.4. I've shown the Genius Office Assistant in Figure 2.4, but you can choose among a variety of Office Assistant personalities, from cats and dogs to William Shakespeare to an animated paper clip with an attitude. (If you're running a system with less than 16 MB, you might want to avoid using Genius—he's a memory hog.) No matter which Office Assistant personality you choose, the Office Assistant delivers the same information.

Figure 2.4

When you ask Office Assistant a question, Word displays choices of relevant help screens.

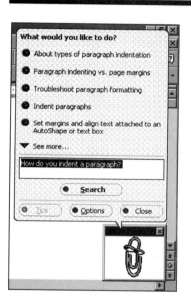

To change the personality of your Office Assistant, right-click on it, and select Choose Assistant from the shortcut menu. Scroll through the available personalities by clicking Next and Back; when you find one you like, click OK.

You can also control how the Office Assistant works, and when "he" or "she" appears, through the Options tab of the Office Assistant dialog box. Any changes you make in Word will also affect the way the Office Assistant behaves in any other Office 97 programs you've installed.

NOTE. *In Word 95, the Question Mark button on the standard toolbar had a different function: if you clicked on it, and then clicked on text, Word would display details about how that text was formatted. This was a Very Cool Feature—and not just for the WordPerfect users who requested it as a substitute for WordPerfect's classic "Reveal Codes" capability. Not many Word users noticed this feature—but the ones who did really became dependent on it. In Word 97, the feature's still there, but it's well hidden. Instead of clicking the question mark, press Shift+F1; then select the text whose formatting you want to see, and voila! There's complete information about your formatting. (See Figure 2.5.) To hide the information, press Esc. You can also get this screen help by choosing Help, What's This?, and then clicking the area of the document whose formatting you wish to review.*

Figure 2.5

To see what formatting
has been applied to a
portion of text, select the
text and press Shift+F1.

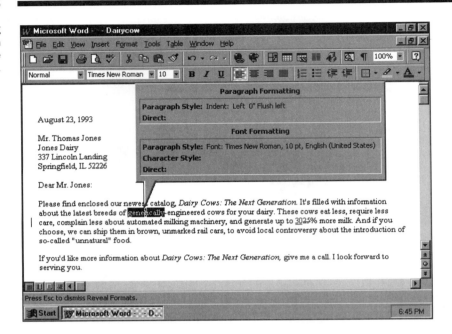

■ Creating a New Document

So now you've admired the Word interface long enough and you'd like to actually *do* something. When Word opens, it displays a new blank document
based on Word's default Normal template. This simply means you have immediate access to the basic styles, margins, page layout settings and other
document characteristics built into a new Word document—all of which you
can change or supplement. (See Chapter 8 for more information on working
with templates and wizards.)

You can always get another blank document based on the Normal template by simply clicking the New button—the button furthest to the left on
the Standard toolbar. You might, however, want to create a document based
on another template. For example, Word comes with additional templates
for resumes, letters, faxes, memos, reports, legal pleadings, publications, Web
pages and a variety of other documents.

Even more templates are hidden in the Office 97 CD-ROM ValuPack
folder, and on Microsoft's Web site: choose Help, Microsoft on the Web, Free
Stuff to get there (assuming you have a Web connection).

If you haven't used any of Word's templates or wizards, check them out: they could save you a lot of time. To use an installed template, choose File, New; select the tab for the category of template or wizard you're interested in, and choose one.

■ Font and Paragraph Formatting

Let's say you've opened a new file. We'll assume you've also entered some text. Now, you're ready to format your text. By default, Word displays text in 10 point Times New Roman—which is about as generic as text can get these days.

To change text formatting, first select the text. Once you've done that, Word provides a variety of ways to change formatting, but the easiest is generally the formatting toolbar, which can control nearly all the text formatting you'll ever want to do (see Figure 2.6).

Figure 2.6

A closer look at the formatting toolbar

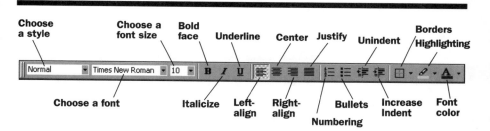

If you want even more control over text formatting, choose Format, Font; the Font dialog box appears, as shown in Figure 2.7.

If you've used Word 6 or Word 95, much of the Font dialog box will look familiar. The Font tab gives you control over font choices and basic font effects. For example, you can specify text as superscript or subscript. Notice that Word 97 introduces effects you never had before, including Shadow, Outline, Emboss, Engrave, and Double Strikethrough.

If you decide you like the way you've formatted text so much that you want *all* your text to use that format, click the Default button. For example, many people find Word's standard 10-point Times New Roman type too small, so they reset it to 12-point type in the Size box, and click Default to set 12 point type as the default for future documents.

The Character Spacing tab of the Font dialog box, shown in Figure 2.8, gives you control over letter spacing. For example, you can expand or compress the space between letters—control that was once reserved for desktop publishers and typesetters. You can also use this tab to control how high or low your superscript and subscript characters appear.

Figure 2.7

The Font dialog box

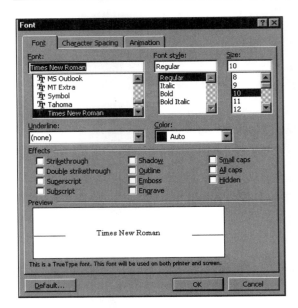

You can use the Kerning for fonts option to adjust the amount of space between combinations of characters when working with TrueType or Adobe Type Manager fonts.

Word 97 also introduces a new Scale feature, which allows you to stretch or compress text horizontally, to any percentage between 1% and 600% of its original size, as shown in Figure 2.9 below. (Incidentally, if all these text effects aren't enough for you, there's more: see the coverage of WordArt 3.0 in Chapter 17.)

Finally, an all-new Font formatting tab, Animation (see Figure 2.10), lets you create Word 97 documents that simulate those Web-based Java applets that are all the rage these days. You can select text and give it a blinking background; or surround it with Las Vegas lights, marching ants (red or black—the choice is yours); or shimmer and sparkle effects. Use these effects sparingly.

Paragraph Formatting

Much of Word's formatting is organized not around characters you select, but around paragraphs. Word defines paragraphs as any block of text that ends with a paragraph mark.

NOTE. *You can actually enter a return in a paragraph without entering a paragraph mark; press Shift+Enter. Word will insert a line break but treat the text that follows as part of the same paragraph.*

Figure 2.8

The Character Spacing
tab of the Font dialog box

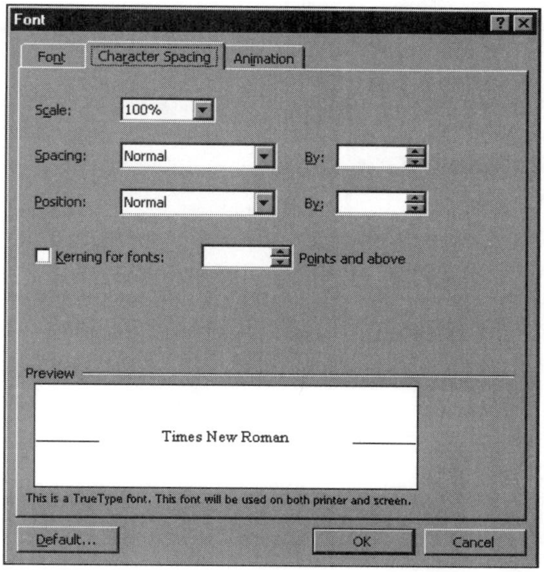

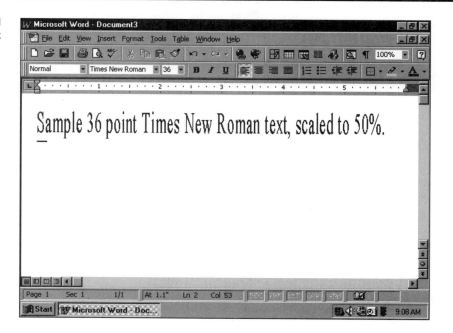

Figure 2.9

Sample text, scaled
to 50 percent

Figure 2.10

The Animation tab of the
Font dialog box

To format a single paragraph, place the insertion point within the paragraph, and apply the formatting you want. To format several paragraphs in one operation, select the paragraphs first. Several of the formatting toolbar buttons you've already seen, such as the indent and alignment buttons, apply paragraph formats. For more control, choose Format, Paragraph; the Paragraph dialog box opens, showing the Indents and Spacing tab, as shown in Figure 2.11. Here, you can control paragraph alignment and indentation; spacing before and after paragraphs; and line spacing.

Indenting Text

Word enables you to indent paragraphs just about any way you want. You can indent only the first line, or create a hanging indent where every line is indented except the first line. You can indent the entire paragraph. You can indent text inward from the right margin. And anything you can indent, you can also outdent—create a negative indent that extends outside the margin.

The simplest, most straightforward indent is the typical paragraph indent—normally an 0.5" indent. The quickest way to indent a single paragraph is to click anywhere within it and then click the Increase Indent button on the toolbar or use the keyboard shortcut Ctrl+M.

Figure 2.11

The Indents and
Spacing tab of the
Paragraph dialog box

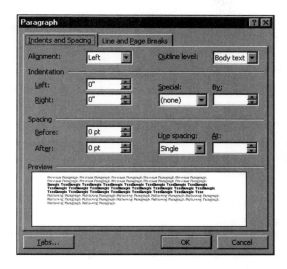

If you want to take more control over your indents, however, you can use the controls in the Indents and Spacing tab of the Paragraph dialog box. For example, you might want to indent both the left and right margins of a specific paragraph by 1"—as, for example, in citing a quote. Type 1" in the Left and Right indentation boxes, and choose OK.

Decreasing Indents

For every indent, there's an equal and opposite unindent—complete with Decrease Indent button on the standard toolbar, and a keyboard shortcut (Ctrl+Shift+M). When the standard indent is set at 0.5", Decrease Indent is also set to 0.5", so when you click Decrease Indent, your indent is reduced by 0.5".

Setting a Standard Paragraph Indent

What if you know that all the paragraphs in your document should start with a standard 0.5" paragraph indent? When you first create the document, choose Format, Paragraph, Indents and Spacing. In the Special box, choose First Line, and in the By box, type 0.5". All paragraphs you type afterwards will start with an 0.5" indent.

If you've already created the document with the appropriate paragraph indents, and you want to add the indents to every paragraph, select the entire document and then set First Line to 0.5".

Creating Hanging Indents

It's common for documents to include a hanging indent, in which the first line of a paragraph is set at the left margin, but all lines beneath it are indented. Word's keyboard shortcut for hanging indents is Ctrl+T. By default, this key combination indents the entire paragraph 0.5 inch from the left margin and then decreases the indent of the first line by 0.5". The result is that the first line remains in its original (unindented) location, but the lines underneath are all indented 0.5". Each time you press Ctrl+T, you add another 0.5" to the hanging indent. Pressing Ctrl+Shift+T reverses the effects of Ctrl+T, gradually eliminating the hanging indent 0.5" at a time.

You can take more control over your hanging indent in the Indents and Spacing tab of the Paragraph dialog box. First select the paragraph or paragraphs you want to apply a hanging indent to. Then, choose Hanging from the Special drop-down list box, and in the By box, specify exactly how wide an indent you want.

Setting Line Spacing for Paragraphs

Word gives you nearly complete control over the space between lines. Typographers call this *leading* (pronounced *ledding*); Word calls it *line spacing*. Word's default is single-spacing, with one point (1/72") of breathing room added between the characters that reach down furthest from one line ("descenders") and the tallest characters on the next ("ascenders").

Single-spacing adds more points when you're using bigger type sizes. It also varies among typefaces, in part because their ascenders and descenders vary. You have three spacing choices instantly available through keyboard shortcuts: Ctrl+1 applies single-spacing; Ctrl+5 sets spacing at 1.5 lines; and Ctrl+2 double-spaces your document. If you want more control than this, you can use the Indents and Spacing tab of the Paragraph dialog box. In addition to single-spacing, 1.5 line spacing and double-spacing, these choices appear in the Line spacing list box:

- *At least:* Sets minimum line spacing but enables Word to handle other line spacing chores automatically.

- *Exactly:* Sets a precise line spacing Word must use regardless of type size or anything else

- *Multiple:* Sets triple-spacing, quadruple-spacing, or any other regular spacing you choose—including fractional spacing.

When you choose one of these options, you must also insert a value in the At box; for example, if you want quadruple spacing, set At to 4.

Setting Tabs

You should know right up front: in many cases where you might once have used tabs, you're now better off with tables (especially for most of those multiple-column lists you've probably struggled with). Word tables are so nifty, they have a chapter of their own: Chapter 3.

The superiority of tables doesn't mean tabs are useless, though. *Au contraire.* As with virtually every Word feature it seems, you have more flexibility than you ever imagined possible, so you can accomplish things you may never even thought about trying before.

You've already been using Word's default 0.5" tab stops with your indent shortcuts (Ctrl+M, Ctrl+N, and Ctrl+T). You can change these default settings. You can add individual tabs wherever you want—in one paragraph or several. You can add tab leaders. And the coup de grace: Word's tabs come in four regular flavors: left-aligned, center-aligned, right-aligned, and decimal tabs (as well as Word's unique "bar tabs," which we'll cover later—no kidding.) Look in Figure 2.12 and in Table 2.2 to see how they behave.

Figure 2.12

Sample left-aligned, center-aligned, right-aligned, and decimal tabs

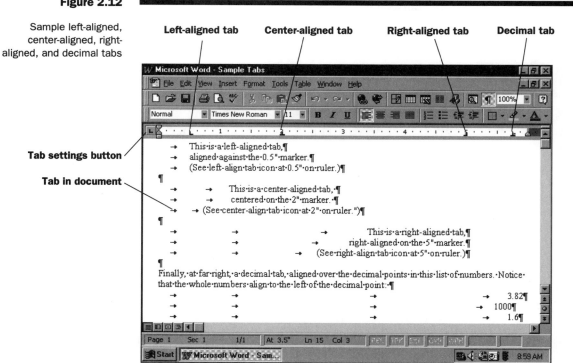

Table 2.2

Word's Available Tabs

TYPE OF TAB	FUNCTION
Left-aligned	Begins tabbed text at tab stop
Center-aligned	Centers text on tab stop
Right-aligned	Ends tabbed text at tab stop
Decimal tab	Centers text over decimal point (for lists of numbers)
Bar tab	Runs a vertical line through a selected paragraph at the tab position

Keep in mind that Word's tab settings are tied to paragraphs. Thus, if you set a custom tab or change the default tab stops, your changes affect only the current paragraph and any other paragraphs that follow the same formatting. If you move elsewhere in the document, the tabs aren't visible or usable. Of course, if you set tabs when you first create a document, those tabs will follow throughout the document until you change them, and if you move text that includes specific tab settings, those tab settings will still apply wherever you paste the text.

To see tabs you've placed in your document, click the Show/Hide Paragraph button on the standard toolbar.

Setting Tabs with the Mouse and Ruler

The easiest way to set tabs is with the ruler. The process involves three steps:

1. Select the paragraphs that are to use the new tab.

2. On the square at the left edge of the ruler, click until you get the kind of tab you want. You move through Word's four kinds of tabs in the following order: left-aligned, center-aligned, right-aligned, and decimal. The decimal tab icon contains a small dot.

3. Click on the ruler at the location where you want the new tab.

To move an existing tab, drag it to the new location. To clear a tab, *drown* it: grab it, drag it underneath the ruler, and let go.

Setting Tabs Precisely with the Tabs Dialog Box

Rulers can set tabs to 1/16" precision—assuming your eyes and hands are that good. You can get better control over your tabs by working in the Tabs dialog box. To open this dialog box, click Tabs from within the Paragraph dialog box, or choose Format, Tabs. The Tabs dialog box appears, as shown in Figure 2.13.

Figure 2.13

The Tabs dialog box

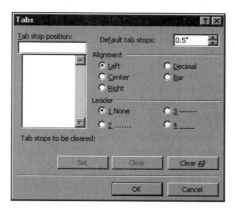

To create a new tab stop in this dialog box:

1. Select the paragraphs that are to use this new tab.

2. Choose Tabs from the Format menu.

3. Type the new tab's location in the Tab Stop position box, using decimal numbers.

4. In the Alignment group, choose the type of tab you want.

5. If you want to add more tabs, choose Set, and then insert another tab.

6. When you've set all the tabs you want, click on OK.

To clear a tab, select it in the Tab stop position list, and click Clear. To clear all tabs, click Clear All. To confirm that you want to clear the tab or tabs, click OK. If you change your mind and decide to keep the tabs, click Cancel.

Changing Default Tab Stops

Word sets default tab stops every 0.5". To change this setting:

1. Choose Format, Tabs.

2. In the Default tab stops box, type or select a new number.

3. Click OK.

Changing Default tab stops affects the entire document, not just selected paragraphs.

Using Tab Leaders

Tab leaders are dots or lines used to connect columns of text, which help readers follow the text more easily. Word enables you to associate a tab leader with a specific tab. If you already have a list of tabs in the Tab stop position box, select one, and choose a leader from the Leader area of the Tabs dialog box. (The default is 1 None.) Click on Set to add the leader; click OK to exit the Tabs dialog box.

Picking Up the Bar Tab

In addition to left, center, right, and decimal tabs, Word offers a fifth kind of tab, the auspiciously named Bar tab. A vertical line runs through any paragraph where a bar tab is set; the line is located at the tab stop position. Figure 2.14 shows an example of a bar tab. You might use this feature to add lines between columns of numbers when you've created the columns with tabs instead of tables.

Figure 2.14

An example of a bar tab

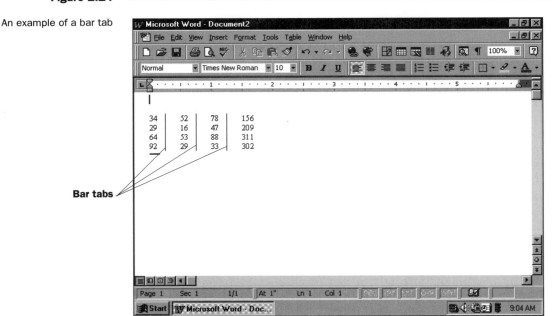

Setting Outline Levels

Before Word 97, the only way to specify relative heading levels in a document was to use Word's built-in heading styles, which are discussed in detail in Chapter 7. For example, if you applied Word's Heading 5 style, Word would know you were creating a fifth-level heading, and carry that information into any outlines and tables of contents you created. This feature had a major disadvantage: You had to use Word's built-in formats for each heading style, or else change them manually—an annoying, time-consuming process.

In Word 97, you can assign any of nine different outline levels to paragraphs without using styles, or you can assign these outline levels to any styles you choose, not just Word's built-in heading styles. You do this by using the Outline level box, in the Indents and Spacing tab of the Paragraph dialog box. (For more information about outline levels, see Chapter 10.)

Controlling the Way Page Breaks Behave

Another option you can control from the Paragraph dialog box is the location of breaks at the end of lines and pages of your document. To control line and page breaks throughout a document, choose the Line and Page Breaks tab (Figure 2.15):

Figure 2.15

The Line and Page Breaks tab

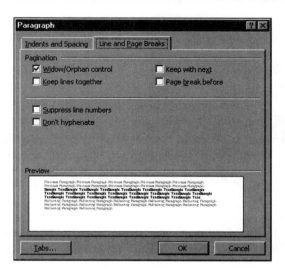

The pagination options listed in the Line and Page Breaks tab (called Text Flow in Word 6 and Word 95) help you control the pagination and line breaks in your document. By default, Word automatically creates page breaks as you fill pages.

Using the pagination options which are summarized in Table 2.3, you can tell Word exactly how to break specific paragraphs at the end of a page. You can apply these options to a single paragraph by simply placing the insertion point there. To affect several paragraphs at once, select them first.

Table 2.3

Line and Page
Break Options

OPTION	INSTRUCTIONS TO WORD
Widow/Orphan control	Don't let a single line appear by itself at the top or bottom of a page. (On by default.)
Keep lines together	Don't split this paragraph onto separate pages, no matter what. (Also useful for lists.)
Keep with next	Keep this paragraph with the next paragraph, no matter what. (Useful for captions, lists.)
Page break before	Place this paragraph on top of the next page, no matter what. (Useful for figures, tables, graphics.)
Suppress line numbers	Don't include any line numbers next to the selected paragraphs, even if they are specified in Page Setup, Layout (see coverage later in this chapter)
Don't hyphenate	Don't hyphenate selected paragraphs

Hyphenation is turned off by default, so you only need to enable the last option if hyphenation has been turned on. Also note that you can turn on more than one option at a time; the Preview box in the Paragraph dialog box always shows you a thumbnail preview of the results.

Using Format Painter

Suppose you've formatted a chunk of text in some unusual way. Let's say it's 16 point Comic Sans MS, Bold, Blue, Engraved, Condensed by 0.2 point, indented by 0.5", with (Heaven help us) the Sparkle effect. Now you have another block of text—either in the same document or another document—that you'd like to format exactly the same way.

You could re-format the new text manually. Or, much easier, you could use Word's Format Painter feature—the paintbrush icon on the Standard toolbar. Select any part of the text that already looks the way you want it to; click the Format Painter button; and then select the text you want to apply the formatting to. Your new text is immediately reformatted. That's all there is to it.

Keep in mind that we've been discussing manual formatting techniques designed to help you format specific chunks of text. In Chapter 7, you'll learn how to use Word's styles and AutoFormat features to ensure that your entire document is formatted consistently, with as little effort as possible.

■ Using Section Breaks

When you open a new Word document, many of the formats you set, such as margins, apply to your entire document. But sometimes, you may want to apply different formats to different parts of your document. What then?

Word's solution is to enable you to format a document in sections. Word uses section breaks to divide a document when you change margins for part of the document. Splitting a document into sections also allows you to specify the following formats for only part of a document:

- Column formatting
- Footnote and endnote appearance and location
- Headers and footers
- Page and line numbering
- Paper size and orientation

To insert a new section break, choose Insert, Break; the Break dialog box opens, as shown in Figure 2.16.

Figure 2.16

The Break dialog box

You have four choices about how Word handles your section break, as indicated in the Break dialog box in Figure 2.16:

This Option	Adds a Section Break, and
Next Page	Starts a new page
Continuous	Continues on the same page
Even page	Starts the new section on the next even page
Odd Page	Starts the new section on the next odd page

After you've chosen one of these types of section breaks, click OK, and the section break takes effect. Section breaks display as double-dotted lines, with the words Section Break and the type of section break centered, as shown in Figure 2.17. To view a Section Break mark, you must enable the Show/Hide Paragraphs button in the standard toolbar.

Figure 2.17

A Next Page section break

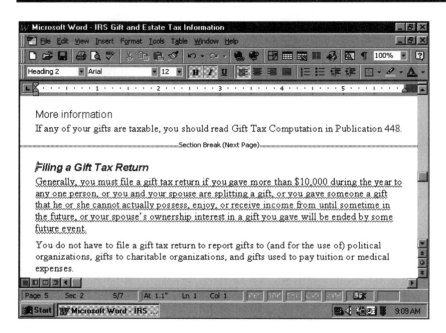

After you insert a section break, you have two sections that contain the same formatting. To change the formatting in one section, click the insertion point anywhere within that section, and make your format changes. Remember that formatting changes that were previously global—such as changing the paper orientation from portrait to landscape—now only affect the section you're in.

■ Page Setup Basics

You've created a document. But before you print it, you want to make sure all your margins and other page settings are right. You can do this from the File, Page Setup dialog box, which controls four main areas of formatting: margins, paper size and orientation, paper source, and layout (see Figure 2.18). Each of these can be controlled for your entire document, or for individual sections you've created.

Figure 2.18

The Page Setup dialog
box with the Margins
tab displayed

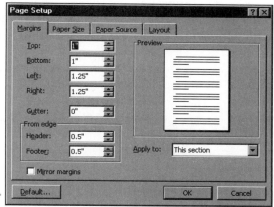

By default, Word uses left and right margins of 1.25" each, and top and bottom margins of 1" each. Note that if you add headers and footers, these appear outside the top and bottom margins.

You can use the Top, Bottom, Left, and Right spin boxes to change margins, or simply type your new margins in the appropriate boxes. When you change a margin, the Preview box shows you a thumbnail image of how your document would change.

To specify how far your headers and footers are placed from the edge of your page, change the Header and Footer settings in the From edge section.

Preparing Pages for Binding: Gutters and Facing Pages

Suppose you're producing a report that will be bound or stapled. You probably want to leave extra space on the left margin of each page to accommodate the binding. File, Page Setup's Margins tab provides a separate setting, Gutter, for this purpose. When you enter a number in the Gutter option, Word adds that value to the left side of your page, in addition to your left margin.

If you're producing a book or booklet, or any other document that will be printed on both sides of every sheet and then bound together, you'll probably want to leave extra space on both the inside margins, near the binding.

First set a gutter, and then check the Mirror Margins box. When you check Mirror Margins, Word changes the Left and Right margin settings to Inside and Outside, and displays a thumbnail sketch of both pages. The effect of this command is that the inside edge of each page will receive the additional margin provided by the gutter.

Using the Ruler to Reset Margins

You can reset top, bottom, left, and right margins for your current document or section without venturing anywhere near the Margins tabbed dialog box. You simply use the ruler.

1. Click the Page Layout view button at the bottom left corner of the Word window. A vertical ruler is added to the left side of the screen, as shown in Figure 2.19, to allow you to control top and bottom margins. (The horizontal ruler you can use to control left and right margins appears in Word 97 by default, but you can display it by choosing View, Ruler.)

Figure 2.19

Displaying the horizontal ruler by positioning the mouse pointer at the top of the editing window

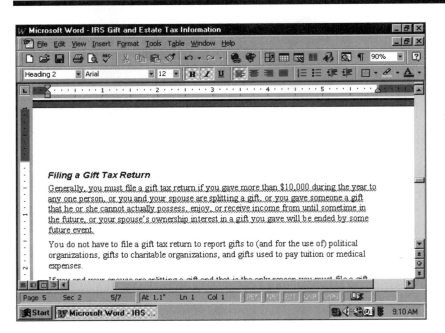

2. Position your insertion point right in the middle of the margin marker, at the intersection of the colored and white parts of the ruler. The mouse pointer will change to a double-arrow, and a ScreenTip will appear indicating that you are controlling the Top, Bottom, Left, or Right margin, depending on where your mouse pointer is located on either the horizontal or vertical ruler.

3. Now drag the mouse pointer to the location where you want your margin to appear.

NOTE. *You can also use the rulers in Print Preview to adjust margins.*

Controlling Paper Size

Word's Page Setup, Paper Size tab in the Page Setup dialog box (Figure 2.20) enables you to specify one of a wide variety of paper sizes.

Word assumes you are using an 8.5" x 11" sheet of paper unless you specify otherwise. In general, your paper size choices depend on the printer you are using. You can see your options in the Paper Size drop-down list box. To choose a custom size, type the measurements in the Width and Height list boxes below Paper Size.

Figure 2.20

The Paper Size
drop-down box

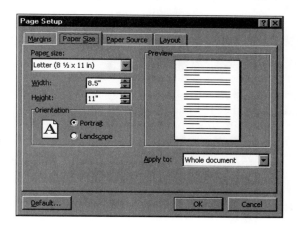

Choosing Paper Orientation

Word's Page Setup, Paper Size tab in the Page Setup dialog box (Figure 2.20) enables you to specify whether your document prints vertically or horizontally. To set the paper orientation, choose Portrait or Landscape from the Orientation box in the Paper Size tab.

By default, Word prints in portrait mode, with the long side of your sheet printing top to bottom. You can switch this orientation so your page prints sideways—in landscape mode. Landscape mode is common for financial reports with wide lists of numbers, and also adds visual interest to proposal documents, newsletters, and many other documents.

Controlling the Paper Source

Many printers enable you to choose the way paper feeds into them. You can control these capabilities through Page Setup's Paper Source tab, shown in Figure 2.21.

Figure 2.21

The Page Setup
Paper Source tab

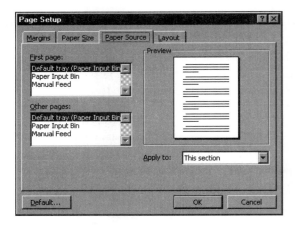

Most business correspondence uses one type of letterhead for the first page, and another (or blank paper) for the following pages. You can specify paper sources in Word, but the options available depend on your printer.

For example, if you have a two-tray laser printer, you can instruct Word to load first-page letterhead from one tray, and the remaining sheets from another.

Or, you may need to specify manual feed if you have only one paper tray, or if you have specified an unusual size of paper that your paper tray cannot handle.

To specify paper source, choose the Page Setup Paper Source tab in the Page Setup dialog box, which includes separate list boxes for First Page and Other Pages.

Changing Document Layout

In the Layout tab of the Page Setup dialog box (see Figure 2.22), Word gives you even more control over the appearance of your pages. Here you'll find ways to alter where sections start, headers and footers, and vertical page alignment.

Section Start

If your document has multiple sections, Section Start gives you a second chance to specify where Word starts each section you've selected; the default is New Page, as discussed earlier.

Vertical Alignment

Vertical alignment determines whether text on a page is pushed to the top margin, centered between top and bottom margins, or justified.

Top is the default setting, good for about 99 percent of the pages you're likely to create.

Figure 2.22

The Page Setup
Layout tab

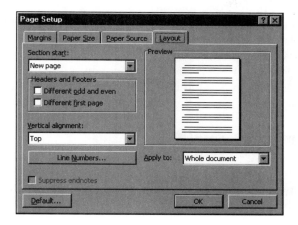

Centered is a real time-saver for document covers, where you might otherwise struggle to figure out how to center the title.

Justified stretches the available text to top and bottom margins. If not
enough text is available, Word leaves large chunks of white space between
paragraphs. You could live a lifetime, and then be reincarnated, without finding a use for Justified.

Line Numbers

The Layout tab's final feature, Line Numbers, places line numbers in the margins of a printed document. To use this feature, click Line Numbers in the
Layout tab of the Page Setup dialog box. The Line Numbers dialog box
opens, as shown in Figure 2.23.

Figure 2.23

The Line Numbers
dialog box

To add line numbers to your document, check Add line numbering. The
three spin boxes and Numbering choices in the dialog box become active.
Start at controls which line number you start with; the default, obviously, is
1. From text sets how far from the left margin your line numbers appear. The

default setting, Auto, sets line numbers 1/4" from the margin (1/8" if you are using more than one column). Count by tells Word whether to show every line number, every fifth line number, or any other increment you choose.

The choices in the Numbering box of the Line Numbers dialog box enable you to control when the line numbers return to your starting number. The default is Restart each Page, but you can also reset numbering with each section, or use continuous numbering throughout your document, regardless of page or section.

Changing Default Page Setup

Once you've made changes in the Page Setup dialog box, you can tell Word to use your new settings as the default for all documents created with the Normal template. Click Default from any tab in the dialog box, and choose Yes to confirm the changes.

■ Using Headers and Footers

A header is text that appears at the top of each page; a footer is text that appears at the bottom of each page. To insert a header or footer in Normal view, choose Header and Footer from the View menu. Word switches you into Page Layout View if you were working in Normal view, makes the header area available for editing, and displays the Header and Footer toolbar as shown in Figure 2.24.

By default you're placed in the Header area at the top of the current page, and Word shows you the visual context in which your header appears. Your document text appears dimmed, in light-gray text, beneath the header box. If you want to work with a footer instead of a header, click on the Switch Between Header and Footer button.

Nearly any editing or formatting you can do in a regular Word editing window, you can do in a header or footer area as well. You have access to all Standard toolbar, Formatting toolbar, and Ruler shortcuts, all basic editing and formatting menu selections, and most keyboard shortcuts.

Word normally styles both headers and footers with left-aligned, Times New Roman, 10-point type. You can change this manually, or by changing the header style in the same way you would change any document style.

NOTE. *Once you've created a header, whenever you're working in Page Layout view, you can double-click on the header or footer pane to edit a header or footer.*

Figure 2.24

A header pane viewed in
Page Layout view; text
has been added

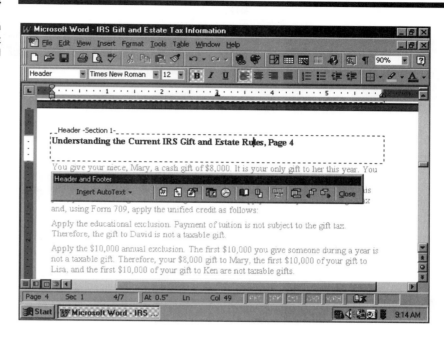

The Header and Footer Toolbar

The Header and Footer toolbar, as shown in Figure 2.25, has been revamped
and improved in Word 97. Each toolbar button is described in Table 2.4.

Figure 2.25

A closer look at the
Header and Footer Toolbar

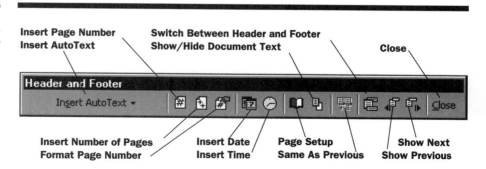

A few of the Header and Footer toolbar's new buttons are worth calling
attention to.

Table 2.4

Header and Footer Toolbar

BUTTON	WHAT IT DOES
Insert AutoText	Allows you to choose from a series of preformatted headers and footers that specify page numbers, author's name, date, filename or other information
Insert Page Number	Inserts a field that displays the correct page number on all pages
Insert Number of Pages	Inserts a field that displays the number of pages in the entire document
Format Page Number	Displays the Page Number format dialog box, which allows you to control page number formatting and numbering
Insert Date	Inserts a field that displays the current date
Insert Time	Inserts a field that displays the current time
Page Setup	Displays the Layout tab of the Page Setup dialog box, where you can specify different headers and footers for odd and even pages, or for the first page
Show/Hide Document Text	Toggles between displaying document text in the background and showing no text in the background
Same as Previous	Specifies that a header (or footer) contain the same text as the header or footer in the previous section
Switch Between Header and Footer	Toggles between displaying the current section's header or footer
Show Previous	Displays the header associated with the previous section, if any
Show Next	Displays the header associated with the next section, if any
Close	Closes the Header and Footer pane

Insert AutoText

Insert AutoText allows you to choose from a series of boilerplate AutoText entries that include much of the information people typically place in headers, such as page numbers, author's name, date, and filename, as shown in Figure 2.26.

When you choose one of these AutoText entries, the information is generally placed in your document as a field, which means that it can automatically be updated as you edit your document. In other words, if the current date changes, it will automatically change in the header, whenever you update your fields. (For more information on using and updating fields, see Chapter 21.)

Figure 2.26

Choices available from
Insert AutoText

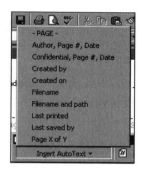

Insert Number of Pages

Word 97 adds a toolbar button that allows you to enter the total number of
pages in your document, making it easy to create headers that say, for example:

Page 13 of 34

Since the number of pages is also entered as a field, when the number of
pages in your document changes, so does the number specified in the heading.

One-Click Access

Word 97 also adds buttons that give you one-click access to two of the dialog
boxes you're most likely to need from within a header or footer:

- The Page Number Format dialog box, where you can specify the appearance and numbering scheme used by page numbers; and

- The Page Setup dialog box, where you can specify different headers and
  footers for odd and even pages, or for the first page of your document,
  and make other page setup changes, as necessary.

Using Different Headers and Footers In Each Section

Many documents require several headers and footers. For example, each
chapter of a book might require its own header or footer. Word gives you
control over multiple headers and footers in documents.

Headers and footers are based on sections. When your document contains only one section, your header or footer appears on every page of the
document unless you specify otherwise.

To allow for different headers and footers within your document, you
must first split the document into multiple sections using Insert, Break
(covered earlier in this chapter). You can then create separate headers and
footers for each section, each with its own text, formatting, and location.

Whenever you divide a document or a section into two sections, the second section starts out with the same header or footer as the first. Word 97 assumes that when you make a change in one section's header or footer, you'll want to make the same change in all your other headers or footers. In other words, by default, all your headers are connected to each other. Similarly, all your footers are connected to their fellow feet.

You can tell when a header or footer is taking its cues from a previous one, because the words Same as Previous appear at the top right of the header or footer area (see Figure 2.27). In addition, the Same as Previous button is depressed on the Header and Footer toolbar.

To change a header or footer without changing others too, de-select the Same as Previous button in the Header and Footer toolbar. Now your header or footer is no longer part of the chain gang. You can edit and format it separately from all your other headers and footers. You can always reconnect a header or footer to the one preceding it in the document, thereby replacing the contents of the current header or footer with the contents of the previous one. To do so, activate the Same as Previous button again. You will be asked to confirm the change; choose Yes.

Figure 2.27

A footer that has been linked to a previous footer

Same as Previous Reference

Same as Previous button

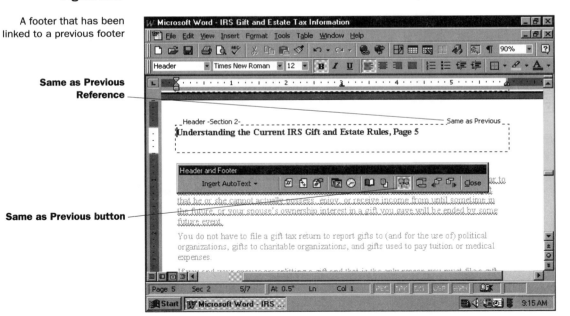

Word's Header and Footer toolbar makes it easy to move through the document, changing headers and footers. The Show Previous button moves you to the end of the previous section and displays its header or footer. The Show Next button moves you to the beginning of the next section and displays its header or footer.

Because Word displays the text associated with each page in the header window, it's easy to decide what should appear in the header or footer. You can also use the scroll bars to move through the page, or to look for a heading to help you decide what text to place in your header.

If, on the other hand, you simply want to make straightforward edits to existing headers or footers, you might want to speed up Word a bit by pressing the Show/Hide Document Text button in the Header and Footer toolbar. When you do this, Word does not redraw the entire new page before showing your header or footer area.

■ Time-Stamping a Document

Word makes it easy to add the time or date to a document. In a header or footer, you can use the Time or Date buttons on the Header and Footer toolbar.

The equivalent keyboard shortcuts are Alt+Shift+D (date) and Alt+Shift+T (time). These keyboard shortcuts can be used anywhere in a document. You might, for example, use Alt+Shift+D to include a date on a memo or on the cover of a business proposal.

When you use the keyboard shortcuts to insert the date and time, they appear in the following format:

```
11/16/96 3:28 PM
```

If you want more control over the appearance of the date and time, choose Insert, Date and Time to display the Date and Time dialog box shown in Figure 2.28. Choose a format from the Available Formats list and click on OK.

If you want Word to update the date and time later, check the Update automatically box, and the Date and Time information will be entered as a field instead of text.

■ Adding Page Numbers to Your Document

From within the header or footer area, you can add page numbering to your document by clicking on the Page Numbers button in the Header and Footer toolbar.

Figure 2.28

The Date and
Time dialog box

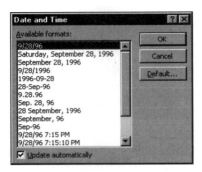

When you add page numbers by using this method, the number 1 appears at your insertion point in the header or footer area. This indicates the page number format and the starting page number Word will use to number this section. You can add text to the page number, reformat it, or move it, using the same text editing techniques you use in a regular document.

Formatting Page Numbers

By default, Word uses Arabic numerals (1, 2, 3), beginning with the number 1. If you prefer a different page numbering format, click the Format Page Number button in the Header and Footer toolbar. The Page Number Format dialog box opens, as shown in Figure 2.29.

Figure 2.29

The Page Number
Format dialog box

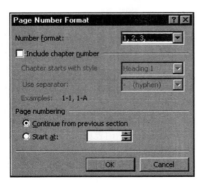

The Number Format drop-down list box gives you the following five choices:

- 1,2,3... Arabic numerals

- a,b,c...Lowercase alphabet

- A,B,C...Uppercase alphabet
- i,ii,iii...Lowercase Roman numerals
- I,II,III...Uppercase Roman numerals

When you choose another numbering scheme, such as A, B, C, this new numbering scheme appears in the status bar where Word displays page numbers, and also in the ScreenTip that shows your current location as you move amongst pages with the vertical scroll bar (see Figure 2.30).

Figure 2.30

If you choose to number your pages using a letter scheme such as A, B, C, then letters will appear in place of page numbers in the status bar, and in the ScreenTips that display as you move throughout the document with the vertical scroll bar.

Screen Tip

Page number, in letter format

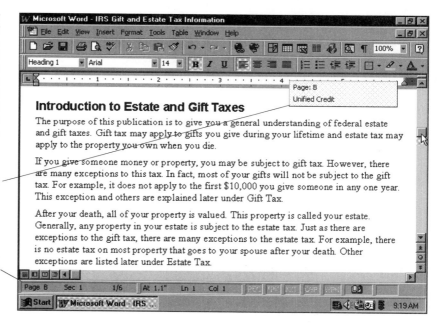

Adding Chapter Numbers to Page Numbering

Word also makes it easy to add chapter numbers to your page numbering. To do so, you first need to enter your chapter number as text anywhere within your document, and set it apart from other text by a paragraph mark. Then format the text by using one of Word's built-in heading styles—or one of your own. (See Chapter 7 for detailed coverage of styles.) In this example, we'll use Heading 1:

1. Select the chapter number in the document.

2. Choose Heading 1 from the Style drop-down list box on the Formatting toolbar.

3. Choose Format, Bullets and Numbering, then click the Outline Numbered tab.

4. Click the last style box in the Bullets and Numbering dialog box, and then click OK.

5. Choose Insert, Page Numbers.

6. Click the Format button.

7. Check the Include Chapter Number check box. The boxes beneath it, Chapter Starts with Style and Use Separator, become usable.

8. In Chapter Starts with Style, select Heading 1 from the list of available heading styles.

9. In Use Separator, pick one of the following characters to separate your heading number from your page number:

   - Hyphen

   . Period

   : Colon

   — Em dash

   – En dash

10. Click on OK.

Having now assigned Heading 1 to chapter numbers, don't use it for anything else, or you will confuse Word unmercifully.

Choosing Starting Numbers

You can control the number Word uses as its starting number when numbering pages. By default, Word continues page numbering from section to section. As already mentioned, if you have only one section, Word starts numbering the pages with page 1. You can, however, start with any page number. Click the Start At option button in the Page Number format dialog box, and then use the spin box to the right to set the page number.

This feature is most commonly used to number a document that is being appended to another document. If you have a 40-page document, for example, you can begin the next document's page numbering with 41.

NOTE. *A problem arises if you want to add a page to a document which has other documents appended to it. All the documents that follow are then numbered inaccurately. There is a solution: Combine several documents into a master document, as discussed in Chapter 13.*

■ Using Bullets and Numbered Lists

Two other very common tasks in creating a document are creating bulleted lists, such as:

Great Elvis Presley Singles

- Heartbreak Hotel
- Don't Be Cruel
- Hound Dog
- Jailhouse Rock
- Suspicious Minds

and numbered lists such as:

The World's Largest Islands

1. Greenland
2. Guinea
3. Borneo
4. Madagascar
5. Baffin Island

Word makes it easy to create either type of list. We'll start with the simplest way to do the job, and then show you how to take complete control of the process.

To create a bulleted list the easy way, select the list of items you want to bullet, and click the Bullets button on the formatting toolbar. To create a numbered list instead, click the Numbering button on the formatting toolbar.

Word 97 is also smart enough to follow behind you and create a bulleted list as you enter text. To take advantage of this feature, type an asterisk and a space at the beginning of the first item you want to bullet. Then enter the rest of the line of text, and press Enter. Word will replace the asterisk with a bullet, and place another bullet at the beginning of your new line, formatting each bulleted item with a hanging indent of 0.25" (unless you specify a different hanging indent in Format, Paragraph). If you don't need a second bullet, either press backspace or enter.

To create a bulleted list using hyphens, enter a hyphen and space at the beginning of the first line; then start entering text and press enter at the end of the first bulleted item.

To create a bulleted list using right-arrow marks, enter the > symbol on the first line. Samples of Word's automated bullets are shown in Figure 2.31.

NOTE. *The Office Assistant may appear, offering you an opportunity to change the text back to its original format, or to learn how to turn AutoFormat off. If you want to do neither, choose Cancel.*

Figure 2.31

Samples of bullets Word can insert automatically

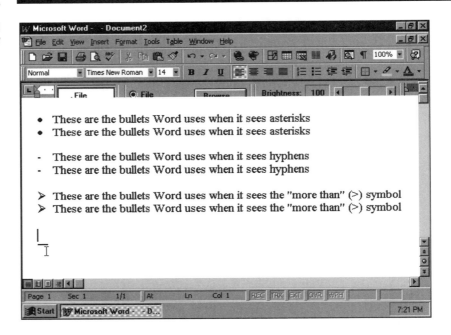

If you go to the end of a bulleted list and press Enter to create a new row, the new row begins with a bullet automatically. Similarly, if you use Enter to create a new row within a bulleted list, it automatically contains a bullet. (You can add new rows to numbered lists this way as well.)

If you *never* want Word to transform ordinary text into bulleted or numbered lists automatically, choose Format, AutoFormat, Options. The AutoFormat as You Type tab of the AutoCorrect dialog box appears. Clear the Automatic bulleted lists check box, the Automatic numbered lists check box, or both, and then click OK.

Changing to Another Bullet Character

You may not want to use Word's default bullets—and you don't have to. Word offers more bullets than your typical Army-Navy store. To create a bulleted list with a different hanging indent or bulleted character, first select the text to be bulleted. Then choose Bullets and Numbering from the Format menu. The Bullets and Numbering dialog box appears. Display the Bulleted tab if it doesn't already appear.

To change the bullet character, choose one of the other seven preset bullets. If you're still not satisifed, *also* choose Customize. The Customize Bulleted List dialog box appears, as shown in Figure 2.32. You can specify another common bullet from the Bullet Character group.

Figure 2.32

The Customize Bulleted
List dialog box

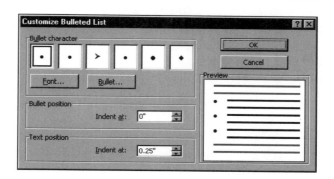

If you don't like any of the bullet formats in the Customize Bulleted List dialog box, you can click the Bullet button underneath the display of Bullet characters in the dialog box. Word displays all the characters available in the Symbol font, Word's default source of bullets. You can choose any of these characters for your bullet by highlighting it.

Still not satisfied? Choose another Font from the drop-down list box in the Symbol dialog box; good candidates to find bullets include Wingdings and Monotype Sorts, if these are installed on your system. Once you've changed fonts, a different set of bullets will appear; select one of those, and click OK.

Once you've chosen a bullet, click OK. Now, click Font and you can format the bullet as if it were any other text. (By the way, here's another chance to use that dreaded Animation tab. Bullets that blink or shimmer would be absolutely dynamite in a document trying to motivate folks to get an eye exam.)

NOTE. *If you use a bullet in a different font, be careful not to reformat the bullet and inadvertently change the font; if you do, you may see a blank space or a character you didn't want, in place of the bullet you inserted.*

If you return to the Customize Bulleted List box again (by choosing Format, Bullets and Numbering, Customize) you can specify an indent for your bullet in the Bullet position box (the default setting is 0"). You can also specify an indent for your text—in other words, how far your bullet and text are separated. The default Text position is 0.25".

Any change you make is immediately reflected in the Preview box.

When you create a new bullet, Word uses it as your default bullet until you choose another bullet, either in the Bullets and Numbering dialog box or in the Customize Bulleted List dialog box.

To remove bullets, select the text containing them, and then click the Bullets button on the Formatting toolbar.

Customizing Numbered Lists

Numbered lists work much like bulleted lists. You've already learned that you can create a numbered list by selecting a list and clicking the Numbering button on the formatting toolbar. You can also start numbering a list manually, using a number followed by a period, hyphen, or closed-parentheses mark. As soon as you press Enter, Word will reformat the list as an automatically numbered list. Word also recognizes numbered lists that start with the letter A or a; or uppercase or lower case roman numeral "I" or "i"; or a letter or number placed between parentheses, such as (1).

If you move paragraphs within a numbered list, Word automatically renumbers them, keeping the numbering consecutive.

For more control over your numbered list, choose Format, Bullets and Numbering, then choose the Numbered tab. The dialog box shown in Figure 2.33 appears.

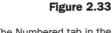

Figure 2.33

The Numbered tab in the Bullets and Numbering dialog box

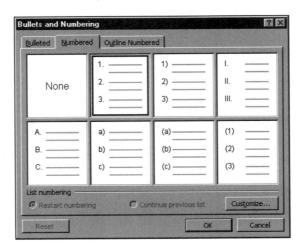

As with bullets, you can choose one of seven standard numbering styles. You can really take control of your numbering options by choosing Customize in the Numbered tab of the Bullets and Numbering dialog box. The Customize Numbered List dialog box opens (see Figure 2.34).

Figure 2.34

The Customize
Numbered List
dialog box

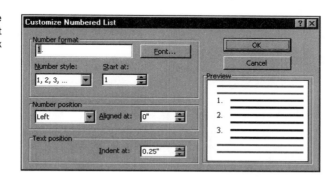

As usual, Word gives you more formatting control than you might know what to do with. You have several choices for the Number style you'll use:

- 1, 2, 3...

- I, II, III...

- i, ii, iii...

- A, B, C...

- a, b, c...

- 1st, 2nd...

- One, Two...

- First, Second...

- 01, 02...

You can also choose no numbering at all, by selecting (none) in the Number style drop-down list box. That's a neat feature. It enables you to type several characters in the Number format box and use them as if they were single bullets—so you could create a numbered list like the following:

```
BONUS! Free software!
BONUS! 30-day free access!
BONUS! CD-ROM packed with sample ideas!
```

You can also specify the text before and text after your number in the Number format box, so you can number a list like this:

```
Chapter 1.
Chapter 2.
Chapter 3.
```

or like this:

```
1st Avenue:
2nd Avenue:
3rd Avenue:
```

You can also specify that your numbers appear with different font formatting from the surrounding text. Choose the Font button in the Customize Numbered List dialog box to see the Format Font dialog box. Here, you can change font, style, size, effects, character spacing and animation of the numbers in your list. Click on OK to return to the Customize Numbered List dialog box.

You can choose a starting number for your numbered list in the Start at box in the Customize Numbered List dialog box. This feature is very helpful if you are presenting a list of numbered steps that must be interrupted by other text, such as figures or Author's Notes.

Finally, as you can see, the Customize Numbered List dialog box also includes the same number and text position settings as Word provides for bullets, so you can specify whether your numbers will be indented, and how far away from your numbers you'll place your text. When you are finished customizing numbers, click OK.

NOTE. *Word's Bullets and Numbering dialog box includes a third tab, Outline Numbered, which controls Word's automatic outline numbering feature. This is covered in Chapter 10, "Outlining."*

In this chapter, you've taken a quick look at the basics of working with Word, with an emphasis on new capabilities in Word 97—and some tips and tricks even experienced Word users may not have noticed.

In Chapter 3, you'll move on to one of Word 97's most useful features—its revamped table feature. Word 97 tables can help you organize virtually any information into neat little cubbyholes—and make those cubbyholes look good. So put away those tabs, and discover a better way to make sure your tabular information stays where you want it, lined up in disciplined rows and columns—just the way you want it to.

- *Creating a Table from the Standard Toolbar*
- *Creating a Table with Insert Table*
- *Editing in a Table*
- *Moving Around within a Table*
- *Selecting Text within a Table*
- *Using the Table Shortcut Menu*
- *Formatting within a Table*

- *Autoformatting a Table*

3

Tables

ONCE UPON A TIME, TABLES WERE NOTHING MORE THAN RIGID rows and columns of information, such as those shown in Figure 3.1. To create a table, chances are you worked with tab settings, and (to put it mildly) there were plenty of opportunities to make mistakes.

Figure 3.1

Typical traditional table

Item	Current	Projected
Horseless carriage	25,000	27,000
Telegraph keys	100,000	110,000
Typewriter ribbons	75,000	125,000
Gramophones	30,000	45,000

Word for Windows 97 has turned the tables—turned them into a feature that is so flexible you will find yourself using tables for tasks you never even thought were related to tables. Figure 3.2 is an extreme example, but you get the point—these are not your father's tables.

Figure 3.2

Word can even turn the tables on tables.

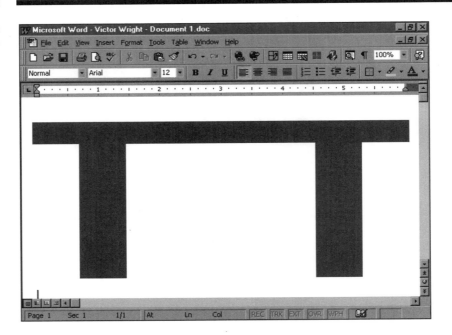

More practically, throughout this book you will learn how Word tables can be used to streamline résumés, forms, scripts, mini-databases, and spreadsheets—and how you can use them to improve your newsletters and other desktop publishing projects. In addition, when all you want is a good old-fashioned table, Word gets the job done lickety-split. Word can even turn the tables on tables.

In this chapter, you'll learn how to create a table from the Standard toolbar and how to create one with Insert Table. We'll cover editing in a table, using the table shortcut menu, formatting within a table, and autoformatting a table. Then, we'll move to inserting and deleting rows and columns, changing column width, specifying row height, adding table borders and shading, and merging cells. Finally, we'll discuss converting text to tables and vice versa, and we'll do a simple table calculation and a simple table sort.

■ Creating a Table from the Standard Toolbar

You say for the moment you will be satisfied with a basic quarterly report table? Here are the steps you need to follow:

1. Click on the Insert Table button in the Standard toolbar. A set of rows and columns appears, as shown in Figure 3.3.

Figure 3.3

The Insert Table button

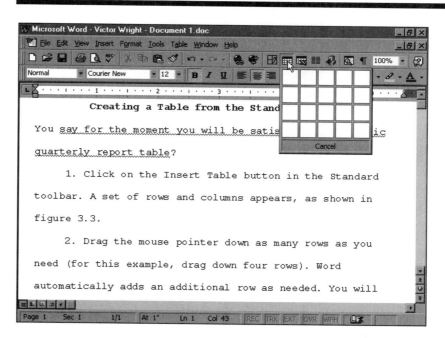

2. Drag the mouse pointer down as many rows as you need (for this example, drag down four rows). Word automatically adds an additional row as needed. You will see the number of rows highlighted as you go (see Figure 3.4).

3. Still pressing the mouse button, drag the pointer across, covering as many columns as you need. Again, you will see the number of columns highlighted (see Figure 3.5).

Figure 3.4

Dragging rows

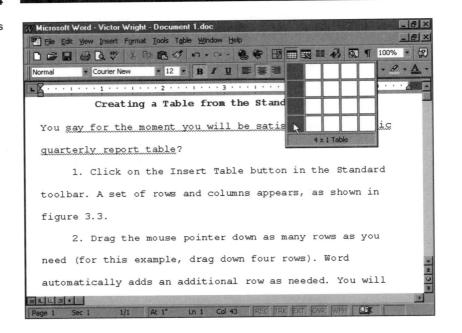

Figure 3.5

Dragging columns

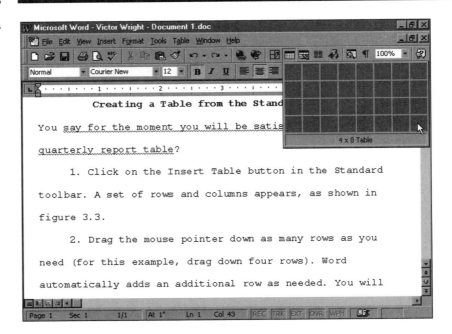

TIP. *Try to have a general idea of how many rows and columns you will ultimately need, but don't worry about it too much. After the table is created, it is easy to add and delete rows and columns.*

4. When you are satisfied, let go of the mouse. Word creates a table, as shown in Figure 3.6.

Figure 3.6

Sample 4x8 table

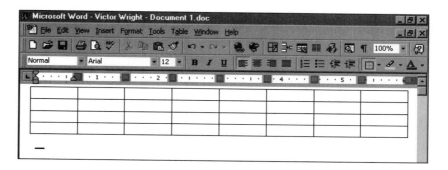

NOTE. *Stealth Tables. If by some chance your tables do not appear, make sure a check mark appears next to Gridlines in the Table menu. This places dotted lines around the borders of each cell, as shown earlier. Otherwise the table might be there, but you can't see it.*

If you start creating a table by clicking on the Insert Table button and dragging to show rows or columns, you can still change your mind and cancel the table insertion. Move the mouse pointer outside the table matrix (the rows and columns appearing beneath the Insert Table button). When the word Cancel appears in the status window, release the mouse button and the table disappears.

TIP. *If you need more rows or columns, use the Table Insert option, which we'll discuss shortly. If you follow the previous procedure, Word changes the menu item to Insert Rows.*

When you create columns within a row, you are creating cells. A cell is the rectangle or box formed by a row and a column (just like a spreadsheet cell). Cells are the basic unit of table formatting. They are similar to paragraphs. Like paragraphs, they have their own markers called end-of-cell markers, as shown in Figure 3.7.

In a blank table, end-of-cell markers appear near the beginning of each cell to indicate that the cell is empty. Notice that another end-of-cell marker appears after the last cell in a row.

Figure 3.7

End-of-cell markers

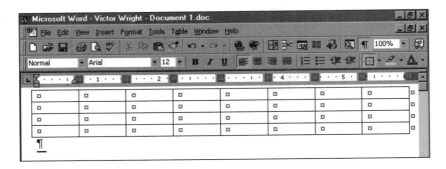

NOTE. *If your paragraph marks appear on-screen, end-of-cell markers also appear. If not, you might want to display them, especially while you are reading this chapter and following the exercises.*

The quick way to display markers is to click the Paragraph Mark button on the Toolbar, but this also places dots between each word. If you find this annoying, follow these steps:

1. Choose Tools, Options.

2. Choose View to display the View tab of the Options dialog box.

3. Check Paragraph Marks in the Non-printing Characters group, and if the All box is checked—uncheck it.

4. Click on OK.

Word now displays end-of-cell markers, paragraph marks, and line breaks.

Table Button Default Settings

Like other toolbar buttons, Insert Table assumes you want default settings. When you use it, all cells are created equal. They each have the same width, divided equally from the space between your margins. If, for example, you are using default margins of 1.25 inches on left and right, that leaves 6 inches of text area. Therefore, if you create a three-column table, Word assigns 2 inches to each column.

Each row also has the same height. Unless you have specified otherwise, row height is one line, based on the line height used in the previous paragraph. Other formatting contained in the previous paragraph carries over, too, including the following:

• Font, size, and character attributes

• Special pagination and line numbering commands

- Tab settings

- Paragraph indents

Stray paragraph indents are some of the most common problems users have with Word tables. A leftover 1.5-inch indent can have the result shown in Figure 3.8.

Figure 3.8

Table with unwanted indents

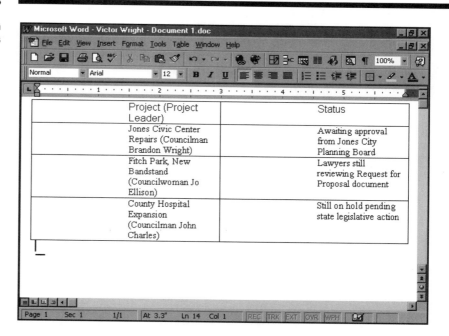

To get rid of the indents, select the entire table, choose Format, Paragraph, and set From Left, From Right, and any Special indents to 0".

Using Word's New Draw Table Feature

Word 97 provides an even more intuitive way to insert tables: now, you can simply draw them. Click the Tables and Borders button on the Standard Toolbar. Word switches you to Page Layout view; the new Tables and Borders toolbar opens displaying all the table and border tools you're likely to need (see Figure 3.9); and the mouse pointer changes shape to resemble a pencil.

Press the left-mouse button and draw the outline of your table. It appears with a ½-point border. Next, draw columns and rows roughly where you want them to appear. Word will automatically extend and straighten lines that you've only drawn partway. If you draw a line where you don't

Figure 3.9

Creating a table
using Draw Table

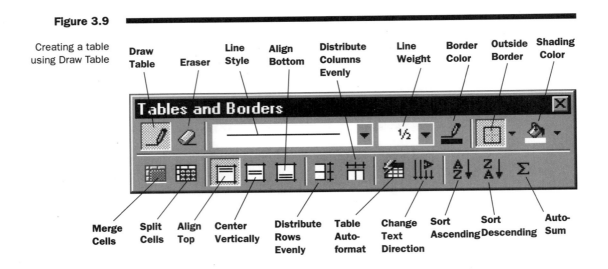

want one, click the eraser tool, and drag across the line until it disappears. When you've finished drawing the table's rows and columns, click the Draw Table button on the Tables and Borders toolbar.

You can now polish your table. For example, if you want several of your columns to be the same width, select them and click the Distribute Columns Evenly button on the Tables and Borders toolbar. Also notice that the toolbar contains several commands that weren't available in earlier versions of Word; for example, you can now align text vertically within a cell, or turn it sideways.

■ Creating a Table with Insert Table

If you want more control over your table while you are creating it, or if you need more rows and columns than the toolbar can provide, place the insertion point where you want the table and choose Table, Insert Table. The dialog box shown in Figure 3.10 appears.

The Number of Columns box enables you to create up to 31 columns. The Number of Rows box enables you to create as many rows as you need. (Remember, you can always add rows later.) The Column Width box enables you to specify the width of all columns. The default setting is Auto, which divides the available space between margins equally among the columns. You can, however, set all columns to a specific width, even if it means they will extend beyond your margins. Columns must be between 0.25" and 10.99" wide.

Figure 3.10

The Insert Table dialog
box

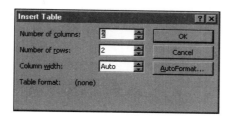

In the section "Changing Column Width" later in this chapter you will learn
how to change the width of a specific column.

■ Editing in a Table

After you create a new empty table, the next step is to put something in it. When
Word creates a new table, it positions the insertion point in the table's first cell.

Typing in a table is similar to typing anywhere else in a document, with
one major exception: When you reach the right edge of a cell, Word wraps text
back to the left edge, as it normally would at the end of a line (see Figure 3.11).

Figure 3.11

Sample table showing
wrapped text

Project (Project Leader)¤	Status¤
Jones Civic Center Repairs (Councilman Brandon Wright)¤	Awaiting approval from Jones City Planning Board¤
Fitch Park, New Bandstand (Councilwoman Jo Ellison)¤	Lawyers still reviewing Request for Proposal document¤
County Hospital Expansion (Councilman John Charles) ¤	Still on hold pending state legislative action¤

NOTE. *You now can see how tables can be used to present side-by-side
paragraphs. These are essential in many kinds of documents. One good
example is video script writing, in which video directions often appear on the
left, and spoken words appear on the right.*

Word also has a very strong multiple-column feature, which is covered in
Chapter 21, "Desktop Publishing and Drawing," but that feature snakes text
down one column and up to the top of the next. Only tables offer a practical
solution for multiple side-by-side paragraphs.

You can enter paragraph marks or line breaks within a cell. These breaks
add lines to the row the cell is in, and to all other cells in the same row, as
shown in Figure 3.12.

Figure 3.12

Sample table with
paragraph marks added

Project (Project Leader)¤	Status¤
Jones Civic Center Repairs (Councilman Brandon Wright)¶ ¶ ¤	Awaiting approval from Jones City Planning Board¤
Fitch Park, New Bandstand (Councilwoman Jo Ellison)¤	Lawyers still reviewing Request for Proposal document¶ ¶ ¤
County Hospital Expansion (Councilman John Charles) ¶ ¶ ¶ ¤	Still on hold pending state legislative action¤

TIP. *Although you cannot have cells in the same row with different heights, you can fake this with borders, as you will see in the section "Using Borders Selectively," later in this chapter.*

■ Moving Around within a Table

To move around with a mouse, click the cell you want to go to. Word also offers many keyboard shortcuts. For example, Tab moves you to the next cell; Shift+Tab moves you back. A complete list follows in Table 3.1.

NOTE. *Within tables, Word appropriates the Tab key for moving between cells. To actually set a tab within a table, press Ctrl+Tab.*

■ Selecting Text within a Table

Within a cell, Word's normal selection methods apply. With the mouse, you can highlight some or all of the text. With the keyboard, you can press F8 and the arrow keys, or press Shift and the arrow keys.

After you reach the end-of-cell marker, things change. When you select the end-of-cell marker, the entire cell is selected. When you extend your selection beyond the end-of-cell marker, Word selects the entire next cell. When you reach the end of a row, Word selects the end-of-row marker.

When you go even further, either extending the keyboard selection or moving the mouse pointer up or down, Word selects entire additional rows. When you go beyond the edge of the table, Word adds other text to your selection.

For any non-table text you add to your selection, the selection process behaves normally; you can add either individual characters or lines to your selection.

Word offers more shortcuts for selecting text in a table Alt+5 (on the number pad) selects the entire table. (That is similar to Ctrl+5, which selects

Table 3.1

Keyboard Shortcuts

THIS KEY	MOVES THE INSERTION POINT
Up arrow	Up one line within a cell. If at the top of a cell, up one cell. If already at the top of the table, moves one line above the table.
Tab	To next cell
Shift+Tab	To previous cell
Down arrow	Down one line within a cell. If at the bottom of a cell, down one cell. If already at the bottom of the table, moves one line below the table.
Left arrow	Left one character within a cell. If at the beginning of a cell, moves to end of previous cell.
Right arrow	Right one character within a cell. If at the end of a cell, moves to start of next cell.
Home	To beginning of current line in current cell
End	To end of current line in current cell
Alt+Home	To beginning of first cell in current row
Alt+End	To end of last cell in current row
Alt+PageUp	To beginning of first cell in current column
Alt+PageDn	To beginning of last cell in current column

the entire document.) In addition, every table cell has its own selection bar. If you move the mouse pointer to the far left of a cell, the pointer changes to a right arrow, as shown in Figure 3.13. Click the mouse, and Word selects the entire cell. Double-click, and Word selects the entire row.

NOTE. *To use the Alt+5 shortcut, you must have NumLock turned off.*

TIP. *Try the keyboard. Because clicking on either the left edge of a cell (its selection bar) or the right edge of a cell (its end-of-cell mark) selects the entire cell, it can be a bit tricky to select the text within a cell without also selecting the cell. You might find it easier to do this with the keyboard, rather than the mouse.*

The normal Word selection bar at the far left of the screen also works. Within a table, the selection bar selects a row rather than a cell, as in Figure 3.14.

Figure 3.13

Using a cell's
selection bar

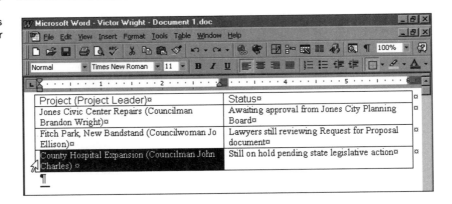

Figure 3.14

Using the Word selection
bar to select a row

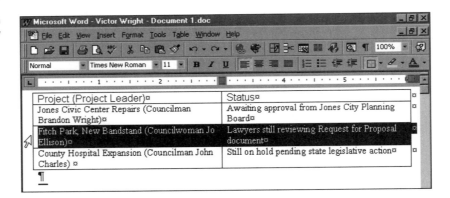

You can select specific columns by carefully positioning the mouse
pointer at the top edge of the column (see Figure 3.15). When the pointer
changes into a down arrow, click the mouse button.

To select more than one column, when the pointer changes into a down
arrow, press and hold the mouse pointer as you move left or right to select
the other columns.

Finally, you can select rows or columns from the menu. To select one row
or column, position the insertion point anywhere in that row or column, and
choose Table, then click on Select Row or Select Column.

To select more than one row, first select individual cells in each row, then
choose Select Row. To select more than one column, first select individual
cells in each column, then choose Select Column. To select the entire table,
choose Select Table.

Figure 3.15

Selecting a column with
the down-arrow mouse
pointer

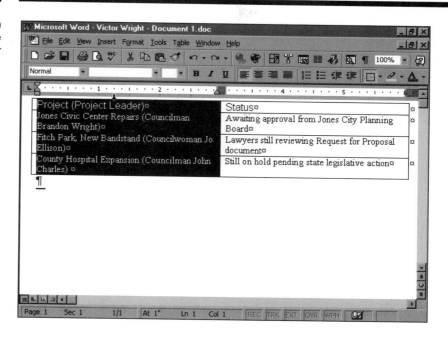

Using the Table Shortcut Menu

Whenever you are in a table, you can right-click to display a shortcut menu of
the commands that Word expects you are most likely to need (see Figure 3.16).

Formatting within a Table

As mentioned earlier, when you create a table, it takes on the character and
paragraph formatting of the paragraph preceding it. In other words, if the
previous paragraph uses Times New Roman 14 point type, double-spaced, so
will your table unless you change it. You can change any of this formatting
by using the same character and paragraph formatting techniques discussed
in previous chapters.

Autoformatting a Table

Word adds a powerful new table feature designed to simplify the creation of
good-looking tables. This feature, called AutoFormat, enables you to pick
whatever elements you want from 39 different formats, as listed in Table 3.2.

Figure 3.16

The table shortcut menus

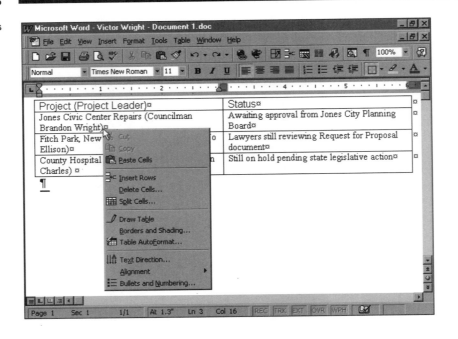

Table 3.2

AutoFormat Table Formats

TYPE OF FORMAT	NUMBER OF VARIATIONS
Simple	3
Classic	4
Colorful	3
Columns	5
Grid	8
List	8
3D Effects	3
Contemporary	1
Elegant	1
Professional	1
Subtle	2

To autoformat an existing table, place your insertion point anywhere inside the table and choose Table, Table AutoFormat. To autoformat a new table, choose Table, Insert Table, set the number of rows and columns (and optionally the column width), and then choose Table AutoFormat. In either case, the Table AutoFormat dialog box appears, as shown in Figure 3.17.

To choose a format, select it from the Formats list box. By default, Auto-Format expects to apply the Borders, Shading, and Font elements from the built-in format. (Font does not change your table's text font to Arial, as implied in the Preview, but it does add bold or italic as shown there.)

AutoFormat also expects to use AutoFit, which shrinks or enlarges each column to fit the widest cell contained in that column.

Figure 3.17

The Table AutoFormat
dialog box

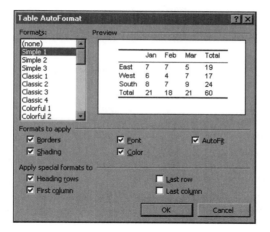

You can turn off each of these features by clearing them. You also can add color in those Table AutoFormats that support it, by checking the Color box. Twenty-two of the formats support color; some of the other formats use more intricate gray or black shading when you choose Color.

Word's Table AutoFormats often include special formatting for Heading Rows, and for the First Column. These are on by default. Word assumes you are actually putting something special in the top row and first column. If you are not, you can turn them off. You might want that special formatting to appear in the Last Row or Last Column—perhaps you are showing a total there. Check the appropriate box to turn these on. Again, the Preview box shows you what to expect. When you have your AutoFormat the way you want it, click on OK.

Inserting and Deleting Rows and Columns

Often, you will have to add a new row or column to your table. In earlier word processors, this was difficult, if you could do it at all. Word makes it much easier.

To add a new row to the bottom of your table, position your insertion point in the last cell and press Tab. A new row appears in the same format as the previous row. To add a new row anywhere else in your table, select the row where you want a new row to be placed and choose Table, Insert Row. A new row appears; other rows are pushed down to make room.

To add a new column within your table, select the column where you want the new column to be placed and choose Table Insert Column. A new column appears, and other columns are pushed to the right to make room. To add a new column at the right edge of your table, select the end-of-row markers, as shown in Figure 3.18, then choose Insert Column.

Figure 3.18

Creating a new column at the right edge of a table

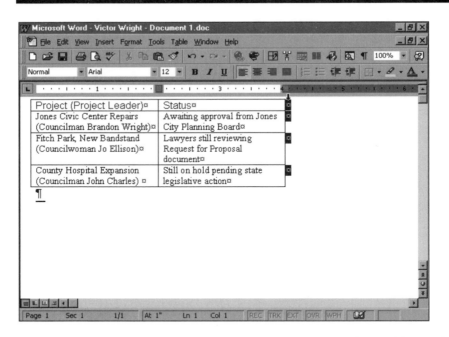

When you insert a row, the new row takes the same height, width, and formatting as the one following it. When you insert a column, it matches the column to its right.

- If you are not in a table, the button assumes that you want to create a table, and it presents you with its row/column matrix.

- If you select a row, the button assumes that you want to insert a row, and it does so.

- If you select a column, the button assumes that you want to insert a column, and it does so.

- If you place your insertion point inside a cell, or select one or more cells, the button assumes that you want to insert cells, and it opens the Insert Cell window, asking you where to move the other cells.

TIP. *You also can add rows and columns with the Insert Table button. Just position your insertion point and click. Word guesses what you want to do:*

Inserting Cells

You also can insert cells anywhere within a table. Position the insertion point at the point you want to add the cell. Then highlight the cell or cells that are currently in the location where you want to add blank cells, and choose Table, Insert Cells. The dialog box shown in Figure 3.19 appears.

Figure 3.19

The Insert Cells
dialog box

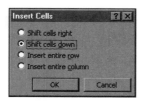

Tell Word where you want to move the cells you are displacing: Shift Cells Right or Shift Cells Down. In either case, Word shifts only these cells—leaving you with a table that has additional cells in some rows or columns, as shown in Figure 3.20.

If you are sure that is what you want, click on OK in the dialog box to confirm. Much of the time, you will want to make changes. You might really want to add an entire row or column, so Word also offers these options.

Cutting and Pasting Cell Contents

As with selecting text, cutting, copying, and pasting within a cell works much the same as it does anywhere else in a Word document. You can use keyboard shortcuts, the toolbar, the menu, or a right-click of the mouse. However, when you select entire cells, rows, or columns, there are a few new behaviors to keep in mind.

Normally, when you cut an entire cell (or multiple cells) into the Clipboard, the empty cell or cells still appear in your table, but the Clipboard

Figure 3.20

Typical table after
inserting a cell and
shifting cells right

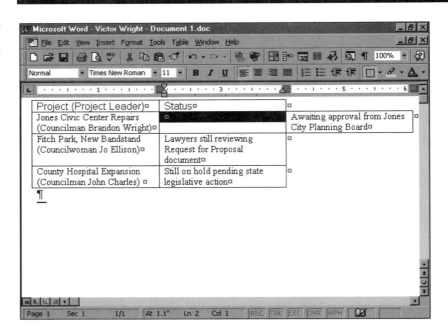

also contains cell borders. If you paste the cell or cells outside the Clipboard, they appear as a "baby" table of their own (see Figures 3.21 and 3.22).

TIP. *If you just want to move the text in one cell, you can avoid this situation if you don't cut the end-of-cell marker.*

If you paste cells into a table, and the cells require more columns or rows than the table already has, Word adds them. Sometimes this means Word creates new empty cells as well.

You cannot paste both cells and regular (non-table) text into a table at the same time, but you can paste text from outside a table into one cell.

TIP. *You also can use drag-and-drop to move rows and columns.*

Clearing Cell Contents

Sometimes, you might want to eliminate the contents of a cell without storing them in the Clipboard. Select the cell and press Delete, or choose Edit, Clear. You also can use Delete or Clear to wipe out entire rows or columns. As with Cut, the cell borders disappear—and the cells are truly gone.

You can retrieve deleted cells by choosing Edit, Undo Clear, or by choosing Clear from the Undo list box on the Standard toolbar.

Figure 3.21

Cut...

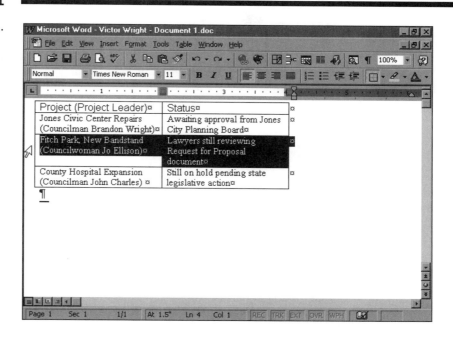

Figure 3.22

...and paste right here

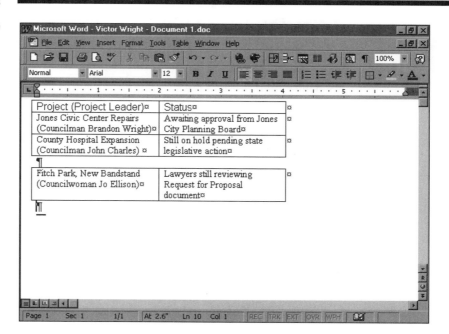

Pasting Cells

After you have cut a cell or cells, there are two ways to paste them. You can position your insertion point at the top left of the space where you want to place the cells. Word simply inserts all the cells in your Clipboard—replacing any existing data that might have been in the way. That is the fastest way, but be careful not to destroy any information you needed.

You also can clear a space for the pasted cells. If you cut a 2x5 matrix of cells into the Clipboard, you can select a 2x5 space as their new home. The cut and paste sizes must be identical, or you will see the message shown in Figure 3.23.

Figure 3.23

Word's Assistant tells you when the Paste command fails

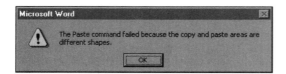

The situation is different if you are pasting a complete row. Then, Word automatically makes room. Insert the pointer where you want the new row, and paste. The existing row is moved down to compensate.

Deleting Rows and Columns

When you select and Cut or Delete a complete row or column, Word also removes the row or column borders—eliminating the row or column entirely, and moving the rest of the table to compensate.

You also can use the menu. Select the row(s) or column(s) you want to delete, then choose Table, Delete Row or Delete Column. Similarly, you can delete an entire table by placing the insertion point in the table and choosing Delete Table.

Changing Column Width

Often, making all cells the same width simply does not work. You might have a descriptive first column followed by many shorter columns of numbers, as in the census statistics shown here:

CITY	1990	1980	1970	1960
New York, NY	7.32M	7.07M	7.90M	7.78M
Los Angeles, CA	3.49M	2.97M	2.81M	2.48M
Chicago, IL	2.78M	3.01M	3.37M	3.55M

CITY	1990	1980	1970	1960
Houston, TX	1.63M	1.59M	1.23M	0.94M
Philadelphia, PA	1.59M	1.69M	1.95M	2.00M

You might also have brief categories followed by lengthier explanations, as shown by this excerpt of a table describing chess moves:

Piece	Moves Allowed
King	One square in any direction
Queen	Any number of open squares in any direction
Rook	Left, right, forward, backward any number of open squares
Bishop	Diagonally
Knight	Any combination of two squares in one direction and one square in a perpendicular direction
Pawn	One square forward, except for its first move, which can optionally be two spaces forward; can capture pieces one diagonal space in front of it

You can, of course, use AutoFit to rearrange this, but you might want to make adjustments. Or, you might not want to take the trouble to clear all the other AutoFormatting elements so that you can use AutoFit.

In either case, as you might be expecting by now, Word offers several ways to change column width without going anywhere near AutoFormat. This section starts with the easiest—the vertical split pointer. To change the width of a column, position the mouse pointer anywhere on the column's right gridline, as shown in Figure 3.24.

Now drag the gridline left or right to the location you want, and let go. The widths of all the following columns change to compensate, so your overall table has the same width. You can, however, change the last column without affecting the others.

Changing Column Width with the Ruler

You also can change column width with the ruler. As you can see in Figure 3.25, when you are within a table, the table's column borders are shown on the ruler.

You can change these column borders by positioning the mouse pointer on the border shown in the ruler (avoiding the indent markers) and dragging to the new border that you want. As you drag a column border, the new measurements are visible on the ruler. The columns that follow shrink or enlarge to compensate, unless you are changing the last column.

Figure 3.24

Vertical split pointer

Vertical split pointer

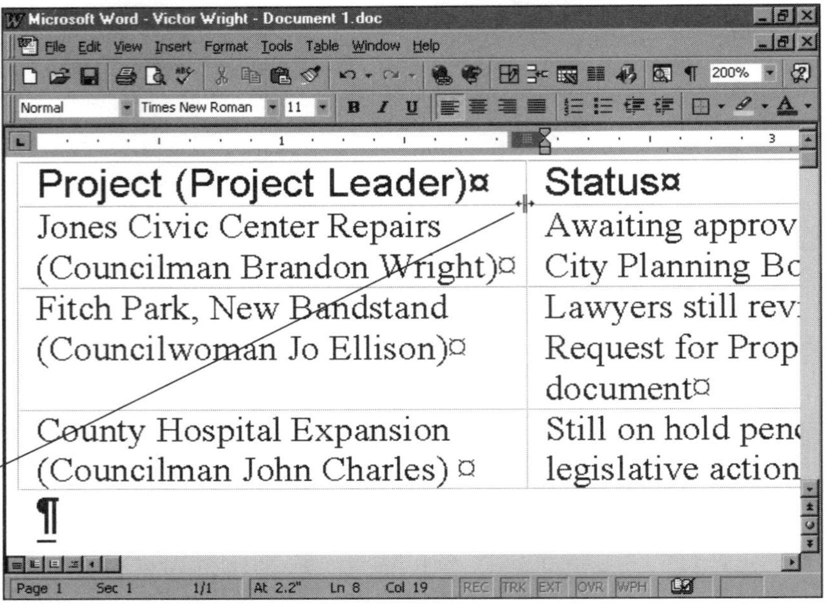

Using Table Cell Height and Width to Change Column Width

If you need more precise control over your column width, if you want to change a column's width without changing the others, or if you want to change the space between columns, work with Cell Height and Width from the Table menu. First, select the column or columns you want to adjust. Then choose Table, Cell Height and Width, and display the Column tab in the Cell Height and Width dialog box, shown in Figure 3.26.

As you can see, the box tells you which column or columns you are working with. Type the new width in the Width of Column box, or click on the AutoFit button to fit the column around its widest text.

If you want to change the width of another column, you do not need to leave the dialog box. Use Previous Column to move to the left, or Next Column to move to the right. When you are satisfied, click on OK.

Changing Space Between Columns

By default, Word places 0.15" of space between the end of one column's text area and the beginning of the next column's text area. Notice that the space is not actually between columns—instead, Word moves the cell borders

Figure 3.25

Ruler and table cells

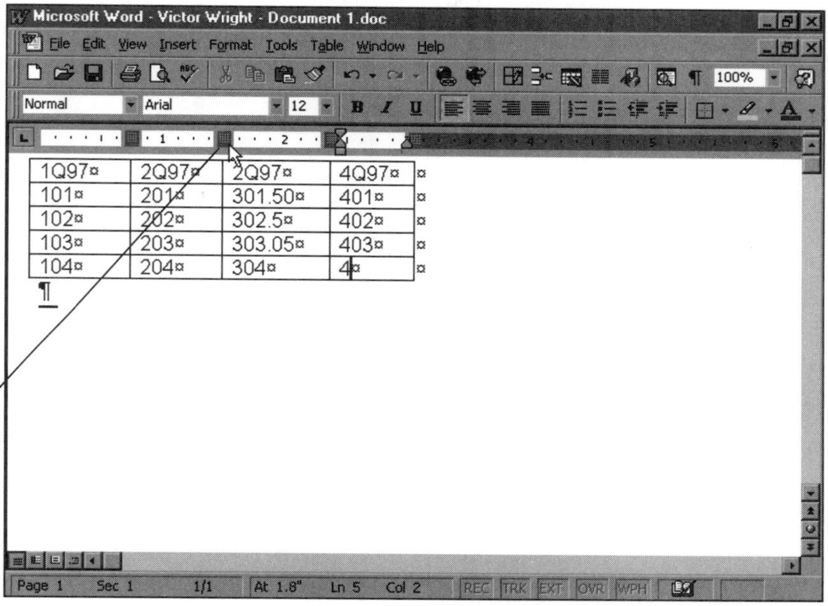

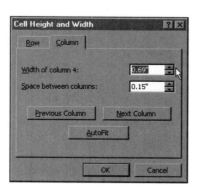

**Move Table Column
pointer on column
border marker**

Figure 3.26

The Column tab in the
Cell Height and Width
dialog box

nearer or farther away from the end-of-cell markers. Because you cannot insert text in a cell after the end-of-cell marker, the result is the same.

The difference in approach shows up more clearly when you use borders.
You do not see a 0.15" space between columns. Rather, you see 0.075" space
between the end of text in a column and the column border. The other
0.075" appears at the beginning of the next column.

In the example shown in Figure 3.27, the space between columns has been extended to 0.8", so you can see the 0.4" blank space reserved on each side of the cell's border. (Space Between Columns can now be set to any measurement; in Word 2, you were limited to measurements between 0" and 0.98".)

Figure 3.27

0. 8" space between
columns

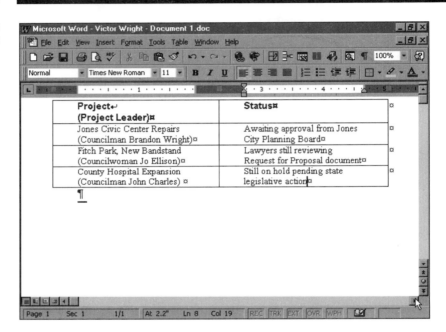

To change the space between all columns, select any column, choose Table, Cell Height and Width, Column, and insert a new value in Space Between Columns. To change the space between all columns in a specific row, place the insertion point in that row, choose Table, Cell Height and Width, Column, and change the value in Space Between Columns.

Specifying Row Height

By default, Word uses a height of one line. "One line" starts out equal to one line in the previous paragraph. As you work within the table, "one line" can grow or shrink depending on the type size you use on each line. Word always leaves a bit of extra room to accommodate your type. In any case, all cells on the same line always have the same row height.

To control row height, choose Table, Cell Height and Width, and click on Row to display the Row tab in the Cell Height and Width dialog box (see Figure 3.28).

Figure 3.28

The Row tab in the Cell
Height and Width dialog
box

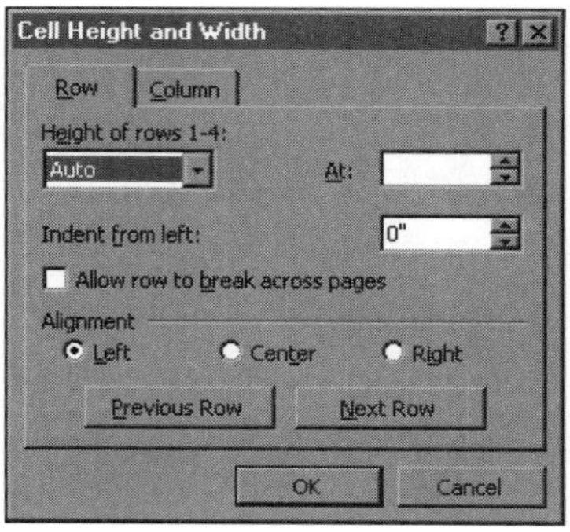

Row height is controlled in the Height of Rows box. The list box tells you the row or rows you are controlling. Height of Row gives you similar choices to those in Line Spacing in the Format Paragraph menu (see Table 3.3).

Table 3.3

Height of Row
Options for Tables

OPTION	DESCRIPTION
Auto	Enables Word to control line spacing, setting it at one line.
At Least	Tells Word the minimum row height it should use; however, enables Word to increase Row Height when necessary.
Exactly	Tells Word exactly what Row Height to use, no matter what the type size is.

In the At box, you can add measurements in lines (li), centimeters (cm), points (pt), or picas (pi).

TIP. *If you tell Word to use a row height greater than one line, Word places the extra space after the text. To add space before the text, set Before spacing in the Format Paragraph dialog box.*

As with column width, you can use Previous Row or Next Row to set the height of adjacent rows without leaving the dialog box to select them. If you use Exactly to set a height shorter than the text in the row, Word cannot display all the text in the row, as shown in Figure 3.29. Using At Least avoids this problem and is generally a better choice unless you have specific typographical or design reasons for setting exact measurements.

Figure 3.29

Bottom gridline
overlaps text that
cannot be displayed.

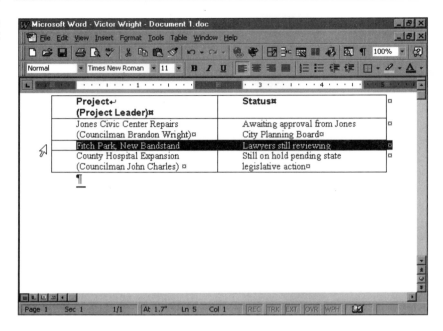

Deciding Whether Rows Can Break across Pages

In Word 2, it was simple: Rows could not break across pages. That simple limitation led to a variety of design restrictions, notably that you often could not use very deep rows.

Now, by default, rows can break across pages. That means you might want to pay attention to the way your page breaks look—widows and orphans in table rows can be even worse than in other parts of your document, especially if you haven't used cell borders to help the reader follow what is going on.

You can select specific cells (or an entire table) and tell Word not to let them break across pages. Choose Table, Cell Height and Width. Choose the Row tab in the Cell Height and Width dialog box, and uncheck the Allow Row to Break Across Pages box.

Indenting and Aligning Tables

You already have seen that existing paragraph indents can affect the location of text within cells. As you will see shortly, you can use the ruler to set indents and tabs within a cell or cells. But what if you want to indent or align the table, or some of its rows?

The Row tab in the Cell Height and Width dialog box contains these goodies, too. First, select the entire table (Alt+NumPad5) or just the rows you want to move. Next, open the Row tab in the Cell Height and Width dialog box. To indent the table, enter a new value in the Indent **F**rom Left list box.

To center the rows, click on the Center radio button in the Alignment group. To right-align the rows, click on the **R**ight button. As shown in Figure 3.30, these buttons have no effect on the alignment of text within an individual cell; they move the table or selected rows. Alignment matters only if your table is narrower than your margins—otherwise, it has no effect.

Figure 3.30

Left-, Center-, and Right-
aligned tables

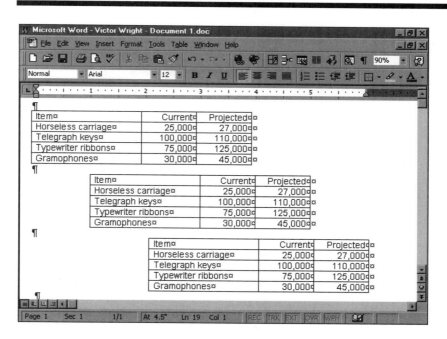

TIP. *One common use for center-aligning tables is to create figures. These figures are often preceded by captions, as shown in this book. To make sure Word always prints the caption on the same page as the table, use the Keep with *N*ext pagination setting in the Format Paragraph dialog box.*

Setting Tabs from within a Table

Why bother with setting tabs within a table? After all, the table looks like tabbed text, and you can even use paragraph alignment to create left, center, and right alignments within a cell. It turns out there are several reasons to use tabs within a table, and one of the best is Word's decimal tab feature, which enables you to line up numbers over a decimal point, as shown in Figure 3.31. Also, you might occasionally have to line up several columns within an individual cell. Often it is easier to use tabs than to add cells and adjust their line widths.

Figure 3.31

Lining up numbers with the decimal tab

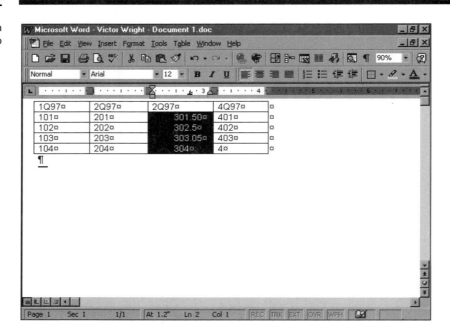

To set tabs in the ruler, select the rows you want to add tab stops for (or press Alt+NumPad5 to select the entire table). Click on the tab box next to the ruler to choose a left, center, right, or decimal tab. Then, as shown in Figure 3.32, click in the ruler where you want the tab to appear.

Adding Table Borders and Shading

In the earlier section "Autoformatting a Table," you already saw how Word's Table AutoFormat feature makes use of borders and shading to make tables easier to read and more attractive. You can use borders and shading not only to make your tables easier to read, but also to fool Word into displaying shapes and sizes that cannot easily be created any other way.

To add a border to an entire table, select the table (Alt+NumPad5), choose Format, Borders and Shading, and choose the Borders tab (see Figure 3.33). To add borders to specific cells, select them before choosing Format, Borders and Shading.

Figure 3.32

Setting a table's tabs
using the ruler

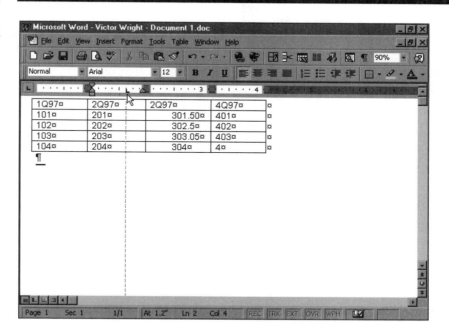

Figure 3.33

The Borders tab in the
Table Borders and
Shading dialog box

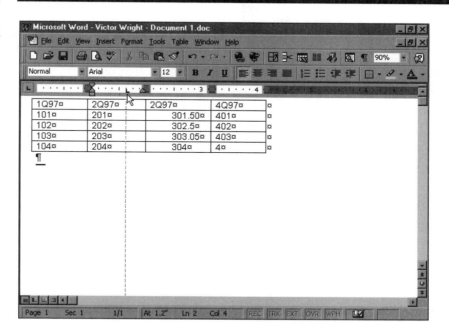

At the left, Word presents the five border approaches it expects you to use most often: None, Box, All, Grid, and Custom. None displays no borders. Box places a ½-point border around the edge of the table, with no border between cells inside. All, the default setting, places a ½-point border around all edges of the table. Grid places a 1-point border around the edge of the table, and a ½-point border around every cell, and Custom creates a custom border using the options you click in the Preview diagram. (Word automatically selects custom if you click on any of the border buttons in the Preview diagram.) When you choose any of these five options, a sketch of the results appears in the Border section at the bottom left of the dialog box.

NOTE. *The Grid box appears only if you choose multiple cells within a table and nothing else. If you choose one cell, or if you choose text inside and outside a table, the Shadow box appears instead, as shown in Figure 3.34.*

Figure 3.34

The Shadow box

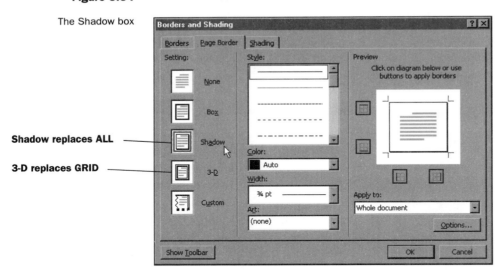

Shadow replaces ALL

3-D replaces GRID

None, Box, All, Grid, Shadow, and 3-D take care of most generic bordering, but you can individually control the left, right, top, and bottom borders of your table—or any cell within it by using the Custom setting.

To set or change the border of only one side of a table, first click the edge you want to border in the Border box. Then click the border you want. You also can choose a color for your border. Click on the Color list box and select from the options in Figure 3.35.

Figure 3.35

Border color choices

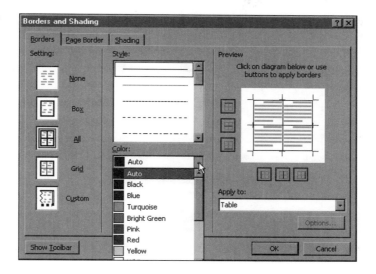

Setting Borders with the Keyboard

With a keyboard, setting borders is clumsy, but still possible. In the dialog box, press the Tab and Shift-Tab keys to move to and from the Borders settings, Styles, Colors, Apply to, and Preview option groups. Press the letter corresponding to the option you want or use the arrow keys. The Preview area includes buttons corresponding to the border sides. These buttons can be used to apply borders to specific sides of an apply to area (see Figure 3.36).

Changing Preset Boxes and Grids

Although Word has default settings for its boxes and grids, you can change them. To change the Box border, first select it, then choose a different border from the Line area.

To change the Grid area, first select it. To change the outside borders, choose a different border from the Line area. To change the inside borders of each individual cell, click in the middle of the thumbnail sketch, then choose a new border from the Line area.

Figure 3.36

Bordering the left edge of
a table using the keyboard

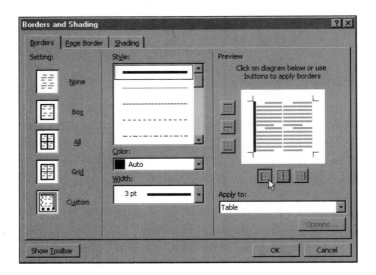

Using Borders Selectively

Remember, you can create individual borders for every cell. This enables
you to perform all sorts of tricks, such as setting up the bowling score form
shown in Figure 3.37. This table is actually a four-line table, with the first and
third lines containing the bowlers' names and pin counts (strikes, spares, and
so on). The second and fourth lines contain the running scores.

Except for the column containing the bowlers' names, the first and third
rows contain twice as many cells as the second and fourth rows, but each cell
is half as wide. That makes it possible to create the small bordered box at the
top right in each frame, where strikes and spares are recorded.

This works only because Word handles Space Between Columns the way
it does. If it actually placed space between every column, instead of just
marking the column edges off-limits for text, the narrower columns would
quickly become misaligned.

After the first small box is bordered, all the others are bordered by using
the Repeat command, F4. When complete, the entire table is bordered by
using the Box button.

Figure 3.37

Bowling form created
with tables

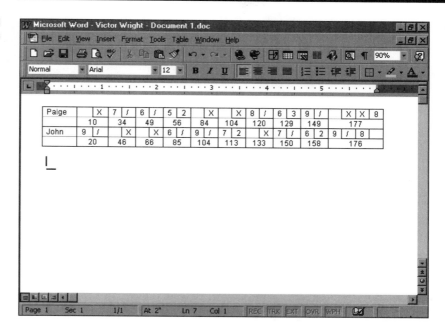

TIP. *You also can use selective borders to imitate placing two tables next to each other, something Word does not normally do. Border some cells at left, then border the cells at right, then select cells between them and eliminate their borders (see Figure 3.38).*

NOTE. *Sometimes you might want your tables to stay in a specific location on the page regardless of what other editing takes place on the page. You might want to place a table on the right-hand side, for example, and have your text flow around it. To do that, Frame your table (see Chapter 17, "Desktop Publishing and Drawing," for more information).*

Shading

As with any other paragraph, you also can create shading in part or all of a table. Select the cell or cells you want; then choose Format, Borders and Shading, and choose the Shading tab, as shown in Figure 3.39. Unless you have a color printer, you might not be too concerned about which colors to change.

NOTE. *Even if you don't have a color printer, you might want to experiment; colors might print differently even on a black-and-white printer.*

Figure 3.38

Turning one table into two

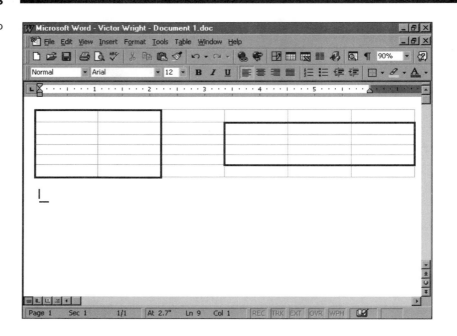

Figure 3.39

Shading tab box

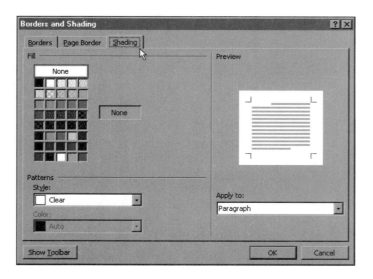

Shading might be more useful than colors on a day-to-day basis. Choosing it enables you to add many different kinds of shading to individual cells. Be careful with shading. Text that is printed over shaded text is much less readable. In general, unless the cell is intentionally left blank (as, for example, some cells on tax forms), don't use more than 20 percent shading for text to be printed on a laser or inkjet printer.

TIP. *The readability of shading depends on the quality of your printer. You can get away with darker shading if your text is sent to a Linotronic or other typesetting machine at 1,200 dots per inch. If you are working with a 9-pin dot-matrix printer, you might want to avoid shading altogether, or limit it to 10 percent, or you might want to boldface the text in a shaded area, so it will stand out more.*

The Shading list box also provides several custom patterns, as shown in Figure 3.40.

Figure 3.40

Custom shading available

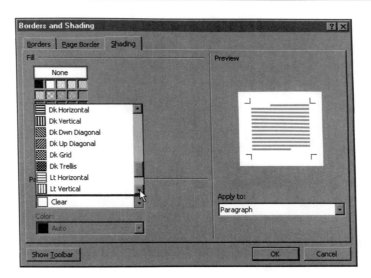

Merging Cells

Occasionally, you will create a table with information in separate cells and later decide the information should be merged into a single cell. You might, for example, realize you don't have enough room (width) to create all those columns—but you do have room to extend them vertically.

Merging cells solves this problem. Select the cells you want to merge, and choose T̲able, M̲erge Cells. Word combines all the selected cells in each row into a single cell. The information that originally was in separate cells is separated with a paragraph marker within each new cell. The new cell is the same width as all the previous cells combined. To narrow it, use the Column W̲idth tools covered earlier. Figures 3.41 and 3.42 show a typical before-and-after example of using Merge Cells.

Figure 3.41

Before Merge Cells

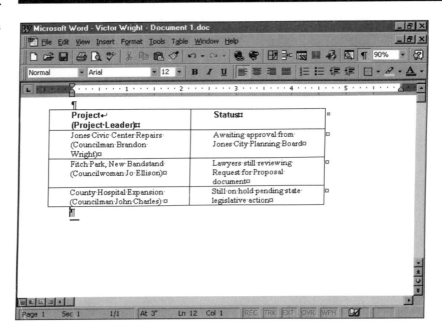

If you decide to split the cells again, select them and choose Split Cells, which appears instead of M̲erge Cells in the T̲able menu. By the way, Word's Split Cells feature can split cells even if they were not previously merged. Select the cell or cells you want to split; choose S̲plit Cells from the T̲able menu. The Split Cells dialog box opens; specify how many columns you want to split each cell into. After you split a cell that was not previously merged, any text that originally appeared in that cell will appear in the first of the smaller cells you've created.

Figure 3.42

After Merge Cells

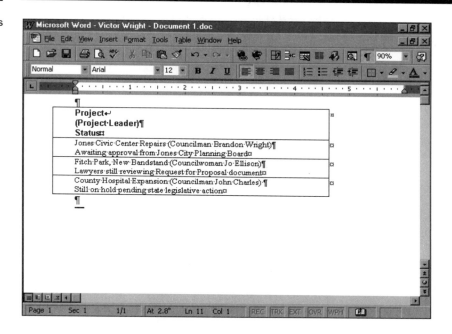

Converting Text to Tables and Vice Versa

Sometimes you might want to convert text into a table format, or the other way around. For example:

- You might have an old table created using tabs; you now want to revise it, and it is easier to make the revisions with the information in table format.

- You might have a print merge or database file that was created or exported in tab-delimited or comma-delimited format.

- You might have text that you decide would simply look better in table format.

To create a table by using existing text, select the text, and choose Table, Convert Text to Table. The Convert Text to Table dialog box appears, as shown in Figure 3.43.

When the dialog box opens, Word shows you its best guess as to the number of columns that will be required and how you want the text to be separated. If, for example, you have selected tabbed material, Word will probably think you want to Separate Text At Tabs. If the only breaks Word can find are paragraph marks, Separate Text At Paragraphs is likely to be marked. You can change this and even specify a custom character of your own.

You can either specify the column width yourself or autoformat the table by using Word's borders and shading features and AutoFit mechanism for specifying column width.

Figure 3.43

The Convert Text to Table
dialog box

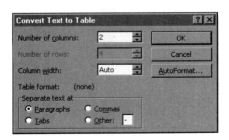

Given a choice, you will generally find it easier to convert text where tabs or commas split cells than where all you have is paragraph marks. First, much of the text you will want to reformat as tables probably was originally created with tabs. (Commas usually are used with exported database files.) A more important reason, however, is the difference in how Word handles the text-to-table conversion.

When you are converting from tabbed or comma-delimited material, Word will recognize a paragraph mark (or line break) as its cue to start a new row. Word also is smart enough to create a table that accommodates the line with the most commas or tabs. All this means you can easily convert long lists of text into tables.

However, if you choose paragraph marks, Word can no longer tell when to end a row. It places each paragraph (or each chunk of text ending with a line break) in its own row. The result is a one-column table.

If you have a table of moderate length, you can use Edit Replace to swap all the paragraph marks (^p) in the selected text for tabs (^t). Then manually restore the paragraph marks where you want each row to end. Finally, use Table, Convert Text to Table.

Text-to-Table Conversions Traps to Avoid

If you are converting from tabbed text, whenever Word sees a tab, it places the text that follows the tab in a new cell to its right. Sometimes people use extra tabs to make sure all the text lines up properly, as in Figure 3.44.

Figure 3.44

Tabbed copy using
uneven tabs, before and
after

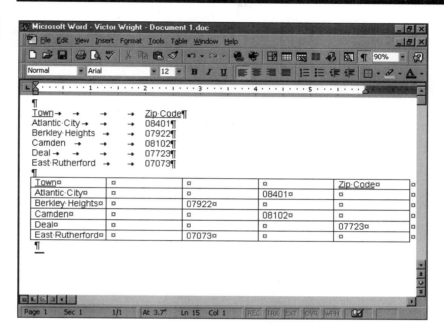

Extra tabs can create havoc when you convert from text to table, because Word will create unwanted empty cells. Of course, this would not have happened if custom tabs were set, rather than using 0.5" default tabs.

If you are converting from comma-delimited text, be careful to make sure that your document contains commas only where you want cell breaks. Sometimes a comma is really just a comma. It is easy to be thrown off by city/state addresses (Fort Myers, FL would be split into two columns) and by numbers (1,000,000 would be split into three columns).

TIP. *Undoing Text-to-Table. If you don't like the results of your Text-to-Table conversion, use Undo Insert Table immediately. If you change your mind later, you can still revert to text by using Convert Table to Text, as described next. But you have to accurately specify whether to divide the table by using paragraph marks, tabs, or commas. If you use tabs, you might also need to adjust the tab settings Word creates, which match the cell borders of the table you just eliminated.*

Converting Tables to Text

Word also can convert tables back to text. Select the table (or rows) you want to convert. (Word does not convert only some of the cells in a row.) Choose Convert Table to Text. The Convert Table to Text dialog box opens, as shown in Figure 3.45. You are asked whether to use paragraph marks, tabs, commas, or another character to divide the information in text. Choose an option, and click on OK.

Figure 3.45

The Convert Table to Text dialog box

Repeating Row Headings on Multiple Pages

What happens when you have several pages of tables, and you would like them all to share the same headings, such as a product list like that shown in Figure 3.46. Word has a Headings feature specifically designed to do the job.

Figure 3.46

Excerpt from product list

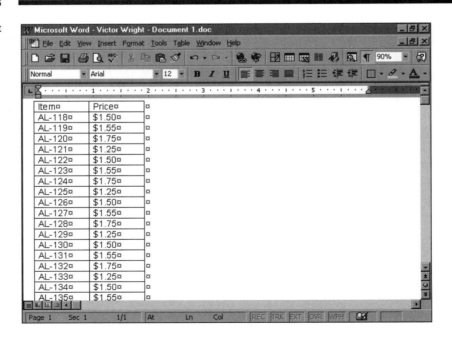

To use Headings, first create your table, including the row you want to repeat. Then select the row, and choose T<u>a</u>ble, <u>H</u>eadings. Now, if the table jumps to a second page, the marked heading repeats at the top of that page.

To tell whether a heading will repeat on multiple pages, select it and see if <u>H</u>eadings has a check mark next to it in the T<u>a</u>ble menu. To stop a heading from repeating, select it and uncheck <u>H</u>eadings in the T<u>a</u>ble menu.

Splitting Tables to Insert Text

What if you want to include non-table text in the middle of a table? Word provides for that, too. Place your insertion point where you want to add text, and choose T<u>a</u>ble, <u>S</u>plit Table. This splits the table into two parts and places a paragraph mark between them, as shown in Figure 3.47.

Figure 3.47

Using the Split Table feature

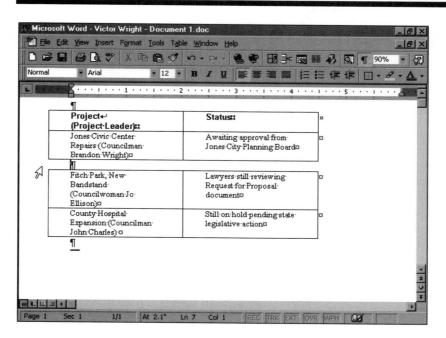

TIP. *What happens when you create a table at the beginning of a document, and you then want to write something before it? You can't move your insertion point in front of the table. Even moving to the beginning of the document (Ctrl+Home) won't do it. The solution? Place your insertion point in the first cell of the table and choose T<u>a</u>ble, <u>S</u>plit Table.*

A Simple Table Calculation

Basic tables look tantalizingly like spreadsheets. In fact, a Word table can actually be made to perform a wide variety of relatively complex calculations. (You can also open Microsoft Excel, if you have it, directly from within Word and perform every imaginable sort of spreadsheet trickery.)

What if you simply want to add up a list of numbers? Imagine you have the table shown in Figure 3.48.

Figure 3.48

Bill of sale

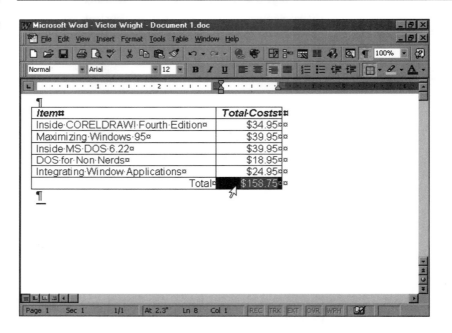

To add the numbers, place your insertion point in an empty cell beneath (or to the right of) the list, and choose Tools, Formula. The Formula dialog box appears, already containing a formula such as =SUM(ABOVE) or =SUM(LEFT) (see Figure 3.49). Click on OK, and Word adds the column or row. You also can choose a Number Format from the list box, which includes dollar and percentage formats.

From here, you also can write your own formula in any table cell. Word cell references are similar to those in Microsoft Excel; the top left cell in a table is called A1. Rows are numbered, columns are lettered. To subtract cell A1 from cell A2, use the following formula: =A2-A1. To multiply cell A1 by cell A2, use the following formula: =A1*A2. To divide cell A1 by cell A2, use the following formula: =A1/A2.

Figure 3.49

The Formula dialog box

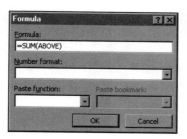

Word offers a variety of functions that also can be used in table formulas. These are available in the Paste Function box.

Finally, your formulas can include numbers from anywhere in your document. Mark the number you want to include as a bookmark. Select it, choose Edit, Bookmark, name the bookmark, and click on OK. Then insert the bookmark in your formula by picking it from the list in Paste Bookmark. (For more on bookmarks, see Chapter 16, "Bookmarks.")

You do not need to be in a table to use the Formula command (although it often simplifies life to work from a table).

A Simple Table Sort

Sorting is another simple trick you can perform anywhere in Word, but you are especially likely to use sorting in tables. Say you wanted to sort alphabetically the list of entertainers in Figure 3.50.

Select the table and choose Table, Sort. The Sort dialog box appears, as shown in Figure 3.51. You can specify up to three levels of sorting. Imagine you have a table in which column 1 includes company names, column 2 includes cities, and column 3 includes names of sales representatives for these companies. You could tell Word to sort first based on company names; after those are in order, to sort based on cities; and finally on the sales representatives' names.

You would get a neatly ordered list of companies, in which each company's listings were sorted by city, and each company's city listings were sorted alphabetically by name.

You also can tell Word to sort a table alphabetically based on text, sort a field based on date order, or sort a field in numeric order. (These sorts can have different results.) You also can specify whether each sort should appear in ascending or descending order.

Word solves an annoying problem: What do you do about the top row? You don't want to sort it, but then you would have to select every line except the top row—a pain in the neck. Now you can tell Word your top row is a Header Row, and Word leaves it alone.

Figure 3.50

List of entertainers

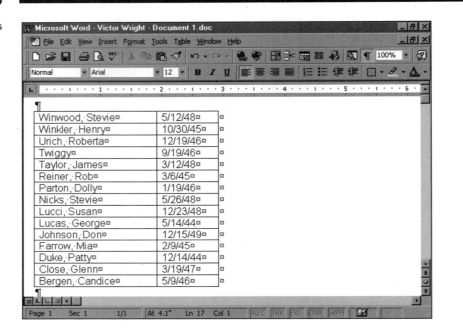

Figure 3.51

The Sort dialog box

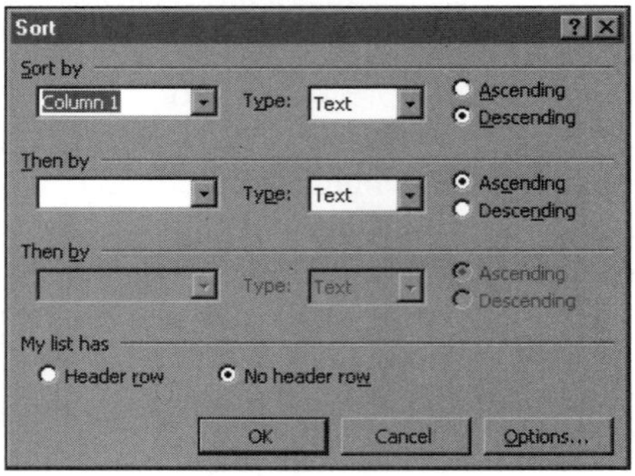

To sort only a single column without moving any text in other columns, select the column, choose Table, Sort, and then choose Options. The Sort Options dialog box appears (see Figure 3.52). Choose Sort Column Only.

Figure 3.52

The Sort Options dialog box

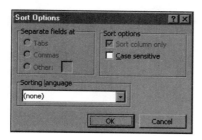

Normally, Word sorts are not case-sensitive: march and March are listed next to each other. If you want Word to separate them, listing all capitalized words before lowercase words, choose Case Sensitive in the Sort Options box.

If you are sorting a list that is not in a table, you have to specify a separator in Sort Options: tabs, commas, or another character.

If you want to alphabetize the names in the first column, A to Z, the settings are right. Click on OK. But what if, for instance, you wanted to find the youngest entertainer? For this example, follow these steps:

1. Select the table (Alt+NumPad5).

2. Choose Tools, Sort.

3. Choose Column 2 from the Sort By list box.

4. Choose Date from the Type list box.

5. Choose Descending.

6. Click on OK.

There you are, youngest to oldest, in Figure 3.53.

In this chapter, you learned how to create tables and then manipulate them in virtually every way imaginable, for virtually every *use* imaginable. Next, in Chapter 4, you'll learn how to use Word's print feature, As with tables, you can do things with Print you probably never imagined. Stick with us: we'll cover just about all of them.

Figure 3.53

Organizing names, youngest to oldest

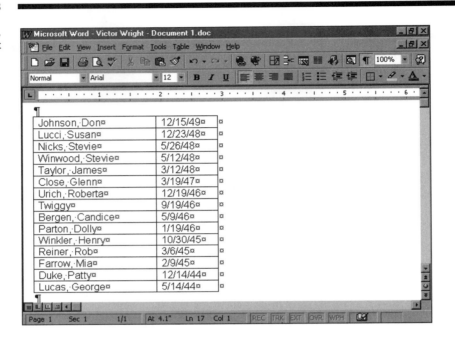

- *Getting Your Printer Ready to Print*
- *Basic Word Printing*
- *Controlling How and What Prints*
- *Printing Envelopes and Labels*
- *Printing Several Files at Once*
- *Printing to File*
- *Using Print Preview*

- *Printing to Fax*

Printing and Faxing: The Complete Guide

W ORD 97 GOES FAR BEYOND THE USUAL CONCEPT OF PRINTING—merely producing a hard copy of a document. Using Word, you can print your document with a single button click, but that's just the beginning. You can also print comprehensive information *about* your documents, or print specific *elements* of your documents, or even print your documents organized in specific views, such as outlines. You can even print postal bar codes that can save you money on postage.

While printing to paper is still critical in most business environments, you can also "print" your documents to fax, to an electronic file, or as e-mail attachments. And with Windows 95 or Windows NT, you can even print Word files from *outside* Word, using the QuickView file viewer or drag-and-drop printing.

In short, Word 97, working with Windows 95 or Windows NT, gives you nearly total control over what you print, and where and how you print it. That's what this chapter is about: taking all the control Word gives you, to get your documents printed as quickly and as well as possible.

■ Getting Your Printer Ready to Print

If you're setting up your computer and printer for the first time, you'll need to make sure they're both working properly together before you can use Word's printing features. To do so, you need to install a printer driver that is compatible with the operating system you are using, either Windows 95 or Windows NT.

The easiest way to install a printer in Windows 95 is to use the Add Printer Wizard. From the Windows 95 Start menu, choose Settings, Printers. The Printers window opens; double-click on Add Printer. The Add Printer Wizard runs as shown in Figure 4.1. Walk through the steps the Add Printer Wizard provides, including:

- Specifying whether you are adding a local printer or a printer that is connected to another computer on your network

- Choosing a printer from the category of printers and manufacturers provided by the Wizard

- Inserting your Windows 95 disk or the driver disk that came with your printer

- Specifying a port your printer will use, commonly LPT1

If you've installed more than one printer, you'll need to tell Word which printer you want to use. Display the Print dialog box, and select the printer you want to use from the Name drop-down box.

■ Basic Word Printing

Now that your printer is set up, basic Word printing is as simple as it gets. Click the Print button in the Standard toolbar (see Figure 4.2). Word sends one copy of your entire document to your current printer (assuming that the printer is turned on and hooked up properly).

Figure 4.1

The Add Printer Wizard

Figure 4.2

The Print button immediately prints one copy of your document, without displaying a dialog box.

Much of the time—maybe most of the time—that's all you need to know about printing. At other times, however, you'll want to take advantage of Word's more sophisticated printing options which require more than clicking on the Print button. The rest of this chapter covers those other times.

■ Controlling How and What Prints

Word lets you control how and what it prints through the Print dialog box, available by choosing the **P**rint option on the **F**ile menu (see Figure 4.3). Or just press Ctrl+P. The Print dialog box was revamped in Word 95 but hasn't changed in Word 97. As always, the simplest thing you can do is print one copy of your document. To do that, just choose the OK button. As you can see, however, you have some other choices.

The choice you may use most often is Number of **c**opies. You can choose to print as many copies as you want. When you print multiple copies, you have another choice to make: Should Word collate the printed copies?

By default, Word automatically collates multiple copies of your document by sending the document to the printer, waiting a moment, and then sending it again. You get output arranged in page order. Because you usually want your document to print in page order, what could be wrong with that?

Figure 4.3

You can control virtually all aspects of printing from the Print dialog box.

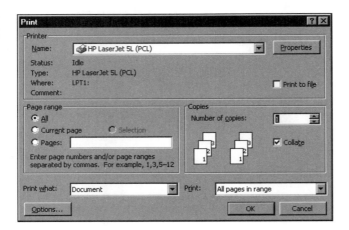

Well, it takes longer. Printers process each page in your document separately. When the second copy of a collated document starts printing, none of the processing for the earlier pages remains in its memory. The processing must all be done over again. This repetitive processing can create significant bottlenecks in your print queue if your documents contain extensive graphics or formatting.

Laser printers can, however, print several *consecutive* copies of the same page without reprocessing them. So if you're willing to manually collate your document—or if you're lucky enough to have someone around to help—you might get your print job done sooner by disabling Word's collating function. To do so, uncheck Collate in the bottom right corner of the Print dialog box.

Printing Part of a Document

Rather than having Word print every page of your document (which it does by default), you can use the Print dialog box to control which pages print. You can print just the page the text insertion point is in by choosing Current page from the Page range section of the dialog box, or you can specify a range of pages to print, or you can print just the text that's selected in the document by choosing the Section option.

The Page range option group on the left side of the Print dialog box enables you to specify the page range you want to print. Specify the pages you want to print in the Pages box. Word understands hyphens and commas in the Pages box as in the following examples:

1–3   prints pages 1 through 3

1,2,6   prints pages 1, 2, and 6

1–3,5,8   prints pages 1 through 3 and pages 5 and 8.

Printing Odd and Even Pages

If you want to print only odd or even pages, you can make this choice from the Print drop-down list. Choose Odd Pages or Even Pages instead of the default, All pages in range.

Printing a Document Outline

In Chapter 10, "Outlining: Get Your Document Organized—Fast!," you'll learn how to organize your document with an outline. Once you've created an outline, it's easy to print your document in outline form, as well. With your document displayed in Outline View, and the outline displayed to the level of detail you want to print, click the Print button.

Printing Accompanying Information

Several other elements are associated with a Word file other than just the document's text and graphics. For example, Word stores Properties—specific information about a document, some of which is tracked automatically by Word, and some of which you can enter. Properties include the document's title, subject, author, and keywords and comments that can help you track the document. You can learn more about Properties in Chapter 6, "File Management: Find What You Need—Now."

Other elements associated with a Word document include a list of the styles used by that document; AutoText boilerplate text entries available to the document; and special keyboard shortcuts the document may have access to. Neither Properties nor these other elements print automatically when you print your document, but Word does provide ways to print them.

In fact, in one of the few changes to printing in Word 97, you can now print *all* of a document's properties, not just the Summary information stored in the Summary tab of the document's property sheet.

You can print Properties and other document elements either with or without printing the accompanying document. To print an element without printing the document, follow these steps:

1. Choose **P**rint from the **F**ile menu.

2. Display the Print **w**hat list box, and choose the element you want to print. The default element is Document, which prints only the document, excluding other document elements.

3. Click on the OK button.

To print an additional element of a file at the same time as you print the document, follow these steps:

1. Choose **O**ptions from the **T**ools menu.

2. Click the Print tab at the top of the dialog box.

3. Check the element in the Include with Document box (see Figure 4.4).

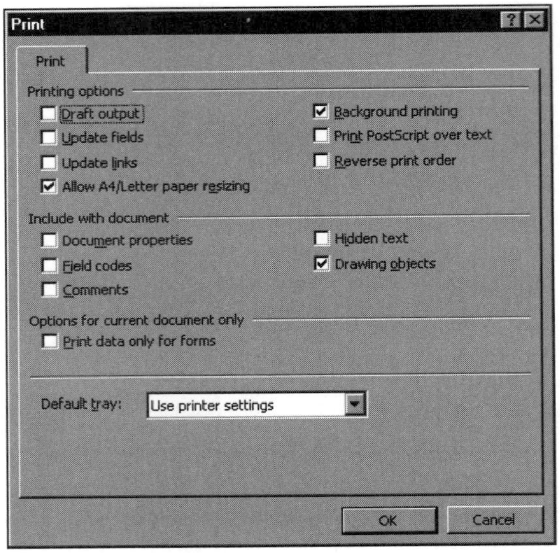

Figure 4.4

The Print Options dialog box allows you to specify the elements you want to print in addition to your document.

Since the controls for printing specific document elements are scattered throughout Word, Table 4.1 lists all the document-related elements you can print, and specifies the command or commands used to print them. In some cases, you must display information in your document before you can print it; these cases are listed in the third column of the table. Since many of these topics have not been covered yet, the first column also shows you where to look in this book for more information.

Controlling Other Printing Options

The Print Options dialog box (Tools, Options, Print) allows you to control virtually all aspects of printing:

- Draft Output—This option prints a document with very little formatting—how little formatting depends on the printer.

Table 4.1

Printing Elements
of Word Files

ELEMENT	INCLUDE WITH DOCUMENT	PRINT SEPARATELY	DISPLAY IN DOCUMENT, THEN PRINT	OTHER
Comments (Chapter 15)	X	X		
AutoText Entries (Chapter 9)		X		
Envelopes (this chapter)				Covered later in this chapter
Field Codes (Chapter 21)	X		X	
Hidden Text	X		X	
Shortcut Key Assignments (Chapter 22)		X		
Changes (Chapter 15)				Tools, Track Changes, Highlight Changes, enable Track changes while editing checkbox, enable Highlight changes in printed document checkbox.
Styles (Chapter 7)		X		
Properties (Chapter 6)	X	X		
Outlines (Chapter 10)				Display Outline View, then print

- **Update Fields**—This feature updates all the fields in your document before printing. See Chapter 21 for more details on fields, which underlie many items Word can insert into your document text, such as dates and times, tables of contents, index entries, and calculations.

- **Update Links**—This feature checks any DDE or OLE connections you've made with other documents or files. If those connections include text that has changed, Word prints the new text.

- **Allow A4/Letter paper resizing**—This new Word 97 feature automatically makes the slight formatting and sizing changes necessary to convert from printing on U.S. standard letter-size paper to the slightly larger European A4 size, or back again. This feature is turned on by default when you install Word.

- Background Printing—As we've already discussed, checking this box enables Word to print in the background, allowing you to go back to work more quickly after you send a print job to the printer, but possibly slowing down the actual printing.

  NOTE. *If you find that Word prints too slowly, try disabling background printing. Follow these steps:*

  1. *Choose **O**ptions from the **T**ools menu.*

  2. *Click the Print tab at the top of the dialog box.*

  3. *Click Background Printing in the Printing Options section to remove the check mark.*

  4. *Click on the OK button.*

  The downside of disabling Background Printing is that Word won't allow you to start working in the file again until it has sent all pages to your printer (or, more precisely, to Windows 95's spooling file). You'll wait a little longer before you can work, but your print job will arrive faster.

- Print PostScript over text—This new Word 97 feature is here for compatibility with Word for the Macintosh documents. It allows PostScript code that may have been placed in a Macintosh Word document to be printed above text, not beneath it. The most common use for this feature is to accommodate watermarks that were created in Word for the Macintosh.

- Reverse Print Order—This feature allows you to print your pages backward.

Changing Paper Sources

Many printers have more than one paper source. For example, many dot-matrix printers can accept pin-fed paper or manual feed. And many laser printers have two or more paper trays: one for stationery, and another for plain paper or envelopes. You can specify a paper source as follows:

1. Choose Page Set**u**p from the **F**ile menu.

2. Click the Paper Source tab (see Figure 4.5).

You can choose different paper sources for the First Page and Other Pages of your document. Most business correspondence uses one type of letterhead for the first page, and another type (or blank paper) for the following pages.

Your choices of paper sources depend on your printer and its accompanying software. Virtually every printer either uses a standard Windows printer

Figure 4.5

The Paper Source tab in the Page Setup dialog box lets you control which paper tray each sheet of your document is printed from and allows you to choose manual feed.

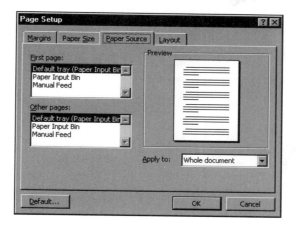

driver or comes with its own driver software, often quite sophisticated, which gives you access to the printer's specific features. If your printer has more than one paper source, your driver software works in tandem with Word and your Windows operating system to allow you to control these paper sources.

If you have a two-tray laser printer, for example, you can instruct Word to load first-page letterhead from one tray, and the remaining sheets from another. Even if you only have one tray, you can specify manual feed for the first page and automatic feed for the remaining pages. You also may want to use manual feed if you have specified an unusual size of paper that your paper tray cannot handle.

Now that you know how to change the paper source for a specific document or part of a document, here's how to change the default paper source Word uses unless you tell it otherwise:

1. Choose **T**ools, **O**ptions, Print.

2. Select the source you want from the Default **t**ray list box.

■ Printing Envelopes and Labels

One of Word's niftiest features is how it automates envelope and label printing—a process that was once tedious and difficult, especially if you were working with large or non-standard envelopes.

In the simplest example, let's assume that you've written a standard business letter, where the recipient's name and address appear at the top, beneath the date.

To print an accompanying envelope, choose Envelopes and Labels from the **T**ools menu. The dialog box shown in Figure 4.6 appears. Word searches your letter for the places that you're most likely to have included an address, and if it finds something that looks like an address, it places this information in the **D**elivery Address box on the **E**nvelopes tab.

Figure 4.6

The Envelopes and Labels dialog box, showing the name and address Word has picked up from your letter.

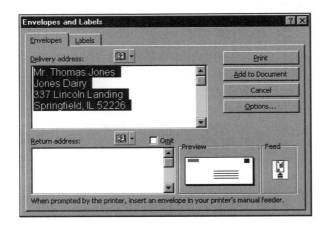

If Word cannot find an address, it leaves the space blank. Occasionally, it may find three other lines that seem to fit the general form of an address but don't. Whether Word's guess is right or wrong, you can edit it in the Delivery Address box.

Word also pulls your own return address from the User Information tab in Tools, Options. You can edit your address in the Return address box in the Envelopes and Labels dialog box, if necessary. If you want no return address, check the Omit box.

NOTE. *You can specify the Delivery and Return Address text yourself if you don't want to let Word find them for you in your document. You can tell Word to flag specific text as the delivery address or return address by using two specific markers (called bookmarks) named EnvelopeAddress and EnvelopeReturn. Follow these steps:*

1. Select the text you want to use as your outgoing or return address.

2. Choose Bookmark from the Insert menu.

*3. In the Bookmark name box, type **EnvelopeAddress** for an outgoing address, or EnvelopeReturn for a return address. (Type these as one word, no spaces.)*

4. Choose Add.

Bookmarks are covered in more detail in Chapter 12.

Getting a Delivery or Return Address from a Personal Address Book

If you have the Microsoft Exchange e-mail client that comes with Windows 95 installed on your computer, or if you have installed Microsoft Outlook, the new personal information manager that comes with Microsoft Office 97, you can also get a delivery or return address from a list of names stored in a Personal Address Book.

Personal Address Books are listings of contacts, phone numbers, fax numbers and other information that is associated with Microsoft's Windows 95 programs designed for sending and receiving messages. In order to use a Personal Address Book from within Word, you must have installed and configured one of these messaging programs, and entered contact information in its Personal Address Book. If you have installed *both* Exchange and Outlook, you may have two address books; if so, you will have to choose the one you want to work with. You may also access information from a Microsoft Schedule+ Contact List.

For either the delivery or return address, click the Address Book icon associated with either the Delivery Address or Return Address areas of the Envelopes and Labels dialog box (see Figure 4.6). The Select Name dialog box appears, as shown in Figure 4.7. The first time you do this, you may first be asked to specify which Microsoft Exchange Profile to use. Microsoft Exchange Profiles are default settings that indicate how messages will be delivered to and from a mailbox, specify server connections and passwords, and list the information services that are available to the user of a program. For example, one Microsoft Exchange Profile might include access to Microsoft Fax for sending faxes through a local modem; another profile might allow faxes to be sent via a faxmodem connected across a network, and also provide access to The Microsoft Network information service.

Profiles may also specify which of several Personal Address Books should be used. When asked which profile to use, select the Profile containing the address book with the addresses you need. (Note that Exchange must not only be installed but configured before you can use this feature.)

Next, select the name you want to appear in the Delivery or Return address box. Word inserts the name as it appears in your Personal Address Book.

As you add names to either the Delivery or Return Address box, Word stores these names, so you don't have to choose from your entire Address Book list the next time you use them. To choose from the list of names Word has already accessed from Exchange or Outlook, click the down-arrow next to the Address Book button, as shown in Figure 4.8. Click the name you want to use. By the way, Word stores different lists of names for the **D**elivery and **R**eturn Address boxes, so adding a name to one box won't add it to the other.

Figure 4.7

Selecting a name from
the Personal Address
Book

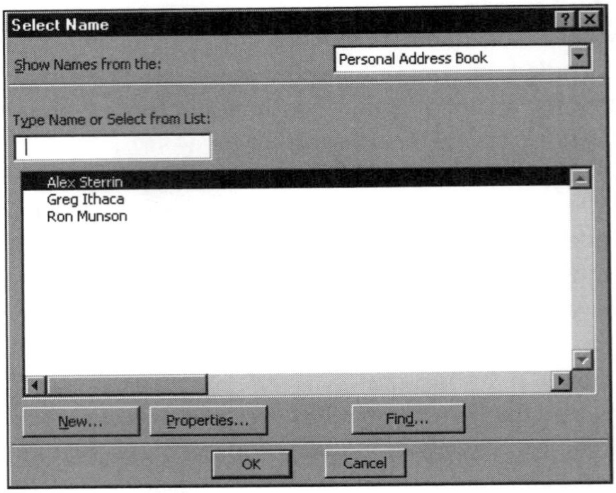

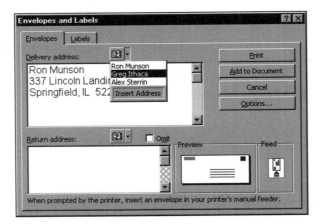

Figure 4.8

Selecting a name by
clicking the down-arrow
next to the Address
Book button

NOTE. *If you have both Exchange and Outlook address books installed, Word 97 can access either of them. When the Select Name dialog box opens, choose Personal Address Book or Outlook Address Book from the Show Names from the box.*

Printing an Envelope—Now or Later

Assuming that you use a standard (#10) business envelope, and that your addresses are correct, you can simply print the envelope by clicking the **P**rint button. Word prompts you to insert an envelope into your printer's manual feed mechanism.

If you're not ready to print yet, you can tell Word to add the envelope to the beginning of your document as a section. Then, when you print the document, Word prompts you to insert the envelope first. To add an envelope to the beginning of your document, choose **A**dd to Document in the Envelopes and Labels dialog box.

Understanding Envelope Printing Options

You've just learned the basics of envelope printing. But that's just the beginning: Word allows you to control all these elements as well:

- What kind of envelopes you use
- How the addresses look and where they appear on the envelope
- Whether the envelopes use postal bar codes
- How the envelopes feed into your printer

Changing Envelope Formatting

To change the formatting of the addresses on your envelope, click the **O**ptions button in the Envelopes and Labels dialog box. The Envelope Options dialog box, shown in Figure 4.9, opens. It provides near-total control over how your delivery and return addresses look and where they print on the envelope.

Figure 4.9

The Envelope Options dialog box is your control center for printing envelopes.

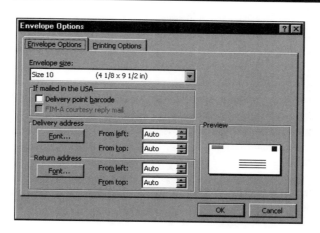

To change the appearance of the typeface used in either the delivery address or return address, choose Font in the appropriate section of the Envelope Options dialog box. If you click the Font button in the Delivery address section of the Envelope Options dialog box, the Envelope Address dialog box opens, as shown in Figure 4.10. It's much like the Font dialog box you've already seen.

You can choose a font, font style, size, and font effects. You also can click the Character Spacing tab to control letter spacing, height, and kerning.

Figure 4.10

You can control the font and character spacing used on envelopes through the Envelope Address and Envelope Return Address dialog boxes, which closely resemble the standard Font dialog box.

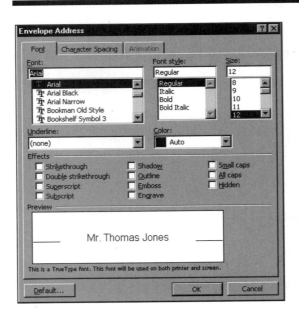

When you have the envelope address formatting the way you want it, choose OK.

NOTE. *If you want all the envelopes you print with your current template to look like the custom envelope design you've just established, choose Default in the Envelope Address or Envelope Return Address dialog box. Then choose Yes to confirm the change (see Figure 4.11). Word changes your current envelope template so that all future envelopes based on it use the new formatting you've specified. For more information on how Word uses templates as the basis for creating both envelopes and other documents, see Chapter 8, "Templates, Wizards and Add-Ins: Smart Shortcuts for Nearly Every Document."*

Figure 4.11

Changing the default envelope address font

Microsoft Word

Do you want to change the default envelope address font to Times New Roman, 12 pt?

This change will affect all new documents based on the NORMAL template.

[Yes] [No]

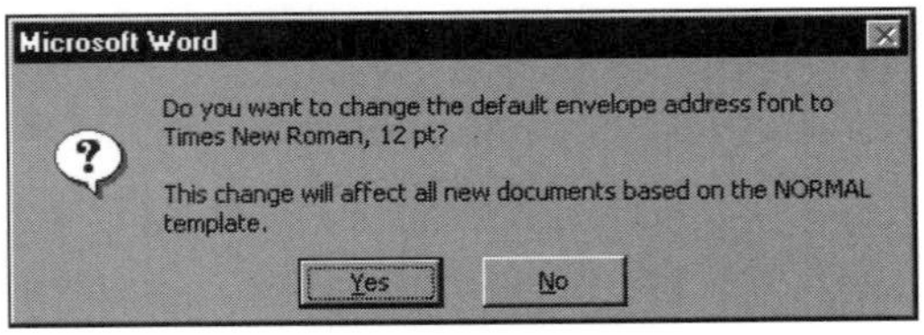

You also can control where the addresses appear by changing the From **L**eft and From Top settings in both the Delivery Address and Return Address boxes by clicking the Options button in the Envelopes tab of the Envelopes and Tables dialog box, and then making changes in the Envelope Options dialog box.

Notice that the default positions for the delivery and return addresses prevent you from selecting settings that go beyond the edges your printer can print, or the edges of the envelope you've specified, or beyond the areas that are acceptable to the U.S. Postal Service. For instance, you can't set the delivery address to be less than 1" from the left edge or less than 1.5" from the top edge of the envelope. You can, however, override these settings by manually entering positions in the From **l**eft and From **t**op boxes in the Envelope Options dialog box.

Changing Envelope Sizes

By default, Word expects you to use a standard business envelope—normally referred to as a #10 envelope. Word previews how your printed envelope should look in the Preview box. If you're using a different kind of envelope, click on the Preview area to get to the Envelope Options dialog box. From the Envelope Size list box, you can choose any of the built-in envelope sizes described in Table 4.2.

Table 4.2

Default Envelope Sizes
Available in Word

ENVELOPE NAME	SIZE
Size #10 (Standard)	4 1/8" x 9 1/2"
Size #6 3/4	3 5/8" x 6 1/2"
Monarch	3 7/8" x 7 1/2"
Size #9	3 7/8" x 8 7/8"
Size #11	4 1/2" x 10 3/8"
Size #12	4 3/4" x 11"
DL	110 mm x 220 mm
C4	29 mm x 324 mm
C5	162 mm x 229 mm
C6	114 mm x 162 mm
C65	114 mm x 229 mm

You also can create a custom-size envelope, which you might need if you're designing a special mailing piece. (If you're looking for a way to spend a great deal of money in a hurry, printing nonstandard custom envelopes will do quite nicely!)

Choose Custom Size, and the Envelope Size dialog box opens, as shown in Figure 4.12. Set the **W**idth and He**i**ght measurements and choose OK. In the Feed Method box located on the Printing Options tab, you can click on the orientation you want. Word also enables you to insert your envelopes Face Down, or in the opposite direction (Clockwise Rotation).

Figure 4.12

The Envelope Size dialog box allows you to control your envelope's height and width.

If, for some reason, you force an envelope orientation that Word doesn't agree with, you'll get a warning message and an opportunity to Reset the orientation to Word's default for your printer. You can ignore this message, if necessary.

If your printer has a special envelope tray, you can feed from that tray, instead of using Manual Feed, by selecting the Envelope feeder in the Feed from list. After you finish, choose OK.

Adding Graphics to an Envelope

Most business envelope stationery includes some form of logo or graphic accompanying the return address. With Word, you can include a graphic next to the return address, without paying for printed stationery. Perform the following steps to add a clip art image to your envelope:

1. Choose **E**nvelopes and Labels from the **T**ools menu.

2. In the **E**nvelopes tab, click the **A**dd to Document button. This inserts the envelope as a new section at the beginning of your document. (The envelope becomes Page 0, so it doesn't affect the page numbering of your document.)

3. Position the insertion point where you want the graphic to be placed.

4. Choose Insert, Picture, Clipart.

5. Select the desired clip art image from the Insert Picture dialog box.

6. Click the Insert button.

7. Resize the graphic, if necessary, by dragging one of the white sizing handles surrounding the image.

You can also import a graphic from another program's clip art library—or a scanned logo. Or you could use Microsoft WordArt to design special type effects. (WordArt and other Word graphics tools are covered in Chapters 17–19.)

After you create a design for your return address, you may want to include it on all your envelopes from now on. To do this, perform the following steps:

1. In your document (Page 0), select all the text and graphics you've designed.

2. Choose Insert, AutoText, New.

3. In the Create AutoText dialog box, type **EnvelopeExtra1.**

4. Choose OK.

Adding Bar Codes to Your Envelopes

By now you've doubtless noticed that much of the mail you receive contains special postal bar codes. Two different kinds of postal bar codes are generally used:

- *POSTNET.* These codes are simply ZIP codes translated into bar code language that the U.S. Postal Service computers can read.

- *Facing Identification Marks (FIMs).* These codes flag different kinds of Courtesy Reply Mail. (Most of us know this as Business Reply Mail, which uses the FIM-A mark.)

Adding bar codes to your mail has two benefits. First, if you're doing mass mailings that qualify, you can get a lower postal rate. Second, bar-coded mail is sometimes delivered more quickly. (That's the theory, anyway.)

All this leads us to a happy ending: Word can handle this bar coding for you. To add a POSTNET bar code, do the following:

1. Choose **E**nvelopes and Labels from the **T**ools menu.

2. Click the Options button.

3. In the If Mailed in the USA group, check Delivery point barcode.

4. Notice that the FIM-A box now becomes available. That's because you can't have a FIM-A bar without a POSTNET code. (You can, however, use POSTNET codes on standard mail that doesn't need a FIM-A mark.)

5. If you're creating Business Reply Mail, check the FIM-A Courtesy Reply Mail box.

6. Choose OK.

7. Click the Add to Document button or the Print button.

Printing Labels

You also can print a label—or a sheet of labels—using either your delivery or return address. To do so, choose **E**nvelopes and Labels from the **T**ools menu; then click the **L**abels tab, shown in Figure 4.13. Word follows the same rules to find an address to include on your labels as it did finding the address for envelopes. If you've already entered a specific name and address in the **E**nvelopes tab, Word places it in the Labels tab as well. Again, you can edit it if you want. And as with envelopes, you can click the Address Book button to insert names from your Microsoft Exchange Personal Address Book or your Microsoft Outlook Address Book.

Figure 4.13

The Labels tab, showing an address borrowed from a letter

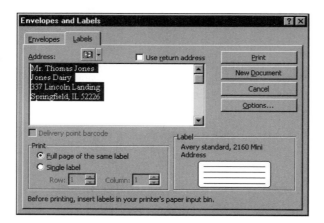

By default, Word assumes that you want the delivery address in the **E**nvelopes, **D**elivery Address box. If you want Word to import your return address, check the Use **R**eturn Address box.

Also by default, Word expects to print a full page of identical copies of the text in the label. Therefore, the **F**ull Page of the Same Label option is automatically selected.

You can, however, click Single label to print only one label. You might want to use this option to create a shipping label for a large envelope or packages, or to create a large return address label.

If you choose to create just one label, Word wants to know which of the labels on your sheet it should print. For example, you might want to print on the second label in the third column of labels.

To print a label in the second row, third column, check Single label. The Row and Column settings become active; enter 2 and 3, respectively.

Word assumes that you manually feed your labels. To tell it otherwise, click the Options button. The Label Options dialog box opens, as shown in Figure 4.14. Select another paper source from the **T**ray drop-down list in the Printer Information section of the dialog box.

Figure 4.14

Select your label, or choose New Label to create a custom label, through the Label Options dialog box.

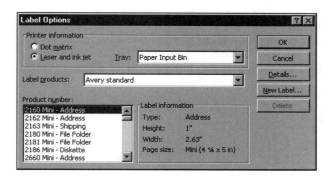

NOTE. *It's always a good idea to spot-check your labels by printing at least some of them on regular paper before using actual labels — which aren't cheap.*

Choosing the Right Label

Unless you're in the label business, you won't believe how many varieties of labels are available. Word supports most popular sizes of labels, especially the Avery brand of computer labels.

The Label **P**roducts box in the Label Options dialog box contains four groups of laser and inkjet labels, as follows:

- Avery Standard
- Avery A4 and A5 sizes
- MACO standard
- Other (includes HP, Inmac, RAJA and UNISTAT labels)

Word also supports the following families of dot-matrix labels:

- Avery Standard
- Avery international (UK)
- Avery international (France)
- CoStar LabelWriter

The laser label choices are displayed by default, even if you have a dot-matrix printer installed as the default printer. To select from the dot-matrix label options, you must first enable Dot **M**atrix in the Printer Information section of the Label Options dialog box.

If none of these label definitions match yours—hard as it is to imagine—you can build your own label. Choose **N**ew Label, and the New Custom Laser dialog box opens, as shown in Figure 4.15. (If you have specified Dot **M**atrix as the printer type, this dialog box is titled New Custom Dot Matrix, and the picture of the label is somewhat different.)

Figure 4.15

The New Custom laser dialog box allows you to control every aspect of a custom label.

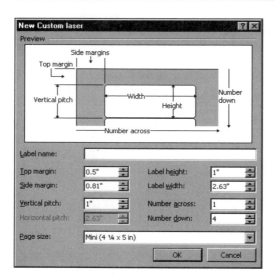

1. Type a name for the label in the **L**abel name box.

2. Select the page size from the drop-down list at the bottom of the dialog box.

3. Set the Number across. This tells Word how many labels are positioned between the left and right margins of the sheet.

4. Set the Number down. This tells Word how many labels are positioned between the top and bottom margins of the sheet.

5. Set the Label height. Notice that Word automatically changes the Vertical pitch setting. (Vertical pitch is the distance from the top of one label to the top of the next label.)

6. Set the Label width. Notice that Word automatically changes the **H**orizontal pitch setting. (Horizontal pitch is the distance from the left edge

of one label to the left edge of the next label. This option will be disabled if your sheet contains only one column of labels.)

7. Adjust the Top margin and Side margin settings, if necessary.

8. Click the OK button to return to the Label Options dialog box. Notice that your custom label is selected in the Product number combo box.

9. Click OK to return to the Envelopes and Labels dialog box.

10. Choose Print or New Document, depending on whether or not you want to send the labels to the printer immediately.

■ Printing Several Files at Once

You can print only one file at a time from the Print dialog box, but Word's File Open dialog box, covered in more detail in Chapter 6, lets you print many files at once.

If you do not have the Word application open, and you want to print more than one Word document in the same folder, here's a quick way to do it: Drag and drop the files to your printer icon (contained in the Printers dialog box that is reachable by clicking Start, Settings, Printers). If you have Word open, it's even easier to print multiple files:

1. Choose **O**pen from the **F**ile menu to open the Search dialog box.

2. Locate and select the first file you want to print.

3. Hold Ctrl as you select the additional files you want to print. All the files will be highlighted.

4. Click the Commands and Settings button or right-click on any of the selected files, and choose **P**rint from the menu that appears (see Figure 4.16).

■ Printing to File

Occasionally you may want to prepare a file to print, but not actually print it. (Perhaps you want to take it to the fancy laser printer at the office, which can print at much higher resolution than your home printer, or has color capabilities whereas your home printer doesn't. Or perhaps you're planning to print a newsletter using your local printing shop. In this case, you may need a file that can be used directly by the shop's typesetting machines, or even a file that can be output "straight to film" — generating materials that can be used to print your newsletter directly, without typesetting. Or maybe you're just out of paper.)

Figure 4.16

Right-clicking on one of the files you've selected displays a shortcut menu.

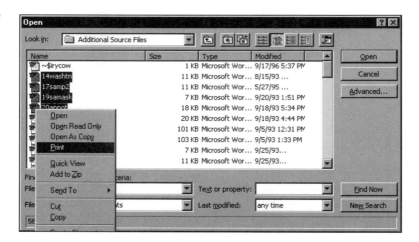

Word allows you to *print to file*—that is, print the document onto a disk that has all the commands a printer needs to print it. To print the active document to a file, perform the following steps:

1. Choose **P**rint from the **F**ile menu.

2. Select the type of printer that the document will actually be printed on. (Word will save the file with the appropriate printer language and instructions.)

3. Check the Print to Fi**l**e checkbox (located on the right side of the dialog box).

4. Choose OK. Word displays the Print to File dialog box, shown in Figure 4.17.

Figure 4.17

In the Print to file box, you can specify the file name and location where you want to print a file containing all printer or PostScript codes that will be needed later to print accurately.

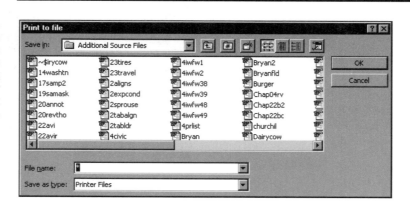

5. Type a name for the file in the File name box.

6. Choose OK.

You now have a file that can be printed. But how? You can't open it in Word and print it—all you get is text interspersed with printer commands. You can't even drag the file to a printer icon, because Windows wants to know what program it should open to interpret the data. If you suggest a program, you're back where you started—text interspersed with printer commands.

The solution is a throwback to the oldest days of MS-DOS: Copy the file to your printer port, from an MS-DOS command session. Here's how:

1. Click Start, choose Programs, and click on MS-DOS Prompt. An MS-DOS window opens, as shown in Figure 4.18.

2. At the command prompt, type the following command (where your file name replaces *FILENAME*):

```
COPY FILENAME.PRN LPT1
```

Figure 4.18

Back to the command line: You can print a .PRN file by copying it to the port your printer is connected to.

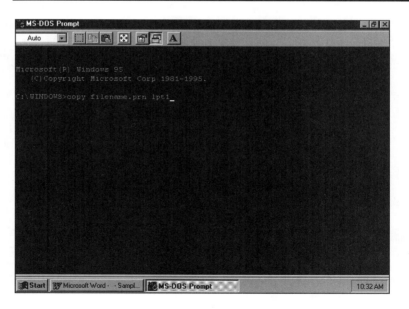

NOTE. *Make sure to include the .PRN extension. If you've used a long file name, use the short file name equivalent, for example, SHOPPI~1.PRN for Shopping List.Prn. You can find the short file name by viewing the file's properties.*

■ Using Print Preview

When you want to preview a document as it will be printed, you can take advantage of Word's highly flexible Print Preview feature. One quick way to get to it is to click the Print Preview button on the Standard toolbar (see Figure 4.19).

Figure 4.19

The Print Preview button

NOTE. *Unfortunately, after you've clicked the Print Preview button, your document might display fairly slowly. One suggestion: If you need to preview the early pages in a long document, make sure to place your insertion point at the beginning of the document, so that Word doesn't take the time to repaginate the whole document before it displays the Print Preview screen.*

You can perform a wide variety of tasks in Print Preview, including viewing, editing, and printing. But first, the basics. Figure 4.20 shows the Print Preview screen. You can see a miniature version of your current document, as well as a toolbar containing several useful options. Whenever you're ready to leave Print Preview, you can click Close, and Word returns you to the view of the document you were using before you selected Print Preview.

Viewing Rulers and Margins in Print Preview

Horizontal and vertical rulers are available in Print Preview, but they are not displayed by default. To see the rulers, choose Rulers from the View menu, or click the View Ruler button on the Print Preview toolbar. When the rulers are displayed, the document's active text margins are displayed in white; nonprinting areas are displayed in gray.

Printing From Within Print Preview

To print one copy of a document from within Print Preview, click on the Print button. If you want more control over how your document prints, choose File, Print to display the same Print dialog box available elsewhere in Word.

Zooming In and Moving Around

While you are viewing the document in Print Preview mode, the mouse pointer becomes a magnifying glass with a plus symbol, as shown in Figure 4.21.

To zoom the document to full size, move the pointer to the region of the page you want to look at more closely, and click. The text enlarges to full

Figure 4.20

The standard Print Preview screen contains the Print Preview toolbar, and, optionally, horizontal and vertical rulers.

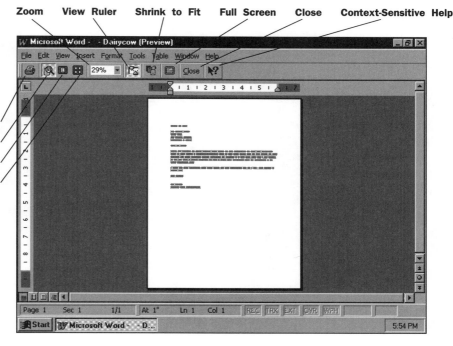

Zoom   View   Ruler   Shrink to Fit   Full Screen   Close   Context-Sensitive Help

Print
Magnifier
One Page
Multiple Pages

size, as shown in Figure 4.22. You can adjust the exact proportion of the text by entering a new percentage in the Zoom box.

If you want to view enlarged text elsewhere on your page, and the text extends beyond the current boundaries of your screen, scroll to it with the vertical or horizontal scroll bars. Keep in mind that the scroll bars take you through the entire document, not just to the top and bottom of the visible page.

NOTE. *To move forward a page in Print Preview, click on the double down arrow button at the bottom of the vertical scroll bar. To move back a page, click on the double up arrow at the bottom of the vertical scroll bar.*

You can make your text area appear a little bigger by hiding screen elements that you might not need. For example, to hide everything except the Print Preview toolbar, click on the Full Screen button on the Print Preview toolbar. Whenever you need a menu, you can make it appear by dragging your mouse pointer up to the very top of the screen and clicking.

When you want to switch from Full Screen view back to the standard Print Preview screen, click the Full Screen button again, or click the Close Full Screen button on the Full Screen toolbar.

Figure 4.21

The magnifying glass
mouse pointer

Mouse pointer

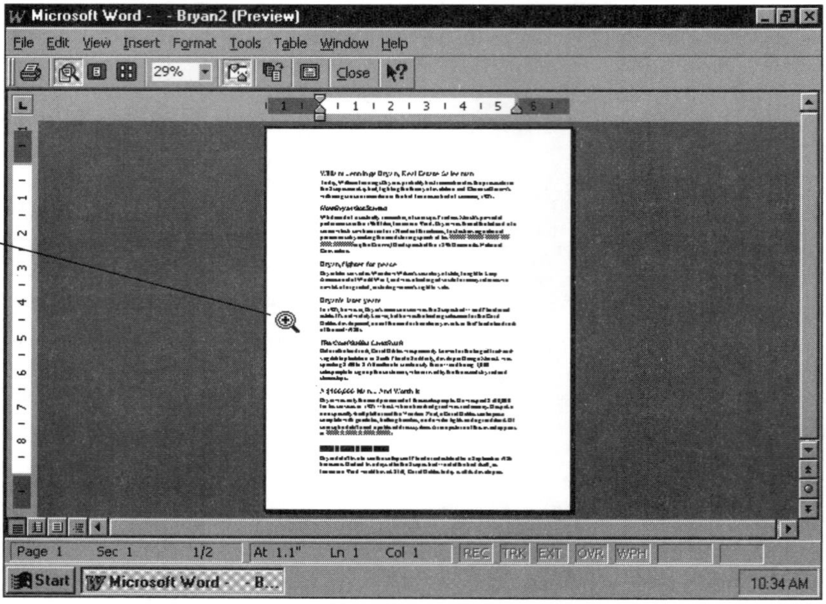

Figure 4.22

Enlarging text with Print
Preview. Notice the
mouse pointer magnifier
contains a minus sign
when the image has been
enlarged. Clicking again
will reduce the size of
your image.

Mouse pointer

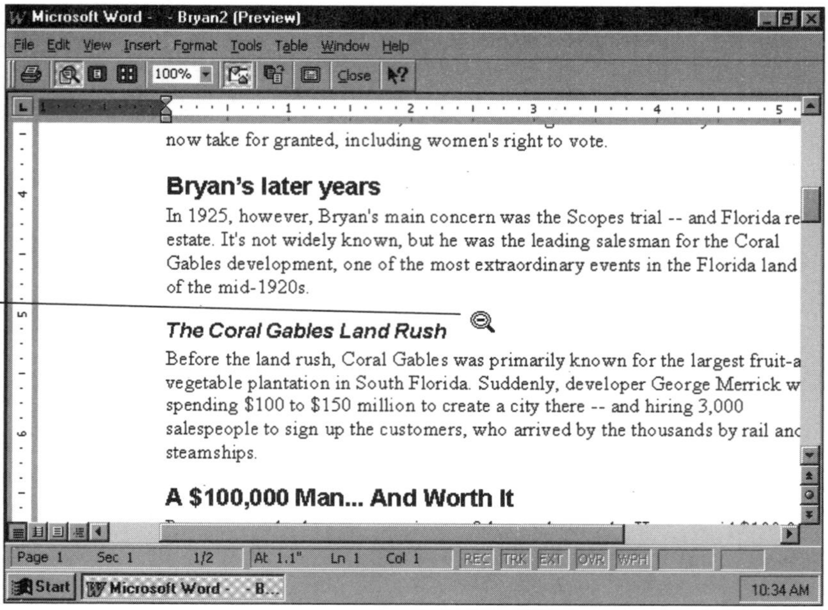

You can view up to 18 thumbnail pages at once in Print Preview. To do so, click the Multiple Pages button in the Print Preview toolbar, and a box opens, as shown in Figure 4.23. (Realistically, you won't see much detail if you display 18 pages, especially if they're text pages. However, showing several pages at once can give you a feel for the high-level organization and appearance of a section of a large document.) Select the number of pages you want to appear by dragging the mouse across the selection grid. You can display up to three rows of pages in as many as six columns. Figure 4.24 shows six pages displayed at once.

To switch back to a single-page Print Preview, click on the One Page button in the toolbar.

Figure 4.23

Using the multiple pages button to display six pages at once

Figure 4.24

Six pages viewed at once

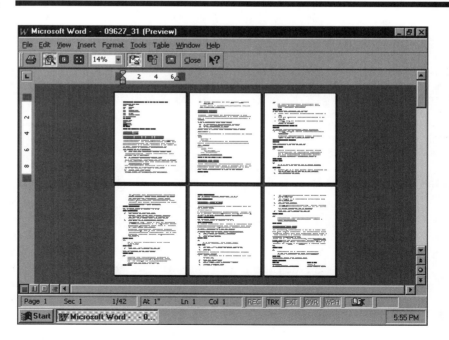

Shrinking Your Document Automatically

At one time or another, you've probably created a document that was just slightly too long. You hoped that report would fit on three pages, but a few lines jumped onto the fourth page. Or someone told you to make your argument in a page, but you just couldn't quite make it fit. In the past, you might have cheated by slightly shrinking the type size and space between lines. Now, Word will do the cheating for you.

Rather than shrinking your document by trial and error, you can have Word calculate the changes needed. Click on the Shrink to Fit button in the Print Preview toolbar.

Be warned, though, Shrink to Fit can be a little like setting the water temperature too hot on your washing machine. Use Shrink to Fit just to save a few lines, or it can shrink things way too much. It can shrink text to 4-point without batting an eyelash. (On occasion, Shrink to Fit gives up and tells you it can't remove a page. But that's rare. It's pretty zealous about trying.)

Editing in Print Preview

You can edit your document in Print Preview. Place the magnifying glass on the part of the page you want to edit, and click to zoom to 100%. Then click on the Magnifier button in the toolbar. This turns the magnifier off, leaving the 100 percent zoom in place. Now you can select text, edit it, move it around, and reformat it as if you were still in **N**ormal or Page Layout standard Word document. (Of course, you don't *have* to increase the size of the type in Print Preview to edit it—if your eyes are that good.)

Most of the usual Word menu items are available while you're editing in the Print Preview screen, including **F**ind and **R**eplace, and nearly everything on the F**o**rmat menu.

Changing Margins and Indents in Print Preview

You can use Word's rulers to change margins and indents in Print Preview, just as you can in the normal document window. To change any of the page's margins, click the Ruler button in the Print Preview toolbar to display the Ruler; then drag the margin boundary with the mouse. (Your mouse pointer will change to a double-headed arrow when it touches the margin boundary on the ruler.) Dragging works for both horizontal and vertical margins, but on the horizontal margins it's easy to inadvertently move an indent instead. Seeing a sample screen helps make this point, so refer to Figure 4.25.

Figure 4.25

Changing margins and indents in Print Preview

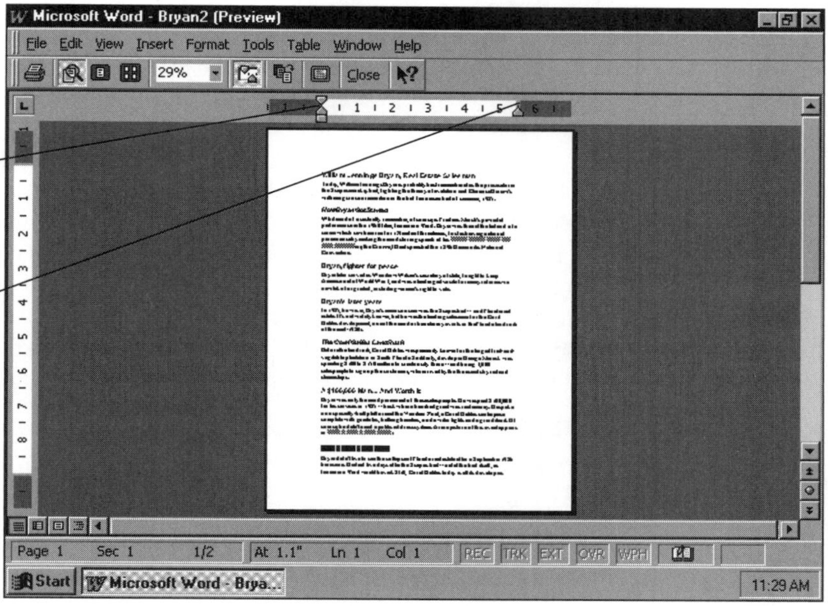

To change the left margin, click *between* the markers and drag.

To change the right margin, click *above* the right tab marker and drag.

■ Printing to Fax

For many people, faxing documents has become as much a way of life as printing them: fax machines and faxmodems have become so commonplace that they now provide a quick and easy way to get information to virtually anyone, virtually anywhere. Microsoft Word, working with Microsoft Fax and Microsoft Exchange, provides extensive support for faxing documents directly from your computer—either via a faxmodem connected to your PC, or via a faxmodem available on your network. You can not only use Word to fax documents to another fax machine, you can fax them to another computer—either for printing out on a printer, or in an editable binary format that can be used by anyone running Windows 95 or Windows NT Workstation.

The most common way to fax from Word is to use the Microsoft Fax driver, which you may have installed during Windows 95 Setup. If you have installed it, this driver should appear in the list of printers available in the Print dialog box.

As we'll discuss in more detail shortly, when you choose the Microsoft Fax driver in place of a printer driver, Microsoft Fax displays the Compose New Fax wizard, which walks you through a series of questions about where and how you want your fax to be sent, and then sends it there, according to the answers you provide.

We'll cover this approach to faxing first; then we'll introduce the new Microsoft Office 97 Fax Wizard, which also utilizes the Microsoft Fax print driver. This new Fax Wizard gives you *more* control over the appearance of your faxed document, but *no* control over issues such as the way your telephone lines are set up, or whether your fax will be sent later, to qualify for lower phone rates.

You may want to use the Compose New Fax Wizard the *first* time you send a fax from Word, to specify the Microsoft Fax settings you'll want to use from now on; *then* use the Microsoft Office 97 Fax Wizard for your day-to-day faxing.

If you did *not* install the Microsoft Fax driver as part of the Windows 95 setup process, or if the Microsoft Fax driver does not appear in your list of printers, you can run a maintenance setup of Windows 95. When you install Microsoft Exchange (as you must), you're asked which information services to include. Choose Microsoft Fax Driver as well as any other options you may need.

NOTE. *If you have trouble using Microsoft Fax, you might have an incompatible modem. According to Microsoft, the following fax/modems won't work with Microsoft Fax:*

Manufacturer	*Model*
AT&T Paradyne	Keep in Touch Card 3761
Best Communications	14496EC
BIT	MX-6, XM124S
Cardinal	14400 V.32bis, MB2296SR
CPV Datensysteme	F-1114HV, StarLine
CTK-Systeme	CTK V.32
Datatronics	Discovery 2496CX
DIGICOM	SNM28, SNM41PC
Digicom Systems, Inc.	Scout Plus
E-Tech Research	E1414MX
EEH GmbH	Elink 301
ELSA	MicroLink, MicroLine
Gateway	Telepath PM144
Hidem	14400 Fax
Kortex	KX PRO 2400
LCE	MiniModem 23

Manufacturer	*Model*
Macronix, Inc.	*Maxfax 9624s, VOMAX 2000*
Megahertz	*P22 Pocket Fax Modem*
MultiTech Systems	*MT932ba*
Nat. Semiconductor	*TyIN 2000*
Neuhaus Mikroelektronik	*Fury 2400*
PNB	*TT9624*
Practical Peripherals	*PM2400 FX96SA, V.32 Pocket*
QuickComm	*Sprint II V.32 Fax*
Sysnet	*SMF44 Fax*
TeleJet	*TeleJet 14400*
US Robotics	*Sportster 28.8 V.FC, Sportster 9600*
Woerlein GmbH	*M288 Fax*
Zoom Telephonics	*FC 96/24, VFX 28.8*

Microsoft Fax may also have trouble with faxmodems that utilize Rockwell Protocol Interface (RPI) compression at speeds greater than 9600 bps, such as the Zoom 14.4 PC Model 110 (internal) and Zoom 14.4 EX Model 160 (external). Contact Zoom for information on possible software or firmware upgrades.

If you can fax from Microsoft Exchange, but you cannot access the Microsoft Fax printer driver from Word or other programs, you may have a missing or damaged Microsoft Fax printer driver. To reinstall it without running a Windows 95 maintenance install, follow this procedure:

1. *Choose Start, Settings, Printers.*

2. *Right-click on the Microsoft Fax icon if it is present, and click Delete to re-move the potentially damaged file.*

3. *Choose Start, Run.*

4. *In the Open box, type the following command, which rebuilds and rein-stalls the Microsoft Fax printer driver: awadpr32.exe.*

5. *Click OK.*

To fax your document, first, select **P**rint from the **F**ile menu, as if you were going to print the document. Then, choose Microsoft Fax from the list of printers in the **N**ame box. Specify any other printing options you wish; then choose OK. The Microsoft Compose New Fax Wizard opens, walking you through the steps required to send a fax. Along the way, you'll have the opportunity to set any options you need to fax successfully. Figure 4.26 shows the Compose New Fax Wizard's opening screen.

Figure 4.26

The Compose New Fax
Wizard's opening screen

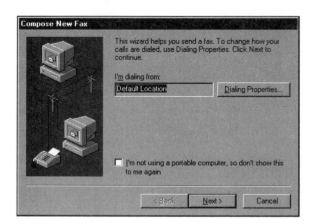

In this screen, you're given an opportunity to specify dialing information—including the location you're dialing from; any digits you use to access an outside line; and calling card and call waiting information if applicable. If you have already specified your dialing information in Microsoft Exchange, just click Next and skip this screen. If you're working from a desktop PC where the dialing information rarely, if ever, changes, you can avoid viewing this screen again, by clicking the **I**'m not using a portable computer, so don't show this to me again check box in the Compose New Fax dialog box. Even if you check this box, you can still change your dialing information later in the Compose New Fax Wizard.

Specifying Dialing Properties

If you do wish to review or change your Dialing information at this time, click Dialing Properties in the Compose New Fax dialog box. The Dialing Properties dialog box opens, as shown in Figure 4.27. Here, you can specify:

- A **N**ew dialing location

- A different default Area code where your PC is located

- A different country

- A dialing prefix for local and/or long-distance calls
  (such as "9" to dial off-premises, or "1" to dial long-distance).

- Whether you use a calling card

- Whether you use call waiting, and if so, which code to use to disable it while you're faxing

- Whether you're using a **T**one or **P**ulse dial phone

Figure 4.27

The Dialing Properties
dialog box

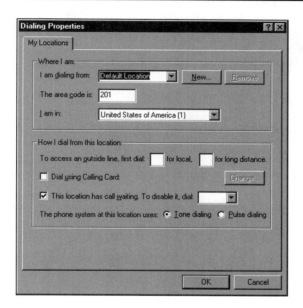

Specify the settings you wish, and choose OK. Note that later in the process of preparing a fax, Compose New Fax Wizard will allow you to specify additional dialing properties, including the number of retries to make on a fax call after an initial failed connection, and how long to wait after each retry.

Addressing a Fax

When you have finished specifying Dialing Properties, choose OK to return to the Compose New Fax dialog box, and choose Next. In the next dialog box (see Figure 4.28), you can specify who will receive your fax. If you only plan to send a fax to this recipient once, the simplest way is to enter the name and phone number of your recipient in this screen, and click Next. However, if the name of your recipient is in your Microsoft Exchange Personal Address Book—or should be—choose Addre**ss** Book. The Address Book dialog box opens (see Figure 4.29). If the recipient you want appears in the list, highlight the name, and click T**o**. If you want to send the fax to more than one recipient, select another name and click T**o** again. If you want to send to a recipient who is not listed in your Address Book, click **N**ew. The New Entry dialog box opens (see Figure 4.30).

Figure 4.28

Specifying a fax recipient

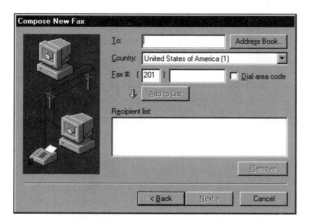

Figure 4.29

The Address Book
dialog box

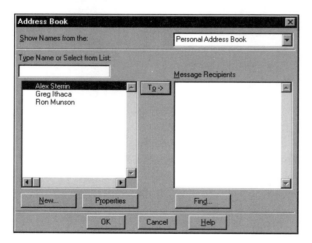

In the New Entry dialog box, choose Fax; then click OK. The New Fax Properties dialog box appears (see Figure 4.31). Enter the name of the recipient as you want it to appear on the fax. In the Fax Number field, enter the fax number. To add this recipient to the list of people who will receive the current fax, click To at the bottom of the dialog box. After you've made your selections in the New Entry dialog box, choose OK, then Next.

Figure 4.30

Adding a new name to the Address Book in the New Entry dialog box

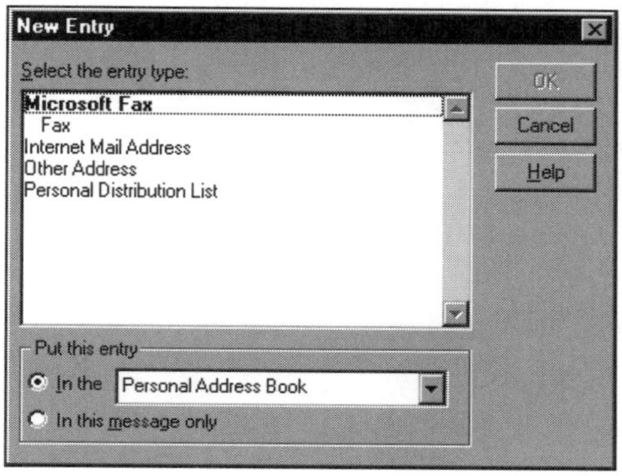

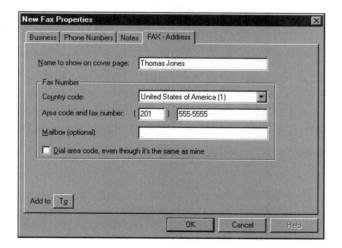

Figure 4.31

Entering information in the New Fax Properties dialog box

Adding a Cover Page

The Compose New Fax Wizard now asks whether you would like to include a cover page. If so, click the Yes radio button, and choose from the four fax cover sheets provided by Microsoft Exchange. (Note that these are not the same fax cover sheets included in Word's library of templates.)

NOTE. *There's a bug in many copies of Windows 95 that makes all your cover sheets unavailable every time you back up your files. To make them available again, search for all the .CPE files in your Windows folder, right-click on each icon to choose Properties, and check the Archive attribute checkbox. Microsoft's Web site now contains a fix for this problem.*

Setting Other Fax Options

You can control many elements of your fax from this second Compose New Fax dialog box by clicking on the Options radio button. The Send Options for this Message dialog box appears (see Figure 4.32). From here, you can define the following:

- When to send your fax

- What form your fax should take (Message Format)

- Additional dialing options such as call retries

- Security options, if any

Figure 4.32

The Send Options for this Message dialog box

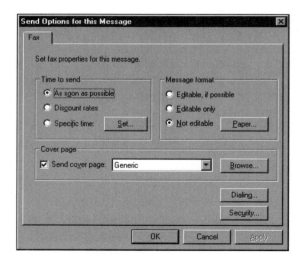

After you've specified all the options you want in the Send Options for this Message dialog box, click Next. The Compose New Fax Wizard moves to the next step—adding a subject and note to your cover page, if you've chosen to include one in the previous window. Subjects and notes are simply the same type of information you would send along with any fax cover sheet: covering information about the contents of the fax you've attached.

Specifying a Time to Send Your Fax

The Compose New Fax Wizard allows you to specify when you want to send your fax: as soon as possible, when your telephone rates are the lowest, or at a specific time. In the Compose New Fax Wizard, on the same page that asks if you want a cover page, click Options. The Send Options for this Message dialog box opens.

To set a specific time, click **S**et, enter the time in the Set Time dialog box, and click OK (see Figure 4.33).

Figure 4.33

The Set Time dialog box

Specifying a Message Format

Compose New Fax Wizard can send a fax in either the standard Group III fax format understood by most fax machines, or in a special editable format called Binary File Transfer (BFT). BFT can be received and understood by computers running Windows 95 and Windows NT, and by the relatively small installed base of fax machines that are compatible with the Microsoft At Work fax specification. Using BFT to send a fax can be a good substitute for sending binary file attachments over the Internet, which can require the use of MIME encoders and decoders at both ends, introducing more complexity than your recipients may want to worry about. If you expect that the fax may be scanned by your recipient at some point, sending with BFT can save them the trouble.

You can specify whether to send your fax in an editable or a non-editable format, or to allow Microsoft Fax driver to choose based on what it learns about the recipient's fax device when it makes a connection.

1. From the Compose New Fax Wizard, click Options on the window that asks if you want a cover page.

2. To specify that you want your message to be able to be edited by the receiver, choose E**di**table, if possible, or **E**ditable only. (If you choose E**di**table, if possible, and Windows 95 can't determine what kind of a fax device the recipient has, it creates multiple formats, making sure that at least one can be used when it establishes a connection.) To specify that you want to send the fax in standard Group 3 format no matter what kind of a fax device is encountered, choose Not editable.

3. Choose OK.

You can also control the image quality, paper size and orientation of the faxes you send. As usual, there is a trade-off between image quality and speed. In the Send Options for this Message dialog box, click Paper. The Message Format dialog box opens (see Figure 4.34). Modify the settings as appropriate, and then click OK.

Figure 4.34

The Message Format
dialog box

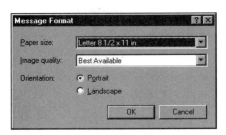

Setting Additional Dialing Properties

Compose New Fax Wizard allows you to designate the number of retries to make on a fax call after an initial failed connection, and how long to wait after each retry. To adjust these settings, click **D**ialing in the Send Options for this Message dialog box. The Dialing dialog box opens (see Figure 4.35).

Figure 4.35

The Dialing dialog box

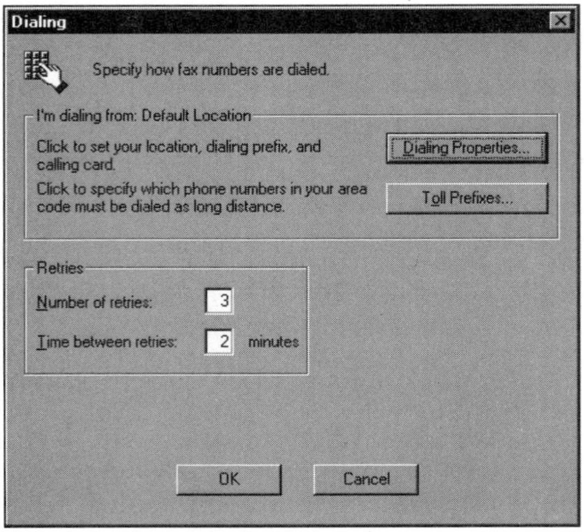

Notice that you can access the Dialing Properties dialog box (discussed earlier in this chapter) from the Dialing dialog box. This ensures that the Dialing Properties dialog box is available even if you instructed the Compose New Fax Wizard to skip over it in its opening screen.

If you live in an area where some of your calls require a long-distance dialing prefix even though they are in the same area code as you, click the T**o**ll Prefixes button in the Dialing dialog box. The Toll Prefixes dialog box opens (see Figure 4.36). From here, you can specify any telephone company exchanges in your area code that require a prefix. When you are finished, click OK.

Figure 4.36

The Toll Prefixes
dialog box

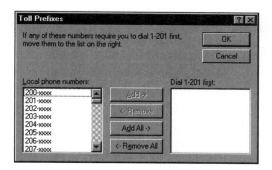

Setting Security for Your Fax

The Compose New Fax Wizard lets you take advantage of the security options built into Microsoft Exchange's fax feature, if you're sending faxes to systems that support Exchange. You can only secure faxes sent in editable format, not those output on a standard fax machine.

From the Send Options for this Message dialog box, choose Sec**u**rity. The Security dialog box opens (see Figure 4.37).

Here, you have four options:

- *None:* The default setting, which provides no security at all

- *Key encrypted:* Allows you to use a public key security system

- *Password-protected:* Allows you to specify a password that travels with your encrypted fax; at the other end, the user must enter the password, or the fax cannot be decrypted

- *Digitally sign all attachments:* A form of security that helps ensure that you, not someone else, sent the fax and its attachments

Figure 4.37

The Message Security
Options dialog box

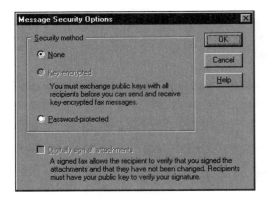

Faxes that carry no security at all are the easiest to manage. Next in line are password-protected faxes. You can simply share your password with the document's recipient, without acquiring or managing a set of public keys. However, password-protected faxes share the drawback of all password systems—passwords have a way of getting misplaced, stolen, or cracked.

Briefly, public key systems work as follows: Two related keys are established: a private key used only by its owner, and a public key available to anyone. To send a message that only a particular person can decipher, you encrypt it using the public key. When the person receives the message, she can decipher it using her private key, but nobody else's private key will do the job.

In the United States, Windows 95's public-key encryption system uses the popular RSA (Rivest-Shamir-Adleman) algorithm—the same algorithm used by the extremely popular Pretty Good Privacy (PGP) freeware package. The encryption generated by PGP is so strong that the United States government prohibits its export.

Briefly, digital signatures work as follows. You run a *hash program* that translates your document mathematically into a unique *digital fingerprint*—a short pattern of data that can only represent a document containing the precise information contained in the original document. Next, you encrypt this digital fingerprint with your private key. The resulting code is your digital signature. Windows 95 sends it with your document.

When the document arrives, your recipient uses your public key to decrypt the accompanying digital signature. She then runs the same hash program on your document, using your public key—expecting to generate the identical digital signature. If the signatures are identical, you sent the document—no other key could have created the same digital signature. If the signatures are different, either someone else sent the document, or it was altered en route.

To use key encryption or digital signatures, you must first establish security in Microsoft Exchange. To do so, open Microsoft Exchange (double-click on Inbox on the Windows Desktop); choose Tools for Microsoft Fax from the **T**ools menu; and choose Advanced Security. The Advanced Fax Security dialog box opens; from there, you can create, exchange, and manage public keys.

Sending the Fax

When you have finished setting options, including any information to be included on a cover page if you specified one, click OK. At long last, you have made it through the Compose New Fax Wizard. (Normally, it goes much faster than this, but we stopped at nearly every possible distraction along the way.) Click Finish, and Windows 95 sends the fax (or processes it for sending later, if you made that choice). When the fax is sent, the Microsoft Fax Status dialog box appears (see Figure 4.38) showing the progress of the fax.

Figure 4.38

The Microsoft Fax
Status dialog box

NOTE. *Some people use faxing as an emergency workaround for getting hard copy when no printer is available. If your printing needs on the road are really light, and you're somewhere with a fax machine and two phone lines, you might get away with carrying a modem instead of a printer. Then, instead of printing to a printer, you can simply print to a nearby fax machine by choosing the Microsoft Fax driver in the Print dialog box, instead of your standard printer driver, and using the Microsoft Compose New Fax Wizard to walk through faxing the document to the fax machine you've chosen. Conversely, if you have hard copy that you need to get into your computer, you can set Microsoft Fax to receive, and then fax the document to yourself. You'll receive a fairly low-resolution copy that may require significant clean-up, especially if you're planning to use optical character recognition to create an editable file, but this trick might still save you a lot of time in a crunch.*

Using the Microsoft Office 97 Fax Wizard

Office 97 provides a second Wizard you can also use to fax documents. The Office 97 Fax Wizard doesn't give you control over minutiae such as whether you need to dial 9 to get an outside line; it relies on the current settings in Microsoft Exchange's Tools, Microsoft Fax Tools, Options dialog box for answers to questions like those. If you've used the Compose New Fax Wizard we've already discussed, you've already created those settings.

Instead, the Office 97 Fax Wizard focuses strictly on the day-to-day issues of faxing:

- What do you want to send?

- Do you want a cover sheet? If so, which of Word's built in fax cover sheet styles would you like to use: Professional, Contemporary, or Elegant?

- Do you want to use Microsoft Fax or another program, or do you simply want a hard copy you can fax from a fax machine?

- Who are you *sending* to?

- What information about *yourself* would you like to include?

To use the Microsoft Office 97 Fax Wizard, choose File, Send to, Fax Recipient. The Fax Wizard opens; click Next (see Figure 4.39). You're asked which document you want to send; the default is your current document. You can specify a different document; you can choose whether to include a cover sheet; you can also specify that you *don't* want to send a document — just a cover sheet. When you're finished, click Next.

Figure 4.39

The Microsoft Office 97 Fax Wizard, asking you to select a document to be faxed.

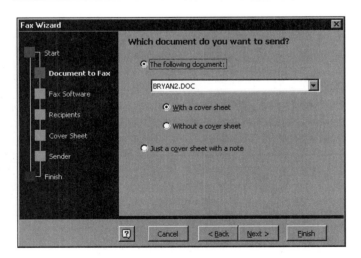

In the next window (see Figure 4.40), you're asked which fax program you want to use to send your fax. Microsoft Fax is the default, but you can specify a different fax program already installed on your computer, or choose to print hard copy of your document for faxing on a separate fax machine. When you're finished, click Next.

Figure 4.40

The Microsoft Office 97 Fax Wizard, asking you to select a fax program to use.

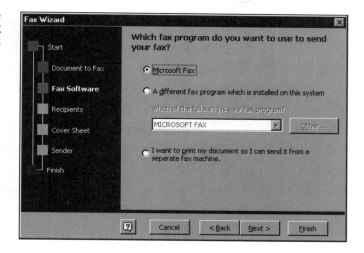

Next, you're asked to specify a recipient or recipients for your fax (see Figure 4.41). You can enter up to five Names and Fax Numbers directly, or you can click Address Book to view the same Select Name dialog box you saw earlier, in Figure 4.6; choose a personal address book; and add names from there. When you're finished specifying recipients, click Next.

Figure 4.41

The Microsoft Office 97 Fax Wizard, asking you to select a fax cover sheet

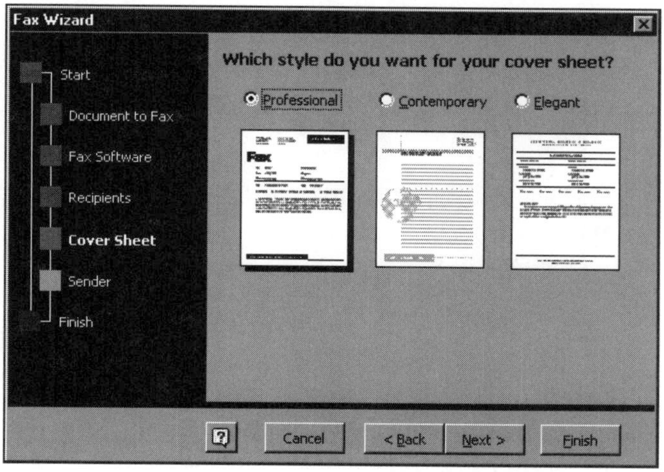

Figure 4.42

The Microsoft Office 97 Fax Wizard, asking you to select recipients

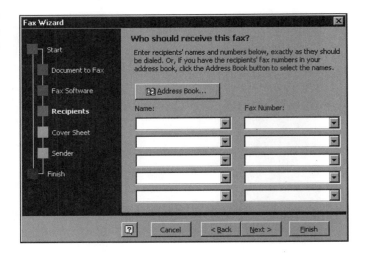

The Microsoft Office 97 Fax Wizard now asks you to choose among Word's three built-in Fax cover sheet styles: Professional, Contemporary, and Elegant. Thumbnail sketches of each are shown (see Figure 4.42). The Wizard skips this screen if you've specified earlier that you don't want to send a cover sheet. Select a cover sheet, and click Next.

In the last step before you're ready to fax, the Microsoft Office Fax Wizard asks you to confirm or enter information about yourself, to be used on the cover sheet (see Figure 4.43). If this information is included in the Tools, Options, User Information dialog box, it will already appear here. You can edit the information manually, or click the Address Book icon to select a different contact name from a Personal Address Book to be named as the file's sender. When you're finished, click Next. Then, click Finish to send the fax.

Other Ways to Fax Word Documents

We've discussed sending faxes through the Word File, Print dialog box, but if you have installed Microsoft Exchange, there are other ways to fax Word documents as well. For example, you can open Microsoft Exchange, and choose Compose, New Fax. The Compose New Fax wizard runs, just as you've learned to use it in Word, with one addition—a window that allows you to specify a file to be added as an attachment.

Or, you can send a Word document as a fax from your Windows desktop, by clicking Start, Programs, Accessories, Fax, Compose New Fax, and then running the Compose New Fax Wizard, which again gives you a chance to attach a document for faxing.

Figure 4.43

The Microsoft Office 97
Fax Wizard, asking you
to provide or confirm
sender information

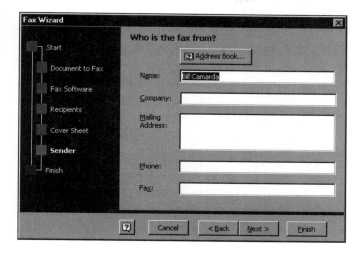

In this chapter, you've learned about virtually every printing scenario imaginable, from printing one copy of a document to sending a document as a binary file attachment to an electronic mail. The point is simple: no matter how you need to communicate the document you've created, Word provides a solution.

In the next chapter, we'll help make sure those documents you're distributing are as perfect as possible, by taking a close look at Word's spelling, grammar, and thesaurus tools.

- *Automatic Spelling and Grammar Check*
- *Running a Spell Check*
- *Controlling Spelling and Grammar Settings*
- *Working with Custom Dictionaries*
- *Using the Thesaurus*
- *A Closer Look at Word's Grammar Check*
- *Understanding AutoCorrect*

5

Spelling and Grammar: Never Be Embarrassed Again!

W ORD OFFERS A COMPLETE SET OF TOOLS TO HELP YOU IMPROVE your writing. Word's spell checker contains well over 100,000 words and can easily be adapted to add or delete words you use in your writing. Word's grammar checker tracks two dozen rules of grammar and style, making recommendations about usage wherever it finds an error. And Word's thesaurus contains 200,000 synonyms for 24,000 key words.

Together, these tools can serve as your personal system for sharpening your writing—especially as you personalize Word's spelling and grammar checkers to meet your specific needs. Best of all, unless you specify otherwise, Word's spelling and grammar checkers will work together on your behalf, 24 hours a day—automatically.

In this chapter, you'll learn how to use Word's built-in, integrated, automatic spell checking and grammar features; how to adapt them for your specific needs; and how to troubleshoot them. You'll also learn how to use Word's thesaurus, and understand the readability statistics Word can generate.

■ Automatic Spelling and Grammar Check

By default, when you open a file in Word 97, Word runs a spell and grammar check and flags all possible errors with wavy underline marks, as shown in Figure 5.1. Word flags all potential spelling errors with a *red* wavy underline—including words not in its dictionary, repeated words, apparent errors in capitalization, and combinations of words with the spaces missing. Word 97 now also flags all potential grammar errors with a wavy *green* line.

Figure 5.1

Word's spelling and grammar checker has flagged potential errors in this document.

Spelling error flagged in red

Potential grammar error flagged in green

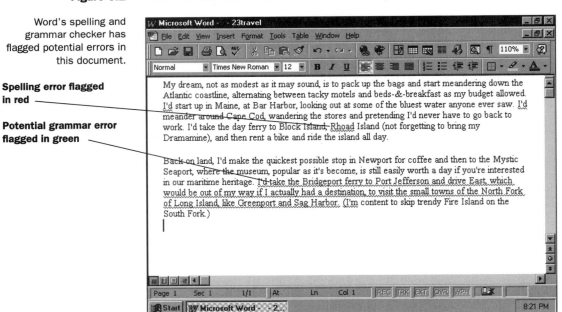

To resolve a potential *spelling* error, right-click on the flagged word. A shortcut menu appears (see Figure 5.2) listing any suggestions Word may have about the correct spelling, as well as a set of choices that depend on the error Word has found. If Word has found a word that does not appear in its dictionary, your choices include:

- *Ignore All*—Tells Word to disregard all occurrences of the spelling within the current document.

- *Add*—Tells Word to add the spelling to your custom dictionary; once you add it, Word won't flag the spelling as an error anymore.

- *AutoCorrect*—Allows you to select a way to correct your spelling, and have Word automatically make the same correction every time you make this mistake from now on—forever.

- *Spelling*—Opens Word's spell checker, which may provide more alternatives than the shortcut menu.

If Word shows a green wavy underline indicating a possible grammar error, right-click to see the grammar shortcut menu. Word may propose choices, as in Figure 5.3; you can also instruct Word to Ignore Sentence—in which case, the green line disappears. Or, you can open the Grammar checker dialog box by choosing Grammar at the bottom of the shortcut menu.

Figure 5.2

The spelling shortcut menu presents Word's best ideas on how to change your possible spelling error.

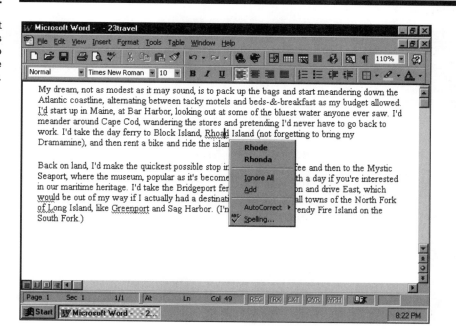

You also can resolve errors without using the shortcut menu by simply editing the text. Word checks the word or sentence again as you move your insertion point away from it, and if the word is now spelled correctly or the sentence uses correct grammar, the wavy underline disappears.

Figure 5.3

Word can propose solutions to potential grammar problems.

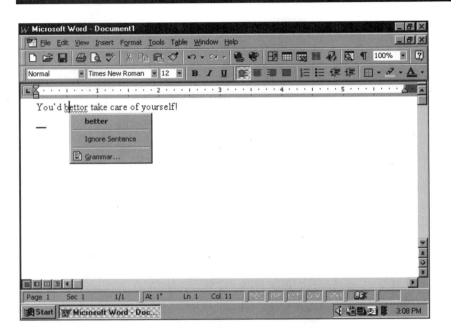

Automatic Spell and Grammar Checking isn't everyone's cup of tea. Many people will appreciate the way it catches typos and other inadvertent errors as they make them—without going through the trouble of a formal spell or grammar check. Others will find this feature distracting and will want to turn it off immediately—especially the grammar checking, which is still far from perfect. The feature also slows down Word slightly.

If you'd prefer not to use Automatic Spell Checking or Automatic Grammar Checking, you can easily turn off one or both of them. Choose Options from the Tools menu; then choose the Spelling & Grammar tab. To disable automatic spell checking, clear the Check spelling as you type check box. To disable automatic grammar checking, clear the Check grammar as you type check box. Choose OK.

You have another option short of turning these features off completely. You can allow Word to track all potential errors, but not display the errors until you're ready. In the same Tools, Options, Spelling & Grammar tabbed dialog box, check one or more of the following boxes: Hide spelling in this document, and Hide grammatical errors in this document.

This Hide feature allows you to deal with all your errors at once—either in the document or through the Spell Check and Grammar Check dialog boxes. You can display your errors immediately by clearing the check boxes you just checked in the Spelling and Grammar tab of the Options dialog box. Word can immediately display the errors without checking your entire document, since it has been checking for errors all along—just not displaying them.

NOTE. *Word offers a keyboard shortcut for moving through a document from one potential error to the next. When you press Alt+F7, Word moves to the next misspelling or grammar error, and displays the shortcut menu of options there.*

■ Running a Spell Check

If you prefer to spell check your documents the old-fashioned way, Word's built-in spelling and grammar checker can be accessed with a button on the Word toolbar, as shown in Figure 5.4. When you click on this button—or when you choose Spelling and Grammar from the Tools menu—Word begins checking both spelling and grammar in the open document, starting at your insertion point. You also can press the F7 key to begin a spelling check.

Figure 5.4

The Spelling and Grammar toolbar button

When Word finds a spelling error, the Spelling and Grammar dialog box opens, as in Figure 5.5. Notice that the word or sentence being questioned appears in the top text box in the dialog box. If Word has flagged a possible spelling error, the incorrect word appears in red, in a box called Not in Dictionary.

If Word has flagged a possible syntax error, the questionable phrase is displayed in green. In this case, the text box is named after the rule it believes you have broken, and you can click the Office Assistant for a detailed explanation of why Word has flagged the sentence—as shown in Figure 5.6.

If Word has flagged a spelling error that is in fact correct, such as a name, you can click Add to add the word to your custom dictionary and not flag it as an error in the future. If you don't want to add the word to your dictionary, but you also don't want Word to flag the problem here, click Ignore. If you want Word to ignore the problem throughout this document, click Ignore All.

If you do wish to make a change, you can edit the word or phrase manually; when you solve the problem to Word's satisfaction, the red or green

Figure 5.5

The Spelling and Grammar dialog box, showing a spelling error and offering suggestions

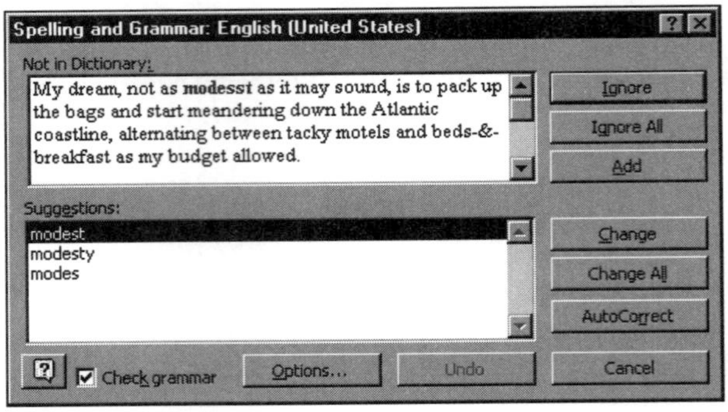

Figure 5.6

Word may also offer suggestions for potential grammar and syntax errors.

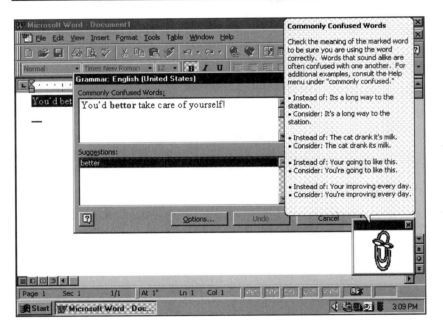

underline will disappear. You can also select one of the Suggestions Word makes in the bottom half of the dialog box.

You can also choose how you wish Word to make the correction. If you click Change, Word will make the correction in this specific location. If the problem recurs later in the document, Word will flag it again. If you click Change All, Word will change all references throughout the document.

NOTE. *Change All only works while the spelling and grammar checker is open. If you close the spelling and grammar checker before checking the entire document, Word won't make changes in the part of the document you didn't check.*

If you choose AutoCorrect as you enter the correct spelling of a word in the spelling and grammar dialog box, Word will add the change as an Auto-Correct entry. This means Word will automatically make the change as you type in all future documents, assuming you have AutoCorrect enabled. This is one of my favorite Word features: it means the longer you work with Word, the smarter and more accurate you get—even if you haven't learned a thing! (AutoCorrect is covered in more detail later in the chapter.)

Disabling Grammar Checking

Word's built-in dictionary is much improved, but the grammar checker is only a little better. You may find that grammar checking improves some of your documents, but not others. Word makes it easy to disable grammar checking at any time during a spell check: simply clear the Che**ck** grammar check box at the bottom of the Spelling and Grammar dialog box. You can also *enable* the grammar checker at any time during a spell check, by checking the Check grammar box.

Undoing One or More Changes

Within Word's spelling and grammar checker, you can always undo your most recent action—except for adding a word to a custom dictionary—by choosing Undo. Once you've finished spell checking your document, you can undo changes one at a time with the Undo command. Remember, however, that Undo doesn't work out of sequence. To undo a fix you made a while back, you have to undo all the fixes in between then and now.

What Word Flags as Misspellings

Word not only flags misspellings, but also repeated words and capitalization that appear to be incorrect. However, Word 97 is smarter than its predecessors about recognizing proper names, including popular first names, names of large companies, cities, and countries. You shouldn't run into embarrassing omissions like "Microsoft" or "Pentium" any more!

■ Controlling Spelling and Grammar Settings

The Spelling & Grammar tab of the Options dialog box (see Figure 5.7) gives you extensive control over how you interact with Word's spelling and grammar checkers. You can display this dialog box by clicking the Options button in the Spelling and Grammar dialog box, or by choosing Tools, Options, Spelling & Grammar. We've already discussed the first two options in the spelling and grammar fields in this dialog box, including Word's check-as-you-type feature, and hiding spelling or grammar errors until you're ready to review them. Now, let's take a look at some of the other controls Word offers you in the Spelling and Grammar dialog box.

Figure 5.7

The Tools, Options, Spelling & Grammar Tab

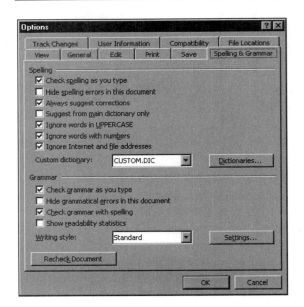

Always Suggest Corrections—Word's spelling suggestions are *often* incorrect in highly technical documents or documents that contain a lot of arcane jargon. For such documents, in the interest of time, you might want to disable Word's suggested spellings to make the spell check run faster.

Suggest from main dictionary only—By default, Word looks in all open custom dictionaries to make suggestions about spelling changes. This can take time. If you're sure your current document won't benefit from words you've added to your custom dictionaries, check this box.

Ignore words in UPPERCASE—Some categories of words cause problems for spelling utilities. For instance, no spell checker understands all acronyms.

Because most acronyms are all caps, you can tell Word not to flag words that are all caps. Choose Options from the Tools menu, and choose the Spelling tab in the Options dialog box. Then check Ignore words in UPPERCASE.

Ignore Words with numbers—Similarly, many product names combine words and numbers. Suppose that you own a 486SX computer, a DX-677 CD player, and a KFE100 fire extinguisher. Word normally flags each of these numbers—driving you stark raving mad if you're proofing a price list. You can tell Word to ignore this by checking Ignore words with numbers.

Ignore Internet and file addresses—Until recently, most spell checkers have choked on Internet file addresses like the Web address http://www.ca-marda.com or the file name c:\camarda\chap12.doc. If you check the Ignore Internet and file addresses box, Word 97 will skip spell-checking addresses like that.

Check grammar as you type—If you clear this box, Word will not display green wavy underlines when it comes across a sentence that may have a grammatical error.

Hide grammatical errors in this document—If you check this box, even if Word is tracking grammatical errors for you, it will not display them in your document with wavy green underlines.

Custom dictionary—If you click on this drop-down list box, Word displays all the custom dictionaries currently active. Select the custom dictionary where you want words added. By default, Word uses the primary custom dictionary, CUSTOM.DIC. (See the "Working with Custom Dictionaries" section for more about working with custom dictionaries.)

Check grammar with spelling—This is checked by default. If you clear it, Word will only check spelling when you run the spell checker.

Show readability statistics—When you check this box, Word compiles a list of readability statistics and displays them upon completion of a spell check or grammar check. See "Using Word's Readability Statistics" later in this chapter for a more detailed discussion of readability statistics.

■ Working with Custom Dictionaries

By default, Word includes one custom dictionary, CUSTOM.DIC, and all the words you add to a dictionary during spell checking are placed there. However, you can create up to ten custom dictionaries, and use each in special circumstances. For example, if you do legal editing only on Tuesdays and Thursdays, you can activate your legal custom dictionary only on those days.

To create a new custom dictionary, choose Tools, Options, Spelling & Grammar, and click Dictionaries. In the Custom Dictionaries dialog box (shown in Figure 5.8), click New. Word then displays the Add Custom Dictionary dialog box (see Figure 5.9). Enter a name for your dictionary and click

Save. The dictionary now appears checked in the Add Dictionaries dialog box. Note that words you add to custom dictionaries during a spell check are placed in whichever enabled custom dictionary is listed first.

Figure 5.8

The Custom Dictionaries dialog box

Figure 5.9

The Add Custom Dictionary dialog box

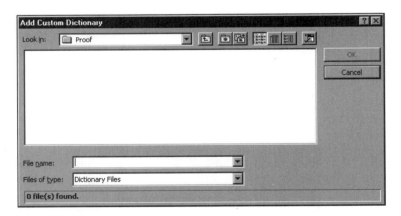

Making Changes Directly to a Custom Dictionary

While you're spell checking, go easy with the trigger finger on the Add button. When you're in a rush, it's all too easy to add words to the custom dictionary that shouldn't be there.

If you do enter words in a custom dictionary by mistake, however, it's easier to edit dictionaries than it used to be. You can also manually add lists of words to a custom dictionary—you don't have to wait for them to show up in your documents.

Word dictionary files are ASCII (text only) lists of words you've added. When you open a custom dictionary, you can add as many words as you want. You can either add words manually or by cutting and pasting them from another location, as long as you save the file as a pure text file with one word on each line.

Word stores words in CUSTOM.DIC in alphabetical order, with all capitalized words appearing before all lowercased words. However, you do not need to store your words in this order—you can edit your custom dictionary to display words the way you want it to. Word will reorganize your list automatically the next time you add a word to this dictionary during a spell check.

To edit a custom dictionary, display the Custom Dictionaries dialog box by clicking on dictionaries in the Spelling and Grammar dialog box. Then highlight the dictionary you want to edit, and click Edit. The dictionary opens as an unformatted Word document, as shown in Figure 5.10. Make your changes in word order—or any other types of changes—and choose File, Save. Word will save your dictionary as a Text file.

Figure 5.10

Editing a custom dictionary

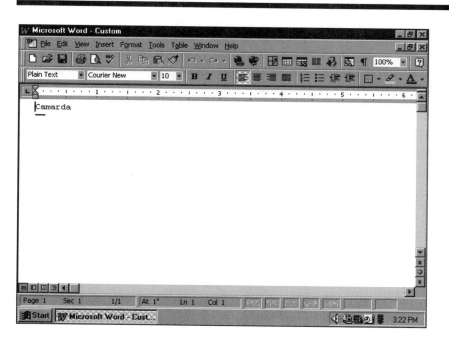

NOTE. *If you are running Word across a network, the network administrator may have set CUSTOM.DIC or its folder as Read Only. If so, you cannot add words to the CUSTOM.DIC dictionary, as indicated by the grayed out Add button. You can, however, create your own CUSTOM.DIC file, store it where you can access it, and then change the location where Word looks for a custom dictionary.*

Removing and Adding Custom Dictionaries

From the Custom Dictionary dialog box, you can also make a custom dictionary unavailable by clearing its check box. To make the dictionary disappear from the list of dictionaries, highlight it and click Remove. Note that this still doesn't erase the file; you can use the Add button to locate the dictionary, place it back on your list, and make it available again.

Spell Checking a Single Word

You've already seen that you can right-click on a word that has been flagged as misspelled to see Word's suggested alternatives. But even if you've turned automatic spell checking off, it's easy to spell check a single word.

Highlight the word by double-clicking on it with the mouse, and press F7. If you spelled the word wrong, Word attempts to provide a list of alternatives. If the word is correct, Word moves to the next spelling error it finds and displays the Spelling and Grammar dialog box with a list of alternatives. You can either continue the spell check or close the spell checker and return to editing your document.

Spell Checking a Text Selection

To spell check part of a document, select the text and click on the Spell Check button on the toolbar. When Word finishes spelling the selected text, it offers to check the rest of the document. To end the spelling check at this point, click on the No button.

Spell Checking Interactively

Often, when you make a spelling change, you notice something else in your document that you want to change at the same time. You don't have to close the spell checker to do so.

Click once in the document (or press Ctrl+Tab to make the editing window active). Word highlights the flagged word. You can format, delete, or replace it using standard Word commands. The title bar of the Spelling and Grammar dialog box becomes grayed out, as shown in Figure 5.11, showing that it is temporarily unavailable. Also, the Ignore button changes to become a Remove button. When you click again anywhere in the document, the insertion point moves there. You can edit the document normally.

When you're finished editing, click on the Resume button in the Spelling and Grammar dialog box, and the spelling check begins again.

Figure 5.11

Editing in the document
with the Spelling and
Grammar dialog box open

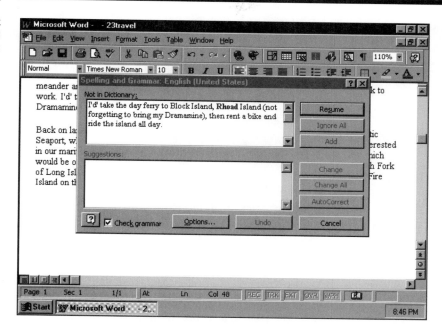

Ignoring Selected Text

Sometimes, you'll want to tell Word to ignore a block of text in its spell
check. You know that the text is accurate, but there are many unfamiliar
words which you know that Word will flag. A list of proper names is a good
example. Here's how to tell Word to ignore a specific block of text:

1. Select the text.

2. Choose Tools, Language, Set Language. The Language dialog box
   appears, as shown in Figure 5.12.

3. Choose the (no proofing) item from the Mark Selected Text As list
   in the Language dialog box (it's at the very top of the Mark Selected
   Text As list box).

4. Click on the OK button.

From now on, Word skips the highlighted text whenever you check the spelling of the document. Word also skips the highlighted text when you run the
grammar check or hyphenation utility.

Figure 5.12

The Language dialog box

Using Foreign Language Dictionaries

Word also can proof your spelling in a wide variety of languages (see Table 5.1). To proof your document in a foreign language, select the text you want to proof, and then select the foreign language in the Language dialog box accessed by choosing Tools, Language.

You can assign text to any language you want. However, there is a catch. For Word to proof in a particular language, you have to install the correct dictionary. In the United States, you use the English (U.S.) dictionary, named MSSP2_EN.LEX. If you bought your software in another country, the proofing tools for the language of that country were most likely the default setting of the Word software.

Many other language dictionaries are available in the United States, through Alki Software at 1-800-669-9673, or outside the United States, through your local Microsoft subsidiary. If you live outside the United States, call 206-286-2600 in the U.S. to find out more. Except as shown in the following table, language files come with a spell checking dictionary, a thesaurus, and a hyphenation file.

NOTE. *When Word is checking text in another language, that language appears in the title bar of the Spelling dialog box.*

Excluding Words from the Dictionary

Occasionally, you might want to have the spell checker flag a word as a possible misspelling even though the word is in its dictionary. Let's say that you've noticed you often mistype liar as lira, both of which are spelled correctly. Because you write crime novels, not reports on European currency exchange, wouldn't it be nifty if the spelling utility would always question lira as a misspelling, instead of assuming that you know what you're doing?

Table 5.1

Foreign Language
Proofing Tools
Available for Word

LANGUAGE	SPELLING	HYPHENATION	THESAURUS	GRAMMAR
Danish	Yes	Yes	Yes	No
Dutch	Yes	Yes	Yes	No
English (British)	Yes	Yes	Yes	Yes
English (American)	Yes	Yes	Yes	Yes
Finnish	Yes	Yes	No	No
French (Canadian)	Yes	Yes	Yes	Yes
French (European)	Yes	Yes	Yes	Yes
German	Yes	Yes	Yes	No
Italian	Yes	Yes	Yes	No
Norwegian	Yes	Yes	Yes	No
Portuguese (European)	Yes	Yes	No	No
Portuguese (Brazilian)	Yes	Yes	No	No
Spanish	Yes	Yes	Yes	No
Swedish	Yes	Yes	Yes	No

You can't remove a word from Word's basic dictionary. You can, however, create a supplemental file, called an exclude dictionary, which includes words you want to flag as misspellings even if they're spelled right.

Like custom dictionaries, exclude dictionaries are ASCII files with one word on each line. Exclude dictionaries use the same file name as the main dictionaries with which they are connected, except they have an EXC extension. They are stored in the same folder as the main dictionary.

If you're using the default dictionary for American English, your exclude dictionary will be MSSP2_EN.EXC. Chances are you'll place it the C:\Program Files\Common Files\Microsoft Shared\Proof folder. To create an exclude dictionary, follow these steps:

1. Create a new document.

2. Type each word you want Word to exclude from spell checking, one per line.

3. Choose File, Save As.

4. Set the Save in list box to the same folder as the main dictionary (probably C:\PROGRAM FILES\COMMON FILES\ MICROSOFT SHARED\PROOF).

5. Select the Text Only option from the Save as type list box.

6. Type the file name that matches the name of your main dictionary, but use EXC as the extension (for example, MSSP2_EN.EXC).

7. Click Save.

8. Close the file.

If, during a spelling check, you tell Word to Add an excluded Word into its main dictionary, this will have no effect: the word will remain in the exclude dictionary unless you remove it manually.

■ Using the Thesaurus

As you write, you may sometimes find yourself getting into a rut—using the same word or phrase repeatedly, when another word might make your point more clearly. That's what a thesaurus is for, and Word comes with a very good one.

To use the thesaurus, position the text insertion point in (or immediately after) the word for which you want synonyms (similar-meaning words). Or, select the entire word by double-clicking on it. Then choose Tools, Language, Thesaurus, or press Shift+F7. Word highlights the entire word or phrase and opens the Thesaurus dialog box, as shown in Figure 5.13.

Figure 5.13

Looking up a word that can be used in several different senses

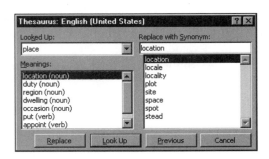

NOTE. *In some cases, Word will recognize a phrase and provide synonyms for it. For example, if you highlight "speed up," Word recognizes it and presents "hasten" and other synonyms.*

Once you have selected your word, it will appear in the Looked Up box. To the right, in the Replace with Synonym box, Word proposes the most likely equivalent term. The example in Figure 5.13 asks for synonyms for the word "place," and Word provides "location" as the most likely synonym. It also provides several additional alternatives in the Replace with Synonym list box.

The thesaurus also allows you to find synonyms for the particular usage of a word which can be used in multiple senses. For example, in the figure above, the word "place" can be used in several senses, which are listed in the Meanings box. Let's say you want to use it as a verb ("He was told to *place* the book on the table"). You would select "put (verb)" in the Meanings box. When you do, new synonyms for "put" will appear in the Replace with Synonym box to the right—"place," "deposit," "settle," and so on.

When Word presents a list of synonyms, you may decide you would like to review the meanings and synonyms of one of those words. To do so, select the synonym and then click the Looked Up drop-down list box. As you can see, sometimes you might follow a trail of several suggested replacements before arriving at the word you want.

If you want to return to a previous Thesaurus request, you can. Click on the downward-pointing arrow on the Looked Up drop-down list box to reveal a list of all the requests you've made since opening the Thesaurus dialog box. Click on the word you want, and the synonyms for that word reappear. When you find the synonym you're looking for, select it, and click on the Replace button. Word substitutes the synonym for the original word in your document.

Sometimes Word can't find a synonym for a particular word. In these cases, Word presents you with an alphabetical list of words with similar spellings, as shown in Figure 5.14.

Figure 5.14

Searching the thesaurus for a word that's spelled wrong—Word suggests words you might mean instead

If you spelled the word wrong, you may be able to pick the correct word from this list and search Word's thesaurus for it. In Figure 5.14 above, you can see that the corrected spelling of "indescribable" appears near the bottom of the alphabetical list.

Finding Antonyms

In many cases, the Word thesaurus can show you antonyms (opposite meanings) of a word or phrase. If a list of antonyms is available, the word Antonyms appears at the bottom of the Meanings list box. Select Antonyms to see them.

Some words in the Word Thesaurus have a number of "related words" that you can review. You may find the related words useful if you're trying to think of an alternative to a word you'd rather not use.

Using Look Up Independently

If you place the insertion point in an area of the screen with no text, and press Shift+F7, Word assumes that you want to look up a word that is not in the document. The Thesaurus dialog box opens with nothing filled into the Looked Up box. Enter the word you want to look up in the thesaurus in the Insert box, and click on the Looked Up button.

■ A Closer Look at Word's Grammar Check

Earlier in this chapter, you learned how to turn Word's grammar checker on and off, and how to use it with Word's spell checker. Now, you'll take a closer look at what the grammar checker actually does, so you can customize it to your best advantage.

Of course, Word's grammar checker doesn't "understand" what it's reading in the sense that people understand it. Word's grammar checker, like all contemporary grammar checkers, simply follows preprogrammed rules. Because the grammar checker cannot really discriminate between "good" and "bad" writing, many "errors" are flagged that are perfectly OK.

On a bad day, Word's grammar checker creates a lot of extra work for you. Every "error" may turn out to be nothing more than a misinterpretation of your text. But on a good day, the grammar checker will pleasantly surprise you—catching things you would never have remembered on your own. Even better, you can personalize the grammar checker so that it only catches the types of errors you actually make—and is less likely to raise false alarms.

Word's grammar checker contains 22 fundamental rules that it can check in your document, ranging from identifying the passive voice in sentences, to recognizing clichés. (In fact, Word has a built-in library of clichés to work from.) Word has incorporated five writing styles into its grammar checker which proof for varying combinations of these rules. These five writing styles are: Standard, Casual, Formal, Technical, and Custom. For example, Word's built-in Casual style only checks documents against five rules; whereas Formal checks for 21 of the 22 rules—excluding only gender-specific usage.

You can change the settings for any of these writing styles to apply a "mix and match" of grammatical rules to the grammar check of your document. The Custom writing style is especially designed to help you find the right settings for the way you like to write.

Choosing Which Writing Style to Apply

The easiest decision you can make about grammar checking—aside from whether to use it at all—is which writing style to apply. Choose Tools, Options, Spelling & Grammar, and in the Writing style drop-down list box, choose Standard, Casual, Formal, Technical or Custom.

Choosing Which Rules of Grammar to Apply

You can edit any of Word's five Writing styles. You might generally like one of Word's existing writing styles, but you want to tweak it a bit. Or you might want to create your own Custom writing style from scratch. To edit a writing style, chose Tools, Options which opens the Spelling & Grammar tabbed dialog box. Then click Settings, which opens the Grammar Settings dialog box, as shown in Figure 5.15. Select the writing style you want to modify, and apply or remove the grammatical rules you want by checking or clearing the boxes next to them.

Figure 5.15

The Grammar
Settings dialog box

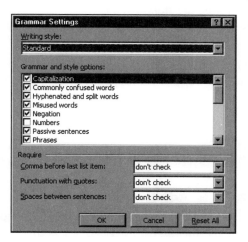

If you want to know more about how Word applies a rule before making your decision, look up "Grammar and Writing Style Options" in Word's help system. The entry under this topic is highly detailed. It even includes a list of 111 pairs of words that are commonly confused and can be caught by the grammar checker.

NOTE. *One strategy for deciding how to deal with the grammar checker is to run a full grammar check on a few of your documents, noticing which types of errors you make most often, and then customize the grammar checker to flag only those errors. I've found the grammar checker especially good at catching passive sentences, subject-verb disagreements, incorrect punctuation and cliches.*

Additional Grammar Settings

Word's Grammar settings include three settings you may be interested in even if you never use grammar checking for anything else. They are listed at the bottom of the Grammar Settings dialog box:

- *Require Comma before last list item*—Some individuals swear by serial commas; others swear against them. You can instruct Word to *always* make sure you use a serial comma before the last item in a list, or make sure you *never* use one, or ignore the issue completely ("don't check").

- *Punctuation with quotes*—You can specify whether you prefer to place punctuation *inside* or *outside* your quote marks, or whether Word should ignore how you punctuate quotes.

- *Spaces between sentences*—If you are of a certain age, your typing teacher taught you always to place two spaces between sentences. Now, in this era of typeset and desktop published documents using attractive fonts, the standard has changed: You should generally use one space between sentences. You can use this setting to specify one or two spaces between sentences, or to instruct Word to ignore the issue.

You might decide that one or more of these three settings are all the grammar you ever want to check. In that case, create a Custom Writing style with all the Grammar and style option boxes cleared, and with the settings of your choice for commas, punctuation and spaces between sentences.

You can always reset grammar checking to its factory setting by clicking Reset All in the Grammar Settings dialog box. Notice that Reset All only resets settings for the Writing style you have currently chosen.

Using Word's Readability Statistics

The Spelling & Grammar tab of the Options dialog box contains a check box that enables readability statistics. If this box is checked, when Word completes a spelling or grammar check, it provides an assessment of your text's readability, as shown in Figure 5.16.

The statistics listed in the Readability Statistics dialog box are based on an estimate of the number of words in an average sentence, and the average number of syllables in each word. The Flesch Reading Ease score in the Readability field of the dialog box rates text on a scale of 1 to 100; the higher

Figure 5.16

Word can report on your
document's readability.

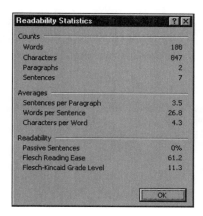

the score, the more understandable the document. You should generally
shoot for at least 60 points.

The Flesch-Kincaid Grade Level score listed in the dialog box rates text
based on the average U.S. grade level needed to understand it. For example, a
score of 7.0 means an average seventh-grader should understand it. If you write
a non-technical document that earns a score much higher than 8 or 9, consider
editing it to make it simpler. (Hey, it's the age of video—that's how it is.)

■ Understanding AutoCorrect

Most people make the same typing errors over and over. For instance, I frequently type "wiht" when I mean "with." Word's AutoCorrect feature can
automatically correct common spelling errors for you, as you work.

AutoCorrect can also watch for common capitalization errors. For instance, you can direct AutoCorrect to always capitalize the first letter of sentences or the names of days of the week. You may not even realize that Word
is following you around, cleaning up your mistakes.

You've already learned how to add AutoCorrect entries to your Word
templates through the Spell Check shortcut menu and dialog boxes. Next,
you'll learn how to take full control over AutoCorrect, to make it as valuable
as possible for you. AutoCorrect isn't just for typos. You can use it to insert
formatted text automatically, or even as "AutoText's smarter brother"—inserting lengthy chunks of text whenever you type a few predefined characters.

To use AutoCorrect, choose Tools, AutoCorrect. The AutoCorrect tabbed
dialog box opens, as shown in Figure 5.17. From here, you can add words to
AutoCorrect—and specify whether the corrected version should appear in

plain or formatted text in your document. To instruct Word about a new change you wish AutoCorrect to make automatically:

1. In the Replace box, type the word you wish to replace.

2. In the With box, type the word or phrase as you wish it to appear.

3. Click Add.

Figure 5.17

The AutoCorrect tabbed dialog box

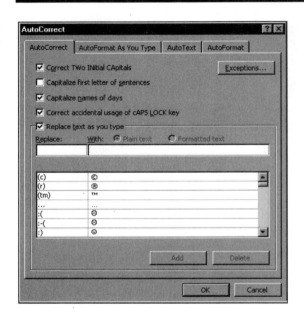

You can also instruct Word to insert formatted text in place of the word you want to replace. For example, you can tell Word to always insert the name of a book as italics. To do so, first format the text in your document, and select it before opening the AutoCorrect dialog box. Then, choose Tools, AutoCorrect. The "corrected" version of the text will appear in the With box. Click the Formatted text radio button. In the Replace box, enter the text you want Word to recognize and change. Finally, choose Add.

The AutoCorrect Library

While you're here in the AutoCorrect dialog box, check out the words and phrases AutoCorrect automatically corrects. By default, AutoCorrect changes a wide variety of "fake symbols," such as (c), into the actual symbols, such as ©. It even replaces e-mail smileys like :) with characters like ☺. But that's just scratching the surface. In Word 97, AutoCorrect automatically corrects nearly 500 words and phrases—far more than ever before. Never again will your documents say "would of been" when they should say "would have been"!

Of course, if you *want* to spell a word or phrase wrong, you can remove it from Word's AutoCorrect list by selecting it and clicking Delete. The entry is instantly deleted. When you exit Word, the NORMAL.DOT template is updated, and the deletion becomes permanent. If you do not want the deletion to be permanent in your template, check the Prompt to Save Normal Template box in the Tools, Option Save tab.

Understanding Other AutoCorrect Options

AutoCorrect offers five additional options that control its behavior. They are all listed as options in the AutoCorrect dialog box. Perhaps the most important, Replace Text as You Type, turns AutoCorrect on and off. If this box is cleared, AutoCorrect won't make any changes automatically. Here are the four other options:

- *Correct TWo INitial Capitals*—A common error is to capitalize the first two characters of a word that normally has only the first letter capitalized. Checking this option tells AutoCorrect to fix this whenever it occurs.

- *Capitalize first letter of sentences*—Another very common error is to forget to capitalize the first letter of every sentence in a document. Checking this box tells Word always to capitalize the first word in a sentence. This is turned off by default, because when it is turned on, Word may sometimes capitalize words that appear after periods, even though they are not at the beginning of a sentence.

- *Capitalize names of days*—The names of days (Monday, Tuesday, and so on) are proper nouns and should be capitalized in most instances. The Capitalize Names of Days option ensures that the days of the week are capitalized properly. Abbreviations such as Tues. and Wed. are not checked by this option.

- *Correct accidental usage of cAPS LOCK key*—By default, Word 97 corrects one additional common error: inadvertently leaving the Caps Lock key depressed. The telltale symptom is a word that starts with a lowercase letter and then becomes all caps. With this option checked, Word changes iNCREDIBLE eDIBLES to Incredible Edibles, and then turns off the CAPS LOCK key.

These AutoCorrect options only affect new text you enter into your document. Existing text is not affected by these options.

Creating AutoCorrect Exceptions

One complaint with Word 6's implementation of AutoCorrect was that it
didn't allow the flexibility to create exceptions. In Word 97, however, you can
exclude specific abbreviations or capitalized terms from automatic correction. To exclude an abbreviation:

1. Choose AutoCorrect from the Tools menu.

2. Click Exceptions.

3. To exclude an abbreviation from automatic correction, choose First Letter (see Figure 5.18). Note that Word already includes a fairly lengthy
   list of abbreviations that it knows enough to leave alone.

4. In the Don't capitalize after box, type the abbreviation you want
   to exclude.

5. Click on Add.

6. Click OK twice.

Figure 5.18

Creating AutoCorrect
exceptions for
abbreviations that should
not be capitalized

To exclude a word with two initial capital letters:

1. Choose AutoCorrect from the Tools menu.

2. Click Exceptions.

3. Choose INitial CAps (see Figure 5.19).

4. In the Don't Correct box, type the word or acronym you want to exclude.

5. Click on Add.

6. Click OK twice.

Figure 5.19

Creating exceptions for words and acronyms that contain more than one capital letter

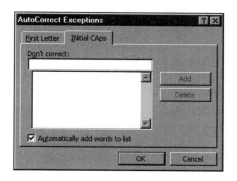

Automatically Creating Exceptions

You can instruct Word to create exceptions automatically as you work. In either the First Letter or Initial Caps tab of the AutoCorrect Exceptions dialog box (or both), check the Automatically Add Words to List box. From now on, whenever Word changes an abbreviation or capitalization you want left alone, press the Backspace key, and edit the word back the way you want it. Word won't dare to change it again.

NOTE. *You'll notice three other tabs in the AutoCorrect dialog box; the two AutoFormat tabs are discussed in Chapter 7, and the AutoText tab is covered in Chapter 9.*

In this chapter, you've taken a close look at Word's proofing tools, and seen how Word 97 now integrates grammar checking with spelling checking. You've discovered how to customize both spell checking and grammar checking to your needs—and learned how Word's increasingly capable AutoCorrect feature can eliminate many errors without your even being aware of it. You've also learned how to make the most of Word's built-in thesaurus.

In the next chapter, we'll step away from the innards of your document, and show you how to manage your files effectively with Word 97 and Windows 95. Never lose a file again—read on!

- *Advanced Techniques for Viewing Files*
- *Saving—In and Out of Word*
- *Retrieving a File That You Recently Worked On*
- *Using the Word 97 Properties Dialog Box*
- *Using the Open Dialog Box to Manage and Locate Files*
- *Using the Favorites Folder*
- *Using Passwords*

- *Creating File Types to Be Recognized by Word*

File Management:
Find What You Need—Now!

Y OU MIGHT ALREADY BE USING WORD FOR WINDOWS REGULARLY, without recognizing its extensive built-in capabilities for working with and managing files. If you learn these capabilities now, you can be more efficient right away. And it really pays off later, when you have hundreds (or even thousands) of documents and need to find a specific piece of information.

This chapter covers Word 97's extensive options for opening, saving, locating, and securing files. You'll learn how to open and work with multiple files at once; save files in different formats, sort file lists, use the Open dialog box to search for files, search by Property, retrieve recently used files, use Word's file security features, and associate non-Word files with Word so that Word loads automatically when you load those files.

■ Advanced Techniques for Viewing Files

It's easy to assume that each document always corresponds to one and only one editing window, but in Word, that's not necessarily true. Using the New Window feature, you can open additional windows containing the same document to make it easier to move through a large document, track what's going on in each part of the document, and make sure your document remains consistent even as you make changes in widely separate locations. Using the split box, you also can visually split a document into two parts and keep both on-screen at the same time.

Using New Window

To open more than one window containing the same file, choose **N**ew Window from the Window menu, and a second window containing your current document opens (see Figure 6.1).

Both windows contain the same contents, and if you change one, the other changes as well. When you close the file, both windows close. Notice that the title bars of these document windows indicate which copy of the document you're working on. In Figure 6.1, the "top" copy is Lodore:2, while the bottom copy is Lodore:1.

You might also want to use **N**ew Window when you want to split a document from left to right to review different parts of a table at once, as shown in Figure 6.2. You'll have to manually arrange the windows to achieve this effect. If you want to split the document horizontally, the split box (see next section) works better than **N**ew Window.

Using the Split Box

The split box is a tiny, nearly invisible 3-D rectangle directly above the vertical scroll bar. Figure 6.3 shows the split box. You can use the split box to split your document horizontally in two so that you can view both parts of the document at once.

To split the document window, move the mouse pointer to the split box; the pointer changes shape; it now appears as two horizontal lines with up and down arrows extending from it. Drag the pointer to the middle of your

Figure 6.1

Two windows containing
the same document

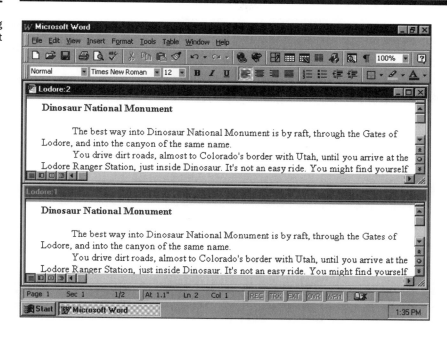

Figure 6.2

Using New Window to
view left and right edges
of a document

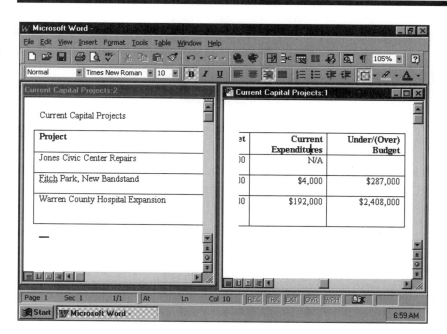

Figure 6.3

The split box

Split box

Split box mouse pointer

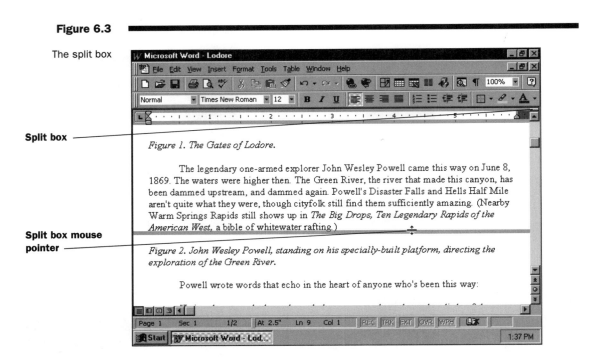

screen, or to the location where you want the screen to split. Figure 6.3 shows how the screen looks while you're positioning the mouse pointer where you want the split to occur. Release the mouse button, and the document window splits into two independent panes, as shown in Figure 6.4. You'll find plenty of opportunities to use the split box. For instance, you may want to copy text from the beginning of a long document to another location near the end of the document, and still view both parts of the document to make sure that the text fits appropriately in both places.

To "un-split" your screen, double-click anywhere along the split bar, or drag the split bar to the top of the screen, above the document window.

Using Window, Split to View Two Parts of a Document

Until now, we've discussed using the split bar to view two parts of the same document, but you can accomplish the same thing using the Window, Split command. When you choose Window, Split, the Split pointer appears in the middle of your editing window. Move it up or down to position it, then click to leave it in position.

You can remove the split the same way you've already learned: Place your mouse pointer on the split box or the dividing line that appears between the two editing windows, and drag them above the top of the editing window.

Figure 6.4

A document split into
two horizontal panes
using the split box
mouse pointer

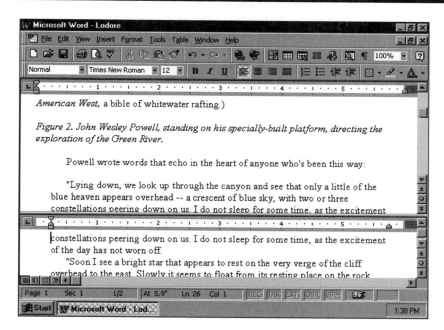

Opening Several Documents at Once

If you are an experienced Windows user, you may already know that you can keep several files open at once, and switch among them by choosing the file that you want to view from the **W**indow menu. (Incidentally, you also can move among windows by pressing Ctrl+F6.)

But you may not realize that you can actually open several files at once, with one command:

1. Choose **O**pen from the **F**ile menu.

2. The Open dialog box lists all Word (DOC) files in your current folder. Select the first file you want to open by navigating to it and clicking on it.

3. To select additional files, press Ctrl while clicking on each additional file name.

4. To open all the files, click the **O**pen button.

If you inadvertently select the wrong file, you can easily deselect it. To do so, point to the file name, press Ctrl, and click.

Arranging Multiple Open Documents

How do you view more than one document simultaneously—for example, if you want to check a reference in one document while you work on another? The quickest way to do this is to divide the available screen equally between all active documents by choosing **A**rrange All from the **W**indow menu. Figure 6.5 shows how **A**rrange All looks when three documents are open.

Figure 6.5

Arrange All with three documents displayed

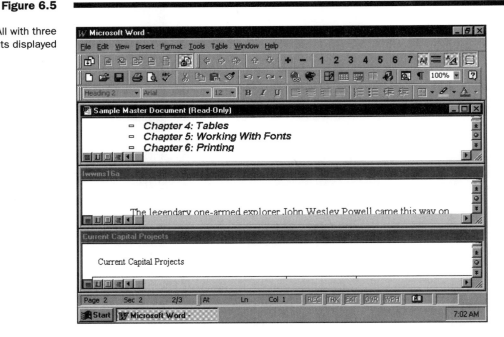

NOTE. *You can cut and paste text between documents just as you can within a document. You also can drag and drop text from one window to another. Also see the coverage of field codes in Chapter 21 to learn how to make one document change automatically because of a change in another.*

■ Saving—In and Out of Word

How much could be involved in saving a file? You just click the Save button on the standard toolbar, and Word stores a current copy of your current file on your hard disk, in the folder that is currently active. Well, some of the time that may be all you need to do, but for those *other* times, Word gives you extensive options and extensive control. For example, you can specify that Word automatically save backups of your files, or embed fonts in your file so people who don't own the same fonts as you do can still see the file as you intended it. You can specify that Word save more quickly than normal by using its Fast Save feature. And you can save files to a dizzying number of formats. In the next few sections, we'll walk through the extensive save options Word provides, and show you how to make the most of them.

The Fundamentals of Saving

When you save a new file—whether by clicking the Save button or choosing File, Save—the Save As dialog box automatically opens. You are prompted to name the file, which is then saved in your current folder unless you specify otherwise. Thereafter, if you click the Save button or choose File, Save, Word will automatically save a new copy of the file to replace the copy you have on disk.

If you wish to make any changes in how the file is saved—for example, to give the file a new name or store it in a different location—choose File, Save As to display the Save As dialog box. To save the file in the same location, but with a different name, enter a new file name in the File name box and click Save. To save the file to a different location, click the Save in box, and browse your computer and your available network or Internet FTP resources, choosing a location where you want to save the file. Once you've specified a location, click Save.

Saving to a Different Format

You may want to save your document to a format other than Word if you want to make the document available to a user who works with a different type of word processor, or to send it across the Internet in text-only format. Word permits you to save files in a wide variety of word processing formats, through the **F**ile, Save **A**s dialog box.

When you save a file in a format other than Word 97 format, the contents of your original Word 97 file still remain in memory, even though the file you've saved to disk may no longer support all your formatting, or other Word 97 features such as hyperlinks. If you then attempt to close the file, Word asks if you want to save changes—even if you just saved the file. This is Word's ambiguous way of reminding you that the file you're editing in memory contains formatting or other elements that will be lost if you close it. If you want to preserve the formatting, *first* save the original file as a Word 97 file, and *then* save a separate copy in the alternate format you wish to use. If the alternate format also uses the DOC extension, as would be the case if you save to Word 6, Word 95, or Word 2 format, use a different file name as well, or store the file in a different location. Otherwise, Word will overwrite your Word 97 file and you will still lose the elements of your file that are only supported in Word 97.

Word can save files in the following formats:

- Word Document (DOC)—This is the default format for Word 97. Note that it is a new format, different from Word 6.0 or Word 95.

- Document Template (DOT)—See Chapter 8, "Templates and Wizards," for more information on templates.

- Text Only (TXT)—This eliminates all formatting, converts line breaks, section breaks and page breaks to paragraph marks, and uses the ANSI character set. Use this format if you're not sure what computer your file will be used on.

- Text Only with Line Breaks (TXT)—Good if you plan to upload the file on an e-mail system, such as MCI Mail, that requires regular line breaks.

- MS-DOS Text (TXT, ASC)—This format uses the extended ASCII character set used by DOS; it's useful for converting files that will be used by non-Windows applications.

- MS-DOS Text with Line Breaks (TXT)—Similar to MS-DOS text, but also converts line breaks, section breaks and page breaks to paragraph marks.

- Rich Text Format (RTF)—A Microsoft standard for exchanging word processing data that preserves most document formatting.

- Unicode Text—This saves your file as a text file that supports Unicode, the international character set standard.

- MS-DOS Text with Layout—Works like MS-DOS text, except that spaces are inserted to simulate Word's indents, tables, line spacing, paragraph spacing, and tab stops.

- Text with layout—Inserts spaces in a document to approximate indents, tables, line spacing, paragraph spacing and tabs.

- Word 2.x for Windows—Saves a file to Word 2.x for Windows format.

- Word 4.0 for Macintosh—This export format often is used for sending files to desktop publishing systems using Macintosh QuarkXpress because, until very recently, Quark has not offered a more current Word document import filter.

- Word 5.0 for Macintosh

- Word 5.1 for Macintosh

- Word 6.0/95—Word 6 or Word 95 for Windows, and Word 6 for the Macintosh. (Word actually saves these files as RTF, as discussed later.)

- WordPerfect 5.0 for DOS—Saves a file to WordPerfect 5.0 for DOS format.

- WordPerfect 5.1 for DOS—The most popular version of WordPerfect for DOS.

- WordPerfect 5.x for Windows

- WordPerfect 5.1 or 5.2 Secondary File

- WordPerfect 5.0 Secondary File

- Microsoft Works 3.0 for Windows

- Microsoft Works 4.0 for Windows

- HTML Document—The format used for documents to be published on the World Wide Web or corporate intranets; these are text files tagged with appropriate style information that will be interpreted by whatever browser opens the files.

If you want to save a file in the HTML format, you don't have to scroll through this entire list of file formats; Word 97 provides the Save as **H**TML command on the File menu, which not only saves the file in HTML format but also displays it using Word's Web Authoring tools. (See Chapter 14, "Word on the Net: Create and Connect With a World of Web Data," for more information on working with HTML files in Word.)

NOTE. *Interestingly, Word allows you to* import *files that were created in some formats that Word does not allow you to* save *files in. WordPerfect 6.x is a notable example. At times Word can be a bit like Roach Motel:* your files get in, but they can't get out!

Some programs that you export to typically expect files to have specific extensions. Word generally assigns those extensions automatically. For example, if you are exporting a file to HTML for use by a Web browser, Word automatically changes its extension from DOC to HTM. In other cases, as with Word-Perfect or Microsoft Word for the Macintosh, the program doesn't require a specific extension, but Word assigns one anyway. For example, files saved in the Word 5.1 for the Macintosh format are saved with an MCW extension.

Because Word displays only Word documents in the Open dialog box by default, files that you save in other file formats may not appear unless you choose All Files in the Files of **T**ype box.

NOTE. *Call Microsoft Customer Service at 800-426-9400 for information about supplementary file conversion filters that are free upon request.*

Additional Save Options

Word also offers many additional Save options that give you better control over backup, recovery, Word's fast save feature, and font embedding. To access these options, click the **O**ptions button in the Save As dialog box, or choose **O**ptions from the T**o**ols menu, and then click the Save tab (see Figure 6.6). When you open Tools, Options, Save, you'll see several options; these will be discussed next.

Figure 6.6

Save Options displayed in Tools, Options, Save

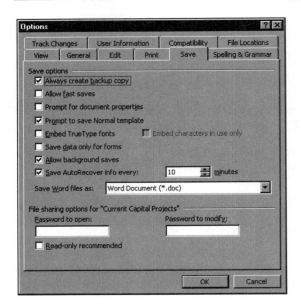

Creating Backup Copies

Always Create **B**ackup Copy tells Word to create a copy of the previous version of the file with a WBK extension every time it saves a file. Note, however, that since the backup is stored in the same folder as the original, you still won't have a copy of your file if your hard drive crashes.

NOTE. *See Chapter 24, "Managing Word: Making Word the Good Corporate Citizen," to learn how to change this default backup extension using the Set Registry Options macro.*

Allowing Fast Saves

Allow **F**ast Saves permits Word to save only the changes in a document, rather than the entire document. You can choose to *allow* Fast Saves, or to *prevent* them, but obviously not both.

Why are Fast Saves so fast? For the same reason that it's faster to throw your clothes on the chair than it is to hang them in the closet. With Fast Saves, Word doesn't actually place the changes in the correct locations within the document. Instead, it creates a list of changes that aren't integrated until the next time you save normally. If you plan to export files, it is a good idea to turn off the Fast Save option since the files may be read by software that doesn't know how to recognize Fast Save information, and therefore cannot integrate it back into your document properly.

NOTE. *Even if you're using Fast Saves, Word occasionally performs a normal save to take care of all the housekeeping that accumulates. Microsoft recommends that you clear Allow Fast Saves and save the document with a full save once you finish working on the document.*

Prompting for Document Properties

As is covered in depth later in this chapter, Word can store a wide variety of information about a document along with that document; this information is accessible from the Properties dialog box. To help make sure that users include information in the Properties dialog box instead of ignoring it, check the *Prompt for document properties* box. When you do, Word will open the Properties dialog box whenever a file is saved for the first time.

Prompting to Save the Normal Template

Word's Normal template stores the settings that are available to every Word document, including margins, default fonts, and many other important document elements. You may change these settings during the course of an editing session. By default, if you make changes in the Normal template, these changes are saved automatically whenever you save a file. However, if you want to be warned whenever Word is about to make changes to this important template, you can check the *Prompt to save Normal template* checkbox.

Embedding TrueType Fonts

This option allows you to include TrueType fonts as part of your document file. This lets others view and print your file as it is supposed to appear, even if they don't have the fonts you used installed on their computer.

As you can imagine, embedding these fonts can significantly enlarge the size of your file. Therefore, Word 97 has added a new option, *Embed characters in use only,* which appears as an additional box next to the *Embed True-Type Fonts* box in the Options dialog box. If you use 32 or fewer characters of a font, Word embeds only the characters you used instead of the whole font.

An example of when you might find this option helpful is a document with a headline in one font and all text in another. In this case, you would only want to embed the headline font information associated with the characters in your headline, and not all the text.

Don't check the *Embed characters in use only* box if you expect a recipient of your file to edit it. If the recipient adds characters that you haven't embedded, Word may not be able to display the new characters properly.

Saving Data Only for Forms

As you will learn in Chapter 20, "Forms: Create Fill-In Forms Your Whole Company Can Use," you can use Word to create forms which may be filled in by many people throughout your organization. When it comes time to compile the information stored in many of these forms, you may want to "throw away" the form's text and formatting, and keep only the information entered by a user. Checking *Save data only for forms* saves the data in your form as a single, tab-delimited record in text-only format, making it easy to import that information into the database of your choice—or use it in a Word mail merge.

Allow Background Saves

Allow background saves allows Word to save documents while you keep working. You always know that a background save is underway because a pulsing disk icon appears in the status bar while Word is writing the file to disk.

Save AutoRecover Info

Word can store information about your file at specified intervals from one minute to two hours, so you will have a backup if your computer crashes or loses power while you're working. This is called AutoRecover. You can choose it and specify the interval in the *Save AutoRecover info every* option listed in the Options dialog box. The disadvantage of AutoRecover is that it forces you to stop working for a few moments while the computer saves this information.

NOTE. *AutoRecover doesn't save a complete copy of your file. It saves only the information you did not have the opportunity to save before your computer failed. In fact, the only time you will see an AutoRecover file is if your Word session ends abnormally. If you save regularly on your own, you may find that your own saved files may be more current than the files AutoRecover generates, so spot-check your AutoRecovered files before you decide to work with them.*

How Word Saves Files to Word 6/Word 95 Format

As already mentioned, Word 97 utilizes a new file format. This file format was designed to accommodate important Word 97 innovations such as Visual Basic for Applications macros that are stored within documents, not only in templates. By default, Word 97 saves all files in this new format.

If you are sharing files extensively with people who do not use Word 97 yet, you may wish to change the way Word saves files by default. You can do this in the Tools, Options, Save tab, by selecting a different format from the *Save Word files as* drop-down list box.

If you choose to save your files as Word 6/95 files, Word does not actually save them in the file format used by Word 6 and Word 95. Rather, it saves them as Rich Text Format (RTF) files, which are text files that contain all your formatting information as formatting tags. RTF files are somewhat similar in concept to HTML files.

When you save a file using this procedure, as opposed to specifically asking Word to save the file as RTF, the file is stored with the Word DOC extension, however, rather than the RTF extension. When a user then opens the file, it is converted back to Word format for display.

In general, you and your colleagues won't care whether files are RTF files or Word 6 files; they open in the same manner, transparently to the user. There are two exceptions, however. If you have checked the Confirm conversion at Open check box in the Tools, Options General tab, Word will ask you to confirm that you wish to open an RTF file whenever you open a file that you *thought* was formatted as a Word 6 or Word 95 file. Just say *yes*.

More seriously, if your file may be run through a third-party batch conversion program that expects DOC files to be Word 6 or Word 95 files, the batch conversion program may not know how to handle them correctly.

When you save a file to Word 6.0/Word 95 format, Word 97 displays a warning that you will lose any macros stored in this file. If you have macros in the file that you want to preserve, first store a copy of the file in Word 97 format and then make a new copy—with a different file name—in Word 6/95 format.

NOTE. *Users working with Word 6.0 or Word 95 can read Word 97 files if they install a special converter that is available free from Microsoft, through its Web page, FTP site, or on disk by mail for a small handling charge. If you purchased Word 97 as part of Microsoft Office on CD-ROM, you already have this converter. Look for the file **Wrd97cnv.exe** in the **\Valupack\ Wrd97cnv** folder. When a user double-clicks on this file, a program runs to install the appropriate converter in the appropriate location. If the user is running Word 6 for Windows 3.1, the converter Msword8.cnv is installed; if the user is running Word 95 or Word 6 for Windows NT, the converter Mswrd832.cnv is installed.*

■ Retrieving a File That You Recently Worked On

Word, like many Windows applications, keeps track of the last four files that you worked on. These appear at the bottom of the File menu. To reopen one of these files, select it from the File menu.

You might want Word to keep track of more (or fewer) of your most-recently used files. For example, you may routinely work with eight or nine files during an editing session; you might want any of the files you worked on in your previous editing session to be available the next time you open Word. Conversely, you might have added commands to your File menu and not even have room for four files without making the menu too long to work with easily.

You can change the number of files that Word tracks by choosing Options from the Tools menu and choosing the General tab. Reset the **R**ecently Used File List box to any number from 0 to 9 files.

Remember that in Windows 95, your last 15 recently used files also are available from the Documents folder on the Start menu, so if a document you want isn't available from the File menu, try Start, Documents before you go searching your hard disk.

If Word already is running, when you open a file from the Start menu, it opens into the same copy of Word that you're already running, instead of starting a new session of Word. This is a sensible change in behavior from Windows 3.1, because it recognizes that most users don't have RAM to waste by opening duplicate copies of the same large application at the same time.

■ Using the Word 97 Properties Dialog Box

As you work, Word compiles information about your document and stores it in the Properties dialog box. The properties contained in the Properties dialog box can include a nearly infinite variety of information about your document—from its size and when it was last edited, to the template it is based on and any keywords you specify to help identify it.

All Windows 95 files and programs have a Properties dialog box; even devices such as printers do. The Properties dialog box for Word documents, however, offers more information than most, and Word 97 gives you unprecedented flexibility in organizing and maintaining that information.

You might use Properties to see when you last worked on your report, and who has worked on it since then. Or you might use it along with Word's file search capabilities to identify all documents with a specific keyword. You might even create custom properties that meet the specific needs of your business, such as properties that identify the department where a document was created, or the manager whose responsibility it is.

If you've used Word 6, you'll find that the Properties dialog box include all the information formerly collected in the Summary Info dialog box—and then some. This information is organized in five categories:

- General
- Summary
- Statistics
- Contents
- Custom

If you're managing document production by a group of people, you should consider enabling the Prompt for document properties checkbox in

Tools, Options, Save, so the Properties dialog box will be displayed automatically when a file is saved for the first time.

You might also become enthusiastic about making sure the properties in your document are complete and up-to-date even if you never have to share a document—especially when you consider that Word lets you locate documents by searching for any property that you choose.

You can view a document's properties by choosing File, Properties and specifying a tab containing the category of properties you're interested in. In the following sections, we'll cover each tab.

General Information

The General tab (see Figure 6.7) displays general information about every document which Word stores on its own—information you cannot edit from within the Properties tab. This information includes:

Figure 6.7

The General Properties tab includes information Windows 95 stores regarding your document.

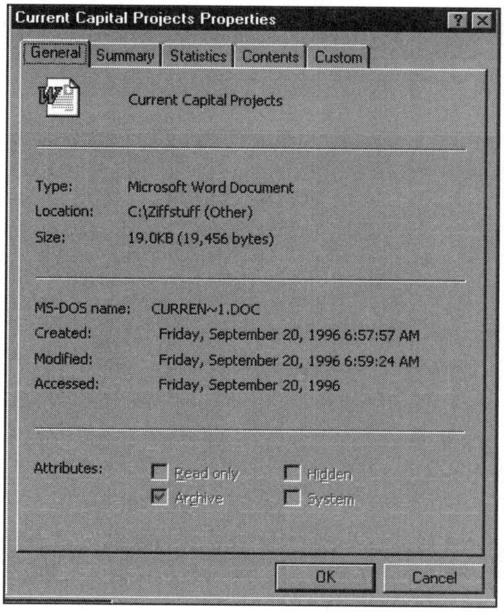

- *Type*—Typically, this entry will be *Microsoft Word Document*. Word gets this information from the document's file extension. Remember, even though file extensions do not appear onscreen in Word 97 or Windows 95 folders by default, they are still attached to documents, stored in the "8.3" short file names that Windows creates so that the files can be accessed by earlier versions of DOS and Windows.

NOTE. *You can open other types of files and view general information about their properties in the General tab as well. For example, a file's MS-DOS 8.3 "short file name" is a property of the document, and viewing the General tab is the easiest way to see that property.*

- *Location*—Word displays the folder where the file is stored.

- *Size*—Word provides file size information both in kilobytes (true kilobytes that are 1,024 bytes each, not the 1,000-byte kilobytes often used by hard-drive manufacturers) and in bytes.

- *MS-DOS Name*—Word provides the file's equivalent short file name—a maximum of eight characters plus a three-character extension.

- *Created*—Word shows the date, time, and second when the file was created.

- *Modified*—Word shows the date, time, and second when the file was last saved. That's useful information, for example, if you have a system crash and need to know whether recent edits were saved.

- *Accessed*—Word shows the date that the file was last accessed.

- *Attributes*—Word stores the current status of the four file attributes associated with every Windows or DOS file: read-only, archive (meaning that the file has been changed since it was last archived), hidden, or system (meaning that the file is a Windows or DOS system file).

No information is stored in the General tab until the first time you save a file. Also, you can't edit any of the information stored in the General tab since Word and Windows keeps track of this data for you.

Summary Information

In the Summary tab of the Properties dialog box, shown in Figure 6.8, Word stores the following Summary information about every document: **T**itle, **S**ubject, **A**uthor, **M**anager, C**o**mpany, Cat**e**gory, **K**eywords, and **C**omments. Each of these entries can be as long as 255 characters.

Using the Title Entry

By default, the first time that you save a document, Word uses the first line of text in the document as the **T**itle of the document, and will list it that way in the *Title:* section of the Summary tab. If you later change the first line of text in the document, however, the **T**itle box does not automatically change. You can edit the document title by placing your insertion point in the **T**itle box and entering new text.

Figure 6.8

The Summary Properties
Tab stores basic
information you provide
about your document, as
well as information
stored elsewhere, such
as the Author's Name.

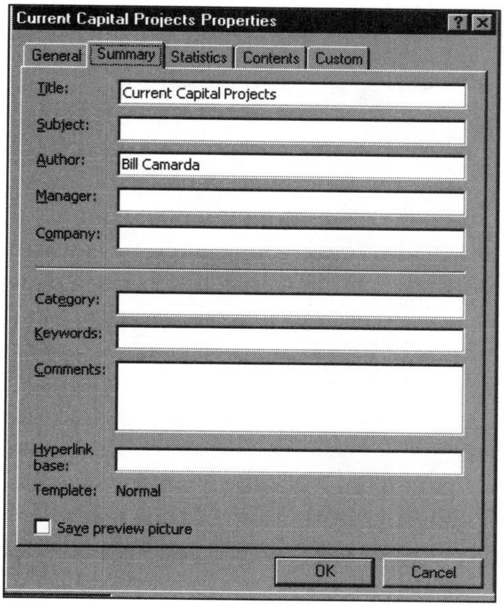

Using the Author Entry

When you open the Properties dialog box, an author's name will probably already appear in the *Author:* box of the Summary tab. It may well be your own name. If, when you installed Word, you included your name as part of the registration information requested by Word, your name was entered into Word's record of User Information and will automatically appear in the *Author:* line of the Summary tab if you created the current document.

All documents created on one computer carry the same author's name. You can change the author's name for a specific document by editing the Author line in the Summary tab of the Properties dialog box. Or, you can change the author's name for all documents you create in the future, by changing it in the Tools, Options, User Information tabbed dialog box, as shown in Figure 6.9.

If you create a file on *one* computer, but save it on *another*, the text in the **A**uthor field will not automatically change. But Word may store a different name in the Last Saved By field, which appears in the Statistics box that will be discussed shortly. The name stored in the Last Saved By field will be the name contained in Tools, User Information on the computer where the file has most recently been saved. In this example, it would be the name stored in Tools, User Information on the *second* computer.

Figure 6.9

In the Tools, Options, User Information tab, you can specify the author's name, initials, and mailing address you want Word to use by default.

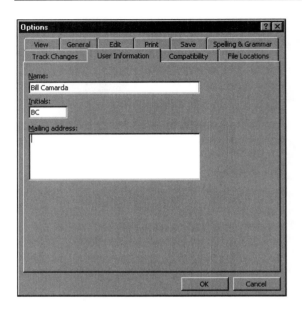

Using Keywords

Keywords are words that represent important concepts or elements in your document, such as the name of a company you're writing to, the product you're writing about, or the nature of a customer complaint. You can include keywords to help you search later for documents containing the same important elements.

For example, you might use Keywords to name all the products included in the document, so you can search for all customer-service letters related to a specific project, possibly discovering patterns. Or, you might use them to search for names of people referred to in each document.

You can use as many keywords as you want, up to a total of 255 characters. Even if you specify multiple keywords in a single document, you can still search for an individual keyword later, if you separate the words with a space and don't use punctuation.

Preview Picture

The Summary tab of the Properties dialog box also now enables you to save a thumbnail picture of the first page of your document for previewing in the Open dialog box. Since the preview picture that Word stores is very small, this function is most useful when the first page of your documents features large items, such as graphics or big headlines, that will be recognizable when displayed in the small print of Picture Preview. If your document features regular-sized text, you might be better off using Word's standard preview option, which shows the first few paragraphs of text in a document. (The preview capabilities built into the Open dialog box are discussed more fully in the section "Choosing Which Files to View," later in this chapter.)

NOTE. *You can also set your document's* hyperlink base *here. See Chapter 12 for detailed coverage of relative and absolute hyperlinks, and hyperlink bases.*

Document Statistics

Word's Properties dialog box also provides detailed statistics about your current document. Click the Statistics tab, and the dialog box shown in Figure 6.10 appears.

Figure 6.10

The Statistics Properties tab tracks word count and other statistics about your current document.

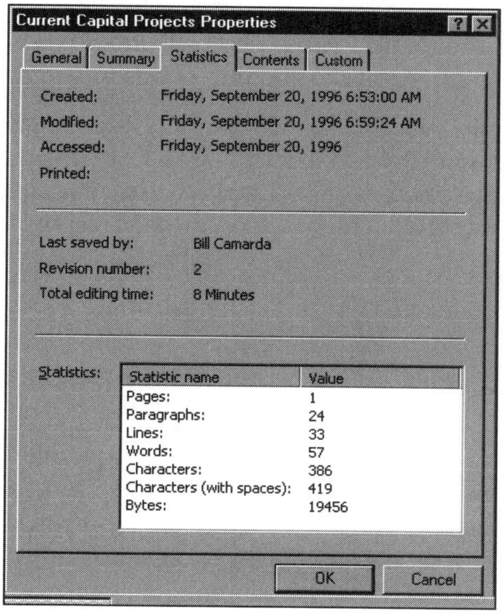

The Document Statistics tab tells you when the document was last printed, as well as the following information:

- *Last Saved By*—Usually the same as **A**uthor in Summary **I**nfo, but can be different if the file was created on another computer, or if you are editing a file created by someone else.

- *Revision Number*—Tracks the number of times that you saved the file, excluding any Word automatic saves. When you save a file for the first time, your current revision number becomes two. Note, though, that

Word counts a revision even if you save a document that hasn't been changed. And if you use Save **A**s to place the file in a new folder, the revision number returns to two.

- *Total Editing Time*—Reflects the amount of time that the document has been open. You can use this feature to track work billed by the hour. Remember that you can always print document properties by selecting Document Properties in the Print what section of the Print dialog box. By the way, if you're working on Document A, and Document B is still open, Word records that you're editing both documents.

- *Statistics*—Tracks the document's page, paragraph, line, word, character, and byte count, as of the last time you saved the document.

Contents Information

The Contents tab (see Figure 6.11) shows the parts of a document. Often there is only one part listed—the document itself, which is represented by its title. However, if you use heading styles in your document and enable the "Save preview picture" checkbox in the Summary tab of the Properties dialog box when you save the file, you will see the headings listed in Document Contents.

Figure 6.11

The Contents Properties tab shows the high-level contents of your document.

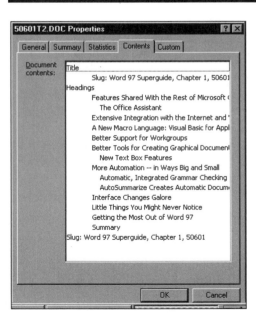

Creating Custom Properties

In Word 6, while the Summary Info feature helped keep track of documents, its categories weren't always appropriate for specialized document tracking.

Word 97 enables you to choose from 27 additional categories, or add categories of your own if Word's don't suffice. To add a category, first choose Properties from the **F**ile menu, and choose the Custom tab, as shown in Figure 6.12. Choose a category from the **N**ame combo box, or place the insertion point in the box and enter a new category name.

Figure 6.12

The Custom Properties tab allows you to create your own properties, or choose from 27 optional properties built into Word.

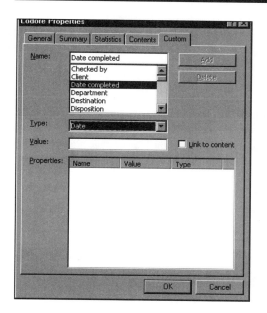

Next, specify a type of data for your new custom category. For example, if you create a custom category named Date Reviewed by Management, you can make sure that nobody can enter anything *but* a date in this category. Next, in the **V**alue box, enter the information that you want associated with this new category. Make sure that the data you enter matches the type you specified. Click on **A**dd and then on OK, and Word adds the new entry.

Later, if you want to edit the value associated with this new category, click on the category name in the **P**roperties box, enter the new text, click on **M**odify, and then click on OK.

To make the most of Custom Properties, you might want to make sure the same custom properties are available for use in all your documents. To do so, add the Custom Property to the Normal template stored in Office95\Templates (or whatever default template you use), and then save the edited template.

To add a Custom Property to the Normal template, enter a placeholder value that users of individual documents will replace. For example, if you add a custom property named Client, you can enter the text Client Name as your value. You can rename this value with the actual name of your client when you use this custom property later.

For more information about editing templates, see Chapter 8, "Templates, Wizards and Add-Ins: Smart Shortcuts for Nearly Every Document."

Linking a Custom Property to Content in a File

You can create a custom property that updates itself when circumstances change. For example, you might use a custom property to update a document containing a table whose values change regularly. Here's a scenario: Each division of your organization sends you a separate quarterly report to management that includes a summary of profits in the form of a Word table. Now you want to use Word's search capabilities to find all the divisions whose profits exceeded $1,000,000—without opening every single file to look. You can bookmark the table cell containing a value for profits, and then use a custom property that reflects the value contained in the bookmark. (See Chapter 3, "Tables," for coverage of table calculations, Chapter 10 for more information on using Word fields, and Chapter 12 for more information on bookmarks. Later, in this chapter's "Choosing a Property" section, you'll learn how to search for documents containing a custom property.)

To create a custom property that can update itself as circumstances change:

1. Enter the information you want to update into the document itself.

2. Select that information, which can include text or fields.

3. Next, mark the selected text with a bookmark.

4. Choose File, Properties, and click the Custom tab if it is not already selected.

5. Check the **L**ink to Content checkbox. (This box is only available if you've added at least one bookmark to your document already.)

6. In the **N**ame box, enter a name for the Custom Property you want to create.

7. Click the down-arrow next to the **S**ource box, and choose the bookmark you've created from the list that appears.

8. Click **A**dd. The new custom property appears with a link icon next to it, as shown in Figure 6.13.

Once you've created a custom property, test it by modifying information in your document, saving the document, and viewing the Custom tab of the Properties dialog box to see if the value has changed properly.

Figure 6.13

A custom property linked
to text via a bookmark

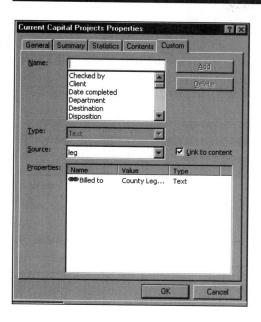

Inspecting the Properties Dialog Box

You can review a document's properties from the Open dialog box while you
decide whether to open the file. To do so, choose Open from the File menu,
and right-click on the document. When the shortcut menu appears, choose
Properties. The Properties tabbed dialog box appears, where you can review
your document's properties before you choose to open it or not.

You don't have to be working in Word to inspect most of the contents of
a Word Properties dialog box. You might, for example, be organizing your
files using the Windows Explorer. Or, you might be looking inside a folder
window containing a series of documents.

In either of the above scenarios, you can right-click on the document
icon and choose Properties from the shortcut menu that appears. Windows
95 then displays the General, Summary, and Statistics tabbed dialog boxes.
You cannot edit this information outside of Word, however.

If the file is a text file that you imported into Word, Summary and Statistics information may not be available from the desktop in Windows 95 or
Windows NT because this information has not yet been compiled by Word.
After you open and resave the file in Word, Summary and Statistics information will become available.

◼ Using the Open Dialog Box to Manage and Locate Files

If you're migrating to Word 97 from Word 6 or an earlier version of Word, you'll discover that the Open dialog box has been completely revamped in Word 97 to take full advantage of Windows's improved file management capabilities—and to go far beyond them, with advanced searching and previewing capabilities.

File, Open now gives you extensive control over the information you can access about the files you're browsing. Using File, Open's shortcut menus, you can copy, delete or rename files from within Word—instead of having to work from Explorer or the Windows desktop. And a highly sophisticated file search mechanism, even better than the one that Word once provided through Find File, is now embedded within the File, Open dialog box.

You'll be using the new Open dialog box a lot, so choose **O**pen from the **F**ile menu and take a quick look around (see Figure 6.14). At the top left, you'll see the Look **i**n box, which shows you which drive or folder you're looking at—and allows you to specify a new one.

To the right of the Look **i**n box, you'll see a set of buttons that you can use to organize how and where your files are displayed. As you'll see later, the last button on the right, Commands and Settings, allows you to perform a wide variety of tasks on your files, including printing and sorting them.

Figure 6.14

Word's Open dialog box, shown in default List view

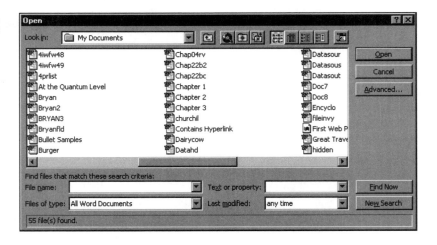

Beneath the Look-in box are the file and folder listings. Right-click on a file or folder, and Word provides a comprehensive list of options—from cutting, copying, and pasting files, to quickly viewing the file's contents in draft font, to e-mailing or faxing the document to a colleague via Microsoft Exchange (see Figure 6.15).

Figure 6.15

Shortcut menu for a file displayed in the Open dialog box

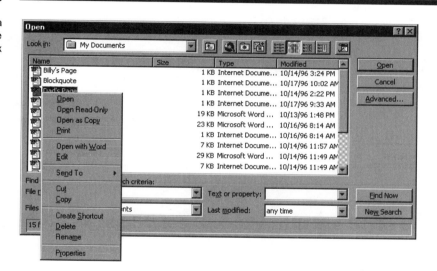

At the bottom of the window in the Open dialog box are basic search criteria that you can use to broaden or narrow Word's search for files in the Open dialog box. You can use these criteria either to weed out files you're not interested in listing now, or to find a specific file.

Word also offers sophisticated search capabilities that you can access by clicking on the **A**dvanced button in the Open dialog box. Word's Advanced Find features are covered later in this chapter.

Choosing a Drive or Folder

Whether you want to open a file or folder, or manage it using File, Open's management capabilities, start by choosing it. With the File, Open dialog box open, click on the Look **i**n drop-down list box at the top left of the Open dialog box (see Figure 6.16) for a bird's-eye view of your computer: the Windows Desktop, each floppy and hard drive, any available network resources, and in Word 97, specific Internet FTP file transfer sites you have made available. (See Chapter 14 for coverage of how to make an Internet FTP site available to Microsoft Word.)

Figure 6.16

The Look in drop-down list box, showing all available locations on your computer and your network, as well as available Internet FTP sites

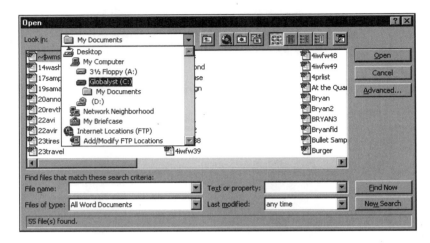

When you first open it, the Open dialog box displays a list of the Word documents in your default Document folder. This folder is typically C:\My Documents, unless you change that default setting through the **T**ools, **O**ptions, File Locations tabbed dialog box.

To look in a different drive now, without changing the default settings, choose a new drive from the Look **i**n drop-down list. To view the contents of a different folder, double-click on that folder icon. To return to the folder one level above, click the Up One Level button to the right of the Look **i**n box.

Changing Your File List Display

Once you display the contents of a folder, Word allows you to choose from a variety of file list formats, each controlled from a button in the toolbar to the right of the Look in box.

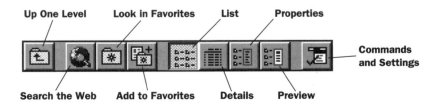

Click on the List button to view a list of file names, their sizes, types, and when they were last modified. This view can help you track different versions of a file, especially in combination with Sorting features (discussed later). Figure 6.17 shows the Open dialog box displaying Details.

Figure 6.17

Details view displays your file's size, type, and last modification date.

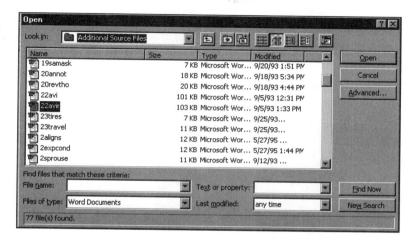

Click on the Properties button to view a summary of the information contained in the currently selected file's Properties dialog box. Figure 6.18 shows the Open dialog box displaying Properties of a selected file.

NOTE. *If you want to see all the properties associated with a file, right-click on the file in the Open dialog box and choose Properties from the shortcut menu that appears.*

Figure 6.18

Properties View, showing selected information from the Properties dialog box

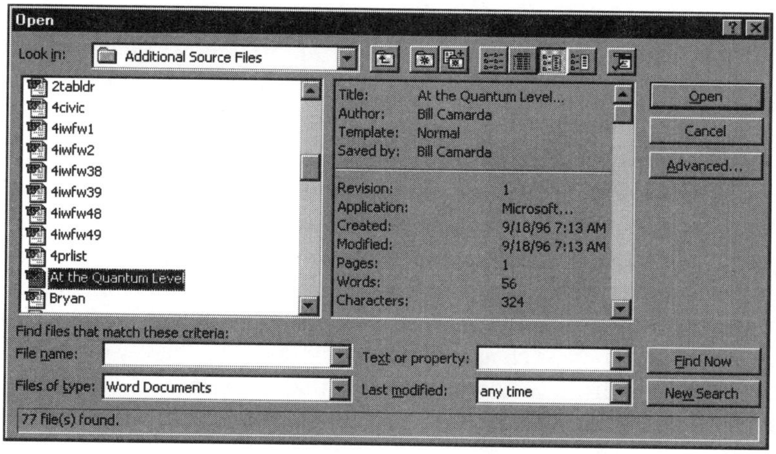

Click on the Preview button to view the first few paragraphs of the document, as shown in Figure 6.19. You can use the vertical scroll bar that appears to the right of the image, to scroll through the document. Unless the file contains a table or other graphic element, Word wraps the document to the width of this window.

Figure 6.19

Preview view displays the first chunk of text in your document.

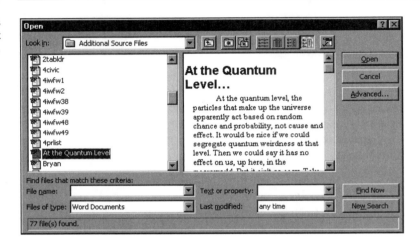

The Preview window displays much formatting information—though not quite all. If you previously saved a thumbnail sketch of the document by checking Save Preview Picture in the Summary tab of **F**ile, Properties, this thumbnail sketch will appear instead of the less-than-WYSIWYG formatting information the Preview window shows by default.

Choosing Which Files to View

As mentioned earlier, Word defaults to viewing only Word documents in the Open dialog box—documents that include a DOC extension. You can, however, tell Word to view any category of files in the current folder. Word's Open dialog box provides powerful winnowing capabilities, allowing you to view and choose from a more manageable selection of files whenever you choose.

To choose to view a different category of document in the Open dialog box, such as text files, click the down arrow next to Files of **t**ype, and choose from the drop-down list that appears.

You can also choose All Files if you want to view every file in the folder, or if you want to view a type of files not listed in the Files of **t**ype drop-down list. For example, say that you want to find a PowerPoint file. There's no PowerPoint category in Files of **t**ype, but you can select All Files and then use the File **n**ame box to specify PPT files. (It's not necessary to enter the "*" wild card.)

Note that Word can use extensions to search for files, even though it does not display those extensions, unless you set your operating system to do so.

NOTE. *Many users still prefer to see the DOS file extensions in their file lists. To display them, double-click My Computer on the Windows 95 Desktop, and choose Options from the View menu. Click the View tab, and clear the Hide MS-DOS file extensions for file types that are registered box.*

As you perform wild-card searches, your searches are stored in the File **n**ame drop-down list box, so you can select them again later without re-entering all the information. Note that Word can use not only the "*" wild card, but also the "?" wild card, which represents one specific character in a file name. For instance, a search for CHAP??MG.DOC finds CHAP02MG.DOC and CHAP12MG.DOC, whereas a search for CHAP0?MG.DOC finds only CHAP02MG.DOC.

Finding Files by Text or Property

You can ask Word to display only files that contain specific text in the Open dialog box. To do so, enter the desired text in the Text or property box in the Open dialog box. Word searches both the document and the Properties you've stored.

This text search is also convenient if you entered keywords that might not appear in the document but would be relevant in helping you find it. For example, a report on the ancient Incas might not include the word "Mesoamerica," but if you included "Mesoamerica" as a keyword in Document Properties, it would show up in this search—along with documents on the Maya, Aztecs, and others stored with the same keyword.

After you specify text to be included as criteria in your search, Word stores that text in case you want to use it again. Display the Te**x**t or property drop-down list to choose this text.

Viewing Files by Last Modification Date

You also can choose a time criteria to display files according to when you created them. The default is "any time," but you also can pick one of these options from the Last **m**odified drop-down list box:

- yesterday
- today
- last week
- this week
- last month

- this month

- any time

You can specify more detailed date and time information by using the advanced searches covered in following section, "Performing Advanced Searches."

Performing a New Search

After you perform a search that displays only a portion of the files in your current folder, you can restore the entire list of files—either for another search, or simply to prevent you from "misplacing" files that are in a folder but don't appear in the file list. To do so, click on New Search, and Word resets the search criteria to All files modified any time—the broadest possible search criteria within the current folder.

NOTE. *Be judicious when selecting drives to search from the Open dialog box. If your network server has a large hard disk, the search can require a long time to perform. Whenever possible, refine the search by selecting specific subfolders on large drives.*

Performing Advanced Searches

If you haven't been able to find the file you're looking for using the basic search capabilities built into the Open dialog box, use the more extensive search features available in the Advanced Find dialog box (see Figure 6.20).

Figure 6.20

You can perform more complex searches from the Advanced Find dialog box.

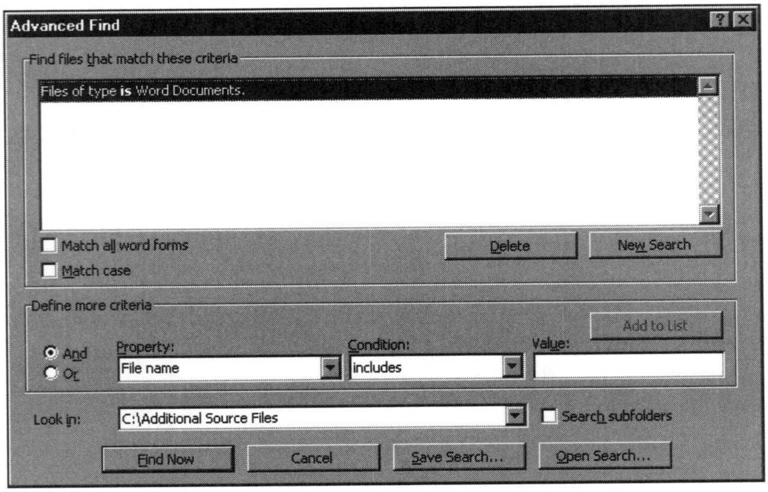

To use Advanced Find, follow these steps:

1. Specify search criteria in the Open dialog box. You might specify only Word documents created during the previous month, for example.

2. Click on **A**dvanced. The Advanced Find dialog box opens, displaying the criteria you already set.

3. Build a search by specifying additional criteria: Choose from the built-in Word properties in the **P**roperty drop-down list box, and specify a condition from the **C**ondition drop-down list box.

As you'll see, the conditions available to each property vary, depending on the nature of the property. If necessary, also specify a value for Word to search for. Also notice that you can define a new criterion using the term "And," which means that Word will only display files which meet this criteria as well as the previous criteria you've set. Alternatively, you can use the term "Or," which means that Word will display all files that meet your new criteria, *as well as* all files that meet other criteria you've already set. Searching with "And" or "Or" is discussed in more detail later in this chapter.

4. Choose **A**dd to List to include this new criteria in your search. A line of text describing your search criteria (in English!) appears in the Advanced Find window. You can add as many separate search criteria as you want.

5. Check the Look in criteria and change the location, if necessary. Also, if you want Word to search the folders below the one specified in the Look in list, enable the Search subfolders checkbox.

6. After you enter all the necessary search criteria, choose **F**ind Now to perform the search. Word displays the files it finds in the Name box within the Open dialog box.

The following sections take a closer look at building a search.

Choosing a Property

The **P**roperty drop-down list in the Advanced Find dialog box contains all the properties available in Word's Properties dialog box, plus many that aren't, such as Number of Slides, which you might use if searching for a PowerPoint presentation file; and Number of Multimedia Clips. (Yes, Word's Advanced Find feature can even search for all documents that contain a specific number of multimedia clips.)

It's important to note that Advanced Find does not limit you to working with properties stored in the document's Properties dialog box. One of the options available from the **P**roperty box is Text or property, which searches the contents of documents as well as their Properties dialog box.

If you want to search for a custom property, type the property in the **P**roperty box. Of course, Word can find a custom property only in those documents in which you have assigned the custom property.

Specifying a Condition

After entering a property, enter a condition in the **C**ondition box. The conditions available to you vary widely depending on the property you specify. If you're searching for specific text in your document, you have a variety of choices, from basic choices like "includes words" to more sophisticated choices like "includes near each other," which you could use to find documents with specified words *only if those words appear in close proximity.* If you're searching based on file name instead, you have three options:

- *includes*—The property must include specific text or a specific numeric value. This is the most flexible criterion, because it enables Word to flag documents regardless of where in the file name the characters are.

- *begins with*—The property must begin with specific text or a specific numeric value. This might be useful if you want to search for documents with their file names in series, such as MEMO1, MEMO2, and MEMO3.

- *ends with*—The file name must end with the characters you specify. This is increasingly useful in an age of long file names, when you might be in the habit of naming files like Jones Report, Stewart Report, and so on.

Or if the property you're searching for contains a numeric value such as total editing time, you'll have the following choices:

- equals

- does not equal

- any number between...

- at most

- at least

- more than

- less than

Finally, if you've specified a property that consists of a date, such as Last modified, you'll have yet another set of choices:

- yesterday

- today

- last week

- this week

- last month

- this month

- any time

- any time between

- on

- on or after

- on or before

- in the last

Specifying a Value

In most advanced searches, you also have to specify a value. However, you won't need to specify a value when you've already given Word enough information to find the designated files. For example, if you've asked Word to search for files created yesterday, Word doesn't need to know what day yesterday was—it can figure that out for itself.

Word is fairly flexible about how it recognizes values. For example, if you ask to search for all files modified between two dates, you can specify the dates in any of the following formats:

- May 8 and June 9

- 5/8 and 6/9

- 5/8/95 and 6/9/95

Notice, however, that you always have to use the word *and* to separate the two values: "&" or a hyphen won't work.

After you enter a property, condition, and value, if necessary, choose **A**dd to List and Word will include the new criteria in the list to be searched.

Using "Or" Criteria

Typically, when you use more than one criterion in an advanced search, you intend to narrow the search. If you ask to find files that were created after June 5, 1995 *and* contain the text "Machiavelli," chances are you'll find fewer files than if you used only one criterion or the other. (You certainly won't find *more* files.)

Word expects you to build searches this way, which is why, in the default setting, the A**n**d option button in the Define more criteria box in the Advanced Find dialog box is checked.

Sometimes, however, you'll want to build a list of *several* kinds of files. You might, for example, want to see both customer service letters and thank-you letters. Or, you might want to see all the presentation files on your disk, regardless of the software used to create them. You can build a search that captures several different kinds of documents by clicking the O**r** radio button each time you establish additional search criteria. When you add the new search criteria, the word "Or" appears at the beginning of the line, as in the following:

```
Application name includes PowerPoint
Or: Application name includes Freelance
Or: Application name includes Harvard Graphics
```

Matching Word Forms and Case

By default, Word searches are not case-sensitive. If you search for documents containing the name "Stone," you might inadvertently also retrieve documents about rocks and gravel. You can choose to make your searches case-sensitive by checking the **M**atch case checkbox in the Advanced Find dialog box.

Word 97 also includes a feature that enables you to liberalize searches so that Word finds the word you're looking for whether it's expressed in past, present, or future tense. If you're searching for documents containing the word "write," you could miss documents that include the word "written." Check the Match al**l** word forms checkbox and Word will catch both.

Note that you can only use these features if you are searching for text in a document; they don't work if you searching by document file name.

Saving and Reusing Searches

Searches can get quite complicated, and recreating them from scratch is a hassle. Fortunately, Word enables you to save searches and then reuse them.

To save a search, create it in either the Open dialog box or the Advanced Find dialog box, and then choose **S**ave Search in the Advanced Find dialog box. The Save Search dialog box opens, as shown in Figure 6.21; enter a name for this search and choose OK.

Figure 6.21

The Save Search dialog box

You can retrieve a saved search in two ways. In the Open dialog box, click on the Commands and Settings button, and choose S**a**ved Searches from the shortcut menu that appears. A cascaded menu appears, listing all saved searches. Click on the one you want. Or, from the Advanced Find dialog box, choose **O**pen Search. The Open Search dialog box appears (see Figure 6.22), also listing all saved searches. Select the search you want, and choose **O**pen.

Figure 6.22

The Open Search dialog box

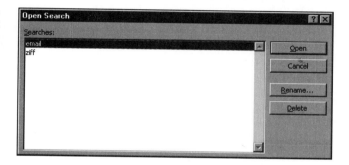

■ Using the Favorites Folder

What do you do when you regularly need to access the same files, but you also need to store them in different folders? For example, say that you need to access monthly reports for all your clients at once—but you store each client's files in separate folders. In Word 6, you would have had to open each folder before accessing the files you wanted—or create a complex search for them.

Word 97's Open dialog box solves this problem by taking advantage of Windows 95 shortcuts. *Shortcuts* are small files that act as pointers to other files (or programs). When you select the shortcut, the file (or program) opens. You might have already created some shortcuts on your Windows 95 desktop. Word 97 can create shortcuts for you and store them in a Favorites folder, which it stores within the Windows 95 folder.

Then you can simply open the Favorites folder to access all your most-used documents. Double-click on a document name, and the document will open—even though the actual document still is stored in the same place it was originally, and only the pointer appears in the Favorites folder. The Favorites feature gives you the best of both worlds—you can organize your files in the way that make the most sense, but still get easy access to the ones you use the most from a central location.

To create a shortcut and place it in the Favorites folder, click on the Add to Favorites button on the row of buttons to the right of the Look in box in the Open dialog box. Word displays a shortcut menu with two choices. The first choice, Add 'Current' Folder to Favorites adds a shortcut to your entire current folder. (The actual name of your current folder appears in the shortcut menu.) The second choice, Add Selected Item to Favorites, adds only the file you select.

Creating Other Shortcuts within the Open Dialog Box

You can use shortcuts for purposes other than just quick access to files. Another common purpose is to gain access to a single file from multiple locations. Consider the example used earlier. Imagine that all of a client's information is stored in a folder with her company's name. Now you want to invoice the client. Should you access the invoices in an invoice folder, or in the client folder? Now, with shortcuts, the file can appear in both places.
To create a shortcut, follow these steps:

1. Select the file you want to create a shortcut for in the Open dialog box.

2. Right-click on the file, and choose Create Shortcut from the menu that appears. Word creates a shortcut in the same folder, adding the words "Shortcut to" to the file name.

   That's all well and good, but a shortcut in the same location as the original file doesn't do much for you. In Word 97, however, you can cut, copy, and paste shortcuts and files in the Open dialog box, just as you would text in a document:

1. Select the shortcut (or file) you want to move.

2. Right-click to view the shortcut menu, and choose Cut.

3. Use the Look in box to move to the drive and folder in which you want to place the shortcut.

4. Right-click in an empty portion of the destination folder, and choose Paste from the shortcut menu. Word pastes the shortcut (or file) in the new location.

Using Commands and Settings

The Commands and Settings button in the Open dialog box gives you control over the way information is displayed in the Name window in the dialog box. When you click on the Commands and Settings button, the shortcut menu shown in Figure 6.23 appears. This menu is something of a catch-all for commands that don't fit elsewhere (though some of these commands are duplicated on the shortcut menu that appears when you right-click on a file or folder).

Figure 6.23

The Commands and
Settings menu

**Commands and
Settings menu**

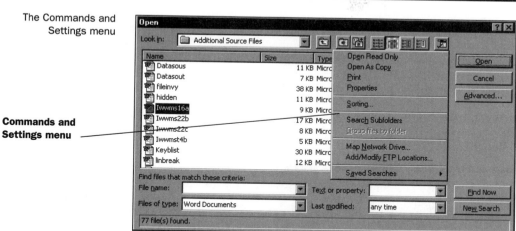

Some of the options in the Commands and Settings shortcut menu are relatively straightforward. **P**rint opens the Print dialog box so you can print the file or files you selected. Propert**i**es displays the Properties dialog box discussed at length in the section "Using Word 97 Properties Dialog Box," earlier in this chapter. The other Commands and Settings options are discussed in the following sections.

Opening a File as Read-Only

Op**e**n Read Only in the Commands and Settings shortcut menu in the Open dialog box opens a file but does not allow changes to be made to the file. Op**e**n Read Only *can* help you or a colleague avoid inadvertently overwriting a file you intended to preserve.

Sorting Files

Choose **S**orting in the Commands and Settings menu to display the Sort By dialog box (see Figure 6.24), which enables you to sort the files in a number of different sort orders displayed in the dialog box.

- *Name*—Sorts files by long file name, disregarding extensions.

- *Size*—Sorts files in order of size.

- *Type*—In order of file type, sorted by extension name. This is the default setting, though you might not notice it because Word's default setting shows only Word documents and no other types of files.

- *Modified*—Sorts files in the order of the Last Modified date stored in the Properties dialog box.

Figure 6.24

From the Sort By dialog box, you can sort files by name, type, size, or last modification date.

An option button controls whether the files are listed in ascending or descending order.

Searching Subfolders

By default, when Word displays the contents of a folder, it shows subfolders first and then individual files. Sometimes, however, you might want to view the files contained in the subfolders at the same time as you see the files contained in the folder itself. To do so, click on the Commands and Settings button in the Open dialog box, and choose Searc**h** Subfolders from the shortcut menu. Word displays all the files as if they were stored in the same folder. If you would like to see the files organized by subfolder, choose **G**roup files by folder. This option is available if Searc**h** Subfolders is selected; it is turned on by default when you enable the Search Subfolders command.

Mapping Network Drives

A mapped drive is a shortcut to a location that exists elsewhere on your network. For example, if you frequently work with a folder that is far down in the folder hierarchy on another drive, such as "F:\DOCS\CLIENTS\D-G\ DISNEY," you could map a drive "Q" that takes you straight to the DIS-NEY folder. Of course, when you map a drive, you must map to a drive letter that has not previously been assigned.

To map a network location to a drive letter on your computer, first click on the Commands and Settings button, and then choose **M**ap Network Drive from the shortcut menu to open the Map Network Drive dialog box (see Figure 6.25). Then, specify the drive name in the **D**rive box. If you want the drive letter designation to represent the same folder in future sessions, you must enable the Reconnect at logon checkbox.

This feature only works if you are on a network.

Sending Files to Disk, E-mail, Fax, or Briefcase

The Send To command on the shortcut menu that appears when you right-click a file in Word 97's Open dialog box can be used to share data with colleagues, via e-mail, fax, or by copying files to disk.

Figure 6.25

You can use the Map Network Drive dialog box to create a shortcut to a specific folder on your network.

To use Se**n**d To, select a file (or files), and then right-click and choose Se**n**d To. A cascaded menu appears with all the choices currently available to you.

If you choose 3 1/2" Floppy or 5 1/4" Floppy, Word copies the files to disk. If you choose Fax Recipient, Word opens the Microsoft Fax Wizard and walks you through the steps required to send a fax. If you choose My Briefcase, Word copies the file to the Windows 95 Briefcase, which is used to synchronize files used on both desktop and portable computers.

Sharing a Folder Across a Network

If you have installed Windows 95's networking capabilities, you can share folders with users on computers connected to yours. To share a folder from within the Open dialog box, click on the folder, and then right-click on S**h**aring. The folder's Properties tabbed dialog box opens, displaying the Sharing tab as shown in Figure 6.26.

Figure 6.26

If your folder is not shared, you can share it from the Sharing tab of the folder's Properties dialog box.

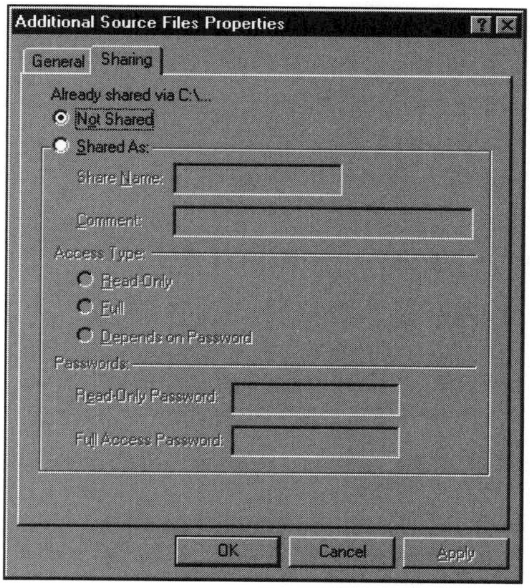

By default, folders are not shared. To change the default setting, click on hared As in the Sharing tab in the Additional Source Files Properties dialog box. Word suggests a share name, the name by which colleagues will recognize this folder. By default, this name is the same as the current folder name, but you can change the name. You also can add a comment about the folder's contents that will be available to other users.

You can provide three types of access to the shared folder: **R**ead-Only, which enables colleagues to read but not edit your files; **F**ull access, which provides the same access that you have to the folder's files; or **D**epends on Password, which enables you to provide full access only to those with the correct password.

If you specify **D**epends on Password, enter a password in the R**e**ad-Only Password box. The password can be up to 15 characters. The Password Confirmation dialog box appears, as shown in Figure 6.27. Type the password again for it to take effect. As you type, Word displays asterisks (*) in place of the password characters, so no one can "shoulder-surf" your password by reading the screen while you type.

Figure 6.27

The Password
Confirmation dialog
box allows you to
confirm a password for
sharing folders.

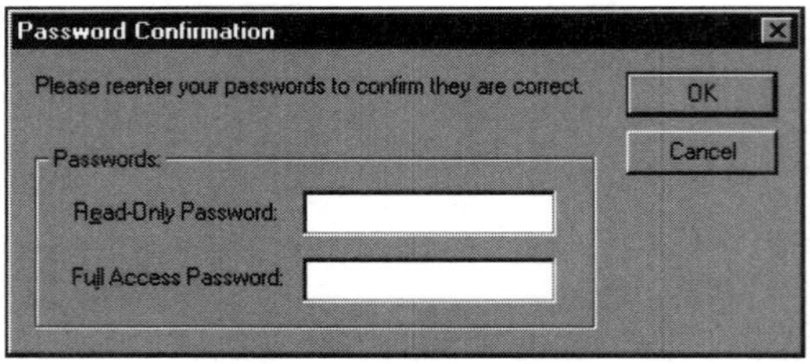

Note that the passwords described here apply only to the folder as a whole. Whether or not you protect a folder, you also can apply passwords to individual files, as discussed next.

■ Using Passwords

Have a file that you don't want anyone to see? Protect it with a password. When you're ready to save a file, perform these steps:

1. Choose Save **A**s from the **F**ile menu.

2. Choose **O**ptions.

3. Type the password in the Password to open box, as shown in Figure 6.28. As you type, Word displays asterisks (*).

Figure 6.28

You can establish
password protection for a
specific file in the Tools,
Options, Save tabbed
dialog box.

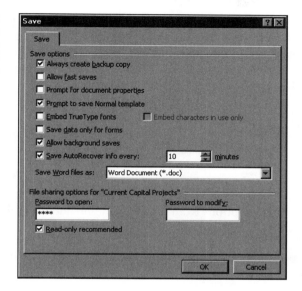

4. Click OK.

5. After Word accepts your password, click the Save button in the Save As dialog box, and the file is saved with the password.

NOTE. *This is serious password protection. Word actually encrypts the file, using a 40-bit encryption algorithm that is the strongest the U.S. government has allowed to be exported. If you open the file with another program that doesn't recognize Word's passwords, all you get is gibberish. WordPad can't display the contents of a Word password-protected file; neither can the Notepad text editor. Make sure you remember your password, without leaving it in plain sight where someone else can find it. And don't use obvious passwords, like your child's name. If you trust yourself not to leave your password where it can be found, you might use a password that serves another purpose as well, such as your CompuServe, MCI Mail, or cash machine password.*

After you password-protect a file, you can change or delete the password only from within the file. To delete a password, follow these steps:

1. Choose Save **A**s from the **F**ile menu.

2. Choose **O**ptions. The Options dialog box opens with the Save tab displayed.

3. Delete the password.

4. Choose OK.

5. In the Save As dialog box, choose **S**ave.

■ Creating File Types to Be Recognized by Word

Windows 3.1 contained a feature called *file association*, which enabled you to associate specific file extensions with specific programs. Windows 3.1 automatically recognizes DOC files as Word documents, for example, so when you double-click on a DOC file, Word opens. That's still the case in Windows 95. However, Windows 95 calls this feature *File Types*.

Say you regularly create reports and want them all to have the extension RPT. You want to place some of these reports on the Windows 95 desktop, and when you double-click on one of these files, you want the file to open in Word. Here's how to associate the RPT file type with Word in Windows 95:

1. Minimize Word and double-click on the My Computer icon on the Windows 95 desktop.

2. Choose **O**ptions from the **V**iew menu, and click the File Types tab, as shown in Figure 6.29.

Figure 6.29

From the File Types tab, you can associate a new file extension with Word, so that Word opens whenever you double-click on a file containing this extension.

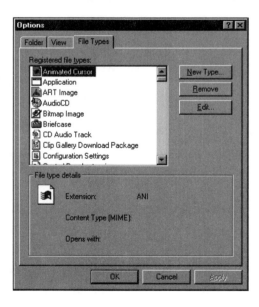

3. Choose **N**ew Type.

4. The Add New File Type dialog box opens (see Figure 6.30). In the **D**escription of type box, enter the name of the file type you want to create; in this example, you might use Report.

Figure 6.30

The Add New File
Type dialog box

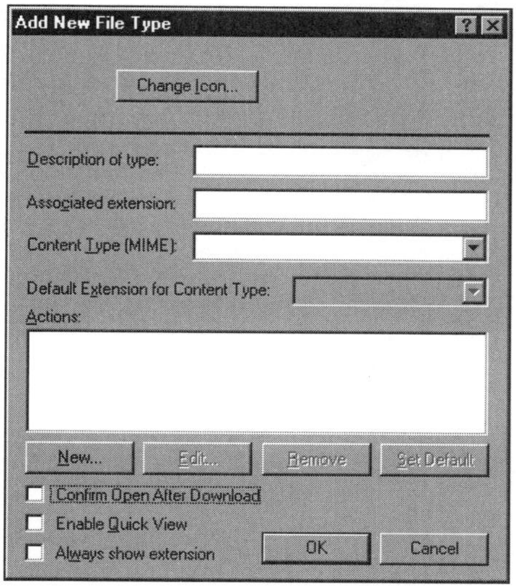

5. In the Associated extension box, type the file extension you want to use; in this example, RPT.

6. Choose **N**ew to specify the action you want to associate with this file. The New Action dialog box opens (see Figure 6.31).

Figure 6.31

Enter Open in the Action
box to make sure that
Word opens when a file
with this extension is
double-clicked.

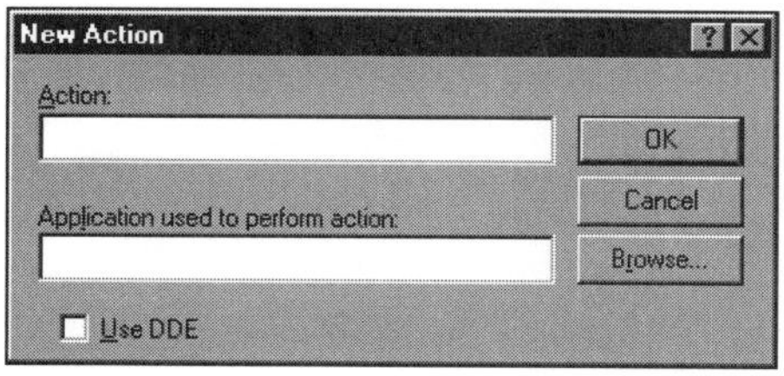

7. In the **A**ction box, type **Open**. (By doing this, you tell Windows that you want to specify what program to open. If you entered Print, you would be specifying which program should print this file when you drag the file to a printer icon.)

8. In the App**l**ication used to perform action box, enter the entire path to the Microsoft Word application (or click B**r**owse and find the Microsoft Word application file in the Browse dialog box).

9. The Add New File Type dialog box reappears with the word Open appearing in the **A**ctions box, and the Word icon appearing to the left of the Change Icon button. Click Close twice.

Now that you know how to manage your documents, in Chapter 7 you'll take a close look at Word's features for automating and streamlining the process of formatting a document.

- *Understanding Styles*

- *Using Word's Default Styles*

- *Applying a Style*

- *Using a Built-In Style That Doesn't Appear in the Style Box*

- *Creating a New Style by Example*

- *Creating a New Style with Format Style*

- *Changing an Existing Style by Using Style by Example*

- *A Word about How Word Interprets Formatting in a Redefined Style*

- *Changing an Existing Style Using Format Style*

- *Copying Styles between Documents*

- *Changing Styles Globally with the Style Gallery*

- *Renaming a Style*

- *Deleting a Style*

- *How Manual Formatting and Styles Interact*

- *Finding Styles Automatically*

- *Replacing Styles Automatically*

- *Keeping Track of Styles*

- *Checking Styles with Help Menu's What's This?*

- *Preparing Style Sheets for Export*

- *Using Word's AutoFormatting Feature*

Styles and AutoFormatting: The Fastest Way to Great-Looking Work

UNTIL NOW, YOU'VE BEEN WORKING RETAIL; THAT IS, YOU'VE made only one edit or one formatting change at a time. The Formatting toolbar and the keyboard shortcuts can make formatting so delightfully easy that many Word users never go any further. But if you always stop at the Formatting toolbar, you're missing out on Word's most impressive productivity tools.

It's time to start working wholesale. By using styles, AutoFormatting, templates, AutoText, and fields, you can magnify the results of your efforts dramatically.

Instead of reformatting a document one paragraph at a time, you can reformat tall documents (in a single bound!) by using styles, AutoFormatting, and templates. Instead of rekeying the same text over and over again, you can insert it automatically (faster than a speeding bullet!) by using AutoText. (This feature is covered in Chapter 9, "AutoText and AutoSummarize.")

In this chapter, you start by learning how to use styles and AutoFormatting—Word's features for wholesale text formatting.

Styles are doubly important in Word 97 because so many other features depend on them. For example, Word can automatically compile a table of contents for your entire document, but only if you've added styles to identify your headings. Word can add chapter numbers to all your document's page numbers, but only if you format your chapter heading with a unique style.

Before Word 6 or Word 7, styles were considered an extraordinary time-saver. Now they're the price of admission to many of Word's most exciting new features.

This chapter will cover understanding styles, using the Normal style, how to apply a style, and creating keyboard shortcuts for applying a style. This chapter also shows you how to create a new style, how to create and modify a style based on an existing style, and how to set an option for automatically following one style with another. You also learn how to copy and move a style between documents, rename and delete styles, clear manual formatting, find and replace styles, and keep track of styles with the Style Gallery and the Organizer. Finally, you're shown how to use AutoFormatting.

■ Understanding Styles

A style is simply a group of formatting instructions that you can name and assign to as much text as you want. Styles offer you three major advantages:

- Instead of individually formatting every attribute of every paragraph or chunk of text, you can do a great deal of formatting with a single command.

- Your document's formatting can remain consistent because you're using a limited number of styles, instead of a virtually infinite number of possible manual formatting combinations

- When you need to change a document's formatting, you only have to change a few styles, not every single paragraph.

The more complex or changeable your document, the more you need styles. Granted, Word isn't quite a desktop-publishing program, but for many complex documents, Word's styles make it better than a desktop-publishing program.

NOTE. *Styles are closely related to templates. Templates are covered in detail in the next chapter; for now, think of a template as the overall starting point for a document, including a default style sheet, macro commands, keyboard shortcuts, and other customization, possibly including toolbar and menu changes. In this chapter, assume that all the style techniques are being used within a single template.*

Saving Time with Styles: An Example

Until they see it for themselves, many people don't believe how much time styles can save them. Here's an example: The *pullquote* paragraph shown in Figure 7.1 is designed to call attention to a quotation and add graphic interest to a page.

Figure 7.1

A sample pullquote

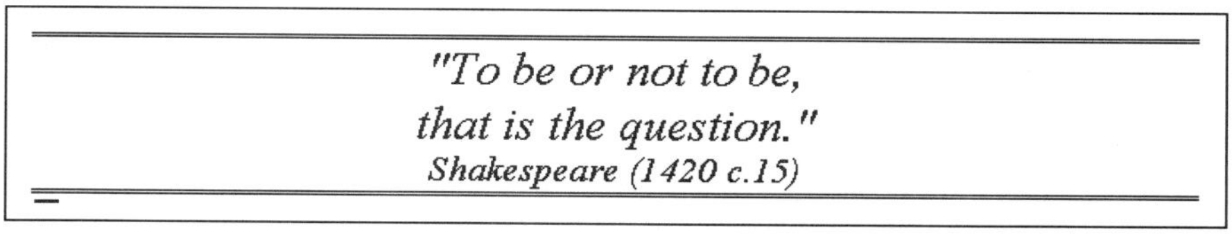

> *"To be or not to be,*
> *that is the question."*
> *Shakespeare (1420 c.15)*

Suppose that you want to make this piece of text appear in a particular font, font size, font style, centered, and with top and bottom borders, but you formatted the whole thing manually. You'd have to use 18-point type for the quotation itself and 14-point type for the quotation's attribution. A double line at the top and bottom adds a border, and three points of space between these borders and the text makes it easier to read. Finally, you'd have to add half a line of blank space between the quotation and the attribution.

This formatting requires 36 mouse clicks and keystrokes. Those 36 clicks and keystrokes would be required every time you created another pullquote. Those ten pullquotes x 36 mouse clicks = 360 actions. That is, unless you use styles.

With styles, all you have to do is select the quotation, including the top border, and type Quote in the Style box on the Formatting toolbar. Then select the quotation's attribution, including the bottom border, and type QRef in the Style box.

This nifty shortcut is called *defining styles by example*, and it enables you to create and name both styles with only 15 clicks and keystrokes. If you want to use both styles, you need to invest only six more clicks. Because this is a total of only 21 keystrokes, you can save 42 percent of your effort the first time you use these styles, and then save 83 percent every time afterward. This way, ten pullquotes = 75 actions.

You can save even more time with styles by telling Word to use QRef automatically as the next style whenever it sees the Quote style. In this real-world example, styles save more than three-quarters of your time and effort.

■ Using Word's Default Styles

Even if you're not using styles, Word is. When you open a document using the default Normal template, Word opens an accompanying *style sheet*—a set of styles. The default style is Normal, which formats your text as in Table 7.1.

Table 7.1

Default Styles of the
Normal Template

ELEMENT	TYPE OF FORMATTING
Font	Times New Roman, 10-point
Language	English (U.S.)
Character Scale	100%
Alignment	Flush Left
Line Spacing	Single
Pagination	Widow/Orphan Control
Outline Level	Body Text

This is the format of your text when you first open Word. Three other styles are immediately available: Heading 1, Heading 2, and Heading 3. Word uses these styles to create three types of headings.

Each heading is based on the Normal style; it uses all the Normal style's attributes except when you specify a different attribute. In essence, any changes you make to Word's default styles are superimposed on the Normal style.

Some 90 additional styles are available in the Normal template, even though they aren't immediately shown on the screen.

These styles are divided into paragraph styles and character styles. In Word for Windows version 2, every style was a paragraph style; that is, it affected the formatting of the entire paragraph to which you applied it. Word 6, Word 7, and Word 97, however, are more precise. You can create and use character styles that apply only to selected text within a paragraph. Tables 7.2 and 7.3 list all the Word styles built into the Normal template.

Table 7.2

Character Styles in the
Normal Template

AS "DEFAULT PARAGRAPH FONT PLUS" STYLE NAME	FORMATS THIS	THIS FORMATTING
Comment Reference	Initials of person making comment	8 pt
Emphasis	Regular body text	Underline
Endnote Reference	Endnote number or custom mark	Superscript
Followed Hyperlink	Text used in a followed hyperlink	Underline, Violet
Footnote Reference	Footnote number or custom mark	Superscript
Hyperlink	Text used in a hyperlink	Underline, Blue
Line Number	Line numbers	No additional formatting
Page Number	Page numbers	No additional formatting
Strong	Regular body text	Bold

Table 7.3

Paragraph Styles in the
Normal Template

AS "NORMAL PLUS" STYLE NAME	FORMATS THIS	THIS FORMATTING
Block Text	Regular body text, Indent: Left 1" Right 1"	Space after 6 pt
Body Text	Regular body text	Space after 6 pt
Body Text 2	Regular body text	Line spacing double, space after 6 pt
Body Text 3	Regular body text	Font: 8 pt, space after 6 pt
Body Text First Indent	Indented body text	Indent: First 0.15"
Body Text First Indent 2	Indented body text	Indent: First 0.15"
Body Text Indent	Indented body text	Indent: Left 0.25", space after 6 pt
Body Text Indent 2	Indented body text	Line spacing double, space after 6 pt

Table 7.3 (Continued)

Paragraph Styles in the
Normal Template

AS "NORMAL PLUS" STYLE NAME	FORMATS THIS	THIS FORMATTING
Body Text Indent 3	Indented body text	Font: 8 pt, Indent Left 0.25", space after 6 pt
Caption	Captions created by Word's Insert Caption feature	Bold, Space before 6 pt, space after 6 pt
Closing	Yours truly, or a similar phrase in the closing of a letter	Indent: Left 3"
Comment Text	Text in a comment pane	No additional formatting
Date	Text in a date	No additional formatting
Document Map	Text used in Document Map headings	Font: Tahoma, Pattern: Clear (Dark Blue)
Endnote Text	Text appearing in endnote pane	No additional formatting
Envelope Address	Addressee's address placed on envelope by Word's Envelopes and Labels Font feature	Font: Arial 12 pt, Indent left 2", Position Center horizontal relative to page, 0.13" From text horizontal, Bottom vertical relative to margin, Width: Exactly 5.5", Height: Exactly 1.38"
Envelope Return	Return address placed on envelope by Word's Envelopes and Labels feature	Font: Arial
Footer	Text placed in footer area	Tab stops: 3" centered, 6" right flush
Footnote Text	Text placed in footnote pane	No additional formatting
Header	Text placed in header area	Tab stops: 3" centered, 6" right flush
Heading 1	1st-level heading	Font: Arial 14 pt Bold, Kern at 14 pt, space before 12 pt after 3 pt, Keep with next, Level 1
Heading 2	2nd-level heading	Font: Arial 12 pt Bold Italic, space before 12 pt, after 3 pt, Keep with next, Level 2
Heading 3	3rd-level heading	Font: 12 pt Bold, space before 12 pt, after 3 pt, Keep with next, Level 3

Table 7.3 (Continued)

Paragraph Styles in the
Normal Template

AS "NORMAL PLUS" STYLE NAME	FORMATS THIS	THIS FORMATTING
Heading 4	4th-level heading	Font: 12 pt Bold Italic, space before 12 pt, after 3 pt, Keep with next, Level 4
Heading 5	5th-level heading	Font: 11 pt, space before 12 pt, after 3 pt, Level 5
Heading 6	6th-level heading	Font: 11 pt Italic, space before 12 pt, after 3 pt, Level 6
Heading 7	7th-level heading	Font: Arial, space before 12 pt, after 3 pt, Level 7
Heading 8	8th-level heading	Font: Arial Italic, space before 12 pt, after 3 pt, Level 8
Heading 9	9th-level heading	Font: Arial 9 pt Bold Italic, space before 12 pt, after 3 pt, Level 9
Index 1	1st-level index entry	Indent: Hanging 0.14", Automatically update
Index 2	2nd-level index entry	Indent: Left 0.14", Hanging 0.14", Automatically update
Index 3	3rd-level index entry	Indent: Left 0.28", Hanging 0.14", Automatically update
Index 4	4th-level index entry	Indent: Left 0.42", Hanging 0.14", Automatically update
Index 5	5th-level index entry	Indent: Left 0.56", Hanging 0.14", Automatically update
Index 6	6th-level index entry	Indent: Left 0.69", Hanging 0.14", Automatically update
Index 7	7th-level index entry	Indent: Left 0.83", Hanging 0.14", Automatically update
Index 8	8th-level index entry	Indent: Left 0.97", Hanging 0.14", Automatically update
Index 9	9th-level index entry	Indent: Left 1.11", Hanging 0.14", Automatically update
Index Heading	Heading separators	Font: Arial Bold (these appear after you compile the index)
List	1st-level item in Word list	Indent: Hanging 0.25"

Table 7.3 (Continued)

Paragraph Styles in the Normal Template

AS "NORMAL PLUS" STYLE NAME	FORMATS THIS	THIS FORMATTING
List 2	2nd-level item in Word list	Indent: Left 0.25", Hanging 0.25"
List 3	3rd-level item in Word list	Indent: Left 0.50", Hanging 0.25"
List 4	4th-level item in Word list	Indent: Left 0.75", Hanging 0.25"
List 5	5th-level item in Word list	Indent: Left 1.00", Hanging 0.25"
List Bullet	1st-level item in Word bulleted list	Indent: Hanging 0.25", Bulleted, Tab stops: 0.25", Automatically update
List Bullet 2	2nd-level item in Word bulleted list	Indent: Left 0.25", Hanging 0.25", Bulleted, Tab stops: 0.50", Automatically update
List Bullet 3	3rd-level item in Word bulleted list	Indent: Left 0.50", Hanging 0.25", Bulleted, Tab stops: 0.75", Automatically update
List Bullet 4	4th-level item in Word bulleted list	Indent: Left 0.75", Hanging 0.25", Bulleted, Tab stops: 1.00", Automatically update
List Bullet 5	5th-level item in Word bulleted list	Indent: Left 1.00", Hanging 0.25", Bulleted, Tab stops: 1.25", Automatically update
List Continue	1st-level item in list continuation	Indent: Left 0.25", space after 6 pt
List Continue 2	2nd-level item in list continuation	Indent: Left 0.50", space after 6 pt
List Continue 3	3rd-level item in list continuation	Indent: Left 0.75", space after 6 pt
List Continue 4	4th-level item in list continuation	Indent: Left 1.00", space after 6 pt
List Continue 5	5th-level item in list continuation	Indent: Left 1.25", space after 6 pt
List Number	1st-level item in numbered list	Indent: Hanging 0.25", Numbered, Tab stops: 0.25"
List Number 2	2nd-level item in numbered list	Indent: Left 0.25", Hanging 0.25", Numbered, Tab stops: 0.50"
List Number 3	3rd-level item in numbered list	Indent: Left 0.50", Hanging 0.25", Numbered, Tab stops: 0.75"

Table 7.3 (Continued)

Paragraph Styles in the
Normal Template

AS "NORMAL PLUS" STYLE NAME	FORMATS THIS	THIS FORMATTING
List Number 4	4th-level item in numbered list	Indent: Left 0.75", Hanging 0.25", Numbered, Tab stops: 1.00"
List Number 5	5th-level item in numbered list	Indent: Left 1.00", Hanging 0.25", Numbered, Tab stops: 1.25"
Macro Text	Text used in macro-editing window	Font: Courier New 10 pt, English (U.S.), Char Scale 100%, Flush left, Line spacing single, Widow/Orphan Control, Body text, Tab stops: 0.33", 0.67", 1", 1.33", 1.67", 2", 2.33", 2.67", 3"
Message Header	Text in Word message header	Font: Arial 12 pt, Indent: Hanging 0.75", Border: Box (Shadowed Single solid line, Dk Horizontal, pt Line Width), Border Spacing: 1 pt, Pattern 20%
Normal	All text not assigned to another style	Font: Times New Roman 10 pt, Language: English (U.S.), Char Scale 100%, Flush (Normal style) left, Line spacing single, Widow/Orphan control, Body text
Normal Indent	Indented text	Indent: Left 0.5"
Note Heading	Text in a note heading	No additional formatting
Plain Text	Text in WordMail messages	Font: Courier New
Salutation	Salutation text in a letter	No additional formatting
Signature	Letter-writer's name, appearing in closing of letter	No additional formatting
Subtitle	Document subtitle	Font: Arial 12 pt Italic, Centered, Space after 3 pt, Level 2
Table of Authorities	Entry text in a table of authorities	Indent: Hanging 0.14"
Table of Figures	Entry text in a table of figures	Indent: Hanging 0.28"
Title	Document title	Font: Arial 16 pt Bold, Kern at 14 pt, Centered, Space before 12 pt, after 3 pt, Level 1
TOA Heading	Heading at the top of a table of authorities	Font: Arial 12 pt Bold, space before 6 pt

Table 7.3 (Continued)

Paragraph Styles in the
Normal Template

AS "NORMAL PLUS" STYLE NAME	FORMATS THIS	THIS FORMATTING
TOC 1	1st-level table of contents entry	Automatically update
TOC 2	2nd-level table of contents entry	Indent: Left 0.14", Automatically update
TOC 3	3rd-level table of contents entry	Indent: Left 0.28", Automatically update
TOC 4	4th-level table of contents entry	Indent: Left 0.42", Automatically update
TOC 5	5th-level table of contents entry	Indent: Left 0.56", Automatically update
TOC 6	6th-level table of contents entry	Indent: Left 0.69", Automatically update
TOC 7	7th-level table of contents entry	Indent: Left 0.83", Automatically update
TOC 8	8th-level table of contents entry	Indent: Left 0.97", Automatically update
TOC 9	9th-level table of contents entry	Indent: Left 1.11", Automatically update

Your current style appears in the Style box (on the Formatting toolbar) unless you've selected paragraphs that have been formatted with different styles. Paragraph styles appear with a paragraph mark (¶); character styles appear with an underlined letter a (<u>a</u>).

■ Applying a Style

You can see all the styles currently in use, including the three heading styles Word includes by default, by clicking on the down arrow next to the Formatting toolbar's style drop-down list, as shown in Figure 7.2. (The keyboard shortcut for access to the style box is Ctrl+Shift+S.)

Word 97's new Style Preview displays the styles in their exact font, size, formatting, and justification in the style drop-down list. What you see in the Style Preview is what you get in your document.

To use a paragraph style to change the style of your current paragraph, place the insertion point in the paragraph or select the entire paragraph. Then choose the new style from this drop-down list.

Figure 7.2

The style drop-down list
and style preview

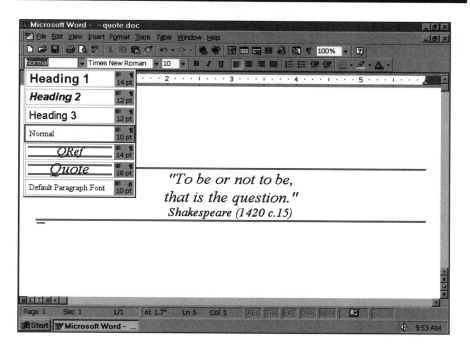

NOTE. *You can also type the style name by positioning your insertion point in the style box and keying the new name. (The keyboard shortcut to open the style box is Ctrl+Shift+S.) Be careful to type the name properly; if you misspell it while text is selected, Word creates a new style based on the current appearance of the selected text. Typos (mistakes in spelling) are common. For this reason, Word includes a feature, called aliases, which enables you to type a brief name that has the same effect as a long style name. Aliases are covered later in this chapter.*

If your Formatting toolbar isn't displayed, you can still choose a style name. Select the paragraph(s), press Ctrl+Shift+S, and choose the style name you want from the Style box in the Format Style dialog box. Then press Enter.

You can change several paragraphs at once by selecting them before applying a different paragraph style. If you want to use a character style, select the text within or across paragraph boundaries, and choose the replacement style from the style box. In either case, the new style appears in the list box, and the text changes.

NOTE. *Each paragraph can have only one paragraph style. Even if you select only part of a paragraph, when you change its style, the entire paragraph's style changes.*

■ Using a Built-In Style That Doesn't Appear in the Style Box

Only the Normal style and three Heading styles appear in the document, but you can use any of Word's 91 built-in styles. Many of those appear automatically when you perform the appropriate task. For example, when you add a table of contents, Word hauls out whatever TOC styles it needs. You can manually access one of these styles in one of two ways:

- Type it in the style box.

- Choose it from the Format Style dialog box.

The Style dialog box is discussed later, but here is a preview. To open it, choose <u>S</u>tyle from the F<u>o</u>rmat menu. The dialog box appears, as in Figure 7.3.

Figure 7.3

The Style dialog box

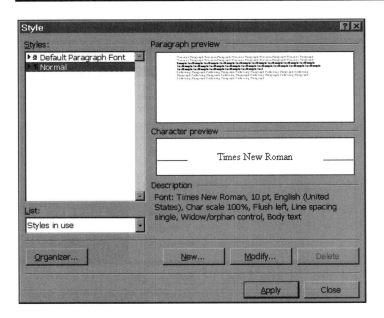

If the Format Style dialog box still only includes Normal and the three Headings (a good name for a New Wave doo-wop group), you can choose All Styles from the <u>L</u>ist box to see all available styles, including the 90+ that Word automatically makes available. Choose a style; then choose <u>A</u>pply. This formats the selected text or paragraph with the style you've chosen.

Using F<u>o</u>rmat, <u>S</u>tyle is slower than simply picking a style from the toolbar, but it compensates by showing you a painfully detailed written description of your style, plus thumbnail sketches of how it might look on your characters and your paragraphs.

When you choose <u>A</u>pply, the style you've just used (but not the entire list) becomes available through the Style box.

NOTE. *If you've created styles of your own, you can tell Word to display only those by choosing User-Defined Styles from the <u>L</u>ist box in the Style dialog box.*

What Can Go into a Style

Most of Word's default styles are relatively simple. Any formatting you can create manually can be included in a style. This includes anything you'll find in any of the F<u>o</u>rmat menu's dialog boxes shown in Table 7.4.

Table 7.4

Formats that Can Be Controlled Using Styles

DIALOG BOX	CONTAINS THESE FORMATS
F<u>o</u>rmat, <u>F</u>ont	Font, Type size, Type style, Underlining, Color, Highlighting, Super/subscript, Type effects, Character scale, Letterspacing, Type position, Kerning
F<u>o</u>rmat, <u>P</u>aragraph	Indentation, Line spacing, Paragraph spacing, Alignment, Pagination, Line numbering
F<u>o</u>rmat, <u>T</u>abs	Tab stop position, Default tab stops, Tab alignment, Tab leaders
F<u>o</u>rmat, <u>B</u>orders and Shading	Edges bordered, Bordering line, Border distance from text, Border color, Foreground shading, Background shading
F<u>o</u>rmat, Bullets and <u>N</u>umbering	Type of bullet used, Type of numbering scheme used, Text included with bullet or number, Multilevel numbering, Bullet/number alignment and indentation
F<u>o</u>rmat, Fra<u>m</u>e	Text wrapping, Size of frame, Horizontal and vertical position, Distance from text
Tools, <u>L</u>anguage	Dictionary to be used, No proofing option

Word even allows you to include formatting for a bulleted or numbered list in your style.

Normally, you decide what a specific element of a document should look like, and then you create a style with the name of that document element.

All the document elements shown in the following list are prime candidates for custom styles, as well as for Word's built-in styles:

Address	Definition	List
Attachments	Enclosure	Pullquote
AutoText Entry	Figure	Quotation
Blurb	Footer	Salutation
Body Text	Header	Sidebar
Byline	Headings	Sidehead
Captions	Headline	State
City	Title	Subhead
Comments	Index	Table of Contents
Date	Initial Cap	ZIP

Word lets you create 4,093 styles for a single document, although you rarely use more than a few dozen. (If your document really needs 4,093 styles, how in the world could you manage without using styles?)

Built-In Keyboard Shortcuts

Word comes with several built-in keyboard shortcuts. You've already seen Ctrl+Shift+S, which opens the Style box. Table 7.5 lists the shortcuts.

Table 7.5

Keyboard Shortcuts for Using Styles

STYLE	SHORTCUT
Normal style	Ctrl+Shift+N
Heading 1 style	Alt+Ctrl+1
Heading 2 style	Alt+Ctrl+2
Heading 3 style	Alt+Ctrl+3
List bullet style	Ctrl+Shift+L
List all styles	Shift+Style box down arrow

If you find yourself using a style frequently, you might want to create a keyboard shortcut for it. Here are the steps:

1. Choose Style from the Format menu.

2. In the Styles list, choose the style to which you want to assign a keyboard shortcut.

3. Choose Modify.

4. Choose Shortcut Key. The Customize Keyboard dialog box appears (as shown in Figure 7.4).

Figure 7.4

The Customize
Keyboard dialog box

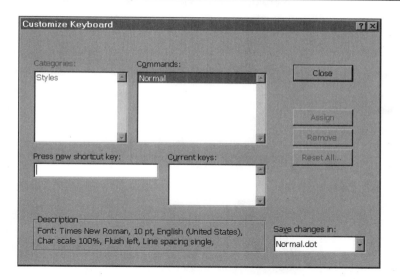

5. In the Press New Shortcut Key box, enter the key combination you want to use. If that combination is already in use, a Currently Assigned To message appears. Press Backspace to delete the shortcut combination and try again.

6. Choose Assign.

7. Choose Close.

Try to keep track of how many shortcut keys you use. You might want to save some for later, when you learn macros. (You can learn more about customizing keyboard shortcuts in Chapter 22, "Customization.")

■ Creating a New Style by Example

You can create a style in one of two ways:

- Create the style by example.
- Use the Style dialog box.

Creating a style by example is the easier of the two methods, because it lets you see exactly what you're doing while you're doing it.

NOTE. *When you create a new style using style by example, Word bases it on the paragraph's previous style.*

To create a new style by example, take the following steps:

1. Format a paragraph or block of characters the way you want your style to appear, and select the paragraph or block (see Figure 7.5).

Figure 7.5

Step 1: Format a paragraph the way you want and select it.

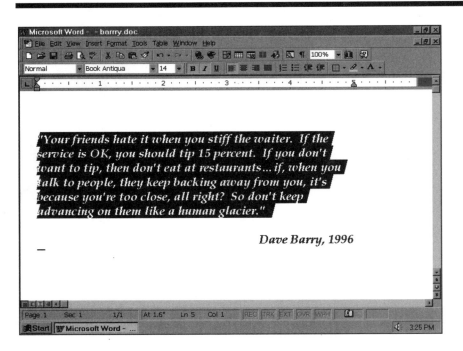

2. Select the Style box from the Formatting toolbar, and type the new style name (see Figure 7.6).

3. Press Enter. Voila, you now have a new style.

Figure 7.6

Step 2: The new style name appears in the Style box.

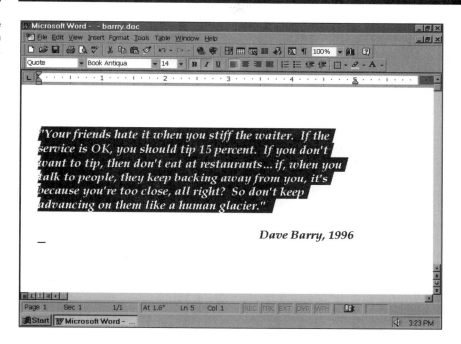

NOTE. *If you plan to change the style drastically, and you already have a style that's closer to the one you're creating, assign that style to the paragraph first. Then, when you make your style changes, you won't have to make nearly as many.*

■ Creating a New Style with Format Style

Using the Format, Style command is a little more complicated than creating a style by example, but gives you direct hands-on control over every part of your style. Start by choosing Style from the Format menu. Next, choose New. The New Style dialog box opens, as shown in Figure 7.7.

Before you format the new style, however, you have some important choices to make, as described in the following sections.

Choosing a Style Name

Type a new style name in the Name box. Style names can be up to 253 characters long. They can be split into several words, but keep away from these four characters:

\ { } ;

Figure 7.7

The New Style dialog box

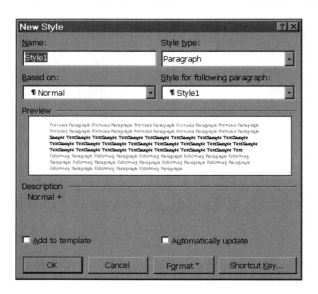

Stay away from commas, too; Word uses them for *aliases*, which you'll read about in a moment.

This means you can now create long, highly descriptive style names. Remember, though, that only about 20 characters fit in the style box, depending on the actual font size. So make sure that you can understand your style name from those first 20 characters.

NOTE. *Name your styles based on the function they serve—not the formatting they contain. For example, use Headline as a style name rather than 48 point Machine Bold. You may want to change the formatting of a style later.*

Using Aliases

If you like to type your style names, yet you favor long style names that clearly explain the purpose of each style, you may want to use aliases. An alias is an abbreviated style name that Word can recognize in place of the long name. To create an alias, type the style's full name in the <u>N</u>ame box of the New Style or Modify Style dialog box, add a comma, and then type your alias. Here's an example: List Bullet,lb.

Both the full name and the alias appear in the style box when you use the style later, but you only have to type the alias to invoke the style. (By using Modify Style, you can add aliases to styles you already have. You will learn about modifying styles later.)

Choosing Between Paragraph and Character Styles

In the Style type box, specify whether you're creating a paragraph or character style.

Choosing Based on Style

In the Based on box, specify which style you want to base your new style on. (You can also base your new style on no style at all.)

Unless you tell it otherwise, Word bases a new style on the Normal style, which is 10-point Times New Roman, flush left, English (U.S.). Often, that makes sense. It helps you build a consistent style because the only elements that vary from the rest of your document are those that you consciously choose to vary. You can, however, base your style on any style in your current document.

But what if your document won't resemble Normal style in the least? Suppose that you're in the business of creating wedding invitations. In the following example, most of the text is centered 20-point type.

If you use the Normal style as the basis for the styles in this document, you must include all those specifications in every new style you create. Instead, create one new style called Normal Wedding. Then build the other styles on it, as shown in Figure 7.8.

Figure 7.8

You can build a series of styles based on a new Normal style you create.

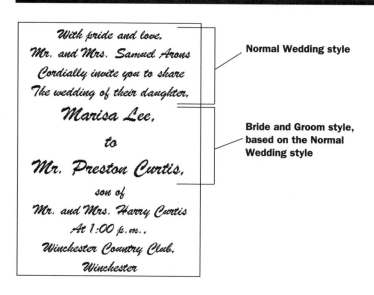

Here, the Normal Wedding style is the primary style, and the other style—the Bride and Groom style—is based on it. The Normal Wedding style centers the text and sets the amount of space between the lines. The Bride and Groom style does the same, but increases the type size to 28 points.

If you're getting ready to create several entirely new styles, each with similar formatting, you'll find it easier to create one new base style first, and use <u>B</u>ased on to build the other styles.

NOTE. *If you know in advance which style you want to base your new style on, choose it in the Style dialog box. It then appears in the <u>B</u>ased on box when you open the New Style dialog box.*

A Word about Global Style Changes

You've already seen how you can assign a Based-on style to any style. In the Normal template, all paragraph styles are based on the Normal style, as you saw earlier. What does this mean? You should be very cautious about making global style changes using the Normal style because the changes ripple through any document you create whenever you use this altered global template. This often creates changes you didn't intend.

Suppose that all the type in your document is in Times New Roman. Most styles are based on a Normal style that uses Times New Roman. (This is the case in the Normal template.) If you change the Normal style to, say, Bookman, almost every element of the document changes. Some headings remain in Arial because they have been specifically designed that way. This, too, can cause a problem, because Arial and Bookman don't work together graphically as well as Times New Roman and Arial do.

A more subtle problem is also possible. Different fonts have different widths. Bookman, for example, sets at least 15 percent wider than Times New Roman. If you change a long document this way, you may find that you've lengthened or shortened it by several pages.

The Based-on feature is powerful. Don't hesitate to use it on custom templates to make quick and dramatic changes to the formatting of a specific type of document. One way to do this is to base one style on another style that is based on yet another style, creating a hierarchy of styles that changes when the style at the bottom changes.

NOTE. *You're limited to nine levels of Based-on styles. For more levels than that, try Nintendo!*

Just be aware of the power of Word's Based-on feature, and leave the Normal style alone if you can. (You learn more about templates in Chapter 8, "Templates, Wizards, and Add-Ins.")

Choosing a Following Paragraph Style

Normally, if you keep typing in a document, Word maintains your current style, applying it to a new paragraph whenever you start one. But what if you want the style to change when you start a new paragraph, and you always want it to change the same way?

This is more common than you might think. For example, most of the time headings are followed by body text; Figure numbers are followed by captions. In the example of the wedding invitation described earlier, paragraphs with the Bride and Groom style are always followed by paragraphs with the Normal Wedding style.

Realizing this, Word's designers created a shortcut you can use to assign a style automatically to a paragraph whenever it follows another style. In the New Style dialog box, this feature is called Style for following paragraph.

In this box, you can choose the style that Word automatically uses for the next paragraph whenever you use the style you're defining. Remember, you can only use Based on or Style for following paragraph if the style you intend to choose already exists.

NOTE. *Style for following paragraph is an example of a style attribute that you can't set when you create styles by example. If you have several styles by example, you might think about editing them by using the Format and Style commands so that you can add a Style for following paragraph.*

Note that Word's AutoFormat as You Type feature, described later in this chapter, can automatically handle some style assignments for you.

Choosing Whether to Include the Style in a Template

By default, when you create a new style, it becomes part of your document, but not part of the template your document uses. This gives you more flexibility, but it can get confusing too. For example, it means different documents using the same template can have varying styles with the same name.

If you believe you will use the new style in other documents that share the same template, check Add to template. From now on, the revised style appears in all documents you create using the current template. If you only use the Normal template, of course, all your new documents will have access to the revised style. (However, the revisions won't automatically appear in documents already created with this template.)

NOTE. *Each Word document file includes the style sheet for its document. Style-sheet edits are just like text edits: They're not permanent until you save the file.*

Choosing Whether to Automatically Update a Style in a Document

By default, when you manually format text with a specific style, Word does not automatically change all the other occurrences of that text to have the same style. However, with Word 97's new automatic style updating feature, you can modify a style in one location in the document and Word will automatically change all the rest of the same style.

Select the Automatically update check box in the New Style dialog box. When you manually format text with the style, Word will automatically update all text in the document with the style.

NOTE. *You can't automatically update Normal style.*

Formatting the New Style

Now you're ready to create the actual formatting that will become part of the style. Choose Format, and a pop-up menu appears, as shown in Figure 7.9.

Figure 7.9

The Format button's
pop-up menu

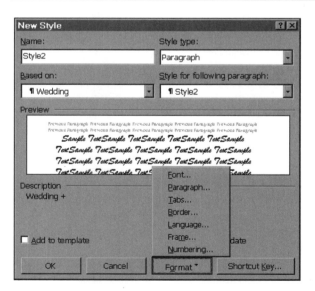

Choosing any of these menu items opens a dialog box that looks identical to the one in the Format menu, but in this case, when you change a format setting, you won't just change the selected text; you may be changing all the text in the document that uses that same style.

If you need to change several parts of a style, make all the changes in one element, such as Font. Then choose OK. This returns you to the New

Style dialog box. Select another item from the Format menu, make the changes there, and choose OK. Each time you return to the New Style dialog box, you can see your revisions reflected in the style description. When you have the style the way you want it, choose OK.

■ Changing an Existing Style by Using Style by Example

The techniques for changing styles are similar to those for creating new ones. To change a style by example:

1. Format a paragraph or selected text the way you want it.

2. Open the Style box and press Enter. Word displays the Modify Style dialog box, as shown in Figure 7.10.

Figure 7.10

The Modify Style
dialog box

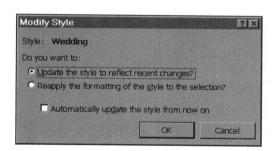

If you want to change the style, be sure to select the radio button marked Update the style to reflect recent changes?, and press Enter.

If you don't want to change the style, you can return the selected text to its current style, eliminating the changes you were toying with. Select the button marked Reapply the formatting of the style to the selection?. To automatically update the text with the modified style in the rest of the document, check Automatically update the style from now on. If you don't want to do anything, click Cancel.

■ A Word about How Word Interprets Formatting in a Redefined Style

Remember that most Word styles are based on paragraphs. What if your paragraph has some stray character formatting that you don't want to include in your redefined style, such as a sentence or two that just happens to be italicized?

Just make sure the first character is formatted the way you want it. If you choose several paragraphs with different paragraph formatting, Word assumes that you want the formatting from the first paragraph.

■ Changing an Existing Style Using Format Style

Once again, the techniques for changing a style with the Format, Style commands are very similar to the techniques for creating one. To change an existing style:

1. Choose Style from the Format menu.

2. Choose the style from the Styles list. (If you've selected text in the style, it will already be selected.)

3. Choose Modify. The Modify Style dialog box opens (see Figure 7.11). It's a dead ringer for the New Style dialog box you've already seen. It contains options for the following:

   - Setting the style's formatting (through the Format button)

   - Naming the style (or adding an alias to the current name)

   - Choosing between Paragraph or Character style (an option that's not always available)

   - Specifying the style on which it will be based

   - Specifying which style will follow it in the next paragraph

   - Specifying whether the style will be added to the template

   - Specifying whether the text containing the style will be automatically updated throughout the document

   - Setting a new shortcut key

4. When you've finished making changes, choose Apply to apply the style to the current text selection, or Cancel to change the style without applying it to anything.

Figure 7.11

Another level of the
Modify Style dialog box

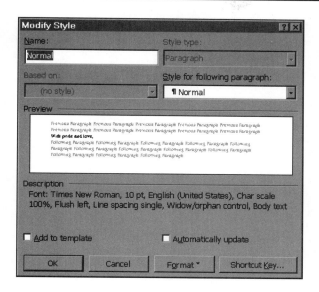

■ Copying Styles between Documents

The easiest way to copy a style between documents is to copy some text with the style into the document where you want the style to appear.

Copying text with a particular style has a few drawbacks, however. First, you may not want the text in your document. Second, if you copy text from one document into another document that already has a style with the same name, the text you copy takes on the new style—not always what you had in mind.

Word provides a tool, called the *Organizer*, which lets you move styles among documents. When you learn how to use the Organizer to manage styles, you'll also know how to manage AutoText entries, toolbars, and macros.

To use the Organizer, choose <u>S</u>tyles from the <u>F</u>ormat menu, then choose <u>O</u>rganizer. The Organizer dialog box opens, as shown in Figure 7.12.

NOTE. *To learn how to use the Organizer in more detail, turn to Chapter 8, "Templates, Wizards, and Add-Ins."*

By default, the Organizer suspects that you may want to move a style you're using in your current document into the NORMAL.DOT template. On this screen, you can copy any style in either direction. To copy a style, choose the style you want to copy. A description of the style appears in the Description box. If you want to copy a style that's in the current document, choose it from the <u>I</u>n Document number list box. If you want to copy a style

Figure 7.12

The Organizer dialog box

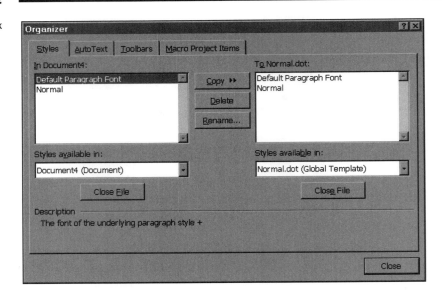

from NORMAL.DOT, choose a style in the To Normal box. If you want to copy a style from another document or template, follow these steps:

1. Choose either Close File button. The list of available styles disappears, and an Open File button appears.

2. Choose Open File. The Open dialog box appears (see Figure 7.13).

3. Choose a document or template the way you normally would. (If you want to move styles from a template rather than a document, choose Document Template from the Files of type box.) Choose OK.

4. Choose the destination document or template where you want to copy it. (This might also mean closing the current document or template and choosing a new one.)

5. Choose the style you want to copy.

6. Choose Copy to copy the style.

7. When you're finished copying styles, choose Close to leave the Organizer.

Figure 7.13

The Open dialog box

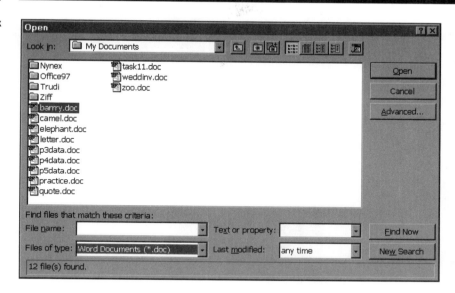

■ Changing Styles Globally with the Style Gallery

Ever wonder how a document would look if it were formatted with the styles from a different template? One of the quickest ways to dramatically change the look of an entire document is to change its template.

Style Gallery lets you manage this feat in an easy, risk-free manner. To use Style Gallery, choose Style Gallery from the Format menu. The Style Gallery dialog box opens, as shown in Figure 7.14.

You can see your current document in miniature in the Preview of box. Choose a Template from the list of those currently available, and Word shows you how your document would look if you imported those styles into your document. You can use the scroll bars on the Preview box to scroll through your document to see how the new styles look.

You can see how the styles look in a Word sample document by choosing Example from the Preview frame. You can also see samples of each style, along with the names of every style, by choosing Style samples. If you decide you want to use the styles from another template, choose OK and Word imports them into your current document.

The Style Gallery doesn't actually change the template attached to your document. Rather, it imports all the styles from the template you choose into the currently open document.

Figure 7.14

The Style Gallery
dialog box

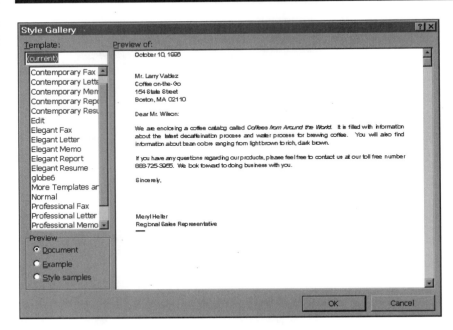

NOTE. *Word replaces any existing styles that have the same name as the new styles you import. If you want to keep both styles, rename one before you enter Style Gallery. See the following section for details.*

■ Renaming a Style

You might want to change a style's name to make sure it's not deleted when you merge styles from another document. Take the following steps to rename an existing style:

1. Choose Format, Style.

2. Choose Modify.

3. In the Name box, type the new name.

4. Click OK twice.

NOTE. *You can't rename or delete any of the 91 styles that are built into Word.*

◼ Deleting a Style

If you find you no longer need a style, you can simply delete it. If any existing text already is formatted with the deleted style, Word automatically reformats that text with the Normal style. Take the following steps to delete an existing style:

1. Select Format, Style.

2. From the Styles box, choose the style you want to delete.

3. Choose Delete. A confirmation dialog box appears.

4. Choose Yes to confirm the deletion.

   If you want to delete many styles at once, use the Organizer as follows:

1. Open the Organizer.

2. Choose the Style tab.

3. Select the first style you want to delete.

4. Press Ctrl and select the next style you want to delete. (If you want to delete several consecutive styles, hold down Shift and select the last style of the group you want to delete. Word highlights all the styles between the first one and the last one you select.)

5. Choose Delete.

6. A confirmation box appears. You can confirm the deletions individually or all at once.

7. Choose Yes or Yes To All. Word deletes the styles.

◼ How Manual Formatting and Styles Interact

You can always add manual formatting to any styled text. The manual formatting is superimposed on the style. If your style calls for 10-point Times New Roman italic, and you boldface it, your type becomes 10-point Times New Roman bold italic. This simple change works the same way for paragraphs, tabs, borders, shading, frames, bullets, numbering, and language.

Manual formatting gets trickier when you start changing your styles. Suppose you change a style from 10-point Times New Roman italic to 10-point Times New Roman bold italic. What happens to the manual boldface formatting you've already added? Should Word keep it bold because that's what you explicitly asked for? Should Word change your bold to regular to maintain the contrast for which you were probably aiming?

Paradoxes like these caused the mental breakdown of the HAL computer in the movie *2001*. You won't have those problems, however, because formatting problems aren't quite as tough, and your PC probably isn't quite as introspective as HAL. When it comes to bold, italic, and underline, Word maintains the contrast, switching your manual formatting when it needs to.

Things change if you actually reapply the style, say, by choosing it again in the Formatting toolbar. Then, the style overrides, eliminating any character formatting that conflicts with it.

Clearing Manual Formatting

Occasionally, you lose track of the manual formatting you've added to an underlying style. Word offers two machete-style shortcuts that let you hack through the underbrush and return to your style.

Ctrl+Spacebar eliminates manual character formatting on selected text. This includes bold, italic, underline, sub/superscript, letterspacing, and everything else in the Format Font tab, plus your Language setting. Ctrl+Q eliminates manual paragraph formatting on selected text. These style commands survive: Font, Based on, and Next style. If the paragraphs you want to clean up have *different* styles, use Ctrl+Q one paragraph at a time. It has the unexpected habit of resetting all your paragraphs to the style in the first paragraph.

NOTE. *Using Ctrl+NumPad5, Ctrl+Q, and then Ctrl+Spacebar unformats your entire document, leaving only the bare styles.*

■ Finding Styles Automatically

Now that you know about styles, you can take advantage of Edit, Find's nifty capability of searching for styles and replacing them.

Suppose you want to search for all major section headings in a document. If they all start with the same letter, no problem. But what if they're numbered? The solution is to format these headings with styles, such as the ones Word includes (Heading 1, Heading 2, Heading 3, and so on). Then you can search for the styles themselves.

1. Select Edit, Find. If necessary, click More to display more options. The Find and Replace dialog box appears, as shown in Figure 7.15.

2. Choose Format. A menu appears, offering several options.

3. Choose the Style option from the menu. The Find Style dialog box appears, as shown in Figure 7.16.

4. In the Find what style list box, choose a style and click OK.

Figure 7.15

The Find and
Replace dialog box

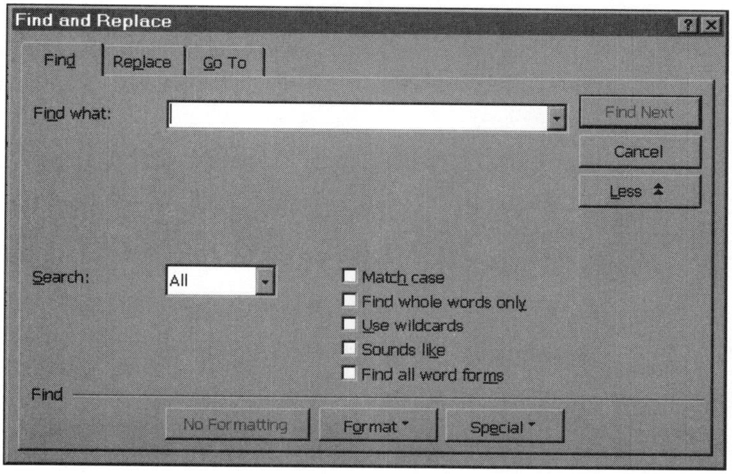

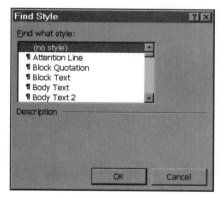

Figure 7.16

The Find Style dialog box

5. Back in the Find and Replace dialog box, make sure that the Find what box is empty (unless you're looking for specific text formatted with a specific style).

6. Click on Find Next.

■ Replacing Styles Automatically

Similarly, you can use _E_dit, _R_eplace to replace a style. Use this when you want to change the formatting of text from one style to another, while preserving the contents of both styles for future use. Take the following steps to replace a style:

1. Choose _E_dit, _R_eplace. If necessary, click _M_ore to display more options.

2. Make sure that the Fi_n_d what box is empty; then click on F_o_rmat.

3. Choose _S_tyle. The Find Style dialog box opens.

4. Choose a style to find and click on OK.

5. Now choose the Re_p_lace With box.

6. Choose F_o_rmat again, and choose _S_tyles again. The Replace Style dialog box appears, as shown in Figure 7.17.

Figure 7.17

The Replace Style dialog box

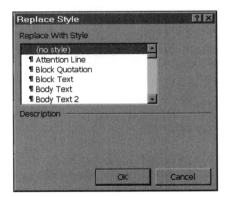

7. Choose a replacement style, and choose OK.

   To replace all examples of the style, choose Replace _A_ll. To replace them selectively, choose _F_ind Next, and then _R_eplace only the ones you want to replace.

■ Keeping Track of Styles

You can always print a style sheet for your document that lists all the styles currently in use. To print a style sheet, take these steps:

1. Choose File, Print.

2. Choose Styles from the Print what box.

3. Click on OK.

If you've been busy redefining keyboard shortcuts, you ought to print those out, too. In Step 2, choose Key Assignments rather than Styles.

Another way to keep track of styles is to keep them visible on-screen, next to the paragraphs where they're used. Word provides the Style Area for this purpose. If you want to activate the Style Area on your screen, take these steps:

1. Choose Tools, Options.

2. Select the View tab in the Options dialog box, as shown in Figure 7.18.

Figure 7.18

The View tab in the Options dialog box

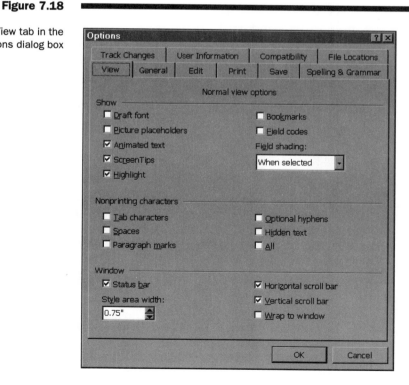

3. In the Style area width box, choose a new width. (The default, zero, means no Style Area. That's why you've probably never seen one.)

4. Choose OK.

Figure 7.19 shows a 0.75" Style Area. 0.75" is a good size because it's wide enough to display most style names without reducing the editing space too much. Any time you want to change the width of the Style Area, you can go back to the View tab and reset the Style Area's width.

NOTE. *The fastest way to change the Style Area's width is to place the mouse pointer on the Style Area's border. When the pointer changes to the vertical split pointer, drag the border to the left or right and let go.*

Figure 7.19

A document window with the Style Area set to 0.75"

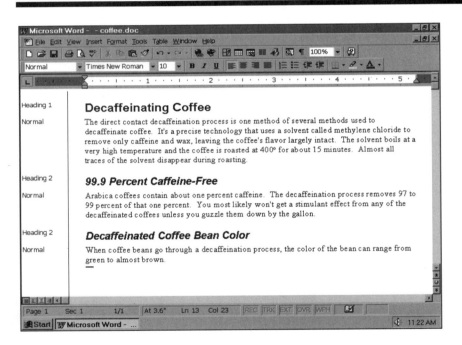

NOTE. *When the Style Area is open, you can select an entire paragraph by clicking on its style name.*

If you have several documents open, setting the Style Area only affects the one you're working in and any additional documents you open during the session.

■ Checking Styles with Help Menu's What's This?

The Help menu feature's What's This? command gives you a nifty shortcut for getting detailed information on the styles that apply to specific text. Press Shift+F1. A question mark (?) appears next to the mouse pointer. Then click on the desired text. Detailed Paragraph Formatting and Font Formatting information appears on-screen, as shown in Figure 7.20. Press Esc to remove the style information box on the screen.

Figure 7.20

Getting detailed style information via What's This?

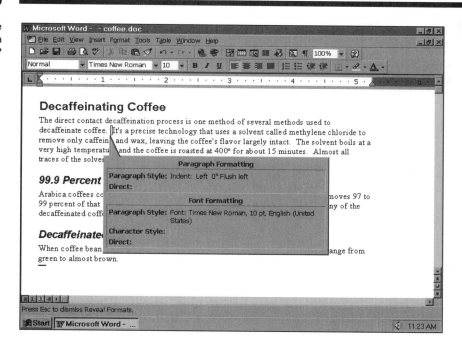

■ Preparing Style Sheets for Export

If you're creating a document that will ultimately be exported to a desktop-publishing program, you may want to prepare a style sheet that can be exported with it.

As of this writing, neither QuarkXPress 3.3 nor PageMaker 5.0 directly converts Word 97 style sheets, but both can convert Word for Windows 2 style sheets. You may have to save your file as a Word for Windows 2 document before converting it, possibly losing some attributes or formatting information in the process.

NOTE. *A preliminary version of a Word 6 import filter for QuarkXPress may be found on CompuServe: GO QUARK.*

Both QuarkXPress and PageMaker use filters to make their style-sheet conversions. These are similar to the import/export filters Word itself uses to bring data in from other word processors, databases, and spreadsheets. The filter in PageMaker 5.0 actually gives you the option of importing Word's tables, tables of contents, index entries, and page breaks.

NOTE. *QuarkXPress imports only the styles actually used in a Word document, ignoring other styles you may have defined but not used. If this is a problem, try saving the Word document as an .RTF file; QuarkXPress imports all the styles associated with these files.*

If the style sheet does not import properly into your desktop-publishing program, first make sure that the filters are installed correctly and are located where the program can find them.

■ Using Word's AutoFormatting Feature

If you simply can't be bothered with styles, Word's AutoFormatting feature will be glad to insert them for you. AutoFormat enables you to take a plain document and have Word format it for you by automatically adding styles. AutoFormat can be a big time-saver for you.

To AutoFormat your document, choose AutoFormat from the Format menu. The AutoFormat dialog box appears, as shown in Figure 7.21. If you want to automatically format your document immediately without reviewing each format change, choose the button marked AutoFormat now and press Enter.

Figure 7.21

The AutoFormat dialog box

If you want to automatically format your document and review each format change that Word suggests, choose the button marked AutoFormat and review each change and press Enter.

By default, Word automatically formats your document using the General document type. You can choose a document type to automatically format your document with more specific formatting changes. If your document contains a letter, you can select the Letter document type. If you have an e-mail message in your document, choose the E-mail document type.

Setting AutoFormat Options

You may want to control AutoFormat's options before you turn it loose. Choose Options, and the AutoCorrect dialog box appears, as shown in Figure 7.22. You can turn on or off every part of AutoFormat. If you click on the AutoFormat tab, Word displays the changes it can make when you run AutoFormat after creating a document. If you click on the AutoFormat As You Type button, Word displays the changes it can make while you work.

Figure 7.22

Controlling AutoFormat
options through the
AutoCorrect dialog box

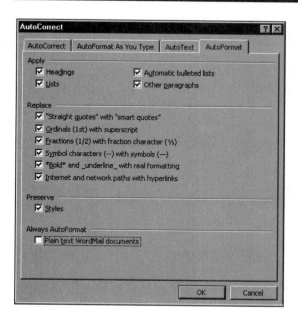

The categories are very similar, but not identical. For example, the Auto-Format As You Type feature can turn a row of hyphens into a border, but the regular AutoFormat feature cannot.

By default, if AutoFormat comes across a style you've added to your document, it leaves that style alone. Word figures you know what you're doing. However, Word's AutoFormat may make substantial changes to your document's styles. In some cases, you may prefer to let Word try to make the entire document consistent, by replacing your styles as well. To do this, clear the Preserve Styles check box in Tools, Options, AutoFormat.

Also by default, AutoFormat applies styles to headings, lists, and other paragraphs. You can tell Word to ignore any of these by clearing the appropriate check box. The following provides more information about the changes Word can make when you run AutoFormat after creating a document:

Headings. With AutoFormat headings turned on, Word automatically applies a heading style to any text that starts with a capital letter, does not end with punctuation, is at least 20 percent shorter than the maximum line length, and is set off from other copy with more than one line of space.

Lists. With AutoFormat Lists turned on, Word automatically starts applying Word's built-in list formats (List, List 2, List 3, and so on) to any list of consecutive lines separated by paragraph marks.

Automatic Bulleted Lists. With Automatic Bulleted Lists turned on, Word automatically inserts bullets in place of characters that are often used to substitute for bullets, such as dashes and asterisks.

Other Paragraphs. With Other Paragraphs turned on, Word formats most other paragraphs as body text, while trying to recognize specialized paragraph formats such as letter salutations and to apply proper formatting to them as well.

AutoFormat can also change specific characters and symbols, if you specify them by choosing Tools, Options, AutoFormat. These changes lead to a more attractive document, but if you plan to send your document to another computer, such as a Macintosh, you may want to turn these features off—the symbols may not translate properly, leading to errors in your document.

Straight Quotes with "Smart Quotes". Word replaces the default apostrophe (') and inch-mark (") quotation marks with the more attractive (") and (") angled quotation marks. This results in a more appealing document.

Ordinals (1st) with Superscript. When Word recognizes that you have typed the word 1st, 2nd, 3rd, and so on, it can automatically replace them with the more attractive 1st, 2nd, 3rd, and so on. This works with any number, but does not work with spelled-out numbers like twenty-eighth.

Fractions (1/2) with fraction character (½). When Word recognizes that you have typed the fraction 1/4, 1/2, or 3/4, it converts the fraction to the special character ¼, ½, or ¾. Note that these are the only fractions Word can

AutoFormat, because these are the only fractions contained in the standard Windows character set. If your document also uses fractions like 5/16, you may want to turn this feature off to maintain consistency.

Symbol Characters with Symbols. When Word recognizes that you type characters that typically are used in place of symbols, such as two consecutive hyphens in place of an em dash (—), it can substitute the proper character automatically.

NOTE. *By default Word changes many other symbols, such as copyright and registered trademark symbols. However, these are controlled through the AutoCorrect feature, which was covered in Chapter 5, "Spelling and Grammar."*

Bold and Underline with Real Formatting. When Word recognizes that you type words enclosed in asterisks (*), it can apply boldface to those words. For example, *extra* would appear as **extra**. Words you type that are enclosed in underscores (_) will be underlined. For example, _better_ will appear as <u>better</u>.

Internet and NetworkPaths with Hyperlinks. When Word recognizes that you type Internet and network paths, such as n:\My Documents\Memos, it can format the paths as hyperlink fields. When you click on a hyperlink field, you jump directly to the Internet or to an item on your network.

By default, Word does not automatically format the plain text in Word-Mail messages when you open them. Word cannot format pasted text or other text files, but it can format WordMail messages. If you want to automatically format the plain text in the message, check the Always AutoFormat Plain Text WordMail Documents box.

Also by default, Word's AutoFormat feature eliminates extra unnecessary paragraph marks, such as empty paragraph marks inserted between text paragraphs. Word also replaces extra spaces with tabs and removes tabs and spaces it doesn't think you need.

When you're done changing AutoFormat options, click OK. To AutoFormat, choose an AutoFormat option, and then choose OK again to close the second dialog box. When Word finishes AutoFormatting, and if you chose not to review the changes, you return to the document. If you chose to review each change, the dialog box in Figure 7.23 appears.

Figure 7.23

The AutoFormat dialog box after AutoFormatting is complete

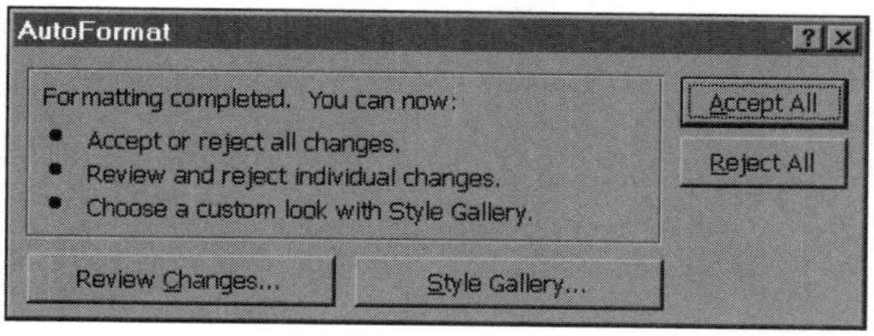

AutoFormat   ?|X

Formatting completed. You can now:

- Accept or reject all changes.
- Review and reject individual changes.
- Choose a custom look with Style Gallery.

Accept All

Reject All

Review Changes...   Style Gallery...

You can either accept or reject all the changes Word made. More likely, you may want to choose Review **C**hanges. Word then displays the changes that have been made, one by one. Additions are marked in blue and with an underline. Blue paragraph marks indicate paragraphs where Word has applied a new style. Deletions are marked in red and strike-through. Every line containing a change also has a black bar to its left.

You can manage the review process from the Review AutoFormat Changes dialog box, which opens when you ask to Review **C**hanges (see Figure 7.24). To find the first change, click on the **F**ind button. Word highlights the first change and explains the change in the Description box.

Figure 7.24

The Review AutoFormat
Changes dialog box

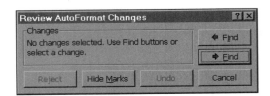

To reject the change, choose **R**eject. (You don't actually accept any changes until you're finished with your review.) If you change your mind after rejecting a Word change, choose **U**ndo.

To continue to the next change, choose **F**ind again. To return to the previous change, choose the **F**ind button. To see how the document would look if you accepted all the changes, choose Hide **M**arks.

When you're finished reviewing the changes, choose Close or Cancel to return to the AutoFormat dialog box. (Close appears as an option if you have rejected at least one change; Cancel appears otherwise.) At this point, you can accept all the changes you haven't rejected during your review, or choose Reject **A**ll to go back to square one.

You also can choose **S**tyle Gallery to open the Style Gallery and see if, somewhere else on your computer, there are some styles you might like better than the ones Word has used.

Word's style assignments stay in place, but Style Gallery can assign new formatting to the styles that have already been assigned. In other words, if AutoFormat specifies Body Text for a paragraph, you can change the look of that body text by importing a Body Text style with different specifications from another template. But Style Gallery won't go back and change the style name AutoFormat has already applied.

AutoFormat As You Type

As if AutoFormatting weren't enough, Word 97 goes even further. AutoFormat As You Type does just that: It makes its changes while you're working, so you don't have to run AutoFormatting separately, and you can decide immediately whether you like the changes Word is making. To specify which types of AutoFormatting you want Word to make while you work:

1. Choose AutoFormat from the Format menu.

2. Choose Options.

3. Choose AutoFormat As You Type to display the options for immediate AutoFormatting (see Figure 7.25). Most of these options are the same as those already discussed in the preceding AutoFormatting section. There are two changes, however. Word doesn't interactively AutoFormat lists or other paragraphs such as salutations. It does, however, automatically add borders in place of rows of hyphens or underlines, and it also creates numbered lists automatically. Even where the options are identical, you can establish different options for conventional AutoFormatting versus interactive AutoFormat As You Type.

Figure 7.25

Controlling AutoFormat
As You Type options

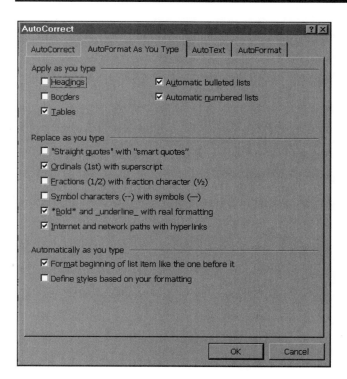

4. Make the changes you want, and choose OK.

From now on, Word keeps track of what you're doing and automatically makes the formatting changes you request.

In this chapter, you've learned how to go beyond manual formatting—and start taking advantage of Word's powerful Styles and AutoFormatting features to control the formatting of your entire document at once. You've learned to use Styles and AutoFormat to make sure your documents don't just look *good*—they also look consistent and professional.

In the next chapter, you'll go a step further. You'll learn how to use Word templates to not only dramatically reduce the time it takes to create and format new documents—but also to make sure that the right tools are always available to you for the specific document you're working in, exactly when you need them.

- *Understanding Templates*
- *Understanding the Normal Template*
- *Creating New Templates*
- *Managing Templates*
- *Using Wizards*

8

Templates, Wizards and Add-Ins: Smart Shortcuts for Nearly Every Document

IF YOU'VE USED WORD FOR WINDOWS AT ALL, YOU'VE COME ACROSS the term *template*. When you create a new Word document, you're asked which template you want to base your document on. At that point, many Word users are relieved to see that Blank Document is already offered up as the default choice. They press Enter and hurry along to the real work.

By doing so, they miss one of Word's most powerful features—and one that can save them an enormous amount of time.

A *template* is a pattern that tells Word what information should already be in a new document when you open it. (Obviously, any information that Word places in your documents *automatically* is information you don't have to put there *manually*!)

Anything you can put in a Word document, you also can store in a Word template, including the following:

- Text

- Graphics

- Automated procedures (macros)

- AutoText (blocks of text that can be called up with a few keystrokes)

- Fields (such as instructions to insert the current date and time)

- Font, paragraph, and page formatting

- Styles

- Customized toolbars, menus, and keyboard commands

If you use templates, you can open your documents with all the boilerplate text and formatting work already done. With templates available, you no longer have an excuse for doing repetitive work to set up a document.

You also can build thoroughly customized work environments into your templates. You can create a template with the built-in text and database connections you need for managing correspondence, for example. Another template might contain the AutoText entries you need to quickly build a new proposal document. As you'll see in Chapter 22, "Customizing Word," each template can even include its own toolbar buttons and menu items.

Templates also are an ideal way of making sure that everyone in your organization prepares consistent documents, and that each Word for Windows user has access to the same shortcuts and macros that you develop over time.

As you build a library of templates, you subtly shape Word to your own work style. At the risk of sounding "cyberpunkish," Word becomes an extension of your personality.

But that's all a bit abstract. Word has another feature, *wizards*, which are anything but subtle. Word wizards are automated procedures that ask you a series of questions, and then build a document based on your responses. You just stand back and watch. Wizards are available for many of the most common kinds of documents, including letters, newsletters, memos, résumés and legal pleadings.

By using the capabilities of Word templates and wizards, you will have to create *very few* documents from scratch.

In this chapter, you'll learn how to create new templates and use the ones in Word's template library; attach a new template to a document; work with global templates; attach global templates permanently; and use the Organizer to manage the contents of your templates. You'll also walk through using some of Word's most important wizards.

■ Understanding Templates

A template is a special type of Word document that can store a wide variety of information and tools which you can then use to simplify the construction of other documents. Word templates can include boilerplate text, custom toolbars, macros, shortcut keys, styles, and AutoText entries.

If you create a template that includes boilerplate text—such as the framework of a memo or a fax cover sheet—whenever you create a new document based on that template, Word automatically includes the text or formatting you've placed in the template. This capability alone can dramatically reduce the amount of time you spend creating routine documents. But it isn't all templates can do, not by a long shot. The other information you can store in a template makes them even more valuable.

If you need to create reports for a specific client, formatted in a specific way, you can store a customized set of styles in a template and open that template whenever you need to create a report for that client.

Or if you're preparing contracts, you can create a template that stores AutoText entries—large blocks of boilerplate text—that correspond to the contract clauses you use most. Then, you can make that boilerplate text available to you whenever you're working on contracts. (See Chapter 9 for detailed coverage of Word's AutoText feature.)

Or, once a month, you may run a mail merge to create a mailing or a catalog. You can write macros (see Chapter 25) that automate the mail merge process, so even inexperienced Word users can manage it. You can then store those macros in a template that you only use when you're ready to run the mail merge.

■ Understanding the Normal Template

You're already using a template, whether you know it or not. It's called the Normal template, and it's stored as Normal.dot in your Templates folder. This is the template you use by default when you create a new Blank Document.

All the default Word styles you learned about in Chapter 7 are collected in the Normal template. So are Word 97's built-in AutoText entries for letters and business documents. Normal is always available to all Word documents, so any changes you make to the Normal template can affect new documents you create with it later.

If you delete or rename the Normal template, intentionally or inadvertently, Word restores it to the original format it had when you first installed the program. This means that deleting or renaming the Normal template is a last resort for salvaging it if you have hopelessly muddled it by adding or deleting characteristics you don't want.

When you delete or rename the Normal template, Word will look for it in its usual place in the User Templates and Workgroup Templates folders, or in another location you've specified in Tools, Options, File Locations. When Word cannot find the Normal template in these locations, Word assumes the file is not present in the system, and creates a new one with standard Word settings. However, the restored Normal template will not have any of the customization you may have added. As you'll see later in this chapter, you can use the Organizer to move any of your customization, including useful Auto-Text entries, styles, toolbars, and macros to safe harbor before you dynamite the Normal template.

■ Creating New Templates

New templates can be created in one of two ways: creating a brand-new template, or saving an existing file as a new template. Each of these options is discussed next.

Creating a New Template from Scratch

To create a new template from scratch:

1. Choose New from the File menu.

2. Select an existing template on which you want to base your new template. (Don't use a wizard.)

3. Check Template in the New box.

4. Click OK.

You now have a new template with the attributes of the template you based it on. Word identifies the new template as Template1 until you save it with a different name.

If you create your new template based on the Normal template, your new template won't include any customized macros or toolbars you may have added to Normal. Typically, you won't notice this deficiency when you use your new template. That's because Normal is a global template; Word is running your new and improved version of Normal concurrently with your new template. So those macros and toolbars that you added to the Normal template are still available to you.

However, if you want to share your template with someone else, the Normal template available on their system will not be your nifty upgraded version of Normal. Therefore, if you want your snazzy new macro and toolbar creations to be available in the new template, you will have to copy them into it, using the Organizer, as will be discussed later in this chapter.

Now that you've created a new template, you can adapt it any way you like, adding or deleting boilerplate text and other customizations. When you're finished, choose **S**ave As from the **F**ile menu. Word opens the Save As dialog box, showing the Templates folder where your other templates are stored. If you store the template here, it will appear in the same General window as Blank Document when you choose File, New.

You may wish to save your new template in another folder within the Templates folder, such as Letters & Faxes, Memos, or one of the other template folders Word has set up. If your new templates don't fit any Word category, or if you're creating a series of custom templates for your company, you might want to create your own folder within the Templates folder to store them in. Once you do, Word displays your custom folder as a tab within the New dialog box.

Creating a Template Based on an Existing Document

The second way to create a new template is to open any existing document and save it as a template. This is the strategy to follow if you have a document that already contains much of the text and formatting you want to duplicate in other documents. To do this:

1. Open the document.

2. Delete any text or graphics that aren't boilerplate and you don't want in your new template.

3. Adjust any formatting or other document attributes to make the document as generic as necessary for your purpose.

4. Save the document using File, Save **A**s.

5. Choose Document Template in the Save as **T**ype box. Word automatically switches to the Templates folder.

6. Specify the file name you want.

7. Click Save.

Changing an Existing Template

Suppose you have created your new template, but now you want to change it. Or, you have another existing template that you want to change. To do so, you will need to first open it directly, as a template. To do so, choose **O**pen from the **F**ile menu. Specify Document Templates in Files of **T**ype. Use the Look in list to switch to the Templates folder. Select the template you want, and click Open. Now, make your editing and formatting changes, and add any styles, AutoText entries, macros, toolbars, menu items, and keyboard shortcuts you want to include in your template. Then, save the template.

Using Style Gallery to Preview a New Template

All documents have access to the Normal template, regardless of the template used to create them.

One way to change a document's formatting quickly and dramatically is to change the custom template attached to it. (Remember, this may also change the macros, AutoText entries, and many other items available to your document.)

Before you do so, you can use Style Gallery to preview how the document will look when it's reformatted, as you learned in Chapter 7. Choose Format, Style Gallery; click the template you want to preview. Word displays how your document would look if you applied the styles in this template. Click Cancel to leave this dialog box. (If you choose OK to apply the styles, Word copies the styles into your current template, which may not be what you want.)

How Template Changes Affect Existing Documents

Suppose you make changes to a template, then open an existing document based on that template. Will your document be suddenly reformatted according to the new template? The answer is no. Your changes to the template (for example, any new styles, AutoText entries, macros, or customized toolbars and menu assignments you may have created), will be *available* in the document. But the document will not suddenly include the changes in formatting or text that you've made to the template.

Using Word 6 and Word 95 Templates

Since Word 97's document formats have changed, templates that were developed for Word 6 or Word 95 will be saved in different formats in Word 97. Specifically, any macros included in these earlier templates will be converted from WordBasic to the new Visual Basic for Applications language, once you save them in Word 97.

In some cases, you may need to edit macros in templates created in older versions of Word to make them work properly in Word 97. If you wish to use a Word 6 or Word 95 template that includes macros, you may want to create a backup copy of it before saving it in Word 97, so you can retain the Word-Basic macro code.

■ Managing Templates

You can choose which templates are loaded into Word at any time, and which are actually attached to your document, controlling its styles and formatting. Templates are managed through the Templates and Add-Ins dialog box (see Figure 8.1), reachable by choosing Tools, Templates and Add-Ins. (Notice that this menu command has moved; in Word 6 and Word 95, you chose File, Templates to reach this dialog box.) The template listed in the Document template box is the one currently attached to your document. The checked templates and add-ins listed in the Global templates and add-ins section of the dialog box are those that are currently loaded into memory. Templates have DOT extensions; add-ins have WLL extensions.

Figure 8.1

The Templates and Add-ins dialog box

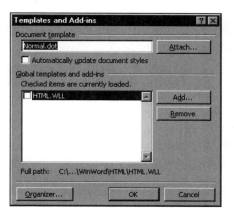

NOTE. *Add-ins are compiled programs written in C or other languages, which interact with Word using Word's Application Programming Interface. WLL, the extension used by add-ins, stands for Word Linked Library. Word add-ins*

*are developed in much the same manner as Windows' Dynamic Link Library
(DLL) files. Add-ins tend to run faster than equivalent macros. Unfortunately,
many add-ins developed for Word 6 or Word 95 are likely to require updating
in Word 97.*

To change the template attached to your document, first open the Templates and Add-ins dialog box; then click the Attach button. The Attach Template dialog box opens, displaying a list of all templates stored in the
Templates folder, and a list of subfolders that may also contain templates
(see Figure 8.2).

Figure 8.2

The Attach Template
dialog box

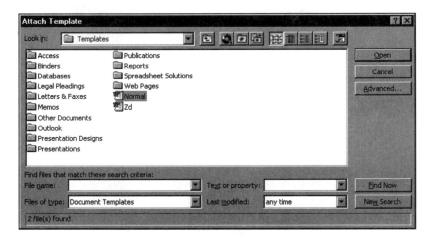

Select the template you want and click Open. If you want Word to automatically reflect the new template's styles in your document, check the Automatically update document styles box. When you're finished, click OK.

When wouldn't you want to update all the styles in a document when
you attach a new template? Perhaps you're attaching the template solely to
gain access to its AutoText entries, toolbars, and macros—not its styles.

Adding a Global Template

Global templates are templates that, once opened, are available to all documents. In other words, while a global template is open, any document you
create or open will have access to its macros, AutoText entries, styles, custom
menus, toolbars, and shortcut keys.

The Normal template you've already learned about is a global template.
However, the Normal template is *permanently* global; other global templates

can be loaded or unloaded whenever you wish—and when you unload a global template, its capabilities become unavailable to your documents.

To manage global templates, first display the Templates and Add-ins dialog box. If more than one global template is already available, check the one(s) you want to use, in the Global Templates and Add-ins list box. If you want to add a global template that isn't displayed in the Global Templates and Add-ins list box, click the A**d**d button. The Add Template dialog box opens (see Figure 8.3). Select the template you want to become a global template, and click on OK. The global template is now loaded for the remainder of your editing session, unless you return to this dialog box and remove it.

Figure 8.3

The Add Template
dialog box

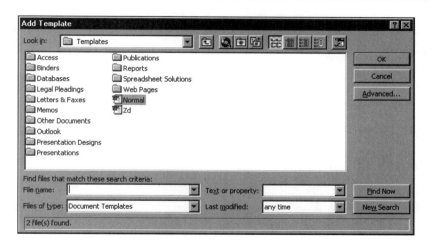

Adding a Global Template Permanently

You may want to add a global template *permanently*, so that it remains available and active for all future editing sessions. To do so, manually copy the template into Word's Startup folder (typically C:\Microsoft Office\Office\Startup). From then on, whenever Word loads, it will automatically load this template as well.

If you want to make the template unavailable to a specific document, uncheck its box in **G**lobal Templates and Add-ins. When you no longer want it to appear as a global template, delete it from the STARTUP folder.

Using the Organizer to Work with Templates

The Organizer brings styles, AutoText, toolbars, and macros together in one place, where they can be copied between templates and documents, or renamed. In other words, the Organizer makes it practical to add specific items associated with one template or document to another template or document.

For example, if you have several large blocks of text recorded as Auto-Text entries in your Letters template and you'd also like them to be available in your Proposals template, the Organizer makes that possible.

Prior to Word 97, the Organizer allowed you to move toolbars, AutoText entries, and macros *only* between templates, although you could move styles among documents as well. Since Word 97 allows you to store toolbars and macros with documents as well as templates, you can now use the Organizer to copy these among either documents or templates. (AutoText entries are still stored only in templates.)

Displaying the Organizer

To display the Organizer, choose Tools, Templates, and Add-ins, and click Organizer. The Organizer dialog box appears, as shown in Figure 8.4.

Figure 8.4

The Organizer allows you to copy styles, toolbars, AutoText entries, and macros among templates and documents.

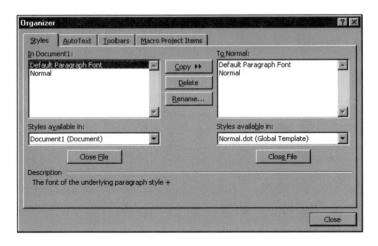

Copying, Renaming, or Deleting Items Displayed in the Organizer

You can copy, rename, or delete items displayed in the Organizer. Once you've opened the Organizer dialog box:

1. Choose the tab corresponding to the item you wish to copy, rename, or delete.

2. Select the specific style, AutoText entry, Toolbar, or Macro Project Item you wish to work with. When you do, a description of the item appears in the Description area of the dialog box. For example, if you select an AutoText entry, the contents of the entry appear there.

3. Select an item in either the left-hand or right-hand window; you can copy items in either direction. (When you open Organizer, the left-hand box displays the Styles, Toolbars, and Macro Project Items associated with your current document, and the AutoText entries associated with the Normal template. The right-hand box displays the styles, AutoText entries, Toolbars, and Macro Project Items with Normal.)

4. Click the Copy button to copy the item to the other template or document you've displayed; or click Rename to rename the item; or click Delete to delete the item.

5. Click Close to close the Organizer.

Copying Multiple Items

You can also copy several items at once. To select several consecutive items to copy, click the first one in the Organizer dialog box; press and hold Shift; then click the last one. To select several non-consecutive items, click the first one; press and hold Ctrl; then click each additional item you wish to select. To complete your copy, click the Copy button.

Copying Items Not Displayed in the Organizer

You may want to copy items to or from templates and documents that aren't currently displayed in the Organizer. To do so, first click on either Close File button in the Organizer dialog box. The list of available items disappears, and an Open File button appears. Click Open File. The Open dialog box appears, displaying the Templates folder, as shown in Figure 8.5. If you want to work with a template, you'll probably find it in this folder, or one of its subfolders.

Figure 8.5

Opening a template in the Organizer to move, copy, or rename its items

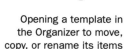

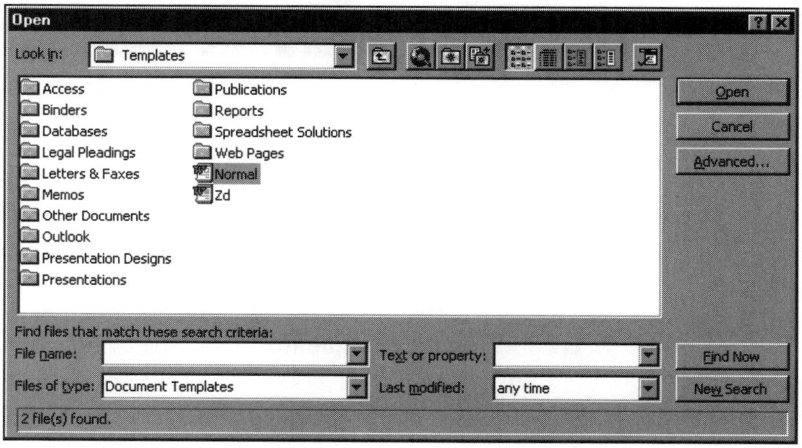

If you want to work with a document that is not displayed in the Organizer dialog box, change Files of type to Word Document, and then browse to the location of the document you want to work with. Choose Open. The Organizer dialog box now displays the items associated with the template or document you've chosen. Once you've opened the window displaying the correct source and destination templates or documents, select the item you want to copy, and click the Copy button.

Renaming an Item

Styles, AutoText entries, toolbars, and macros tend to grow like weeds. You may occasionally want to go through your garden and put things in order. For example, you can make sure all related items share similar names and are located in related templates. To rename an item, select it and click Rename. The Rename dialog box opens (see Figure 8.6). To rename the item, enter a new name and click OK.

Figure 8.6

You can rename styles, AutoText entries, toolbars, and macro entries in the Rename box.

Deleting an Item

You can also use Organizer to eliminate styles, AutoText entries, toolbars, or macros you no longer use. To delete an item, select it, click Delete, and then click Yes to confirm the deletion.

Browsing Word's Alternate Templates

Word comes with more than 20 templates that offer internally consistent styles for most kinds of documents. In Word 97, these are organized into categories, and Word takes advantage of long file names to provide a good description of each template. Better yet, you can preview the templates in Word's New dialog box.

The templates are also organized into three graphical approaches: contemporary, elegant, and professional. If you choose one of these styles and use it consistently for all your documents, you'll have created a consistent set of corporate graphic standards with little or no work.

Many of these templates, such as the Fax cover sheets and letter templates, already include text. All you need to do is substitute your appropriate information. The boilerplate text Microsoft provides even gives you guidance, sometimes as much as several pages, on using the template.

■ Using Wizards

Word's *wizards* are built-in programs that ask you questions about how you'd like your document constructed and then build a document based on your answers. Depending on the wizard, when you're done you may have a finished document, or just a well-designed framework into which you can add your specific text.

Nearly all the wizards that appeared in Word 95 have been revamped in Word 97. Some, such as the Fax Wizard, have been dramatically improved. For example, whereas the Word 95 Fax Wizard only generated cover sheets, the Word 97 Fax Wizard also walks you step-by-step through the process of actually transmitting the document and cover sheet.

NOTE. *If you're using Word to develop legal documents, be sure to try out the Pleading Wizard, which provides a quick and easy way to structure legal pleadings of many kinds.*

Browsing Word's Wizards Library

To open a wizard, choose **N**ew from the **F**ile menu, choose the category of document you want by clicking on its tab, and select the wizard icon from the box displaying all templates and wizards in that category. Then wait a few moments as Word prepares the wizard for use. (Unfortunately, wizards are among Word's slower features, especially if you have limited memory installed in your computer.)

NOTE. *One ingenious way to use a wizard is to have it help you create a template which you can use in the future instead of the wizard. To do so: First run the appropriate wizard. As you develop your document with the wizard, to save time add only the skeleton information. Then when Word displays the document and you can once again work at the speed of Word rather than the wizard, make any text or formatting changes you need. Then save the document as a template so that you can base new documents on it without running the wizard again. You might even want to go one step farther, and turn the document into a form that can be edited only in the spaces you mark—something you'll learn to do in Chapter 20.*

In Word 97, many wizards have been redesigned to follow a common format. As a result, when you've worked with one wizard, you have a fairly good idea of what to expect from the others. To show you how wizards work, the next section walks you through the Résumé Wizard in detail, displaying each screen and pointing out items common to most wizards.

Using the Résumé Wizard

To display the Résumé Wizard, choose File, New; click the Other Documents tab, and double-click on Résumé Wizard. The Résumé Wizard opens, as shown in Figure 8.7.

Figure 8.7

The Word 97 Résumé Wizard's opening dialog box

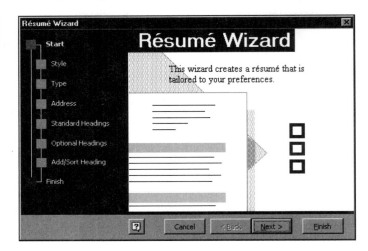

At the left, the Wizard displays a "map" showing you where you are. You can skip back and forth among steps by clicking on them. The last step, marked with a red square, is Finish. Whenever you're ready, you can click this step to finish the Wizard and generate your document.

At the bottom of the Wizard's dialog box, Cancel, Back, Next, and Finish buttons appear. There's also a question mark Help button that displays the Office Assistant, who can provide help with using the Wizard.

If you've ever used the Wizard before, your previous settings are saved, and you can simply click Finish to generate an identical document again. Or you can walk through the document step-by-step, viewing your previous choices and adjusting them as necessary.

To begin walking through the Résumé Wizard, click Next. In the dialog box shown in Figure 8.8, you're asked which style of Résumé you would like to create. Make a choice and click Next.

In Figure 8.9, Word asks you to pick a type of Résumé: professional, entry-level, chronological, or functional.

In the next dialog box (Figure 8.10), you're asked to insert your Name, Address, Phone, Fax, and e-mail address. Much of this information may already be filled in, if you've included it in the Tools, Options, User Information tabbed dialog box. Make sure the correct data appears, and click Next.

Figure 8.8

You can choose
the appearance
of your Résumé.

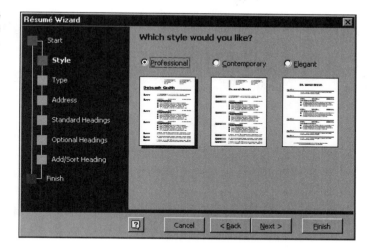

Figure 8.9

Specifying a type of
Résumé

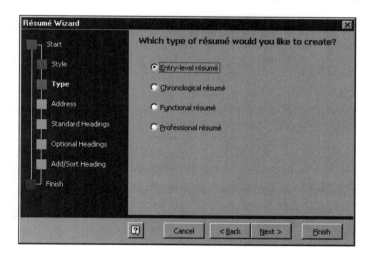

Next, the Resume Wizard recommends several headings that typically accompany the type of Résumé you've chosen (Figure 8.11). Adjust these
choices as you wish, and move on. Next, as shown in Figure 8.12, the Résumé
Wizard suggests some optional headings you might like to include.

Next, in Figure 8.13, you're asked if there are any custom headings you
want to include and if you wish to reorganize the order in which your current
headings appear or remove any headings. (If you now decide you want to
include more of the headings Word suggested earlier, you can always return

Figure 8.10

Filling in name, address and other contact information in the Résumé Wizard

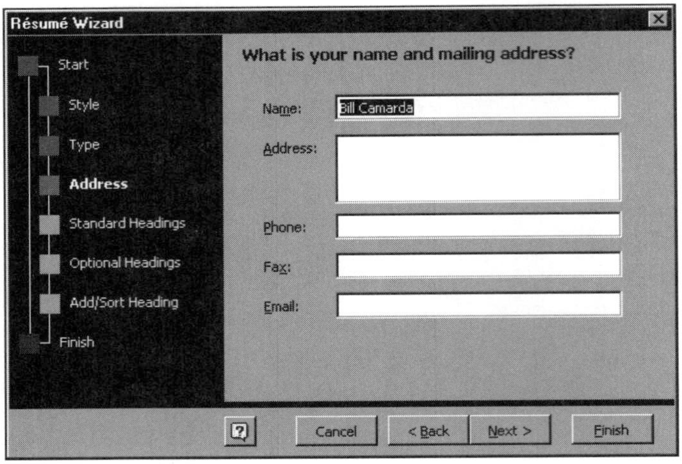

Figure 8.11

The Résumé Wizard recommends specific headings for the style of Résumé you've chosen.

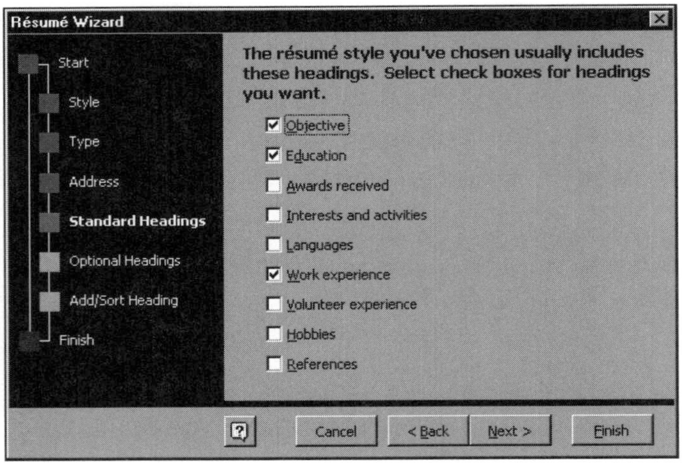

to earlier dialog boxes.) When you've finished specifying the contents of your Résumé, click Next.

Word now displays the last screen of the Wizard. Here's your chance to take a breath and make sure you've included everything you wanted to. When you're ready, click Finish, and Word will generate your Résumé document. This may take a few moments, depending on the speed of your computer and the complexity of the document. Word then displays the document in Page Layout View, and the Office Assistant gives you options as to what you might want to do next (Figure 8.14).

Figure 8.12

Adding optional headings
to your resume

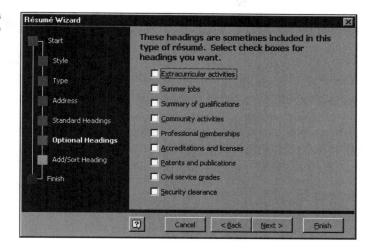

Figure 8.13

Adding custom headings
to your resume

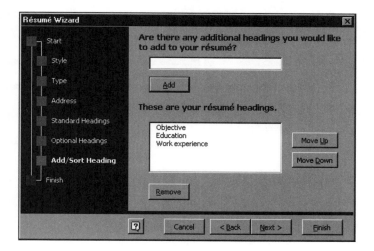

You can choose one of the options offered by the Office Assistant or click Cancel to return to your document. You can now edit your Résumé if you wish.

Notice that all placeholders in brackets are actually fields. If you click on them and enter your text, the placeholder text disappears.

Since your Résumé may include more than one job or degree, you can copy blocks of placeholders, creating the space you need. Notice, also, that most of your Résumé is formatted as a table. If you plan to modify it significantly, you might want to choose Table, Show Gridlines to get a better idea of the document's formatting and structure, as shown in Figure 8.15.

Figure 8.14

When the Wizard is finished, the Office Assistant asks what you want to do next.

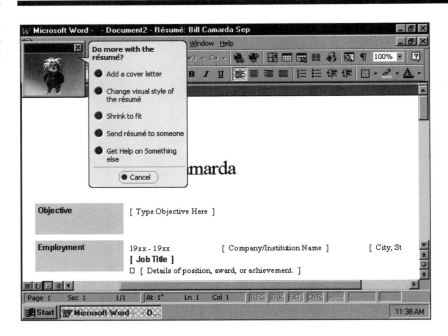

Figure 8.15

Part of a Wizard-generated Résumé with table gridlines. Note that selected placeholder text is a field.

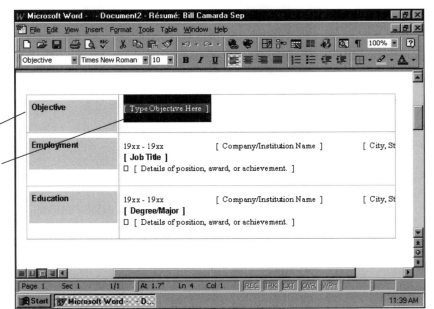

In this chapter, you've learned how templates can streamline your work by making exactly the right tools available to you at exactly the right time. You've also learned how to manage your templates, and taken a quick look at Word's built-in library of templates and wizards that can simplify the creation of the documents you're most likely to need.

In the next chapter, you'll learn about two Word 97 features that can simplify your work even more: AutoText, which allows you to enter large blocks of boilerplate text with just a few keystrokes, and AutoSummarize, which allows you to create executive summaries and abstracts automatically.

- *Understanding AutoText*
- *Creating AutoText Entries*
- *Using Previously Defined AutoText Entries*
- *Printing AutoText Entries*
- *Using AutoText Field Codes*
- *Introducing the New AutoSummarize Feature*

C H A P T E R

9

AutoText and AutoSummarize: Spend Less Time Typing and Editing

NOTHING IS MORE MIND-NUMBING AND ERROR-PRONE THAN TYPING the same boilerplate text over and over. With Word 97's AutoText tool for reusing text and graphics, you never have to do this again. With just a few keystrokes, you can insert anything you want—text, graphics, field codes, macros, you name it—into a document. Your AutoText entries can be of any length, provided you have the disk space and memory.

Word 97 AutoText has been revamped to make it an even more useful feature. It now has dozens of the most common phrases built in—even your name and company name. It's more accessible and more flexible than ever before. Bottom line, it's a nifty feature.

Here's another nifty new feature: AutoSummarize. With AutoSummarize, you can actually instruct Word 97 to summarize a document, either one that you've created or one you're reading online. (Why waste time reading lengthy documents that aren't worth the trouble?) You can even create an Executive Summary of your document automatically. Word doesn't do a perfect job, but if you have a fairly well-structured document, you may be surprised by how well it can do. With AutoSummarize, it's conceivable you'll only have to make final touch-ups on your summary, instead of creating it from scratch.

■ Understanding AutoText

Word's AutoText feature provides a quick and easy way to store text or graphics and then paste them into documents later as needed. AutoText maintains a database of frequently used text or graphic objects that you can quickly and easily drop into your documents.

You can use AutoText to insert long company names, complex scientific terms, or graphics into your documents. For instance, using AutoText, you can replace "ZD" automatically with "Ziff-Davis Press."

AutoText entries are stored in document templates, which means that different AutoText entries can be made available from different templates. AutoText entries stored in Word's default NORMAL.DOT template are available whenever you use Word.

■ Creating AutoText Entries

In Word 97, the AutoText feature has been revamped and relocated, but the basics remain roughly the same as ever.

To create an AutoText entry, begin by keying in the text, then add any special formatting, and inserting any graphics or other special elements. If you add a phrase or a sentence, be sure to add a space after it—that way, you won't have to do it manually every time you use the AutoText entry. Then select the material you want to save as an AutoText entry. Next, choose AutoText from the Insert menu, and then choose New from the cascaded menu that appears. The Create AutoText dialog box appears, with Word's suggestion as to what to name your AutoText entry, as shown in Figure 9.1. Edit the AutoText entry's name as you like, and click OK to store it. That's all there is to it. Unless you choose to make a bigger deal out of it, which you may sometimes *want* to do, as we'll describe in the next section.

Figure 9.1

The Create AutoText window shows a truncated version of your text selection that will become an AutoText entry.

Naming AutoText Entries

A word to the wise about naming AutoText entries: In general, use names that are short enough to save you time, but not so short and generic that you can't remember what they stand for. (Well, maybe you can get away with a few really short ones, like the stock ticker symbol T, which stands for American Telephone & Telegraph Corporation.) Of course, the longer or more complex the text contained in the AutoText entry, the less you mind a few extra characters in its name.

One final tip on naming AutoText entries: If you have several related AutoText entries, give them names that make it obvious they're related. For example, in writing this book, when I want to insert a figure caption, I use the AutoText entry FCP; when I want to insert a figure description, I use FDS.

Specifying Where Your AutoText Entry Should Go

As we've already mentioned, AutoText entries are stored with templates. You can choose which template to store an AutoText entry with—and this capability comes in handy. For example, if you work with different clients whose fields are completely unrelated, you might want to organize a separate set of AutoText entries for each of them. To store an AutoText entry with a particular template, first enter and format the text you want to transform into an AutoText entry; then choose AutoText from the Insert menu. Then, choose AutoText from the cascaded menu. The AutoText tab of the AutoCorrect dialog box appears, as shown in Figure 9.2. To specify which open template to place your AutoText entry in, choose it from the Look in drop-down list box at the bottom of the dialog box. Choose OK. (Templates are covered in depth in Chapter 8.)

Managing AutoText Entries

While you're in the AutoText tab of the AutoCorrect dialog box, have a look around. Notice that you can preview your AutoText entry here, in the Preview box. Notice that this dialog box doesn't attempt to suggest a truncated

Figure 9.2

The AutoText tab of the
AutoCorrect dialog box

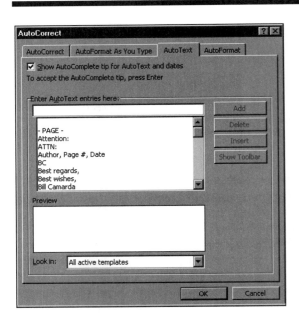

version of your AutoText entry—it simply allows you to edit your own. Notice that you can also select an existing AutoText entry from the list shown
here and delete it.

Using AutoComplete Tips With AutoText

The AutoText tab of the AutoCorrect dialog box also controls another Word
97 innovation, AutoComplete. If you leave the check in the box for Show AutoComplete tip for AutoText and dates, whenever a user types at least four
characters of a word or phrase that match the beginning of an available Auto-
Text entry, Word will display a ScreenTip showing the AutoText entry, as
shown in Figure 9.3. Pressing Enter will insert the entire AutoText entry.

AutoComplete is turned on by default. It works only for AutoText entry
names that are at least four characters long.

Yet another enhancement is worth noting: If you click the Show Toolbar
button on the AutoText tab of the AutoCorrect dialog box, the AutoText toolbar appears, as shown in Figure 9.4. It may contain only three buttons, but
hey, they're powerful!

The AutoText icon button, on the left side of the AutoText toolbar,
displays the AutoText tab of the AutoCorrect dialog box. The All Entries
button displays all available AutoText entries, organized into categories.
(More on this in the next section.) If you place your insertion point on text
formatted with a style that has corresponding AutoText entries, the name

Figure 9.3

Word can display an AutoComplete tip, which shows you at least a portion of the entire text associated with an AutoText entry.

Screen Tip

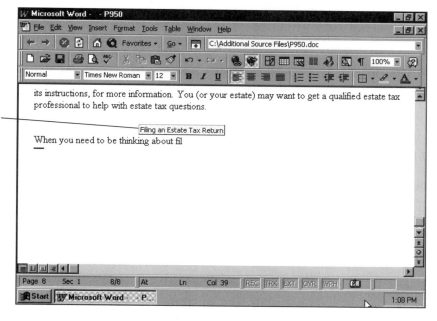

Figure 9.4

The AutoText toolbar allows you to create, choose, or manage AutoText entries.

All Entries will change to the style you have selected, and clicking the button will display only the entries associated with that style.

The New button, located on the far right of the toolbar, gives you a shortcut for creating new AutoText entries. Click it, and it displays the Create AutoText dialog box, where you can create a new AutoText entry. The New button is only active when you select text.

■ Using Previously Defined AutoText Entries

The easiest way to use text or graphics saved as an AutoText entry is to type the name of the AutoText entry into the document, and then press F3. If AutoComplete is turned on, Word may display the contents of your Auto-Text entry before you finish typing. If it does, you can press Enter to insert the entry. Otherwise, Word will find the AutoText entry name and automatically insert the corresponding AutoText entry text and/or graphics in its place in your document.

NOTE. *AutoText isn't case-sensitive. Word ignores distinctions between uppercase and lowercase letters.*

If you don't remember the name of the AutoText entry, you can display a list of all available AutoText entries. Place your insertion point on a part of your document formatted in Normal style or one of Word's built-in heading styles, then choose Insert, AutoText. A cascaded menu appears, showing all categories of AutoText entries available to you, as shown in Figure 9.5.

Figure 9.5

The cascaded menu shows built-in options for the Mailing Instructions category. The category QQ includes all AutoText entries that use the custom QQ style.

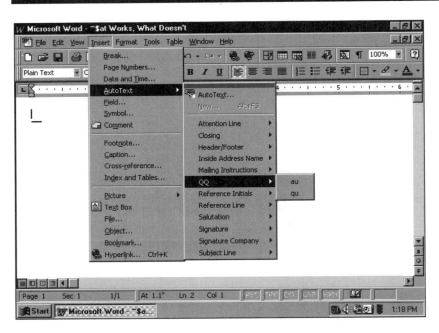

If you've used Word's AutoText feature before, you'll quickly notice two changes in Word 97. First, dozens of AutoText entries come built in: your name, the name of your company, sample headers and footers, a wide variety of common business letter openings and closings, and phrases often used in business memos. Some of these entries, such as Author, Page #, Date in the Header/Footer category, use field codes to update themselves as you update your document. In Word 6 and Word 95, there were no built-in entries; you had to create them yourself.

Second, the AutoText entries you create are *organized by style*. All the AutoText entries associated with a specific style are listed together, in a cascaded menu item named after that style.

For example, let's assume you often create business reports with the same headings, such as Executive Summary, Proposed Course of Action,

Opportunities and Risks, or similar phrases. Since they're all headings, you usually style each of them as Heading 1. If you create AutoText entries for them, they will all be stored together, under the cascaded menu listing Heading 1.

NOTE. *Once you've inserted an AutoText entry, you can edit it the same way you edit anything else in your document.*

Formatting AutoText Entries

By default, Word preserves the character formatting that you give an AutoText entry. When you insert the AutoText into another document, the formatting given to the AutoText in its original document is preserved, no matter how the document into which you insert the AutoText entry is formatted. The preservation of an entry's formatting is a major advantage. This feature relieves you of the job of duplicating the complex formatting of a foreign document, which might not be readily created by Word styles—such as text with many different character attributes in the same paragraph.

Editing Existing AutoText Entries

Occasionally, you might want to change an existing AutoText entry. For example, you may have an AutoText entry representing your phone number. What if you change phone numbers? Here's how to change your AutoText entry:

1. Insert your existing AutoText entry into your document.

2. Revise the entry's contents as you want.

3. Select the revised entry.

4. Choose Insert, AutoText, New, or click the New button on the AutoText toolbar.

5. Enter the same AutoText name you used previously.

6. Select the OK button or press Enter.

7. You'll be asked to confirm whether you want to redefine your existing AutoText entry. Choose Yes.

Renaming an AutoText Entry

You also can rename an AutoText entry, although the procedure is a bit complicated.

1. Choose Tools, Templates and Add-Ins.

2. In the Templates and Add-ins dialog box, click **O**rganizer.

3. The Organizer dialog box opens with the **S**tyles tab selected. Choose the **A**utoText tab to reveal the AutoText options (see Figure 9.6).

4. Select the AutoText name you want to rename and click the **R**ename button.

5. The Rename dialog box (see Figure 9.7) pops up over the Organizer AutoText tab.

6. Enter the new name for the AutoText entry in the New name text box and choose OK or press Enter.

7. Close the Organizer dialog box.

Figure 9.6

The Organizer's AutoText tab allows you to rename AutoText entries.

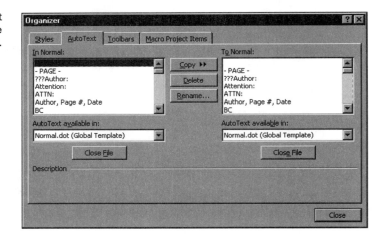

Figure 9.7

The Rename dialog box allows you to specify a new name for an AutoText entry.

Deleting an AutoText Entry

If you no longer need an AutoText entry, you can easily delete it, as follows:

1. Choose AutoTe**x**t from the Insert menu, and then click on AutoText in the cascaded submenu.

2. Select the AutoText entry to be deleted.

3. Click on the **D**elete button.

4. Click OK.

Word does not ask you to confirm the AutoText deletion. Once you choose Delete, the entry instantly disappears from your list and you cannot get it back. The next section tells you how to recover accidentally deleted AutoText entries.

Recovering Deleted AutoText Entries

AutoText entries are stored by default as part of NORMAL.DOT, the global document template, although you can specify a different template for their storage. When you delete AutoText entries, unless you specify otherwise, you make changes to NORMAL.DOT. Since NORMAL.DOT is automatically saved by default, when you exit Word you lose forever the AutoText entries you deleted during your Word session.

You can tell Word that you want to be prompted before Word saves changes to NORMAL.DOT. This can save you a great deal of trouble and prevent you from accidentally deleting valuable AutoText entries.

To institute the prompt, you must turn off the NORMAL.DOT "autosave" feature, since it's turned on by default. To ask to be prompted, select **O**ptions in the **T**ools menu, then click on the Save tab. This tab, shown in Figure 9.8, contains all the various save options for Word, including the ones for changes to NORMAL.DOT.

Figure 9.8

The Save tab of the Options dialog box allows you to confirm changes to the NORMAL.DOT template.

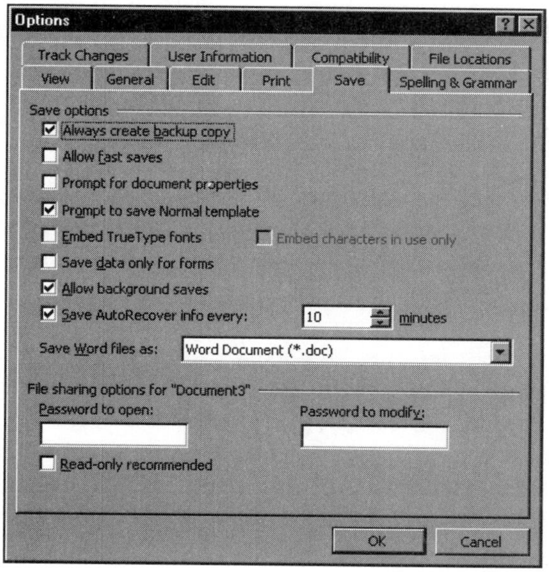

With the Pr**o**mpt to save Normal template box checked, any time you make a change to the document template during an editing session (including changes to styles, macros, or AutoText), Word asks if you want to save NORMAL.DOT when you exit Word. This option gives you a chance to recover AutoText entries you delete by accident.

■ Printing AutoText Entries

Nobody's memory is good enough to remember every AutoText name and its contents. You might want to occasionally print out your AutoText entries and share them with anyone else who uses them.

1. Choose **P**rint from the **F**ile menu.

2. In the Print **w**hat list box, select AutoText Entries.

3. Choose OK or press the Enter key.

If your document uses a custom template, Word prints out the AutoText entries in both the document template and NORMAL.DOT—in other words, all AutoText entries that are available to the document.

■ Using AutoText Field Codes

AutoText entries are also ideal partners for field codes (Chapter 21) and macros (Chapters 25–28). You can use an AutoText entry to insert text that includes field codes—such as figure reference numbers that can update themselves automatically. In particular, Word 97 contains two field codes that make the AutoText feature even more powerful.

Whenever you change it once, the { AUTOTEXT } field code changes a block of text that appears repeatedly throughout a document. It's ideal for situations where you know you will have to repeat text often throughout your document, but you expect that text to change as you edit the document.

Instead of inserting the text as an AutoText entry, you can insert your AutoText entries into your document as fields. So when you change the entry once, the text is automatically updated throughout your document.

For example, let's say you've created an AutoText entry named FC. To ensure that any changes you make to FC will always be made wherever it appears in your document, you would insert the following field into your document:

```
{ AUTOTEXT FC }
```

To insert this field code, choose Insert, Field. The Field dialog box opens, as shown in Figure 9.9. Select AutoText from the list of Field names, type the name of your field after the word AUTOTEXT in the text box below the Categories and Field names, and click OK.

Figure 9.9

The Field dialog box, with the { AUTOTEXT FC } field entered

There's more. Imagine you're in the cheese business and you have an Auto-Text entry FC, which enters the text Farmer's Cheese. Suddenly, your market for Farmer's Cheese dries up; you decide to sell Fontina Cheese instead. Redefine your AutoText entry, update your fields, and voila! All your fields now display Fontina Cheese where they previously displayed Farmer's Cheese.

Equally powerful, and brand new in Word 97, is the { AUTOTEXTLIST } field code. It allows you to place a drop-down list box anywhere in your document, containing available AutoText entries. You can display directions along with your drop-down list. For example, "Right-click here to make a selection." Then when the user selects an entry from the inserted list, that entry replaces the directions.

Let's walk through an example. Imagine you're developing a proposal, and you've create three different paragraphs to be used depending on which schedule your client wants: regular, rush, or extreme rush. You've styled all of these paragraphs as Body Text Schedule, and assigned each one an Auto-Text entry name: reg, rush, xrush. Now, using the Insert Field dialog box discussed above, you can create the following field code:

```
{ AUTOTEXTLIST "Click here for schedule choices" \s "Body Text Schedule" }
```

When a user clicks anywhere on the phrase "Click here for schedule choices," the list of options appears, as shown in Figure 9.10. Choose one, and its text replaces the directions you had placed there, as shown in Figure 9.11. (Notice that the switch \s indicates the style your replacement options are formatted in.)

Figure 9.10

The AUTOTEXTLIST field allows you to choose text from within a document.

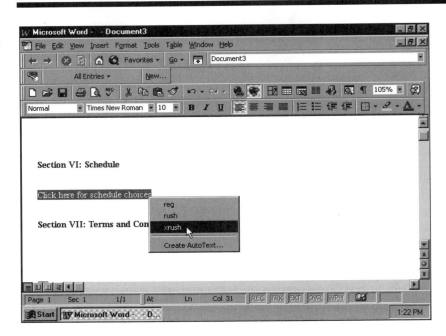

Whenever a user's mouse pointer hovers over the field code in the document, a ScreenTip appears, providing instructions for displaying the list.

■ Introducing the New AutoSummarize Feature

Who would have imagined a few years ago that your word processor would be able to read your document and summarize it? Well, if you have a fairly well-structured document, Word 97's new AutoSummarize feature can do a pretty respectable job. You can use it either on your own documents or for online documents you may not wish to read in their entirety.

AutoSummarize analyzes each sentence in your document, assigning a score to each sentence. For instance, if a sentence uses several of the words that appear most often throughout the document, chances are it's relatively important, so it receives a higher score.

Figure 9.11

When you choose an
AutoText entry,
it replaces the
directions that had
appeared in
the document.

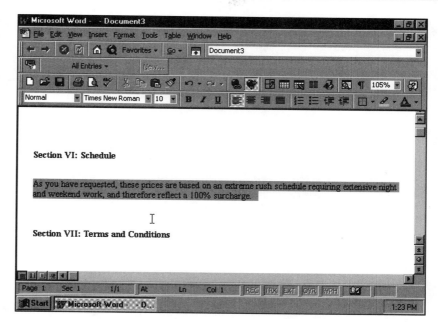

Using AutoSummarize

To use AutoSummarize, choose Tools, AutoSummarize. Word examines
your document and then displays the AutoSummarize dialog box, as shown
in Figure 9.12.

You now have four choices about how you would like to display your summary. These four choices let you decide where you want your summary placed
and how you want to view it: highlighted within your document, or displayed
by itself with no other document text showing, or as an abstract at the beginning of your document, or in a new document.

Summarizing within Your Original Document

Your first choice is *Highlight key points* (in the upper left quadrant of the AutoSummarize dialog box). An example of this type of summary is shown in
Figure 9.13. When you select Highlight Key Points, Word displays your document with the most important sentences in yellow. The AutoSummarize toolbar appears, as shown in Figure 9.14.

Figure 9.12

The AutoSummarize dialog box allows you to specify exactly how you want to use this feature.

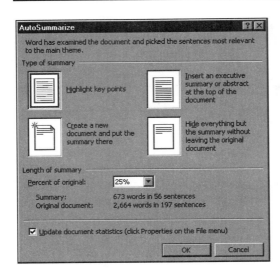

Figure 9.13

A document with AutoSummarize sentences highlighted

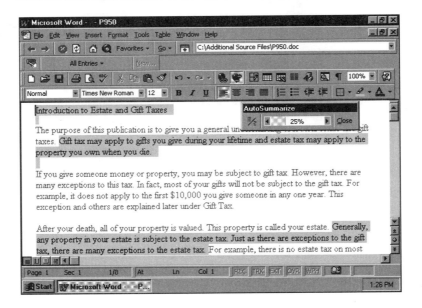

Figure 9.14

The AutoSummarize toolbar

The AutoSummarize Toolbar

The Highlight/Show Only Summary button (on the far left of the AutoSummarize toolbar) toggles between displaying the most important sentences highlighted in yellow, and displaying *only* the most important sentences. When you choose the Show Only Summary option of the toggle button, the text in your document that's not part of the summary is temporarily treated as hidden text (if you've set hidden text to display, this text will still be visible, with a dotted underline). Choosing Show Only Summary is equivalent to choosing Hide everything but the summary without leaving the original document.

When you choose the Highlight option of the Show Only Summary/ Highlight toggle button, the entire document will be visible, with less important sentences displayed in light gray.

The AutoSummarize toolbar also lets you decide what percentage of the document length you want the summary to be. By default, AutoSummarize summarizes your document to 25% of its original length. However, you can drag the slide to the specific percentage you wish. The lower the percentage, of course, the fewer sentences will appear in the summary—and the more likely it is that your summary will consist largely of headings.

Create an Executive Summary or Abstract

Another of the options in the AutoSummarize dialog box is to have Word place its summary of your document at the beginning of your document as an Executive Summary or Abstract. You can access this option by displaying your document, choosing Tools, AutoSummarize; then choosing Insert an executive summary or abstract at the top of the document, and clicking OK. The summary information will appear under the heading Summary, starting on page 1 of your document.

Create a New Document and Put the Summary There

Another of the four ways of summarizing your document is to create a new document and put the summary there. To use this option, open the document you wish to summarize; choose Tools, AutoSummarize; choose Create a new document and put the summary there; and click OK.

AutoSummarizing Web Pages

Ever get on the Web, come across a very long document, and wonder if it's worth reading? You can use AutoSummarize to find out. In this example, we'll start out in Word, move to the Web via Internet Explorer 3.01, capture a document, and AutoSummarize it from within Word.

First display the Web toolbar, and click Search the Web. Microsoft Internet Explorer opens. Connect to the document you want to AutoSummarize and click the Edit button, as shown in Figure 9.15. (For more information on using Explorer and the Web, see Chapter 14.)

Figure 9.15

In Microsoft Internet Explorer 3.01, click Edit to copy your current Web page to Microsoft Word for AutoSummarizing.

Edit Button

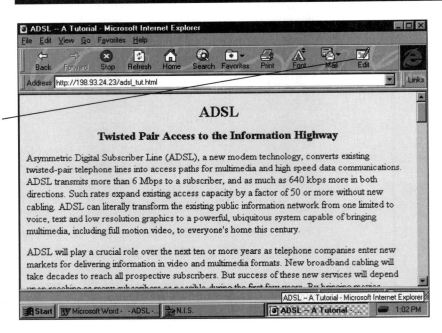

Word opens (perhaps a bit slowly), showing a converted version of the HTML page you were visiting (see Figure 9.16).

Choose Tools, AutoSummarize. All the same options for displaying summaries that are available to you in Word documents are available here. We'll choose Hide everything but the summary without leaving the original document. The results are shown in Figure 9.17.

In this chapter, you've learned about two more Word features that can dramatically reduce the time required to create documents. AutoText allows you to quickly enter boilerplate text—and Word 97 even provides some of the boilerplate text you're likely to need most. AutoSummarize does a courageous job of summarizing documents for you—and if your document is well-organized, it does a reasonably good job.

Next, in Chapter 10, you'll learn about Word's powerful outlining tools, which can help you make short work of organizing your document in the first place.

Figure 9.16

The Word conversion of the Web page in Figure 9.15

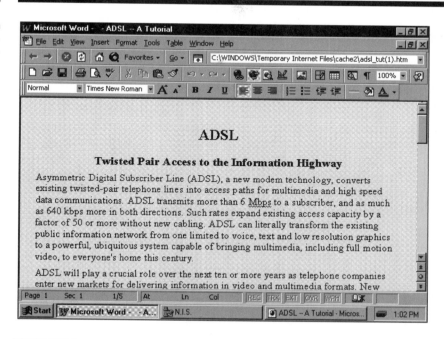

Figure 9.17

An AutoSummarized version of the Web page, shown in Word.

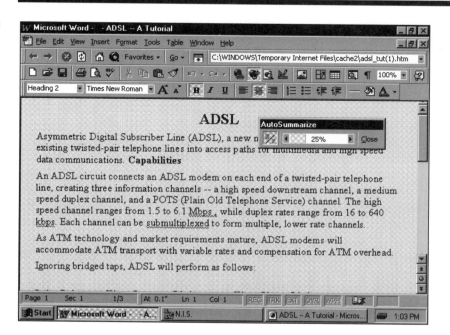

- *Word's Outlining Tools*
- *Looking at a Document in Outline View*
- *Creating an Outline from Scratch*
- *Printing an Outline*
- *Adding Outline Numbering*

10

Outlining: Get Your Document Organized–Fast!

Even if you've never cared to write from an outline, you will find Word's outlines extremely valuable. They make it easy to see a bird's-eye view of your document. They make it easy to move large chunks of text, quickly restructuring even a very long document. Outlining also offers a convenient way to apply the styles that Word uses to automate many of its features, such as tables of contents—as you'll learn in Chapter 11, *Tables of Contents and Indexes: Let Word Do the Hard Work.*

You can even convert Word outlines into PowerPoint presentations, using Word's File, Send to, PowerPoint menu command, which automatically translates each first-level heading into a separate slide and displays your document in PowerPoint's own Outline view.

And if you *do* like to write from an outline, welcome to hog heaven. With Word 97, you can easily create an outline and then build your document around it, effortlessly modifying your outline whenever you want. You get all the structure you could possibly want.

In this chapter, you'll learn how Word outlining works—and how to create, edit, number, view, and print your outline. Most of all, you'll learn how to use Word outlining to create a skeleton for virtually any document—one that's flexible enough to build on, no matter how you choose to flesh things out.

■ Word's Outlining Tools

In Word, an outline is not separate from the rest of a document; rather, it is simply a different view of the same document—a view that takes into account the headings or outline levels you may have already applied, and provides an easy way to organize your document with headings or outline levels whether you've previously applied them or not.

To work with an outline, switch to Outline view: choose **O**utline from the **V**iew menu, or click on Word's Outline view button on the horizontal scroll bar (see Figure 10.1). A new outlining toolbar appears, as shown in Figure 10.2.

Figure 10.1

Click the Outline view button, to the left of the horizontal scroll bar, to view your document in Outline view.

The Outline view toolbar contains your tools for working in Outline view. These tools are listed below, along with a brief explanation of their functions. A more in-depth walk-through of each function follows later in the chapter.

Tools for Changing Heading Levels

The first three buttons on the left of the Outline view toolbar enable you to increase or decrease a heading's level in your document, thereby changing the relative importance you give to it in your outline. Changing the level of a head is called *promoting* or *demoting*. You can promote or demote a single heading, or you can change the level of many headings all at once, by selecting them all and then using the promote or demote buttons, or the keyboard shortcuts, shown below in Table 10.1.

Figure 10.2

When you switch to Outline view, the Outline view toolbar opens, providing tools for organizing and restructuring your outline.

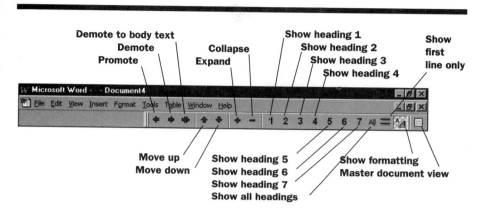

Table 10.1

Promoting and demoting headings

BUTTON	KEYBOARD EQUIVALENT	NAME	WHAT IT DOES
	Alt+Shift+Left Arrow	Promote	Raises a heading one level (making it more important)
	Alt+Shift+Right Arrow	Demote	Lowers a heading one level (making it less important)
	Alt+Shift+5 on the numeric keypad with NumLock off	Demote to Body Text	Changes the contents of a heading to body text

Tools for Moving Elements of an Outline

The next two buttons on the Outline view toolbar with upward and downward facing arrows enable you to move outline headings, and the subordinate headings or body text associated with them, thereby rearranging your document. (Notice that, in contrast to typical outlines you may have created manually, you can view body text in a Word outline. Any body text you view, you can also change into headings—and you can change headings into body text.)

Tools for Expanding and Collapsing Outlines

Expanding an outline means viewing all of its subordinate headings and body text. *Collapsing* an outline means hiding all of its subordinate headings and body text. With the two buttons on the Outline view toolbar showing a + and a -, you can expand or collapse your outline, or any part of it you select.

Table 10.2

Moving elements of an outline

BUTTON	KEYBOARD EQUIVALENT	NAME	WHAT IT DOES
⬆	Alt+Shift+Up Arrow	Move Paragraph Up	Moves the current outline element (heading or body text) ahead of the previous one
⬇	Alt+Shift+Down Arrow	Move Paragraph Down	Moves the current outline element after the next one

The tools are shown in Table 10.3. To use the buttons on the numeric keypad, first turn NumLock off.

Table 10.3

Expanding and collapsing outlines

BUTTON	KEYBOARD EQUIVALENT	NAME	WHAT IT DOES
➕	Alt+Plus	Show Subtext	Completely expands any outline element you select
➖	Alt+Underscore	Hide Subtext	Completely collapses any outline element you select

Tools for Displaying Specific Outline Levels

The group of buttons on the Outline view toolbar showing numerals are called the Show buttons. They enable you to control just how much of an outline is displayed. Pressing the button marked 1, for example, tells Word to display only first-level heads; pressing the button marked 2, first- and second-level heads; and so on. Pressing the All button on the toolbar expands the entire document, showing all headings and body text. On the keyboard, Alt+Shift+A toggles between showing all body text and none of it; you can also press * on the numeric keypad.

Sometimes you may want to view a little more of a document's content than is visible in its headings alone, but you don't want to view all the body text. Word's Show First Line Only button (see Figure 10.3) provides the solution. Press the button on the Outline view toolbar with two thick horizontal lines on it, and Word will display the first line of each paragraph of body text. You can switch between displaying all text and just the first line of each paragraph by pressing the Show First Line Only button on and off. (Alt+Shift+L does the same thing from the keyboard.)

Figure 10.3

The Show First Line Only button allows you to view the first line of text underneath a subhead—without showing so much that you can't see the rest of your outline.

The Show/Hide Character formatting button on the Outline view toolbar is the one with two letter As on it, as shown in Figure 10.4. It is used to display or suppress character formatting in your outline. In some cases, especially when many large headlines and subheads are included, outlines can be easier to follow with the formatting temporarily hidden.

Figure 10.4

When the Show Character Formatting button is toggled on in Outline view, Word displays all elements of the outline in the default font and point size.

NOTE. *Master documents use Word's outlining feature to streamline the assembly of multiple documents. The Master Document View button is the last button on the right side of the Outline view toolbar. This topic is covered in Chapter 13, "Master Documents: Manage Even the Longest Documents."*

■ Looking at a Document in Outline View

Let's look at a typical document in Outline view—as shown in Figure 10.5. You can see some of the differences between Outline view and Normal or Page Layout view right away.

Word presents you with a somewhat stylized version of a typical outline you might have learned in school. When subheadings are displayed, they appear indented underneath their major headings. Body text also appears indented under its subheading. In place of the numbers associated with normal outlines, however, each paragraph of a Word outline has a plus sign, minus sign, or small square next to it. A plus sign tells you there are subheadings and body text beneath this line or paragraph; a minus sign tells you there aren't any. A small square tells you the paragraph is body text. The plus and minus signs don't tell you which level of heading you're in, but you can always tell by looking at the style box.

Figure 10.5

A typical document, with headings and body text, shown in Outline view

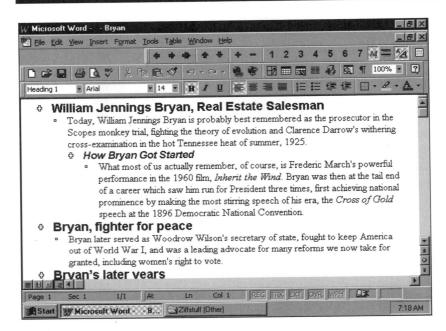

NOTE. *You can also tell Word to display a breakdown of your outline's heading structure in an area on the left side of the screen called the Style Area. To do so, choose Tools, Options, View, and specify a style area of approximately .75"; Word lists each heading's style to the left of the heading. By the way, this feature works in Normal view, too.*

Moving Around in an Outlined Document

Word 97's new Document Map (see Figure 10.6) makes it significantly easier to navigate through outlined documents, by compiling all the headings in a separate window to the left of the document window. To display the Document Map, choose View, Document Map. Then, to move to a specific location in the document, just click on that location's heading in the Document Map.

You can use the Document Map alongside *any* view of a document, including Normal, Online Layout, Page Layout and Outline view. However, since the Document Map resembles a document outline showing all headings, if you switch to Outline view while Document Map is open, Word assumes the outline will be sufficient for your needs, and closes Document Map view. Word gives you two more navigational tools for moving from one heading to the next in your document. Either click the double up-arrows or down-arrows at the bottom of Word 97's vertical scroll bar, or use the

Figure 10.6

Word's Document Map feature makes it easier than ever to move throughout an outlined document.

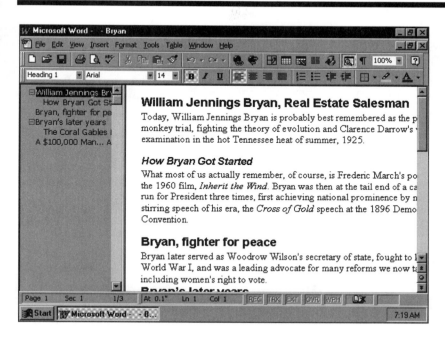

Browse by Object technique to move from one heading to the next. Start by clicking the Browse by Object button at the bottom of the vertical scroll bar, between the Previous Page and Next Page buttons. Then click the Browse by Heading button, the fourth button from the left on the bottom row of the toolbar that appears (see Figure 10.7). The arrows on the Previous Page and Next Page buttons at the bottom of the vertical scroll bar change color to let you know that you are working in the Browse by Object mode. Now when you click those buttons, the insertion point will move from one heading to the next. The advantage of using this technique is that you don't have to display the Document Map to quickly move from one heading to the next.

■ Creating an Outline from Scratch

Next, let's create an outline from scratch. Start by opening a new document, and then choose **V**iew, **O**utline, or click on the Outline view button.

You're presented with an insertion point that follows a minus sign, as in Figure 10.8. The minus sign tells you that no copy appears under this heading. Word assumes that you want to type a first-level heading, such as a chapter name, and use Word's built-in Heading 1 style. This is a reasonable assumption in Outline view, since you're probably intending to create the

Figure 10.7

Word's Browse by Object feature allows you to move from one heading to the next without displaying the Document Map.

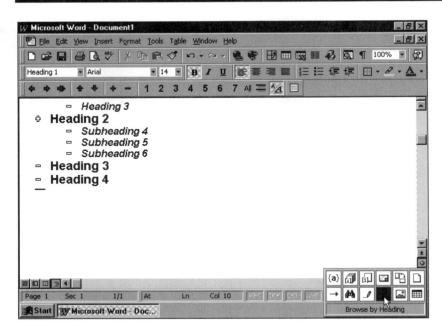

structure of a new document. However, starting off your document with a heading may not be what you're used to, especially if you're accustomed to working in Normal or Page Layout view, which assumes you want to type Normal (body) text unless you specify otherwise.

Creating a New Document in Outline View

To begin entering your outline, start typing just as you would in Normal view. When you're finished entering a heading, press Enter. Word starts a new paragraph—again, expecting the new line to be a first-level heading.

Entering Subheadings in a New Outline

Now let's say you want to create some subheadings under the main heading you already have. With your insertion point positioned in the line underneath the main heading, click the Demote button, or use the keyboard shortcut Alt+Shift+Right Arrow.

As you can see in Figure 10.9, two things happen immediately. The first heading now displays a plus sign (+), meaning there's now subordinate text below it (your new subhead). And the second-level head is now indented and formatted in Heading 2 style.

Figure 10.8

In Outline view, the minus sign tells you that no copy appears under a heading.

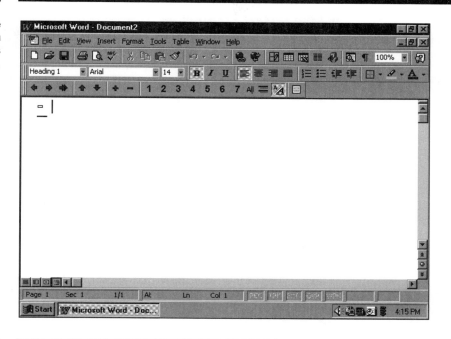

Figure 10.9

When you add a second-level heading in Outline view, the first-level heading is now marked with a plus sign to show that it has subordinate headings and/or body text.

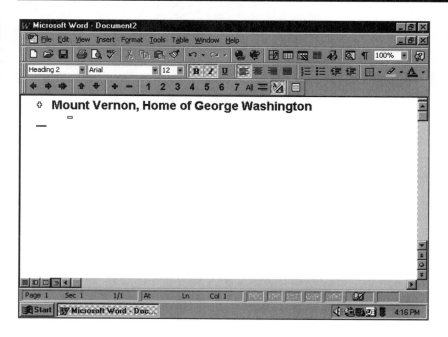

If you press Enter again, Word anticipates another second-level heading. (Word always expects the next heading to be identical to the last.) However, you can always change heading levels (and their accompanying styles) before or after you enter text. This means you can always add another heading or body text paragraph in Outline view by placing the insertion point at the end of the previous one and pressing Enter.

Entering Body Text in a New Outline

Okay, you've got some headings; now let's say you want to add some body text. It's unlikely you're going to edit your entire document in Outline view, but it's *quite* likely that you might have the beginnings of some ideas about what you intend to cover. Why not add those ideas right now, in Outline view, while they're on your mind?

To add body text, click the Demote to Body Text button, or press Alt+Shift+5, using the "5" key on the numeric keypad. (Remember that NumLock must be off to use the keyboard command.) A square box appears next to your insertion point in the outline, and a plus sign appears in the previous subheading, indicating that the subheading now has subordinate text. You can see this in Figure 10.10.

Figure 10.10

Inserting body text in an outline

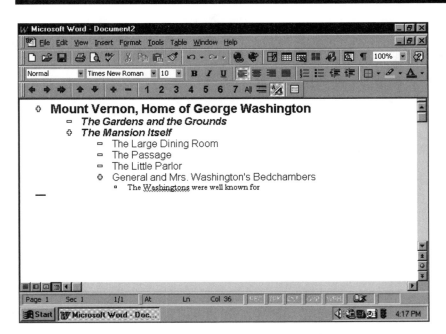

You can type text at the insertion point, paste text from another document, import a graphic, use a field code to generate a result, or use character formatting.

NOTE. *You can use the Shortcut menu in Outline view, just as you can elsewhere in Word. Just right-click on any text in your outline. (See Figure 10.11.) You can cut, copy, format, paste, and—if you select the menu while you are in a heading—you can change indents. Note that increasing and decreasing indents has no effect on how the text is displayed while in Outline view. You will see the effects of the indents only if you switch to Page Layout or Normal views or if you print the document. Note, also, that most formatting commands are unavailable from within Outline view.*

Figure 10.11

The Shortcut Menu in
Outline view

Shortcut menu

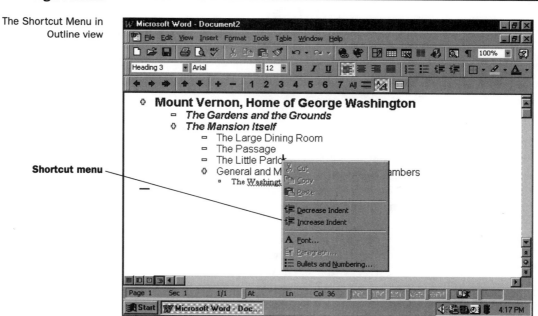

Creating and Editing Headings

You've added your body text, and now you're ready to insert another first-level head. Press Enter to start a new line. Then click the Promote button. Your text is now formatted as a third-level heading. Your outline's structure should now resemble the example in Figure 10.12.

NOTE. *You can also apply heading styles directly from the Style list on the Formatting toolbar. This is especially useful if you want to promote or demote a heading by several levels.*

Figure 10.12

Inserting another first-level heading

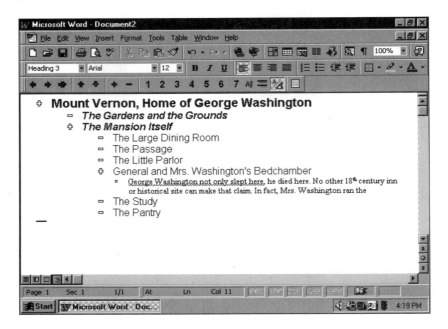

Changing Headings and Subheadings Together

If the heading you're changing contains subheads, those subheads do not necessarily change levels when you change the heading's level. For example, if you promote a second-level head to first-level, all of its third-level heads normally stay at the same level. Likewise, if you want to move heading text, its subordinate text does not automatically follow along. To move a heading with its subordinate text, you must first select the heading and its subordinate text. As you'll see next, that's easy.

Selecting Text in an Outline

If you are promoting, demoting, or moving one heading, it is not necessary to select the text first; you just need to make sure the insertion point is within the text. However, to change the level or position of more than one heading—or a heading and its subordinate text—you must first select the text.

To select all the headings and body text that are subordinate to a specific heading, just click on its plus sign. (Your mouse pointer changes to a four-headed outline pointer when you're in the right place.)

When you select multiple headings, you can promote or demote them all at once. If you realize that your document needs to cover a high-level topic before moving on to detail, you can subordinate all your existing headings with a single click on the right-arrow button. Your styles change automatically. If you've used Word's automatic heading numbering feature (covered later in this chapter) to number your headings, those will change automatically, too. If you've used Word's table of contents feature to compile a table of contents, that too can automatically be updated.

One powerful feature of Word outlines is that when you cut or paste multiple headings, you also move all the text subordinate to them, whether or not it is displayed in the outline. This makes incredibly quick work out of reorganizing a large document. This feature comes in even handier once you start using outlining techniques with Master Documents (Chapter 13), moving entire chapters, and managing entire book-length projects with aplomb.

NOTE. *When you promote or demote multiple headings, the body text underneath them remains body text. To turn body text into a heading, you must select it individually and then promote it. (You can select and promote multiple paragraphs of body text at once, as long as you haven't selected headings along with them.)*

Displaying All or Part of an Outline

Until now, you have been adding new headings and body text to an outline with the entire outline displayed. But one of the advantages of Outline view is that you can view your document at any level of detail you like.

Think of Word's outline display option as a microscope. You can use it to view only the most important topics in your document (first-level headings), or you can zoom out to view the entire document, looking at second-level, third-level, or additional headings. You also can zoom in on a specific part of a document, displaying it fully (including body text), while showing only top-level headings in the rest of the document.

To show only first-level headings, click the Show Heading 1 button or press Alt+! (see Figure 10.13). Notice the thick, gray underline beneath each heading in Figure 10.13. That tells you the headings contain body text or subheads that are not displayed. You are looking at the top-level view of this document. Even though the document could be dozens or hundreds of pages long, you can see the most important topics in the entire document at a glance. If you're working on a long document in Normal view, try occasionally switching to Outline view and displaying only high-level headings. This allows you to step back and place yourself in context. It's a great way of remembering the forest when you're surrounded by trees and underbrush.

NOTE. *You can always switch quickly back to displaying the full Outline view of all heads and text by clicking the Show All Headings button on the Outline view toolbar, or by pressing * on the numeric keypad.*

Figure 10.13

A sample document
with only first-level
headings displayed

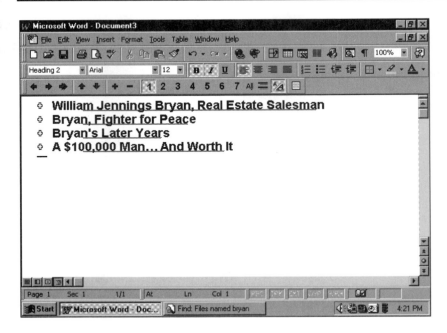

Expanding a Heading to Display All Its Contents

To see all the subheads and text underneath one main heading, select that heading and click the Expand button (or Alt+Plus). Your document should look something like Figure 10.14. If you have a great deal of body text in some sections of your document, there are times when you might want to see only the first line of each body text paragraph to remind you of its content. With all body text displayed, click on the Show First Line Only button, or press Alt+Shift+L. Word abbreviates each paragraph, as in Figure 10.15.

Hiding All Character Formatting

In some cases, you might be using Outline view primarily as a method of easily organizing styles for a document that will later have a table of contents added, or will become part of a larger master document. In this case, you don't care about seeing the varying Arial-based font formats Word uses by default to display headings. In fact, you might find them distracting. You can turn them off with the Show Formatting button in the Outline view toolbar, as shown in Figure 10.16.

The look of Word's default styles might not be what you want in the final printed document. For example, many publishers want to see all text, including

Figure 10.14

Zooming in on the
contents of one
main heading

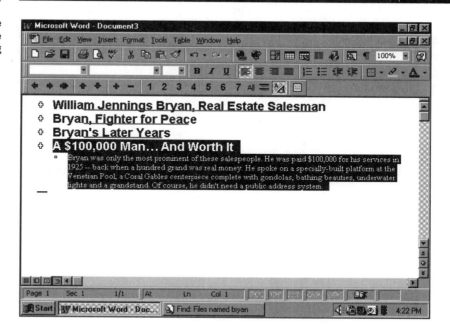

Figure 10.15

Displaying the first line of
each paragraph

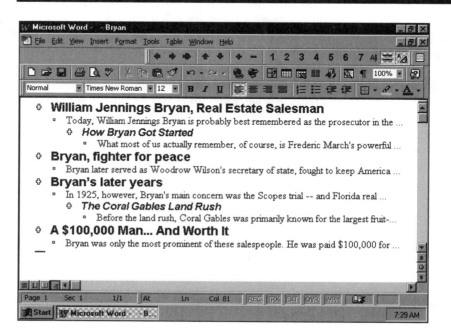

Figure 10.16

Turning character
formatting off in Outline
view: Word displays the
entire outline in the
default font for all
text formatting.

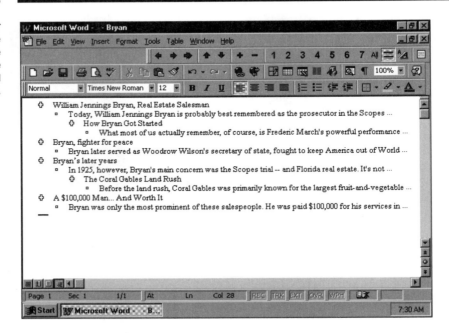

headings, submitted in a typewriter-style font such as Courier. Word's built-in heading styles, on the other hand, display text in a variety of sizes and formats, none of them basic Courier. While Word 97 now allows you to specify outline levels separately from heading styles, you may still find heading styles more convenient to work with. You can change the heading styles to look any way you wish—even change them so they create text that all looks alike. Then, you can keep using Word's outline tool to organize your document and its headings, but when you submit the document, your headings will look the way your editors want them to.

Outline View and Word Styles

So far you have been creating a new document in Outline view. But what if you already have a document? Good news! If your document is properly set up, your outline will already be there. One of the nice features of Word is that if you create your document using Word's built-in heading styles (heading 1 through heading 9), Word recognizes them when you switch to Outline view. This means you get all the easy document navigation and restructuring that Outline view provides—without having to consciously create an outline as you write.

Word lets you decide which approach to take—whether to use an outline to build a document, or build a document that includes an outline. In many ways, the end result is the same. But there are subtle differences. For example, if you create the document in Outline view, the correct styles are built into the document when you promote and demote headings. If you build your document in Normal view, you assign the heading, and Word displays the correct heading levels when you switch to Outline view.

■ Printing an Outline

When you print from Outline view, Word prints the outline as it appears on-screen, not the entire document. You can select exactly what part of the outline you want to print, then choose File, Print, and click on OK.

■ Adding Outline Numbering

If you've spent too many hours trying to insert the proper heading numbers in every heading in your document—and worrying about maintaining the right numbers as your document is edited—you'll love Word's Outline Numbering feature.

After you have promoted and demoted all the headings you want, and the document is organized the way you want, you can delegate the actual outline numbering to Word. With your document displayed in any view you prefer, choose Format, Bullets and Numbering, and click the Outline Numbered tab. The dialog box shown in Figure 10.17 appears. To quickly number your documents, all you need to do is select one of the seven commonly used options Word provides, and click OK. Word automatically numbers all your headings, and once they are numbered, Word automatically renumbers them as you edit and rearrange your document.

You may want more control over your outline numbering, however—and Word provides plenty of it, as you'll see in the following sections.

Creating Custom Heading Numbering

As you've already seen, the Outline Numbered tab of the Bullets and Numbering dialog box allows you to choose one of seven preset Outline Numbering formats, reflecting several of the most common document structures. For example, one format displays Section and Chapter names; another is structured like many typical contracts. If you prefer, however, you can adapt a format of your own. In the Outline Numbered tab, select the document structure that appears closest to what you'll need, and then choose Customize. The Customize Outline Numbered List dialog box appears, as shown in Figure 10.18. In the bottom right corner, Word previews any changes you propose in this dialog box.

Figure 10.17

The Outline Numbering tabbed dialog box is your gateway to near-total control over automatic heading numbering.

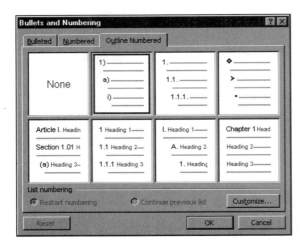

Figure 10.18

The Customize Outline Numbered List dialog box allows you to control the appearance, content, position, and relationships among nine different levels of headings.

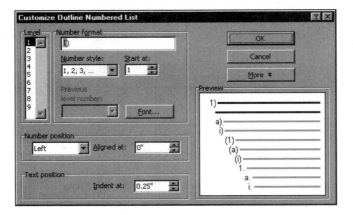

The Level box, in the upper left-hand corner of the dialog box, allows you to specify which level of heading you want to modify. The Number format box shows the current format that will be applied to your headings, based on the standard style you're intending to customize.

The gray text in the Number format box shows the style of numbering, for example: I, II, III; 1, 2, 3; or A, B, C. You can change this style in the Number Style box immediately below.

Any text or punctuation you want to place around the heading number can be added in the Number format box. For example, say you want your first-level headings to read Main Idea #1, Main Idea #2, and so on. Type

Main Idea # in the Number format box, just to the left of the grayed-out number. Or, if you want to surround your heading numbers with parentheses, just add parentheses before and after the grayed-out number in the Number format box.

You also can set a font for each level of heading in your outline. When you click <u>F</u>ont, the <u>F</u>ont dialog box opens, similar to the one used to apply font formatting elsewhere, with a couple of minor exceptions. For example, you can't apply font effects like superscript, shadows or embossing to your headings. You *can*, however, click the Animation tab and specify an animation like Las Vegas Lights and Shimmer—giving your headings that faux Java look which seems to be everywhere on the World Wide Web this season.

As briefly mentioned already, the Number style box lets you specify the numbering series Word uses to number your outline headings, including numbers, letters, roman numerals, bullets, ordinal numbering, and other choices, some new to Word 97. It also allows you to control what number, letter, or symbol to begin with. For example, if you're writing Chapters 18 through 20 of a book, you can specify that your first-level headings start with Chapter 18, not Chapter 1.

Outline heading numbering schemes accommodate all kinds of uses. A playwright could use "First, Second, Third" numbering, for example, to number the different acts and scenes.

NOTE. *If you want the same text to recur at every heading—with no numbers—just enter the text in Number format (in the Customize Outline Numbered List dialog box) and choose (none) in the <u>N</u>umber style list box.*

Formatting Other Heading Levels

When you format a heading level in the Customize Outline Numbered List dialog box other than Heading 1, an additional option becomes available: <u>P</u>revious level number. If you want previous heading letters or numbers to be part of your subhead numbering (for example, if you want a heading to read A1), choose the level here. If you want to specify more than one level of heading to be included in your number format, you can: Just position your insertion point where you want the heading to appear in the Number format box, and choose another heading from the Previous level number list box.

Here are some examples of headings with numbers (or letters) included from previous levels:

- I.A.1.

- 4.c.iii.

- First Act, Second Scene

Custom-Positioning Your Heading Numbers

The Customize Outline Numbered List dialog box also allows you to control where your outline numbers are positioned, and how much of an indent separates them from each heading's text. To do so, start by specifying in the Number position box where you want the outline number to appear relative to your margin. By default, Word assumes you'll want to left-align your outline numbers, but you can center or right-align them as well.

Also, you can specify different indents for the numbers associated with each level of heading by choosing values in the Aligned at box. For example, one of Word's most commonly used outline numbering styles indents the numbers associated with each heading level by an additional 0.25", giving the outlines an upside-down-staircase effect.

Once you've specified where your outline numbers will appear, you may want to change where the heading text appears next to them. You can specify this in the Customize Outline Numbered List dialog box as well, in the Text position box. Keep in mind that your heading text and your heading number can't overlap.

Advanced Outline Numbering Features

We've discussed the outline numbering features you're likely to use most often. There are a few additional features you may rarely need—but if you ever do need them, they're lifesavers. In the Customize Outline Numbered List dialog box, click More to display these features, as shown in Figure 10.19.

Figure 10.19

Clicking More displays advanced options for customizing your outline numbering.

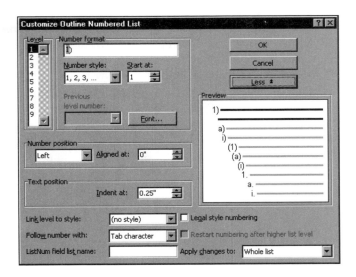

Creating Outline Numbers Without Using Heading Styles

Before Word 97, if you created your outline with styles other than Word's built-in heading styles, there was no way to build an outline based on them, short of replacing all your style names with ones that Word could recognize. While it still generally makes sense to use Word's built-in styles, Word 97 recognizes that there will be times you can't, or prefer not to. Perhaps you were given the document by someone else who didn't use Word styles, or you need to use Word's built-in heading styles for another purpose.

You can now link any style name present in your document, or any of Word's built-in 80+ styles, to any outline level—and then build your outline numbers with those styles.

To do so, first display the Customize Outline Numbered List dialog box, and click More. In the Level box, specify the level of heading you want to link a style with; then in the Link level to style box, select a style to link with the current outline number. You can repeat the process for up to nine heading levels, choosing a different style for each.

NOTE. *Once you've done this, you can use your styles in Outline view as if they were heading styles—promoting or demoting them at will. Let's say you link Outline Level 1 to a style called* **Extremely Important** *and Outline Level 2 to a style called* **Fairly Significant.** *Now, when you promote a heading styled* **Fairly Significant,** *it will be restyled* **Extremely Important.**

In this chapter, you've reviewed Word's extensive tools for outlining documents, and discovered how those tools can help you quickly organize—or reorganize a document. You've learned how outline levels and headings are the basis for many of Word's features—and you've learned how one of those features, automatic outline numbering, can dramatically reduce the amount of time you spend keeping track of headings, especially in large documents. You've also learned how to use headings to quickly navigate a document in a variety of ways, including Word's convenient new Document Map feature.

In the next chapter, you'll build on what you've learned here, seeing how Word can use your heading or outline numbers to build tables of contents automatically. And once you've learned how to build tables of contents, you'll find it easier to understand Word's powerful indexing features, which can automate the creation and maintenance of even the most complex document indexes.

- *Building a Table of Contents from Styles*
- *Updating a Table of Contents*
- *Using Table of Contents Entry Fields*
- *Tables of Figures and Captions*
- *Using Word's Caption Feature*
- *Citations and Tables of Authorities*
- *Understanding Indexes*

- *Marking All References to Specific Text*
- *Creating Helpful Index Entries*
- *Compiling an Index*
- *Taking Even More Control of Your Index*
- *Updating Indexes*
- *AutoMarking and Creating Concordance Indexes*

Tables of Contents and Indexes:
Let Word Do the Hard Work

THE CREATION OF TABLES OF CONTENTS AND INDEXES USED TO strike fear into the hearts of document preparers. Today, Word largely automates the process. In many cases, Word can do nearly the entire job without getting your hands dirty, and if you want to make your table of contents or index a real work of art, Word gives you the flexibility to do so.

When you need specialized tables to accompany your Table of Contents, Word offers specific Table of Figures and Table of Authorities features that work much like Table of Contents, but are customized to your specific needs. You can use Word's Caption feature to create captions that Word places automatically in its Table of Figures.

In this chapter, you'll learn how to build a table of contents from styles—either Word's built-in heading styles or any other style you've inserted in your document. You'll learn how to compile and format your table of contents, include chapter numbers in its listings, update your document as it changes, and include special entries that don't correspond to styles. You'll learn how to use tables of figures, tables of authorities, and Word's powerful caption feature.

Once you've learned how to create tables of contents, you'll use some of the same techniques to mark, compile, edit and format indexes. You'll learn how to create quick-and-dirty indexes in very little time; how to customize your index and its contents; and how to use Word's predefined index formats (or new ones you create). You'll learn how to index parts of a document—or create a concordance that indexes every single word in the document. You'll even learn how to let Word 97 mark your index entries for you.

■ Building a Table of Contents from Styles

Before you compile a table of contents, you have to create table of contents entries. This can be done in two ways:

- With styles
- With fields

Styles are much easier to use, and fortunately they'll handle most of your needs.

NOTE. *Once, the only way to create tables of contents was to manually insert Word field codes (as discussed in Chapter 21). Those days are long gone, but there are still a few tricks you can play using Word's TC and TOC field codes that aren't available through Word's hand-holding Table of Contents dialog box. For example, you can use them to create table lists other than tables of contents, figures, and authorities, or to build a table of contents that includes both styles and custom-marked table entry fields.*

By default, Word recognizes its first three built-in heading styles, Heading 1 through Heading 3, as likely table of contents entries. The style Heading 1 corresponds to a first-level head, Heading 2 to a second-level head, and so on.

You also can add other styles to your table of contents. Typically, these will be additional heading styles, such as Heading 4 through Heading 9, but you can include any style used in your document. If you want to use a Word style that doesn't exist yet, select and format some text with that style before compiling your table of contents.

NOTE. *If you use the Normal template, only Headings 1 through 3 may appear in the Style box on your formatting template, but all nine are available.*

Once you've assigned a style name to every heading you want to include in your table of contents, place your insertion point where you want the table of contents to appear. Then, select Inde**x** and Tables from the **I**nsert menu, and choose the Table of **C**ontents tab from the Index and Tables dialog box (see Figure 11.1).

Figure 11.1

The Table of Contents tabbed dialog box gives you nearly complete control over the format and contents of your table of contents.

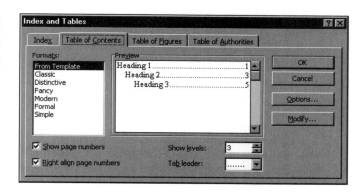

Basic Table of Contents Formatting

You now have some choices. First of all, you can choose from among six built-in table of contents Forma**t**s: Classic, Distinctive, Fancy, Modern, Formal, and Simple. Generic versions of these tables of contents appear in the Preview box when you select them. (By the way, *Distinctive* was called *Elegant* in Word 6, but it's the same style.)

Other Tables of Contents Options

By default, Word includes page numbers in its tables of contents. You can omit them by clearing the **S**how page numbers box. In each preformatted style (except Modern and Simple), page numbers are displayed flush-right. You can override the default by checking or clearing the **R**ight align page numbers box.

Also by default, Word shows three levels of headings. You can change this by selecting or typing a new number in the Show **l**evels box.

NOTE. *If you add more levels, Word assumes that you want to use additional heading styles, such as Heading 4 and Heading 5, as the source of these levels. If not, you'll need to tell Word where else to look, as described shortly.*

Except for Distinctive and Formal, Word does not automatically include a tab leader in its table of contents formats. You also can control this by choosing a leader from the Ta**b** leader box, which is available for all styles except Modern or Simple.

Customizing a Table's Style

Word provides a common procedure for customizing the appearance of tables of contents, figures, and authorities. Select the From Template option from the Forma**t**s box, and then choose **M**odify. (From Template was called Custom Style in Word 6 and Word 7, but it's the same feature.)

A Style dialog box opens (see Figure 11.2). You're presented with the built-in base styles that Word provides for the kind of table you modify. Each style is previewed in Paragraph preview and Character preview and described in exhaustive detail in the Description box. To change a style, select it from the **S**tyles box, and choose **M**odify. The Modify Style dialog box opens (see Figure 11.3). The Modify Style dialog box enables you to specify the style you want the new style to be **B**ased On (right now, the styles are based on the Normal style). Choose F**o**rmat, and you're presented with a list of all the editable elements of a Word style: Font, Paragraph, Tabs, Border, Language, Frame, and Numbering. In short, you can edit a style here much the same way you'd normally edit a style elsewhere in Word (as described in Chapter 7, "Styles and AutoFormatting").

After you finish, you can decide whether to add this style permanently to your template, which will make it available to other documents based on the same template. If so, check **A**dd to template. You can also tell Word whether to automatically redefine the style based on any manual formatting you add to it, by checking the A**u**tomatically update box.

Choosing Where Table of Contents Entries Come From

Now that your table of contents *looks* the way you want, you can decide where its entries will come from. Choose **O**ptions from the Table of **C**ontents tab from the Index and Tables dialog box. The Table of Contents Options dialog box appears (see Figure 11.4). Here, you choose the styles that Word looks for when it generates entries for your table of contents. You can choose any style in your document as a table of contents item. You also can rearrange your table of contents entries by typing new order numbers in the TOC **l**evel box for specific styles.

Figure 11.2

You can specify custom table of contents formats in the Style dialog box.

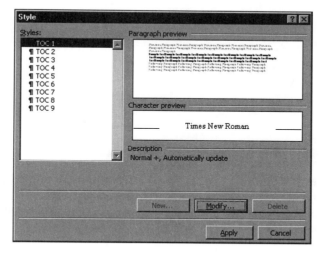

Figure 11.3

The Modify Style dialog box works the same way here as it does anywhere else: use these controls to specify the overall behavior of your style, and click Format to control individual formatting elements.

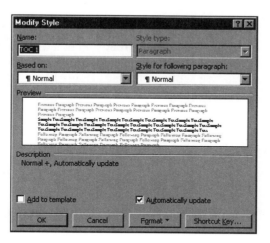

Most likely, you'll specify heading levels starting with 1, but you don't have to. If all your second-level heads were product names, for example, you could compile a list of the products covered in a document by choosing only heading level 2 and clearing the rest. If you also want to add fields to your table of contents, check the Table entry fields box.

To reset the Build table of contents from list to Word's default settings (Headings 1 through 3 only), select **R**eset.

Figure 11.4

The Table of Contents Options dialog box lets you specify which styles to compile in your table of contents, and whether to compile custom table entry fields.

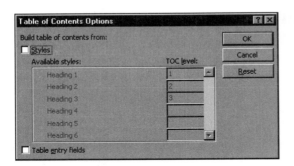

NOTE. *If, after compiling a table, you want to keep it permanently, select it and press Ctrl+Shift+F9 to unlink the fields underlying it. This turns the list into ordinary text. The next time you compile a table of contents, this list of headings won't be updated.*

Including Chapter Numbers in a Table of Contents

To include chapter numbers in a table of contents, first include them in your document's regular page numbering:

1. If your chapter names are already included in your document, format them with a style that will only be used for chapter names. Often, that will be Heading 1, but you can use any of Word's built-in heading styles.

2. Choose Page Numbers from the Insert menu.

3. Choose Format.

4. Check the Include chapter number box.

5. In the Chapter starts with style box, select the style that you've used for your chapter number.

6. In the Separator box, select a separator character; a hyphen is the default character.

7. Choose OK.

■ Updating a Table of Contents

Tables of contents are fields. You can update a table of contents the way you update any field: select it and press F9.

In previous versions of Word, you were permitted only one table of contents in a document. Now, if you already have one, and you attempt to create another one, Word will ask whether you wish to replace your existing table.

If you say no, Word will add a second table of contents adjacent to the first one. You might use this feature if you want to create a separate table of contents based on different heading levels, or a second table based strictly on table entry fields (discussed next).

■ Using Table of Contents Entry Fields

Most of the time you'll pick up your table of contents entries directly from styles, as we've discussed. However, there may be times when you want to compile a table of contents that includes—or is composed entirely of—listings that don't correspond to headings. For example, you might want to:

- Include a table of contents entry that doesn't correspond to specific text in the document, such as a paraphrase

- Include a table of contents entry without assigning it a style that Word will flag everywhere it appears

Suppress the page numbering for a specific table of contents entry. The table of contents entry field is named *TC*. Do not confuse this field with *TOC*, which compiles the table of contents. (TOC is discussed later.) To insert a TC field:

1. Select Fi**e**ld from the **I**nsert menu.

2. Select TC from the Field **N**ames box.

3. In the Field Codes box, type the text you want to appear in the table of contents entry. Place the text between quotation marks, as in this example:

```
TC "Why Projects Fail"
```

4. Specify the level of the entry. Choose **O**ptions, select **\l** from the Switches box, and choose Add to Field. Then add a number from 1 to 9 corresponding to the table of contents level you want Word to use when it compiles the table. For example:

```
TC "Why Projects Fail" \l 3
```

5. Choose OK to insert the entry, unless you need to add an option:

   - Option 1: If you don't want a page number to print with the entry, add the switch **\n**.

   - Option 2: If you want the entry to appear in another list, not the table of contents, choose **O**ptions and add the switch **\f**, along with a letter that corresponds to that list. Here is an example:

```
TC "Why Projects Fail" \f i
```

This example can be used to identify a table list for compilation in a table of illustrations. The letter "i" at the end of the field will be used in all other TC field codes flagging entries for the same table of contents.

NOTE. *You also can enter the field by pressing Ctrl+F9 and keying the field text between the { } brackets that appear. See Chapter 21 for more information on using field codes.*

Compiling a Table of Contents Using the TOC Field

The Table of Contents tab in the Index and Tables dialog box contains most of the gizmos you need for compiling a table of contents. But you might use the TOC field to compile an alternate table list, such as a table of illustrations, that isn't covered by Word's Table of Figures and Table of Authorities features—or to compile a table of contents for only part of a document, as is covered next.

Compiling Only Part of a Document

Suppose, for example, that you're working on a document, and someone asks you which points you plan to cover on a specific topic. To create a *partial* table of contents, follow these steps:

1. Select the text you want to cover.

2. Select **B**ookmark from the **E**dit menu, and type a one-word bookmark name. Click on OK.

3. Position the cursor where you want the table of contents to appear, and then create a TOC field with the \b switch and the bookmark name. The following is an example:

```
{TOC \b vietnam}
```

4. Update the field by pressing F9 to see the new table of contents.

You can add other switches to the TOC field, as described in Chapter 10. In the preceding example, you can use the \o switch if you want to print a table of contents for the Vietnam section, but only include heading levels 1 and 2:

```
{TOC \b vietnam \o 1-2}
```

Notice the double hyphens used to indicate a range of heading levels.

Several additional switches are available; use Insert Field to see all your options.

NOTE. *What if you want to compile the table of contents for an entire book, but each chapter has its own file? Build a* master document *that creates a table of contents based on all the separate files. Chapter 13 discusses master documents in detail.*

■ Tables of Figures and Captions

As with tables of contents, Word's Table of Figures feature also builds lists based on a style you assign to all your figures. You can decide in advance that all your figures will use a style called Figure. You then format the style and compile it much as you would a table of contents.

However, there is a very pleasing alternative: Word can automatically create your figures and figure numbering for you, using its Caption feature.

■ Using Word's Caption Feature

To insert a caption anywhere in a document, select Caption from the **I**nsert menu. The Caption dialog box opens, as shown in Figure 11.5. By default, Word assumes your captions will be associated with figures. The words **Figure 1** appear in the Caption box. You can add any text you like, but you can't edit the text Word has already displayed—you have to change that elsewhere.

Figure 11.5

From Word's Caption dialog box, you can control virtually all elements of captioning.

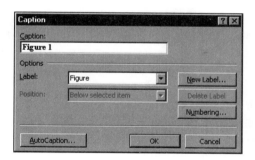

If you want a numbered equation or a table, choose these alternatives from the **L**abel list box. If you want to use another label, create it by pressing the **N**ew Label button. The New Label dialog box appears (see Figure 11.6). Key the label in the **L**abel box; then click on OK.

Figure 11.6

If you want your captions to be named something other than figure, equation or table, enter a new caption name here.

By default, Word uses the numbering scheme 1, 2, 3... for captioning. You can choose another numbering scheme by choosing N**u**mbering. The Caption Numbering dialog box opens (see Figure 11.7). This closely resembles the Page Number Format dialog box you've seen in Chapter 2 and elsewhere. Choose a numbering scheme from the **F**ormat list box. If you want to include a chapter number, first place the chapter number in your document and assign it a unique style that doesn't appear elsewhere in the document.

Figure 11.7

The Caption Numbering dialog box. If you choose to include chapter numbers, Word will ask you to specify which style your chapter numbers are formatted with.

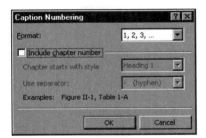

Then return to the Caption Numbering dialog box, and check Include **c**hapter number. In Cha**p**ter starts with style, choose the style name. In Use S**e**parator, choose the character you want to appear between the chapter number and the figure number. Finally, click on OK.

Telling Word to Caption Automatically

If you regularly caption imported objects such as Excel graphs, CorelDRAW! illustrations, or Equation Editor equations, Word can insert your captions for you whenever you add the object to your document. Set up AutoCaptioning when you create a new document. Word can't go back and AutoCaption objects you've already imported.

To set up AutoCaptioning, follow these steps:

1. Select Capt**i**on from the **I**nsert menu.

2. Choose **A**utoCaption. The AutoCaption dialog box appears (see Figure 11.8).

3. In the **A**dd caption when inserting box, choose an object type from the list of objects available on your computer.

Figure 11.8

The AutoCaption dialog box allows you to tell Word to automatically create a caption every time you import any object registered with Windows 95.

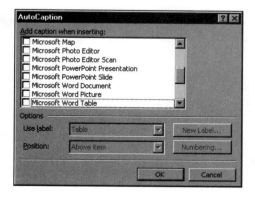

NOTE. *This list includes object types that appear in your OLE registration database; in other words, programs that registered their OLE support with Windows when you installed them, or had their OLE information migrated to Windows 95 when you installed Windows 95 over an older Windows 3.1 installation.*

4. In the **P**osition box, specify whether you want the caption to appear above or below the object you will be inserting.

5. In the Use **L**abel box, specify the label you want to appear when you insert one of these objects. Choose **N**ew Label if you need to create another label.

6. Click on the N**u**mbering button to set a numbering scheme, unless you're happy with 1, 2, 3....

7. After you've finished with any **N**ew Label-making or N**u**mbering changes, click on OK to activate AutoCaptioning.

Creating a Table of Figures

You can create as many tables of figures as you want in the same document. You can have one table for figures, another for illustrations, and another for tables—you name it!

To create a table of figures, choose Index and Tables from the Insert menu, and select the Table of Figures tab from the Index and Tables dialog box (see Figure 11.9). Much of this will look similar to tables of contents. You can choose to show page numbers, right align page numbers, and include a tab leader. As with tables of contents, Word provides several standard table of figures formats: Classic, Distinctive, Centered, Formal, and Simple. Each style and any change you make to the style is previewed in the Pre**v**iew box.

Figure 11.9

The Table of Figures dialog box allows you to control all aspects of formatting and content for a table of figures, including whether figure labels and numbers should be included.

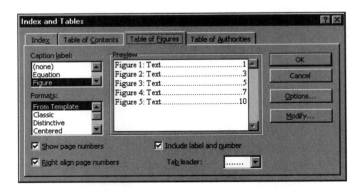

One important addition to the Table of Figures dialog box is Include label and **n**umber. In this box, you choose whether to use a caption you've created using Word's Caption feature.

If your captions weren't created using Word's caption feature, clear the Include label and **n**umber check box, and then choose **O**ptions. The Table of Figures Options dialog box appears (see Figure 11.10). If all your figures have been assigned a specific style, check **S**tyle and choose the style from the accompanying list box. If you include the list figures you created as TC entry fields, check Table **e**ntry fields. In Table **i**dentifier, specify the initial you've used for compiling this list. Click on OK to return to the Table of Figures dialog box. Click on OK again to compile your list.

Figure 11.10

The Table of Figures Options dialog box allows you to specify where Word will look for figures, either based on specific styles or on table entry fields.

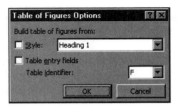

Adding a TC Entry Field to Your Table of Figures

You rarely need to enter field codes directly to create table of figures entries, or to compile a table of figures.

Occasionally, you might want to include a table entry field in your table of contents. For example, if you want to suppress page numbering for one or only a few items in a table of figures, you'll need to use a field.

In those cases, how do you make sure that the TC entry field appears in the correct table of figures? Add the \f switch. Before you add the switch, the basic TC entry field looks like this:

```
{TC "Text you want to appear in your table"}
```

To this, add the \f switch, followed by an initial representing the table in which you want the text to be included. Word's default is F, for figure. In that case, your table entry field might read:

```
{TC "Text you want to appear in your table" \f f}
```

If you don't include an **\f** switch, the TC entry field appears in your table of contents, not in a table of figures.

■ Citations and Tables of Authorities

Word also provides a Table of Authorities feature specifically designed to streamline the preparation of legal briefs and other documents that must refer to statutes, rules, and judicial decisions.

Tables of authorities are designed to list all citations made in a document, in alphabetical order within category. Before you can compile your citations, however, you have to mark them.

Marking Citations

To build a table of authorities, first edit your document as you normally would, including citations wherever appropriate. Then scroll through the document, looking for citations.

NOTE. *If all your citations follow a specific format, such as Jones v. Smith, you can search for v. to find the citations.*

Whenever you find a citation, select it and press Alt+Shift+I. This opens the Mark Citation dialog box (see Figure 11.11) with the citation already appearing in it. Edit the Selected **t**ext box so that it includes all the detailed information that should appear in a first reference. Your edits don't appear in the document itself, but they do appear in the table of authorities.

In the **S**hort citation box, edit that text; the edited version appears as a follow-up reference in your table of authorities. Also assign the reference to a **C**ategory. Word provides the following seven built-in categories:

- Cases

- Statutes

- Other Authorities

Figure 11.11

Mark Citation allows
you not only to mark
citations, but to
categorize them and
create abbreviated
versions for convenient
reference in a Table of
Authorities.

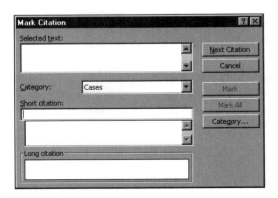

- Rules

- Treatises

- Regulations

- Constitutional Provisions

Word also provides nine other categories, numbered 8 through 16, which you can replace with real category names. To create a new category name, choose Category. The Edit Category dialog box opens (see Figure 11.12).

Figure 11.12

Use the Edit Category
dialog box to manage the
categories assigned to
your citations.

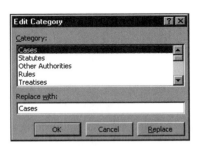

NOTE. *Choose a category that you want to replace, and type a new name in the Replace with box. Choose Replace, and click on OK.*

Now you have a choice. You can mark this citation by choosing **M**ark, or you can mark all identical citations throughout the document by choosing Mark **A**ll. Mark **A**ll marks the first reference with the full citation you created in Selected text; any following references to the same case use the **S**hort citation.

Pardon the pun: legal citations are *case*-sensitive. The capitalization and text have to be identical for the Mark A̲ll option to flag it.

After you have created your citations, you can move from one to the next by opening Mark Citation and choosing N̲ext Citation.

Compiling a Table of Authorities

When you finish creating your citations, you can compile them into a table of authorities by using the following steps:

1. Place your insertion point where you want the table to go.

2. Select Index and Tables from the Insert menu.

3. Choose the Table of Authorities tab from the Index and Tables dialog box (see Figure 11.13).

Figure 11.13

The Table of Authorities dialog box allows you to generate a custom Table of Authorities. Note that you can control whether Word will use the *passim* abbreviation in place of references that appear repeatedly in the document.

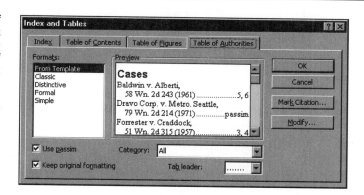

As with tables of contents and figures, Word provides several formats to choose from. There's also a custom style you can adapt by selecting this option and then choosing Modify.

4. In Category, you can choose the types of citations you want to compile; the default is All. In Ta̲b leader, you can specify whether you want a tab leader; different Forma̲ts have different default tab leader settings.

5. You can also control two other options that are specific to tables of authorities:

   • *Use p̲assim*—If Word finds references to the same authority on five or more pages, it can substitute the word *passim*, rather than list the pages. This option is on by default.

- *Keep original formatting*—Word retains any formatting applied to the citation in the document itself. This option is also on by default.

6. After you set the table of authorities the way you want, click on OK to compile it.

■ Understanding Indexes

The best indexes are works of art that have been created by people with a wonderful sensitivity to nuance and a finely honed judgment about what's important.

Word 97 doesn't change that. How good an index will be is still up to the indexer. (This chapter gives you a few clues, though.) For many documents, a down-and-dirty index is all that's needed. Either way, Word does a masterful job of taking care of the basics: the actual compilation of an index.

As with tables of contents, the idea is simple: you mark index entries, and when the document is finished, you tell Word how you want the index to look. Then you compile the index.

Creating Index Entries

To mark an index entry:

1. Position your insertion point where you want the index entry. If you want to copy words from the document into the index entry, select the text.

2. Press Alt+Shift+X. The Mark Index Entry dialog box opens, as shown in Figure 11.14.

Figure 11.14

The Mark Index Entry dialog box is accessible via the keyboard shortcut Alt+Shift+X or via the Index tab available through Insert, Index and Tables.

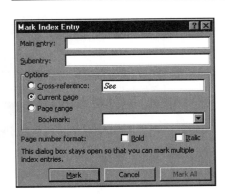

3. If you've chosen text, that text appears in the Main entry box. If not, type in your index entry, or revise what's already there.

4. If the text that you selected contains a colon, Word adds a backslash in the index entry. That's because, as you'll see, Word reserves colons as its way of flagging subentries. (If you *want* a subentry there, delete the backslash, and Word treats the words that follow the colon as a subentry to the words that precede it.)

5. Choose **M**ark.

Word places a hidden {xe} field in your document, with the index entry text in quotes:

```
{xe "Complementarity"}
```

That's as basic as it gets. You'll wind up with an index such as the following:

```
Classical physics, 36
Complementarity, 253
Confucius, 117
Consciousness, 406, 432, 477
Copenhagen Interpretation, 43, 45, 51
Copernicus, 227
Decay, 46
Doppler effect, 352
```

As you can see in the preceding example, all index entries carry equal weight. No subentries are included; no page numbers are boldfaced or italicized; and all references are to single pages.

The Mark Index Entry dialog box lets you change these elements. When you specify an entry, Word inserts a hidden {xe} field in your document. Later, you'll learn how to control other elements of your index entries by directly editing these {xe} fields, and the {index} fields Word uses to compile its indexes.

Boldfacing or Italicizing Page Numbers

Later, when you compile the index, you might want to call attention to a specific entry's page number by using italics or boldface. Select the entry, open the Mark Index Entry dialog box, and click on **B**old or **I**talic in Page number format. Note that clicking on **B**old or **I**talic doesn't boldface or italicize the text itself—only the page number.

Inserting Page Ranges in Index Entries

Often, you may want to create a page range for an index entry, as in the following example:

```
Double-slit experiment, 52–55
```

Before creating the field entry, select all the text you want to include in the entry and create a bookmark. Then open the Mark Index Entry dialog box. Check the Page range button and choose your bookmark name from the list box beneath Page range. You also can type the bookmark name there yourself, as long as you also click on the Page range button.

Creating Multilevel Indexes

After you catch on to indexing, you'll see that some topics fit naturally as subentries beneath other topics. The process of building an index is similar to building an outline: not everything is a main topic.

Take, for example, the following multilevel index. In that example, "Detergents" is a second-level subentry, and "Dishwashing detergent" is a third-level subentry:

```
Amway Corporation

    Detergents, 52–54

            Dishwashing detergent, 52

            Laundry detergent, 53

            Soap, 57

Shaklee Corporation

    Cereal, 112

    Vitamins, 39
```

To create a subentry, first type the main entry that you want the subentry to appear beneath. Then type the subentry itself. If you would like multiple levels of subentry, place them all in the **S**ubentry box, separated by colons:

```
Detergents:Dishwashing detergent
```

NOTE. *Because the Mark Index Entry dialog box stays open as you move around the document, you can move to the document, select text that you want to be included in an index entry, and copy that text into the Subentry box.*

You can specify up to seven levels of index entry this way. (That's an awfully cumbersome index, however. You should rarely have to use even four levels.)

If you don't create any entries specifically for the main index entry, the main index entry appears in your index without a page number, as in the example index shown earlier.

Using Text instead of a Page Number

Until now, all the index entries have referred the reader to a page number or a range of pages. But sometimes you come across an index entry such as the following:

```
Alice, see Looking Glass
```

Word refers to this as a *cross-reference*. You can add a cross-reference by opening the Mark Index Entry dialog box, and then clicking on the **C**ross-reference button. The word "See" is already there; type the entry you want to cross-reference. (If you want to use a different word, delete "See" and type the word that you prefer.)

NOTE. *These cross-references are not the same ones you get by choosing Insert, Cross-reference.*

■ Marking All References to Specific Text

Word's Mark Index Entry dialog box contains a shortcut for marking all references to specific text:

1. Select the text that you want to index.

2. Press Alt+Ctrl+X to open the Mark Index Entry dialog box.

3. If necessary, edit the Index Main Entry and Subentry to read the way you want them to appear in the finished index.

4. If necessary, select a **C**ross-reference or a Page **r**ange Bookmark.

5. Choose Mark **A**ll.

Word searches the document, looking for references to the precise text you've marked, and then flags each of the references with an index entry.

NOTE. *If you want to mark all references to several text items at once, use Word's AutoMark feature, described later in this chapter.*

NOTE. *When Mark A̲ll begins running, it immediately displays all nonprinting and hidden characters. If you want to hide them again, you'll have to do that manually after you finish using it.*

■ Creating Helpful Index Entries

In many cases, your index items might be identical to the text you've selected. But you might want to make your index more interpretive. Think about your reader. How would he or she search for information? Consider the ways a reader might think about the following paragraph:

Miserable in a loveless marriage, Marie Antoinette threw herself into a life of pleasure and careless extravagance. The old story—that upon hearing about peasants without bread, she said, "Let them eat cake"—is most likely false. But scandals such as the Affair of the Diamond Necklace were all too real.

Of course, the preceding paragraph should be indexed under *Marie Antoinette*. But you also might want to flag the quote *Let them eat cake*, perhaps as a subentry under Marie Antoinette. You also can mark the paragraph as an entry in *French Revolution, causes,* or under *ancien regime.* Those three subjects might not explicitly appear in the text, but they might be what your reader is looking for. Similarly, think of synonyms for the index entries you're presenting. (Word enables you to create as many index entries for a passage of text as you like, of course.)

Be sensitive to the relative importance of entries, and use Word's subentry feature wherever appropriate. Even if you create many specific entries, you will help the reader if you also add a broad, conceptual entry that includes them as subentries.

In indexing names, remember that last names should appear first. Word does not invert them automatically. (*Marie Antoinette* is an exception.) Think about phrases that should also appear in inverted form, including the following:

```
burial masks

masks, burial
```

Finally, when you create index entries that refer to items that can be abbreviated, spell out the entire name. Then include a separate entry, using the acronym or abbreviation, pointing to the main entry:

```
Confederate States of America, 37, 52, 69, 84

CSA, see Confederate States of America
```

■ Compiling an Index

Remember, your index will be created using Word's current pagination. Before you compile your index, make sure that you do the following:

- Complete every aspect of your document. That includes last-minute items such as the table of contents and Figure lists.

- Hide all hidden text. (Select **T**ools, **O**ptions, **V**iew; clear the **H**idden Text box in Nonprinting Characters.)

- Hide all field codes. (Make sure that there's no check mark next to **F**ield Codes in **T**ools, **O**ptions, **V**iew.)

When you're ready, place your insertion point where you want the index. Most likely, that's the end of the document. Then select Inde**x** and Tables from the **I**nsert menu, and choose the Inde**x** tab (see Figure 11.15).

Figure 11.15

You can control how your index will compile through the Index tab of the Index and Tables dialog box.

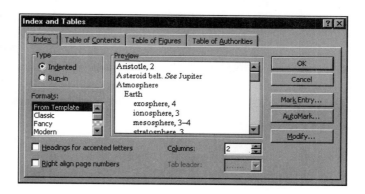

If all you want is a standard index using Word's default settings, click OK now. However, from this dialog box, Word offers almost total control over the formatting of your index.

Word offers two main **T**ypes of indexes. By default, Word creates an In**d**ented Index: each new entry appears on its own line. You can, however, choose a Ru**n**-in Index to save space. The following is an example of what that will look like:

```
Amway Corporation: Detergents, 52-54; Dishwashing
detergent, 52; Laundry detergent, 53; Soap, 57

Shaklee Corporation: Cereal, 112; Vitamins, 39
```

Notice that main entries are separated from subentries with a colon; subentries are separated from each other with a semicolon; the next main entry still appears on a line of its own. In addition, whenever you create an index, Word inserts an index field in your document; if you create a run-in index, Word adds the \r switch. You also can tell Word to place all page numbers flush right by clicking on **R**ight align page numbers.

You can divide your index page into multiple columns by selecting a number from 1 to 4 in the C**o**lumns box; the default is two columns.

Now that you've made a few basic formatting decisions, Word enables you to choose from six basic index styles: Classic, Fancy, Modern, Bulleted, Formal, and Simple. (These are consistent with the table of contents formats you saw in Chapter 13, "Tables of Contents," except that Bulleted replaces Distinctive.)

As with the table of contents, you can create your own style by selecting Custom Style from the Forma**t**s box in the Index and Tables dialog box. Then choose **M**odify. The Style dialog box opens. Select an index style that you want to modify, and choose **M**odify again. Both the Style and Modify Style dialog boxes work as discussed in Customizing a Table's Style, earlier in this chapter (and in Chapter 7's coverage of styles). You can use Modify Styles to change any aspect of the style you've chosen, and to preview the changes before they take effect. Click on OK when you're finished.

Including Chapter Numbering in an Index

Suppose that you have a document containing multiple chapters, and you want to include the chapter numbers in your index entries, as in the following example:

```
Elks, 2-9

Kiwanis Club, 4-8

Lions Club, 3-12

Rotary Club, Chapter 6-3; 6-8
```

Word automatically includes those page numbers in your index, if you use **I**nsert, Page N**u**mbers to add them to your document's numbering.

Indexing Part of a Document

Word's Index and Tables dialog box still doesn't provide a way to index only part of a document. But fields provide three ways to do it. Whenever you insert an index into a document, Word inserts an {index} field. You can modify one that Word inserts, or insert one of your own.

To index only part of a document, do the following:

1. Select that portion of the document.

2. Create a bookmark for that text:

   a. Choose Book**m**ark from the **E**dit menu.

   b. Type a one-word bookmark name.

   c. Click on OK.

3. Next, after deselecting text, insert the **{ INDEX }** field:

   a. Choose Fiel**d** from the **I**nsert menu.

   b. Choose Index from Field **N**ames.

   c. In the Field Codes box, after INDEX, type **\b** followed by the name of the bookmark.

   d. Click on OK.

4. Press F9 to update the field.

Creating Indexes that Contain Specific Entries

By default, Word indexes contain all the items in the pages being indexed. You can, however, create an index that only contains items that you specify. For example, perhaps you're sending a large document to a reviewer who is an expert on a specific topic; you might use this capability to call attention to only the pages that contain information related to his or her field of expertise.

After you insert the index entry {xe} fields, display them and add the \f switch to them, followed by an initial. Your field could look like the following:

```
{XE "Bryan, William Jennings" \f x}
```

Add the same switch and initial to every {xe} field that you want to compile. Then, when you want to compile these special index entries into an index, insert an INDEX field with the same \f x switch:

```
{INDEX \f x}
```

Keep in mind a few important points about working with these special index entries:

- Don't use the initial *I*. That's Word's default setting; it'll simply include all the index entries in your index.

- Index entries using \f identifiers other than *I* won't appear in your overall index—only in an index created with {index \f}.

Compiling Only Some Letters of an Index

You can use the \p (partial) switch to tell Word to compile an index containing only certain letters. (Perhaps your index will be split between two reviewers, each taking half the alphabet.) The following example shows an INDEX command specifying that only letters N through Z be printed. Note the *double* hyphen between N and Z:

```
{index \p n--z}
```

■ Taking Even More Control of Your Index

If you're willing to edit the {index} field that Word enters when you use the Index and Tables dialog box, you can control the following conditions:

- How (and whether) all the index entries under one letter of the alphabet are separated from the entries for the next letter

- Which character is used in page ranges (normally, it's a hyphen, as in: 36-42)

- How an index item is separated from its page number

- Whether sequential references such as figure or table numbers are included in the document

For more information about these options, open Insert Field, select Index, and choose Options.

Customizing the Way Word Separates Each Letter's Entries

You've already seen that the Index and Tables dialog box enables you to choose a blank line or a letter to separate your A entries from your B entries (and C, D, and so on). You can specify more detailed formatting by using the \h switch.

Place what you want to include between quotation marks. For example, if you want to place dots between each letter, type the following:

```
{index \h "........"}
```

To place a letter at the beginning of those dots, type:

```
{index \h "A........"}
```

When you type **{index \h "A........"}**, the resulting index displays separators such as the following:

```
A.........
Alphabet, 28
Animals, 36
```

```
B.........
Barracuda, 52
Bell, 46
C.........
Chimpanzee, 73
```

NOTE. *Any A-to-Z letter you use after an \h switch is interpreted as an instruction to insert alphabetical letters at every separation. So if you specified something such as the following:*

```
{index \h "A entries"}
```

you'd be rudely surprised by:

```
A AAAAAAA
Alphabet, 28
Animals, 36
B BBBBBBB
Barracuda, 52
Bell, 46
C CCCCCCC
Chimpanzee, 73
```

All alphabetical characters are capitalized by default. However, you can use the switch * lower to specify lowercase:

```
{index \h "AAA" \*lower}
```

You can also tell Word to insert one *blank* line between letters with the following field:

```
{index \h " "}
```

Changing Page Range Separators

Page ranges usually appear in indexes, as shown in the following example:

```
Home on the Range, 37-39
```

On occasion, you might want to change the separator, which is controlled by the \g switch. To display a colon instead of a hyphen, type the following:

```
{index \g :}
```

Changing Page Number Separators

Normally, a list of page numbers is separated by a comma:

```
Elective surgery, 346, 362, 377, 403
```

You can change this separator with the \l switch. To specify a semicolon, type the following:

```
{index \l ";"}
```

To add a space after the semicolon, type the following:

```
{index \l "; "}
```

This field command *does* require quotation marks.

Changing the Way Index Entries Are Separated from Page Numbers

Normally, an index entry is separated from its page number by a comma:

```
British Telecom, 36
```

You can change this by using the \e switch, and up to three characters of your choice, including tabs. Type the following to add three dots:

```
{index \e "..."}
```

You end up with the following:

```
British Telecom... 36
```

■ Updating Indexes

Even though Word automates the compilation of an index, that doesn't mean that the index it creates will be perfect. You may find when you read your index that certain entries aren't quite right.

Perhaps you indexed MacArthur in one place and McArthur in another. You now realize they should all be MacArthur. Or, more likely, you created a main index entry that, upon reflection, really should be a subentry in another index listing.

In any case, you'll most likely want to proceed systematically through your index, to clean up errors like these. You can do this by setting up two windows on your document: one to view the index and one to scroll through the document (see Figure 11.16). Choose Window, New Window to open the second window.

NOTE. *Word's Wrap to Window feature is invaluable for this kind of work. Select it from the View tab in the Tools, Options dialog box.*

First, display hidden text, so your index entries will be visible. Then, begin moving through the index. Whenever you see an entry that needs

Figure 11.16

Revising an index by
displaying both the index
and the document in
separate windows

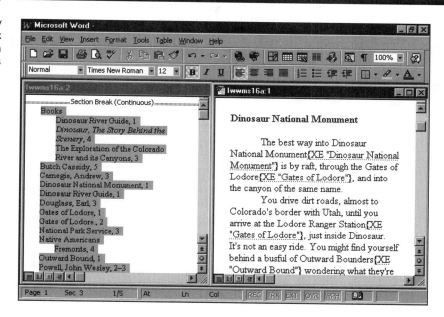

editing, switch windows. In the document window, search for the text of the
index entry (or Go To the entry's page). Edit the {xe} field. Switch windows
and continue to move through the index.

When you've made all the changes you want, you can update the entire
index to reflect them. Select Inde**x** and Tables from the **I**nsert menu. Select
the Inde**x** tab. Click on OK. You'll be asked if you want to replace the current index (see Figure 11.17). Choose OK.

Figure 11.17

Confirming an
index update

■ AutoMarking and Creating Concordance Indexes

A concordance index (sometimes simply called a concordance) is an alphabetical index of all the words in a text, and it shows every occurrence of each word.

Concordance indexes are most well-known in Bible studies, where—for example—if you're feeling especially put upon, such an index could point you to every reference to Job. Concordance indexes also often are used by academic specialists to study literature, ancient and otherwise.

Word for Windows contains a feature that's capable of creating something very much like a concordance index: AutoMark. To use AutoMark, you open a new file (which Word calls your AutoMark file). Create a two-column table in that file. In the first vertical column, list all the words that you want to index all references to. (Note that unlike a true concordance, this list probably won't contain every single word in your document.)

In the second column, key the index entry the way that you want it to appear. If you want it to appear as a subentry, key the entire entry—including the main entry—separating each part with a colon. Here's an excerpt from an AutoMark file for indexing Bruce Springsteen lyrics:

Entry	Subentry
Cadillac	Car:Cadillac
fever	Fever
highway	Street:Highway
night	Night
river	River
road	Street:Road
street	Street

Save and close the file. Then, in the file that you want to index, select Index and Tables from the Insert menu. Select the Index tab and choose AutoMark. The Open Index AutoMark File dialog box opens (see Figure 11.18). In File name, find the AutoMark file that you just created. (Change folders or drives if necessary.) Then click on OK. Word generates an index of all references to each word in your AutoMark file.

A few notes about AutoMarking: First, if Word finds more than one reference to your specified text in a paragraph, it will only create an index entry for the first reference. Also, AutoMarking is case-sensitive; both lowercase and uppercase must match to be indexed. If you want to AutoMark river and River, you need to include them both in your AutoMark file.

Figure 11.18

The AutoMark File dialog box allows you to choose a specific file that Word can use as its guide in automatically marking index entries throughout your document.

Creating True Concordance Indexes

If you did want to create a *true* concordance index of *every* word in your document, Word can do it. Here's how: First use search and replace to change every space to a paragraph mark (^p); then use Word's Table, Sort Text feature to alphabetize all the words. Next, write a macro that finds and eliminates duplicate words. You now have a document listing every word in your document.

Use Word's Table, Convert Text to Table feature to convert it to a one-column table; copy the entire table to a new second column. You now have a document that can be used as an AutoMark file which will create a true concordance.

- *Understanding Footnotes*

- *Viewing Footnotes*

- *Finding Footnotes*

- *Moving, Copying, and Deleting Footnotes*

- *Changing Footnote Formatting*

- *Introducing Bookmarks*

- *Introducing References and Cross-References*

- *Introducing Hyperlinks*

Footnotes, Bookmarks, Cross-References, and Hyperlinks

WITH WORD 97, IT'S EASIER THAN EVER TO HELP YOU AND YOUR readers find the right information in your printed—or electronic—documents. In addition to the supercharged document navigation tools covered in Chapters 1 and 2, Word offers a wide range of features that help you call attention to specific information in both printed and electronic environments.

Footnotes and endnotes help readers locate and evaluate information that supports the points you're making in your document.

Bookmarks allow you to mark specific blocks of text and then locate them virtually instantly, by picking them from a list. Used with field codes and macros, they offer an exceptionally powerful way to automate and manage changes to your document.

Cross-references allow you to tell readers where else in your document they will find information of importance to them—and put Word in charge of keeping your cross-references straight, no matter how your document changes.

Finally, and perhaps most exciting, Word 97 introduces *hyperlinks*, which allow readers of your electronic documents to click and be connected to other related information, even if that information is stored on the Internet.

■ Understanding Footnotes

If you've ever tried to leave the correct number of lines at the bottom of a typewritten page for footnotes, you know it's not easy. And, if you even remember trying, you're beginning to show your age. In any case, it's now time you delegated tasks like that to Word.

Word will put your footnotes in the right places, and will keep them numbered and arranged properly, no matter how many editing changes you make. Just tell Word how you want them numbered, and where you want them to go, and then you can pretty much forget about the process.

If you're willing to do a little footwork, you can even refer to a footnote in text, and have Word update your reference for you if the footnote's number changes. And Word lets you insert both footnotes and endnotes.

Inserting Footnotes and Endnotes

If all you want is a straightforward numbered footnote or endnote, place your insertion point where you want it, and press Alt+Ctrl+F for a footnote or Alt+Ctrl+E for an endnote.

Word inserts a numbered footnote reference mark in your text and opens a footnote or endnote pane, where you can edit your footnote, as shown in Figure 12.1.

If you've chosen a footnote, your footnotes will be numbered 1, 2, 3, and so on. If you've chosen an endnote, the note will be numbered i, ii, iii, and so on.

NOTE. *If you're in Page Layout view, the footnotes pane doesn't appear. Instead, a footnote editing area appears on the bottom of the page (unless you've already moved your footnotes elsewhere). Depending on your cursor's position on the page, you might need to scroll down the document to see this area. You can see this in Figure 12.2.*

Figure 12.1

The Footnote Pane appears at the bottom of your screen.

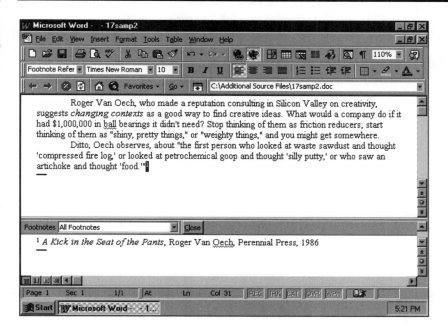

Figure 12.2

The default footnote editing area in Page Layout view

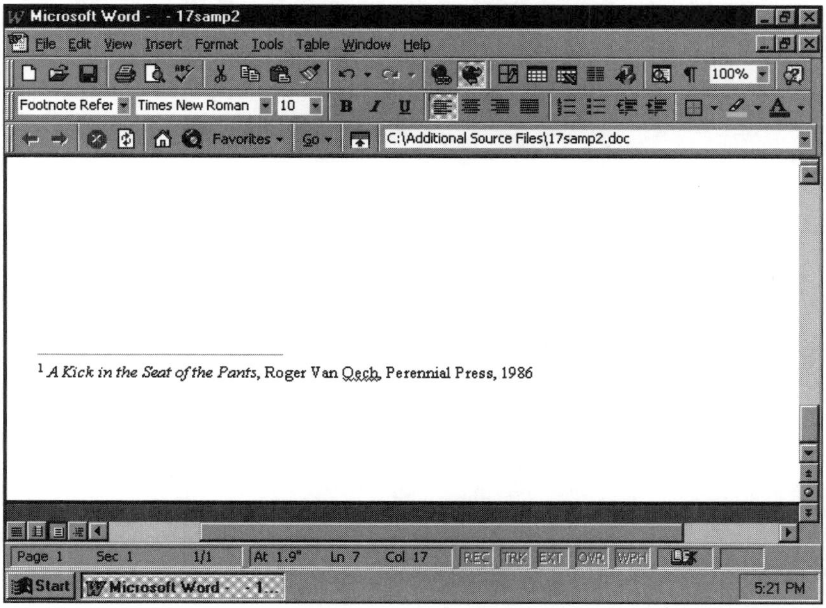

Editing Footnotes

Assuming you are in normal view, you can type your footnote text into the footnote pane, or copy it from another document. You can use REF fields to bring in footnote information from elsewhere in the document, and you can link or embed information from other documents—even across a network. A footnote can include almost anything your document can, including images, sound, and video. When you're done with the footnote text, you can close the footnote pane by choosing Close or pressing Alt+Shift+C.

NOTE. *A few fields can't be placed in a footnote pane. These include table of contents entries (TC), index entries (XE), and some mail merge fields (such as NEXT and NEXTIF).*

Getting More Control over Your Footnotes

If you want something other than a simple numbered footnote or endnote—say you want a custom mark, such as §—choose Foot**n**ote from the **I**nsert menu. The dialog box shown in Figure 12.3 opens. In the Insert box, choose either a **F**ootnote or an **E**ndnote. Then, in numbering, choose either:

- *AutoNumber*—This inserts a numbered footnote that Word keeps track of as you edit the document.

- *Custom mark*—Word inserts any symbol you want.

Figure 12.3

The Footnote and
Endnote dialog box

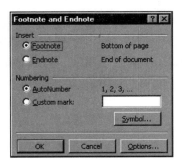

If you select a custom mark, choose **S**ymbol, and Word displays the standard Symbol dialog box, where you can pick any symbol available in any of your currently available fonts, including great sources of symbols such as Wingdings and Zapf Dingbats. Word places the symbol you choose in the **C**ustom mark box. If you use numbered footnotes and custom reference marks in the same document, the numbered footnotes will number consecutively, ignoring any custom marks.

Controlling How and Where Footnotes Appear

By default, Word footnotes appear on the bottom of the page, and Word endnotes appear at the end of the document. You can change this if you need to. Choose **I**nsert, Foot**n**ote and then select **O**ptions. The Note Options dialog box opens (see Figure 12.4).

Figure 12.4

The Note Options dialog box allows you to control the location, format, and numbering of your footnotes or endnotes.

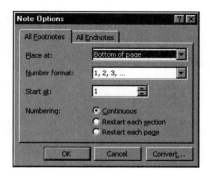

Footnote Options

To set options for footnotes, choose the All **F**ootnotes tab. Here, you can do the following:

- Set the location of your footnotes in the **P**lace at box: consistently at the bottom of every page, or directly underneath the last of your text.

- Set a **N**umber Format from among these choices:

```
1, 2, 3...
a, b, c...
A, B, C...
i, ii, iii...
I, II, III...
*, _, _, §...
```

If you use custom reference marks, the last choice—numbering with symbols—may be ideal for you. It allows Word to maintain its footnotes in order, and saves you the trouble of specifying a symbol each time you add a new footnote.

If you later change your mind and decide to use numbers, Word can display them in order—you don't have to replace each individual custom reference mark.

By the way, after Word inserts these four symbols (*, †, ‡, §), it doubles them, so your fifth footnote is **, your sixth is † †, and so on.

- Set a starting footnote number in the Start at box.

- Set a Numbering approach: either continuous numbers through the entire document, returning to the Start at number for each new section, or returning to the Start at number on each new page.

Endnote Options

To set options for endnotes, choose the All **E**ndnotes tab, as shown in Figure 12.5.

Figure 12.5

The All Endnotes
tab of the Note
Options dialog box

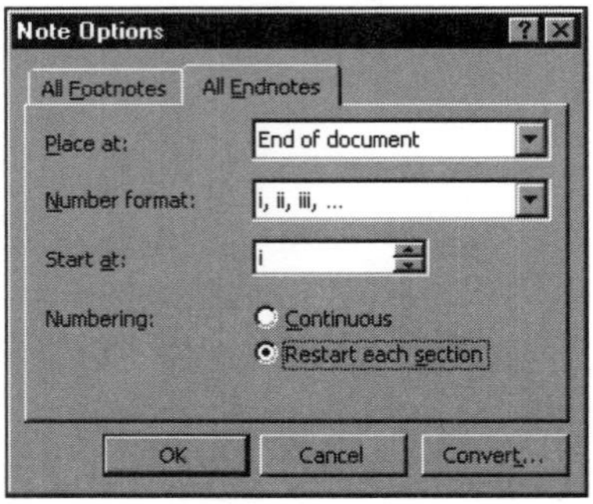

There are several choices in the Note Options dialog box:

- Set the location of your footnotes in the **P**lace at box: at the end of your document, or at the end of each section.

- Set a **N**umber format. These choices are the same as for footnotes.

- Set a starting footnote number. This option is in the Start **a**t box.

- Set a numbering approach: either continuous numbers through the entire document, or returning to the Start **a**t number for each new section.

Converting from Footnotes to Endnotes and Vice Versa

You can convert your document's footnotes to endnotes, or the other way around. Choose Insert, Footnote, click the Options button, and then click the Convert button. The Convert Notes dialog box opens (see Figure 12.6). Choose the option you want. (If you only have footnotes or endnotes, but not both, only one option is available.) Choose OK in the Convert Notes dialog box, click OK in the Options dialog box, and then click Close in the Footnote and Endnote dialog box.

Figure 12.6

The Convert
Notes dialog box

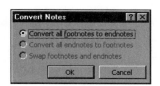

■ Viewing Footnotes

Word 97 introduces a new way to view your footnotes: just position your mouse pointer over the specific footnote or endnote you want to view, and wait a moment: A ScreenTip will appear, containing the text of the footnote.

If you need to take a closer look at your footnotes, they're accumulated in the footnote and endnote editing panes. To open a footnote or endnote pane and view or edit its contents, double-click on any footnote or endnote reference mark.

You can also choose **F**ootnotes from the **V**iew menu, assuming that you already have footnotes to view. With the pane open, you can scroll through your footnotes or endnotes, editing them as you want. As you move throughout your footnotes or endnotes, your document scrolls to the locations where the footnotes appear in text. You can switch between viewing endnotes and footnotes by choosing All Footnotes or All End notes from the Notes drop-down list box located at the top of the footnoteendnote pane.

To move between footnote pane and body text, you can click on the pane you want, or press F6. You can copy or move text between panes using any of Word's cut, copy, and paste techniques.

NOTE. *You can also open the footnote pane by pressing Shift and dragging the split bar down. If you have no footnotes, Word displays an error message. Once your footnote pane is open, you can make it larger or smaller by dragging the split bar up (or down).*

■ Finding Footnotes

You can always find a specific footnote or endnote by pressing F5, which opens the Go To tab of the Find and Replace dialog box (see Figure 12.7).

Figure 12.7

Going to a specific footnote through the Go To tab of the Find and Replace dialog box

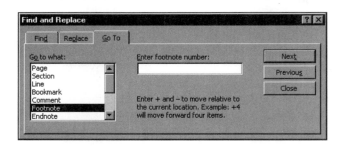

When it opens, choose Footnote or Endnote in the Go to **w**hat box, then do one of the following:

- Go to the next immediate note by choosing the Nex**t** button, or the previous note by choosing the **P**revious button.

- Key in the number of the note you want to see in the **E**nter footnote or **E**nter endnote box.

- Go forward a specific number of notes (enter + and the number).

- Go back a specific number of notes (enter - and the number).

In Word 97, you can always move to the next footnote in a document by clicking the Select Browse Object button at the bottom of the vertical scroll bar, and clicking the Footnote button.

■ Moving, Copying, and Deleting Footnotes

The footnote reference marks that appear in your body text are permanently attached to their corresponding footnote text in the footnote pane. You can move a footnote reference mark, and the footnote text moves as well, automatically renumbering if necessary. You can copy a footnote reference mark, and a duplicate footnote (including footnote text) appears wherever you paste the mark. If the marks are numbered, the new entry receives a new number. If you copy a custom reference mark, the same character appears in both places.

You can delete a footnote reference mark in body text, and its corresponding footnote text disappears from the footnote pane. (You can't delete a footnote mark from the footnote pane, but you can delete all its text. The footnote mark remains until you delete its reference from the body text.)

When you copy, move, or delete blocks of text that contain footnotes, the footnotes themselves are also copied, moved, or deleted. So pay attention when you're deleting large blocks of text that might have footnotes.

■ Changing Footnote Formatting

The normal font for footnote reference marks is Times New Roman superscript; footnote text is Times New Roman—in other words, the same default text Word uses for normal body copy. Since the Footnote Text style is based on the Normal style, if you change the font used by the Normal style, footnote text will change as well.

Of course, if you change your body text font without using styles, the footnote text won't change—but you may well want to manually reformat it to match the changes you've made elsewhere in the document.

Positioning Footnotes on a Page

Word keeps track of the length of your footnotes. By default, it attempts to leave space for them at the bottom of the same page where they appear in text. If this means jumping body text to the next page, Word does that—following any special Forma**t**, **P**aragraph Pagination commands you may have given elsewhere.

By default, Word normally separates your footnotes from text with a line that stretches two inches from your left margin. For footnotes, this is called the *footnote separator*; for endnotes, quite reasonably, it's called the *endnote separator*.

Occasionally, a footnote is so long that it must be continued on the following page despite Word's best efforts. In these cases, Word normally separates text from footnotes with a line that stretches from the left to the right margin. This is called the *continuation separator*—there's one for footnotes and another for endnotes.

Finally, Word lets you add a *continuation notice*—text that informs the reader that footnotes or endnotes will continue on a following page.

You can change or eliminate any of these separators and notices. To change any or all of them, open the footnote or endnote editing pane. (The quickest way is often to double-click on a footnote or endnote reference mark; you can also choose **F**ootnotes from the **V**iew menu.)

Then, in the Footnotes drop-down list box, choose the item you want to change. If you want to change a footnote separator or notice, but you find yourself in an endnote pane, choose All Footnotes first. Then, choose the footnote item you want.

Word displays the current footnote separator or notice; by default, the notice is blank. Now, you can edit any of these elements as you wish, in the footnote pane. You could even replace the default separator border line with text, as in Figure 12.8.

Figure 12.8

Changing the appearance of a footnote separator

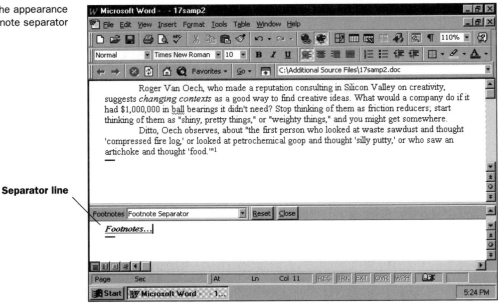

Separator line

When you've finished editing the separator or separators, close the pane. The changes take effect immediately.

Referencing Footnotes in Text

You may occasionally want to refer to a footnote in text, as in the following example:

```
For Eisenhower's reaction to MacArthur's observations, see footnote 12.
```

Word's NOTEREF field lets you do this. To use it, follow these steps:

1. Place the footnote in the document.

2. Select the footnote reference mark in the document.

3. Choose **B**ookmark from the **I**nsert menu, and name the bookmark and then click Add.

4. Place the insertion point where you want the reference to appear.

5. Choose Insert, Field, select the Links and References category, and then select NoteRef in the Field names list.

6. Place the insertion point after NOTEREF in the Field codes text box and type the name of your bookmark.

7. Click OK.

Another nice thing about NOTEREF is that it lets you reference the same footnote or endnote in as many places as you want, using the same footnote or endnote number or symbol. To create a common footnote or endnote:

1. Create a footnote or endnote as you normally would.

2. Bookmark its reference mark.

3. Place the field {NOTEREF *bookmarkname*} wherever you want to reference the same footnote.

4. Format the field result in footnote reference style, so that it looks like other footnotes.

Remember, though: If you delete the footnote you've bookmarked, none of the references will work.

■ Introducing Bookmarks

Sometimes, Word's find and replace function just isn't enough to find what you're looking for—especially in a long document. That's where bookmarks come into play.

With a bookmark, you can name a specific location in a document or a selected portion of a document. When you want to find that location or selected material, you just go to the bookmark.

Use bookmarks to flag any document element you might otherwise have trouble finding easily—for example, an unattributed quote. Use bookmarks to help guide another reader through a document, or perhaps, to flag parts of a document that need more formatting attention.

These are some of the ways bookmarks can help you directly, but bookmarks also can help you indirectly. They mark text, so that fields can act upon it, and they can simplify many aspects of document preparation, including creating internal cross-references and inserting material from other documents. To place a bookmark at a location (or on selected text) in a document:

1. Position the insertion point at the location you want to mark (or select the text).

2. Choose **B**ookmark from the **I**nsert menu. The Bookmark dialog box appears, as shown in Figure 12.9.

3. Type a name in the Bookmark dialog box.

NOTE. *You can also insert a bookmark from the status bar by pressing Ctrl+Shift+5 and typing the bookmark name.*

Bookmark names can't exceed 20 characters: letters, numbers, or underscores (_). They must start with a letter, and can't include spaces or punctuation. Also, don't use a name that's already the name of a field that returns document information, such as comments or title.

4. Choose **A**dd.

Figure 12.9

Using the Bookmark
dialog box to insert a
footnote

Finding a Bookmark

Once a bookmark has been created, you can find it by using Word's Go To feature. If you know the name of the bookmark, press F5; type the bookmark's name; and press Enter. If you don't know the name of the bookmark, choose the **G**o To option on the **E**dit menu (or press F5), and then choose a bookmark from the list.

For the first time, Word 97 enables you to view all your bookmarks at once. Choose **O**ptions from the **T**ools menu, then click the View tab and check Boo**k**marks in the Show box. All bookmarks now appear in your document surrounded by thick gray brackets, as shown in Figure 12.10.

Deleting a Bookmark

If you use a bookmark for temporary purposes, such as helping to find a part of a document that needs more work, you will probably want to delete the bookmark at some point. Perform the following steps to delete a bookmark:

1. Choose **B**ookmark from the **I**nsert menu.

2. Select a bookmark from the list, or type its name.

3. Choose **D**elete.

Figure 12.10

Displaying all bookmarks in a document

Bookmarks in the text

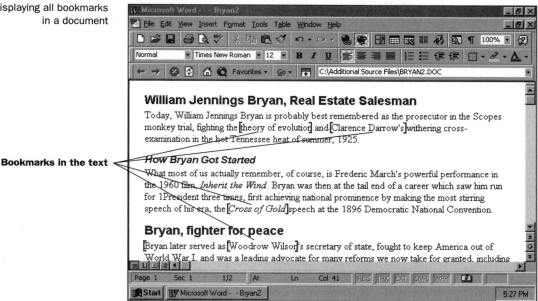

4. Choose Close to return to your document.

You also can redefine a bookmark by creating a bookmark with the same name as one that already exists. Word does not prompt you that you're about to overwrite an existing bookmark, though, so be careful.

NOTE. *If you delete text that includes an entire bookmark reference, the bookmark disappears. So, if you're using bookmarks to flag text for editing, select* all *the text that might be related to the reference you want to establish, not just a phrase or sentence that might inadvertently be deleted.*

■ Introducing References and Cross-References

When you quote text that appears elsewhere in your document, you're *referencing* it. But that's only the most basic example of a reference. You might also reference the page number where the text appears. That way, if the page number where your reference appears changes, Word can automatically change the page number to the new number.

Word helps you automate the process of creating and tracking cross-references, and also provides field codes that allow you to customize your cross-references in just about any way you choose.

Creating a Reference

A single dialog box manages your cross-references to numbered items, headings, bookmarks, footnotes, endnotes, equations, figures, and tables. You'll probably most often reference the following:

- *Headings,* to identify sections of your document

- *Bookmark,* to identify any specific text you want

- *Figures,* to include text references to figures elsewhere in your document

NOTE. *Word's features work together very closely—maybe more closely than you expect. For example, Word's Cross-Referencing feature recognizes headings only if you've identified them with one of the built-in heading styles, Heading 1 through Heading 9. It recognizes heading numbers only if you've used Word's Outline Numbering feature. It recognizes figures only if you've created them with Word's Caption feature.*

To create a cross-reference, place your insertion point where you want the cross-reference to appear. Type any introductory text you might want, such as **For background, see...** or **This is covered in more detail in....**

Then choose Cross-**r**eference from the **I**nsert menu. The Cross-reference dialog box opens, as shown in Figure 12.11. To create a reference to a heading, choose Heading from the Reference **t**ype box. In the For **w**hich heading box, choose a heading from the list Word displays. This list includes the beginning text of any paragraph styled as a Word heading—other text won't be marked. You may know it's a heading, but Word doesn't—unless you say so.

Figure 12.11

The Cross-reference
dialog box

In the Insert **r**eference to box in the Cross-reference dialog box, Word invites you to choose which aspect of the heading you want to reference. For headings, you have six choices.

You can insert the heading text itself. In the following reference, what Word has inserted is underlined; Word itself uses the base style of the surrounding text:

`For more information, see Bryan's later years.`

Or you can insert the page number where the heading may be found. For example:

`This is covered in more detail on page 26.`

You have to add the word **page**—Word doesn't do it for you. (You're forgiven for expecting otherwise.)

You can also select the heading number, but only if you've used Word's Outline Numbering feature to set it, as discussed in Chapter 10. For example:

`See I.A.2 for more about this.`

Word 97 gives you new flexibility in how you specify outline numbers. If you choose Heading number, Word displays the paragraph number of the heading you're cross-referencing, using the following rules: If the heading is in the same section as the cross-reference will be placed, an abbreviated version of the heading will be included. For example, if you're in section **2.A.**, and you insert a cross-reference to section **2.B.**, Word will display the reference **B**. However, if you requested the same reference to be placed in section **3.A**, Word will insert the reference **2.B**, helping readers understand not only which paragraph the cross-reference is in, but also which section that paragraph is in.

The abbreviated reference is called a *no context* reference; the detailed one is called a *full context* reference. If you always want a cross-reference to be included without context, you can specify Heading number (no context); if you always want the context included, you can choose Heading number (full context).

Word 97 also allows you to specify that instead of text or a number, a cross-reference will simply say "above" or "below." A sample above/below cross-reference might read:

`see page 22, above.`

If you later move the text containing the cross-reference to a location *above* the cross-reference, the reference will change to:

`see page 22, below.`

In most cases, you can either specify Above/Below in the Insert reference to drop-down list box, or you can add it to the other information you've asked to include in your reference, by checking the Include above/below checkbox. So, for example, you could insert a combined reference that says:

```
See page 22, below.
```

If you choose another Reference **t**ype, such as a Footnote, your options will be different. Table 12.1 lists what kind of reference **I**nsert Cross-**r**eference can create for each Reference **t**ype.

Table 12.1

Reference Types and Choices

REFERENCE TYPE	REFERENCE	OR...	OR...	OR...	OR...	OR...
Numbered item	Page number	Para-graph number	Paragraph number (no context)	Paragraph number (full context)	Para-graph text	Above/below
Heading	Heading text	Page number	Heading number	Heading number (no context)	Heading number (full context)	Above/below
Bookmark	Bookmark text	Page number	Paragraph number	Paragraph number (no context)	Para-graph number (full context)	Above/below
Footnote	Footnote number	Page number	Above/below	Footnote number (formatted)		
Endnote	Endnote number	Page number	Above/below	Endnote number (formatted)		
Equation	Entire caption	Only label and number	Only caption text	Page number	Above/below	
Figure	Entire caption	Only label and number	Only caption text	Page number	Above/below	
Table	Entire caption	Only label and number	Only caption text	Page number	Above/below	

NOTE. *By default, Word 97 inserts cross-refernces as hyperlinks, which means that if someone reads your document on-screen, they can click the cross-reference and Word will move to the referenced page, heading, bookmark, or other text. You'll learn more about hyperlinks later in this chapter.*

If you do not want Word to insert your cross-reference as a hyperlink, clear the Insert as hyperlink checkbox in the Cross-refernce dialog box.

Looking under the Hood

Because cross-references are fields, you can update them the same way you update any other field: by selecting them and pressing F9.

Cross-references are usually {REF} fields. They are {PAGEREF} fields when you ask for a page number; they are {NOTEREF} fields when you reference a footnote or endnote. When you ask to insert a header's text, Word inserts a field that looks like this:

```
{ REF _Ref273159031 \* MERGEFORMAT }
```

The number is purely random, but the * MERGEFORMAT command is Word's way of telling itself that the reference should use the same style as the text surrounding it.

You can display your reference field codes and edit them in any way you want. For example, you can use the Word field-formatting command `\* upper` to specify that a code will insert its text reference in ALL CAPS. (These field-formatting commands are covered in Chapter 21, "Field Codes.")

Using the {ASK} Field to Create References

You've already seen how you can create a reference to specific text by marking the text as a bookmark. But you don't need a preexisting bookmark to create a reference to specific text. You can set up your document so that it actually requests information from the user, assigns that information a bookmark, and inserts that information throughout your document. To do this, use the {ASK} field.

In the following example, the user is asked for a client's name, and the client's name is assigned the bookmark *clientname*.

```
{ASK clientname "What is your client's name?"}
```

NOTE. *You can instruct Word to insert default text into the document if the user doesn't type any. Use the \d switch, and place the default text in quotation marks:*

{ASK clientname "Who is your customer?" \d "Client"}

Now use Word's Cross-Reference feature to insert {REF} fields wherever the client's name should be added to the document. Press F9 to update your fields. Then, enter text in the {ASK} field, as shown in Figure 12.12.

Figure 12.12

A typical ASK dialog box

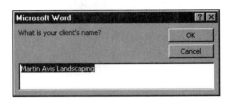

In Figure 12.13, notice how the {ASK} text and {REF} field codes have been added throughout the document. Each time you select your ASK field and update it, the ASK dialog box reappears, containing the current text. If you want to keep the text you've already added, press Enter.

Figure 12.13

A sample document with REF field codes and ASK

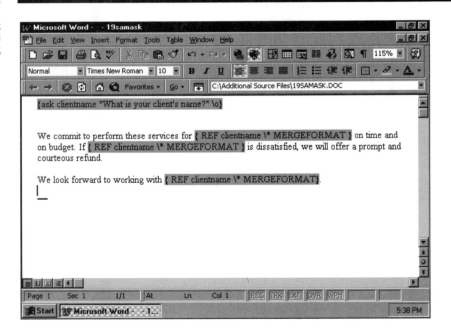

A Variation: The {SET} Field

If you don't want the user to be prompted for text, you can use the {SET} field instead. Here, you place both the text you want and the corresponding bookmark into the field code. In the following example, the bookmark name is *state*, and the text you want to include is *New Jersey:*

```
{SET state "New Jersey"}
```

As with the {ASK} field described earlier, the words *New Jersey* will be placed in the document wherever you insert the field {REF state}—either directly or through the Insert Cross-reference dialog box. If the inserted reference appears as a field instead of the value New Jersey, select the field and press Shift+F9 to view the value.

Notice that the {SET} field enables you to create a bookmark without including the corresponding text in your document until you're ready. Because you're setting the reference, you don't need to provide an alternate in the event no input is provided.

Choosing Your Reference Based on Events Elsewhere

What if you want one reference to appear in your document if certain conditions are met and another reference if different conditions are met? You can do this by using both the {SET} and {ASK} fields, combined with the {IF} field, which enables Word to make a decision based on what it finds.

Let's use this scenario: You're writing order confirmations. Customers ordering more than 5,000 units automatically qualify for your Frequent Buyer Club, in which they earn credits toward gifts. Customers ordering fewer than 5,000 units don't qualify, but you'd like them to know about the Club. Maybe they'll place larger orders later.

Start by creating an {ASK} field to input the size of the current order, as in the following example:

```
{ask ordersize "How many units in this order?"}
```

Remember, when the user inputs this information, it's also stored in a bookmark. Here, the bookmark is named *ordersize*.

Now that you have a bookmark that always contains current information about the size of an order, you can build a field that acts on this information. Use an {IF} field, which contains the following:

- The test you want to perform

- The result if the conditions are met

- The result if the conditions are not met

In the example, the test is: *are there at least 5,000 orders?* You know how many orders there are—that number is stored in the bookmark ordersize.

Therefore, you can write the test as follows:

```
if ordersize >= 5000
```

Now you have to specify what happens if the order is at least 5,000. In this example, these big orders should trigger the appearance of the following text:

```
Congratulations! You've earned points in our Frequent Buyer Club.
Call 1-800-555-5555.
```

If the order is less than 5,000, you want the following text to appear:

```
Have you heard about our Frequent Buyer Club? Call 1-800-555-5555.
```

So the field looks like this:

```
{if ordersize >= 5000 "Congratulations! You've earned points in our Frequent
Buyer Club. Call 1-800-555-5555." "Have you heard about our Frequent Buyer
Club? Call 1-800-555-5555."}
```

The size of each order determines what's displayed in this field.

Now for the final touch. Suppose that you want this information to appear repeatedly throughout the document. (Maybe you want it on the cover, in each footer, and at the end of the document.)

Select the field discussed, and mark it as a bookmark. Call this bookmark *buyerclub*. Now, wherever else you want this text to appear, use this field:

```
{ref buyerclub}
```

That's it. It took a little doing, but you've taken the first step toward building customized documents that present a message tailored precisely for each of your customers.

■ Introducing Hyperlinks

Now for the icing on the cake: Word 97 introduces a powerful hyperlink feature that lets you connect your lowly Word document to anywhere on Earth. You can create hyperlinks to other parts of your document; to other documents on your hard disk (whether or not they were created in Word); to your company's network or intranet; or if you have a modem and an Internet connection, to files on the World Wide Web. There are several ways to do it:

- You can choose Insert, Hyperlink, and specify the location of the document you want to link with, or any specifically marked location in the document.

- You can simply type the names of files, intranet or Internet locations—and let Word change those names and locations into hyperlinks.

- You can create a cross-reference, as just discussed—but insert a hyperlink instead of a standard cross-reference.

Once the link is established, anyone who views your document can link to the location by simply double-clicking on the hyperlink.

The applications are endless:

- Include hyperlinks in your reports, so people can link to statistical support in one of your Excel worksheets.

- Include hyperlinks to your competitors' Web sites as part of your marketing research.

- Give all new employees Word documents containing hyperlinks to bene-fits information on your corporate intranet.

- Launch a product with a CD-ROM containing hyperlinked documents: It's easier than traditional multimedia, you can include sound, images and movies, and anyone with a Web browser can view it. You can even distribute the Microsoft Explorer Web browser, free, along with your presentation.

Wow! These hyperlinks do everything but cook your dinner. All that's left is to learn how to use them. Let's start with the basics.

Inserting Hyperlinks with the Edit Hyperlink Dialog Box

To insert a new hyperlink into your document, choose Insert, Hyperlink. The Insert Hyperlink dialog box opens, as shown in Figure 12.14. In the Link to file or URL box, enter the file name or Internet/intranet location of the file you want to connect with. If you've inserted a link to the same file recently, click the down-arrow next to the Link to file or URL box, and select the file name from there.

If you haven't linked with this file before, and you don't know the file's name or location offhand, you can browse for it. Click Browse; a standard Word File Open dialog box opens. From here, you can browse for any file on your computer or your network, and select it to be hyperlinked.

When you've finished typing the file name (or browsing for it), click OK. A blue hyperlink reference appears in your document; when you point to it, it displays the complete file name.

NOTE. *If you're distributing a document to readers which contains hyperlinks to documents on a network, make sure your readers have sufficient rights to access the document location on your network.*

Figure 12.14

The Insert Hyperlink dialog box allows you to create new hyperlinks, either to entire files or to locations in files.

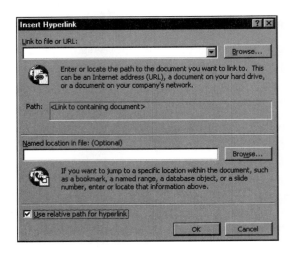

Hyperlinking to an Internet FTP Site

When you browse the Link to File dialog box, you may notice a surprise in the Look in drop-down list box. You won't just see the usual suspects—"My Computer," "Network Neighborhood," "My Briefcase," etc.—you'll also see Internet Locations (FTP sites).

These are Internet sites that specialize in storing and transferring files; FTP stands for *file transfer protocol*, in fact. As an example, ftp://ftp.microsoft.com connects you to Microsoft's FTP site, just as http://www.microsoft.com connects you to Microsoft's Web site.

To make an FTP site available for hyperlinking, select Add/Modify FTP Locations. The Add/Modify FTP Locations dialog box opens. In Name of FTP site, include the name of the site you want to hyperlink with. For most cases, choose Anonymous as your log-in. Most public FTP sites extend the courtesy of allowing users to log on as Anonymous, but request that you use your e-mail address as the password.

Some private FTP sites—such as those your company may maintain for its own employees—require a "real" password. Click Add to include the FTP site in the FTP sites list at the bottom of the dialog box.

Once you've made an FTP site available for hyperlinking, add the hyperlink to your document as follows:

1. Choose Insert, Hyperlink.

2. Click Browse to select a Link to file or URL.

3. In the Open dialog box, click in the Look in drop-down box, and select Internet Locations (FTP).

4. Select the location you want, and click OK.

5. In the Insert Hyperlink dialog box, click OK.

Adding a Hyperlink to a Named Location in a File

If you are creating hyperlinks to files created by other Microsoft Office 97 applications, you can link directly to specific locations in those files. For example, you can link to:

*   A bookmark marked in another Word 97 file

*   A specific slide in another PowerPoint 97 file

*   A named range in an Excel 97 file

*   A database object in an Access 97 file

Once you have specified in the Insert Hyperlink dialog box the file you want to hyperlink with, enter the Named location in that file. Or, click Browse next to the Named location in the file box, and Word will show you the bookmarks or other marked information you can hyperlink to, if any exist in that document. In Figure 12.15, Word is browsing another Word document for bookmarks that are available for hyperlinking.

Figure 12.15

Choosing among bookmarks to select a hyperlink location

When you have completed creating the hyperlink, click OK, and the hyperlink will appear in your document as blue underlined text (see Figure 12.16). Then, when you click the hyperlinked text, Word closes the current document (warning you to save first), and opens the hyperlinked document. After you've clicked the hyperlink once, the hyperlink changes color to magenta.

Figure 12.16

A typical hyperlink as it
appears in a Word
document

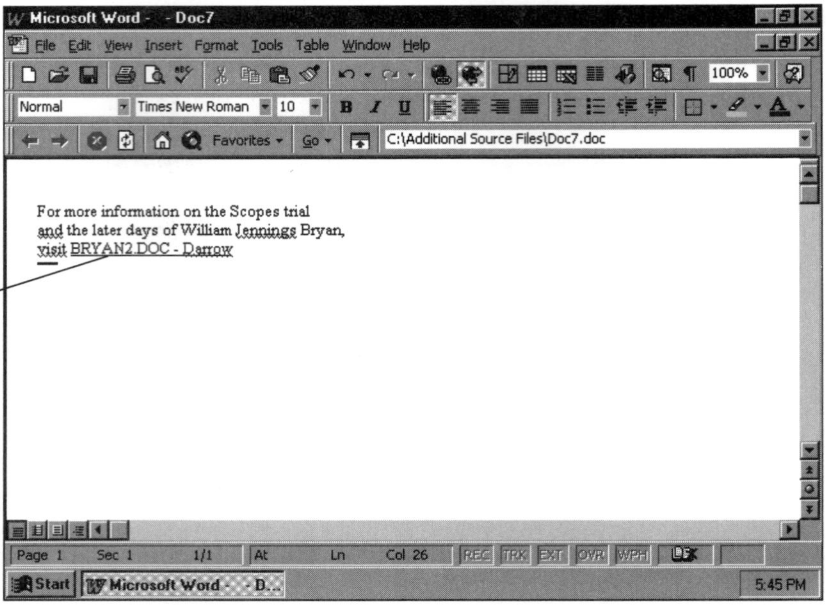

Understanding Relative and Absolute Links

What happens if you create a hyperlink and then move the file you're hyper-linking to? For example, what happens when you copy both the source and destination files to a network drive or an intranet?

If you've used a specific file and path name—what Word calls an *absolute hyperlink*—that hyperlink will break when the destination file moves.

The solution (if you do not want the link to be broken) may be to use a relative link. When you specify a relative link, if both files are in the same folder now, as long as they stay in the same folder the hyperlink will stay intact. Similarly, if you link to a file one folder above your current folder, and you move both folders without changing their hierarchy, the hyperlinks will stay intact.

To specify a relative link, create your hyperlink by using Insert, Hyper-link. In the Hyperlink dialog box, check the Use relative path for hyperlink box. (This is the default setting.)

Automatically Reformatting Text as a Hyperlink

If you use many hyperlinks, you can set Word's AutoCorrect feature to insert them automatically. Choose Tools, AutoCorrect, and click the AutoFormat As You Type tab. Then make sure the Internet and network paths with hyperlinks box is checked. (Again, this is the default setting.) Now, when you type an Internet address or a file name that includes a network path, Word will automatically transform that text into a hyperlink. Here are some examples of file names Word will recognize and turn into hyperlinks:

```
www.camarda.com
http://www.camarda.com
ftp://camarda.com
\\dell\d:\camarda\decweb.doc
```

However, Word *won't* AutoFormat a file name that doesn't include a network address, such as c:\camarda\decweb.doc. If you want to create a hyperlink to another file on your local disk, you'll have to do that manually.

Creating Hyperlinks with Word 97's Cross-Reference Feature

Earlier in this chapter, you learned how to create cross-references that help people locate information in other parts of a printed document. The next step for cross-references was obvious: Turn them into hyperlinks. Now, you can create cross-references that don't just tell you where a reference can be found, they'll take you there.

To create a hyperlinked cross-reference, choose Insert, Cross-Reference; specify a reference type and what you wish to Insert the reference to; check the Insert as hyperlink box, and click OK.

Pasting Hyperlinks from Another Word or Office Program

Sometimes the easiest way to create a hyperlink is to simply copy the information you want to link from its source file to the location where you want the link to appear. All Office 97 applications support cut-and-paste hyperlinking. In the following example, you copy a selected range of cells from Excel to Word, but instead of simply pasting the cells, you paste them as a hyperlink. (However, this would also work with selected PowerPoint slides shown in Slide Sorter view, Access database objects, or even text selections in other Word documents.)

First, select a range of cells in an Excel worksheet, as shown in Figure 12.17.

Next, click on Word, display your Word document, and position your insertion point where you want the hyperlink. Then, choose Edit, Paste as Hyperlink. The range of cells now appears in your document, formatted as blue underlined text, as shown in Figure 12.18. If you click this text, Excel opens, displaying the selected cells.

Figure 12.17

Selecting a range of
cells in Excel

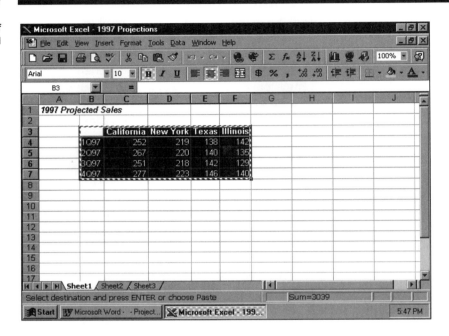

Figure 12.18

Cells pasted as hyperlink
from an Excel worksheet

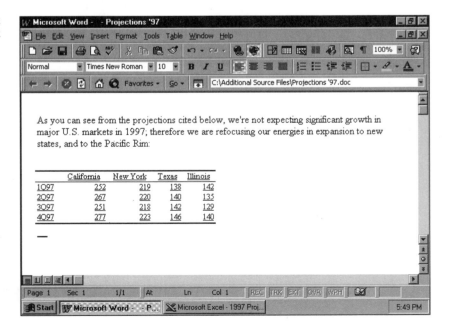

Using the Hyperlink Shortcut Menu

When you right-click on a Hyperlink, Word displays a shortcut menu that includes the Hyperlink command. Click Hyperlink, and a cascaded menu appears, as shown in Figure 12.19.

Figure 12.19

The Hyperlink
shortcut menu

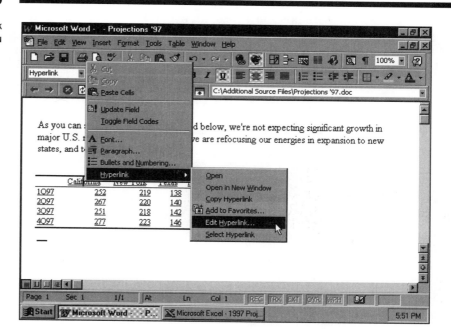

This menu includes the following choices:

- *Open* opens the file you've hyperlinked to, and closes the file you have open.

- *Open as New Window* opens the file you've hyperlinked to, using a new window. The file that contained the hyperlink remains open.

- *Copy Hyperlink* allows you to copy the hyperlink to a new location, either in this Word document, another Word document, or another Office document.

- *Add to Favorites* copies a shortcut to the hyperlinked file into your Favorites folder, where you can store shortcuts to all the files you use most.

- *Edit Hyperlink* allows you to change your hyperlink so it specifies a connection to a different file and/or a different location in a file.

- *Select Hyperlink* allows you to select the entire hyperlink for editing or formatting.

NOTE. *The hyperlink commands don't appear on the shortcut menu if the hyperlink has been flagged as a spelling or grammar error.*

Until now, all the hyperlinks we've placed in Word documents either appear with the name and location of the file being hyperlinked, or (as in the Excel example above) displaying the full contents of the selection being linked. But what if you want your hyperlinks to say something different? For example, on a Web site, hyperlinks typically describe the page being linked to—rather than simply showing the name of that file.

You can easily change the text in a hyperlink. First, select the entire hyperlink. The easiest way is to right-click on the hyperlink, and choose Hyperlink, Select Hyperlink from the shortcut menu. See the example in Figure 12.20.

Figure 12.20

One hyperlink selected for editing, and others edited to present more interesting text than simply a file name

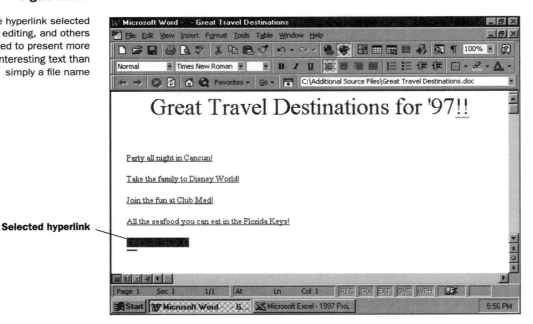

Selected hyperlink

Once you change the text associated with a hyperlink, how can you tell what you're hyperlinking to? Hover your mouse pointer over a hyperlink, and a ScreenTip will appear showing what it links to (Figure 12.21).

Figure 12.21

A hyperlink ScreenTip can
always show you the
contents of a hyperlink
even if the text in your
document doesn't.

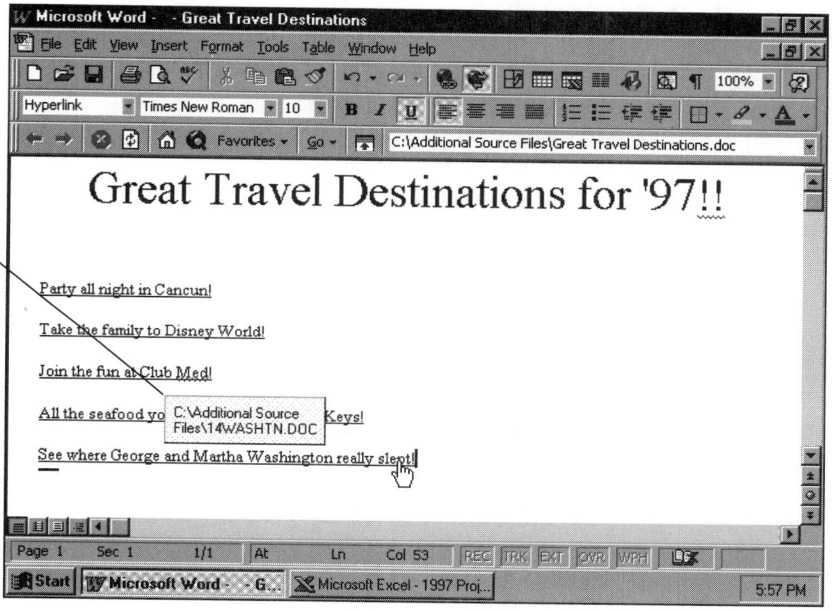

Screen tip

Changing the Appearance of All Hyperlinks At Once

All Word hyperlinks use the character style Hyperlink when they are inserted. Once they have been used, the style changes to Followed Hyperlink.
The fastest way to change the appearance of all your hyperlinks is to change
the Hyperlink or Followed Hyperlink style. You can change these styles the
same way you change any other style—through the Format, Styles dialog
box, which is discussed in detail in Chapter 7.

Here's a brief overview of how to change the style of your hyperlinks:
With the Styles dialog box open, choose the style you want to change; click
Modify; then click the Format button. You can modify only the font, border,
and language information associated with a hyperlink, not the paragraph,
tab, frame, or numbering formats.

Now that you've learned about hyperlinks, in Chapter 13, you'll learn
how Word 97 uses them in Master Documents, to help streamline and simplify the process of working with large documents—no matter how complex
those documents are. Then, in Chapter 14, you'll see hyperlinks at work yet
again, in the biggest hyperlinked environment on Earth—the Internet.

- *Creating a New Master Document*

- *Creating a Subdocument*

- *Saving a Master Document*

- *Opening a Subdocument*

- *Printing Master Documents and Subdocuments*

- *A Word about Styles in Master Documents and Subdocuments*

- *Transforming an Existing Document into a Master Document*

- *Adding an Existing Document to a Master Document*

- *Adding an Index, Table of Contents, or Other Table*

- *Working with Others on the Same Master Document*

- *Managing Read-Write Privileges*

- *Reorganizing Your Master Document*

- *Merging and Splitting Subdocuments*

- *Renaming or Moving Subdocuments*

- *Removing a Subdocument*

- *Insert File: Another Way to Combine Word Files*

13

Master Documents:
Manage Even the Longest Documents

A MASTER DOCUMENT GIVES YOU A BIRD'S-EYE VIEW OF THE
contents of many small documents that together form a book or
other large document. A master document closely resembles an
outline, except that the material being outlined can come from
many different documents, which are called *subdocuments* when
they are part of a master document.

You can use master documents to:

- Quickly see where elements appear in a large document

- Reorganize a large document, even though its components are in different files

- Make sure that all parts of your document are formatted consistently, even if they're in different files

- Create cross-references, tables of contents, and other tables that encompass multiple documents

- Send one command that prints the entire document, even though the document is split into several files

Master documents can help you work faster, because Word slows down when processing extremely large individual documents. By using master documents, you can work with subdocuments within the context of the entire document—allowing you to use smaller files that Word can process more quickly.

You can create a master document by building it from the ground up or by bringing existing documents into a master document, transforming the imported documents into subdocuments. These subdocuments behave much like Word document sections. They can have their own headers, footers, margins, page size, page orientation, and page numbers. But you can override these differences in sectional formatting by editing and printing from the master document, where the formatting follows a single consistent template.

■ Creating a New Master Document

In this section, you'll create a new master document and learn about the Master Document toolbar, from where you can centrally control your master document. To create a new master document:

1. Open a new Word Document and choose Master Document from the View menu. Your document is displayed in Outline view, and the Master Document and Outline toolbars appear.

2. Now begin to outline your document. Use Word's outlining tools and heading styles. Review Chapter 10 if you need to refresh your memory on how to do this.

3. Keep developing your outline until you're ready to divide your document into subdocuments. For example, if you're writing a book, you might want to finish the entire book outline, get it approved if necessary, and then break apart the outline into subdocuments for each chapter.

You now have the makings of a master document. But so far, all your text still appears in a single document. Your next step will be to specify which text should be placed in subdocuments, which can be edited separately yet still be managed as part of the same master document. In order to work with subdocuments, it will help to first take a closer look at the Master Document toolbar, shown in Figure 13.1. Table 13.1 describes what each of these toolbar buttons do. (If you're not familiar with hyperlinks, which the table mentions, see Chapter 12. Later in this chapter, you'll learn how Word 97 can display hyperlinks in place of subdocument text, so you can simply click a master document hyperlink to display a subdocument at any time.)

Figure 13.1

The Master
Document toolbar

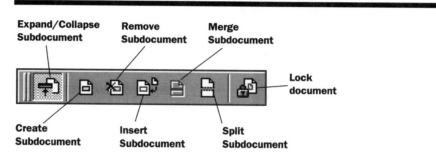

Table 13.1

Master Document Toolbar

BUTTON	WHAT IT DOES
Expand/collapse subdocument	Toggles the display of subdocuments on and off. The name of the button changes depending on the current status of the document. When the subdocuments have been collapsed, hyperlinks containing their file names appear in their place.
Create subdocument	Converts selected outline items into individual subdocuments
Remove subdocument	Removes a subdocument from a master document
Insert subdocument	Inserts an existing document as a subdocument into the document
Merge subdocument	Combines two or more adjacent subdocuments into one subdocument
Split subdocument	Splits one subdocument into two separate subdocuments
Lock document	Locks a subdocument so that it cannot be changed. When you click the button a second time, it unlocks the document.

■ Creating a Subdocument

Now that you've created an outline as the framework for your master document and learned about the Master Document toolbar, you can begin to create subdocuments. Figure 13.2 shows an outline before subdocuments have been added; the figures that follow will show the master document as it appears with subdocuments.

Figure 13.2

Preliminary outlining without subdocuments

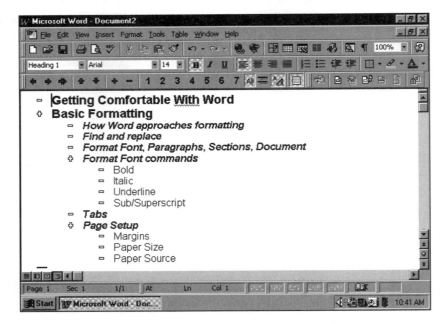

To create a subdocument of your Master Document, select the headings or text you want to incorporate into the subdocument and click on the Create Subdocument button in the Master Document toolbar. A small document icon appears at the top left of the area you select, and a light gray box appears around the selected text (see Figure 13.3).

Word allows you to create many subdocuments at once. In the outline we've been working with, for example, we've created first-level headings that we want to use as the dividing lines between subdocuments; in other words, each first-level heading should start a new subdocument. To break the document into subdocuments that begin at each first-level heading, take the following steps:

1. Click on button 1 of the Outline toolbar to display only first-level headings.

2. Select the entire document (Ctrl+A).

3. Click on the Create Subdocument button.

Figure 13.3

A subdocument
viewed as part of the
master document

**Grey rectangle
indicates sub-
document's borders**

Subdocument icon

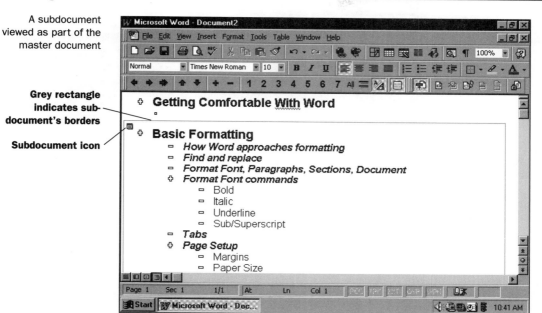

4. Each first-level heading has now become a subdocument.

■ Saving a Master Document

When you save a master document, Word also saves all of its individual sub-documents. Word assigns names to these subdocuments based on the first let-ters of each one's top heading and using the default Word DOC extension, as shown in Figure 13.4.

If the names of more than one chapter would otherwise be identical, Word inserts consecutive numbers as part of the names. For example, if all your chap-ters start with the word "Chapter," Word will automatically name the first sev-eral subdocuments CHAPTER1, CHAPTER2, CHAPTER3, and so on.

After you save a subdocument, its text is contained in that subdocument, not in the master document. This has two important implications: First, you can edit subdocuments individually, as if they were regular documents. Sec-ond, if you delete a subdocument or move it, its text disappears from the main document.

If you want to edit a subdocument in a way that affects the master docu-ment, open the subdocument from within the master document. For exam-ple, edit your subdocument from within the master document if you want

Figure 13.4

Word assigns names to subdocuments in master documents based on their top headings.

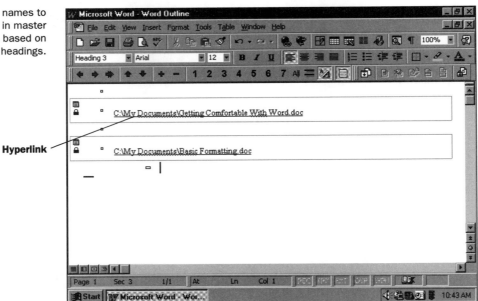

Hyperlink

to add elements to your subdocument that will reference the contents of other subdocuments, such as fields, a table of contents, or an index. Unless the master document is open, the subdocument will not have access to the other files it needs, and error messages are likely to be displayed in place of the information you want.

■ Opening a Subdocument

If you've just created a new subdocument, you can edit it in a number of ways. First, you can edit it in the master document. You're not restricted to Outline view; you can switch to Normal view if you prefer. Second, you can double-click on its document icon. That opens a new window that contains only the subdocument.

After you save your master document for the first time and file names are created for each subdocument, you also can close the master document and open the subdocument individually by using its new file name.

In Word 97, when you close a master document and then reopen it, your subdocuments will appear as hyperlinks, as shown in Figure 13.4. As covered in the previous chapter, a hyperlink is a block of colored, underlined text that a viewer can click to move to another specified location—in this case, a subdocument connected to the master document where the hyperlink appears.

To edit a subdocument, click the hyperlink in the master document. Word opens the subdocument in its own window. To edit the subdocument within the master document, click the Expand Subdocuments button on the Master Document toolbar. All subdocuments will now appear as they did when you set them up—in other words, instead of seeing a hyperlink, you'll see the text and heading associated with each subdocument. If you now decide you want to edit a subdocument in its own window, you can double-click on the subdocument icon at the top left of the bordered gray rectangle containing the subdocument.

■ Printing Master Documents and Subdocuments

To print all the contents of a master document, open the master document, switch to Normal view, and print from there. To print only selected contents, or an outline at only specified levels, use Word's Outline view tools.

You can print individual subdocuments by opening them from within the master document or by opening them separately.

NOTE. *If you print from Normal view, Word places a section break between subdocuments. By default, this section break is also a page break. If you want the next subdocument to start printing on the same page as the previous one, change your section formatting in the Insert, Break dialog box.*

■ A Word about Styles in Master Documents and Subdocuments

Remember that if you open a subdocument from within the master document, it will use the master document's styles. If you open the subdocument separately using Word's File, Open command, it will use any styles associated with the subdocument.

Imagine that your master document is based on the Normal template and uses the Normal template's default styles; for example, 14-point Arial boldface for Heading 1 styles. Now you divide the master document into subdocuments and create a new Heading 1 style while working in the subdocument. When you return to viewing the subdocument from within the master document, it will be displayed using the Normal template's styles, not the custom style you created.

Some users are surprised at changes in a subdocument's formatting from one editing session to the next—this is usually the explanation. In general, it makes the most sense to work on your subdocuments from within the master document whenever that's practical, and maintain consistent formatting and styles that are all managed from the master document rather than individual documents.

■ Transforming an Existing Document into a Master Document

You might have already started the Great American Novel without waiting for the new version of Word to arrive. So you now have a large document you want to transform into a master document. Easy, as long as you used Word's heading styles when you wrote your novel. If so, you can simply switch to Master Document View and divide the document based on the heading levels you already specified.

Styles dramatically simplify the process of creating subdocuments, because they give Word a way to automatically divide your document for you—just tell Word which style represents the beginning of a new subdocument, and as you'll see, Word can handle the rest. Before Word 97, you had to use Word's specific heading styles (Heading 1 through Heading 9), but now any style will do. As you learned in Chapter 10, Word 97 allows you to assign levels to any style, through the Format, Bullets and Numbering, Outline Numbering tab, as discussed in Chapter 10. Once you've done this, Word can create subdocuments based on levels.

If you never assigned styles at all, but your document contains text blocks that look like headings, chances are you're still in luck. Say you've formatted all your text manually, in boldface, and set the text blocks apart from body text with extra paragraph marks. You can try Word's AutoFormat feature (covered in Chapter 7), which will automatically assign heading styles based on Word's best guesses. Spot-check the results, though, before you split the document.

Yet another way to change manually formatted headings into styles is to use Edit, Replace to find all text with your manual formatting, and replace it with the same text using the style you want. This only works if your heads and subheads are formatted differently from the other text elements in your document.

Okay, let's assume that, one way or another, you now have workable styles in your document, and you're ready to split your document into subdocuments. To do this:

1. Open the document.

2. Choose Master Document from the View menu to display it as a master document.

3. Select the text or headings you want to make into a subdocument, using the same outlining tools discussed earlier in Chapter 10.

4. After you make the changes you want, choose Save As from the File menu to save the file under a new name. Word creates individual files for your subdocuments and assigns names to them.

■ Adding an Existing Document to a Master Document

What if you want to add an existing subdocument to a master document you're constructing? Follow these steps:

1. Open the master document. The Outlining and Master Document toolbars appear.

2. Place the insertion point where you want to insert the new document.

3. Click on the Insert Subdocument button. The Insert Subdocument dialog box appears (see Figure 13.5).

4. Find and select the document you want to insert. Click on Open. The document appears in a box in your master document.

Figure 13.5

Insert Subdocument allows you to convert an existing Word document into a subdocument of your master document.

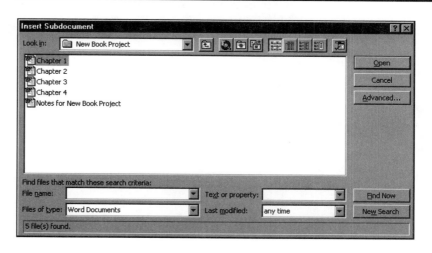

When Word saves a file that has been inserted into a subdocument, the file keeps its original name.

■ Adding an Index, Table of Contents, or Other Table

Master documents make it possible, even easy, to add an index, table of contents, table of figures, or table of authorities that encompasses multiple documents. Use the following steps:

1. Open the master document. (Make sure that all subdocuments are present and accounted for. For example, if someone else is using a subdocument, you won't be able to edit that subdocument.

2. Switch to Normal view.

3. Place the insertion point where you want the index or table.

4. Choose Index and Tables from the Insert menu, and insert your table of contents as you normally would. (For more information on inserting tables of contents, see Chapter 11.)

■ Working with Others on the Same Master Document

Because Word master documents are likely to be used by many people, each responsible for a different component, Word makes special provisions for keeping track of the components of master documents.

When you open a master document, you can edit any subdocument that you created. You can read the ones someone else created, but you can't edit them without unlocking them first.

To unlock a subdocument, expand the subdocument, then place the insertion point inside it and click on the Unlock Document button. You can't open and edit a file someone else is currently editing, unless you've specified that changes can be made by more than one user at once, as discussed in the previous section.

To determine who created a file, Word checks the Author information in the Summary page of the file's Properties. If you change that information, you can change the subdocument's read-write behavior.

■ Managing Read-Write Privileges

As with any Word document, you can protect a master document with passwords, and assign read-write privileges. Follow these steps:

1. Open the master document or subdocument and save it by choosing Save As from the File menu.

2. Select Options. The Save tab of the Options dialog box opens (see Figure 13.6).

3. If you want to prevent unauthorized individuals from even opening the file, insert a Password in the Password to open box.

4. If you want to allow anyone to view the file, but restrict authorization to modify it, insert a Password in the Password to modify box.

5. Press Enter. Word will ask you to confirm any passwords you've added.

6. Type the password again and click OK.

If you want to discourage, but not prevent, changes by others, you can check Read-Only Recommended. When the file is opened, Word encourages users to open the file as read-only, but doesn't require them to do so.

Figure 13.6

Here is where you create passwords that prevent unauthorized users from reading or modifying your master document.

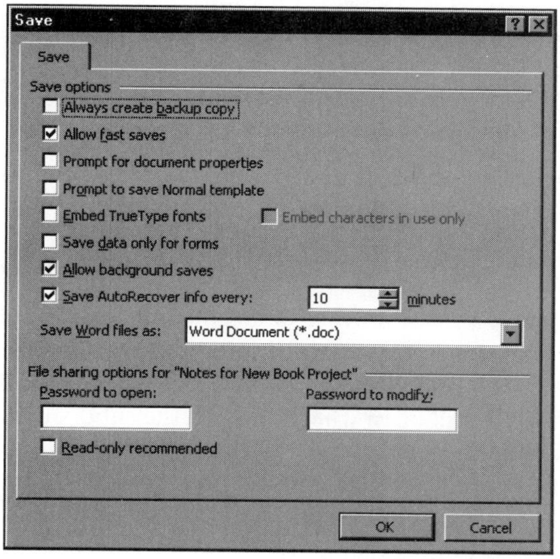

■ Reorganizing Your Master Document

All the outlining tools covered in Chapter 10 work in master documents as well—once you click Expand Subdocuments to see your document outline. You can move body text and/or headings within a subdocument or between subdocuments. You can promote or demote headings. You can select and move large blocks of copy by displaying only high-level headings and cutting and pasting those. (To select all the contents of a subdocument to be moved or reformatted, click its subdocument icon.)

■ Merging and Splitting Subdocuments

You can combine two subdocuments into one. Or, perhaps you would rather split one subdocument into two, when it gets too big or when you want to delegate parts of it to another author.

To combine two subdocuments, follow these steps:

1. Move both subdocuments next to each other in the master document.

2. Select both subdocuments.

3. Click on Merge Subdocument.

4. Save the master document. When Word saves the merged subdocument, it uses the name of the first subdocument contained in it.

To split one subdocument into two, follow these steps:

1. Place the insertion point where you want the subdocument to split.

2. Click on Split Subdocument.

3. Save the master document.

■ Renaming or Moving Subdocuments

You can rename or move a subdocument and still maintain its connection to the master document. Just open the subdocument from within the master document by double-clicking on its subdocument icon. As long as the master document is still open when you save the subdocument, the connection will be preserved. If you're using Windows NT or have Windows 95 configured to support peer-to-peer networking, you can use this process to save a subdocument to another workstation on your network, and it will still appear as part of your master document. You might have to log onto a remote drive to find it, however.

■ Removing a Subdocument

To remove the subdocument, but keep its text in the master document, click on the subdocument icon, and click on the Remove Subdocument button.

To remove the subdocument and also remove its text, click on the subdocument icon and press Delete. The document file remains on the disk, but no longer is attached in any way to the master document.

■ Insert File: Another Way to Combine Word Files

If you want to combine several Word files, and you don't need them to remain as independent files afterwards, use the Insert, File command instead of the Master Document feature:

1. Place your insertion point where you want the file to appear.

2. Choose File from the Insert menu. The File dialog box opens; it resembles the standard Open dialog box.

3. Select the file you want to open. If it's a Word file, the file is inserted. If it's not a Word file, or if it is a file from an early version of Word, Word attempts to convert and insert it—assuming the proper conversion filter is installed on your system.

The more you work with long, complex documents, the more you need tools to manage them. Word provides several long document management tools; you've learned in this chapter about one of the most important, master documents. With master documents, you and your colleagues can edit parts of a document separately, whenever it's more convenient to work that way. But you can manage them together—making sure they're consistently formatted, share the same table of contents, index, and other features.

In the next chapter, you move from traditional print documents to today's revolutionary electronic documents, learning how Word 97, Microsoft Office and Microsoft Internet Explorer work together to provide a comprehensive solution for World Wide Web access and authoring.

- *A Very Brief Introduction to the Internet*

- *Introducing the World Wide Web*

- *Installing Microsoft Explorer*

- *Getting to Know Explorer*

- *Using Explorer with Microsoft Word 97*

- *Creating Web Content*

- *Adding New Formatting to a Web Page*

- *Including Multimedia in Your Web Pages*

- *Working with HTML Source Code*

- *Posting to Your Internet Service Provider's Web Server*

- *Additional Internet Tools Provided with Office 97*

Word on the Net: Create and Connect with a World of Web Data

THE INTERNET HAS REACHED CRITICAL MASS, AND IT'S CHANGING everything. Suddenly, research that once required days in the library is taking only minutes online. Suddenly, entirely new virtual communities are springing up, practically overnight. Suddenly, your company's brochures can be available to every potential online customer on earth, 24 hours a day—even if you're a one-person shop. Suddenly, electronic publishing is making sense for virtually every organization—and practically everyone who prepares documents is having to come to terms with the most revolutionary changes since Gutenberg.

And suddenly, for the first time, Word 97 and Office 97 can help you make the most of this revolution. There's no bigger improvement in Word 97 than its connectedness. Word, together with Internet Explorer and the rest of Microsoft Office, now represents an excellent solution for creating, formatting, and testing Web content. You'll even find a Web Page Wizard that can automate the creation of several of the most common types of Web pages.

In Word 97, you can even access the Web from your Word desktop. You can insert hyperlinks in your Word documents that connect readers directly to sites on the Internet or on other networks. Suddenly, it's child's play to transform Web documents into Word documents, and vice versa. If you purchased Microsoft Office on CD-ROM, you even have a personal Web server for testing your files before you publish them—and a Web Posting Wizard to automate placing them on your Web site.

We'll walk through nearly all of Word's new Internet capabilities in this chapter—showing you exactly how to make the most of them. But first, the basics.

■ A Very Brief Introduction to the Internet

If you're already familiar with the Internet and the World Wide Web, you can skip the next few pages—but if you're one of the majority of PC users who is only now getting connected, this brief introduction is for you.

What is the Internet? Quite simply, it's a network of computers that virtually any computer can connect with, provided that it uses the correct protocols. Those protocols are the Transmission Control Protocol (TCP) and the Internet Protocol (IP), usually referred to as TCP/IP. TCP/IP handles all the nasty details of disassembling your communications into small packets called datagrams, scattering them across the Internet, and then reassembling them as they arrive from various locations at the other end.

This approach to communications is called *packet switching*. As is now the stuff of legend, the Internet harks back, at least in part, to the United States Defense Department's need to make sure computers could stay connected in the event of a nuclear war. With packet switching, if part of a transmission gets lost because one connection fails—whether due to a thermonuclear explosion or any other reason—that data can be quickly resent along other pathways.

TIP. *If you're interested in the real origins of the Internet, you'll find an excellent account in* Where Wizards Stay Up Late, *by Katie Hafner and Matthew Lyon (Simon & Schuster, 1996).*

Much as the federal interstate highway system helped make possible the growth of the suburbs, the Defense Department's investment in computer networking research helped lay the foundation for today's extraordinarily vibrant Internet marketplace and communities. Building on the strong foundation of TCP/IP, Internet users began building a wide variety of services on the Internet. These services include:

- Electronic mail, connecting anyone with Internet access

- Usenet newsgroups and Internet mailing lists, which compile messages about specific topics, and make them available to anyone interested in them—either from a central location or through free "subscriptions" delivered via e-mail

- FTP sites, which store libraries of files, and are generally open to the public for downloading

Each of these services has proven remarkably useful to millions of people. But the service that put the Internet on the front page of *Time* and *Newsweek*—the one that most people think of first these days—is the World Wide Web.

■ Introducing the World Wide Web

Unlike the Internet, which was built on the contributions of thousands of people, the World Wide Web was largely invented by one man: Tim Berners-Lee, then of CERN, Europe's high-energy physics laboratory. He envisioned it as a way to link research information stored at various locations and make it easy for researchers to move between those locations, finding related information quickly and easily.

While the World Wide Web has grown dramatically in sophistication, its underlying elements are still the same. The Web consists of text files ("pages") located on many computers, all prepared using a common set of codes called *Hypertext Markup Language* (HTML). Groups of related files are known as *Web sites*; the first page you see when you enter a Web site is called a *home page*.

Web sites can include virtually any kind of content, from slick advertisements by auto manufacturers to detailed compilations of techniques for electron microscopists. Later in this chapter, we'll point you to some Web sites of specific interest to Word users.

To make Web sites accessible, they are stored on a computer that is connected to the Internet and is running software designed to deliver Web documents. This computer and software are called a *Web server*. The software on your computer which requests Web documents is called a *Web browser*. Microsoft Explorer is a Web browser; so is Netscape Navigator.

The Role of HTML

HTML provides a way of tagging elements of text in a document so that browsers reading these documents can display them consistently. Typically, some of these codes also specify *hypertext* links to other locations, which can either be pages within your site, or other pages elsewhere on the World Wide Web, regardless of where they are physically stored. These codes may also specify links to graphics, sound, or other multimedia elements. When a user clicks on the text associated with these links, they access the new location, image, or multimedia element.

In other words, HTML documents are simply text documents containing HTML tags, as you can see in Figure 14.1 and Figure 14.2, which show a document as it appears on the Web, and the underlying code used to create it. So, underneath all the glitz, creating Web pages simply means creating text files which contain the built-in HTML code needed to make them display properly, and then link to the other locations you want.

Figure 14.1

A page as it appears on the Web

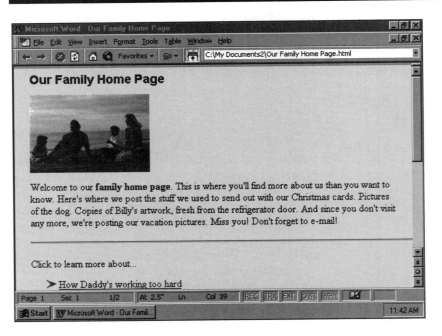

The trick is: How do you create these codes easily and efficiently, without becoming a programmer? And once you've created them, how do you publish them on your Web server? As we'll get to later in this chapter, *that's* where Word 97 and Office 97 come in.

Figure 14.2

The underlying code that makes that page possible

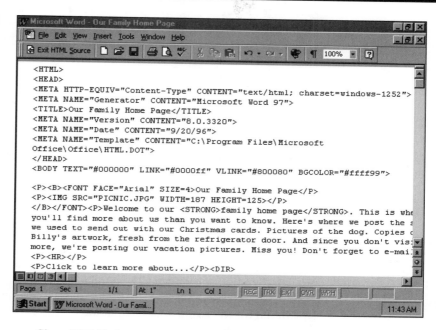

Since HTML documents are unencumbered by formatting information that's specific to one word processor, they can be read by *any* Web browser, using *any* computer connected to the Web—Windows, Mac, UNIX, or whatever. That's the beauty of it: While HTML isn't perfectly standardized, you can create basic HTML pages without worrying too much about the hardware and software capabilities of the people who are accessing your Web site. (Admittedly, things *do* get more complex when you start adding bells and whistles, however.)

Imagine you're a corporation: You can now create an internal Web site, called an *intranet*—and store all your current policies, forms, and other company information there. Then, you can give a Web browser to everyone that works for you, and they can access this information through your corporate network, regardless of what other software they have, or which computer they're running it on.

Because HTML is free, and Microsoft's Explorer 3.01 Web browser is free, and so is Microsoft's Internet Information Server, the full-featured Web server included with Windows NT Server 4.0, your start-up software and hardware costs can be minimal. (*People-related* costs are another story, needless to say.) And you've finally found a solution to the perennial problem of delivering all the current information your people need, without inundating them with paper. It's no wonder businesses have become so excited about the Internet.

Incidentally, the Web's platform-independence is exactly why it worried Microsoft so much: If people began using browsers as their predominant applications, who would need Windows? Microsoft's answer has been twofold: to make Windows and Microsoft applications the best way to use the Web—and to give away extensive Web capabilities at little or no cost, undercutting the business of its competitors.

■ Installing Microsoft Explorer

OK, all of you people who skipped those Internet basics: we're back.

Word 97 connects to the Web through Microsoft Explorer 3.01, so in order to take advantage of Word's Web tools, you'll need to install Internet Explorer.

As we've mentioned, Explorer is essentially free: The only question is how to get your hands on it. If you've purchased Microsoft Office on CD-ROM, the answer is easy: You already have it. (Otherwise you can download it from Microsoft's Internet site if you already have a Web or FTP connection; you can get it from commercial information services such as MSN, CompuServe or AOL; or you can purchase it inexpensively at retail.)

On the Microsoft Office CD-ROM, you'll find Explorer in the folder \Valupack\Iexplore. Double-click the file Msie301.exe, or double-click on the icon Setup for Microsoft Internet Explorer 3.01 that may appear on your desktop. The installation process begins immediately; Explorer doesn't install through a separate setup program the way most Microsoft applications do. By default, Explorer installs in the \Program Files\Microsoft Internet folder.

■ Getting to Know Explorer

Now that you've installed it, let's take a quick look around Internet Explorer, as shown in Figure 14.3. As you work with Explorer, keep in mind that Microsoft's ultimate goal is to integrate Explorer-like functionality into Windows 95 itself—so learning Explorer gives you a head start on the future of the operating system itself.

In Explorer, you can always see where you are on the Web in the Address box. If you've installed Explorer from the Office CD-ROM, when you connect to the Internet, Explorer will display the Microsoft Office Home Page, shown in Figure 14.3.

You can move to another location by entering the Web address in the Address box, or by clicking a blue or purple *hyperlink* in your current Web document. (By default, hyperlinks are blue if you've never followed them before; purple if you have already followed them at least once.) If you'd like to take advantage of some interesting links that Microsoft has built in, click the Links button to the right of the address line: It displays links to several locations Microsoft has developed to help Explorer users find their way around (see Figure 14.4).

Figure 14.3

Explorer's default Start
Page, the Microsoft
Office Home Page

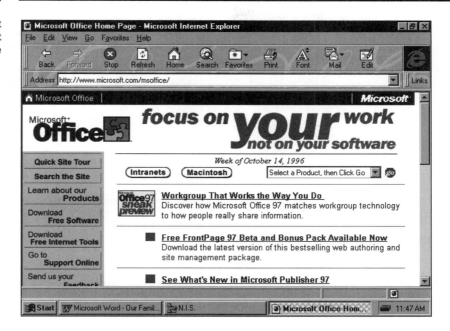

Figure 14.4

Displaying Microsoft's
built-in Links

Built-in links

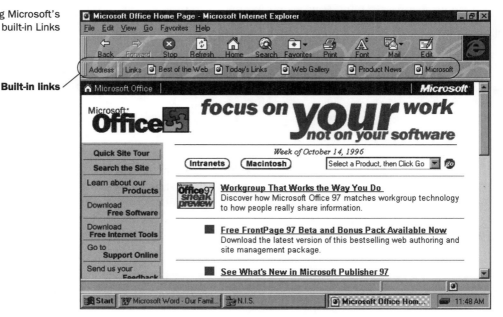

Most of the tools you'll need to use Explorer can be found in the Explorer toolbar, shown in Figure 14.5.

Figure 14.5

The Internet
Explorer toolbar

Back takes you to the Web page you were looking at previously. When you move back, the *Forward* button becomes available to return you to the following Web page. *Stop* instructs Explorer to stop loading a page; perhaps you've decided the graphics are taking too long to load, or you don't want to go to this destination after all. *Refresh* tells Explorer to load the same page again. Clicking Refresh occasionally delivers more up-to-date information, but more often it's used to simply try again to load a page you're having problems with.

The *Home* button takes you to the Web page that Internet Explorer opens when you first start it. By default, this is the Microsoft Office Home Page, but you can change your start page. Choose View, Options, Navigation, and specify a new address for the Start Page.

The *Search* button takes you to a Web page designed for Web searching. By default, this page is **http://www.msn.com/access/allinone.asp**, a page stored on the Microsoft Network site, from where you can connect to many Web search resources. However, if you prefer to use a specific Web search site, like Yahoo, you can set Explorer to always go there when you click Search. Display View, Options, Navigation. Choose Search Page from the Page drop-down box. Then, in the Address box, enter the Web address of your preferred Search page. When you finish specifying the search page, click OK.

Clicking *Favorites* on the Explorer toolbar lists all the sites you've told Explorer you want quick access to. When you choose a Favorite, Explorer connects you directly to that location. (If you've used Netscape Navigator, Favorites are the equivalent of Navigator Bookmarks.)

If you're at a location you like, you can make it a Favorite by clicking Favorites, Add to Favorites. Explorer asks you to confirm or edit the name of the location (see Figure 14.6). Choose OK, and the new location is added to your Favorites list. Favorites are the Internet equivalent of Windows 95 shortcuts; in fact, they're simply text files containing two lines of text in the following format:

```
[InternetShortcut]
URL=http://www.sitename.com
```

Favorites are stored in the \Windows\Favorites folder alongside any non-Web Favorites you may have placed there.

Figure 14.6

Creating a new Favorite

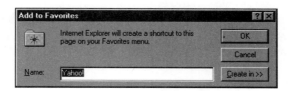

Let's cover a few more Explorer toolbar buttons. The *Print* button displays the Print dialog box, from where you can print either the entire current Web page you're currently accessing, or the specific text you've selected. *Font* allows you to enlarge or shrink the text and headline fonts used by Explorer. *Mail* displays a menu of options that utilize Microsoft Outlook or your other compatible e-mail program. Finally, *Edit* displays Microsoft Word—opening it, if necessary—and copies your current Web page there, so you can edit it.

Organizing Your Favorites

As you start creating more and more Favorites, your list may begin to get quite unwieldy. Fortunately, Explorer makes it easy to organize your Favorites into folders much like the ones you're already accustomed to in Windows 95. To organize some or all of your Favorites into folders, choose Favorites, Organize Favorites. The Organize Favorites dialog box opens, as shown in Figure 14.7.

Figure 14.7

The Explorer Organize Favorites dialog box

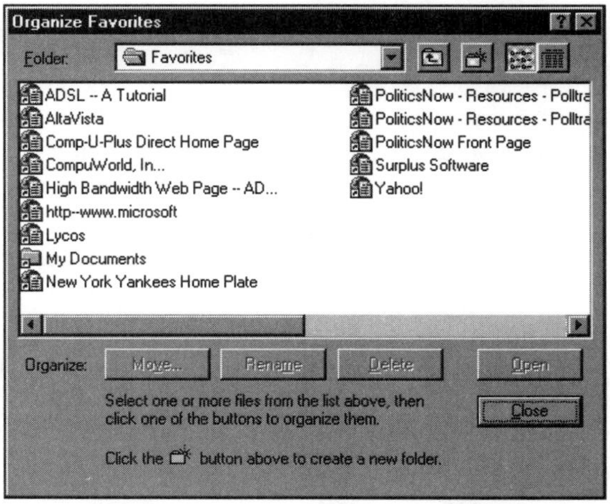

To create a new folder, click the Create New Folder toolbar button. A new folder appears in the Folder window; type a name for the folder and press Enter. Now, you can drag other Favorites into this folder. When you display Favorites from Explorer, the folder will appear as a cascaded menu item, as shown in Figure 14.8.

Figure 14.8

Displaying shortcut folders

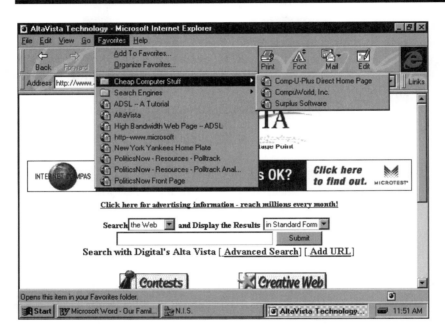

Working Off line in Explorer

Many Internet users don't realize it, but you can do much of your Internet work *off line*—and maybe save a few bucks. While you're connected, Internet Explorer stores the pages it downloads in a special hard disk location called a *cache*. This has two benefits. It means Explorer can display a page much more quickly when you request a connection to it, because that page is already stored on your hard disk. It also means you can access that page even when you aren't connected to the Internet. You can use this to your advantage—especially if you aren't blessed with a second telephone line, an unlimited-usage Internet account, and an Internet service provider who's only a local phone call away. Establish your connection; quickly visit all the sites and pages you're interested in; then get off-line, and use the Forward and Back toolbar buttons to read the pages at your leisure. The hyperlinks still work: Click on one, and Explorer will re-establish your Internet connection and take you there.

By default, Explorer sets aside at least 2 percent of your hard disk space for its cache, using a higher percentage if you have less hard drive space available. The default cache is stored in the \Windows\Temporary Internet Files folder. You can increase or reduce the cache size, depending on your needs. You can also move your cache to another hard disk where you may have more space.

To make these changes, choose View, Options, Advanced, and click Settings. The Settings dialog box appears (Figure 14.9). You can use the slider to control how much disk space is used. To move your cache, click Move Folder. The Browse for Folder dialog box appears (Figure 14.10); select a folder, and choose OK.

Figure 14.9

The Settings dialog box

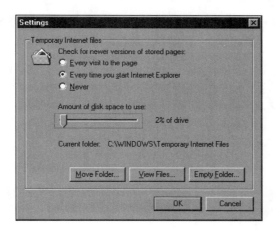

Figure 14.10

The Browse for
Folder dialog box

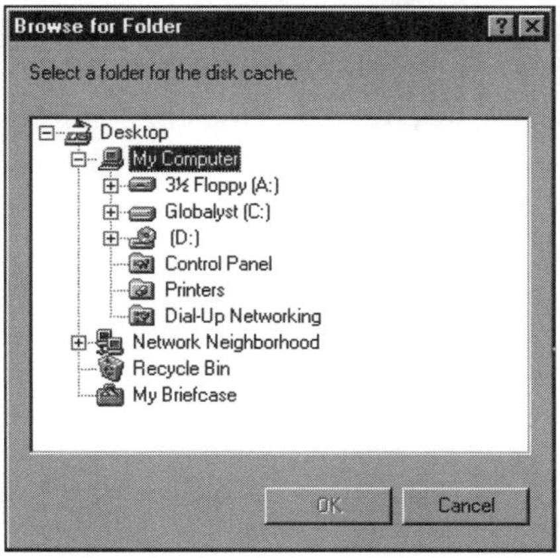

Viewing HTML Source Files in Explorer

We've mentioned that all those highly graphical Web pages you've seen are, underneath their fancy trimmings, simply HTML-encoded text files. The fastest way to get familiar with what HTML code looks like is to strip those pages bare, and view the underlying code. To do this in Explorer, choose View, Source. A Windows Notepad window will appear, displaying the underlying HTML source codes associated with the page you're viewing (see Figure 14.11).

Figure 14.11

Viewing HTML source in a Notepad window

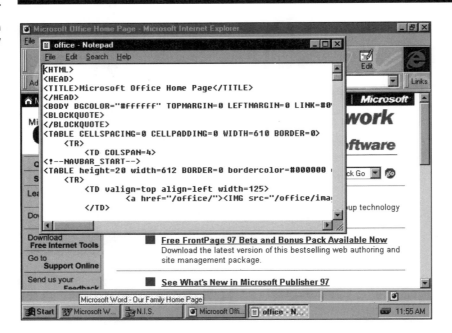

You can save the file either by choosing File, Save from the Notepad window, or by choosing Save As File in the Explorer window. From the Explorer Save As dialog box, you have two choices:

- *Save as HTML*, which saves the file with the HTML codes intact, or

- *Save as Plain Text*, which eliminates all the codes and stores only the document text.

■ Using Explorer with Microsoft Word 97

You may be wondering: All this is very nice, but when do we start using Word? *Now.*

Microsoft has made it easy to access Explorer through Word, and several of Explorer's features, such as Favorites, are closely integrated with Word.

NOTE. *The integration between Word 97 and Internet Explorer 3.01 isn't as tight or as consistent as it might be. To draw the contrast, if you were to embed an Excel worksheet in a Word document, and then double-click to edit that worksheet, Word's menus and toolbars change to Excel's; if you then click outside the worksheet, the menus switch back. In contrast, when you click a Web toolbar button to display a Web site, a separate full-screen copy of Explorer loads. There's a little more integration in the opposite direction: If you create a Start Page that's a Word document on your local hard disk instead of a Web document, loading that Start Page loads a copy of Explorer with Word menus and toolbars added. In any event, Microsoft's direction is clear: Future versions of Explorer will be ever more tightly integrated with Word, Office, and Windows 95.*

To access the Web from Word, first display the Web Toolbar, as shown in Figure 14.12. Choose View, Toolbars, Web.

Figure 14.12

Word's Web toolbar

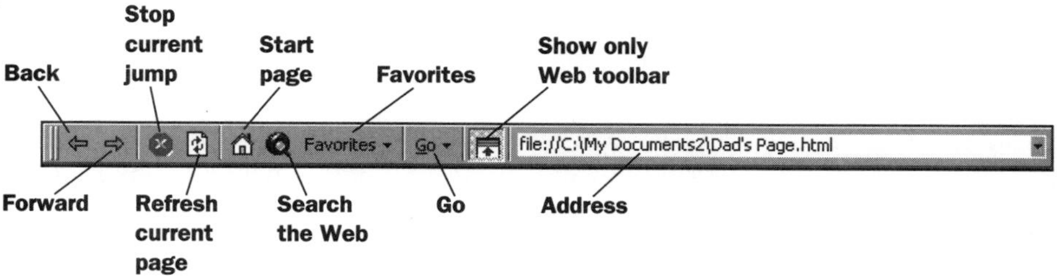

You'll see some familiar suspects here. The four buttons at the left, which are usually grayed out and unavailable, are navigation tools, comparable to buttons you've seen in Explorer. These buttons can help you move among Word documents that contain hyperlinks. For example, if you are creating a Web site containing several pages, and you want to move among them to make sure the links work properly, you can use these buttons. This will be discussed later in the chapter; you can also learn more about hyperlinks in Chapter 12.

WARNING. *Be careful with the Refresh Current Page button. This button becomes usable when you open a document and then make changes to it. When you click Refresh Current Page, you're asked whether you want to discard your edits and reload the document as it exists on your hard disk or network. It's all too easy to discard document changes this way.*

The *Start Page* button establishes a Web connection, displays Explorer, and takes you to the Microsoft Office Home Page, or whatever page you have specified as your Start page.

The *Search the Web* button also connects you to the Web and displays Explorer; then it takes you to Microsoft's Search page. From here, you can search Microsoft's resources on the Web, or search the entire Web using any of six leading search engines:

- *Alta Vista*, which attempts to catalog all individual Web pages and newsgroups.

- *Excite*, which specializes in independent reviews of Web sites.

- *Infoseek*, which shows Web pages matching your search criteria and provides lists of related pages.

- *Lycos*, an extremely large compendium of Web page outlines and abstracts.

- *Magellan*, which reviews and rates sites.

- *Yahoo*, one of the first prominent search engines; organized by category, it provides site summaries, current news, and special search areas for children and for residents of some major cities.

The *Favorites* button on Word's Web toolbar displays the same list of Favorites you created in Explorer—including any Favorites folders you created.

The *Go* button displays a menu of options. Open displays the Open Internet Address dialog box (see Figure 14.13). Enter the address where you want to go, and Explorer will open to take you there. Other options include *Set Start Page* and *Set Search Page.* When you change the Start Page or Search Page in Word, you've changed it for both Word and Explorer. However, you don't have as much flexibility from within Word: You can only change the Start Page or Search Page *to the current document you have open,* not to another site on the World Wide Web. The Show Only Web toolbar hides all other toolbars, leaving more space to view whatever you're viewing in Word—whether it's a Web page or a regular document.

Finally, the Address box displays your current Word document, and all the recent Web pages you've visited. When you select an HTML file stored on your computer or network, or if you select a Web site, Explorer opens and connects to that location.

Figure 14.13

The Open Internet
Address dialog box

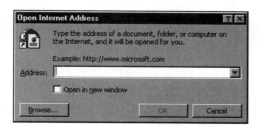

Internet Resources For Word Users

Now that you know how to use Explorer and Word to get where you want on
the Internet, umm, where do you want to go today?

Any discussion of Internet resources for Word users has to begin with all
those menu items hanging off of Help, Microsoft on the Web (see Figure
14.14). Each of them connects you to a specific page on Microsoft's Web site.

Figure 14.14

Microsoft on the Web
commands

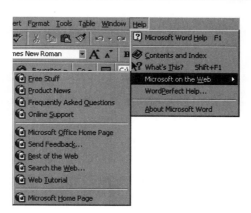

Table 14.1 shows a current list. Keep in mind that, as always, Internet addresses are subject to change.

Independent Sources of Information about Word

As you would expect, there are a lot of people talking about Word on the
Internet—and there are many independent sources of information to be
found there. In this section, we'll highlight some of the best.

Table 14.1

Microsoft on the Web
(Web addresses should
be entered on one line.)

THIS MENU COMMAND...	CONNECTS YOU TO...	WHERE YOU CAN DO THIS...
Free Stuff	http://www.microsoft.com/word/fs_wd.htm	Connect to upgrades, templates, and other Word freebies
Product News	http://www.microsoft.com/word/default.htm	Get up-to-date news about Word and Microsoft Office
Frequently Asked Questions	http://www.microsoft.com/MSWordSupport/content/faq/	Get the answers to frequently asked questions about Word
Online Support	http://www.microsoft.com/MSWordSupport	Access the Microsoft Knowledge Base, a database of thousands of technical articles about Word, Office, Windows 95, Windows NT, and other Microsoft products
Microsoft Office Home Page	http://www.microsoft.com/office/default.htm	Get information about Microsoft Office
Send Feedback	http://www.microsoft.com/office/feedback/fb_ofc.htm	Send Microsoft a message
Best of the Web	http://www.microsoft.com/default2.asp	See Microsoft's Best of the Web page, with regularly updated links to Web sites worth visiting
Search the Web	http://www.microsoft.com/access/allinone.asp	Access Microsoft's combined Search page, discussed earlier in this chapter
Web Tutorial	http://www.msn.com/tutorial/default.html	Access a Web page containing basic information about using the Web
Microsoft Home Page	http://www.microsoft.com	Access Microsoft's home page, from where you can get information about any product or service

WordInfo (www.wordinfo.com) (see Figure 14.15) is a site maintained by Alki Software Corporation, a company that specializes in add-in products for Microsoft Word. The site compiles current news about Microsoft Word, How To techniques and user tips, as well as links to other sites with Word-specific information. WordInfo's WebIndex page also contains an excellent Reference Shelf with links to a wide variety of online reference materials for writers.

Figure 14.15

WordInfo site sponsored
by Alki Software

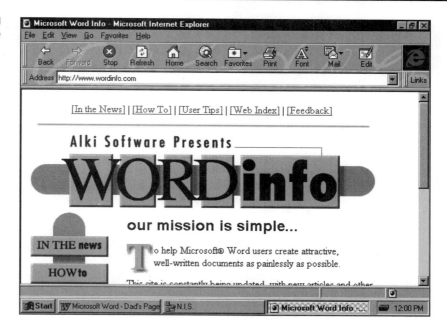

The Unofficial Word for Windows Home Page (www.nd.edu/~crunge/word.html) compiles information and links about Word updates, bug fixes, Web publishing, and legal applications for Word.

Baarns Publishing for Microsoft Office (www.baarns.com) compiles frequently asked questions, developer's information, and software solutions for Microsoft Word and Office (see Figure 14.16).

WordCentral for Microsoft Word for Windows (www.inetnow.net/~hacker/WordCentral/index.htm) compiles add-on software for Microsoft Word for Windows, including an extensive library of both shareware and freeware (see Figure 14.17).

KnowHow on the Web On-Line Guide: Word for Windows (www.knowhow.com/winword.htm) compiles essays about various advanced Word features.

Woody Leonhard's Welcome to Woody's Office Power Pack site (www.wopr.com) brings together insider's information and Office-related software. At this site, you can subscribe to Woody's Office Watch, a free weekly newsletter for power users of Word and Office.

Figure 14.16

Baarns Publishing site for
Microsoft Office

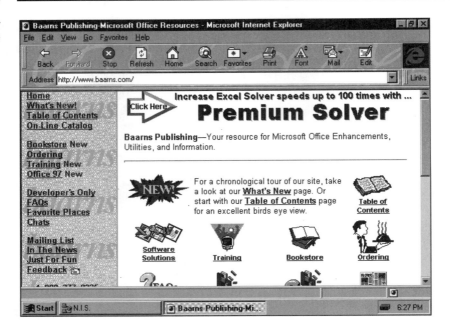

Figure 14.17

WordCentral site

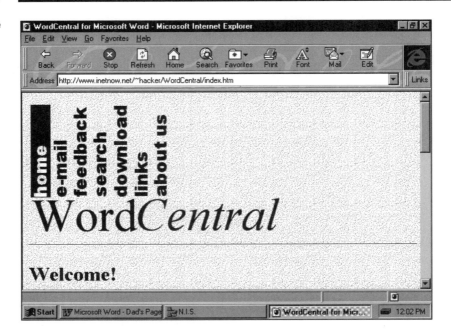

Word-Related Mailing Lists and Newsgroups

In addition, there are several Usenet newsgroups and Internet mailing lists focused specifically on Microsoft Word. These include newsgroups Microsoft has established to replace the forums it previously operated on CompuServe.

Most mailing lists contain a database of Frequently Asked Questions; check those databases before you ask a question of your own. Mailing lists have two addresses. One address is the name of the list; the other, called the *listserv* address, is the address from where the list is managed. To subscribe to a list, send a one-line e-mail message to the listserv address, using the following format:

```
SUB nameoflist yourname
```

Table 14.2 contains a list of Word-related mailing lists.

Table 14.2

Word-Related mailing lists

NAME	WHAT IT COVERS...	LISTSERV ADDRESS
WORD-PC	Mailing list covering Word for Windows and Word for DOS	LISTSERV@ufobi1.uni-forst.gwdg.de
TECHWR-L	Mailing list with information for technical communicators, with extensive coverage of Word	TECHCOMM@LISTSERV.NCSU.EDU

Within a day, you will normally get confirmation of your subscription, along with details about the list you've subscribed to. Thereafter, your e-mail box will be filled with copies of messages sent to the mailing list. If you later decide to unsubscribe, send another e-mail message to the listserv address:

```
SIGNOFF nameoflist
```

To access a newsgroup, you need to install a newsgroup reader program. Fortunately, that's free, too. (Heck, you could get used to this.) Unfortunately, it's not in the Office ValuPack: You'll have to download the file mailnews.exe from Microsoft's Web site at http://www.microsoft.com/ie/download/ieadd.htm. To install Internet Explorer's Mail and News Readers, just double-click mailnews.exe once you've downloaded it. Then, choose Go, Read News in the Internet Explorer to walk through the process of getting access to newsgroups. Since there are thousands of newsgroups, this will take a few minutes, but once you're done, you'll have access permanently. If the newsgroup you're interested in doesn't show up on the list that appears, check to make sure your Internet Service Provider carries it on their servers. Word-related newsgroups are listed in Table 14.3.

Table 14.3

Word-Related Newsgroups

NAME	WHAT IT COVERS...
comp.os.ms-windows.apps.word-proc	Overall coverage of Word and other Windows word processing software
bit.mailserv.word-pc	Overall coverage of Word
microsoft.public.word.general	General Microsoft Word issues not covered in other Microsoft newsgroups
microsoft.public.word.applicationerrors	Errors, error messages, and potential bugs
microsoft.public.word.conversions	Importing and exporting files and graphics among file formats
microsoft.public.word.formattinglongdocs	Formatting, styles, master documents, and other issues related to working with long documents
microsoft.public.word.mailmergefields	Mail Merge and all Word fields
microsoft.public.word.OLEinteropq	OLE and DDE as used by Word
microsoft.public.word.printingfonts	Printing and fonts
microsoft.public.word.programming	Programming Word with VBA (and programming previous versions of Word with WordBasic)
microsoft.public.word.setupnetworking	Using Word in a networked environment

■ Creating Web Content

Until now, we've focused on ways you can use Word and Office to access Web content and resources that already exist. Now it's time to learn how to use Word to create *your own* documents for posting on the World Wide Web.

First, you'll learn about the process of creating Web documents with Word; then, you'll learn to transform existing documents into HTML files. After that, you'll learn how to create HTML files from scratch—and take advantage of Word's built-in Web Page Wizard. After that, you'll take a closer look at the HTML code itself, so you can refine your documents to look exactly as you want them to. Finally, we'll take a look at the Office Web Page Posting Wizard, which helps you place your Web pages on a Web site where others can see them.

Understanding the Process of Creating a Web Page with Word

Creating a Web page with Word is typically an iterative process that moves back and forth between several views of the document:

- Edit the content of the page in Normal view or one of Word's other views, including Online Layout, Page Layout, or Outline view;

- Preview the way it will look by clicking Web Page Preview; Word opens Internet Explorer 3.01 and your page in it;

- Look over your page in Explorer; then exit Explorer and return to Word to make any necessary changes. Some of these changes may require editing HTML code directly; if so, choose View, HTML Source to view the HTML text file which underlies your document.

Of course, before you actually publish your page, you should test it on competitive browsers—particularly the market share leaders, Netscape Navigator 2.0 and 3.0—to make sure that it will display properly for viewers using those browsers.

You should also plan for the server where your Web pages will ultimately be posted. If you will be posting files on your Internet Service Provider's server, speak with them about how to structure your files, and about the type of systems they will be run on.

Your first challenge will be to make sure that all the hyperlinks you create will still work when you move your files to the server. To do so, create a single folder for all your Web pages and associated images; if your Web site begins to get large, create subfolders within that folder.

As described later, make sure that when you create hyperlinks to other files on your own Web site, you use relative links, rather than absolute hyperlinks that depend on files being in the same location *on your hard drive.* If you create relative hyperlinks, you can move all your Web pages, images, and subfolders together, and they will still work when they arrive.

Conversely, if you are establishing links to other, existing Web sites, use absolute links that include the specific Web site Uniform Resource Locator (URL) address. So, if your Web site takes a political stand, and you want to encourage people who agree to share their opinions with the president, you can create an absolute link such as **http://www.whitehouse.gov**, which always delivers Web users straight to the White House, no matter where your files are located.

Just as important, be aware that long file names and hyperlinks which make perfect sense in a Windows 95 compliant environment may not work if you're posting to a server that doesn't recognize them—for example, a UNIX or Macintosh server, which can only read the truncated short file names that accompany Windows 95 files. This may require you to rename files before posting them.

One final thing to watch out for: As will be stressed repeatedly in this chapter, HTML files are text files—straight ASCII. If you inadvertently save them using the standard Word format, they won't work.

Converting a Word Document to HTML

Let's start with the simplest case: you already have a Word document open, and you'd like to transform it into HTML. Choose Save As HTML from the File menu; Word saves the file with an HTM extension, and displays the HTML version in your editing window.

You'll notice the Word interface changes immediately, to indicate that you're now editing an HTML document. You're now in Word's Web Page Authoring Environment (see Figure 14.18).

Figure 14.18

Word's Web Page Authoring Environment

Web toolbar —

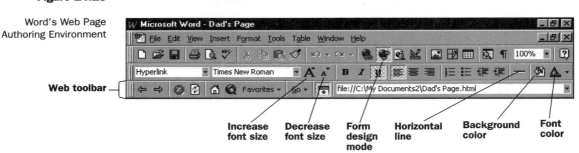

Increase font size   Decrease font size   Form design mode   Horizontal line   Background color   Font color

For example, on the standard toolbar, two new buttons appear: the Web Page Preview button, and the Form Design button. On the formatting toolbar, the Outside Border button is replaced by a horizontal line button, and while the Font Size drop-down box disappears, it is replaced by buttons that allow you to increase or decrease the size of fonts. There are even more significant changes to Word's menus, as we'll discuss later.

Many of these changes reflect the realities of working with HTML. For example, HTML's device-independence—its ability to run on any computer with any browser—means that you can't assign a specific font size to HTML text. Rather, you assign one of seven font size *levels*, and the browser which reads the file will translate those to the specific fonts and sizes it happens to use.

How Your Document's Appearance May Change When Converted to HTML

When you convert a Word document to HTML, Word closes the original document and opens a new text file formatted with HTML. In Figure 14.19 and Figure 14.20, a sample document is shown before and after conversion to HTML.

Figure 14.19

A sample Word
document before
conversion to HTML...

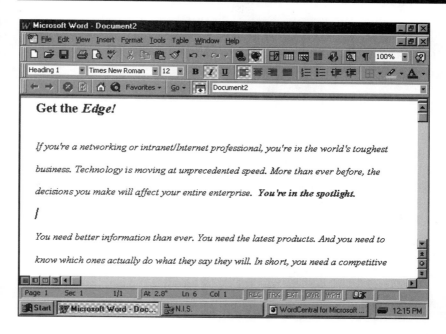

You're likely to see several changes between your original document
and the new HTML document.

For one thing, it's common to discover that Word's HTML formatting
has added more space between paragraphs than you would like. The easiest
solution is to use styles in your original Word documents, which contain extra
space after each paragraph—and to use Shift+Enter to specify line breaks instead of paragraph breaks wherever appropriate. Later, you'll also learn an
easy way to fix this problem in the HTML source code.

If your document is complex, you may find that much of your formatting
hasn't survived the move from Word to HTML. In some cases, HTML simply
doesn't offer an equivalent option to the formatting that Word can do in its
native format. For example, highlighting, page borders, and margins are lost
when you convert a file to HTML. Your document styles are converted to direct formatting, assuming HTML can support that formatting. Field codes disappear; your HTML documents include the information those fields were
displaying when you converted the file. Tabs are converted to spaces—which
is yet another reason *never* to use tabs to design tabular information.

In other cases, Word formatting disappears because it's meaningless in a
Web environment. For example, by definition, every HTML file is equivalent
to one Web page, so who needs page numbering? In still other cases, Word

Figure 14.20

...and the same
document after
conversion to HTML

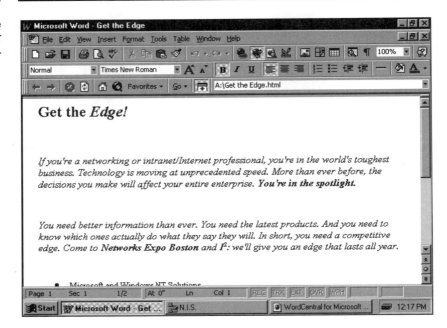

simply hasn't implemented a conversion. For instance, Word drawing objects such as AutoShapes disappear when converted into HTML.

Despite these limitations, many Word formatting features *are* retained. For example, bold, italic and single-underline text is converted properly; left, center, and right-alignments are maintained (though justification is not). Indents are also maintained. Moreover, you can select these features in the Web Page Authoring Environment using the same toolbar buttons and menu items as you do elsewhere in Word—even though Word is actually entering HTML codes in your Web pages instead of its own formatting codes.

Graphics stored in your document are automatically converted to Web-compatible GIF files (unless they are already JPEG (JPG) files, which can also be read by Web browsers.)

Finally, Word tables are still displayed as tables when you convert them to HTML—assuming they are displayed on a browser that can show tables. Some earlier browsers couldn't. However, some table formatting, such as varying table widths and table borders, is lost.

Creating a New Web Page from Scratch

To create a new Web page instead of converting an existing Word document, choose File, New, Web Pages. To create an empty Web page—that is, open an empty text file and display Word's Web Page Authoring Environment—choose Blank Web Page and click OK. To create a Web page based on one of Word's built-in formats, choose Web Page Wizard and click OK. The Web Page Wizard dialog box opens, as shown in Figure 14.21.

Figure 14.21

The Web Page Wizard dialog box

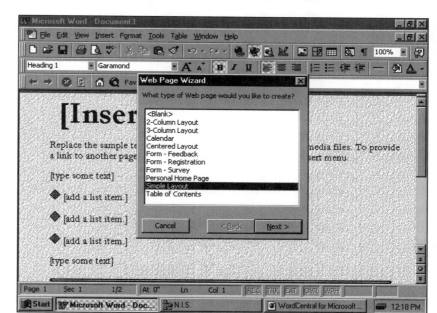

In the background, you can see your current settings; by default, Word displays a Simple Layout. Choose the type of Web page you want; Word displays the new layout in the background.

Click Next. You're asked which style you wish to use for your Web page (see Figure 14.22). Based on the style you choose, Word will include appropriate background textures and clip art for bullets and borders. If you are creating several Web pages, apply the same style to all of them, and you'll have a consistent, professionally designed Web site without hiring a professional designer.

Click Finish, and the Web Page Wizard will generate your Web page. Now that Word has created the framework, you can replace Word's boilerplate text with your own.

In most cases, Word generates pages with boilerplate hyperlinks; you'll need to specify where you want those links to connect. However, if this is the first Web document you're creating for your site, you won't be able to create those links yet: There won't be any other pages to link with.

Figure 14.22

Choosing a visual style from Word's built-in Web page formats

First, create each of the pages you're planning, and save them all in the same folder. If you insert graphics, Word saves them as GIF image files in the same folder when you save your file. Then, start creating the links. To create a link, choose Insert, Hyperlink. The Insert Hyperlink dialog box opens, as shown in Figure 14.23. (You can find more detailed discussion of hyperlinks in Chapter 12.)

Figure 14.23

Inserting a hyperlink

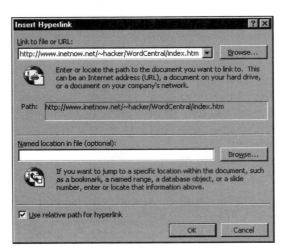

Click Browse to find the file you want to link with in the Link to File box. Choose OK. You're returned to the Insert Hyperlink dialog box. Make sure the Use relative path for hyperlink box is checked; this ensures that when you move all the files in the folder to your Web site, the links will remain intact. Choose OK, and the hyperlink appears in your document.

■ Adding New Formatting to a Web Page

As mentioned earlier, many (but not all) of Word's standard formatting capabilities are available through Word's new Web Page Authoring Environment. Word's formatting menus and dialog boxes are revamped to reflect the capabilities and limitations of HTML.

Formatting Text

To format text, choose Format, Font. The Font dialog box appears, as shown in Figure 14.24. You can choose a font; one of seven specific font sizes; a font color, and basic font effects, including bold, italic, underline, strikethrough, superscript, or subscript. Remember that choosing a font in Word does not necessarily guarantee that viewers of your Web site will have that font—or that their browsers will display it properly.

Figure 14.24

The Font dialog box as it appears in Word's Web Page Authoring Environment

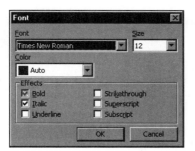

TIP. *If you simply must maintain fonts and formatting precisely, consider authoring your Web pages using a plug-in program like Adobe Acrobat, which embeds precise formatting information in documents. Users will then need to use the Acrobat Reader to display the documents, but that reader is widely available, and you can easily provide a link to Web sites where it can be downloaded at no charge. Alternatively, you can provide free Word viewers that Microsoft has created, which allow Word documents to be viewed from Netscape-compatible browsers without being converted to HTML documents first.*

Adding Graphical Bullets

To insert bullets into text, select the paragraphs you want to bullet, and click the Bullets buttons on the formatting toolbar—just as you would if you were working on a standard Word document.

However, there are a few tricks up Word's sleeve when you're working in the Web Page Authoring Environment. For example, you can use images in place of bullets. To change Word's standard round bullet into an image, or to use an image in the first place:

1. Select the paragraphs you want to format with bullets.

2. Choose Format, Bullets and Numbering. The Bullets and Numbering dialog box appears, as shown in Figure 14.25. This is a much more streamlined dialog box than you're accustomed to in Word. The bullets shown are not characters from the Windows 95 Symbol font. (You wouldn't want them to be—many of the people viewing your Web site won't have this font.) Rather, most of them are separate GIF files.

3. Choose a bullet. Or, if you want to see more choices, click More to view the Insert Picture dialog box (Figure 14.26). Select a bullet there.

4. Click OK. (If you are selecting a bullet from the Insert Picture dialog box, click Insert.)

Figure 14.25

The Bullets and Numbering dialog box as it appears from within the Web Page Authoring Environment

Once you've inserted a custom bullet, if you press Enter at the end of a list to add a new item, the following line will display another copy of the same custom bullet.

Adding Numbering

To number a list of items, select it and click the Numbering button on the formatting toolbar. The items will automatically be numbered, and (as elsewhere in Word), if you add or insert new items in the numbered list, all numbering will be updated accordingly.

Figure 14.26

Choosing among
more bullets

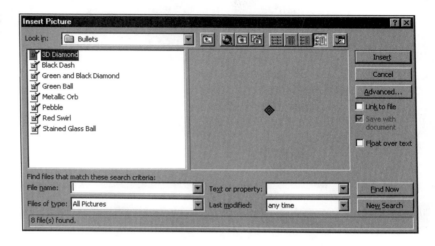

Formatting Text Colors

To change the color of text, select text in the paragraph you want to reformat, and choose one of 16 standard text colors available for Web pages. Note that HTML only supports "colorizing" entire paragraphs—so you can't select and add color only to a specific phrase.

You can, however, specify the colors that will be used by hyperlinks, or hyperlinks that have already been followed. To do so, choose Format, Text Colors. The Text Colors dialog box opens, as shown in Figure 14.27. Choose a Hyperlink color from the Hyperlink drop-down box; choose a followed hyperlink color from the Followed hyperlink drop-down box. Note, however, that Word's default colors are the ones that most Web users expect to see; other colors might confuse them.

Figure 14.27

Text Colors dialog box

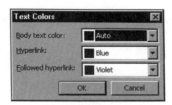

Using Background Colors and Fill Effects

It's common for Web pages to use color or textures as background elements to add visual interest. In Word's Web Page Authoring Environment, you can add a color by clicking the Background button (the paint can icon) on the formatting toolbar. If you want to choose a different color, click More Colors; the Colors dialog box opens. Here, you can select a color from the palette that appears, or choose Custom to create a custom color. (Choosing colors, and creating custom colors are covered in more depth in Chapter 17.)

To use one of Word's built-in background textures, click the Background button on the formatting toolbar, and click Fill Effects. The Fill Effects dialog box opens, showing a library of background textures you can use (see Figure 14.28). Choose one and click OK. For more information on Word's textures, and on additional textures that may be available from the Office CD-ROM or other sources, see Chapter 17.

Figure 14.28

Choosing a texture background

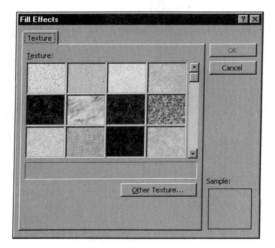

The more colors and textures you use, the more important it becomes to test your Web site on different browsers and different types of computers. If you're not careful, a texture that appears to add an attractive highlight on one system can make the accompanying text unreadable on another.

Inserting Horizontal Lines

HTML doesn't support the wide variety of left, right, top, and bottom borderlines that Word normally provides. However, you *can* insert a wide variety of decorative horizontal lines to separate areas of text or images on your Web pages. To insert Word's default decorative borderline, position your insertion point where you want it to appear, and click the Horizontal Line button on the formatting toolbar. The results are shown in Figure 14.29.

Figure 14.29

Word's standard
decorative horizontal line

Horizontal line

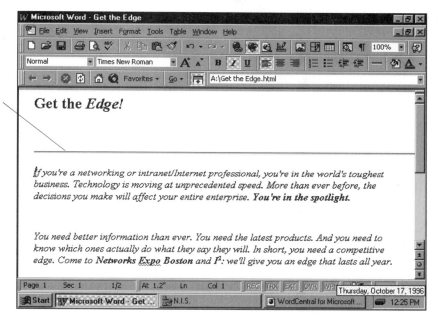

To choose from a broader selection, choose Insert, Horizontal Line. The Horizontal Line dialog box opens, providing ten choices (see Figure 14.30); select one and click OK. If you want additional choices, click More; Word displays other borders in the Insert Picture dialog box. When you select a border, Word previews it, as shown in Figure 14.31. Choose Insert to place it in your Web page.

Figure 14.30

The Horizontal
Line dialog box

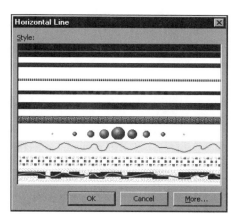

Figure 14.31

Choosing from additional decorative horizontal lines in the Insert Picture dialog box

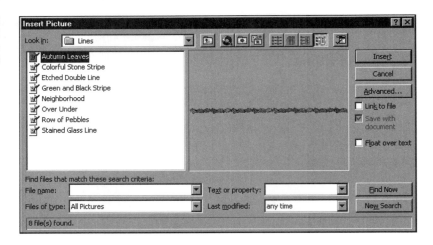

Using HTML Styles Built into Word

When you edit a document using Word's Web Page Authoring Environment, the style choices associated with ordinary documents are supplemented with new style choices that correspond to formatting which is supported by HTML, and understood by Web browsers. You can see that the styles correspond to the types of text that HTML's developers expected to be most commonly used in Web pages; if you use them, you build a document with a loose but fairly well-defined structure. These styles, along with their corresponding functions and HTML tags, are shown in Table 14.4.

You can select styles the same way you normally do, from the Style box on the formatting toolbar. If you select a standard Word style rather than an HTML style, when you save the document Word will attempt to convert your style formatting into HTML formatting. If you create or modify a style to include formatting elements that HTML can't understand, they will be lost in the HTML document.

Changing HTML Table Properties

Earlier, we mentioned that tables translated from Word to HTML documents lose the heights and widths you specified in Word. However, you can create *new* tables with custom heights and widths, using the same table design tools Word provides elsewhere. You can insert a matrix of table cells of equal width and height using the Insert Table button. Or you can draw a table by clicking the Draw Table button and drawing your table with the pen-shaped mouse pointer. Once you have a table—whether you created it your-

Table 14.4

HTML Styles
Built into Word

STYLE NAME	WHAT IT'S USED FOR	EQUIVALENT HTML TAG
Address	Italicizes the address of the document's author	\<ADDRESS>
Blockquote	Indents and italicizes a quotation from another source	\<BLOCKQUOTE>
CITE	Defines text as a citation from another source	\<CITE>
CODE	Defines text as computer code for instance, a line from a sample program	\<CODE>
Comment	Turns the text into a comment that only appears when viewing HTML source code	\<COMMENT>
Definition	Defines text as an italicized definition; might be used in a glossary	\<DD>
Definition List	Defines text as part of a definition list, containing both a definition term and definition text	\<DL>
Definition Term	Defines text as a definition term	\<DT>
Emphasis	Emphasizes text; most browsers interpret this command by italicizing	\<EM>
H1 through H6	Heading levels 1 through 6	\<H1> through \<H6>
HTML Markup	HTML code you want to insert manually	Not applicable
Keyboard	Keyboard input text	\<KBD>
Preformatted	Preformatted text using the viewer's current text settings	\<PRE>
Sample	Used to show sample output text	\<SAMP>
Strong	Strongly emphasizes text—most browsers use boldfacing to interpret this command	\<STRONG>
Typewriter	Formats text as typewriter-style text	\<TT>
Variable	Defines text as a text variable	\<VAR>

self or saved it from a Word document—you can use all of Word's standard tools for working with rows, columns, and individual cells, including changing height, width, borders and background colors. These will be translated into the corresponding HTML 3.0 codes.

Word's Web Page Authoring Environment provides three new Table menu commands for working with tables: Table Properties, Cell Properties, and Borders.

Table Properties, shown in Figure 14.32, controls

- Text wrapping around an HTML table

- The background color used by an HTML table

- The space between columns of an HTML table

Figure 14.32

The Table Properties
dialog box

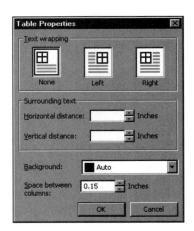

Cell Properties, shown in Figure 14.33, controls

- The vertical alignment of the contents of a selected cell or cells (top, middle or bottom)

- The background of the cell(s)

- The width and height of the cell(s)

Table Borders, shown in Figure 14.34, controls whether the table cells you have selected will have a border or not, and if so, how thick the border will be. The actual appearance of the table border—for example, whether it will appear in 2D or 3D—will vary depending on the browser viewing the table.

Figure 14.33

The Cell Properties
dialog box

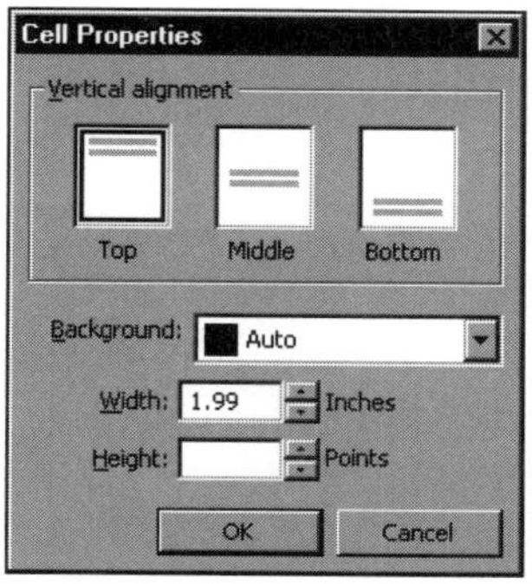

Figure 14.34

The Table Borders
dialog box

TIP. *Earlier, we mentioned that borders surrounding text disappear when you convert a Word file to HTML. If you want to border a paragraph, place it within a one-cell table, and apply borders using the Table Borders dialog box.*

■ Including Multimedia in Your Web Pages

Word 97 offers complete tools to add both audio and video to your Web pages. Before you go overboard, however, you need to carefully consider your audience, and the types of computers and browsers they are most likely to have.

Multimedia is the future of the Web, or so everyone says. Someday, the experience of browsing the Web will be as easy as watching network television is today. Of course, there's one catch: Digital multimedia files are enormous, and downloading them through even the fastest modem is a bit like trying to drink Niagara Falls through a straw. So use audio—and especially video—judiciously. The following two sections show how to embed audio or video clips into your Web documents.

Embedding Audio in Your Web Documents

To add an audio clip to your Web files, position your insertion point where you want your audio clip to appear—in other words, where you want viewers to click in order to hear it. Choose Insert, Background Sound, Properties. The Background Sound dialog box opens, as shown in Figure 14.35. To select an audio file, click Browse and choose the file you want from the File Open dialog box.

Figure 14.35

The Background Sound dialog box

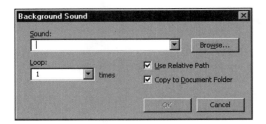

By default, when you insert a link to a sound file in your document, Word creates a relative link. As discussed earlier, this allows you to move an entire folder full of documents and linked audio, images, and other files *together*, with the links intact. By default, Word also automatically copies the sound file to the same folder that contains your other Web documents. This is a valuable feature, since many sound files are likely to be stored on CD-ROMs that can't be provided to the people who manage your Web server. You can, however, change these behaviors by clearing the Use Relative Path or Copy to Document Folder check boxes.

By default, Word specifies that when a user clicks a sound, they will hear it once. However, in the Loop drop-down box, you can specify that the sound repeat up to five times—or infinitely, if you want the sound to be a permanent backdrop whenever people are working in your Web site.

Be aware that Word allows you to insert sounds in most of the leading Internet sound formats, including WAV, MID, AU, AIF, RMI, SND, and MP2 (MPEG audio). However, not all browsers support all these types of sound. For example, WAV files are Windows-specific and have traditionally rarely been used on the Internet.

RealAudio support, which allows users to hear sound files as those files "stream" onto their computers, isn't included with Word 97. (To create and use RealAudio files, you need a special RealAudio server, available from Progressive Networks.)

Also, remember that all Word is really doing is entering the appropriate HTML commands to play a linked file. No more, no less. So if you want to link a file that Word can't insert automatically, you can always do it yourself by inserting raw HTML code.

Inserting Video into Your Web Document

Inserting video into your Web document is similar to inserting audio, with just a few added twists. Choose Insert, Video; the Video Clip dialog box appears, as shown in Figure 14.36.

Figure 14.36

The Video Clip dialog box

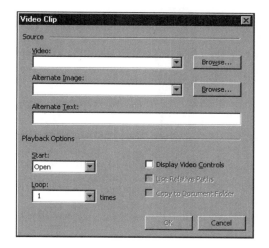

The first step is to browse for the video file you want to include. By default, Word allows you to insert AVI files, Windows's standard video format; the Office CD-ROM contains a library of generic AVI video clips in the Clipart/Mmedia folder.

As with sound, however, you'll need to make sure that your audience can view AVI files. In other words, do they have browsers that have helper applications which recognize AVI files? Arguably, the Video Clip option may be most useful for corporate intranets where you have control over your environment, high-bandwidth networks, and standardized computing platforms.

Since many users won't bother to load video files—they're too big and slow—Word allows you to select an alternate still image for users to see instead. Word also allows you to enter text that will appear if users don't choose to display graphics. These features allow you to make sure your message is communicated no matter what browser users have, or how they choose to use your site.

As with sound, you can control the looping of your video file, looping from one to five times, or continuously. Also, in the Start box, you can control when a video clip runs: either when the page is opened or when the mouse is positioned over the image (Mouse-over), or both.

■ Working with HTML Source Code

Typically, when you work in Word's Web Page Authoring Environment, you format your HTML document much as you would format a regular Word document—using toolbar buttons, keyboard shortcuts, menu commands, and dialog boxes. Word handles the behind-the-scenes HTML code for you. However, there are times when you may want to insert code directly. For example, HTML is evolving rapidly, and you may want to use an HTML command not supported by Word 97. You might, for example, want to use Netscape extensions that allow for formatting not permitted by the official HTML standard—but which can only be read by Netscape-compatible browsers. Or you might want to insert a reference to an interactive multimedia Java applet that Word cannot insert directly.

Whatever your reason for inserting HTML source code directly, Word offers two ways to do it. First, you can enter the codes you want, and format them with the HTML Markup style. As soon as you apply this style, the code disappears from view. If Word supports the formatting or other command you've entered, you can instead see the result generated by the code—for example, formatted text.

Alternately, you can view source code directly. With a Web page displayed, choose View, HTML Source. Word closes your Web page window and displays the HTML source code file, as shown in Figure 14.37. Notice that your Formatting toolbar has disappeared because you can't format an HTML file—it's pure text. However, you can use editing commands such as cut, paste, and copy.

The Structure of an HTML Document

Let's take a brief look at the structure of an HTML document. All HTML commands are bracketed; for example, an HTML document begins with the tag <HTML>.

The first section of an HTML document is called the Head, and begins with the tag

```
<HEAD>
```

The Head includes information useful to both Web browsers and anyone involved in managing Web pages. For example, it details how the document

Figure 14.37

Viewing HTML
source code

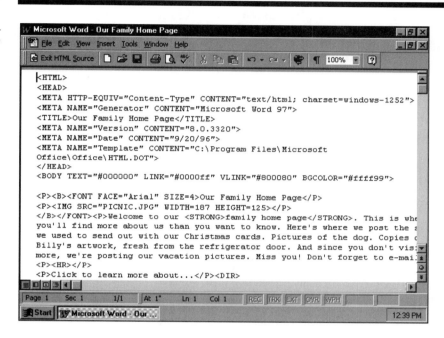

was generated, and specifies the Name of the page (which doesn't have to be
the same as the file name—thankfully, since many Web servers will only support old-fashioned 8.3 file names). In the Head, only the <TITLE> command actually appears when the document displays; all the other commands,
each of which use variations of the <META> statement, indicate text that is
not displayed.

You can tell when you're at the end of the Head section by the tag

```
</HEAD>
```

This syntax applies repeatedly throughout Web documents. Since many,
if not most, HTML commands either impact the way selected text is formatted or have a specific beginning and end of their own, HTML provides a standard syntax for marking these beginnings and ends:

```
<COMMAND> Stuff that goes in the command </COMMAND>
```

Commands that follow this format are called *container* commands.
Notice that containers can overlap; you can have several containers within
a single "larger" container. In fact, an entire HTML document is a container
that starts with <HTML> and ends with </HTML>.

Let's say you're formatting a specific phrase as <STRONG>—which translates to boldface in most browsers. Your document might have an HTML container tag like the following:

```
Welcome to our <STRONG> Family Home Page</STRONG>.
```

After the Head of an HTML document comes its Body, the part of the document that contains the information you're delivering—text, graphics, and other elements. As you would expect, the body begins with the command

```
<BODY>
```

and ends with the command

```
</BODY>
```

Within the Body of an HTML document, you'll see the text you've inserted, typically blocked off by <P> and </P> paragraph marks. If you've used extra paragraph marks to separate paragraphs, you'll see them here: a paragraph mark at the end of a paragraph, and another blank line with *only* paragraph marks and HTML coding, such as

```
<P> </P>
```

To remove the extra paragraph marks, you can use Word's Find and Replace feature to replace lines like these with nothing at all. (Don't worry about   it's simply an escape sequence that indicates a paragraph mark was entered in the document.)

You may also come across commands like <LI>, which specifies a line break (as distinct from a paragraph break). <LI> is an example of an *empty* tag. Unlike container tags, empty tags stand by themselves; they don't have to contain anything.

If you've used images or multimedia in your files, you'll also see lines containing HTML statements like the following:

```
<P><IMG SRC>="Bullet7.gif" WIDTH=15 HEIGHT=13> <A HREF="Dad's Page.html">How
Daddy's Working Too Hard!</A></P>
```

This is a lot less intimidating than it looks. Let's walk through it.

<P>, as you've seen, simply indicates the beginning of a new paragraph. <IMG SRC> tells a browser two things. The IMG (image) portion of the command tells HTML that an image file (IMG) is about to be referenced— in other words, the source code is telling a Web browser that an image should be displayed here. (The file Bullet7.gif happens to be one of the sample bullet images that comes with Office. Notice that if you have a bulleted list, each item can use the same image file; you don't need to store multiple copies of it.)

The SRC (source) portion of the command tells HTML where to look for that image. You'll notice that in this statement there's only a file name—not a complete path name. This is a *relative link*: The file can be loaded as long as it's in the same folder as the HTML document.

Immediately following the image reference, HEIGHT = and WIDTH = statements tell a Web browser how large the image should appear; Word enters this information automatically, based on the proportions of your image file. If you need to size your image file more precisely, one way to do so is to edit the HTML source. Note, however, that if you resize height and width disproportionately, browsers will distort your image instead of cropping it.

Following the height and width commands, the statement continues as follows:

```
<A HREF="Dad's Page.html">How Daddy's Working Too Hard!</A></P>.
```

<A HREF="Dad's Page.html"> specifies what follows the bullet: a hyperlink to another HTML file named Dad's Page.html. The beginning of this phrase, <A, specifies an HTML *anchor*: It tells a Web browser that everything which follows until </A> is part of the same instruction.

Once again, the file name is specified with no path: This is another relative link. The text following the > bracket is the text that will appear in the hyperlink. Finally, as mentioned above, </A> tells your Web browser that the hyperlink command is finished—and </P> says the paragraph is finished as well, so a paragraph mark should be displayed.

The result of this command is shown in Figure 14.38; when you click on the text *How Daddy's Working Too Hard!,* a Web browser displays Dad's Page.html.

Of course we've just scratched the surface of HTML syntax and commands. Table 14.4 earlier in this chapter presented many other important HTML commands. You won't be surprised to learn there are also a wide variety of online sources for more information about using HTML. Some of the best include:

- *A Beginner's Guide to HTML* http://www.ncsa.uiuc.edu/General/Internet/WWW/HTMLPrimer.html

- *HTML Quick Reference* http://kuhttp.cc.ukans.edu/lynx_help/HTML_quick.html

- *Crash Course on Writing Documents for the Web* http://www.pcweek.ziff.com/~eamonn/crash_course.html

- *A Basic HTML Style Guide* http://guinan.gsfc.nasa.gov/Style.html

Figure 14.38

A hyperlink: the results of
an HREF command

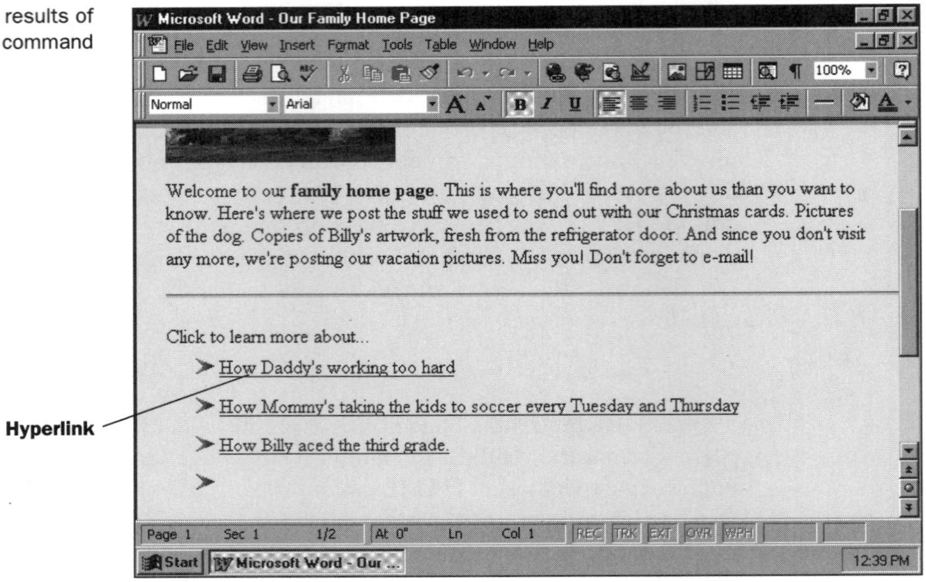

Hyperlink

■ Posting to Your Internet Service Provider's Web Server

If you've purchased Microsoft Office on CD-ROM, you also have a separate utility program, the Web Publishing Wizard, that walks you through posting your Web pages on another computer that will act as your Web server. This program can be installed from the folder \Valupack\Webpost. Double-click the Webpost icon: the program is installed. To run it, choose Start, Programs, Accessories, Internet Tools, Web Publishing Wizard. The opening screen appears; click Next. From the next window (Figure 14.39), you can browse to find specific folders or files you want to publish.

Click Next; the Web Publishing Wizard asks the name of your Web server. Two options are built in: CompuServe's Our World server, and SPRY-NET's SPRY Society server. If you do not have an Internet service provider or internal Web hosting resources, you can arrange with CompuServe for hosting services and then use one of these servers. To choose a different Web server, click New (see Figure 14.40).

In this window, you can enter a name for your Web site. If you're not using CompuServe or SPRYNet, choose <Other Internet Provider>, and click Next. You can now enter your Web site's URL address (see Figure 14.41); for example, http://www.yourname.com.

Figure 14.39

Using the Web Publishing
Wizard to find the files
you want to publish

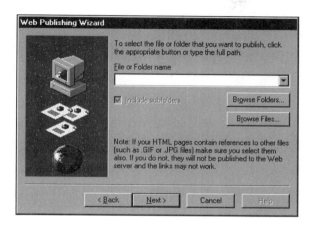

Figure 14.40

Choosing a new
Web server

Click Next; the Web Publishing Wizard asks if you will connect to the Internet via a local area network or via Dial-up Networking with a modem (see Figure 14.42). If you choose Dial-up Networking, you can select one of the dial-up networking connections you already use to access the Internet, or you can create a new one by clicking New Dial-Up Connection.

Click Next; the dialog box that Windows normally uses to establish an Internet connection appears (see Figure 14.43). Click Connect. Depending on how your connection is configured, a terminal window may appear where you will have to enter your log-on commands.

Once you establish the connection, the Web Publishing Wizard will complete the process of uploading your files.

Figure 14.41

Entering your Web
site's URL address

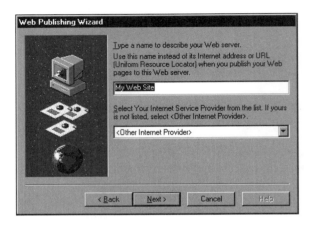

Figure 14.42

Choosing an Internet
connection

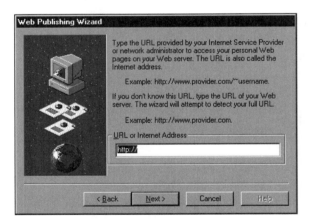

■ Additional Internet Tools Provided with Office 97

If you have purchased Microsoft Office on CD-ROM, you'll find additional
tools that make it easier to use Word to create and access Web documents.
Two of these tools are especially worth mentioning.

First, Microsoft has provided Netscape-compatible plug-ins that allow
Web users to view Word, Excel, or PowerPoint documents *in their native format* on the Web, from Netscape Navigator. You can post these viewers on your
Web site and create links that make it easy to retrieve them, or you can create
links to Microsoft's Web site where the viewers may also be downloaded.

Figure 14.43

Making the connection

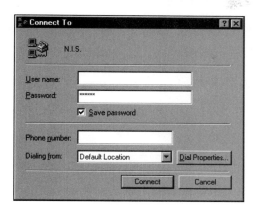

Since Navigator is still the most widely used browser, this is invaluable when you want to make available documents without converting them into HTML—especially heavily formatted documents that won't translate properly.

Second, if you are on a corporate intranet based on Windows NT 3.51 or 4.0, you can use Web Find Fast, which extends the power of Word's Find feature, so you can quickly search for any Web or Office document anywhere on your intranet.

■ Summary

When it comes to Web connectivity, Word and Office have come a long way in a hurry. You've learned how to use Word and the companion program Internet Explorer 3.0 to travel the Web, and how to retrieve documents for editing on your own system. You've learned about a world of Word-related resources on the Web—both those provided by Microsoft and third parties. You've been introduced to Word's new Web Page Authoring Environment, and discovered how to use it to create Web pages with text, graphics, sound, and video. You've taken a quick look at the underlying HTML code that makes the Web work—and learned how to move your pages onto the Web itself, using the Web Publishing Wizard. Finally, you've learned about some additional Web tools Microsoft has provided to make Word work even better on the Web. In short, you've learned everything you need to know to start creating your own Web pages. Give it a try!

- *Using the Reviewing Toolbar*
- *Options for Controlling the Track Changes Feature*
- *Protecting a Document for Revisions*
- *Using Compare Documents to Mark Tracked Changes Automatically*
- *Using Document Highlighting*
- *Creating a Microsoft Outlook Task*

- *Sending a File to a Colleague*

15

Comments, Changes, and Versioning: Streamline "Writing by Committee"

THE WRITER STILL WORKS ALONE, BUT THESE DAYS, MOST documents are—to at least some degree—a collaborative effort. Several Word and Office features have been specifically designed to help you manage the process of collaborative writing. In this chapter, we'll focus on four of these features: Comments, Track Changes, Versioning, and Highlighting.

The *Comments* feature, formerly called Annotations, enables you and other reviewers to mark a document with comments that don't appear when the document is printed. Since it's easy to find and read comments, this feature makes it easy to respond to the concerns of your reviewers.

The *Track Changes* feature enables you to propose specific changes in a document's text, which can then be accepted or rejected. (You can also use a closely related feature, *Compare Documents*, to check changes made between two versions of a document, so you can determine where a problem arose, or whether a change was missed.)

Word 97 also introduces *Versioning*, which allows you to save multiple documents in the same file. That means no more worrying about finding multiple files to compare, or about keeping track of the history of changes that mysteriously disappear.

Last but not least, *Highlighting* is exactly what you think it is: the electronic equivalent of that transparent yellow pen you may have used in high school.

In this chapter, you'll learn how to create comments—both written and spoken; edit or view the comments that others make; and prevent others from making any changes to your document other than comments. You'll learn how to track changes in your document, view them, and decide whether to accept them. You'll learn how to merge comments from several reviewers, and how to compare two versions of a document. You'll also learn how to store and manage several versions of a document in the same file.

Finally, if you have Office 97, you also have Outlook, Microsoft's new Personal Information Manager—so we'll briefly show you how Word can use Outlook to help track your progress in reviewing files, or to send them to colleagues who must review them.

■ Using the Reviewing Toolbar

If you're planning to thoroughly review a document, or respond to someone else's comments or proposed changes, you may want to open Word 97's new Reviewing Toolbar, which brings together all the tools you're likely to need. The Reviewing Toolbar is shown in Figure 15.1; to open it, choose View, Toolbars, Reviewing.

As we walk through Word's Comments and Track Changes features, we'll point out opportunities to use the Reviewing Toolbar—as well as equivalent ways to get the job done without it.

Creating Comments

How do you make a comment on someone's document without adding text that will need to be deleted manually at some point? How do you make comments on an entire document, in a way that makes those comments easy to manage and respond to? Use Word's Comments feature.

Figure 15.1

The Reviewing Toolbar

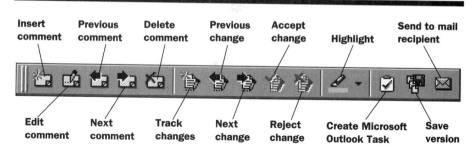

Inserting an comment places a mark in the document and opens a separate *comments pane* where you can type comments, and others can review them. (If you've used Word before, you may have used annotations; comments are the same feature, with a slightly friendlier name.) To create a comment:

1. Place the insertion point where you want the comment to appear, or select the text you want to comment upon.

2. Click the Insert Comment button on the Reviewing Toolbar, or choose Insert, Comment. Your initials and the comment number appear in the document as hidden text; Word uses the initials you've stored in the Tools, Options, User Information tab. At the same time, the comment pane opens, as shown in Figure 15.2.

3. Type and format your comments in the comment pane.

4. If you want to close the comment pane, click on **C**lose or press Alt+Shift+C. If you want to create another comment, press F6 to switch panes (or click in the editing pane). Place your insertion point where you want the next comment, and repeat these steps.

You can enter just about anything in a comment pane, including graphics, sound annotations, and most fields (with a few exceptions such as table of contents and index entries). You can also copy text or graphics from the editing window to a comment pane, and vice versa.

The number that appears in the document reflects the sequence in which comments appear in the document. Word does not number each individual's comments separately. When you insert, move, copy, or delete comments, all the existing comments are automatically renumbered as needed.

Viewing and Editing Comments

Word uses yellow highlighting to mark text in a document that has associated comments. In Word 97, you can see the contents of a comment instantly, by positioning your mouse pointer above text that has been highlighted to indicate a comment. The comment appears as a ScreenTip, as shown in Figure 15.3.

Figure 15.2

The comment pane,
displaying comments

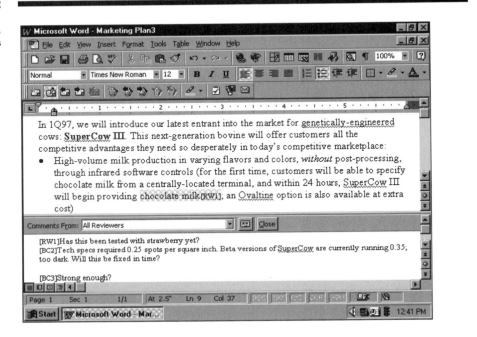

Figure 15.3

Comment displayed as
ScreenTip

ScreenTip

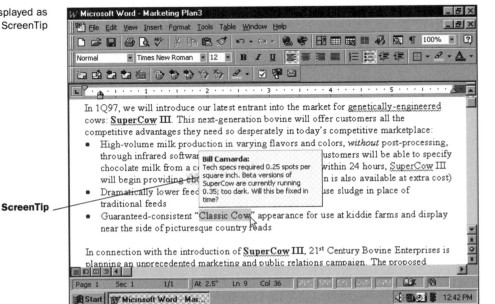

Numbered comment markers are visible in the editing pane when the Show/Hide button is turned on.

To edit a comment or review many comments at once, open the comment pane by double-clicking on a comment marker in the document. The comment pane shows all the comments in a document; you can scroll through them. When you position your insertion point on a comment in the comment pane, Word scrolls the document to the matching position.

If you have many comments, you might want to enlarge your open comment pane. To do so, position the mouse pointer on the split bar that appears between the comment pane and the editing window, and drag the split bar up (or down) to move the border between these two windows (see Figure 15.4).

Figure 15.4

Resizing a comment pane

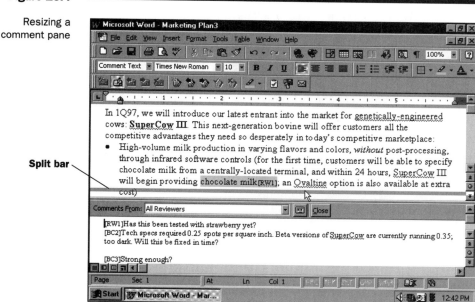

Split bar

The easiest ways to move between comments are to click the Next Comment or Previous Comments buttons on the Reviewing Toolbar, or to use Word's new Select Browse Object feature. To use Select Browse Object, first click the ball icon on the editing window's vertical scroll bar. Then click the Browse by Comment icon, and Word moves to the next comment (both in the document and in the comment pane if it's open).

If you want to review all comments by a specific reviewer, press F5, or choose Edit, Go To to display the Go To dialog box. Then select Comment in the Go to What box. You can then use the Enter reviewer's name box to review comments by a specific reviewer, or by Any reviewer. To move to the Next comment, click Next; to move to the previous comment, click Previous.

Reviewing Selected Comments

By default, when you open a comment pane, Word displays all the comments in your document. But you can tell Word to display only the comments made by one reviewer. Open the comment pane. Click on the Comments From drop-down list box, and select the name of the reviewer whose comments you want to see.

Deleting a Comment

Once you've responded to a comment in your document, you may want to delete it. To delete a comment, select the entire comment mark in your document (but don't include the highlighted text associated with the comment), and then click Delete Comment on the Reviewing Toolbar, or delete the comment mark as you would any other text in your document.

Locking Documents for Comment

The Comments feature gives reviewers a way to comment *about* your document without actually changing the text *in* the document. That way, you have complete control of what actually makes it into the document. You can go one step further and prevent reviewers from making any changes to your document *except* for comments:

1. Select Protect Document from the Tools menu. The Protect Document dialog box opens (see Figure 15.5).

2. Choose Comments.

3. Type a password.

4. Retype the password to confirm it, as requested by Word. Remember that passwords are case-sensitive.

5. Click on OK.

Figure 15.5

Protecting a document for comments

Inserting a Voice Comment

If you have a sound board and a microphone, you can insert voice comments in your document.

1. Place your insertion point where you want to make the comment.

2. Select Comment from the Insert menu.

3. After the comment pane opens, click on the Insert Sound Object (cassette tape) icon. A cassette tape icon appears next to the comment mark in your comment pane.

4. The Windows 95 Sound Recorder opens, as shown in Figure 15.6. Click the Record button (the red button at the right), and record the comment.

5. If you're asked to update the object, do so.

6. Close the comment pane.

Figure 15.6

Adding a voice comment with the Windows 95 Sound Recorder

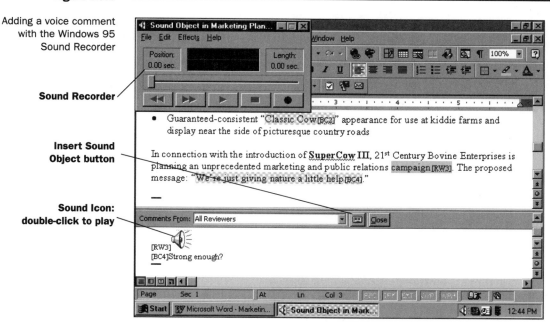

Because you're using the standard Windows 95 Sound Recorder, you have access to all of its features. For example, you can choose Insert File from the Sound Recorder's Edit menu and include a sound file you've already recorded or stored elsewhere.

Listening to a Voice Comment

If you have a sound board, you can listen to any recorded voice comment:

1. Select Comments from the View menu.

2. Double-click on the microphone icon that appears next to the comment you want to hear.

3. Close the comment pane after you finish.

Printing Comments

You can print comments in two different ways. First, you can print the document with its comments. This method prints the comment markers, so you can see the locations that correspond to each comment. (Because comment markers are hidden text, this means other hidden text also appears.) The comments appear on a separate page. To print the document with comments:

1. Select Print from the File menu.

2. Select Options.

3. Check Comments. Hidden Text is automatically checked as well.

4. Click on OK.

5. Select File, Print; enter any print settings, and click OK.

   Alternatively, you can print *only the comments:*

1. Select Print from the File menu.

2. Select Comments from the Print what box.

3. Choose Print.

Understanding the Track Changes Feature

Comments are well-suited for observations about a document, but less well-suited for specific corrections. For this, Word offers another feature: *Track Changes.*

With track changes, you can propose a revision, which will appear in underlined text; all your proposed revisions will appear in the same color. You can also propose deletions; your deleted text does not disappear, but rather appears in color, with strikethrough formatting added. Later, the original author can decide whether to accept or reject your corrections—all at once, or one at a time.

To begin marking revisions, double-click TRK in the status bar; TRK is highlighted, and all changes you make are tracked. Or, choose Tools, Track Changes, Highlight Changes. The Highlight Changes dialog box appears, as shown in Figure 15.7. Check the Track changes while editing box, and click OK. Word begins tracking changes until you tell it to stop. You can turn off Track Changes whenever you want; either by double-clicking the TRK box in the status bar, or by choosing Tools, Track Changes, Highlight Changes, and clearing the Track changes while editing dialog box.

Figure 15.7

The Highlight Changes dialog box

Viewing Revisions

Figure 15.8 shows a sample page with revisions marked. To the far left, vertical *revision bars* appear, extending top-to-bottom next to each line that has revisions. This makes it easier to tell where revisions have been made.

Figure 15.8

A sample document with proposed changes marked

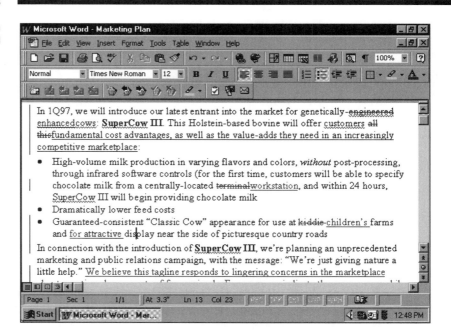

Tracking Revisions in the Background

If you expect to make substantial changes in a document, you might find it distracting to watch all the colored text, underlines, and strikethroughs pile up in your document. To have Word track revisions without showing them on-screen:

1. Right-click on the TRK button in the status bar and choose Highlight Changes from the shortcut menu (or, instead, choose Tools, Track Changes, Highlight Changes).

2. Clear the Highlight changes on screen check box.

3. Choose OK.

Choosing Whether to Print Revisions

By default, the changes you enter in a document are displayed in any printouts you make; if those changes are highlighted on screen, change marks appear as well. You might not want that. For example, perhaps you're proposing revisions, but it hasn't been decided whether to accept them. If you want Word to print the original unrevised copy, clear the Highlight changes in printed document check box in the Highlight Changes dialog box.

■ Options for Controlling the Track Changes Feature

Word 97 gives you complete control over the way Track Changes works.

For example, as you've learned, text that you insert while Track Changes is turned on appears in your document with an underline; text that you delete appears in strikethrough. You've seen that Word automatically assigns a color to each document reviewer. Word also marks lines that have been changed with vertical bars on the outside border of each page—in other words, on the left margin of even-numbered pages, and on the right margin of odd-numbered pages. *You can change every one of these behaviors, and more.*

Controlling How Insertions and Deletions Are Marked

To control how insertions and deletions are marked, display the Highlight Changes dialog box, and choose Options. The Track Changes dialog box appears, as shown in Figure 15.9.

To change the way inserted text is marked, choose either Underline, Bold, Italic, Double Underline, or (none) in the Inserted text Mark drop-down box. Whenever you make a change, its effects are displayed in the Preview box to the right of the drop-down boxes you're changing.

You can control the way deleted text appears in the same way: in the Deleted text area of the dialog box, choose a Mark. If you wish, choose a Color as well, as is discussed next.

Figure 15.9

The Track Changes
dialog box

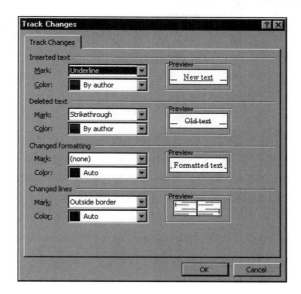

Controlling How Word Assigns Colors to Reviewers

One reviewer per document might be ideal, but in the real world, it's not unusual for several people to review one document. Whenever a reviewer turns
on Track Changes, Word searches the Tools, Options, User Information settings to identify the reviewer. If this reviewer hasn't worked on the document
before, his or her revisions appear in a different color. Word has eight colors
available in its Color drop-down box, but it only automatically assigns colors
to the first eight reviewers. If a document has more than eight reviewers, the revisions can still be tracked separately, but some will have to share a color.

To specify a color manually for your changes instead of allowing Word to
automatically assign you one, choose it from the Color drop-down box.

Controlling How Changed Lines Appear

As we've mentioned, Word flags changes in a document by displaying vertical lines along the outside border of the page, on every line containing a
change. Using the Changed Lines area of the Track Changes dialog box, you
can control where these lines appear, and how they look. In the Mark drop-
down box, you can specify that they always print along the left border, the
right border, or not at all. By default, the color of these lines is Auto, which is
typically black; you can specify a color manually as well.

Controlling How Formatting Changes Are Marked

In previous versions of Word, there was no way to track formatting changes. If you changed formatting while Word was tracking revisions, the change would not be marked in any way.

Word 97 now tracks formatting changes. By default, however, formatting changes are not marked in your document, even though vertical lines do appear in the margins next to them. This can be *very* confusing: when you review a document that includes tracked formatting changes, you'll see that changes have been made, but you'll have no idea what those changes were.

The Track Changes tab of the Options dialog box allows you to specify a mark for Changed formatting: either Bold, Italic, Underline, or Double Underline. (You'll probably want to use a mark that isn't used elsewhere. If you haven't customized your other settings, Double Underline may be your best option.)

■ Protecting a Document for Revisions

Earlier in this chapter, you learned how to protect your document so the only changes a reviewer can make are to add comments using Word's Comments feature. You can do the same thing with tracked changes. With Protect Document for Tracked changes turned on, no editing will be allowed unless it is made with the Track Changes feature turned on, or unless the reviewer enters the correct password. To protect your document this way:

1. Choose Tools, Protect Document.

2. Click the Tracked changes button.

3. If you want to protect your document with a password, enter it in the Password box.

4. Click OK.

5. If you've entered a password, enter it again in the Confirm Password dialog box, and click OK again.

■ Using Compare Documents to Mark Tracked Changes Automatically

The world is full of people who don't know Word as well as you do, and they don't use all of its features. Imagine you've given a colleague a document for review, and they chose not to use Word's Track Changes feature. Back comes your document, full of changes—but *what* have they actually changed? *How* can you evaluate the changes?

Or perhaps you have made changes in a document, and now you need to recall which specific changes were made—but you didn't use Track Changes.

Easy. Have Word compare the two documents and mark the differences for you.

1. Open the document where you want the change marks to be placed— typically, the most recent version.

2. Select Tools, Track Changes, Compare Documents.

3. Select Compare Documents. The Select File to Compare With Current dialog box appears, as shown in Figure 15.10.

Figure 15.10

The Select File to Compare With Current Document dialog box

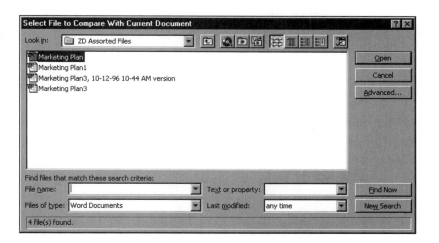

4. Choose the file that you want to compare to the file that's already open.

5. Click on OK.

Word moves through the document, adding change marks wherever additions or deletions were made in the document. This can take a while in a long document. In the status bar, Word tells you what percentage of the document has been compared.

Once Word finishes, you can work with these change marks the same way you would if you had created them using the Track Changes feature.

TIP. *In a long document with many changes, using Track Changes can slow down Word. Instead of using Track Changes, you might deliberately choose to use Compare Documents, marking all your changes at once after you've edited the document.*

Merging Revisions

If you've been handed revisions from several reviewers, each of whom has saved their file separately, you can merge these separate files into a single document where you can decide how to resolve all of their concerns at once. Follow these steps:

1. Open the file where you want all your colleagues' changes to be placed.

2. Select Tools, Merge Documents.

3. The Select File to Merge Into Current Document dialog box appears (see Figure 15.11).

4. Select the file you want to merge into your current file.

5. Click on OK.

Figure 15.11

The Select File to Merge Into Current Document dialog box

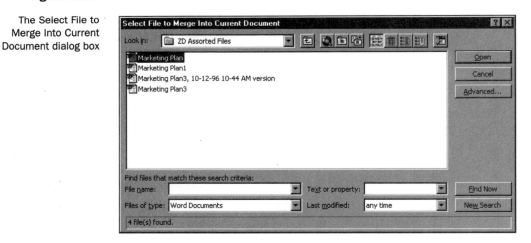

One by one, you can repeat the process with each set of revisions; all revisions will display in the same document, with each reviewer's changes appearing in a different color.

Resolving Proposed Revisions

Now that you (and your colleagues) have marked up a document with recommended changes, the next step is to decide what to do with each of those changes. To walk through a document containing tracked changes, first open the document; then display the Reviewing toolbar. Click the Next Change button; Word selects the first change in your document. To accept the change, click Accept Change. To reject it, click Reject Change; the change will disappear from the document, and the original text will be restored. (Of course, you always have the option of accepting or rejecting a change and then editing the text to reflect the reviewer's concerns in your own way.)

You may often want to see who made a change: for example, you might have to pay more attention if it came from the CEO than if it came from Dilbert in the next cubicle. Place your insertion point over the change, and Word displays a ScreenTip showing *who* made the change, *when* they made it, and *what kind* of a change they made (Figure 15.12).

Figure 15.12

ScreenTip showing the source of a change

ScreenTip

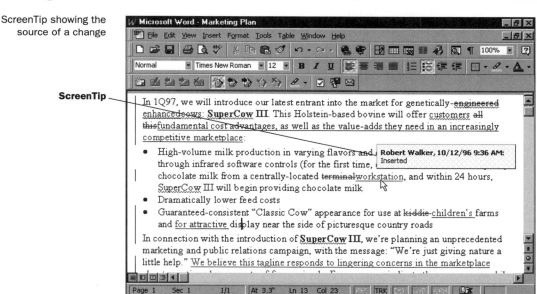

Taking More Control Over the Way You Resolve Changes

As you review changes, you might want to change the way you're viewing the document. For example, you might want to see what the document would look like if *all* changes were accepted, or what it looked like before *any* changes were made. To make changes like these, right-click on the TRK button on the status bar, and choose Accept or Reject Changes from the shortcut menu. The Accept or Reject Changes dialog box appears, as shown in Figure 15.13.

To view changes with Word's underline, strikethrough, or other markings, click Changes with highlighting. To view the document as it would look if all changes had been accepted, click Changes without highlighting. To view the document as it would look if all changes were rejected, click Original. Choose Close.

Figure 15.13

The Accept or Reject
Changes dialog box

Accepting or Rejecting All Changes at Once

It's rare, but it happens: You may want to accept or reject all of a reviewer's
changes at the same time. To do so, open the Accept or Reject Changes dialog box, and select Accept All. A confirming dialog box appears (see Figure
15.14). If you click on OK, all proposed additions and deletions are incorporated into the document. The previous text no longer exists, unless you've
kept another copy of the file. Rejecting all proposed revisions is equally
straightforward (and equally rare). Select Reject All. After you confirm that
you really mean it, Word eliminates the revisions. If you change your mind,
you can click the Undo button in the Accept or Reject Changes dialog box.
When you're happy withg the results, close the dialog box.

Figure 15.14

Confirming that you want
to accept all changes

NOTE. *After you incorporate your revisions and leave the Accept or Reject
Changes dialog box, Word's Undo feature cannot bring them back.*

Using Word's New Versioning Feature

Have you ever searched for an old version of a document; or been uncertain
which version was most recent? With Word 97's new Versioning feature, you
can store all versions of a document together, in the same file. Since Word
only stores the changes among versions, the file sizes remain smaller than
they would if you had saved separate files.

To use Versioning, click the Save Version button on the Reviewing Toolbar. The Save Version dialog box opens, as shown in Figure 15.15. You're
asked to make comments as to the nature of the version you're saving; for example, why the draft was created, or whose input it reflects. Word automatically records the date and time the draft was created, and who created it.

Figure 15.15

The Save Version
dialog box

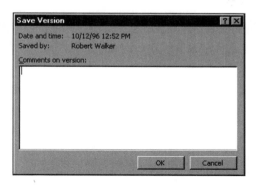

If you want more control, choose File, Versions. The Versions dialog box opens, as shown in Figure 15.16. You have several options. You can choose Save Now to save a separate version immediately. If you do, the Save Versions dialog box will open, and you'll be invited to make a comment that will accompany the saved version.

Figure 15.16

The Versions dialog box

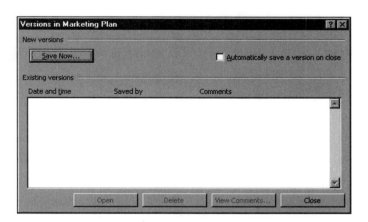

If you don't want to worry about saving versions manually, you can tell Word to save a new version whenever you close the file. In the Versions dialog box, check the Automatically save a version on close check box. Word inserts the comment "Automatic version" whenever you save a version using this automatic save feature.

Opening an Older Version of a File

By default, Word assumes you want to work with the most recent version of your file. This helps prevent you from inadvertently editing older versions.

At times, however, you may want to view an older version—perhaps to retrieve some language that had been deleted, but is now useful again. To view an older version of a file, choose File, Versions; choose the version from the Existing versions window; and choose Open. Word opens the second version in a separate window, tiling both windows, as shown in Figure 15.17. In the title bar of the window containing the older version of the file, Word displays the date and time this version was saved.

Figure 15.17

Displaying two versions at once

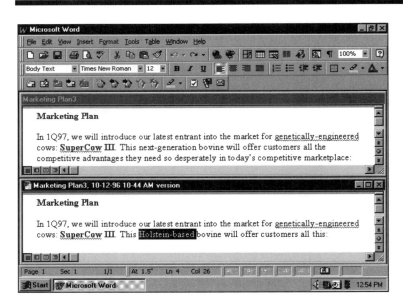

You can only open additional versions while you're working in the window containing your most current version. Word can open several versions at once, but it only displays two in the editing window. You can reorganize the screen so all versions are visible by choosing Arrange All from the Window menu.

Viewing Comments about a Version

If you've stored comments about a version, the first few words of those comments are visible in the Versions dialog box. However, if you need to read a comment that's longer than the space available, click View Comments. The View Comments dialog box opens, as shown in Figure 15.18. Notice that comments on older drafts can only be viewed—*not* edited.

Figure 15.18

The View Comments
dialog box

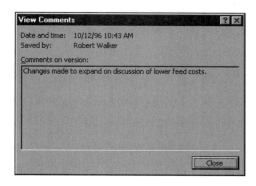

Saving a Version as a Separate File

Unfortunately, you can't use Word's Compare Documents feature to compare two versions stored in the same file. However, you *can* save each version as a separate file, and *then* compare them.

To save a version as a separate file, first open it. Then, while the version's
editing window is selected, choose File, Save As. Word will suggest a new file
name that includes the time and date the version was originally saved; you
can use that name or any other name. Finally, click Save, and Word will store
the version as a separate file.

■ Using Document Highlighting

Many people learned in school to highlight important parts of a document
with a transparent highlighting pen. You can do this in Word as well, even
without inserting formal comments into your document.

Select the text you want to highlight, and click the Highlight button that
appears on both the Formatting and Reviewing toolbars. Word can highlight in
any of 15 colors; if you don't want to use the default yellow color, click the
down-arrow next to the highlight button and choose a color (see Figure 15.19).

Another way to use highlighting is to first select your hightlight color;
then drag across the text to be highlighted. You can highlight several separate blocks of text this way, before clicking the Highlight button again to
turn highlighting off.

Figure 15.19

Choosing a color with
Word's highlighting tool

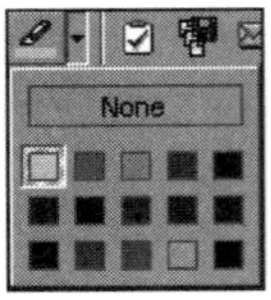

■ Creating a Microsoft Outlook Task

If you purchased Word 97 as part of Office 97, you may also be using Outlook, Microsoft's new personal information manager. Outlook can track a wide variety of important information, including calendars, tasks, and contacts.

In the process of reviewing a document, it's common to realize that you need to perform a task. For example, let's say you're developing a marketing plan. In reviewing a document, you realize that by a certain date, you'll need to check with a colleague about the advertising program contained in that plan.

In Word 97, it's easy to attach your Word document to an Outlook task, so you can easily access the file from within Outlook whenever you want to work on that task. Once you've stored a file as an Outlook attachment, you can then track and manage it from Outlook as well. For example, you can tell Outlook to remind you when the task is due to be complete; you can track the amount of time it takes you to complete the task; you can even use Outlook's phone dialing features to call the people you need to discuss the task with.

To attach a Word document to an Outlook task, first open the document and display the Reviewing Toolbar. Then click the Create Microsoft Outlook Task button; Word displays Outlook's task window, as shown in Figure 15.20. The Word file you're working on appears as a shortcut icon, so whenever you double-click the icon, Outlook can open the file.

You can now specify a start date and a due date, the status of the task, and its priority. In the Status tab, you can also store additional information about the task—such as the automobile mileage you've run up in connection with it.

When you've completed filling out the Task information, click Save and Close to return to Word. You can now continue to edit the document. If you open the document later from Outlook, Word will display the latest version—unless you move the document. In that case, the shortcut will no longer work.

Figure 15.20

A Word document
displayed as a
shortcut from
Outlook's task window

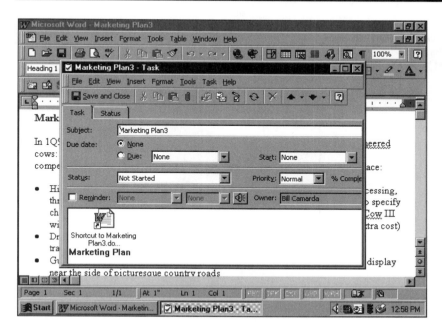

■ Sending a File to a Colleague

Often, it's not enough to tell yourself to take care of a task: you have to tell someone else. If you're using Microsoft Outlook or another MAPI-compatible e-mail client, it's easy to send a file to a colleague for review.

Open the document you want to send; then click Send to Mail Recipient on the Reviewing Toolbar (or choose File, Send To, Mail Recipient). Your e-mail client software appears; Figure 15.21 shows the Microsoft Outlook client. Notice that the Word document appears in the editing pane as an attachment, not simply a shortcut: in other words, the entire file will be sent.

To specify a recipient for the file, click the To… button, and choose a recipient from the Select Names address book. Enter your cover note in the editing pane; set any options in the Options tab; and click Send.

Managing a review process that involves many people and constituencies will never be easy—but Word 97 helps make sure that the logistics won't get in the way. In this chapter, you've learned how to mark up a document—with comments, with proposed changes, or with highlighting. You've learned how to manage changes proposed by others. You've learned how to store multiple versions of a document together. Finally, you've learned how Word and Outlook work together to make sure you can track your projects closely—and get your files where they're needed.

Figure 15.21

Sending a Word file to a colleague for review. (This screen appears if you have selected Word as your e-mail edotor.)

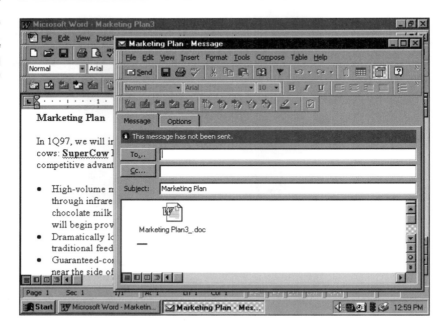

Now that you and your workgroup have created the perfect document, Chapter 16 will show you how to broadcast it to the world—using Word's extraordinarily powerful mail merge capabilities.

- *Understanding Word's Mail Merge*
- *Printing Accompanying Envelopes and Labels*
- *Using Word Fields*

16

Mail Merge: Creating Intelligent Merges

WHETHER YOU CREATE DIRECT MAIL PIECES BY THE HUNDREDS or thousands or just want to mass-mail a family Christmas letter, Word 97's mail merge is for you.

Mail merge traditionally has been one of the most complex, error-prone facets of word processing, and perhaps the most frustrating, especially after you discover you've printed that whole stack of letters incorrectly. Each version of Word for Windows, however, has made mail merge a little bit easier.

Using the feature still isn't exactly easy, but now if you pay reasonably good attention and understand the overall concepts, you've got a pretty good chance of succeeding the first time. That's the goal of this chapter: for your next mail merge to come out of the printer perfectly, the first time.

Once you manage a simple mail merge, plenty more power awaits you under the hood. You can, for example, tell Word to make choices about which records to merge or which text to include in a mail merge. And you can create mail merge envelopes and labels, or even a catalog in which one merged record follows another on the same page.

In this chapter, you'll learn how to use Word's Mail Merge Helper to walk through the process; how to create mail merge main documents and data sources; how to use merge fields, preview a mail merge, make decisions about what records to merge, and run the merge—both to hard copy, and to e-mail or fax.

■ Understanding Word's Mail Merge

Here's the one fundamental concept you need to understand to create a mail merge: You need a *main document* and a *data source.*

The main document contains the text that you want to remain constant. The main document also contains instructions about which changeable text Word 97 should import, and where it should place it.

You then need a data source that contains the changeable text. We'll spend most of our time working with data created or imported to Word tables, but we'll also show you how to use a database file or a Microsoft Exchange or Microsoft Outlook Address Book.

If you use a Word table, each column in the table should have a header—a top row—that tells the main document what kind of data the column contains. This allows the main document to decide whether to merge that information, and if so, where to merge it.

While you work in mail merge, Word can put a friendly *front end* on your data source table, with dialog boxes that make it easier to use. But underneath it all, it's still nothing more or less than a table.

NOTE. *You can also use tab-delimited text, such as that which can be imported from a wide variety of other programs. In general, if you import tab-delimited text, you'll find it easier to work with if you convert it to a Word table. There's one exception: If your data consists of more than 31 columns, Word cannot display it as a table; it will have to stay tab-delimited.*

Accessing Word's Mail Merge Helper

To help simplify the mail merge process, Word provides the Mail Merge Helper, which guides you step-by-step through a mail merge, structuring the process for you. To open the Mail Merge Helper, choose Mail Merge from the Tools menu. In Word 97, you can also run the Letter Wizard from File, New, and specify that you want to Send letters to a mailing list. Either way, the Mail Merger Helper dialog box appears, as shown in Figure 16.1.

Figure 16.1

The Mail Merge Helper as it appears when you first begin the merge process

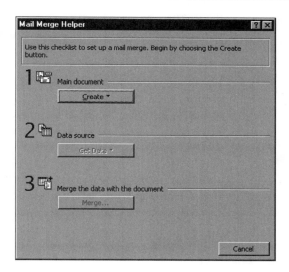

Take a quick look around. The Mail Merge Helper shows the three main tasks you need to perform: creating a main document, creating or getting a data source, and merging the two. Only the tasks you're ready to perform are available. If you haven't prepared a main document and a data source, for example, Word doesn't allow you to use the Merge button.

Creating a Main Document

The first step when you perform a mail merge is creating a main document. (If you want to use an existing document as a mail merge main document, open it before you choose Mail Merge.) To create a main document for a mail merge, follow these steps:

1. Choose Mail Merge from the Tools menu.

2. In the Main Document section of the Mail Merge Helper dialog box, choose Create. A list of options opens: Form Letters, Mailing Labels, Envelopes, or Catalog.

3. Choose the type of main document you want to create. If you want to print letters, for example, choose Form Letters.

4. From the next dialog box that appears (see Figure 16.2), choose Active Window to use the existing open document, or choose New Main Document to use a new document.

5. Whether you choose Active Window or New Main Document, a new button appears in the Main Document portion of the mail merge window: Edit. When you choose Edit, a list of open main documents appears. (If you've just started creating a new window, only that new window document is available. If you're starting the mail merge process for the first time in your current session, you probably have only one choice.)

6. Choose a document from this list to return to that document. You then can edit the new or existing document to include the boilerplate text you want to appear in all copies of the letter.

Figure 16.2

You can choose Active Window to create your main document in, or you can open a new main document.

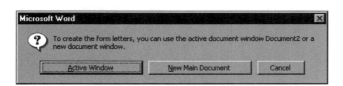

Before you can tell Word where to place the information to merge in, you need a data source.

Choosing a Data Source

The easiest way to create a data source is to go back into Mail Merge Helper from your main document. This time, choose Get Data from the Data Source box. You now have four more choices: Create Data Source, Open Data Source, Use Address Book, or Header Options.

If you already have a data source, choose Open Data Source. The Open Data Source dialog box appears (see Figure 16.3). Locate your data source, select it, and choose OK. (For the moment, we'll assume you have a data source; we'll return later to the issue of creating one from scratch.)

Using a Microsoft Exchange Address Book

In Windows 95, Microsoft Exchange replaced the Microsoft Mail program that accompanied Windows for Workgroups. Office 97 introduces Microsoft Outlook, a streamlined messaging client that also includes personal information management capabilities. Both Exchange and Outlook contain centralized

Figure 16.3

Select an existing data
source through the Open
Data Source dialog box.

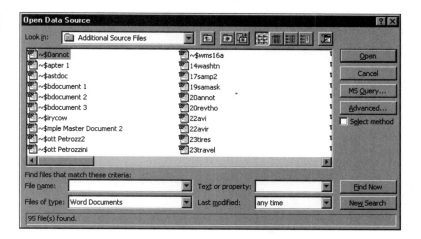

Address Books that other programs can use, including Word 97. If you're running either of these programs, you can merge postal, e-mail, and fax addresses
from your Address Book into your mail merge documents. You also can use a
contact list from Microsoft Schedule+ as a data source.

To specify that your data source is an Address Book, click Get Data
in the Mail Merge Helper and choose Use Address Book. Then, select the
address book you want to use from the Use Address Book dialog box
(see Figure 16.4).

Figure 16.4

If you want to use a
Schedule+ Contacts List,
Microsoft Exchange
Personal Address Book,
or Microsoft Outlook
Personal Address Book
as your data source, you
can select it here.

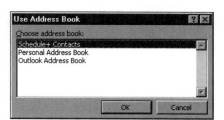

The Choose Profile dialog box may appear (see Figure 16.5). A Microsoft Exchange profile is a set of configuration options that includes data
on the information services you use; the location of your inbox, outbox, and
address lists; and personal folder files you use to store and retrieve messages
and files. Choose MS Exchange Settings or a custom profile you may already
have created. Then, choose OK.

Figure 16.5

Choose the standard MS
Exchange Settings profile
or another profile you
have created.

NOTE. *If you want to create a new Microsoft Exchange profile at this stage, click on New to run the Microsoft Exchange Profile wizard, which walks you through the process. If you want to set a default profile so Word doesn't ask you for a profile again, just click on Options and enable the Set as default profile check box.*

NOTE. *If you plan to merge e-mail to an information service such as the Microsoft Network, you may want to view information about the connections available in your current profile. To do so, after you click on Options, enable the Show logon screen for all information services check box.*

If you specify a data source before you actually enter any data fields in your merge document, Word opens the dialog box shown in Figure 16.6. To begin entering data fields in the main document, choose Edit Main Document.

Figure 16.6

Here you can begin
entering data fields in
your main document.

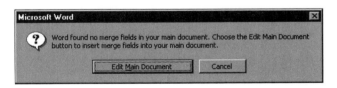

Creating a New Data Source

As mentioned earlier, there will be times you need to create new data sources. To do this, choose Create Data Source from the Get Data button in the Mail Merge Helper dialog box. This will open the Create Data Source dialog box (Figure 16.7).

Choosing Categories for the Data Source

You now can choose which categories of data to include in your data source or, as you'll see later, create your own new categories. As do most database programs, Word calls these categories *fields*.

Figure 16.7

You can create a new
data source by
choosing field names
from Word's built-in list
or adding your own.

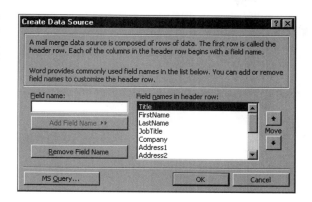

These fields are not the same as the fields you learn about in Chapter 21, "Field Codes." Instead, they're comparable to the fields in a database program. But, as with other Word fields, they do offer a way for Word to include varying input in a document, depending on other factors, in this case, the differing information contained in different records.

When you create a new data source, Word automatically includes the categories of information you're most likely to use when you merge letters, labels, and envelopes. (As you can see, Word's default data form is set up to track people. After all, that's who generally gets mass mailings. But you could equally well use the form to track products in a catalog by creating new categories of data.)

Your job now is to winnow out the categories you don't need, add new categories, and move the categories to match the order in which you want them.

To remove a category, select it in the Field Names in Header Row box. Then choose Remove Field Name. To add a category, type a new category name in the Field name text box, and then choose Add Field Name. Each of these category names must be one word of no more than 40 characters with no spaces. The word must start with a letter, although you can include numbers. You can use underscore characters to connect words, as in the following example: Last_Called_When?

To move a category, select it in the Field names in header row box, and then use the up or down arrows to the right of the box to place it elsewhere in the list.

Specifying Records for the Data Source

After you finish using the Create Data Source dialog box, choose OK. Word displays the Save As dialog box, prompting you for a file name. Enter a file name and choose OK. This saves the data source file and displays the dialog box shown in Figure 16.8.

Figure 16.8

Word prompts you to save the data source you've created.

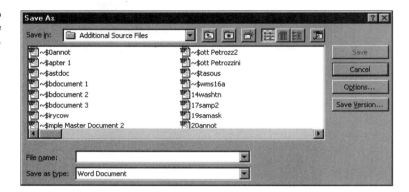

Because you now have a data source to accompany the main document you've already created, you could at this point go back to the main document and tell it which data to pull when you run the print merge. This step is called *inserting merge fields*. To insert merge fields, you choose Edit Main Document. For more information on this process, see this chapter's section "Inserting Merge Fields."

Or you could stay in your data source, adding new records to it. To add new records to your data source, choose Edit Data Source. A blank *data form* appears (see Figure 16.9) that includes the fields you specified a little while ago. Unless you delete several of the default fields, you have to scroll to see them all.

You're presented here with the first *record*. A record is a collection of information about a specific person or thing. To fill in the record, click on the field you want to enter (or press Tab to move to it). Then start typing. To move from one field to the next, press Enter or Tab.

After you finish, if you want to create another record, choose Add New and a new blank record appears. If you don't like the edits you've made to the current record, choose Restore to revert this record to its contents before you edited it (in this case, a blank record). If at some point you no longer need a record, choose Delete. The record is gone with no further ado.

Figure 16.9

The Data Form dialog box

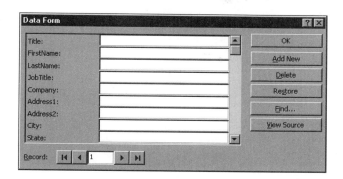

NOTE. *Restore doesn't bring back a deleted record, and Word's Undo feature isn't accessible from a data form. Therefore, the only way to bring back a record you just deleted is to close your file without saving the changes you just made, in which case you'll also lose any other changes you made since the last time you saved. The more often you save, of course, the less information you lose. On the other hand, if you set Automatic Save to save very frequently, it might save your changes before you have a chance to close the file, in which case your deleted record will be gone for good!*

Finding Information in Records

You can use the Record box, which always displays your current record, to move quickly among records (see Figure 16.10). You also can search for specific information within the data form. To do so, choose Find. The Find in Field dialog box opens, as shown in Figure 16.11.

Figure 16.10

Move among records by using the Record box.

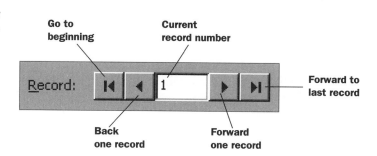

Figure 16.11

Use the Find in Field
dialog box to find
specific information in a
specific field.

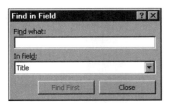

Type the information you want to find in the Find what box. Specify the field you want Word to search in the In Field list box. Then choose Find First. Word finds the first reference and displays the Find Next button. To find another reference to the same text, choose Find Next.

Working with the Underlying Data Table and the Database Toolbar

The data form is only a friendly front end patched onto a standard Word table. Not surprisingly, you can do some things from the table that you can't do from the form. Viewing the table also is the only way you can see your data in tabular format, with many records showing at once.

Here's a good example: You can search from within the form, but you can replace only from within the table. Suppose that an area code has changed, and you need to walk through the database, finding references to (212) and deciding whether they should change to (718). That task would be clumsy within the data form. You'd have to find a reference, choose Find and make your edit, choose Find again to locate the next reference, and so on. In the Word table, however, you can just use Shift+F4 to select the next reference, and overtype the new area code whenever you need to.

To work in the underlying data table, choose View Source from the Data Form dialog box. The table appears and the Database toolbar appears (see Figure 16.12). As you can see, the table might be too wide for your screen, and even so, many words wrap inauspiciously. The aesthetics leave something to be desired, but all your information's there.

The Database toolbar, meanwhile, contains the shortcut buttons you're likely to need while you work on the data source table. These shortcut buttons are listed in Table 16.1. The following paragraphs briefly discuss some of these buttons.

NOTE. *If you plan to work at length in the source table, you might consider turning off Automatic Spell Checking. It probably will display many names, street addresses, cities, and other data as if they were spelled wrong, because these are not included in Word's dictionary. Automatic Spell Checking can be turned off by choosing Options from the Tools menu; then selecting the Spelling & Grammar tab; then clearing the Check spelling as you type check box.*

Figure 16.12

An underlying table
stores the database
information you're
working with.

Database toolbar

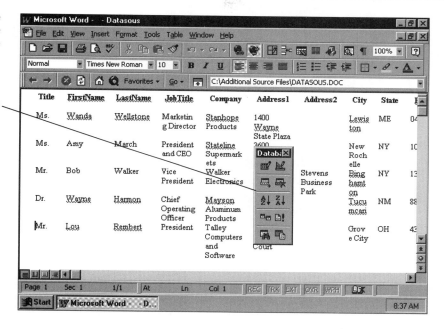

Table 16.1

Database Toolbar Buttons

BUTTON	FUNCTION
Data Form	Returns you to the data form, where you can edit a record
Manage Fields	Adds/deletes a database field
Add New Record	Adds a new record to a database at the insertion point
Delete Record	Deletes a selected record from a database
Sort Ascending	Sorts selected records in A to Z and/or 0 to 9 (ascending) order
Sort Descending	Sorts selected records in Z to A and/or 9 to 0 (descending) order
Insert Database	Gets information from elsewhere and places it in the current document
Update Fields	Updates the results of fields you select
Find Record	Locates a specific record in a mail merge data source (opens the Find in Field dialog box)
Mail Merge Main Document	Switches to the main document

Manage Fields enables you to insert, delete, or rename fields. It opens the dialog box shown in Figure 16.13, which works like the Create Data Source dialog box, except that you also can choose an existing field and re-name it. New Record and Delete Record do the same thing as inserting a table row or selecting a row and deleting it.

Figure 16.13

The Manage Fields dialog box allows you to add, delete, or rename fields on the fly.

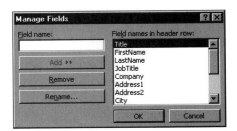

Sort Ascending and Sort Descending buttons sort rows, based on the contents of the first column. (In other words, you can't select a column and ask Word to sort all the rows by the contents of that column.) These buttons ignore the first line, which contains Word's field headings.

Insert Database imports information from other Word documents or database programs. Update Fields does just that—updates fields. You'll learn where you might use fields in merge letters later, in the section "Using Word Fields," but here's a brief example now. You can include a field to add up numbers that are placed elsewhere in your database.

NOTE. *You can format and print the data source table the same way you would any other table. It still functions as a data source. You also can use Word's table features (such as the Table shortcut menu) to edit the table. You could, for example, use Delete Column to get rid of a field you no longer need.*

Inserting Merge Fields

Once you have your data source under control, it's time to return to the main document and insert *merge fields*—the instructions that tell Word what to pluck from the data source and where to put it.

In the Database toolbar, click on the Mail Merge Main Document button, and Word switches to the main document attached to the data source. This document has its own Mail Merge toolbar, shown in Figure 16.14. For more information about this toolbar, see the next section, "Using the Mail Merge Toolbar."

To insert your first merge field, place your insertion point in the document at the spot where you want the field. Then click on the Insert Merge Field button. A list appears showing the category fields available in the data source document you're going to use (see Figure 16.15).

Figure 16.14

The Mail Merge toolbar is your control center for all Mail Merge activities.

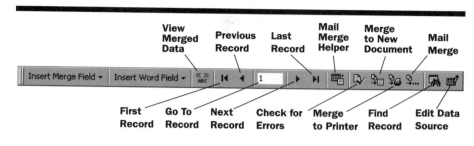

Figure 16.15

The Insert Merge Field list gives a list of fields available for merging.

You then choose a merge field from the list, and it appears in your main document, as shown in Figure 16.16. If you see a field code such as {MERGEFIELD LastName} instead, select it and press Alt+F9 to display the field result.

Each merge field starts and ends with chevron symbols: << >>. You can't insert a merge field from the keyboard; you have to use Insert Merge Field. Place each of your merge fields in the correct location. Don't forget to include spaces between merge fields if they are separate words. And remember the punctuation that needs to appear in the finished document.

Look, for example, at this standard letter introduction:

```
Mr. Thomas Walker
Vice President
Walker Corporation
Suite 40832 Industrial Drive
Mission Hills, ND 45881


Dear Mr. Walker:
```

To get this type of introduction in your merge letter, you need the merge fields and punctuation shown in Figure 16.17.

Figure 16.16

A merge field, inserted
into a main document

Merge field

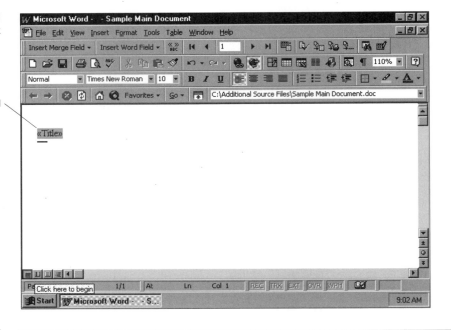

Figure 16.17

The merge fields needed
to create and punctuate
a typical letter opening

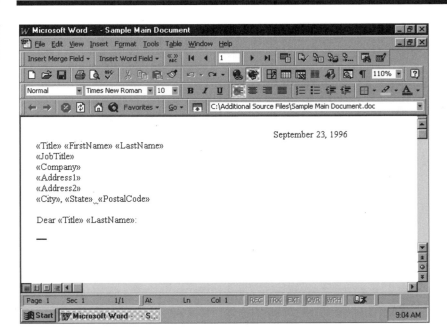

NOTE. *When you start developing a letter, the Office Assistant may appear to ask if you would like help with your letter. If you click Yes, the Letter Wizard will appear. While the Letter Wizard won't streamline the Mail Merge process, it can help you structure and automate the assembly of your letter.*

Using the Mail Merge Toolbar

The Mail Merge toolbar contains several tools to help you manage the merge. Table 16.2 summarizes what's in the Mail Merge toolbar.

Table 16.2

Mail Merge
Toolbar Buttons

BUTTON	FUNCTION
View Merged Data	Displays the merge document as it will appear after you merge it, with the contents of a specific record rather than merge fields
First Record	Shows the first record in the data source
Previous Record	Shows the preceding record in the data source
Go to Record	Shows the current record in the data source; type a new number to go to another record
Next Record	Shows the next record in the data source
Last Record	Shows the final record in the data source
Mail Merge Helper	Opens the Mail Merge Helper dialog box
Check for Errors	Previews the results of your mail merge before you run it so you can identify errors
Merge to New Document	Merges data source and main document to a new file, which appears on-screen
Merge to Printer	Merges data source and main document and prints the results
Mail Merge	Opens the Merge dialog box, in which you can specify where to merge the document (including e-mail) and select from many other options
Find Record	Finds records that contain specific information you choose (opens the Find in Field dialog box)
Edit Data Source	Switches to the data form so you can edit records

Keep in mind that the Merge to New Document and Merge to Printer buttons perform default mail merges, to a document or to your printer, based on your current mail merge settings. Chances are, you'll use these buttons only after you're confident that your mail merge will work the way you want.

The first time around use the Mail Merge button, which leads you to the climax of this whole enterprise: merging your data source with your main document.

Merging the Data Source with the Main Document

Now that you have your data source and main document in shape, you're just about ready to merge. If you're in the main document, click on the Mail Merge button or choose Merge from the Mail Merge Helper to open the Merge dialog box (see Figure 16.18).

Figure 16.18

Finalizing the way you
want your merge to work

Merging to a Document or Your Printer

Your first option is where you want to merge to. You can see Word's default setting, New Document, in the Merge to box. New Document places all the merged documents in a single new document, *Form Letters1*. A section break that starts the next page separates each merged letter from the others. After you merge the new document, you can easily print your letters from it.

NOTE. *You also can browse the Form Letters1 document to see whether you want to add other personal comments to the letters. Form Letters1 behaves just like any other Word document.*

Obviously, you also can merge directly to the printer. If you prefer to do so, choose Printer in the Merge to box.

Merging to Electronic Mail or Fax

In the Merge to box, there are also options for electronic mail and electronic fax. If you have the appropriate network connections or fax/modem, you can use this option to broadcast documents to others from your e-mail network or fax machine anywhere in the world.

Electronic Mail is designed for internal electronic mail and fax systems based on either the Messaging Application Programming Interface (MAPI) or the Vendor Independent Messaging (VIM) standard. MAPI and VIM are competing standards. Electronic mail systems compliant with the same standard can exchange messages with each other.

Microsoft's messaging products are MAPI products; Lotus cc:Mail and some other competitive products support VIM. The standard Windows 95 messaging client, Microsoft Exchange, also has a fax feature designed to work with Word 97's Mail Merge to electronic fax.

If you choose the Electronic Mail or Electronic Fax option, you need to make sure that your data source has a field that contains the electronic mail or fax addresses you plan to use. You can use an external data source that already contains these addresses, such as a Microsoft Exchange Personal Address Book. Another option is to add an e-mail address field to a new data source; when you're ready to merge, tell Word to use that field as its source of e-mail addresses.

To merge to e-mail or fax, follow these steps:

1. Choose Mail Merge from the Tools menu.

2. Click the Merge button.

3. Choose Electronic Mail or Electronic Fax in the Merge to list box.

4. Click on the Setup button that becomes available. This opens the Merge To Setup dialog box (see Figure 16.19).

5. Choose Data Field with Mail/Fax Address, and choose the appropriate data field from the list box.

6. If you send e-mail, in the Mail message subject line text box, type in a summary of the contents of the message.

7. Most e-mail systems let you choose between sending the text of your file and sending the document itself as an attachment that the recipient can store and edit. If you want to send a document as an attachment, select the Send Document as an attachment check box.

8. Choose OK.

Using Word with Microsoft Outlook or Exchange for Broadcast Fax

Broadcast fax means sending the same (or similar) faxes to multiple recipients at once. Word and Microsoft Outlook or Microsoft Exchange can work together to do just that; you can even use Word's mail merge features to personalize the fax each recipient gets. Because all these programs support Win-

Figure 16.19

In Merge to Setup, you can set up a merge to electronic mail or fax.

dows 95's improved multitasking, you can even send faxes in the background while you work on other projects.

To use Microsoft Outlook or Exchange with Word for a broadcast fax, first create your mail merge main document and establish your Exchange or Outlook Address Book as the data source, as discussed earlier in this chapter in the section, "Using an Address Book." When you're ready to send the fax, follow these steps:

1. Choose Mail Merge from the Tools menu.

2. Click the Merge button.

3. Choose Electronic Mail in the Merge to list box.

4. Click on the Setup button that becomes available. This opens the Merge To Setup dialog box.

5. Choose Data Field with Mail/Fax Address, and choose the Personal Address Book data field that contains your fax numbers (it'll probably be Primary Fax Number).

6. Choose OK.

Specifying Records to Merge and Blank Lines to Print

In the Merge dialog box (Figure 16.18), you also can specify which records you want to merge. Word numbers by rows. The first row beneath a field heading is record #1. The default setting is All; if you want to specify records, choose From, and specify records in a range from a certain record to a certain record.

By default, Word doesn't print blank lines in empty data fields. Why? Some letters have two-line addresses; others have only one. Some recipients might have titles; others might not. Leaving a blank line in an address or other field is a dead giveaway of a computer-generated letter.

On the other hand, you might want the blank line to appear. Perhaps you're printing a form, and you want the reader to know that the information is incomplete. (Maybe you want them to complete it.) In such a situation, in the When merging records frame, select Print blank lines when data fields are empty.

Using Query Options to Refine Your Selection

Query Options in the Merge dialog box gives you more sophisticated control over which data you output. Choosing Query Options opens the Filter Records tab shown in Figure 16.20.

Figure 16.20

The Filter Records tab gives you extensive control over which records merge.

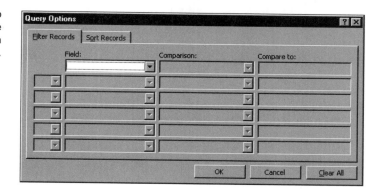

The first tab, <u>F</u>ilter Records, enables you to keep some records from printing based on criteria you specify. First, you tell Word the field on which you want to base your selection. Then you tell Word which comparison to make to decide whether to include a record. You can make several kinds of comparisons. Choose one of the following from the Comparison list box:

- Equal to
- Not equal to
- Less than
- Greater than
- Less than or equal to
- Greater than or equal to
- Is blank
- Is not blank

In most cases, you not only need to provide a comparison, but you also must tell Word to what it needs to compare the text or number to. (Equal to what?)

Here are a few examples of how filtering records works, first in English, and then in Word's language:

"Print letters for all records where the company name is AT&T."

Field	Comparison	Compare to
Company	Equal to	AT&T

"Print letters for all records where the order size is less than $1,000."

Field	Comparison	Compare to
Order Size	Less than	$1,000

"Print a letter for every record except those that don't have a name."

Field	Comparison
Name	Is not blank

The list boxes at the far left of the dialog box allow you to add comparisons by specifying And or Or. You can make up to six comparisons at the same time in the same query. Here's an example using the And operator: "Print a letter for all records where Postal Code is greater than 11700 but less than 11999." (This query would print only letters addressed to Long Island, New York.)

Field	Comparison	Compare to
Postal Code	Greater than or equal to	11700
And		
Postal Code	Less than or equal to	11999

Here's another example, this time using the Or operator: "Print a letter for all records where the addressee's company is AT&T, IBM, or General Electric."

Field	Comparison	Compare to
Company	Equal to	AT&T
Or		
Company	Equal to	IBM
Or		
Company	Equal to	General Electric

If you tell Word to print only records that meet one condition and another condition, you almost always get fewer records than if you select records that meet one condition or the other. A bit more subtle tip: the order in which you use And and Or does make a difference. When Word sees an And, the program performs that selection immediately, before doing anything else. Only after the results of that selection are firmly in place does Word handle any additional qualifiers. An example might be useful here. Suppose Word sees this query:

Field	Comparison	Compare to
Job Title	Equal to	Vice President
Or		
City	Equal to	Cincinnati
And		
Title	Equal to	Mr.

Word finds all the vice presidents in your database, adds to it everyone from Cincinnati, and then subtracts all the women. But swap things around a bit, and it's a different story:

Field	Comparison	Compare to
Job Title	Equal to	Vice President
And		
Title	Equal to	Mr.
Or		
City	Equal to	Cincinnati

Word first finds all the vice presidents in the list, next excludes the women vice presidents, and then adds anyone from Cincinnati, without regard to gender.

NOTE. *If you create a set of filtering rules that doesn't work, you can start over again by choosing Clear All.*

Deciding the Printing Order for Your Letters

A point or two about sorting is in order. The second tab you can access from the Query Options dialog box is Sort Records (see Figure 16.21). Here you specify the order in which the records should print.

In the basic sort, you choose the field on which you want to sort from the Sort by list box. You also can choose whether to sort in ascending or descending order. Both are relatively simple if your list contains just text or just numbers. *Ascending* sorts from 0 to 9 and then from A to Z. In other words, any entries starting with a number appear before entries starting with a letter. *Descending* sorts from Z to A and then from 9 to 0. In other words, letters appear before numbers.

Figure 16.21

The Sort Records tab gives you extensive control over the order in which your records merge.

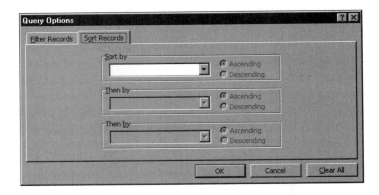

Word sorts non-alphanumeric characters by their position in the ANSI character set where numbers appear before letters. However, as you can see by choosing Insert, Symbol, and viewing the character set, some symbols appear even before numbers:!, @, and #, which appear at the top of your keyboard. Many other symbols, such as copyright and registered trademark symbols, appear after the letters in the ANSI character set.

You can sort up to three levels, using Sort by and Then by. Word first sorts by the field in Sort by. When that sort is complete, Word sorts by the field in the first Then by box and finally by the second Then by.

Previewing the Mail Merge to Check for Errors

The last step before you merge your document is to check for errors. Errors in field names, such as spaces between words, can prevent a successful merge. Error checking also flags discrepancies between merge fields in the main document and field names in the data source.

To run error checking, choose Check Errors from the Merge dialog box, or click on the Mail Merge Check button in the Mail Merge toolbar. This opens the Checking and Reporting Errors dialog box (see Figure 16.22).

Figure 16.22

Checking and Reporting Errors helps you track and fix errors in your merge.

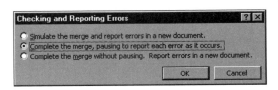

You have three choices. The first and third choices list your errors in a new document, named Mail Merge Errors1. The middle choice runs the merge, displaying a message on-screen each time an error takes place. After you complete error checking, choose <u>M</u>erge to run the merge.

■ Printing Accompanying Envelopes and Labels

If you have a data source, Word enables you to print envelopes or labels along with your letters. You can print matching envelopes or labels for your merged letters by using the same data source with the same selection and sorting options.

Printing Merged Envelopes

To print envelopes, follow these steps:

1. Choose <u>M</u>ail Merge from the <u>T</u>ools menu.

2. In the Main Document box, choose <u>C</u>reate; then choose <u>E</u>nvelopes.

3. Choose <u>N</u>ew Main Document.

4. Choose <u>G</u>et Data. Select or create a data source.

5. Set up your main document for envelopes by choosing Setup Main Document from the Mail Merge Helper dialog box. The Envelope Options dialog box appears (see Figure 16.23). You can set envelope size, envelope bar codes, fonts, and location where addresses print. In the Printing Options tab, you can control the way your envelopes feed into your printer.

6. Choose OK. The Envelope address dialog box opens (see Figure 16.24).

Figure 16.23

The Envelope Options
dialog box

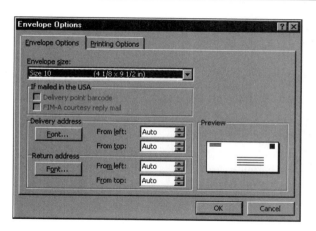

Figure 16.24

The Envelope address
dialog box

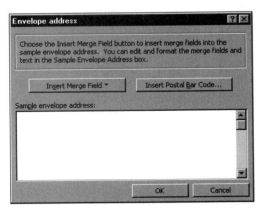

7. Create your envelope address by choosing merge fields from the Insert Merge Field box, as if you were working directly in a main document.

8. If you also want to add a POSTNET bar code to streamline mail handling, choose Insert Postal Bar Code. The dialog box shown in Figure 16.25 appears.

Figure 16.25

Word can automatically
bar code your mailing.

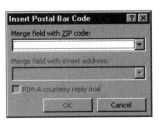

9. To add the postal code, specify which of your merge fields contains the ZIP code and the street address. Choose OK.

10. Choose Mail Merge from the Tools menu. Then, in the Mail Merge Helper screen, choose Edit your main document. Your envelope appears in page layout view (see Figure 16.26).

11. If necessary, move the text box that contains your delivery address merge fields. The return address is that shown in Tools, Options, User Information. If you don't need a return address, select and delete it. If the name and address are wrong, you can edit them.

12. To print, click on the Merge to Printer button on the Mail Merge toolbar.

Figure 16.26

An envelope in
Page Layout View

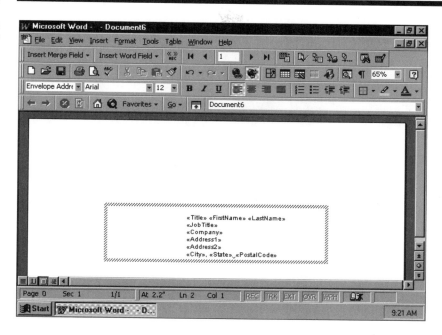

Printing Merged Labels

To print labels, follow these steps:

1. Choose Mail Merge from the Tools menu.

2. In the Main Document box, choose Create, then choose Mailing Labels.

3. Choose New Main Document.

4. Choose Get Data. Select or create a data source.

5. Set up your main document for labels by choosing Set Up Main Document from the Mail Merge Helper. The Label Options dialog box appears (see Figure 16.27).

Here, you can choose a standard label or define a custom label and also specify how you want your label to print. (Chapter 4 covers the Label Options dialog box in depth.)

6. Choose OK. The Create Labels dialog box opens (see Figure 16.28).

7. Create your label address by choosing merge fields from the Insert Merge Field list box as if you were working directly in a main document.

Figure 16.27

The Label Options
dialog box

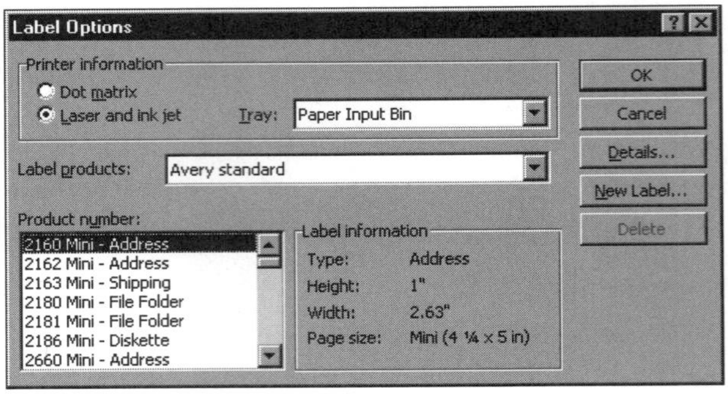

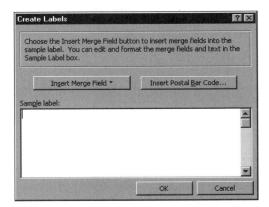

Figure 16.28

The Create Labels
dialog box

8. If you also want to add a POSTNET bar code to streamline mail handling, choose Insert Postal Bar Code.

9. To add the bar code, specify which of your merge fields contain the ZIP code and the street address. Choose OK.

10. If you want to check the formatting of your labels, choose Edit your main document. Your label fields appear in Page Layout view (see Figure 16.29). Note that you see the fields, not the finished mail merge.

11. To print the labels, click on the Mail Merge button, set your options (including Merge To Printer), and choose Merge.

Figure 16.29

A page of labels in
Page Layout View

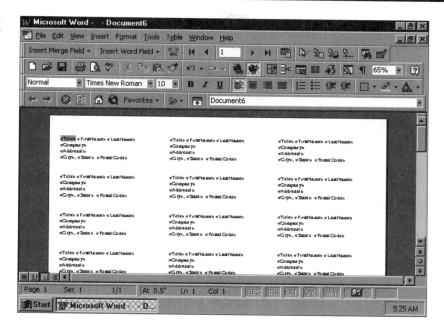

Creating a Separate Header Source

Normally, Word takes its merge field names from the top row of your data
table or from the field names in the database to which you connect. Occasionally, however, using these merge field names might be inconvenient. You
might, for example, want to merge several different data sources that have
different field names into a single main document. Or you might use a read-
only data source.

For such times, Word enables you to use a separate header source. To do
this, follow these steps:

1. Choose Mail Merge from the Tools menu.

2. Choose Get Data.

3. Choose Header Options. The Header Options dialog box opens, as
   shown in Figure 16.30.

4. Choose Create from the Header Options dialog box. The Create Header
   Source dialog box opens (see Figure 16.31).

5. Edit Word's proposed field names by adding new ones in Field name
   and removing any unnecessary ones from Field names in header row.
   Use the Move keys to rearrange them in the order you want.

Figure 16.30

The Header Options dialog box

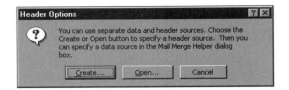

Figure 16.31

The Create Header Source dialog box

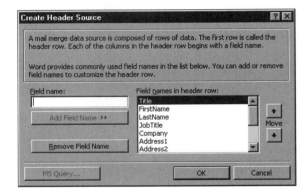

6. Choose OK. The Save Data Source dialog box opens.

7. Save the data source with its own file name.

After you establish the header source, you can then create or get your data source and proceed with the rest of your mail merge. Later, you can open and use this header source whenever you need it. This helps you retain the same main documents without having to worry about changing the merge fields.

■ Using Word Fields

Until now, this chapter has discussed using merge fields in a Word mail merge main document. But you also can use the other fields available to Word documents. You can add the current date, for example, by using { DATE }.

You also can perform a calculation. In the simplest case, suppose that your merge field categories contain dollar amounts. Perhaps you're sending a letter confirming a customer order. You can place these dollar amount fields in a table and use Word's AutoSum field to tally them in each letter.

Finally, several Word fields are designed especially for mail merge. These are listed in Table 16.3.

Table 16.3

Word Fields Designed
For Mail Merge

FIELD	FUNCTION
Ask	Asks the user for input and assigns that input to a bookmark. With the Set field, you can use that bookmark throughout your document.
Fill-in	Asks the user for input at each new mail merge document and places that input in the document
If...Then...Else...	Specifies text to print if a certain condition is met, and different text otherwise
Merge Record #	Inserts the number of your data record in your main document
Next Record	Tells Word to print the next record without starting a new page. Often used with labels
Next Record If...	Starts the next record on the same page only if certain conditions are met
Set Bookmark...	Marks text as a bookmark that you can insert repeatedly throughout a document
Skip Record If...	Skips printing the current record if a specified condition is met

These Word fields appear in the document enclosed in chevrons, like merge fields, as in <<Merge Record #>>. If you choose to view field codes, however, you still see the raw code, as in {MERGEREC}. You place a Word field in a main document by clicking on the Insert Word Field button on the Mail Merge toolbar. The list of available fields appears (see Figure 16.32).

Figure 16.32

Choosing a Word field

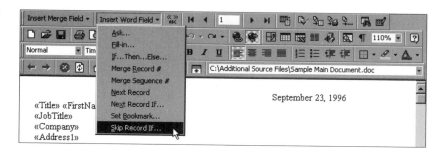

Using the Fill-in Field

Perhaps the most straightforward Word field is Fill-in. When you insert a fill-in field, Word stops before printing each document and asks the user for input to place in the location specified by the fill-in field.

To insert a fill-in field, click on Insert Word Field and choose Fill-in. The Fill-in dialog box opens (see Figure 16.33).

Figure 16.33

The Fill-in dialog box makes it easy to create fill-ins.

In the Prompt box, insert the question you want to ask whoever is running the mail merge. For example, "Would you like to include a special offer in this letter?"

If you want the same text in every letter, check the Ask Once box. Then, after the user inserts the information once, Word repeats that information in all letters that the mail merge generates.

To specify default text that prints unless you choose different text for a specific letter, type your text in the Default fill-in text box. When Fill-in runs, a dialog box like the one shown in Figure 16.34 prompts the user to type information in the box beneath the text you've added.

Figure 16.34

The Fill-in prompt dialog box

Using the Ask Field

The Ask field takes this concept one step further. Instead of placing your response directly in text, the Ask field transforms your response into the contents of a bookmark. Wherever you place that bookmark in your text, these contents appear. Therefore, Ask is ideal for inserting the same text repeatedly throughout a letter.

When you choose to insert an Ask field, you also must choose or name a bookmark (see Figure 16.35).

Figure 16.35

Inserting an ASK field

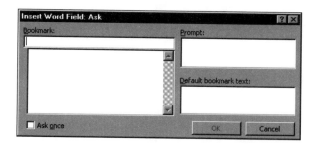

Because all Ask does is create a bookmark, it doesn't place anything in your letter by itself. You have to place a bookmark field wherever you want the text. You can insert this field manually by pressing Ctrl+F9. The field brackets appear, and then you type the bookmark name between them, as in {offer}.

Using the Set Bookmark Field

The Set Bookmark field (known to field code aficionados as *Set*) also sets the contents of bookmarks. But the user isn't prompted for the contents of these bookmarks during the mail merge; you set them ahead of time.

Other fields often use bookmarks you created with Set, especially the If...Then...Else field, to decide whether to perform certain actions. Here, the Set field creates a bookmark called *threshold* and places the number $50,000 in it:

```
{set threshold "$50,000"}.
```

Now you can compare individual records with that number and specify different text for those over and under the number. The following example uses a nested field that also includes If...Then...Else to tell Word to change its response depending on the current contents of the threshold bookmark. Here, if the contents of the year sales field for this record are less than $50,000, the advice "We have some ideas that could help you increase your sales" is given. If they've sold more than that, they don't need any advice, so they don't get any.

```
{if {mergefield yearsales} < {threshold} "We have some ideas that could help
you increase your sales" ""}
```

NOTE. *Here's how to create a nested field. First display the field rather than the field result. Select the field and press Alt+F9, then place the insertion point where you want the nested field to appear and choose the field you want to nest from the Insert Word Field list. Chapter 21 covers nested fields in more detail.*

Using the If...Then...Else Field

The preceding section discussed If...Then...Else. In this section, you learn a bit more about it. This field uses the following syntax: If such-and-such happens, Then do this. Else do something different.

This syntax becomes visible when you choose the field from the Insert Word Field list and then see the IF dialog box shown in Figure 16.36.

Figure 16.36

The IF dialog box

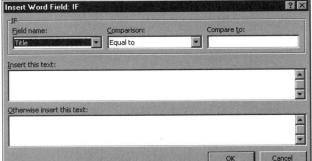

In the area at the top, you create the If part of the comparison. First, choose a Field name from the list box. This field is the category of information you want to compare in each record. Then choose the kind of comparison you want to make. The comparisons are the same ones available in Query options: Equal to, Not equal to, Less than, Greater than, Less than or equal to, Greater than or equal to, Is blank, or Is not blank. Finally, unless you've chosen Is blank, or Is not blank, you also need to add (in the Compare to box) the number or text with which you're comparing the field.

Now for Then. In Insert this text, type the text you want to appear if the condition is met. Else is handled next. In Otherwise Insert this Text, type the text you want to appear if the condition is not met.

Using the Merge Record # and Merge Sequence # Fields

Inserting a Merge Record # field tells Word to insert a consecutive number in each merged document, starting with 1. The fourteenth document to print would include the number 14. Inserting a Merge Sequence # field tells Word to include the total number of records merged into the current printout or file. You could use these fields together to get something like this: Item 34 of 56. In this example, the underlying Word fields are Item <<Merge Record #>> of <<Merge Sequence #>>.

Using the Nextif and Skipif Field

These two commands are leftovers from Word 2. They determine whether Word should include a given record in the merge. In general, you should use Query Options instead.

Using the Next Field

You can use the Next field to tell Word to print the next record on the same page. But in Word, the Next field has generally been supplanted.

One of the most common applications for this field is catalogs. Accordingly, Word 97 provides a fourth choice, Catalog, for new main documents. When you choose Catalog, Word doesn't jump to the next page when it moves to the next merge record.

Merging with a Microsoft Access 97 Database

Word 97 makes merging with Access databases easier than it's ever been—but if you're primarily a Word user, you may not realize that the easiest way to start the process is from within Access. First, open the Microsoft Access database you want to merge with; the Access switchboard displays, as shown in Figure 16.37. In this example, we'll use the sample database NORTHWIND.MDB that's included with Microsoft Access 97. (If you haven't installed it, you may wish to do so for practice.)

From the Access switchboard, open the table containing the fields you wish to use. In our example, we'll use the Customers table, since we're sending letters to customers. The Table opens. This is a matrix in which columns display the contents of fields and rows display individual data records (see Figure 16.38).

Choose Tools, Office Links, Merge It With MS Word. The Microsoft Word Mail Merge Wizard opens, as shown in Figure 16.39. You have two choices: Link your data to an existing Microsoft Word document, or create a new document and then link the data to it. Since you may not know the exact names of the fields in your Word database, we'll create a new document.

Word opens, with the Mail Merge toolbar showing. Now, as you can see in Figure 16.40, you're on familiar turf. You can prepare your main document, inserting merge fields from the list of Access data fields available to you.

Figure 16.37

The Access switchboard, displaying the options available in the database

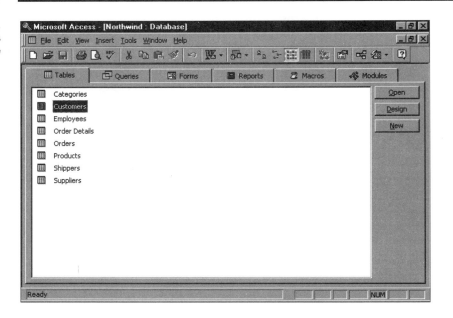

Figure 16.38

The Customer Table in the NORTHWIND.MDB database

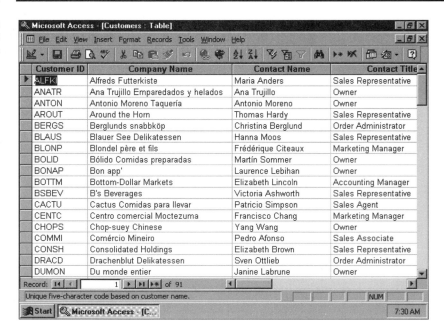

Figure 16.39

The Microsoft Word Mail Merge Wizard

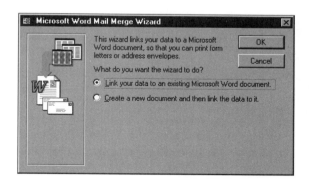

Figure 16.40

The Access Mail Merge Wizard opens Word and enables you to choose merge fields from a table in Access.

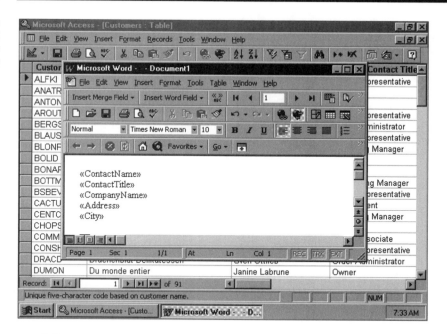

When you're ready to move on, click the Mail Merge Helper button within Word. As shown in Figure 16.41, you'll see that your data source is Northwind!Table Customers.

Set any query options you wish, click Merge to specify where and how you want to merge, and when you're ready, click Merge.

Figure 16.41

Word's Mail Merge
Helper, showing the
NORTHWIND.MDB
customer table as the
data source

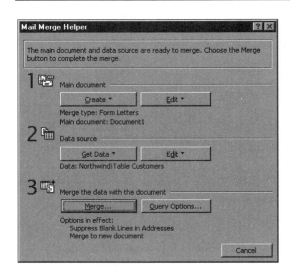

Merging with Another Database File

It's true: not everyone uses Access 97. The world is full of database files, and the majority of them started life in a database other than Access. For example, many database files use the .DBF format first developed for dBASE and used by Microsoft FoxPro and many other database programs. Another example is that quite a few database users work with Lotus Approach as a front end, because it's a very easy database to learn and work with. Approach can store its data in .DBF format, making it highly accessible to other programs.

Office 97 comes with optional Open Database Connectivity (ODBC) drivers that, when installed, allow you to connect with .DBF files and use them for Word mail merges. We'll walk you through an example of creating a merge using one of the sample .DBF files included with Office 97. If you chose to install them, you will probably find them in the C:\Program Files\ Common Files\Microsoft Shared\Msquery folder.

To merge with a .DBF file, first choose Tools, Mail Merge, and create your Main document, as you've already learned. Next, click Get Data, and choose Open Data Source. Select dBase files in the Files of type box, and browse for the location of the data source you want to use. Select it, and click Open. The Confirm Data Source dialog box opens, as shown in Figure 16.42; choose dBASE Files via ODBC (*.dbf). (While you're here, if you would like to see a list of all data source drivers that are currently installed, click Show all.)

Figure 16.42

The Confirm Data
Source dialog box

When you're finished, click OK. Word invites you to insert merge fields
in your main document; when you do so, you'll find the fields from your
.DBF file listed as your options. Now you can finish organizing and running
your mail merge, just as you've already learned.

In this chapter, you've learned how you can use mail merge to create
form letters, labels, envelopes and catalogs, to send customized faxes and
e-mail messages, and how to create a data source or use data that may be
stored in Microsoft Access 97 or another database.

Now that you know how to spread your words far and wide, we'll show
you how to make them look as good as possible. Chapter 17 introduces
Word's sophisticated page design features, including Word 97's powerful new
text boxes, which give you much of the same flexibility for designing publications that you once had to pay several hundred dollars to get in a dedicated
desktop publishing program.

- *Working in Page Layout View*
- *Working with Multiple Columns*
- *Using Borders and Shading*
- *Using Text Boxes*
- *Formatting Your Text Box*
- *Linking Text Boxes*
- *Controlling Hyphenation*

- *Getting Images into Your Documents*
- *Using WordArt 3.0*

17

Word Desktop Publishing: Newsletters and Much More

W HAT PROGRAM COMES WITH THE CAPABILITY TO IMPORT graphics from any Windows application, create multi-column layouts, use drop caps, embed TrueType fonts for delivery to a typesetting machine, and provide built-in brochure and newsletter designs, custom fonts, clip-art images, and built-in drawing and font effects software? Yes, Word 97 does all that.

Word isn't quite a desktop publishing (DTP) program—-no color separations here. But if you know your way around Word, you can do a pretty fair newsletter or brochure. In this chapter, you learn about several features you can use in any document, but that are most frequently used in newsletters, brochures, and other DTP documents.

For example, you'll learn how to work with multiple columns, use borders and shading, work with Word 97's flexible new text boxes, import pictures, and use Word's new drawing and font effects tools.

■ Working in Page Layout View

If you're planning to create a publication with multiple columns, or use graphics and wrap-around text, you'll quickly find yourself in Page Layout view. Many of the Word drawing tools that you'll see later in this chapter switch you to Page Layout view automatically—they won't work any other way. If you'd like to go voluntarily, just click the Page Layout View button to the left of the horizontal scroll bar (see Figure 17.1).

Figure 17.1

Page Layout View button

■ Working with Multiple Columns

To many people, desktop publishing means newsletters—and newsletters mean multiple columns. Word gives you extensive control over columns. You can create uneven columns, specifying exact widths for each. You also can add a new column to existing columns.

TIP. *Before you create your newsletter manually, see if Word 97's built-in Newsletter Wizard can save you some or all of the trouble. Also, if you need to control the way text moves between columns—say, to create jumps from page 1 to page 4 of your newsletter—read about Word's brand-new text box feature, covered later in this chapter.*

If you simply want to create multiple columns of the same size, click on the Columns toolbar button. (If you want to create multiple columns for only part of the document, select the text you want to split into columns, and then choose the Columns toolbar button.)

When you choose Columns, a box appears, displaying four columns (see Figure 17.2). Click on the box and drag across until the number of columns you want is highlighted. Then release the mouse button. Word applies the columns either to your entire document, or if you have selected text, to only that text. Word also displays your document in Page Layout view, so the columns are immediately visible. You can, however, switch back to Normal (or another) view, and work there, if you choose.

Figure 17.2

Selecting columns from the standard toolbar

If you're creating multiple columns for only a portion of your document, Word inserts section breaks before and after the text you've selected.

NOTE. *Although the Columns button displays four columns when you open it, you can use it to create up to six columns.*

Getting More Control from Format Columns

You may want more control than the Columns button can give you. You might want columns of different sizes, for example. You might want to change the exact spacing between individual columns, or add a line between columns. To do any of these things, choose **C**olumns from the **Fo**rmat menu. The Columns dialog box opens (see Figure 17.3).

Figure 17.3

The Columns dialog box

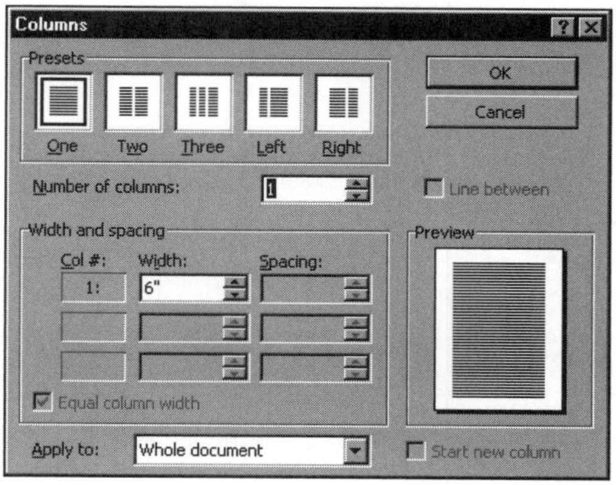

Columns comes with five preset column formats: basic **O**ne column, **Tw**o-column, and **T**hree-column formats, as well as two-column formats in which the **L**eft or **R**ight column is larger.

You also can specify the number of columns directly, using the **N**umber of Columns spin box. Word won't create columns narrower than 0.5 inch, so if you're using Word's default formatting of 1.25-inch left and right margins on an 8.5-inch page, you can specify up to 12 columns. Check Line **B**etween to tell Word to place a line between each column.

In the **A**pply To box, choose whether you want your column settings to apply to the Whole Document or from This Point Forward. If you choose This Point Forward, Word inserts a section break at your insertion point unless you're already at the start of a new section.

If you've selected text before opening the Columns dialog box, your choices here are Selected Text or Whole Document. As already mentioned, if you create columns for selected text, section breaks are added before and after the text. As you make changes, Word shows their effects in the Preview box.

Changing a Column Width Using the Ruler

To change a column width from the Ruler, switch to Page Layout view if you aren't already there. If your ruler isn't displayed, hover your mouse pointer on the gray border at the top of your editing window. Notice the column markers that appear in the horizontal ruler (see Figure 17.4) when the ruler displays.

Figure 17.4

Column markers displayed in the ruler

Column markers

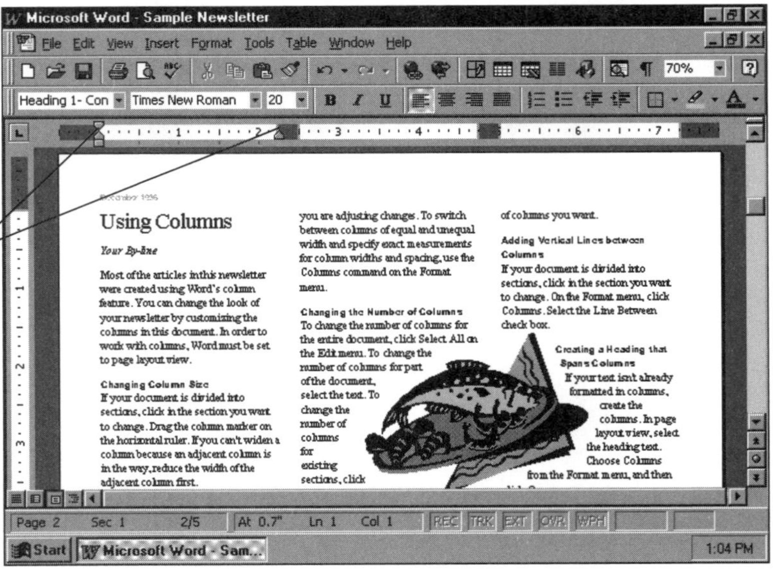

To change a column width, drag the column marker to where you want it. If all your columns are equally wide, this changes them all. If your columns vary in width, this changes only your current column. (You can't drag one column marker into the space reserved for another column. You have to narrow that column first.)

Getting More Control over Individual Column Widths

You can set precise column widths in the Format, Columns dialog box. If your current settings are for columns of equal width, first clear the Equal Column Width check box. This allows you to work on any column listed in the Width and Spacing area.

Then for each column, set Width and Spacing. (You can move from one box to the next by pressing Tab.) If you have more than three columns, a scroll bar appears to the left of the Col. # list; use it to scroll to the columns you want to set.

Starting a New Column

To begin a new column at your insertion point, either choose Insert, Break, and select Column Break from the Break dialog box; or, select Format, Columns, apply the column settings to This Point Forward, and check the Start New Column box.

Evening the Bottoms of Columns

Sometimes you'll want a document in which all the bottom columns line up. This is called *balancing* your columns, and it isn't always easy to do in a way consistent with your paragraph pagination commands. If you've specified that two paragraphs must stay together (Keep With Next), for example, you limit Word's capability to move a few lines around to even things out.

To tell Word to balance the columns on a page, choose a Continuous Section Break at the end of the column you want to balance. (Use Insert, Break.) This allows Word to end the section wherever necessary to balance the columns.

■ Using Borders and Shading

You can apply borders or shading to any paragraph in a Word document—or to table cells, text boxes, WordArt type effects, and graphics. To border or shade text, first select it, and then apply the bordering or shading you want.

Word 97 has revamped its bordering and shading feature to make it easier to access the borders and shading you'll need most—and to give you more flexibility in the types of bordering and shading you can use.

In most cases, the quickest way to border text is to use the Outside Border button on the formatting toolbar. Select the text you want to border; then click the right arrow next to it, and choose among the borders available (see Figure 17.5). The Outside Border button gives you most of the choices you'll ever need, and you may find it more convenient than its predecessor. For example, in Word 95, you had to click two boxes to border all the cells in a table—one to border the outside edges of the cells, and another to place borders between the inside cells. Now you only need to click one.

Figure 17.5

Bordering text using the Outside Border button

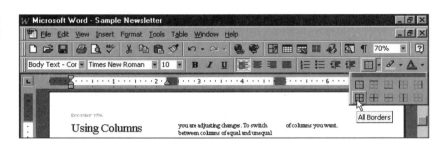

If you want a little more control over your borders—or if you want quick access to Word's shading capabilities—click the Tables and Borders button on the standard toolbar (see Figure 17.6). The new Tables and Borders toolbar appears. Figure 17.7 highlights the toolbar buttons we're most interested in now.

Figure 17.6

The Tables and Borders button on the standard toolbar

Figure 17.7

The Tables and Borders toolbar

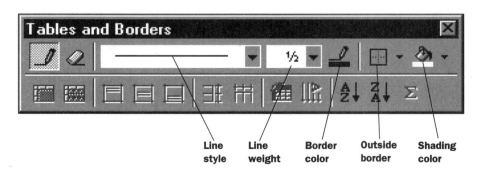

Line style   Line weight   Border color   Outside border   Shading color

When you click on the down-arrow next to any of these buttons, or when you click on the Border Color button, Word displays the default choices available to you. For example, when you click Line Style, you can scroll among 24 built-in line style choices to pick the one you want (see Figure 17.8).

Figure 17.8

Choosing a line style from the Tables and Borders toolbar

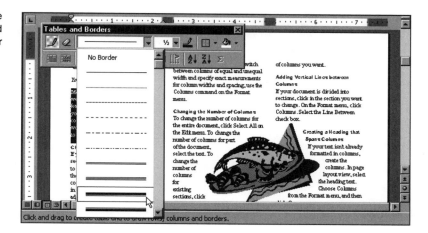

Once you make a choice, the choice is marked in the toolbar button; for example, if you choose to use red shading, the Paintcan button will display a red line under it.

Many of these border choices, such as the patterns, should rarely, if ever, be used over text. They're ideal, however, for blocking off empty space to help the eye move across the page.

Setting Shadows, Colors, and Other Border Elements

For more control over your borders and shading, select the text elements you want to border, and choose Format, **B**orders and Shading. The dialog box shown in Figure 17.9 opens.

Word 97 now offers four preset borders: None, Box, Shadow, and Three-D, along with a new Custom border feature you can use to create your own border, which will remain available whenever you need it. To choose one of these border styles, click on it.

In the Style box, you have access to the same line styles, colors, and line widths you've already seen; you can adjust any or all of these. If you want to change only *one* edge of the border you're working with, set the Style, Color, and Width settings for that edge, and then click on the edge in the Preview box.

If you want to specify how far from text your border lines will appear, click Options, and make changes in the four spin boxes that appear (Figure 17.10). As you make changes, the Preview box displays their impact.

Figure 17.9

The Borders and Shading
dialog box with the
Borders tab displayed

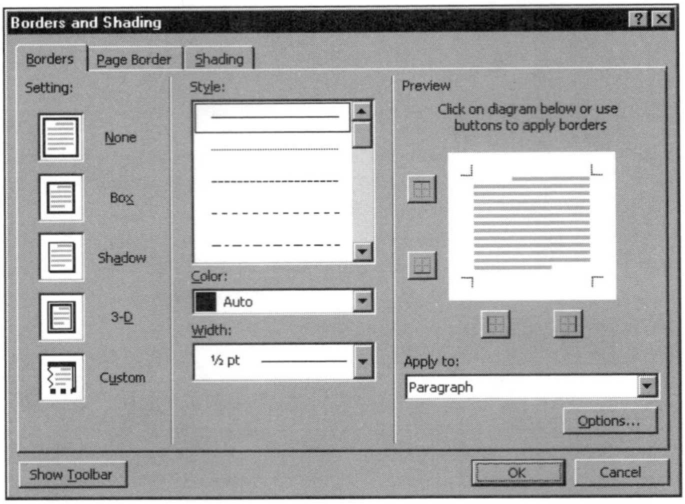

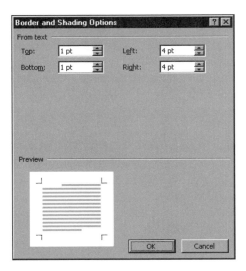

Figure 17.10

The Border and Shading
Options dialog box as it
appears when you're
working with paragraphs
or selected text

Bordering Entire Pages

For the first time, Word 97 allows you to border entire pages. Click the Page
Border tab of the Borders and Shading dialog box; you'll see choices quite
similar to the ones you've been working with already. There's one additional
option, Art, which allows you to choose from over 160 custom borders—

things like apples, ice cream cones, stars, and art deco frames, as shown in Figure 17.11. (Now you can really say goodbye to your desktop publishing program: this stuff's *perfect* for creating the tacky ads you see in those free weekly newspapers!)

Figure 17.11

Using one of Word's Art borders around your page

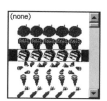

In bordering entire pages, you'll face a couple of issues that don't typically apply to bordering paragraphs and text.

First, you'll have to decide which pages to apply the borders to. The Page Border tab's Apply to box gives you four choices: Whole Document, This section, This Section First page only, or This section All except first page.

Next, you'll have to specify not just margins, but whether those margins will be measured from the edge of the page, or from your document text. Click Options to display the Border and Shading Options dialog box, shown in Figure 17.12.

Edge of page is the default setting. If you want the borders to be measured from the text instead, you have a few more issues to consider. You can choose to Align paragraph borders and table edges with the page border. You can also decide whether your page border should surround your document's header or footer.

One additional option, Always display in front, specifies that your border be visible even if text or graphics overlap it. This option is turned on by default.

Using the Shading Dialog Box

To set shading, choose the Shading tab of the Borders and Shading dialog box (see Figure 17.13). Pick the color you want from the Fill box; the small gray *fill color label* to its right describes the color that is currently selected.

Normally, when you create text, your text is black against a white background. When you set a shading pattern—whether it's a percentage of gray or a pattern such as diagonal lines—Word creates the shading by adding dots against a white background. You can control the pattern you overlay on your fill, specifying both the style of the pattern and its color. To change the style, make a selection from the Style box. To change the color, make a selection from the Color box.

Figure 17.12

The Shading tab of the
Borders and Shading
dialog box

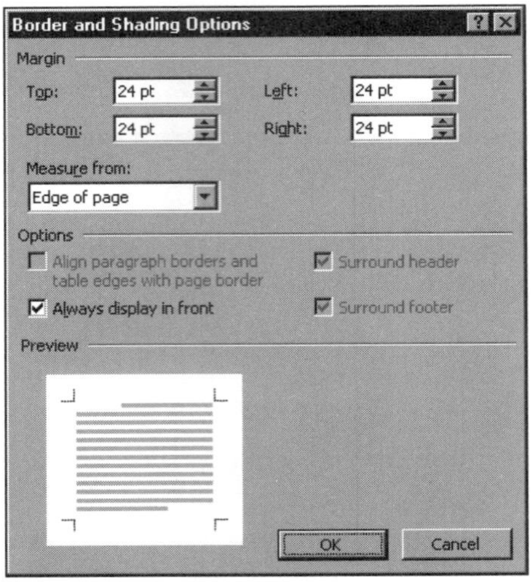

Figure 17.13

The Borders and Shading
dialog box as it appears
when you're working with
Page borders

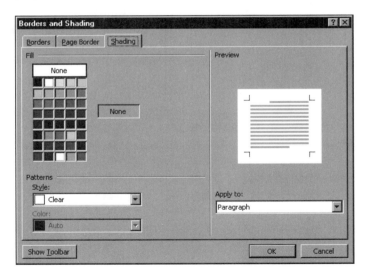

NOTE. *You can use borders and shading together to create a sidebar—a chunk of text that discusses material relevant to the main discussion, but which might interrupt the flow of that discussion. To best control where your sidebar is located, place it within a text box.*

■ Using Text Boxes

Normally, when you work in Word, your text adjusts up, down, or sideways when you make other editing changes. But sometimes you want something—either text, a graphic, a table, or some other document element-to stay where it is, no matter what. Or, perhaps, you want to include "sidebar" text in your document, and make sure that the other text flows around it. Or, perhaps you want to create copy that flows between one location and the next—as you would if you were producing a newsletter with a story that "jumped" from one page to another. These are just some of the many uses you'll find for text boxes, Word 97's smarter, more flexible replacement for frames.

NOTE. *Like your coccyx or your appendix, Word 97 contains an ever-so-small vestige of its frame feature, which once served a purpose deep in the evolutionary past, but which you're only likely to notice now if something goes wrong. If you want to include text or graphics containing footnotes, endnotes or annotation (comment) marks, you still have to use a frame. Similarly, if you open a Word 6 or Word 95 file with frames, Word 97 will convert the frames to text boxes—except those containing text or graphics that include a footnote, endnote, or comment mark.*

Inserting a Text Box

As you might suspect, the easiest way to insert a text box is to choose Insert, Text Box. Your mouse pointer turns into a crosshair; drag it until you have a rectangle in the shape you want. Word switches you into Page Layout View, and displays a text box with shaded borders, as shown in Figure 17.14.

Notice that your text box has a separate insertion point; you can now enter text in it. You can also insert graphics, tables, fields, or virtually anything else Word can place in a document, with the following exceptions:

- Page and column breaks
- Comment marks
- Footnotes and endnotes
- Indices and tables of contents (note that while index and table of contents entries can be placed in text boxes, they won't automatically be found when you compile your index and table of contents)
- Columns
- Drop caps

You'll also notice that Word displays the Text Box toolbar, as shown in Figure 17.15. Most of the buttons here relate to linking multiple text boxes;

Figure 17.14

A typical text box

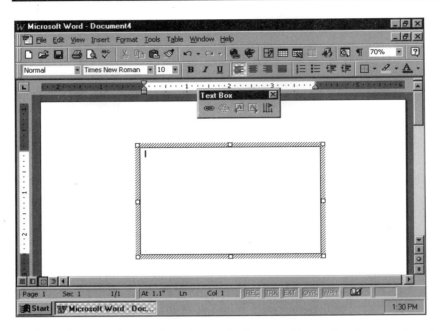

we'll get into that later. There is one button worth mentioning now, however. You can use the Change Text Direction button to turn text in a text box sideways. As you click, the direction toggles; first to 3:00, and then to 9:00. You can't turn text upside down, nor can you turn only some of the text in a text box—it's all or nothing. But hey, don't look a gift horse in the mouth: before Word 97, you couldn't turn text at all, except extremely clumsily, by inserting it as WordArt. The Change Text Direction feature, which is available in text boxes and in table cells, has a wide variety of uses; for example, it simplifies the presentation of columnar data when you have several columns, each with long column headings.

Figure 17.15

The Text Box toolbar

Other Types of Text Boxes

In Chapter 18, you'll walk through Word's drawing tools in detail, but here's one thing you should know now: Word text boxes aren't limited to rectangles. Word 97 provides roughly 100 AutoShapes that allow you to include practically any shape in your document, from flowchart symbols to starbursts to cartoon-style callouts. You can easily transform any of these to a text box (except for lines and arrows that don't have an inside area where text could be entered).

Start by displaying the Drawing toolbar; the easiest way to do that is to click the Drawing button on the standard toolbar. Now click AutoShapes; select a category of shapes and choose the shape you want to insert. As you've already seen, your mouse pointer changes to crosshairs; drag the shape to the size and proportions you want. Now, right-click to display the shortcut menu, and select Add Text. Word turns the shape into a text box, and displays an insertion point inside it.

■ Formatting Your Text Box

Once you've inserted a text box, you have exceptional flexibility in formatting your text box. You can:

- Change the color of the border, or the inside of the text box

- Change the style and thickness of the text box borderline

- Resize or rotate the text box

- Specify the precise location of the text box on your page, or set a precise location that moves when your margins or adjacent paragraphs move

- Decide how text will wrap around your text box

- Create internal margins for your text box

You can also format text inside a text box using any of Word's Font and Paragraph formatting tools.

Working With Text Box Colors and Borders

You can reach all the formatting controls that relate to text boxes by selecting a text box and choosing Format, Text Box. You can also select the text box, right-click, and choose Format Text Box from the shortcut menu. Either way, the Format Text Box tabbed dialog box opens, as shown in Figure 17.16. (Some formatting controls are also accessible from the Drawing toolbar that will be covered in depth in Chapter 18.)

Figure 17.16

The Format Text Box
dialog box with the Colors
and Lines tab displayed

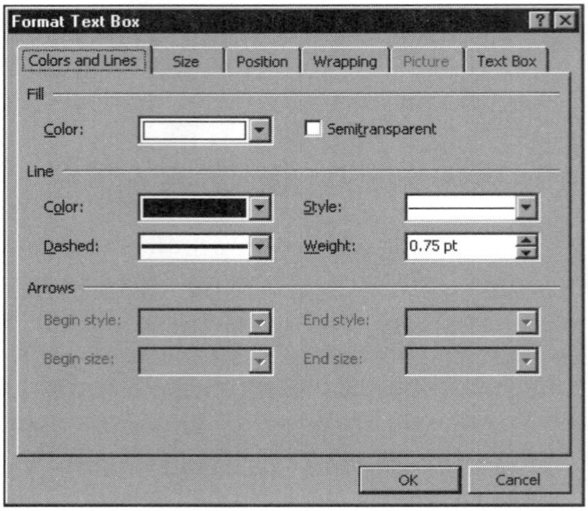

The first tab, Colors and Lines, controls the background (fill) color used inside the text box, as well as the color and other attributes of the bordering line that surrounds the text box.

To control fill color, click the down-arrow next to the Color drop-down box, and choose a color from the options available (see Figure 17.17).

Figure 17.17

Choosing a fill color

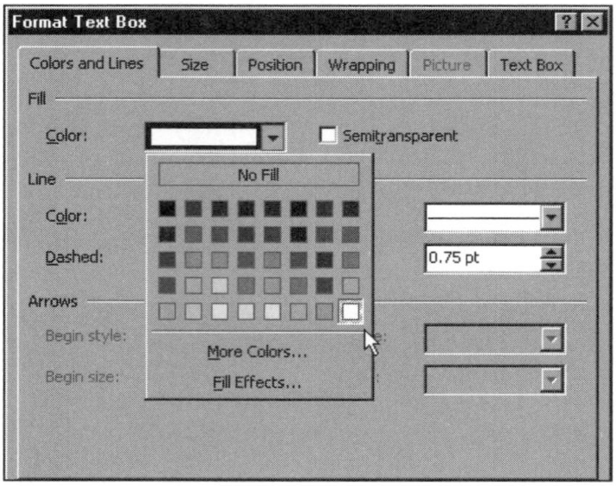

Notice that you're not limited to Word's basic palette of 40 colors. To choose another color, click More Colors; the Colors tabbed dialog box opens (see Figure 17.18). In the Standard tab, you can pick from a wider palette of 124 colors, as well as 15 shades of gray. If that still isn't enough, you can manufacture a custom color through the Custom tab (see Figure 17.19).

Figure 17.18

The Colors tabbed dialog box

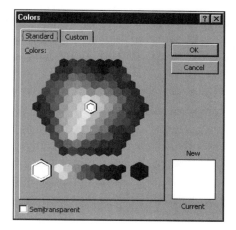

Figure 17.19

Specifying a Custom Color using the Custom tab

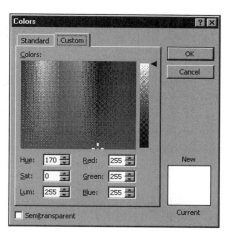

To start, click a color in the Colors box. The color will now appear on a slider, in varying shades from very light to very dark. You can drag the slider triangle to get the shade you want.

Dragging the slider bar is equivalent to changing luminescence (Lum) in the boxes beneath the color box. Of course, using the 3-digit luminescence settings can be more precise. Similarly, changing hue is equivalent to dragging your color selection to the left or right in the Color box, and changing saturation (Sat) is equivalent to dragging your color selection up or down.

The colors available to you will depend on the colors displayed on your monitor. If you create a custom color on a system that can display 16-bit "high color" or 24-bit "true color," and then display the file on a system limited to 16 or 256 colors, Word will display the nearest color available, which will probably not be what you intended. Also, be aware that Word does not offer the built-in color precision or color matching of a desktop publishing program like QuarkXpress, so if you're planning to print a Word document professionally, your printed document may not maintain the precise colors you saw on screen.

Once you've chosen a color, either through the Standard or Custom tab, click OK. The color will now appear in your Color box, and in the text box in your document. Notice that any text or illustration in your text box shows through the color you've chosen (unless it's very dark). You can lighten the color and allow text or graphics to show through more clearly, however, by checking the Semitransparent checkbox next to the Color box.

Selecting a Fill Effect

Until now, you've worked only with solid colors, but Word also provides *fill effects* that allow you to add gradients, textures, paterns, even images, as backgrounds to your text box. To choose a Fill Effect, click the down-arrow next to the Color box, and choose Fill Effects. The Fill Effects tabbed dialog box opens, as shown in Figure 17.20. Notice the Sample box at the bottom right; any fill effects you apply are previewed here first.

By default, the Gradient tab displays. You can choose among four gradients, each of which fades from the color you've already selected, to black. For example, you can fade from light to dark, from dark to light, or from dark to light and back again. However, if none of the default settings catch your fancy, you can change virtually any aspect of your gradient.

To keep the color you've already chosen, but control the darkness of the fade, click the One color button. A slider appears; as you drag from left to right, the fade color changes from black to gray to white. You're likely to use this feature often: it helps you make sure black text stays readable even through the gradient you've chosen. Notice that when you select One Color, the Color 1 box appears, making it convenient for you to change the base color you're working with, if you choose.

Figure 17.20

The Fill Effects tabbed dialog box, showing the Gradient tab

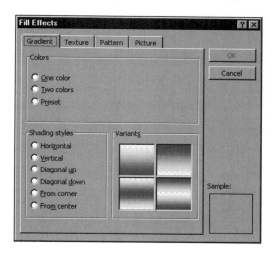

What if you don't want the second color in your fade to be black, gray, or white? Click Two colors, and the Color 2 box appears; you can now specify two separate colors.

Gradients Without the Hard Work

What if you want an interesting gradient without doing the hard work of customizing one? Choose Preset and select one of Word's 24 built-in color schemes, such as Early Sunset, Daybreak, Fog, Brass, and Silver.

Controlling Shading Styles

Whether you create a One-color, Two-color, or Preset gradient, you can also control how your gradient's fade works: in other words, where the second color appears, and how it changes. The default setting is Horizontal: all four variants change from one color to another as you move from top to bottom or vice versa. However, you can also create vertical or diagonal fades, start the fade in any of four corners, or create a fade that starts in the center. A fade that's lightest in the center is shown in Figure 17.21.

Using Textures in Text Boxes

Word 97 comes with 24 textures—the same ones that are available as backgrounds for Web pages, as discussed in Chapter 14. To select one, click the Texture tab, and choose from the textures displayed (see Figure 17.22).

If none of Word's 24 textures meet your needs, you can use your own—any Windows Bitmap (BMP or DIB), or Windows Metafile (WMF or

Figure 17.21

A fade that's lightest in the center

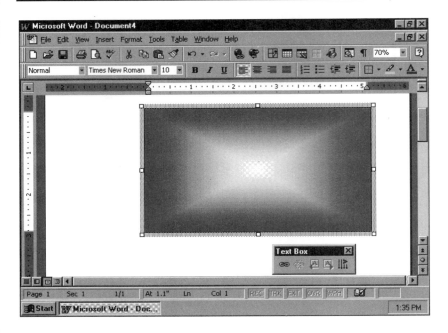

Figure 17.22

The Texture Tab of the Fill Effects dialog box

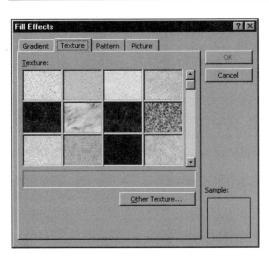

EMF) will do. You can also use any other graphic you've installed an import filter for. With the widespread popularity of textures for multimedia and Web applications, there are now many third-party texture clip art packages to choose from.

To add another texture, click Other Texture; the Select Texture dialog box opens (see Figure 17.23). Browse for the texture you want, and choose OK. Notice the globe icon on the Select Texture toolbar: You can use it to display Internet Explorer 3.01 (if you've installed it) and search the World Wide Web for new textures. Once you find the texture you're looking for, click OK; the image is previewed in the Sample box. If you want to use the picture, click OK twice.

Figure 17.23

The Select Texture
dialog box

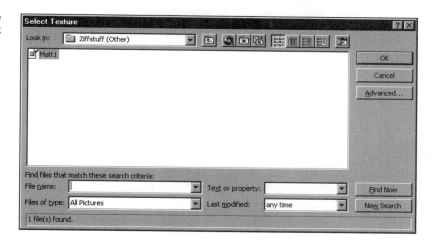

NOTE. *When you insert a texture, Word tiles (repeats) the background as many times as necessary to fill the text box. As a result, Word does not allow you to insert a very large image file as a texture. However, you can insert the same image into a text box as a picture that will appear once, filling the text box. This is discussed later in the chapter.*

Using Patterns in Text Boxes

You can apply any of 48 patterns to a text box, choosing both the foreground and background colors. Choose the Pattern tab (see Figure 17.24); select a pattern from the Pattern box. By default, the foreground color is black and the background color is white; however, you can change both of these.

Using a Picture as a Fill Effect

You've already seen how you can use an image as a texture that appears behind your text; you can also insert images as pictures. To do so, choose the Picture tab from the Fill Effects dialog box (see Figure 17.25), and click Select Picture. The Select Picture dialog box opens; as with Select Texture, you

Figure 17.24

The Pattern tab of the Fill
Effects dialog box

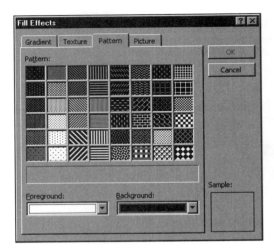

can search your computer, or click the Search the Web icon to load Internet
Explorer and search for images on the Web. Once you find the picture you're
looking for, click OK; the image is previewed in the Picture box. If you want
to use the picture, click OK twice.

Figure 17.25

The Picture tab of the Fill
Effects dialog box

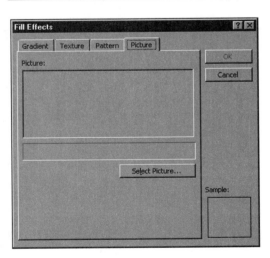

Controlling the Size of Your Text Box

When you first drew your text box, you sized it using the text box sizing handles. But you may need to size your text box more precisely. For example, if you are using a text box as part of a newsletter layout, you may need a text box that is precisely 5" by 1 2/3"—no more, no less. You can specify size precisely, by displaying the Format Text Box tabbed dialog box and choosing the Size tab (see Figure 17.26).

Figure 17.26

The Size tab of the Format Text Box tabbed dialog box

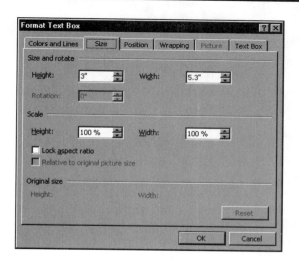

Here, you can specify the precise Height and Width of a text box, to 1/100th of an inch. If you prefer, you can also set the size of your text box with the Scale controls. For example, you can leave the width setting at 100%, but set Height to 200%; Word would then double the height of the text box without changing the width. If you want to shrink or enlarge the text box proportionally, check the Lock aspect ratio box; then, when you change the proportion of either Height or Width, the other setting will change as well.

Specifying the Position of a Text Box

Next, you can specify exactly where a text box appears. In doing so, you establish horizontal and vertical reference points—the starting locations from where Word can mark off the distance you specify.

When you open the Position dialog box, as shown in Figure 17.27, Word displays the current position of the text box on your page. You can create horizontal reference points that tell Word to measure a specific distance from the margin, page, or column. Or you can set vertical reference points that tell Word to measure a specific distance from the Margin, Page, or previous Paragraph. Each of these settings affects your text box differently.

Figure 17.27

The Position tab of the Format Text Box dialog box

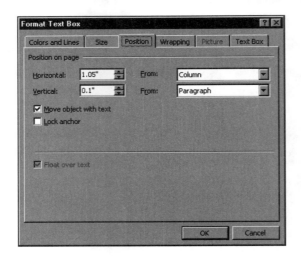

By default, when the paragraph before a text box moves, the text box moves as well. In other words, the text box is *anchored* to the paragraph. If you want to change this behavior so the text box stays where it is, regardless of what happens to the adjacent paragraph, set the text box position relative to a margin, or the page itself, rather than a paragraph. The Move object with text check box is automatically cleared.

In other cases, you may not only want the text box to stay next to a specific paragraph, you may also want to make sure it always stays on the same page as that paragraph. Word handles this through a feature called Lock Anchor. Check the Lock anchor check box, and the text box moves to any new page where the paragraph to which it's anchored goes.

Wrapping Text Around a Text Box

Text boxes are ideal for copy elements such as sidebars, the short blocks of text that often accompany longer articles. They can also be used for holding graphics. Depending on how you've used a text box, you might want the surrounding text to wrap around it in a variety of ways. For example, you might want Tight wrapping, where the text comes very close to the edges of the text box.

Conversely, you might not want text to wrap around the text box at all—you might simply want the surrounding text to appear above or below the text box. Or you might want the text to wrap tightly on one side, but not at all on the other. Word gives you all this control and more, through the Format Text Box Wrapping tab (see Figure 17.28).

Figure 17.28

The Wrapping tab of the Format Text Box dialog box

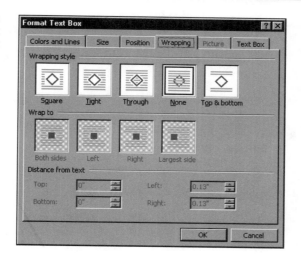

First, specify a wrapping style. The default is None, which means the text box is simply superimposed over any text in its way, hiding that text. Other options are:

- *Square*, which creates a rectangle of white space around the text box;

- *Tight*, which wraps the text as closely as possible to the text box, following its contours;

- *Through*, which is similar to Tight, except that it wraps inside any parts of the object that are open; and

- *Top and Bottom*, where, as mentioned earlier, text doesn't wrap around a text box—it appears above the text box and then jumps beneath it.

Once you've set a Wrapping style (other than None), you can use the Wrap to options to specify whether the Wrapping will occur on both sides of the text box, or only on one side. You can also specify how far away from the text box the wrapped text appears—in other words, you can set margins between the text box and the text that wraps around it. For example, if you use Top & Bottom wrapping, you can specify how much space above and below the text box stays empty.

Setting Internal Text Box Margins

We've just discussed setting margins between a text box and the text outside it. But you can also set top, bottom, left and right margins for text or graphics that appear *inside* the text box. To do so, display the Format Text Box tabbed dialog box, and choose the Text Box tab (see Figure 17.29).

Figure 17.29

The Text Box tab of the Format Text Box dialog box

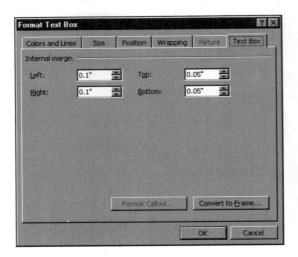

■ Linking Text Boxes

If you've ever tried to create a newsletter in an earlier version of Word, you know that it can be difficult to manage the "jumps" from one page to another within an article—especially if you're still editing that article. You may have found yourself moving small chunks of copy manually from one page to the next—and then having to do it again after making more edits. With linked text boxes, that's no longer necessary. As you edit an article to become longer or shorter, the contents of each linked text box will adjust accordingly—automatically.

To link text boxes, start by placing two text boxes in your document. Select the first text box, and click the Create Text Box Link button on the Text Box toolbar. The mouse pointer changes shape to resemble a pitcher, as shown in Figure 17.30.

You can create links between as many text boxes as you want. Then, when you start entering text in the *first* text box, if you run out of room, the text will flow into the *next* text box, and continue flowing from one linked

Figure 17.30

Pitcher mouse pointer, preparing to create a link among text boxes

Pitcher mouse pointer

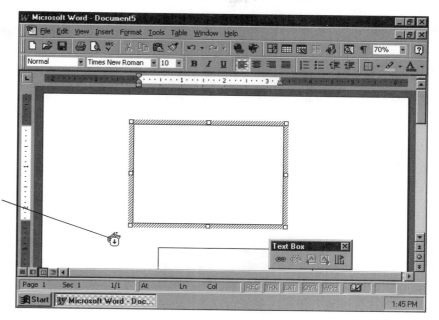

text box to the next. If there's not enough text to fill them all, the text boxes at the end of the chain will remain empty.

You can edit the contents of all linked text boxes at the same time. For example, you can press Ctrl+A within one text box, to select *all* the text in *all* text boxes linked to it. Then, you can apply formatting to all the linked text boxes at once. (Conversely, if you press Ctrl+A to select all text *outside* a text box, no text inside any text box will be selected.)

Once you've linked text boxes, you can easily move from one text box to the next by clicking the Previous Text Box or Next Text Box buttons on the Text Box toolbar. You can also break links between text boxes whenever you want.

Breaking Links Between Text Boxes

To break a link, choose the text box you want to unlink, and click the Break Forward Link button. All the text that *previously* appeared in the linked text box is now stored with the previous text box. Of course, the excess text that *had* appeared in the text box you've now unlinked will not be visible in the previous text box unless you expand that text box or reformat the text to make it smaller.

■ Controlling Hyphenation

If you've worked with captions, or with narrow text boxes, you may have noticed that some of your words may be spaced oddly—or, if you've left-aligned your text, there may be large, unsightly gaps at the end of some lines. When typesetters and designers encounter similar situations, they often make the necessary adjustments by hyphenating the document. Word's automatic hyphenation features offer you the same flexibility. To hyphenate a document, choose Tools, Language, Hyphenation. The Hyphenation dialog box opens, as shown in Figure 17.31.

Figure 17.31

The Hyphenation dialog box

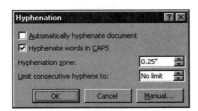

To automatically hyphenate the entire document, check Automatically hyphenate document, and choose OK.

TIP. *You can hyphenate any part of a document by selecting it before you display the Hyphenation dialog box.*

Taking More Control over Automatic Hyphenation

You may find that Word's automatic hyphenation is hyphenating more—or fewer—words than you'd like. For example, when you left-align text, there's a trade-off between the raggedness of the text and the number of words you hyphenate.

Word automatically considers words for hyphenation if they fall within the last 0.25 inch of a line. Word calls this the *hyphenation zone*; some typographers call it the *hot zone*. If you shrink the hyphenation zone, Word will tend to hyphenate more words, but the right-edge of your copy will be less ragged—or if you are justifying text, you'll be less likely to see distracting "rivers" of white space flowing through your document.

You might also find it distracting to encounter several hyphenated lines in a row. You can specify how many consecutive lines can be hyphenated by setting a value in the Limit consecutive hyphens to box.

Finally, if your document contains many acronyms or capitalized product names, you may want Word to skip those when you hyphenate a document. If so, clear the Hyphenate words in CAPS check box.

Manually Hyphenating a Document

Finally, if you really want control, you can manually hyphenate your document. In the Hyphenation dialog box, enter the hyphenation settings you want, and click Manual. Word moves to the first word it wishes to hyphenate, and displays where it recommends placing the hyphen, as shown in Figure 17.32. In the background, you can view the document as it would appear if you accept Word's hyphenation.

Figure 17.32

The Manual
Hyphenation
dialog box

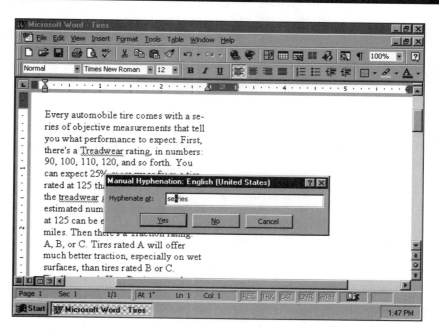

You can choose to hyphenate the word, or skip it, or move the hyphen anywhere within the word, using your mouse or left/right arrow keys. When you make a decision, Word skips to the next word it wishes to hyphenate.

■ Getting Images into Your Documents

There's more to desktop publishing than words, so Word 97 and Office 97 give you an unprecedented range of options for getting images into your documents. You can:

- Choose an image from your Word or Office clip art library, which can include as many as 3,000 images

- Insert an image from a file on your disk, your network, or on the Internet

- Create an image from text, using the WordArt program

You can also insert AutoShapes (covered briefly earlier in this chapter, and in more detail in Chapter 18), or charts (covered in Chapter 19), or scan an image directly into Word using your scanner (see Chapter 23).

Using the Microsoft Office 97 Clip Art Gallery

To open an image from the Microsoft Clip Art Gallery, place your insertion point where you want the image, and choose Insert, Picture, Clip Art. The Microsoft Office Clip Art Gallery opens, as shown in Figure 17.33.

Figure 17.33

The Microsoft Office
Clip Art Gallery

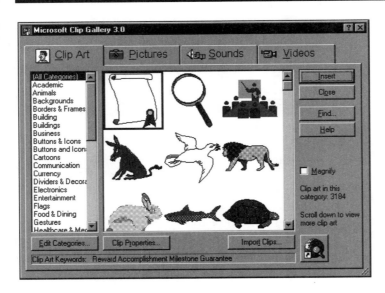

Select a clip art image, or choose a category and select from the images available in that category. You can also click Find to display the Find Clip dialog box (see Figure 17.34), where you can search for a specific clip by keyword relating to the clip's contents, or by file name, or by file format. Once you've found the file you want, choose Insert to place the image in your document.

Figure 17.34

The Find Clip dialog box

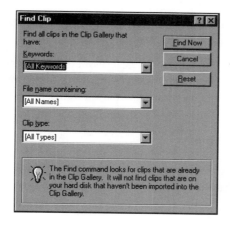

Notice that in Word 97, the Clip Art Gallery has separate tabs for built-in Clip Art, other pictures, sounds, and videos; however, the default Office installation only includes clip art. If you purchased Office on CD-ROM, however, you can find significantly more clip media on your disk. To install the Microsoft Clipart Extra library, you need to run a separate setup program, which can be found in the Clipart folder on your CD-ROM. When you do, you'll wind up with more than 3,000 pieces of clip art, over 140 photos, 31 sounds, and 20 brief video clips.

Notice, also, the Connect to Web button on the bottom right of the Clip Art dialog box; if you have installed Microsoft Explorer, clicking this button connects you to Microsoft's online clip art library, where you can download even more images.

Since the Clip Art Gallery is free and convenient, you might want to use it to store thumbnails of other clip art you own, whether this clip art is stored on your hard disk or on CD-ROM.

Using Other Clip Art

You can use a wide variety of images with Word, whether or not you choose to organize them through Word's Clip Art Gallery. In Word 97, the available file import filters have been beefed up considerably. Notably, you can now use JPEG and GIF files, the Internet's two standard image formats. The list of built-in Word image filters now includes:

```
JPEG File Interchange Format (JPG)
Portable Network Graphics (PNG)
Windows Bitmap (BMP, RLE, DIB)
Windows Enhanced Metafiles (EMF)
Windows Metafiles (WMF)
```

You can also import a wide variety of additional image files if you have installed the appropriate filters, which are included with Word but are not automatically installed. (You can rerun Word's Setup program to add filters at any time.)

```
AutoCAD Format 2-D DXF)
Computer Graphics Metafile(CGM)
Corel Draw 3.0 through 6.0(CDR)
Encapsulated PostScript(EPS)
GIF(GIF) .
Kodak Photo CD(PCD)
Macintosh PICT(PCT)
Micrografx Designer/Draw(DRW)
PC Paintbrush(PCX)
Tagged Image File Format(TIF)
Targa(TGA)
WordPerfect Graphics(WPG)
```

To insert a picture from a file, choose Insert, Picture, From File. The Insert Picture dialog box opens (see Figure 17.35), displaying the Clip art directory on your hard disk. Notice that there's a shortcut to Clip art on Office CD, which makes it easy to find clip art stored on your Office CD-ROM. Browse for a file on your computer or network, or click the Search the Web toolbar button to look for an image on the Internet. When you've found the file you're looking for, click Insert; the file will be inserted in your document at the insertion point.

Inserting Graphics Without Dramatically Increasing File Size

There's no way around it: graphics are *large*. Even though Word 97 compresses graphics, documents with many graphics can get very cumbersome, very quickly. One solution is to insert a *link* to the images, rather than inserting the images themselves. Then, Word can find the images when they're necessary for viewing or printing, without storing duplicates of the images in your

Figure 17.35

The Insert Picture
dialog box

**Search the Web
toolbar button**

Link to file button

**Shortcut to
Clipart on Office CD**

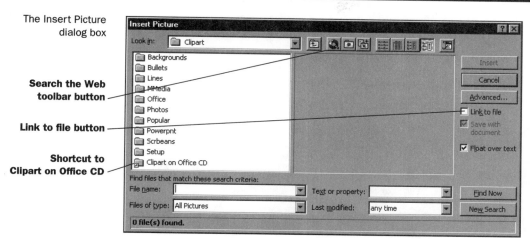

Word files. To insert a picture file as a link, choose Insert, Picture, From File; select the image you want to link; check the Link to File box; and click Insert.
When *wouldn't* you choose to link a picture?

- When you're planning to move your file or the picture

- When the picture is stored on a network resource or on the Internet, and might become temporarily unavailable when you need it

TIP. *Graphics formats can be surprisingly complex. If a file doesn't import the way you expect it to, you can find out more about Word's file filter by displaying the Help window* Graphics file types Word can use.

■ Using WordArt 3.0

A picture may be worth a thousand words, but sometimes you can get almost the same payoff by transforming your words into a picture. That's what WordArt is for: it places a breathtaking variety of text effects at your fingertips. If you've ever used WordArt with previous versions of Word or Office, you'll find that it's been completely revamped—and you'll probably find it much easier to get the results you're looking for.

To use WordArt, choose Insert, Picture, WordArt. The WordArt Gallery opens, as shown in Figure 17.36. Here, you can choose among 30 pre-styled effects.

Choose an effect and click OK; the Edit WordArt Text dialog box opens (see Figure 17.37). Enter your text; choose a font; italicize or boldface the text if you choose; when you're finished, click OK. The text appears in your document, along with the WordArt toolbar (see Figure 17.38).

Figure 17.36

The WordArt Gallery

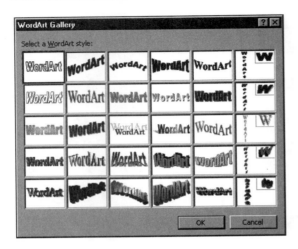

Figure 17.37

The Edit WordArt Text
dialog box

Now that you can see how your text looks, you can use the WordArt toolbar to make adjustments to get exactly the effect you're looking for. (If you're not at all satisfied with the effect or text you already have, you can use the WordArt toolbar to change it entirely. Click the Edit Text button to return to the Edit WordArt Text dialog box and change your text, or click the WordArt Gallery button to choose a different pre-styled effect.)

For example, you can change the fill and line color, size, position, and wrapping of WordArt text, much as you learned to do with text boxes earlier in this chapter. Click Format WordArt to display the Format WordArt dialog box (see Figure 17.39).

Figure 17.38

WordArt text in your
document, with the
WordArt toolbar displayed

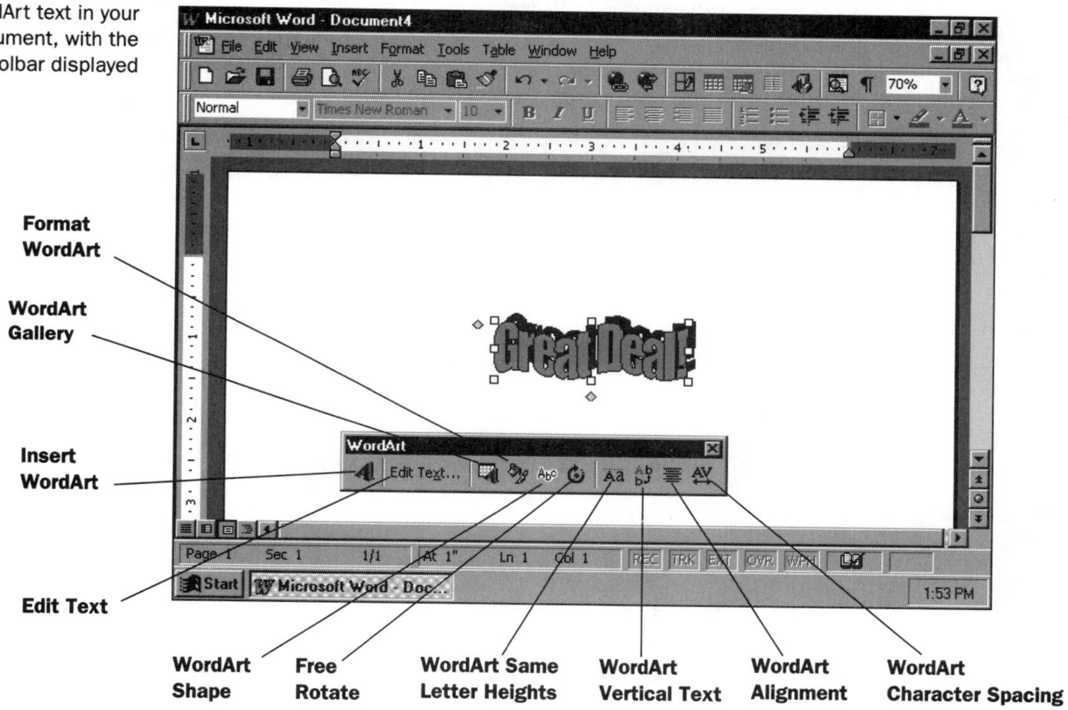

Format
WordArt

WordArt
Gallery

Insert
WordArt

Edit Text

WordArt   Free   WordArt Same   WordArt   WordArt   WordArt
Shape   Rotate   Letter Heights   Vertical Text Alignment   Character Spacing

Figure 17.39

The Format WordArt
tabbed dialog box

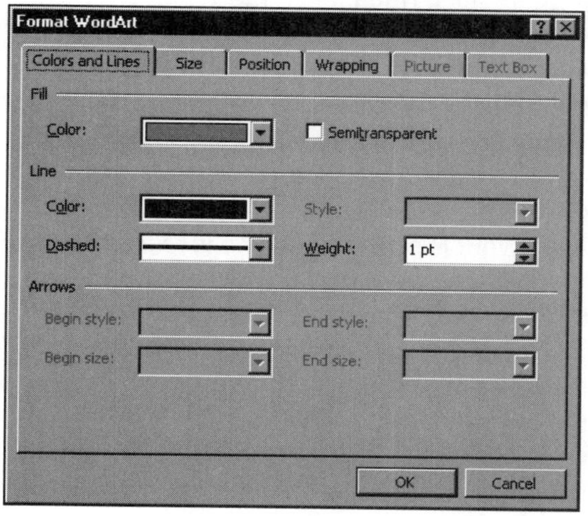

You can also change the shape your text is warped into, by clicking the WordArt shape button and choosing among the 40 shapes provided there (see Figure 17.40).

Figure 17.40

Choosing a
WordArt shape

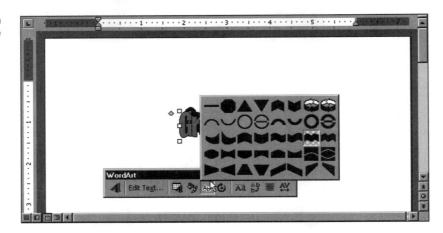

You can rotate WordArt objects to any angle you wish. Click the Free Rotate toolbar button; the object's selection handles change to green circles, and your mouse pointer changes to resemble the Free Rotate icon (Figure 17.41). Click on a selection handle and drag the object to the angle you want. When you're satisfied, click the Free Rotate button again to finish.

If you simply want to rotate your text 90 degrees, stacking the letters one on top of each other, click the WordArt Vertical Text button instead (see Figure 17.42).

WordArt provides a few more options for adjusting the appearance of text. You can click WordArt Same Letter Heights to make your lowercase letters as large as your capital letters, as shown in Figure 17.43. You can align or stretch your text using the options that display when you click the WordArt alignment button (see Figure 17.44). Finally, you can control the letterspacing used by your WordArt text by choosing among the options displayed when you click the WordArt Character Spacing button (see Figure 17.45).

In this chapter, you've taken a close look at several Word 97 features specifically designed to make it easier to create heavily formatted documents such as newsletters or brochures. You've learned how to create documents with multiple columns, use borders and shading, and work with Word 97's extremely powerful and flexible text boxes. You've also learned how to make the most of graphics in your Word documents, whether those graphics come

Figure 17.41

Rotating a WordArt object

**Free rotate
mouse pointer**

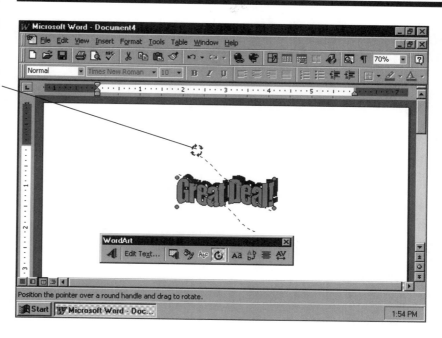

Figure 17.42

Stacking WordArt
text vertically

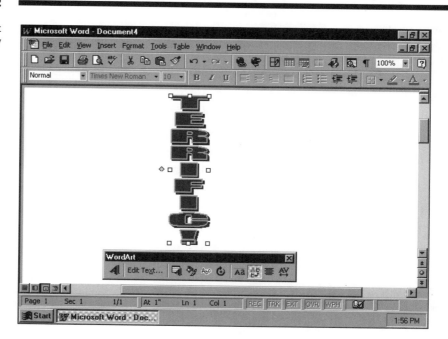

Figure 17.43

Using WordArt Same
Letter Heights

Figure 17.44

Choosing how to align or
stretch your text

Figure 17.45

Setting character spacing
for WordArt text

from the Office 97 clip art library or your own images, or WordArt's cornuco-
pia of text effects.

In the next two chapters, you'll go a step further, taking a look at Word
97 drawing tools, which for the first time rival some full-featured drawing
programs—and learning how to create professional charts more easily than
ever before. By the time you're done, you'll wonder how anyone was ever
satisfied with a mere *word* processor!

- *Creating Lines, Rectangles, and Ovals*
- *Using AutoShapes*
- *Using Text Boxes and Callouts*
- *Controlling Colors*
- *Shadowing and 3-D*
- *Backgrounds and Textures*
- *Grouping and Ungrouping*

Drawing:
Imagine It, Then Draw It (Maybe)

THIS BOOK HAS FREQUENTLY ALLUDED TO ADDING GRAPHICS TO
your document. There are two ways to do this:

- Import a clip art graphic
- Create your own graphic, using Word's powerful
  drawing tools

It's all well and good to import an illustration if you already have one that will do the job. But sometimes you need to create a new one. That's where Word's drawing features come in handy.

Word is a *drawing* program, which means it builds its images from lines. (Sometimes drawing programs are called *vector* programs.) This contrasts with *bitmapped* painting programs that splash dots across the screen as you create your image.

You already own a painting program—Microsoft Paint, which comes with Windows 97. With Word's drawing features, you can draw as well. Painting programs are traditionally a bit easier to work with, but drawing programs create images that can be printed on any kind of printer at any resolution.

Introducing Word 97's Drawing Toolbar

To draw in Word, first display the Drawing toolbar (see Figure 18.1). To show the Drawing toolbar, click the Drawing button on Standard toolbar, and the Drawing toolbar appears at the bottom of the Word application window.

Figure 18.1

The Drawing toolbar

The Drawing toolbar contains Word's tools for drawing. You'll find some of these—such as callouts—valuable even if you never create an image from scratch. Table 18.1 lists and describes Word's drawing tools.

To draw, you need to be in Page Layout view. If you're not in Page Layout view and you choose a drawing tool from the Drawing toolbar, Word automatically switches to Page Layout view.

To create a line or shape, choose the drawing tool you want, and click where you want the shape to begin. (Your mouse pointer now looks like a crosshair.) Then drag the drawing tool to where you want the shape to end (see Figure 18.2). When you release the mouse button, the shape appears.

You'll see small square boxes (*handles*) at the ends or corners of the shape. These indicate that the shape is *active*. You can delete an active shape by pressing the Backspace key. You can move the entire shape by dragging it. You can move one end, shrinking or enlarging the shape, by dragging its handle. You also can add color to the line or the inside of the shape, add patterns, and change the line style.

Figure 18.2

Dragging a drawing tool

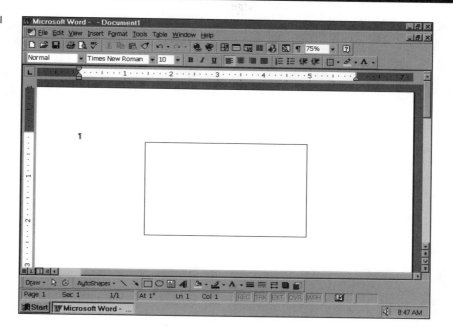

■ Creating Lines, Rectangles, and Ovals

With the Line tool, you can draw straight lines in your choice of colors, weights, and styles. Lines can begin and end in a variety of arrowheads, as explained in the section on Drawing Arrows later in this chapter.

With the Rectangle and Oval tools, you can draw rectangles, squares, ovals, or circles. By default, the tools draw rectangles and ovals. In the next section you learn how to draw squares and ovals with the Rectangle and Oval tools.

Making Exact Squares, Circles, and Angles

It's not often easy to draw an exact square or circle using typical drawing tools. Word offers a shortcut. If you want an exact square or circle, choose the Rectangle or Oval button and press Shift while you drag the mouse.

The same Shift key works to make straight lines that are precisely horizontal, vertical, or diagonal. If you press Shift while you drag the Line tool, you're limited to the following angles: vertical, horizontal, and 30°, 45°, and 60° angles in all four quadrants.

Table 18.1

Word's Drawing Tools

BUTTON	WHAT IT DOES
Draw	Enables you to group, ungroup, and regroup objects, arrange the stacking order of objects, align objects on a grid, nudge objects, align and distribute objects, rotate and flip objects, reshape a curve or freeform object, change to a different AutoShape, and set AutoShape defaults.
Select Objects	Selects one or more objects for editing.
Free Rotate	Rotates selected object to any angle and direction.
AutoShapes	Enables you to choose freeform shapes.
Line tool	Draws straight lines.
Arrow tool	Draws arrows.
Rectangle tool	Draws rectangles and squares.
Oval tool	Draws ovals and circles.
Text Box	Enables you to insert text into text boxes and callouts.
WordArt	Enables you to manipulate fonts such as stretch, squeeze, bend into a shape, add a shadow and border, and add other effects.
Fill Color	Enables you to choose a fill color.
Line Color	Enables you to choose a line color.
Font Color	Enables you to choose a font color.
Line Style	Enables you to choose a line style.
Dash Style	Enables you to choose a dashed-line style.
Arrow Style	Enables you to choose an arrow style.
Shadow	Enables you to choose a shadow style.
3-D	Enables you to choose a 3-D style.

Drawing Arrows

You've already seen how to draw a line. Wouldn't it be neat if that line had an arrow at the end of it? Then you could draw a pointer connected to anything you wanted.

Word offers this feature. Click on the Arrow Style button, and a variety of arrow styles appear, including arrowheads, diamonds, circles, and arrows going in either or both directions (see Figure 18.3).

Figure 18.3

The Arrow styles

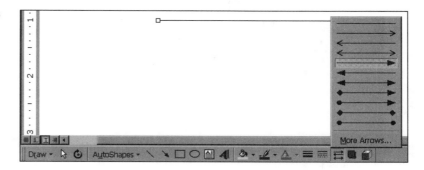

You can choose one of these, and then choose the Arrow button to draw the arrow. Or, to get more control over your line or arrow, choose More Arrows. The Format AutoShape dialog box opens, showing the Colors and Lines tab (see Figure 18.4).

Figure 18.4

The Colors and Lines tab in the Format AutoShape dialog box

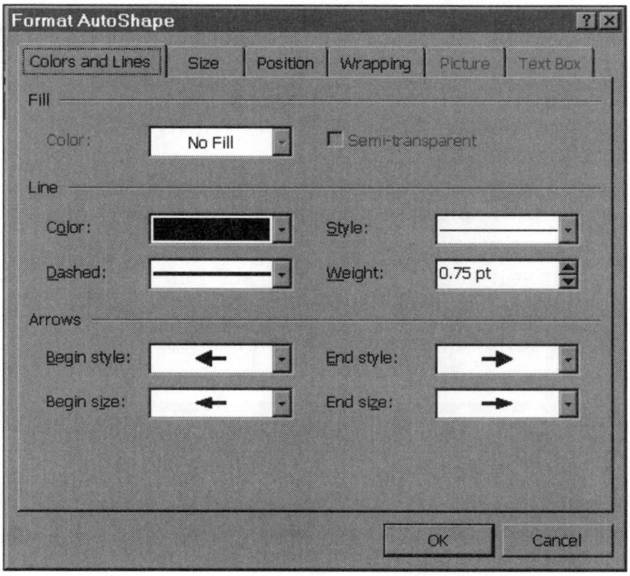

If you want to change the arrow style and size, choose any option you want from the **B**egin Style, **E**nd Style, Begin Si**z**e, and End Si**z**e options in the Arrows area.

Changing Line Style

When you draw a line, rectangle, or oval, it appears in the default fill color (no fill color), line color (black), and line style (thin). The general process for creating an object is to select the colors and line styles you want to use, click the drawing button you want to use to select it, and draw an object on the page.

To change the line style, click on the Line Style button, and an assortment of line styles appear, including several thicknesses of regular lines, and double and triple lines (see Figure 18.5).

Figure 18.5

The Line styles

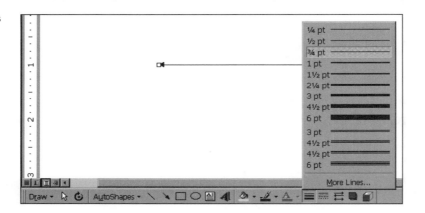

To customize your own line style, choose More Lines. The Format AutoShape dialog box opens, showing the Colors and Lines tab. From here, you can specify a line color and weight (defaults are black, 0.75 point).

If you want a broken or dashed line, click on the Dash Style button, and an assortment of line styles appear, including several thicknesses of regular lines, dotted lines, and broken lines (see Figure 18.6).

Figure 18.6

The Dash styles

After you select a line style, choose the Line button to draw the line. If you've already drawn a line or box, you will see that the object contains the line style you specified.

NOTE. *To change the color of a line (or the edges of a shape), you can also click on the Line Color drop-down arrow to display a color palette. Select a color from the palette.*

■ Using AutoShapes

With Word's new AutoShapes feature, you can add predesigned freeform shapes to your drawing. You have a multitude of freeform shapes to choose from: lines, basic shapes, block arrows, flowchart symbols, stars, banners, and callouts (see Figure 18.7).

Figure 18.7

The AutoShape lines

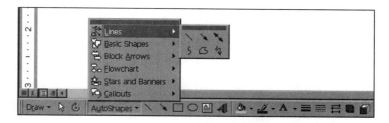

To insert a freeform shape, choose the AutoShapes drop-down arrow, choose an AutoShape category from the menu, and then click the shape you like. In your document, click and drag to create the shape (see Figure 18.7).

Do you see the little yellow diamond on the AutoShape button? This is an adjustment handle that enables you to change the feature that stands out the most on the shape. For instance, you can adjust a rounded square to be more or less rounded.

You can resize, rotate, flip, or add color to these ready-made shapes, or even combine them with other shapes to make fancier shapes.

NOTE. *What if you want a different AutoShape instead of the one you selected? No problem. You can select the AutoShape you want to change, click Draw on the Drawing toolbar, choose Change AutoShape, select a category, and then click the shape you want.*

■ Using Text Boxes and Callouts

You might want to include text in your drawing. To do so, choose the Text Box button. Click and drag where you want the text box to appear (see Figure 18.8).

Figure 18.8

A text box

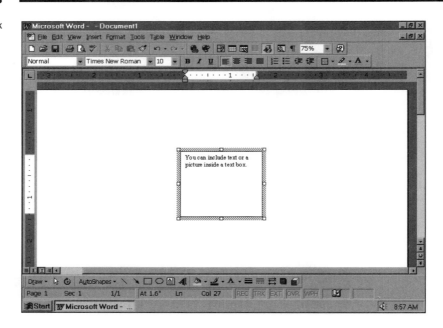

The text box appears, surrounded by a diagonal-line border. An insertion point appears. You also see the Text Box toolbar, as shown in Figure 18.9. The Text Box toolbar contains buttons for linking and unlinking text boxes, moving between linked text boxes, and changing the direction of the text in a text box.

Figure 18.9

The Text Box toolbar

NOTE. *If you don't see the Text Box toolbar on-screen, don't worry. Choose View, Toolbars, Text Box to redisplay the Text box toolbar.*

You can edit and format inside a text box as you can anywhere else in Word. Choose any of the formatting buttons on the Formatting toolbar to boldface, italicize, and underline the text, as well as to change the font and font size. You also can copy material into a text box.

If your text extends beyond the text box, it won't all be visible. But you can expand the text box by clicking on its border to select it, and then dragging its sizing handles.

Linking Text Boxes

If you want to make text flow in a continuous story on multiple pages in your document, you can place this text in text boxes and link the text boxes. This is a new feature in Word 97.

NOTE. *The text box links don't have to be adjacent in the document; they can be in different locations throughout the document. The links don't have to be set up in a forward direction—they can go backward, forward, or in any direction.*

One example of using linked text boxes is making an article flow from page 2 to page 5 in a news bulletin.

Here is how you create linked text boxes:

1. Click in the document where you want the first linked text box to appear. Draw a text box in your document.

2. Create additional text boxes where you want the text to flow.

3. Click the first text box.

4. Choose Create Text Box Link on the Text Box toolbar. The mouse pointer changes to an upright pitcher.

5. Click in the text box that you want the text to flow to. The mouse pointer changes to a pouring pitcher which indicates that the text box can receive the link.

6. To create a link to the other text boxes, click in the text box that you just created the link to. Then, repeat steps 4 and 5 to create the links.

After you link the text boxes, click in the first text box and type the text. Notice that as the text box fills up, the text flows into the other text boxes that you linked.

To move among linked text boxes, click the Next Text Box button or Previous Text Box button on the Text Box toolbar.

If you want to break a link in the series of linked text boxes, first click the text box you no longer want linked. Then, click the Break Link button on the Text Box toolbar. Word automatically rearranges the text flow in the remaining linked text boxes.

NOTE. *If you add text to a linked text box, the text will flow forward into the next text box. If you delete text from a linked text box, the text in the next box moves backward.*

Creating Callouts

Arrows plus text boxes equal callouts. A callout is a label that you can use to point out specific information on a graphic, a drawing object, or a figure in a document. Word now offers 20 callouts that you can choose from the AutoShapes Callouts palette (see Figure 18.10).

Figure 18.10

The AutoShapes Callouts

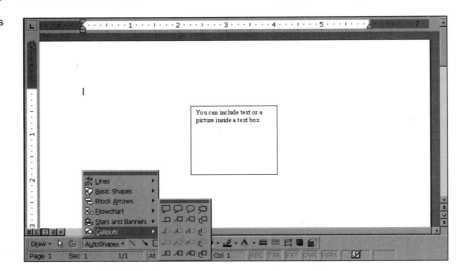

To add a callout, click the Autoshapes drop-down arrow, choose the Callouts category, and click on the callout you want. Next, click on the spot where you want the arrow or line to begin. Then drag the crosshair mouse pointer to where you want to type the callout. Release the mouse button; a text box appears there (see Figure 18.11).

If you move the text box, the callout line still ends at the same spot where you put it, unless you select it and move it manually. You can use the yellow diamond adjustment handle to adjust the position of the pointer on the callout. For example, drag the callout pointer so that it points to a higher and lower position on the object.

■ Controlling Colors

By default, there is no fill color in an object. However, you can have a heyday choosing fill colors. Initially, line color is black, but you can change the line color in an object to anything your heart desires. You can also change the font color for text in a text box, linked text box, and callout.

Figure 18.11

A sample callout

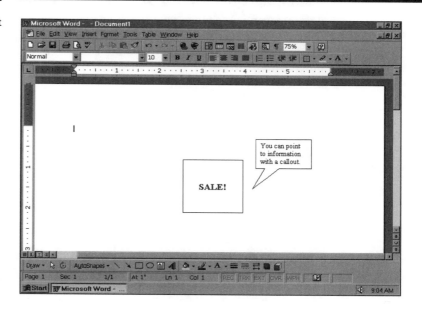

Changing the Fill Color of a Drawing Object

Shapes, like free time, exist to be filled. You can tell Word to fill a shape
with a solid color or pattern by selecting the shape to be filled, clicking the
Fill Color drop-down arrow, and choosing a color from the available palette
(see Figure 18.12).

Figure 18.12

The Fill Color palette

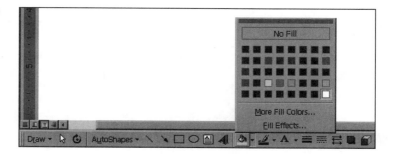

If you don't want any fill color, choose No Fill Color from the palette. To
customize a fill color, choose More Fill Colors. The Colors dialog box opens.
Choose the Standard tab to select a specific color from the palette. Choose
the Custom tab to select a gradient color.

Changing the Line Color of a Drawing Object

Not only can you change the fill color of any object, but you can also change the color of the lines. To change the line color, click the Line Color drop-down arrow, and pick a color from the Line Color palette. If you want to remove a line, choose No Line in the palette (see Figure 18.13).

Figure 18.13

The Line Color palette

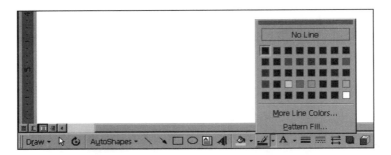

Customizing a line color is similar to customizing a fill color. Choose More Line Colors. It's deja vu. This Colors dialog box is exactly the same as the Colors dialog box for fill colors. The Standard options let you select a specific color from a palette. The Custom options contain gradient colors.

Changing the Font Color of Text in a Text Box

To add pizzazz to your text in a text box, select the text in the text box that you want to change. Choose the Font Color drop-down arrow. Notice that the default font color is Automatic (black). Select a color from the palette to change the font color (see Figure 18.14).

Figure 18.14

The Font Color palette

■ Shadowing and 3-D

You can instantly add a 50-percent gray drop-shadow to the border of a line or shape. The shadow appears on any side of an object, on top of the object, or surrounds the object like a picture frame. As shown in Figure 18.15, drop-shadows add an interesting three-dimensional effect to lines, rectangles, and ovals, and any other shape you have drawn.

To add a drop-shadow, select the object, choose the Shadow tool, and then pick a Shadow style from the Shadow palette (see Figure 18.16).

Figure 18.15

A drop-shadow below and
to the right of the object

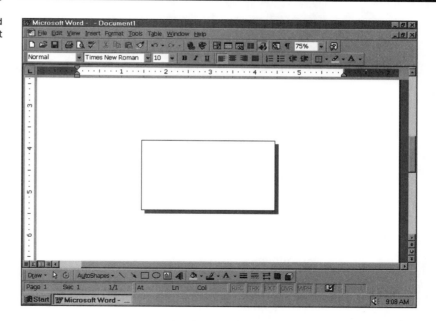

Figure 18.16

The Shadow palette

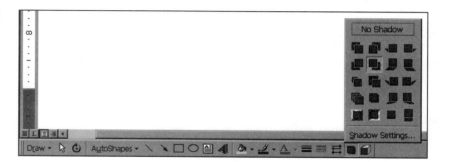

If you don't like the way the shadow looks, you can choose a different shadow. Or, if you decide that you don't really want a shadow for the object, then choose No Shadow from the Shadow palette to remove the shadow.

You can change the shadow style settings by clicking the <u>S</u>hadow Settings button on the Shadow palette. The Shadow Settings toolbar appears, as shown in Figure 18.17. From this toolbar you can choose several shadow options that can change the look of a shadow.

Figure 18.17

The Shadow
Settings toolbar

To add or remove a shadow, click the Shadow On/Off button. You can even move the shadow a little bit at a time in a particular direction. Choose the Nudge Shadow Up, Nudge Shadow Down, Nudge Shadow Left, and Nudge Shadow Right buttons. You can nudge the shadow up, down, left, or right on the selected object in small increments.

What if you want to change the shadow color? You can click the Shadow Color drop-down arrow and find the color of your choice. If you want to customize the shadow color, click the More Shadow Colors button on the Shadow Color palette. Doesn't this Colors dialog box look familiar? You know the drill. The Standard colors and Custom colors are yours for the asking.

You could probably show off your drawing with two-dimensional objects, but wouldn't it be impressive if you could add more depth, perspective, and elevation to the objects? Word can help you add a third dimension (without going into the Twilight Zone) with its 3-D styles.

To add a three-dimensional effect to an object, select the object, and then choose the 3-D tool. The 3-D palette opens, as shown in Figure 18.18.

Figure 18.18

The 3-D styles

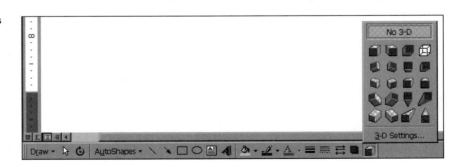

Pick a 3-D style, any 3-D style, and watch how the object takes on a whole new look. It almost looks like the object is popping out the screen (see Figure 18.19).

Figure 18.19

A sample 3-D object

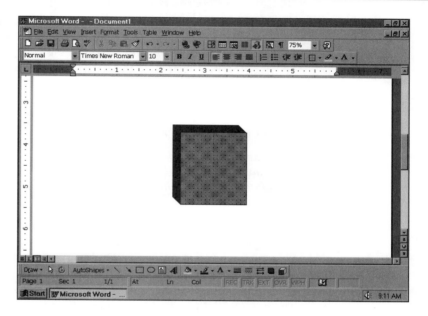

If the 3-D effect doesn't add any value to your object, choose a different 3-D style or get rid of it altogether by choosing No 3-D in the 3-D styles palette. You can fine-tune the 3-D style settings clicking the **3**-D Settings button on the palette. You see the 3-D Settings toolbar (see Figure 18.20).

Figure 18.20

The 3-D Settings toolbar

You can use this toolbar to add to or remove the 3-D style from an object. Click the 3-D On/Off button.

Try experimenting with the Tilt Down, Tilt Up, Tilt Left, and Tilt Right buttons to tilt the 3-D on an angle until you see the object's best view. Each time you click the Tilt Down or Tilt Up button, Word rotates the 3-D effect six degrees around a horizontal axis. Likewise, each time you click the Tilt Left or Tilt Right button, Word rotates the 3-D effect six degrees around a vertical axis.

NOTE. *If you want to rotate the 3-D effect to the next 45-degree point, hold down Shift and click a tilt button to move the effect in the direction you want.*

By default, the depth of the 3-D effect is set to 72 points, which defines the distance from the front to the back of the object. Click the Depth button and choose a depth perspective. Depth is measured in points ranging from zero to infinity. You can also specify the number of points you want in the Custom box. It's a good idea to test out the various depth amounts to see how deep the object looks and get it to look the way you want.

To get a new perspective on the object, click the Direction button, and choose an Extrusion Direction style from the palette.

The Perspective (default) projection option makes the 3-D effect protrude toward a single viewing point. Therefore, it looks as though you are looking at the object from a single location. The object looks almost real.

NOTE. *Be careful when you use the Depth Perspective option because it might make similar 3-D effects look different on adjacent objects. In this case, you might want to use the Parallel option instead.*

The Parallel projection option is good for technical drawings and gives consistency to multiple objects in a drawing. Word extends all sides of the 3-D effect parallel to one another instead of toward a single viewing point.

Selecting lighting to put on a 3-D object is similar to using a dimmer switch to control lighting in a living room. Click the Lighting button, choose a Lighting Direction type, and a Lighting type.

The default Lighting Direction shines light from the left. You may find that shining the light from the right, top, bottom, or center will make part of the object disappear. Keep playing with the lighting directions until you get the results you like.

There are three lighting types: Bright (default), which adds the most white to the color or shade of the 3-D portion of the object; Normal, which adds some white; and Dim, which adds the least amount of white.

You can give your 3-D object another type of look by changing its surface. The surface is the outer appearance of the 3-D portion of the object. Word gives you four surfaces to choose from: Wire Frame, Matte, Plastic, and Metal. The wire frame surface shows only the underlying structure because Word removes all the outer surfaces from the object. The matte surface has a dull finish to it. The plastic surface looks like plastic, and the metal surface looks like shiny metal.

To bring attention to the 3-D effect on an object, you can change its color. Click the 3-D Color drop-down arrow and choose a color. Voila. The 3-D portion of the object appears in a different color from the rest of the object.

■ Backgrounds and Textures

You can add some pretty fancy backgrounds to a selected object such as gradients, textures, patterns, and even pictures that you created yourself. Word refers to these backgrounds as fill effects.

The color you choose from the Standard or Custom color options may be replaced by a fill effect or blend in with the fill effect, depending on what fill effect you choose. For instance, if you choose the Granite texture, Word displays only the granite fill effect in the object (see Figure 18.21).

Figure 18.21

Granite texture

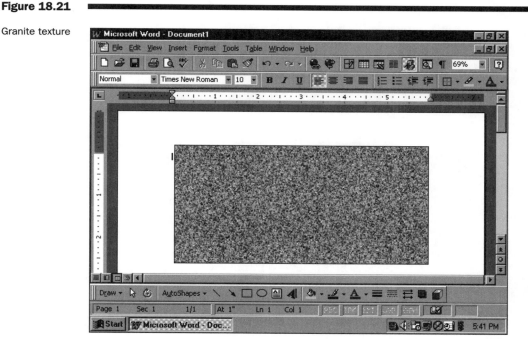

If you choose a color from the Standard color options and a pattern, Word displays the fill color in the fill pattern you chose. For example, if you select bright green for the fill color and the vertical stripe pattern, the result is bright green vertical stripes in the object (see Figure 18.22). In other words, the fill color is the primary color and the fill pattern color is the secondary color.

Adding Gradients, Textures, and Patterns

To add a fill effect, you can select Fill Effects from the Fill Colors palette. The Fill Effects dialog box appears.

Figure 18.22

Vertical stripes pattern

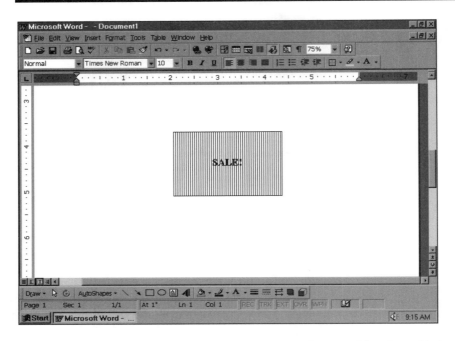

A gradient color can have one or more colors in a combination of light and dark shades and various shading styles. Choose the Gradient tab to custom blend a special gradient, as shown in Figure 18.23.

In the Colors area, you can specify the number of colors. In the Shading Styles, choose how you want the shading to appear—horizontally, vertically, diagonally, from a corner, or from the center. In the Variants area, select a variant: light to dark, dark to light, light to dark to light, or from dark to light to dark. Figure 18.24 shows a sample Gradient fill effect.

Textures come in one color or a blend of colors. They contain attractive and elaborate patterns such as marble, granite, parchment, tissue paper, and newspaper. Choose the Texture tab to select a texture.

Word offers simple, two-color patterns with a small design that is repeated many times. For example, you can choose from vertical, horizontal, and diagonal stripes, bricks, plaid, diamond-shaped patterns, and much more. Choose the Pattern tab to select a pattern.

Figure 18.23

The Gradient options in
the Fill Effects dialog box

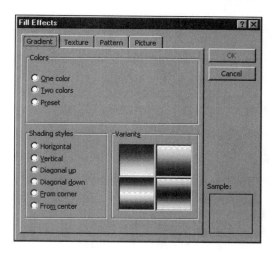

Figure 18.24

Sample gradient

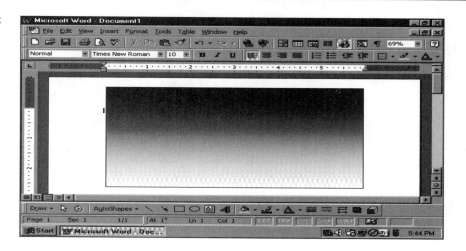

Placing a Picture in Your Drawing

Sometimes you might want to insert a picture as the background of an
object. You can insert any of Word's clip art pictures into a drawing object.
For more information on Word Clip Art, see Chapter 17.

To place a picture in your drawing, place your insertion point where you want the picture, and then click on the Fill Color tool. Choose Fill Effects and click the Create Picture tab. Choose Select Picture and choose a clip art file.

The picture that appears in the Preview box is the original picture and the picture in the Sample box shows what it will look like as a background for the object (see Figure 18.25).

Figure 18.25

Sample picture

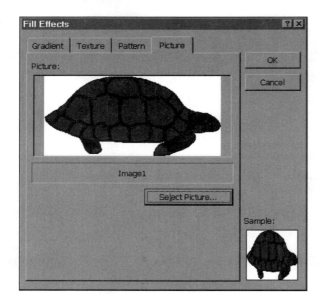

Click OK to insert the picture into the selected object's background.

■ Grouping and Ungrouping

At some point, you might have several shapes and lines you'd like to move, style, or remove together. Most individual drawings are made up of several components, grouped together. A drawing of a house, for example, might include a grouping for each window, another for the door, another for the chimney, and so on. The Group command enables you group the objects together as one unit.

To select them, choose the Select Objects button, and extend a rectangle around them. Next, click the Draw button, and choose Group. Notice the selection handles surround the group of objects, not each individual object, as shown in Figure 18.26.

Figure 18.26

Grouped objects

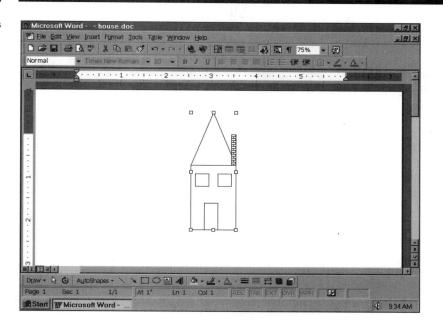

Then move or restyle the group of objects, or press Backspace to delete all the objects in the group.

To edit a part of the drawing, you'll first want to separate the part (ungroup it) from the rest. To ungroup part of an image, select it using the Select Objects button, click the Draw button, and then choose Ungroup.

Conversely, you may want to regroup several objects together, making them easier and faster to move and display. To group drawing objects that were originally grouped together, select one of the objects, click the Draw button, and choose Regroup.

Layering Your Drawing

Word enables you to create layers in your drawing. Each object that you draw exists on its own layer. This means that some objects (those that are closer to the top of the pile) can appear to cover up parts of other objects (those toward the bottom of the pile). Figure 18.27 shows a set of three objects arranged in different orders from front (the top of the pile) to back (the bottom of the pile).

New objects are always drawn at the very front of the picture (on top of the pile). Because objects toward the front of the pile can cover up those toward the back, it is often necessary to change the order of the objects. Fortunately, there are commands on Draw's Order menu for just that purpose.

Figure 18.27

Examples of
layered objects

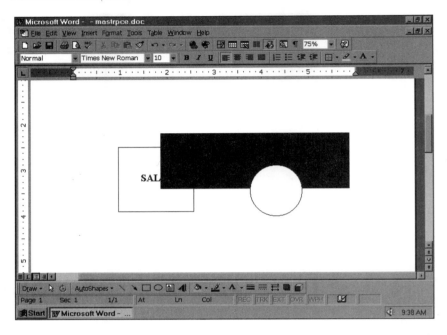

To specify whether a shape, line, or text box appears in the front or back, select it, click the Draw button, and then choose Order.

If you want an object to appear behind all of the other objects (so that those objects can hide part of the object in the back), choose Send to Back. On the other hand, if you want an object to appear at the very front of the pile, (so that all of it is visible and it covers up parts of the objects behind it), choose Bring to Front. In general, you want to have text appear at the very front of the pile.

You exercise even greater control over the order of objects in a pile by using the Send Backward and Bring Forward commands on Draw's Order menu. If you want to move the selected object one step closer to the bottom of the pile, choose Send Backward. If you want to move the selected object one step closer to the top of a pile of objects, choose Bring Forward.

There are two other Order commands that you can use to manipulate objects and text. The Bring in Front of Text command moves an object in front of the text. The Send Behind Text command moves an object behind the text.

Rotating Your Illustration

Word offers features for rotating a shape or an illustration. To turn an image 90 degrees to the left or right, click the Draw button, and choose Rotate or **F**lip. Then, choose Rotate **L**eft or Rotate **R**ight. If you want to rotate an image to any angle, click the Free Rotate button on the Drawing toolbar. The mouse pointer changes to an arrow that curls around to the right. You see rotation handles (small circles) on each corner of the object. Drag a corner of the object in the direction you want to rotate it (see Figure 18.28).

Figure 18.28

Example of a free rotated object

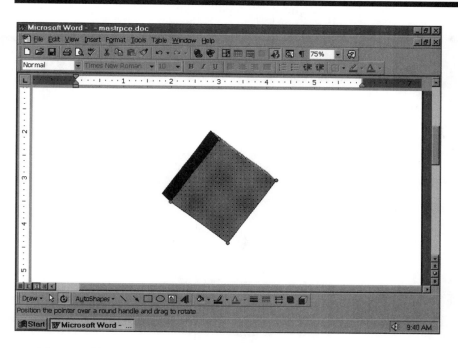

You can flip an illustration to create a mirror image effect. To flip an illustration, click the Draw button, and choose Rotate or **F**lip. To flip the image from left to right, choose Flip **H**orizontal. To flip the image from top to bottom, choose Flip **V**ertical.

NOTE. *You can rotate a text box, but the text in it will stay right side up. Use WordArt to create upside-down and sideways text. WordArt is covered in Chapter 17: Word Desktop Publishing.*

Aligning Elements of Your Drawing

Often, you'll want to line up two or more elements of your drawing. You can align objects to the left, right, and center, top, middle, and bottom. Also, you can distribute the objects so that they are at an equal distance from each other horizontally or vertically.

Aligning and Distributing Objects

To align and distribute objects, select them, click the Draw button, and choose Align and Distribute.

Choose how the objects will align: horizontally, vertically, or by their edges (see Figure 18.29). You can use the Distribute Horizontal or Distribute Vertical commands to line up the objects equal distances from each other.

Figure 18.29

Example of objects aligned left

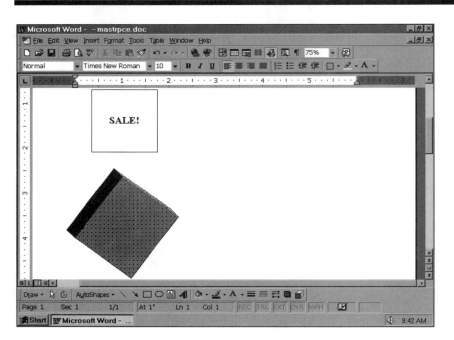

By default, Words aligns the objects relative to each other. However, you can line up the objects in relation to the page by choosing Relative to Page.

Lining Up Elements with the Grid

Word contains a built-in invisible grid that aligns drawing objects to the nearest 1/10th inch. This makes it much easier to line up objects. You can change the fineness of the grid, or turn it off altogether, by clicking the Draw button and choosing Grid. The Grid dialog box opens (see Figure 18.30).

You can change the Horizontal or **V**ertical Spacing. You also can change what Word calls the Horizontal **O**rigin and the Vertical O**r**igin. These set the grid's beginning point; in other words, you can specify no grid on part of your screen, and a grid on the rest of it. To turn off the grid entirely, clear the **S**nap to Grid check box.

Figure 18.30

Grid dialog box

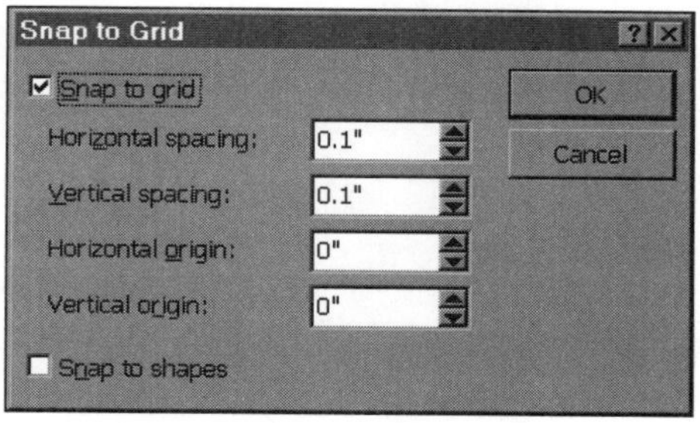

If you want to automatically line up objects with gridlines that go through the horizontal and vertical edges of other shapes, check the Snap to Shapes check box.

- *Understanding Graphs and Charts*
- *Using Microsoft Graph 97*
- *A High-Level Look at Charting in Word*
- *Creating Data to Be Graphed*
- *Opening Microsoft Graph*
- *Selecting a Chart Type*
- *Specifying Chart Options*

- *Setting Chart Options*
- *Formatting Chart Elements*
- *Adding Pizzazz to Your Charts*
- *Quickly Changing a Chart*
- *Creating Your Own Custom Chart Type*
- *Revising Charts*

19

Creating Graphs:
Make Sense of Your Data,
No Matter Where It's From

W ORD MAKES IT EASY TO INTEGRATE BUSINESS GRAPHS AND charts into your documents. Word and the other Microsoft Office applications share a powerful, newly enhanced graph-making program called Microsoft Graph 97. You can create your data in Word (or Excel), build a graph from it, and adjust your graph's formatting any way you like from within Microsoft Graph.

In this chapter we'll look at:

- Using graphs and charts
- What is Microsoft Graph 97
- Selecting a chart type
- Formatting charts manually
- Inserting new chart elements
- Adding arrows, titles, and labels
- Working with the datasheet
- Creating custom chart types
- Using 3D charts
- Revising a chart
- OLE and chart embedding

■ Understanding Graphs and Charts

Considerable merit attaches to the old idea of a picture being worth more than a thousand words. This is just as true about numbers. Tables or columns of numbers often appear dry, uninteresting, and difficult to understand—but a chart that shows a graphical representation of the same information can impart instant understanding.

Suppose you look at sales figures for a company with four regional offices over four financial quarters. Discerning who's doing well and who's not can be tougher than it ought to be. Put the same figures into a comparative 3D bar chart and you see patterns instantly that reveal who deserves credit and which offices need to pull up their socks.

■ Using Microsoft Graph 97

Charts and graphs have been used quite commonly to design reports in spreadsheet packages, but recently they've become a feature of word-processing applications. Microsoft Word for Windows was one of the first mainstream PC word-processing applications to include a charting/graphing module, called Microsoft Graph. Microsoft Office 97 includes an updated version of Microsoft Graph 97, which makes it easier than ever to create and edit your charts. The charting capabilities provided by Microsoft Graph to Word are also available from Microsoft Excel and PowerPoint.

■ A High-Level Look at Charting in Word

Word 95's Graphing program contained the Chart Wizard, which walked users through the process of building a graph. Word 97's graphing program offers many more options, especially for creating highly visual charts. Unfortunately, the Chart Wizard has disappeared, so you'll have to organize the process of building a graph yourself. Here's a high-level overview of the process:

1. First, select the values in your Word document that you want to graph. This step is optional; you can skip it if you want to create the source information for your graph in Microsoft Graph. However, we'll assume that in most cases you've already created the data you want to graph, so we'll make that assumption as we walk through the process of building a graph.

2. Second, choose Insert, Picture, Chart, to run Microsoft Graph.

3. Third, set the Chart Type—tell Word what kind of chart you want.

4. Fourth, set Chart Options—what elements you want the chart to include, such as titles, gridlines, legends, and data labels.

5. Fifth, format the chart and its elements, selecting fonts, colors, backgrounds and other attributes.

6. Sixth, take another look at the chart and make any changes you want, using Graph's editing, formatting, and drawing tools.

7. Finally, click outside the chart area to return to Word.

Now, we'll take a closer look at each step of the process.

NOTE. *Microsoft uses the terms graph and chart interchangeably throughout Microsoft Graph.*

■ Creating Data to Be Graphed

The easiest way to create data in Word for charting by Microsoft Graph is to first enter your data in a Word table, as shown in Figure 19.1.

NOTE. *Creating your data with tabs neatly lined up will also work, but if Word cannot interpret the information you want it to graph, it opens Microsoft Graph and displays a chart with dummy data instead of placing your data in the graph it inserts.*

Now select the cells—or the entire table—that you want to chart. (If your table includes a cell, row, or column that contains totals, you will probably not want to select those totals. Doing so skews the scale of your graph, making all the other data points look small in relation to the data point or points that contain the total. If you're creating a pie chart, exactly half the pie will contain your total. This probably is not the result you had in mind.)

Figure 19.1

A Word table containing data to be charted

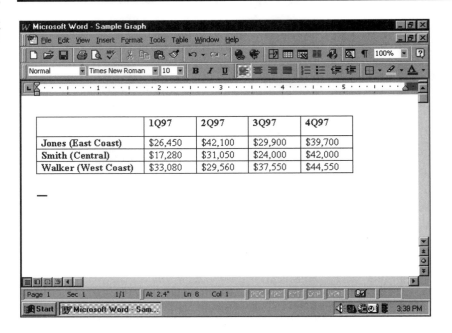

■ Opening Microsoft Graph

Once you create the table and select the cells you want to chart, the next step is to build a default chart with that information, as follows:

1. Select Insert, Picture, Chart.

2. Word inserts its default chart in your document, directly beneath the table you based it on, as shown in Figure 19.2. Superimposed over the chart is the Microsoft Graph datasheet, which contains the values in your table. As you'll see later, you can edit these values in the datasheet. (For now, however, you may wish to hide the datasheet; click the View Datasheet button on Graph's standard toolbar to toggle it on and off.)

Unless you've changed Microsoft Graph's default settings, Graph inserts a 3D bar chart in your document. The chart is selected so you can make changes to it. Whenever a chart is selected, the menus on your menu bar and the buttons on your toolbars change to reflect Microsoft Graph's commands rather than Word's. Microsoft Graph's commands allow you to do all this, and more:

- Format the chart, or elements of it.

- Change data that the chart graphs.

Figure 19.2

When you insert a
chart based on
existing data from a
Word table, Word
displays a 3D chart
and superimposes a
datasheet above it,
containing a copy of
your data.

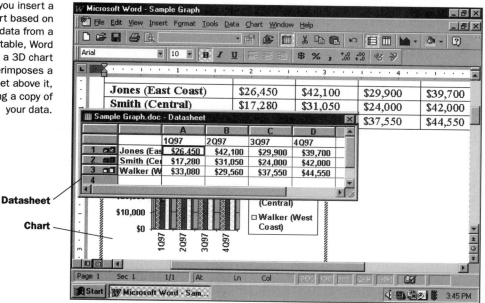

Datasheet

Chart

- Add or change elements to the chart, such as data points, legends, or labels.

- Add a background pattern, shading, or a picture to the chart—or to individual chart elements, or the chart area itself.

Figure 19.3 shows the Microsoft Graph toolbars.

A few of the toolbar buttons shown in Figure 19.3 will come in handy later, when you start formatting and editing elements of your chart. For example, the Chart Objects list box allows you to select a specific chart element, so you can format or edit that element. You'll find it especially valuable when you need to select something that's hard to click on, like a narrow gridline.

The Import File button allows you to open a Microsoft Excel or other file and add information from that file to the chart you already have open. The Chart Type button gives you a quick way to switch among the most popular types of charts. And on the formatting toolbar, the Currency Style, Percent Style, Increase Decimal, and Decrease Decimal toolbars give you a quick new way to make sure your axes and other elements display the way you want them to.

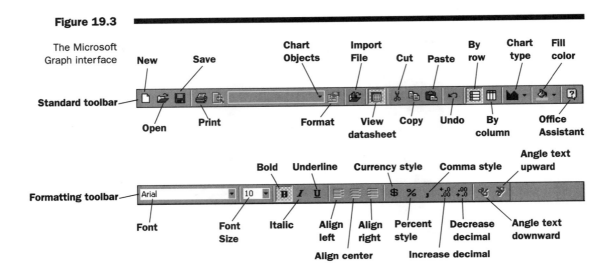

Figure 19.3

The Microsoft Graph interface

■ Selecting a Chart Type

Once you've opened Microsoft Graph 97 and displayed your information in its default chart format, you'll probably first want to decide what kind of chart you really want. Graph's default 3D bar chart will make sense in quite a few situations, but there will be many times you want something else.

Graph 97 provides almost an infinite number of possible permutations—more than ever before. These are available from the Chart Type dialog box. To display this dialog box, either choose Chart Type from the Chart menu, or right-click on an empty area of your chart and choose Chart Type from the Shortcut menu. The Chart Type dialog box opens, as shown in Figure 19.4.

In the Standard Types tab, choose the type of chart you want. Once you do, Word will provide options as to how you want the chart to appear. Select one in the Chart sub-type box. In Microsoft Graph 97, you don't have to guess how a sub-type will actually look with your data. You can preview it. Click and hold the Press and hold to view sample button.

Figure 19.4

The Chart Type dialog box

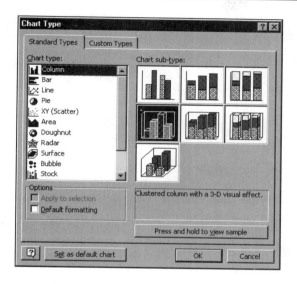

Word's Library of Standard Charts

A wide variety of chart types is supported within Microsoft Graph. Each type is particularly suited to a given set of data, although you can display any single set of data in various ways. Microsoft Graph's chart types include:

- *Column chart.* Each data point corresponds to a vertical line; each series of data uses vertical lines of the same color (see Figure 19.5).

- *Bar chart.* This is probably the most popular type of chart; it shows data as a series of horizontal bars (see Figure 19.6). It can be used effectively with three or four series of data over a period of time (such as monthly sales figures from four different regions).

- *Line chart.* This is most useful for sets of data with large numbers of data points and several series. Data appears as a series of points connected by a single line (see Figure 19.7).

- *Pie chart.* This chart can be used only with a single series of data. However, it's particularly well-suited for showing the percentage distribution of expenses, revenues, or any other single-series data (see Figure 19.8).

- *Scatter chart.* This chart is particularly useful for showing the relationship or degree of relationship between numeric values in separate groups of data (see Figure 19.9). You can use a scatter chart to find patterns or trends and determine whether variables are dependent on or affect one another.

Figure 19.5

Column chart

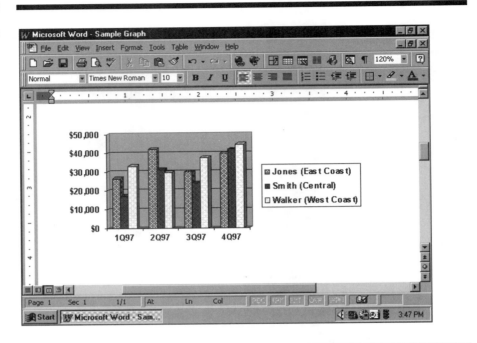

Figure 19.6

Bar chart

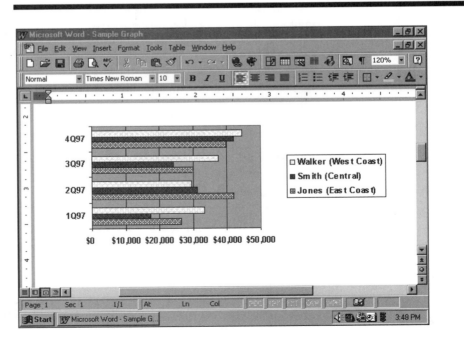

Figure 19.7

Line chart

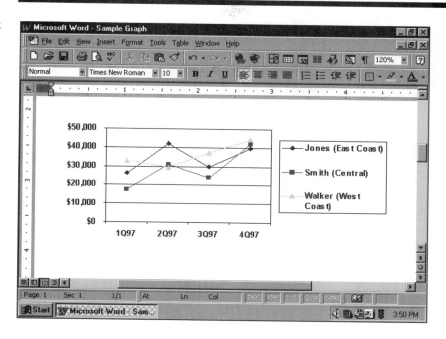

Figure 19.8

Pie chart

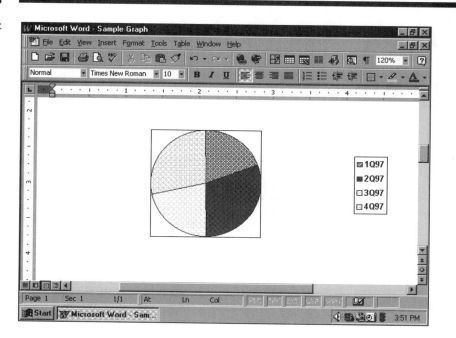

Figure 19.9

XY (Scatter) chart

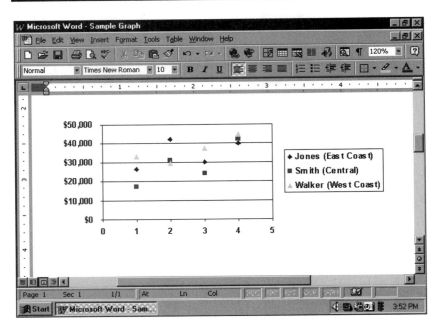

- *Area chart.* This chart shows data as areas filled with different colors or patterns (see Figure 19.10). It's best suited for charts that don't have large numbers of data points and that use several data series. Area charts look particularly dramatic in 3D form.

- *Doughnut chart.* This is basically a pie chart but with more flexibility and a hole in the middle. Each ring of the doughnut chart represents a data series. Use this chart to compare the parts to the whole in one or more data categories.

- *Radar chart.* This chart resembles a cobweb and shows changes in data or data frequency relative to a center point. Lines connect all the values in the same data series.

- *3 D Surface chart.* This chart resembles a rubber sheet stretched over a 3 D column chart. 3 D surface charts can help show relationships between large amounts of data. Colors or patterns delineate areas that share the same value. Use this chart for finding the best combinations between two sets of data.

- *Bubble chart.* This is similar to an XY scatter chart. The bubble size is a third value type that is relative to the x-axis and y-axis data. Use this for depicting the relationship between two kinds of related data.

Figure 19.10

Area chart

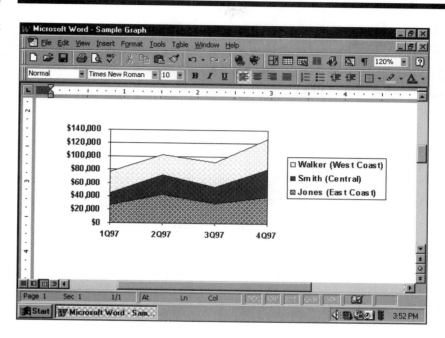

- *Stock chart.* This is similar to a column chart but adds the high-low-close information commonly used in stock charts; you must provide these values to use a stock chart effectively.

- *3D cylinder, 3D cone, and 3D pyramid charts.* Cylinder, cone, or pyramid data markers can spice up your 3D column and bar charts. These charts have a dramatic look to them.

Word's Library of Custom Charts

In addition to Word's standard charts, there's a library of built-in custom charts that are already formatted and ready to use. There are 19 custom charts available. If you select one, you'll save yourself the time and effort of formatting a chart a single element at a time. To choose a custom chart, click the Custom Types tab, shown in Figure 19.11, and select the chart type you want; when you're satisfied, click OK.

Setting a Default Chart Type

As we've mentioned, Word's default chart type is a 3D bar chart. However, you may prefer to use a different standard or custom chart type as your default for all charts from now on. To set a different default chart, first select

Figure 19.11

From the Custom Type
tab, you can create a
custom chart.

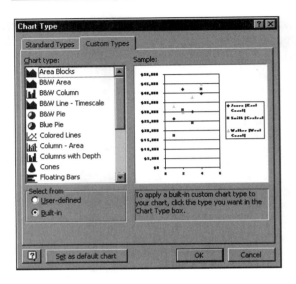

the chart type and sub-type from either the Standard Types or Custom Types
tab, and then click Set as Default chart. When Word asks you to confirm the
change, click Yes.

■ Specifying Chart Options

Now that you've decided what type of chart to create, you can set a wide variety of options for your chart. For example, you may want to annotate the
chart with a title, a legend, and titles for each individual chart axis, depending on the number of axes the chart has.

Before you start working with chart options or with chart formatting,
however, it will help to take a look at the elements that can appear in Word
charts, and the nomenclature Word uses to describe these elements—which
may not always be familiar.

Inspecting a Word Chart

Figure 19.12 shows a typical 3D column chart. This chart's elements include
the *plot area* (the main part of the chart), which is bounded by the *axes:* the
x-axis, y-axis, and possibly a *z-axis* in some three-dimensional charts.

NOTE. *To view the elements of a chart, move the mouse pointer to an element
on the chart, and Word displays a ScreenTip. The ScreenTip shows you the
name of the chart element to which you're currently pointing.*

Figure 19.12

Typical Microsoft
Graph chart

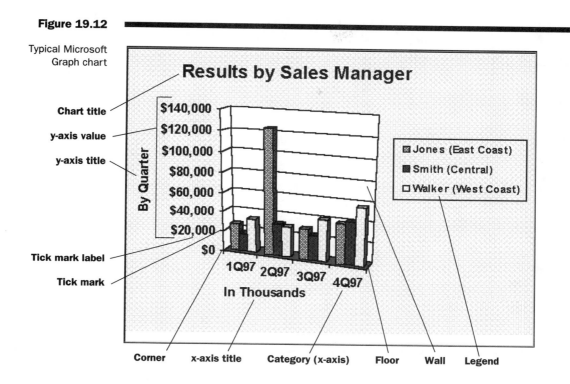

Within the plot area, the chart depicts one or more *data series*, each representing a row or column of data from your Word table or other source. The individual *bars, columns*, or other elements representing each data point within the data series are called *data markers*. The plot area can also contain several optional text elements, such as axis *titles* that describe what each axis is measuring and *data labels* that show exact values (or names) for each data marker. *Gridlines* are used to help the eye keep track of multiple lines.

A *chart title* appears at the top of the chart. In this example, the *y-axis* is the scale Microsoft Graph uses to generate the chart. This is true with most charts, with the notable exception of pie charts. If all your data points are beneath 500, for example, Graph places 0 at the bottom of the scale and 500 at the top.

Each increment on the y-axis is called a *tick mark*. Graph also features a *y-axis title* that you use to tell your audience what you're measuring. Some examples might be Profit, in millions of dollars; Commissions, by percentage; Hard disk speed, in milliseconds; Land, in square miles.

The x-axis normally tells which data series is being measured. Often, the x-axis displays the passage of time. For example, it might show four quarters in a year or monthly results. It might show results from various locations or divisions.

By default, Graph displays each data series in a different color, with like information displayed in the same color. Graph maintains contrast between adjacent bars, pie slices, and so on. This contrast enables you to understand the data clearly, even when it's printed in black and white. As you'll see later, however, you can change color, add patterns, or change the background Graph normally uses.

In 3D charts, such as the one shown in Figure 19.12, Graph also includes a *wall, corner,* and *floor,* that make up the 3D background to the "room" where the chart appears. Walls and floors can each be formatted separately.

Finally, most charts (except those that use only one data series) also contain a *legend*—the explanation of what each color or pattern represents. Graph inserts a legend by default.

■ Setting Chart Options

To control the options available for your specific chart, select the chart and choose Chart Options from the Chart menu; or right-click on an empty area within the chart, and choose Chart Options from the Shortcut menu. The Chart Options dialog box appears, as shown in Figure 19.13.

Figure 19.13

The Chart Options dialog box, showing the Titles tab

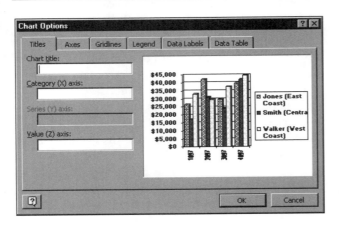

Keep in mind that the options available to you will depend on the chart you've chosen. For example, a column chart has two axes that can be titled, whereas a radar chart has none. Most charts have gridlines; pie charts and doughnut charts don't.

Some controls are available no matter what kind of chart you have, however. For example, you can always specify a title for your chart in the Titles tab. Use the Legend tab to create a legend and specify where it will appear.

Enter data labels that show the actual values or names associated with each data point you are plotting. As you work in these tabs, you can see the effects of your changes in a generic preview that appears inside the dialog box.

In the next few sections, we'll cover some of the most commonly used chart options.

Inserting a New Title

To add a title to your chart, display the Chart Options tab, and select the Titles tab. Graph displays the titles options, as shown earlier in Figure 19.13. Here, you can specify which titles you wish to add: a chart title, and in most cases, titles for at least one axis. Type the titles in the text boxes, and click OK. Graph now displays the titles in the chart, as shown in Figure 19.14. Here, you can edit or format them manually, using toolbar buttons like cut, copy, and paste; and menu commands like Format, Font, each of which works the same way it does in Word.

Figure 19.14

Editing a title in the chart

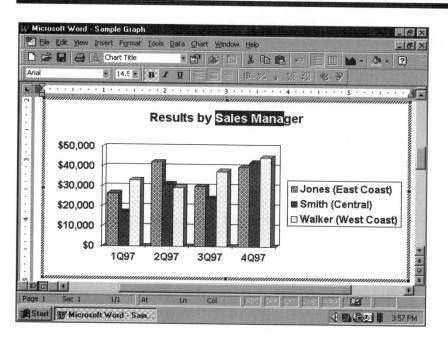

Inserting New Data Labels

By default, Graph inserts a chart without including the specific values or names associated with each data point. However, if your readers need to know specific values or names, you can add them. Display the Chart Options dialog box and select the Data Labels tab (see Figure 19.15). You can either display the value associated with each selected data series or data point (Show value) or the name of that data series or data point (Show label). For pie charts, you also have the option of displaying a percentage (Show percent). If you already have data labels and want to remove them, choose None.

Figure 19.15

The Data Labels tab in the Chart Options dialog box

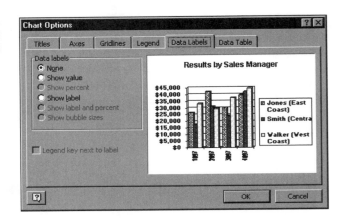

Inserting New Gridlines

Recall that you can toggle vertical or horizontal gridlines on and off using toolbar buttons. If you want more control over your gridlines, however, choose the Gridlines tab in the Chart Options dialog box. The Gridlines tab appears (see Figure 19.16).

Figure 19.16

The Gridlines tab in the Chart Options dialog box

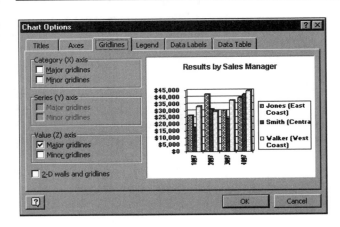

By default, Graph places gridlines perpendicular to the data being charted at the same points where values are shown along the axis. For example, if you create a bar graph where the columns appear horizontally, the value axis is the x-axis, and the gridlines are displayed vertically from that axis, as shown in Figure 19.17.

Figure 19.17

Default gridlines for a horizontal bar graph. Gridlines run vertically from the x-axis.

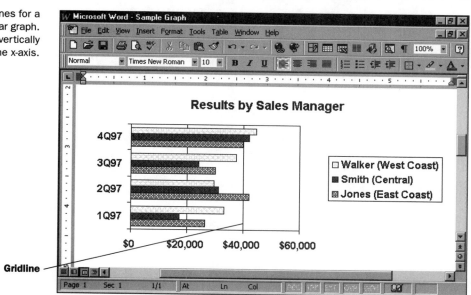

Gridlines placed at the same points as values are called *major gridlines*. If you want additional gridlines to appear between major gridlines, add *minor gridlines*. By default, Graph does not display gridlines parallel to the data being charted, but you can add these as well—both major and minor gridlines.

■ Formatting Chart Elements

Any element of a chart you can insert, you can also format.

In some cases, as mentioned earlier, you can format a chart element directly. For example, you can select text in a title and apply font formatting to it. You can also move elements, such as your chart's legend or plot area, by dragging them with the mouse. However, in most cases, you'll work with dialog boxes to access the formatting controls you need. To format a chart element, double-click on it; or right-click on it, and choose the format command that appears at the top of the Shortcut menu. For example, if you click on an empty space within the chart, but outside the plot area, the Format Chart

Area command will appear, and selecting it will display the Format Chart Area dialog box, as shown in Figure 19.18.

Figure 19.18

The Format Chart Area dialog box

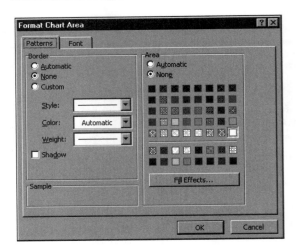

Table 19.1 describes the chart elements that can be formatted, and the formatting categories available to you through tabs in the chart element's formatting dialog box.

■ Adding Pizzazz to Your Charts

Graph 97's standard graphs are quite functional, and many of its custom graphs are downright attractive. But sometimes you'll want to add more pizzazz to your chart. You've already taken a high-level look at the formatting tools available to you. In the next few sections, we'll take a closer look at some of the more interesting options you have for making your chart more visually interesting—and helping it communicate your message more effectively.

Working with Patterns

In Chapter 17, you learned how to use Word's new backgrounds and fill effects in your documents. Many of these features are available in Microsoft Graph 97 as well. Let's say you want to add a background pattern for your chart area. Double-click on the chart area to display the Format Chart Area box, and select one of the colors Graph provides in the Patterns tab. Or, from the Patterns tab, click Fill Effects, and specify a gradient, texture, pattern, or even a picture to use with your graph. Samples of what you can do are shown in Figures 19.19 and 19.20.

Figure 19.19

A chart area using one of
Graph's built-in textures

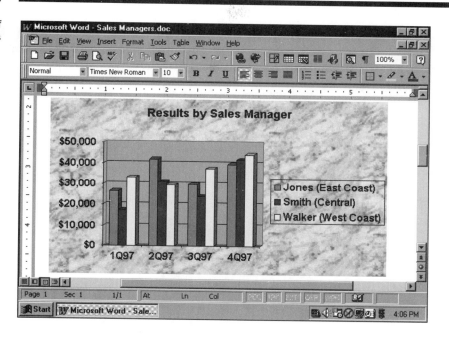

Figure 19.20

A plot area using a
picture as a background

Table 19.1

Chart Elements and
Available Formatting

CHART ELEMENT	AVAILABLE FORMATTING
Axis	Patterns, Scale, Font, Number, Alignment
Chart Area	Patterns, Font
Chart Title	Patterns, Font, Alignment
Data Labels	Patterns, Font, Number, Alignment
Data Point	Patterns, Data Labels, Options
Data Series	Patterns, Axis, Y Error Bars, Data Labels, Options (varies with chart type)
Data Table	Patterns, Font
Error Bars	Patterns, Y Error Bars
Floors	Patterns
Gridlines	Patterns, Scale
Legend	Patterns, Font, Placement
Legend Entry	Font
Plot Area	Patterns
Trendline	Patterns, Type, Options
Walls	Patterns

Adding Callouts with Graph's Drawing Tools

In Chapters 17 and 18, you learned about Word's graphics and drawing tools, including AutoShapes. These tools are available within Microsoft Graph as well. So you can, for example, insert a callout that calls attention to a specific data point, as shown in Figure 19.21.

To insert a callout:

1. Choose View, Toolbars, Drawing to display the Drawing toolbar.

2. Click AutoShapes, Callouts, and select a callout from the cascaded menu.

3. Position your mouse pointer where you want the callout to begin, and drag the mouse to extend the callout.

4. At the insertion point that appears inside the callout, type the text you want to include in the callout.

Figure 19.21

A sample chart
with a callout

Callout

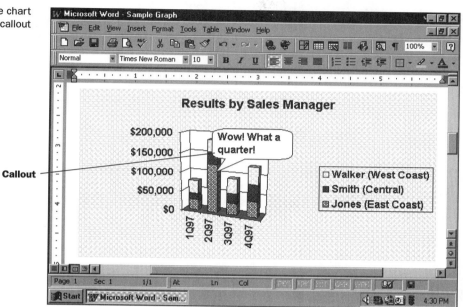

Of course, you can use Graph's Drawing tools to add text boxes, arrows, and any other shape you can think of to embellish your chart.

■ Quickly Changing a Chart

If you create a chart and later decide that a different type of chart will communicate your information more accurately, Graph gives you several ways to make the change. If you want an entirely different presentation, activate the chart you want to change, click on the down-arrow next to the Chart Type button, and choose the chart you want. If you want more control, choose Chart Type from the Chart menu. The Chart Type dialog box opens, as shown in Figure 19.4 earlier in this chapter.

Click the Standard Types tab, highlight a specific type of chart, such as bar or column. If you're satisfied with a generic chart, choose OK, and Graph will reformat your chart accordingly.

NOTE. *To get a sneak preview of how your chart looks with the chart type you select, choose Press and hold to view sample.*

If you want more control, take a look at the Chart sub-type box, which presents the chart appearance options Microsoft Graph has available within the Chart type you choose. The options in the Chart sub-type box vary depending on the chart type you've chosen. For example, if you choose a bar chart, Graph gives you the option of using a stacked bar chart, wherein all data points for the same time period are stacked on the same bar.

If you want to reformat the entire chart, click the Custom Types tab. Graph provides many ready-to-use built-in charts that are preformatted. In the Chart Type box, choose the chart type you want. The formatted chart appears in the Sample box. Choose the chart that most closely resembles what you're seeking. Choose OK, and Graph automatically formats the chart.

Using Trendlines and Error Bars

Trendlines and error bars are statistical tools that help your audience evaluate the meaning and implications of your data. Trendlines show apparent trends in a data series, and Microsoft Graph can map these trends into the future by using regression analysis techniques. Error bars show degrees of uncertainty relative to each data marker in a series. They're often used in engineering applications.

To create a trendline, select a data series and choose Add Trendline from the Chart menu. The Add Trendline dialog box opens, as shown in Figure 19.22. Choose the type of trendline you want, set any options, and choose OK.

Figure 19.22

The Add Trendline
dialog box

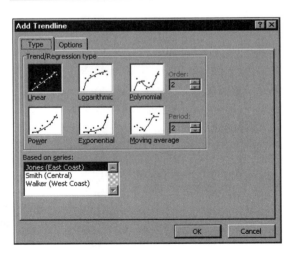

Similarly, to create an error bar, select a data series and then from the Format menu, choose Format Data Series. This brings up the Format Data Series dialog box. Click the Y Error Bars tab, and the Y Error Bars options appear (see Figure 19.23). Choose the type of error bar you want, set any options, and choose OK.

Figure 19.23

The Format Data Series dialog box allows you to format data series.

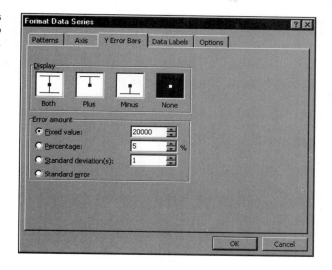

Working in the Datasheet Window

At some point, you may want to change manually the values your chart is based on. Graph includes a datasheet window for this purpose. The datasheet looks much like a basic spreadsheet, except that you can enter only numbers and letters in it. It cannot handle formulas. The only purpose of the datasheet is to control the data that creates a chart in Microsoft Graph. To view the datasheet, click on the View Datasheet button or choose Datasheet from the View menu (see Figure 19.24).

If you create your chart from data in a Word document, that data also appears in the datasheet when you open it. To change a value, click in its cell and enter the new value. When you change a value in the datasheet, the chart reflects the change immediately.

NOTE. *Keep in mind that changes you make in the datasheet are not automatically reflected in the table or Word text you may have used as the original source for the chart. If you make changes in the datasheet, Graph updates your chart to reflect the change you made.*

To link the values in your document to the contents of your chart automatically, see "Establishing an OLE Link between Word and Graph" later in this chapter.

Notice that each row of the datasheet also contains a data series graphic, which is a chart icon showing the color and pattern of the corresponding data series as it now appears in the chart.

Figure 19.24

The datasheet

Column heading

Select All button

Row heading

Data Series graphic

Scroll bar

Active cell

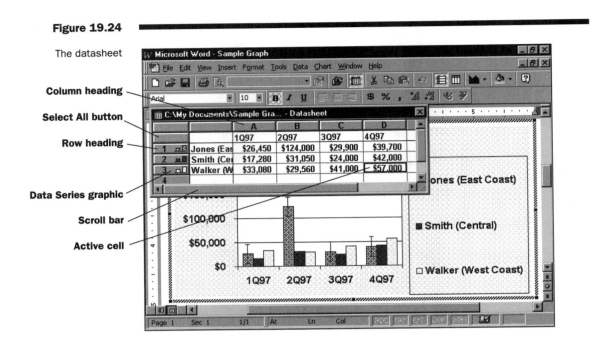

Moving Data in the Datasheet

If you've used Excel, working in the datasheet will seem familiar. You can select a row by clicking on the row number box to its left; you can select a column by clicking on the column letter above it. You can select the entire
datasheet by clicking on the gray box in the top left-hand corner. You have
access to pop-up menus for cutting, pasting, copying, and deleting cells, rows,
and columns. (Keyboard shortcuts and toolbar buttons are also available for
cutting, copying, and pasting.) You can also use drag-and-drop to move data
from one location in the datasheet to another. If drag-and-drop doesn't
work, choose Options from the Tools menu, click the Datasheet Options tab,
and make sure Cell Drag and Drop is checked.

Formatting Data in the Datasheet

Although the text formatting of the datasheet generally doesn't affect the
formatting of either the chart or your original Word document, you do have
the ability to change fonts, font size, and column widths. Select the cells,
rows, or columns you want to change, and choose Font from either the Format menu or the Shortcut menu. A Font dialog box opens, much like the one
in Word itself; from there you can choose fonts, font styling, font size, and
other font formatting.

NOTE. *A quick way to change the font, font size, font style, or other font formatting is to select it right from the Graph Formatting toolbar.*

To change column width, select the column(s) you want to adjust and choose Column Width from either the Format or Shortcut menu. You also can position the mouse pointer above the column, at the edge of the next column, and drag the pointer until the column is the width you want.

In one case, the formatting you apply in the datasheet does affect the chart. To specify how numbers are formatted, you can use Format, Number or choose Number from the Shortcut menu. The Format Number dialog box appears (see Figure 19.25). Microsoft Graph enables you to specify a wide variety of number formats. For example, you can specify that numbers be formatted as dollars and cents, or with scientific notation, or precisely to a specific number of decimal places. As soon as you make a change in number formatting, that change is reflected in the chart as well.

Figure 19.25

The Format Number
dialog box

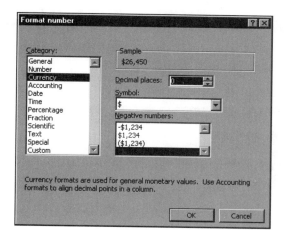

■ Creating Your Own Custom Chart Type

Your organization may standardize on a certain custom look for charts. Is there an easy way to make all your charts look the same without manually re-formatting every one? Yes, there is, by creating your own custom chart. Here's how to do so:

1. Format a chart the way you want it, applying the appropriate chart type, subtype, options, and manual formatting.

2. Select the chart.

3. Choose Chart Type from the Chart menu. The Chart Type dialog box opens.

4. Choose the Custom Types tab.

5. Choose the User-Defined option. (If you're doing this for the first time, there will be no User-defined custom charts—only the Default chart.)

6. Choose Add. The Add Custom Chart Type dialog box opens (see Figure 19.26). Enter a custom chart type name of no more than 31 characters and a description with a maximum of 255 characters. Choose OK.

7. The custom chart name and a thumbnail sketch now appear in the Custom Types Sample box. Choose OK.

Figure 19.26

The Add Custom Chart Type dialog box

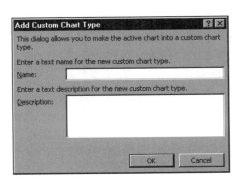

NOTE. *If you no longer want a user-defined custom chart, you can delete the chart. Choose User-defined from the Custom Types options, and in the Chart Type list, click on the chart you want to delete. Choose Delete, and then choose OK.*

■ Revising Charts

If the data used to create a chart changes, as it often does when you report on fluid business situations, you need to be able to alter your charts quickly. Microsoft Graph is well-suited to enabling you to make quick changes, because it holds the data for the chart in the datasheet. If you change the information in the datasheet, you update the chart accordingly.

You can make your changes by entering new data directly into the datasheet and overwriting the old data in the process; or, if the data is held in a spreadsheet that's continually revised, you can re-import the spreadsheet data every time it changes.

However, if you want your chart to update automatically when you make a change in your document, there's a better solution: an OLE link.

Establishing an OLE Link between Word and Graph

If you want tight and permanent links between your chart and your Word document, so the chart changes when data changes in your document, establish an OLE link between the Word document's original chart data and the contents of the chart itself. Then, whenever you open the chart, it automatically is updated to reflect changes you may have made in the document. Here's how to do this:

1. Select and copy the Word data you want to graph.

2. Open Microsoft Graph.

3. If the datasheet does not appear, click on the View Datasheet button to view it.

4. Click your insertion point in the top left cell of the datasheet.

5. Choose Paste Link from the Edit menu.

6. Graph displays the chart, as well as the datasheet window containing the data you pasted.

Once you establish the link in this way, when you make changes to the Word table, the accompanying graph is automatically updated.

Establishing a Link with Microsoft Excel

Essentially the same procedure can be used to establish a link with Microsoft Excel and other programs that support Microsoft's OLE 2.0 specification. To create an OLE link between an Excel worksheet and a Microsoft Graph chart appearing in a Microsoft Word document, follow these steps:

1. In Excel, open the Excel worksheet you want to link.

2. Copy the cells you want to include in a chart in Word.

3. Open or switch to Word, and open the document where you want the chart.

4. Place your insertion point where you want the chart.

5. Open Microsoft Graph by choosing it in Insert, Object or clicking on the Insert Chart button.

6. If the datasheet does not appear, click on the View Datasheet button to view it.

7. Click your insertion point in the top left cell of the datasheet.

8. Choose Paste Link from the Edit menu.

9. Graph displays the chart, as well as the datasheet window containing the data you pasted.

Now, when a change is made in the Excel worksheet, that change is reflected in the Word chart as well.

NOTE. *If you close both the Word and Excel documents, when you reopen the Word document containing the chart, you may need to double-click on the chart to update it.*

In this chapter, you've learned how to use Microsoft Graph 97, the sophisticated charting tool that is included with Word 97 and Office 97. You've learned how to insert charts, choose what kind of chart to use, specify the elements to include in your chart, and format your chart for maximum effect.

In Chapter 20, you'll take a look at another feature that takes Word far beyond traditional word processing. You'll discover how to use Word to build interactive forms that can be filled out online by anyone in your organization. Hey, you never know—enough features like that, and maybe we'll arrive at the paperless office someday!

- *Using Word Features to Create a Form*
- *Using the Forms Toolbar*
- *Adding Text Form Fields*
- *Placing a Number, Date, or Time in a Text form Field*
- *Adding Check-Box Form Fields*
- *Adding Drop-Down Form Fields*
- *Advanced Features for All Form Fields*

- *Protecting a Form from Unwanted Change*
- *Saving a Form*
- *Filling In Online Forms*
- *Creating Printed Forms*
- *Distributing Your Forms*

20

Forms: Create Fill-In Forms Your Whole Company Can Use

Y OU'D THINK THE PC WOULD BE A NATURAL FOR CREATING FORMS. After all, both form design and form filling are well within a PC's technical capabilities. Surprisingly, until recently, few people responsible for forms have used the PC as well as they might have. And they've had their reasons.

Using the PC to create forms often meant purchasing a separate program designed especially for forms. And filling in the forms was probably still a paper task—unless you provided a form-filling program to everyone who was likely to use them.

But now Word—a program with wide distribution—has sophisticated forms capabilities. You can create forms that enable users to choose from lists of options. Forms that provide online help. Forms that guide the user from beginning to end. Best of all, users can fill in these forms without changing the underlying form itself. If you're networked, you can even use your network server rather than some distant warehouse as a central repository for forms. All in all, maybe it's time to take another look at how you handle forms.

In this chapter, you'll learn how to use Word's formatting features to create a framework for your form; how to use the Forms toolbar and shortcut menu to add check boxes, list boxes, fill-in fields, and online help to your form; and how to use macros with your form. You'll learn how to protect your forms against unauthorized changes, how to distribute and fill them in, and how to store the data you capture in a way that's easiest to use elsewhere.

■ Using Word Features to Create a Form

Your first step in creating a form is to create a new template, which should contain the basic information you want to include in every form. Include any list boxes, check boxes, dialog boxes, and Help features you might add to the form. Then add any macros and AutoText entries you may have created (or will create) to streamline filling out the forms later. (See Chapter 9 for coverage of AutoText entries, and Chapters 25–28 for coverage of macro procedures.)

As you learned in Chapter 8, you create a new template by choosing New from the **F**ile menu. Click on the T**e**mplate button in the New dialog box, and click OK.

You can then use Word's formatting techniques to lay out the basic elements of the form. You'll probably find tables, text boxes, borders, and shading especially useful here. For example, you can use tables to quickly create the matrix of columns and rows that typifies invoices, purchase orders, and similar forms.

If you already have the basic contents of a form in a file, you can save that file as a template. Be aware that Word's File, New dialog box also contains a wide variety of documents you may be able to use as the basis for your form.

NOTE. *When you create a new template, your form is unprotected, which means you can make any changes you want. But if you need to revise an existing form, its original designer may have protected it from changes. To unprotect the form, choose Un**p**rotect Document from the **T**ools menu, choose **F**orms, and choose OK. For more information, see the section "Protecting a Form from Unwanted Change," later in this chapter.*

At this stage of developing your form, don't include any of the options used to fill out the form. Simply put the structure in place, as shown in Figure 20.1.

Figure 20.1

The first step in creating a form is to block out where everything will fit.

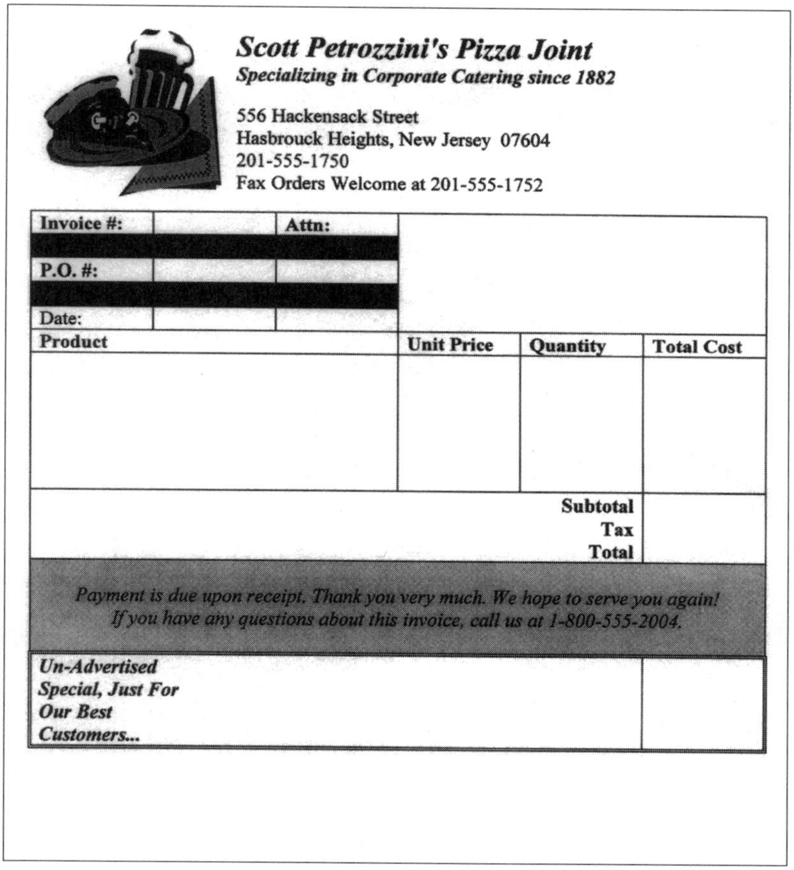

Scott Petrozzini's Pizza Joint
Specializing in Corporate Catering since 1882

556 Hackensack Street
Hasbrouck Heights, New Jersey 07604
201-555-1750
Fax Orders Welcome at 201-555-1752

Invoice #:			Attn:				
P.O. #:							
Date:							
Product				Unit Price	Quantity	Total Cost	
				Subtotal			
				Tax			
				Total			
Payment is due upon receipt. Thank you very much. We hope to serve you again! If you have any questions about this invoice, call us at 1-800-555-2004.							
Un-Advertised Special, Just For Our Best Customers...							

■ Using the Forms Toolbar

As soon as you start creating a form, open Word 97's Forms toolbar (see Figure 20.2). It contains shortcuts you may well want to use, such as the Draw Table, Insert Table, and Text Box buttons, and it also contains all the controls you'll need to make your document behave as an electronic form using Word's special form fields. (In Word 6 and Word 95, you could access those controls from an Insert, Form Field menu command, but that command is gone in Word 97, so you'll have to use the toolbar.)

Let's go through the functions of the toolbar buttons, from left to right. Text Form Field creates a space where the form's users can insert text. Check Box Form Field creates a check box that users can check or clear. Drop-Down Form Field allows users to select from several predefined choices. Form Field Options allows you to control any form field you have selected. Draw Table allows you to draw a table. Insert Table allows you to insert equally sized table rows and columns. Text Box allows you to insert a text box. Form Field Shading allows you to add shading to a form field. Protect Form allows you to protect all areas of a form from change, except for those that users are intended to fill in.

Figure 20.2

Word 97's revamped toolbar is now essential for building forms.

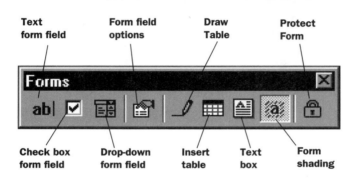

NOTE. *For access to Word's borders and shading capabilities, which are often used to help make tables and forms easier to understand, you can display the Tables and Borders toolbar as well.*

Inserting Form Fields

Now we'll move on to what makes forms different from other Word documents and templates. Word allows you to specify exactly where users may enter text in their forms, and how they may do so. You do this with form fields. Word offers three kinds of form fields, each with different associated options:

1. Text form fields allow users to enter text, numbers, symbols, and spaces. You can also use text form fields to make calculations based on entries that users make in other form fields.

2. Check box form fields place a check box in your form, as shown in Figure 20.3.

3. Drop-down form fields allow you to give your user a list of alternatives, as shown in Figure 20.4.

Figure 20.3

A check box form field

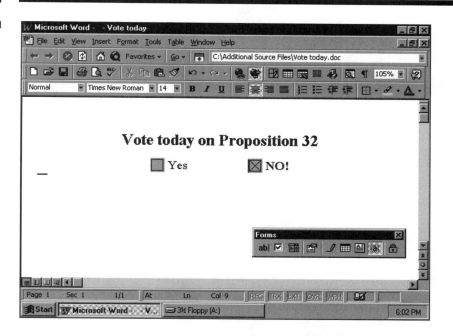

Figure 20.4

A drop-down list box form field in a finished form

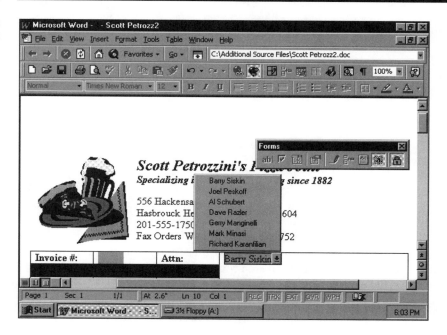

■ Adding Text Form Fields

To enter a standard text form field, display the Forms toolbar, position your insertion point where you want the field to appear, and click the Text Form Field button. You've just inserted a Text Form Field button; it appears shaded in your document.

The generic Text Form Field button you've just placed in your document allows users to insert any text, of any length. But you may want to restrict what users can enter here—and give them some help in entering the information you need.

You control the options associated with a text form field through the Text Form Field Options dialog box, shown in Figure 20.5. This dialog box can be reached in two ways. You can select the field you want to edit and click the Form Field Options button on the Forms toolbar. Or you can right-click on the field and click Properties from the Shortcut menu that appears.

Figure 20.5

The Text Form Field Options dialog box

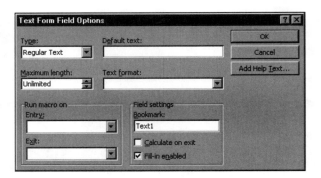

■ Placing a Number, Date, or Time in a Text Form Field

The first aspect of the text form field you can control is whether it should be text at all. You can use the Type drop-down list box in the Text Form Field Options dialog box to specify several alternatives, including Regular Text, Number, Date, Current Date, Current Time, and Calculation.

One of the most useful options is Number. Specifying Number takes you one small step toward data integrity: nobody can fill in alphabetical characters, for example, in a field that requires a dollar amount.

If you choose Number, you also can specify the format in which the number appears. Make a choice from the Number format drop-down list box.

(The title of the Text format drop-down list box you see in the figure changes depending on the format you choose.) Then, even if the user enters another format, Word automatically changes it to be consistent with all the other forms you're collecting.

In the example invoice shown in the figures in this chapter, Number form fields have been added to each of the table cells under Unit Price. Unit prices have been set to appear in dollars-and-cents format (see Figure 20.6).

Figure 20.6

Dollars-and-cents formatting appears in the Unit Price column

Unit Price in dollars and cents

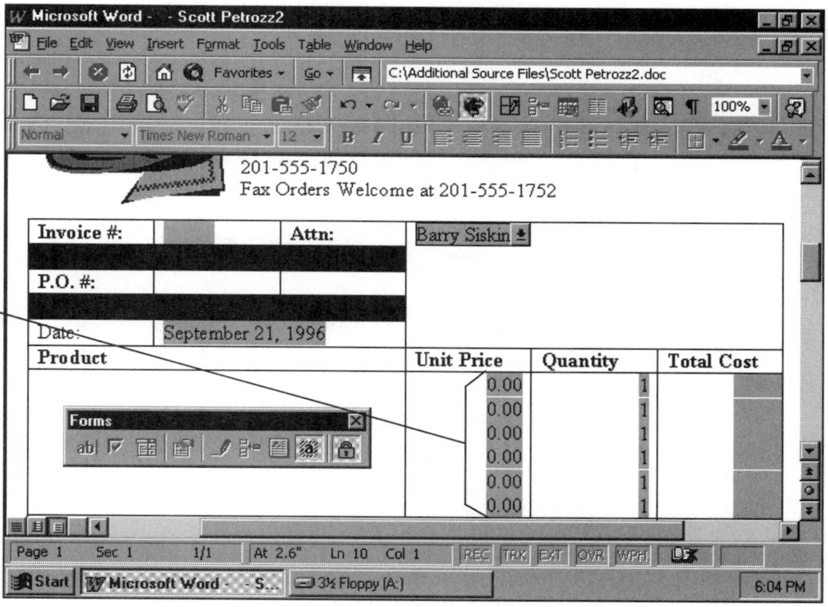

NOTE. *You can go beyond standard numeric formats by adding a numeric picture in the Number format box, as you might in Insert Field. The numeric picture ###.###, for example, tells Word to round off any entry to thousandths. Chapter 21 covers numeric picture formatting.*

Another useful option is *time stamping.* You can specify that the form field automatically display the date when the form is filled out. Alternatively, you can specify that it always display the current date or current time. You can choose a date/time format from the Date format list box, or use Word's date/time picture feature to create your own (see Chapter 21 for more information). Later, when users work with this form, they can't change the date; Word sets this information automatically.

NOTE. *Remember that a user can still circumvent your time and date settings by resetting the system clock, thereby making it appear that a form was filled out sooner than it really was.*

You can see these fields in your template if you choose to view field codes (check the Field Codes box in **T**ools, **O**ptions **V**iew).

NOTE. *You might think that you can use Word's standard date and time fields here, but you can't. Standard date and time fields don't update when they're used in a form. When you place a text form field in your template, Word places a new kind of field there that is unavailable from Insert Field. It's {FORMTEXT}. When you specify the date, Word creates a nested field: {FORMTEXT {DATE}}.*

Whether you insert text, a number, or a date, you can provide default information that appears in the form unless a user changes it. Enter this default information in the Default text box shown in Figure 20.5. Remember, the name of this box will change if you change the type of data Word will accept in the form.

In the invoice example shown earlier, since users generally purchase one of any item, **1** has been specified as the default number in each cell under Quantity.

Similarly, it was assumed that no entry under Invoice # will be longer than four digits, so that value has been specified in the **M**aximum Length option in the Text Form Field Options dialog box. (A text form field can be up to 255 characters in length unless you specify a shorter limit.)

TIP. *When you need to create several identical rows, create one row containing all the form fields you need, formatted the way you want them. Then copy that row as often as needed.*

Finally, you can insert a calculation in your form by choosing Calculation from the Ty**p**e box. The D**e**fault Text option changes to **E**xpression, and an equal sign appears in the **E**xpression text box. Here, you can create a calculation just as you might in Table Formula or Insert Field. Again, however, a calculation doesn't work in a form unless you build the calculation here, in the Text Form Field Options dialog box.

In the example shown earlier, a calculation field has been inserted to multiply automatically a product's Unit Price by the Quantity purchased to arrive at the Total Cost in each row. Then these values are added together to arrive at a Subtotal; 7 percent tax is added; and a Total is created.

Calculations also appear in the document as nested field codes, such as{FORMTEXT {=(b7*c7) \# "$#,###.00"}}. Unfortunately, you have to create fields like these one at a time, because they're all different—they reference different cells. Unlike Excel, Word has no Fill Down feature, and no relative cell references.

Adding Character Formatting to a Text Field

Most of the text formatting you apply to form fields is done the same way as other text formatting—by manually applying it to characters or paragraphs, or by using styles. However, the Text Form Field Options dialog box does allow you to control the case to be used in entries: Uppercase, Lowercase, First Capital, or Title Case.

NOTE. *When applying character formatting in a form, make sure you use fonts that will be available on all the computers using your form. If you're using TrueType fonts, select Embed True Type fonts in the Tools, Options, Save tab. Don't choose the Embed characters in use only option: You don't know which characters users will add to your form. If you use fonts that aren't available to your users, Windows 95 may substitute fonts that look unattractive or are difficult to read.*

■ Adding Check-Box Form Fields

Check box form fields allow you to accommodate situations where a user can select among one or several options. You might, for example, build a list of options as shown in Figure 20.7. To insert a simple check box with no options, click the Check Box Form Field button on the Forms toolbar.

Figure 20.7

An example of how check boxes are used in a form

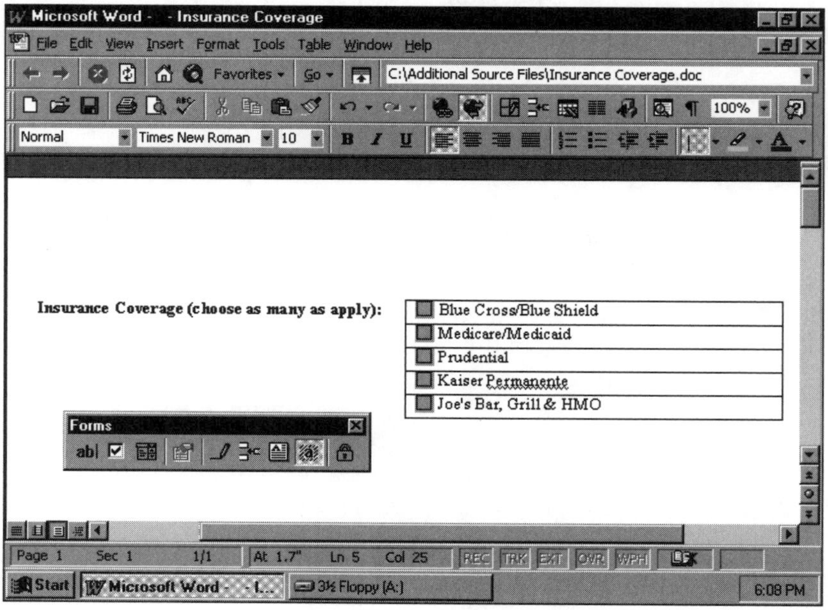

By default, Word displays boxes unchecked. If you want a box to appear checked, or to change other options associated with a check box, display the Check Box Form Field Options dialog box, shown in Figure 20.8. To view it, either select the check box field you want to edit and click the Form Field Options button on the Forms toolbar; or right-click on the field and click Properties from the Shortcut menu.

Figure 20.8

The Check Box Form Field
Options dialog box

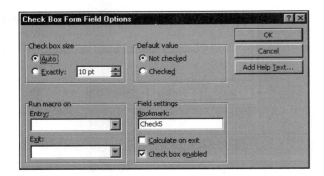

To specify that the box appear checked by default, choose Checke**d** in the Default value box. While you're here, you may want to consider some other settings as well.

By default, Word keeps your check box the same size as the text that follows it; if that text changes size, so does your text box. The Check Box Form Field Options dialog box, however, enables you to change the size of the check box without changing the size of any surrounding text. For example, you could enlarge a box for emphasis.

NOTE. *In the Insurance Coverage example above, the larger boxes that enclose the check boxes are text boxes. Text boxes hold the check boxes in place while the promotional copy "wraps around" them. Text boxes are covered in more detail in Chapter 17.*

To specify the precise size of a form field check box, choose the **E**xactly option button in the Check Box Size frame; then enter the new size in points in the combo box.

Occasionally, you might want to display a box checked or unchecked and prevent users from changing the setting. To do this, select the initial state of the check box using the option buttons in the Default value frame; then in the Field settings frame, clear Check box e**n**abled.

■ Adding Drop-Down Form Fields

You can add drop-down list boxes to a form to give your users a set of choices. (Unlike some Word drop-down lists, list boxes don't enable a user to type a selection that's not on the list.)

To add a drop-down list box to a form, display the Forms Toolbar and click the Drop-Down Form Field button. If that's all you do, however, your form will contain a drop-down form field with no options. Chances are, you'll want to supply your users with some options, and you can do that from the Drop-Down Form Field Options dialog box, shown in Figure 20.9. To display this dialog box, either select the field you want to edit and click the Form Field Options button on the Forms toolbar; or right-click on the field and click Properties from the Shortcut menu that appears.

Figure 20.9

The Drop-Down Form
Field Options dialog box

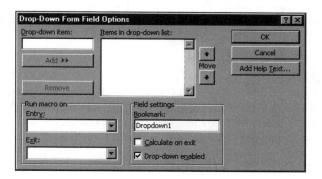

To add an item, type it in the **D**rop-Down Item text box and choose **A**dd. The item then appears in the **I**tems in Drop-Down List list box. You can place up to 50 items in a drop-down list box.

Word treats the first item in your list as your default choice—it's the one that appears selected when the user opens the form. To change the order of a list, select the item you want to move, and click on either the Move up or down arrow.

Suppose you no longer need one of your options; let's say you've discontinued a product. You can delete the option from your form by selecting it and choosing **R**emove.

As with check box form fields, there may be times when you want to specify choices but not allow users to access them; perhaps you plan to make them available later, but for the time being, users are stuck with your default option. To disable the drop-down list box while still displaying the default option, clear the Drop-down e**n**abled check box.

■ Advanced Features for All Form Fields

Until now, we've discussed form field options specific to the type of form field you're using. However, Word provides some capabilities you can use regardless of whether you've inserted a text form field, a check box form field, or a drop-down form field. These include:

- Adding help to your forms
- Associating form fields with bookmarks
- Running macros when users enter or exit a form field

Adding Help to Your Forms

If you're in charge of helping people fill out their forms, you can cut down dramatically on the support you need to provide by adding built-in help to your online forms. Word's built-in help for forms can provide more detailed explanations than your form itself may have room for. You can use it to elaborate on the options you're offering, or the information you wish to collect, or on how to use the form itself.

NOTE. *If you plan to use Form help, your form itself should include information on how to access that help. Otherwise, your users may not know how to get the help you've worked so hard to include. Your language might read something like this:* To get help about any item, move to it with the mouse or the keyboard and press F1.

To add help text, create the form field, display its Options dialog box, and choose Add Help **T**ext. The dialog box shown in Figure 20.10 appears.

Figure 20.10

The Form Field
Help Text dialog box

You now have two sets of choices to make: where your help message appears, and where its contents comes from. You can display help messages in the Word status bar, in a dialog box that appears when a user presses F1, or both. In fact, you can include two different messages. For example, you might provide abbreviated help in the status bar, ending the status bar message with "Press F1 for more," which displays more detailed information in a special Help dialog box, as shown in Figure 20.11.

Figure 20.11

A sample Help dialog box

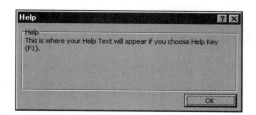

An advantage of displaying help in the status bar is that your message appears automatically whenever a user selects that field. A disadvantage is that many Word users never look in the status bar.

Next, you can decide whether the help message will come from an Auto-Text entry you've already created, or from a message you insert here in the Help Text dialog box, by choosing **T**ype your own and then typing the message. To select an AutoText entry, choose the **A**utoText Entry list box and select from the available AutoText entries.

Chances are, though, you'll want to type your own message, for two reasons. First, neither the Help dialog box nor the status bar displays graphics or tables, even though AutoText entries can store them. Second, when you want to edit the help message, you may find it easier to do so if you can edit it right here, rather than displaying an AutoText entry, editing it, and then having to open AutoText to reassign the edited entry.

Running Macros from Form Fields

You can instruct Word to run a macro whenever a user enters or leaves a field. In either case, you can select from all macros available in your current document or template. (Of course, you'll probably be creating the macro within a new template, and saving the macro there.)

A simple example of how you might use this feature is shown in Figure 20.12. In this example, a macro, PrintForm, has been recorded. PrintForm simply sends the file to your default printer. Whenever a user enters the Click Here to Print File field, the file prints automatically.

Figure 20.12

Using Run macro on Entry to place a print command in a document

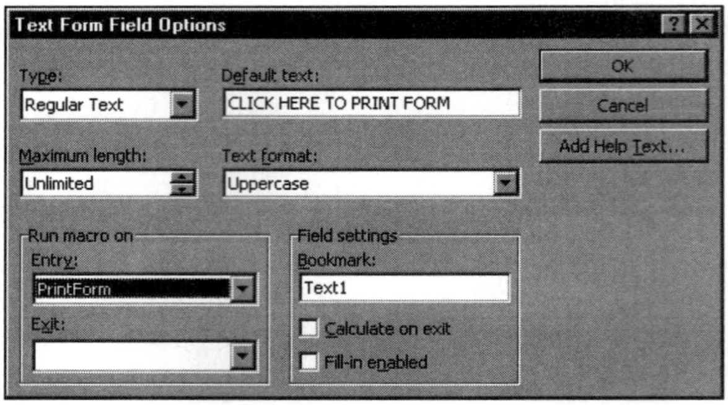

NOTE. *One drawback to this example is you can't protect this field from revision. The user can select only fields he or she can actually edit.*

You also can set a form field as a bookmark that a Word macro can recognize and act upon. Simply use the controls in the Run macro on group frame. You could, for example, create a macro that checks the current contents of a bookmark and, based on what Word finds, places corresponding contents in other fields.

This feature has many applications. When you insert a name, the form could automatically insert a corresponding company and address. When you insert a check box, the macro could fill in information in other locations. Finally, you can set a form field to display specific information all the time. This information is read-only. The user can't edit it.

You might, for example, require customers to purchase one specific item before they become eligible to buy other products. You could insert a checked check box for that item and disable it, as discussed earlier in this chapter.

Changing a Form Field

You can't change a form field from a document based on your form template. You have to change the form field from within the template itself. To do so, follow these steps:

1. Open the template. (After you choose **F**ile, **O**pen, you need to specify Document Templates in the List Files of **T**ype box.)

2. Unprotect the document so you can edit it. Choose Un**p**rotect Document from the **T**ools menu.

3. Double-click on the form field. The Options dialog box for the field you've chosen appears.

4. Make your changes.

5. Click on OK.

■ Protecting a Form from Unwanted Change

Until now, we've briefly mentioned protecting and unprotecting form templates. Word gives you extremely tight control over the changes that can be made to a form. When you protect a template, a user can't make any changes in documents based on that template, except where you've inserted form fields. In fact, a form doesn't behave like a form until you protect it.

When you protect a form, some form fields that provide specific information can't be changed either. In a text form field that makes a calculation, for example, the user can't override the calculation. And, as you've seen, unchecking the E**n**abled check box in a form's Options dialog box also prevents a user from making changes in that field.

To protect a form, first open the form template, and then choose **T**ools, **P**rotect Document. The dialog box shown in Figure 20.13 appears.

Figure 20.13

Protecting a form through the Protect Document dialog box

If you want, you can add a password. Including one probably makes sense if your form will be used in a large organization where someone might feel like editing it inappropriately. (You don't want sabbaticals in Siberia added to your benefits options form.)

Unlike the protection available to entire documents, form passwords don't encrypt the document. Users can still open a password-protected form template; they just can't unprotect and edit it. When a user does try to unprotect such a document, the Unprotect Document dialog box opens, as shown in Figure 20.14.

Figure 20.14

Unprotecting a document through the Unprotect Document dialog box

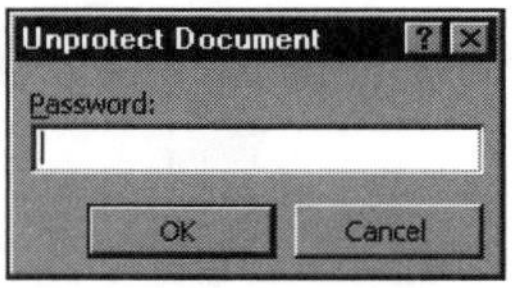

All the usual password safeguards apply; choose a password you'll remember but nobody else can figure out. Don't leave it in an obvious location. And remember, after you create and confirm a password, you have no way to unprotect the document without the password.

To remove a password, first open the document (using its password). Then unprotect it using the Un**p**rotect Document option on the **T**ools menu. Then protect it again by choosing **P**rotect Document from the **T**ools menu. Choose **F**orms in the Protect Document dialog box. No password appears in the **P**assword box. If no password is what you want, choose OK. Once you save the file, it no longer requires a password.

■ Saving a Form

After you create a form, save it as a template under a new name, preferably a descriptive one. If your organization numbers its forms, you might include the new form number in the name.

■ Filling In Online Forms

To fill in an online form, create a new document based on the template that contains the form. Each form field is shaded in gray. The first field is shaded in deeper gray. That's where your insertion point is (see Figure 20.15).

Figure 20.15

Filling in a form

Darker grey indicates active field for editing

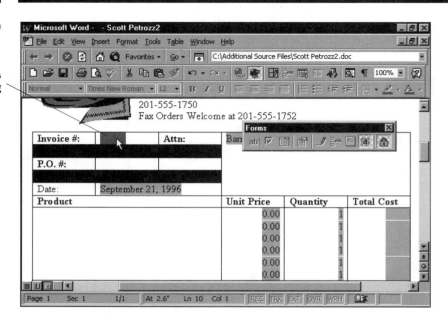

Unless you specified that the field consist of very few characters, the gray area will extend as you type. If the field is located in a text cell, the text simply wraps when you reach the end of the cell.

NOTE. *This word wrap can wreak havoc with a form design. That's one reason to set a maximum length when you create the form, especially if you ultimately plan to print it.*

After you fill in a form field, press Enter, Tab, or the down-arrow key—they all move you to the next form field in which you may make an entry. (Word skips over form fields that it automatically calculates and fields in which you disable user input.)

Table 20.1 shows Word's editing and navigation keys for editing forms. As you can see, some keys work a little differently in forms compared with other documents.

Table 20.1

Word's Form-Editing
Commands

TO DO THIS	USE THIS KEY OR COMBINATION
Move to the next editable field	Enter, Tab, or down arrow
Move to the previous editable field	Shift+Tab or up arrow
Show the contents of a drop-down list	F4 or Alt+down arrow
Move up or down in a drop-down list	Up arrow or down arrow
Make a selection in a drop-down list	Enter
Mark or unmark a check box	Space bar or X
Show help for a form	F1 (if you've specified that Word display a dialog box to show help; otherwise help appears in the status bar
Insert a tab	Ctrl+Tab

■ Creating Printed Forms

Your users will often need hard copies of blank forms, which are easy to generate. Simply print the template or an empty document based on the template.

Sometimes, you might want to print only the data in the form, not the form itself. To print only the data, follow these steps:

1. Choose **T**ools, **O**ptions.

2. Choose Print tab.

3. In the Options for current document only box, choose Print data only for Forms.

4. Click on OK.

■ Distributing Your Forms

You have several choices about how to distribute your forms. The simplest is to use Word primarily as an easy way to create paper forms. This method allows you to print forms only as needed and to revise them quickly, rather than store large quantities of forms that risk obsolescence as your needs change.

A step beyond this is to compile all your forms on a floppy disk and provide a copy of the disk to everyone who shares your forms. This approach has the advantage of largely eliminating printed forms (well, at least in theory). Of course, it assumes everyone is running a version of Word that understands form fields. (If you're working with people who use Word 6 or Word 95, you can save your files to their format, or provide them a free file converter that can allow their software to read Word 97 files.

Before you distribute your forms electronically, you should seriously consider password protecting them. If you're networked, you can place your protected form templates in a common folder available to everyone on the network.

If you have a form that you want everyone to fill out, you can send the template as an attachment on your electronic mail network. (Remember to add instructions on what to do with the form.) If you're using Microsoft Exchange or another MAPI- or VIM-compatible e-mail system, you can just use the Send to Mail Recipient, Send to Routing Recipient, or Send to Exchange Folder commands on Word's File menu. Send to Routing Recipient makes it easy to send a form to as many people on the network as is necessary, either one at a time or all at once.

In this chapter, you've learned how to use Word's forms creation features to develop electronic forms, complete with built-in guidance, which any of your colleagues can fill out.

The form fields you've learned about here foreshadow Chapter 21—where you take a closer look at Word's *fields* feature, which allows you to automate many elements of your document, keeping it up-to-date with virtually no effort on your part.

21

Field Codes: 70+ Ways to Automate Your Documents

Fields are your executive assistant. you can delegate many of the most annoying details of assembling a document to your computer. (Hey, it's a computer—it thrives on that stuff.) Meanwhile, you can do the thinking.

Say that your document has figures and tables that need to be numbered consecutively. You can do it manually—and redo the numbering every time you insert or delete a figure or table. Or you can use a field code, and let Word track it all for you.

Word disguises many of its field codes as friendly dialog boxes. When you insert a cross-reference, numbered caption, or table of contents, or tell Word to insert a date and time that can be updated automatically, you're inserting a field code.

But it's still a good idea to become acquainted with the underlying field codes themselves. You can do many things with field codes that haven't yet been built into neat and clean menu items, buttons, and check boxes. Even some Word features that have been slicked up with dialog boxes can perform extra tricks if you know how to use field codes. If those tricks perform tasks you really need, you'll be glad to know about them.

As with styles, templates, and AutoText entries, fields require a little more forethought—but they pay off handsomely in time savings. And you certainly don't have to understand all of Word's 70+ fields to make good use of them. A dozen might be all you ever need.

This chapter shows you how fields work, how to insert and view them, how to update them, and how to format them so they deliver the precise results you want. We'll also direct you to the fields you're most likely to find useful.

■ Understanding Fields

A *field* is a set of instructions that you place in a document. Most often, these instructions tell Word to find or produce some specific text and stick that text where you have inserted the field. In other cases, fields may be used to mark text, such as index entries, which you want Word to keep track of. In a few cases, Word fields can also tell Word to take an action that doesn't place new visible text in your document, such as running a macro that saves a file.

NOTE. *Experienced field users will want to know that Word 97 introduces four new fields:*

{ AUTOTEXTLIST } which allows you to insert text in a document and at the same time format the text in any style available to the document;

{ DOCVARIABLE } which allows you to insert the value of a document variable created with Visual Basic for Applications;

{ HYPERLINK } which allows you to insert a hyperlink to another location in your document, on your hard disk, on your network, or on the Internet; and

{ LISTNUM } which allows you to generate a set of numbers anywhere in a paragraph and update them automatically, just as Word's automatic outline numbering feature can update headings and outline levels.

Result Fields

Fields that specify instructions which Word can use to determine which text to insert in your document are called *result fields*, and the information they generate is called *field results*. These "result field field results" can come from many sources, including the following:

- Information stored in the document's Properties or Statistics dialog boxes (such as the author's name)

- Information Word calculates from sources you specify, such as adding a column of numbers

- Information Word requests later

- Information Word produces based on what it finds in your document (such as page counts)

- Information found in other files

- Information found elsewhere in your document

Because your document includes the field instructions, not the actual information, Word can find and insert new information whenever a change occurs. That's the magic of field codes—they handle the details you can easily forget.

Marker Fields

Some fields simply mark text so that you (or another field) can find it later. For example, the TC field marks entries that later can be compiled into tables of contents.

Action Fields

Finally, some action fields tell Word to perform a specific action that doesn't place new visible text in your document. For example, the Macrobutton field places a button in the text; when the button is clicked, Word runs a macro you choose. You might include a Macrobutton that saves an open file whenever it is clicked.

■ Fields That Might Already Be in Your Document

You've come across several field codes already, although you may not have realized it. When you place the date, time, or page number in a header or footer, Word places a field code in the document. The Date field code checks your computer's built-in clock and inserts the date and time that it contains. You can insert many fields quite easily if you use the specific Word menu commands or toolbar buttons instead of field codes (see Table 21.1 for a list).

Table 21.1

Menu Command Shortcuts for Some Fields

THIS FIELD COMMAND	CORRESPONDS TO THIS MENU COMMAND, TOOLBAR BUTTON, OR KEYBOARD SHORTCUT
={ Formula }	T**a**ble, **F**ormula
{ AutoText}	**I**nsert, **A**utoText
{ BarCode }	**T**ools, **E**nvelopes and Labels
{ Bookmark }	**I**nsert, Book**m**ark
{ Date }	**I**nsert, **D**ate and **T**ime{ Time }
{ DDE }	**E**dit, Paste **S**pecial (Paste **L**ink)
{ Embed }	**I**nsert, **O**bject
{ FormCheckBox }	Forms Toolbar
{ FormDropDown }	Forms Toolbar
{ FormText }	Forms Toolbar
{ IncludePicture }	**I**nsert, **P**icture, **F**rom File
{ IncludeText }	**I**nsert, Fi**l**e
{ Index }	**I**nsert, Inde**x** and Tables
{ Hyperlink }	**I**nsert, Hyperl**i**nk
{ NoteRef }	**I**nsert, Foot**n**ote
{ Page }	**I**nsert, Page N**u**mbers
{ Ref }	**I**nsert, Cross-**R**eference
{ Seq }	**I**nsert, Capt**i**on
{ Symbol }	**I**nsert, **S**ymbol
{ TOA }	**I**nsert, Inde**x** and Tables
{ TOC }	**I**nsert, Inde**x** and Tables
{ XE }	Mark Index **E**ntry (Alt+Shift+X)

Even if you enter a field code using a menu command, you might still want to edit it later for precise formatting. But that's still easier than creating it from scratch.

■ Viewing Fields

Rarely do you see the fields in your document—what you see is the information the fields find or create. Sometimes, however, you *want* to see your fields. For example, you might want to edit a field so that it presents different information, or presents it in a different format. Or maybe a field isn't behaving the way you expect, and you'd like to know why.

To view all field codes, press Alt+F9, or do the following:

1. Select **O**ptions from the **T**ools menu.

2. Select the **V**iew tab dialog box.

3. Check the **F**ield Codes box in the Show area.

Field Code Shading

In early versions of Word, it often was difficult to tell whether text was a field code or just plain old text (that is, until you tried to backspace into it, and your computer beeped).

Word now gives you some help. By default, field codes are now shaded in gray, but only when you select them. In the Fi**e**ld Shading list box (Tools, Options, View), you can also choose Never, or Always (field codes always shaded, even when not selected). It's a matter of taste, and now you have a choice. Field shading doesn't appear in Print Preview, and it doesn't print.

NOTE. *If you see field codes rather than field results, press Alt+F9 to toggle them off, or clear the **F**ield Codes box in **T**ools, **O**ptions, **V**iew.*

You might occasionally want to view your field codes and field results at the same time. (You might, for example, want to check whether you've formatted a field the way you want.) Open a second window on the same document, as follows:

1. Select **N**ew Window from the Window menu.

2. Select Arrange All from the **W**indow menu. Both windows are displayed horizontally.

3. In one window, select Tools, Options, View and check the Field Codes box. In the other window, make sure the Field Codes box is cleared.

Your screen displays field codes in one window and field results in the other, as shown in Figure 21.1.

Figure 21.1

Two windows, one with
field codes and one
with field results

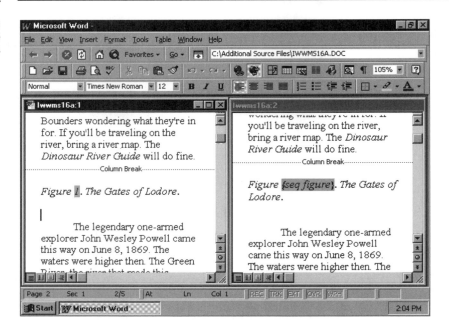

■ Inserting a Field Using Insert Field

Although you can enter a field directly, you'll generally prefer to use the
Field dialog box. Select Fi**e**ld from the **I**nsert menu (see Figure 21.2).

Figure 21.2

The Field dialog box is
where you will insert
most fields that
don't have dialog
boxes of their own.

Field syntax information
appears here ———

Enter your field
information here ———

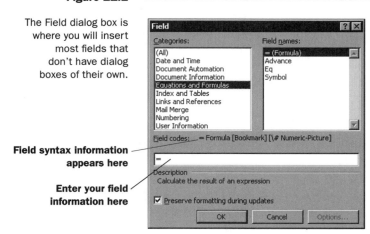

The Field dialog box helps you build the field syntax that Word understands and acts upon. Step one is to select a field code. Select the field code from a list of available fields in the Field **n**ames box, or if you know exactly what you want, type it directly into the box. (Unless you're creating a formula, delete the equal sign first.)

If you're not sure of the name of the field code, select a category of fields from the **C**ategories list, and Word lists your choices for you. Word organizes its field codes into nine categories, described respectively in the following minitable:

Field Category	What It Covers
Date and Time	Fields that include the current date or time, or the date or time that an event relevant to your document took place (for example, the last time you saved or printed)
Document Automation	Compares values and takes an action: runs macros, jumps to new locations, sends printer codes
Document Information	Inserts or stores information about your document
Equations and Formulas	Creates and calculates the results of formulas; inserts symbols
Index and Tables	Creates entries in, or builds, indexes and tables of contents, figures, and authorities (which list by category all citations made in a document)
Links and References	Inserts information from elsewhere in your document, from AutoText entries, or from other documents and files
Mail Merge	Imports information from a data source for a Word mail merge
Numbering	Numbers your document's pages or sections, inserts information about your document's page numbers or sections, or inserts a bar code
User Information	Stores your name, address or initials, or inserts them in a document or envelope

Notice the check box in the lower left hand corner of the box. If you mark this box, and later make manual formatting changes to the field's contents, Word won't eliminate those manual formatting changes when it updates your field.

NOTE. *If you actually look at the field code Word generates when you check this box, you'll see that the * mergeformat switch has been added. We'll cover * mergeformat later in this chapter; it's just one of the many ways you can control how your fields appear in your document.*

With some fields, once you've chosen them, you can just click OK—you're done. For example, if you want Word to find the user's name stored in the User Information tab of the Options dialog box (accessible by choosing **T**ools, **O**ptions), simply insert the following field, and choose OK:

USERNAME

More often, however, you must tell Word more. You can tell whether you need to tell Word more by looking at the syntax information provided in the Insert Field box, just above the box where you can enter your field information (refer back to Figure 21.2).

To get online help about a specific field, select it in the Field dialog box, and press F1 or click the "?" help icon. You can also get Field help from anywhere in Word, as follows:

1. Select Contents and Index from the **H**elp menu.

2. In the Type the word(s) you want to find box, enter the name of the field you're interested in.

3. In the **C**lick a topic, then click Display box, select the topic that refers to the field code.

4. Click **D**isplay.

What Goes into a Field

This section briefly covers what can go into a field. A more detailed discussion appears later in the chapter.

In the Username field, *USERNAME* is obviously the name of the field—or, as Word puts it, the field type. In this example, Username searches for the name recorded in the User Information tab of the Options dialog box (accessible from **T**ools, **O**ptions), and then inserts it into the document.

But you can also use Username to place a new name in the document and store the same name in the User Information dialog box, as follows:

{ USERNAME Robert Smith }

The text after USERNAME is a simple example of *field instructions*. Often Word helps you create these field instructions—through a specific menu item, or through **I**nsert, Fi**e**ld.

In field codes in which you ask Word to refer to text elsewhere in your document, you have to add a *bookmark*—a name that you have already assigned to that text. (See Chapter 12 for a detailed discussion of bookmarks.)

If you want to specify text that you want Word to add to the document verbatim—as opposed to text that Word will find elsewhere in the document—you generally need to specify this text in quotation marks.

Often, you will also have to specify a *switch*—a command that starts with a backslash, and tells Word to modify the behavior of the field.

Specifying Field Options

If you need to add a switch, or another option, to your field, select **O**ptions from the Field dialog box. The Field Options dialog box appears (see Figure 21.3). Say hosannas for this dialog box: it's where Word saves you the trouble of memorizing hundreds of switch names.

Figure 21.3

The Field Options dialog box gives you easy access to all the field-specific switches associated with the field you're using, as well as some general switches that affect field appearance.

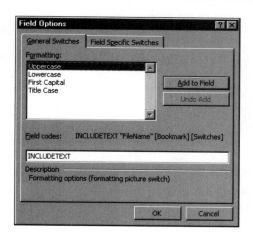

Many fields have both *general switches* (which determine how your field will be formatted), and *field-specific* switches, which change field behaviors that are unique to the field you're working with. If Word expects that you will need both kinds of switches, the Field Options dialog box will present them in separate tabs, as shown in Figure 21.3 above. Note, however, that you may occasionally need a general switch, and have to add it manually because it does not appear in the Field Options dialog box. We'll return to general switches in much more detail later. For now, it's enough to recognize that there are four kinds of general switches:

Switch	Name	Does
*	Formatting	Lets you decide how to format inserted text
\#	Numeric picture	Lets you decide how to format inserted numbers
\@	Date-time picture	Lets you decide how to format a date
\!	Lock result	Lets you decide *not* to update a specific field even as others are being updated

Not every field can use all four of these general switches. For example, you can't create a date-time picture for a paragraph of text. Conversely, many fields have switches that only make sense in their specific context. For example, if you use \t in an XE index entry field, Word knows not to include the page number with the index entry, but to include text instead. This would be a meaningless instruction in most other fields.

To add a switch to your field, select it from a box. After you select the switch, a description of it appears in the description box. If you like what you see, choose **A**dd to Field.

Some switches require you to add more information manually. For example, if you're using the Seq field to create a sequence of numbers, you can use the \r switch to tell Word to "reset" your sequencing back to a specific number. But Word won't know what number to use until you add the number after the \r switch.

After you finish, choose OK to return to the Field dialog box, and choose OK again to insert the field into your document.

Inserting a Field Using Field Characters

Using Insert, Field usually makes sense, because it walks you through inserting fields that you don't use every day and may not remember exactly how to work with. However, sometimes you may know exactly what you're planning to do—especially if the field is so simple that all you need to enter is its name. For those instances, here's how to insert fields directly into your document without using **I**nsert, Fi**e**ld.

Press Ctrl+F9 to tell Word you want to edit a field. Word places two curly brackets around your insertion point and colors them gray to indicate that you're now in a field (see Figure 21.4).

Figure 21.4

When you press Ctrl+F9 to insert a field in your document, the field appears as two curly brackets; by default, these are highlighted in gray.

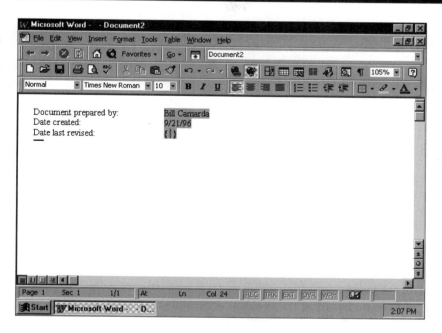

These curly brackets are called *field characters*. The curly brackets on your keyboard don't do the job, however. (If they did, how would Word know when all you wanted was curly brackets? To paraphrase Freud, sometimes curly brackets are just curly brackets.)

Word also adds an extra space after the opening bracket and before the closing bracket. That's why field codes inserted by Word look like this:

```
{ FILENAME }
```

The fields work fine without those extra spaces, and the field names don't have to be all uppercase.

Once you have your curly brackets, you can type your field names, bookmarks, quoted material, switches, or anything else you need, inside the brackets. (You can also cut and paste text into or from the brackets, as long as the brackets are visible—in other words, as long as the field codes are displayed.)

NOTE. *Another way to repeatedly insert the same field code is to create an AutoText entry that contains it. Simply select the field; choose **I**nsert, **A**utoText, **N**ew; enter the name you want to use for the AutoText entry, and click OK. Now whenever you type the AutoText name and press F3, the field will be inserted.*

■ Updating Fields

One of the best things about fields is that you can update them without manually changing the text they represent. It's easy, but for most fields, not quite automatic. F9 is the magic key!

To update a single field, place your insertion point within it, and press F9.

To update more than one field, select them and press F9.

To update all the fields in a document, press Ctrl+A and then press F9. In a long document with many fields, this can take a little while. You can always stop an update by pressing Esc.

When you insert a field using Insert, Field, the field updates automatically when you click OK to leave the dialog box. When you insert a field using Ctrl+F9, Word doesn't update the field until you select it and press F9.

NOTE. *Updating with F9 doesn't affect the following fields: Autonum, Autonumgl, Autonumout, EQ, Gotobutton, Macrobutton, and Print.*

At one time, Word updated all your fields whenever you printed your document, but no longer. If you want to update fields whenever you print, do the following:

1. Select **O**ptions from the **T**ools menu.

2. Select the **P**rint tab.

3. Check **U**pdate Fields in the Printing Options area.

Locking, Unlocking, and Unlinking Fields

Suppose you want to temporarily prevent a field from being updated, even as you update fields surrounding it. Say you use an Includetext field to display the first quarter results from a table in another document. You might want to update that table at some point, but the first quarter results that appear in your current document aren't likely to change—they're history. So you lock the field, which prevents updating.

You might recall that the \! switch enables you to lock a field. But it is easier to lock a field as follows. First, place your insertion point in the field (or if you want to lock several fields at once, select text that includes them all). Then, press Ctrl+F11 or Alt+Ctrl+F1.

When you try to update this field, a message appears in the status bar that it cannot update locked fields. (By the way, the \! switch does not appear in a field you lock this way.)

To unlock a field so that it can again be updated, place your insertion point in the field and press Ctrl+Shift+F11 or Alt+Ctrl+Shift+F1.

You might decide you never want to update a field. For example, you've absolutely finished your document, and you're exporting it to a desktop publishing program that displays Word field codes as gibberish. Word lets you permanently replace the field codes with the most recently updated field results. This is called *unlinking*. Before unlinking a field, you will probably want to manually update it to make sure that it is current: Word does not automatically update a field before you unlink it. To permanently unlink a field, first place the insertion point in the field, or select text, including the field(s) to be unlinked. Then, press Ctrl+Shift+F9.

After you unlink a field, the field is gone forever, unless you use Word's undo feature or close the document before changes are saved. Just to be safe, before unlinking all the fields in a complex document, you may want to save a duplicate copy of the file with its fields still in place.

■ Word's Field Shortcut Menu

When you right-click on a field, a shortcut menu appears (see Figure 21.5), including commands for two of the most common tasks you may need when working with fields: Update Field and Toggle Field Codes. (Toggle Field switches between field codes and field results.)

Figure 21.5

The shortcut menu that appears when a field is highlighted

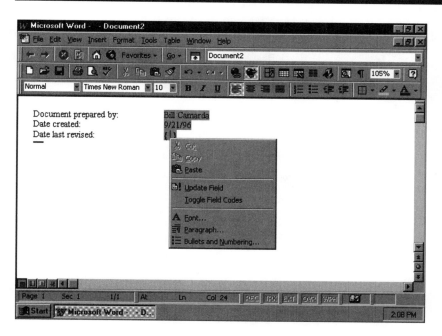

Word Keyboard Field Shortcuts

You've already learned some of Word's keyboard shortcuts for using fields.
They're collected in Table 21.2.

Table 21.2

Field Key Combinations

TASK	KEY COMBINATION	WHAT IT DOES
Insert Field	Ctrl+F9	Inserts field characters { } and awaits your field instructions
Update Field	F9	Produces a new field result
Go to Next Visible Field	F11 (or Alt+F1)	Moves to next visible field
Go to Previous Visible Field	Shift+F11 (or Alt+Shift+F1)	Moves to previous visible field
View/Hide All Field Codes	Shift+F9	Toggles between displaying field codes and their results
Lock Field	Ctrl+F11	Prevents a field from being updated until you unlock it
Unlock Field	Ctrl+F11	Allows a locked field to be updated again
Unlink Field	Ctrl+Shift+F9	Replaces a field with its most recently updated results, eliminating the field code
Update Source (Works with Includetext field only)	Ctrl+Shift+F7	Updates selected text in another document that is connected to the current document by an Includetext field
Perform Field Click (works with Macrobutton or Gotobutton fields only)	Alt+Shift+F9	Performs whatever actions you've programmed into a Macrobutton or Gotobutton field
Insert Date Field	Alt+Shift+D	Inserts Date field with default format (06/02/97)
Insert Page Field	Alt+Shift+P	Inserts Page field with default format (1,2,3...)
Insert Time Field	Alt+Shift+T	Inserts Time field with default format (04:29 PM)

■ Finding and Replacing Field Contents

When field codes are displayed, you can also search and replace their contents. This might be useful if you need to change many field codes at once. For example, let's say your document contained several { USERINITIALS } field codes that display a user's initials, and you decided to replace them with { USERNAME } field codes that display the user's full name instead. Press Alt+F9 to display the field codes; use search and replace to make the changes; then press Alt+F9 to hide the field codes again.

Word's Replace feature is also ideal if you want to change the formatting of a specific kind of field that recurs throughout your document. For example, if you decided that references to calculations should appear in the format used on checks, you could replace all references to { =profit } with { =profit * dollartext}—and Word would change the way it displays the results of every formula accordingly, to use this format: *Twenty-seven and 00/100*.

■ Moving Among Fields

Word offers shortcuts for moving among fields. F11 (or Alt+F1) moves to the next field and selects it. Shift+F11 (or Alt+Shift+F1) selects the previous field. You can also move among fields by using Word 97's Select Browse Object's Browse by Field button. Select Browse Object is covered in more detail in Chapter 6.

Some fields, such as index entries, are automatically formatted as hidden text. Word's next-field and previous-field keyboard shortcuts normally skip these fields. (Using **F**ind and R**e**place from the **E**dit menu skips them, too.) You can show hidden text as follows:

1. Select **O**ptions from the **T**ools menu.

2. Select the **V**iew tab.

3. Check H**i**dden Text in the Nonprinting Characters group.

■ A Closer Look at Field Instructions and Formatting

Now that you've reviewed the elements of a typical field code, let's go into greater detail about how you can control your field codes and make their results appear in your documents exactly as you intend.

Field instructions—when necessary at all—can include any of the following elements:

```
Arguments
Bookmarks
Expressions
Identifiers
Switches
Text
```

Arguments

Arguments are text, numbers, or graphics that help a field decide how to act, or what information to insert. For example, the following line tells Word to insert "How to Succeed in Advertising" where you place the field, and also in the Summary Info box:

```
{ TITLE "How to Succeed in Advertising" }
```

Note that the field instruction is surrounded by quotation marks. Technically, that's only necessary if the instruction is longer than one word, but it's a good habit to develop.

Once in awhile, you might need to tell Word that you actually want real quotation marks to appear in the document. To indicate this, use backslashes, as in the following example:

```
{ TITLE "Start \"Loafing"\ Around" }
```

You might wonder: What if I need to include a document path, which already uses backslashes? The answer: Use two backslashes wherever you would have used one:

```
{ INCLUDETEXT c:\\reports\\income.doc }
```

Bookmarks

Bookmarks are markers you place anywhere in a document. They identify a location or selected text. You can add a bookmark to some fields, which tells Word to go to that location, or to insert that text. The bookmark name can be only one word, so you never have to worry about quotation marks when you insert a bookmark name in a field. For example:

```
{ REF jones }
```

This tells Word to insert text about Jones that you've flagged elsewhere in the document.

Formulas

You can include a formula as a field code; Word does the math and displays the results. Word formulas start with the = symbol. For example, { =24-8 } displays 16.

But that's an awfully convoluted way of doing math in Word. The real benefit of expressions is that you can base them on other information in your document—and when that information changes, the expression updates itself in your document. The example

```
{ =joesales - bobsales }
```

tells Word to look for a bookmark named *bobsales* which already contains a value, and subtract it from another bookmark named *joesales*, which also contains a value.

You can use the If field to tell Word to display one kind of information if it finds one mathematical result, and different information otherwise. Using the joesales/bobsales example, bookmark the expression field. Call it *joevbob*.

This field pats Joe on the back if he outsells Bob. If not, it quietly lets the occasion pass.

```
{IF joevbob > 0, "Congratulations, Joe, you've made it. Top salesperson of the month!"}
```

Notice that the expression is now embedded in the field instructions, after If. You can also use cell names (A1, A2, and so on) in place of bookmarks, so that a table can perform many of the tasks of a spreadsheet.

Identifiers

Identifiers tell Word's action fields to recognize specific text to be acted upon. The best example of how identifiers work is the Seq field, which creates and updates sequences of figures, tables, and other elements of your document.

Word's Insert Caption feature has automated Figure lists, but let's suppose you want to number some other kind of item scattered throughout your document. You can insert a Seq field everywhere you want a consecutive number to appear.

Text

In the context of this discussion, *text* can be words (or images) that you want to appear in the document or on the screen. As with arguments, text should appear between quotation marks if it's more than one word.

The Fillin field offers a good example of using text. It enables you to display a dialog box that prompts the user to type something:

```
{ FILLIN "What's your sign?" }
```

You may use Fillin often if you plan to use Word for forms development.

Switches

You may want to change the way a field acts, or the way a field result looks. That's what *switches* do. We've already discussed inserting switches through the Field Options dialog box. Note that all Word field code switches start with a backslash and appear after your other instructions. For example, \! ensures that a field doesn't change its contents even when all the others are updated, as in the following example:

```
{ INCLUDETEXT january.doc \! }
```

Some switches only work with one type of field, but general switches work with nearly all fields. Earlier, we presented a brief overview of general switches, and showed the overall categories of general switches in Table 21.1. Now, you'll learn how to actually use general switches to control field formatting in as much detail as you need.

Formatting Field Results

Suppose you've made an important point somewhere in your document. You've formatted it in boldface for emphasis. Now you want to bring the same sentence into your executive summary, but your executives are a staid bunch: you don't want the information to be boldfaced in *this* context.

You *could* reformat or edit your field result manually—but then, unless you checked Preserve formatting during updates in the Field dialog box when you created it, the field might revert to the bold formatting anytime you update your fields. You *could* lock that field—but if you ever want to update the *substance* of the field, then what? The best solution is to use one of Word's many field formatting options. This is where Word's formatting field text options come in.

Formatting Field Text

If you use a field that consists only of the field name, such as NumChars, it's easy. Format the first character of the field name to look the way you want your text to appear. If you want bold italic underlined text, your field should look like this:

```
{ NUMCHARS }
```

If the field also contains instructions, things get a bit more complicated. Again, format the first character of the field name the way you want it. Then, add the following switch to the end of your field code:

```
\* charformat
```

For instance:

```
{ INCLUDETEXT report.doc \* charformat }
```

Using * mergeformat

You do have an alternative. You can manually format your text, and tell Word not to change the formatting no matter what. You do that with the * mergeformat switch.

The catch is, when you use * mergeformat, Word counts words and takes their formatting literally. If the fourth word in your field result happens to be italicized now, then your fourth word will always be italicized—even if you change the contents of your field result, and it's no longer appropriate to italicize that particular word. Let's say the field you insert consists of the following:

From Paul Dickson's collection, *Words*, comes the word **culacino**, Italian for the mark left on a tablecloth by a wet glass.

Let's say that you edited it a bit. You could wind up with:

Paul Dickson's collection, Words, *includes* the word culacino, **which** is Italian for the mark left on a tablecloth by a wet glass.

This literalism limits * mergeformat to times when you know the order of words in your field results won't change.

Setting the Case of Field Results

Word also enables you to choose the case of your field results by using the options shown in Table 21.3:

Table 21.3

Setting the Case of Field Results with the * Switch

THIS SWITCH	DOES THIS	LOOKS LIKE THIS
* caps	Capitalizes each word	Sample Text
* firstcap	Capitalizes first word	Sample text
* lower	Makes all text lowercase	sample text
* upper	Capitalizes all text	SAMPLE TEXT

Formatting Field Numbers

You can use * charformat and * mergeformat to format numbers as well. But numbers present some unique issues. What if a number should appear one way in one place, but another way where a field places it?

The predefined numeric formats in Word's Field Options dialog boxes can handle many of your needs, but this section will help you understand what's going on "under the hood" so you can troubleshoot problems, or edit formats directly without using Insert, Field.

For instance, let's say that your source is a numbered list:

Sherby's Laws of Consulting (source: Gerald M. Weinberg)

1. In spite of what your client may tell you, there's always a problem.

2. No matter how it looks at first, it's always a people problem.

3. Never forget they're paying you by the hour, not by the solution.

Now let's say that you want to use a field to refer to this rule elsewhere in the document, in another context:

Remember Sherby's third rule of consulting: Never forget they're paying you by the hour, not by the solution.

How can you transpose "3" into "third"?

Or, let's say you have a dollar amount, $32.50, that needs to be placed elsewhere in check format:

Thirty-two and 50/100

Word offers several field formatting options that can change a number from the way it appears in its source location, or establish an altogether new formatting for a number created by a Word field. These numerical options use the * switch, as shown in Table 21.4.

Table 21.4

Numeric Formats Controlled by the * Switch

THIS SWITCH	CREATES THIS	LOOKS LIKE THIS	YOU MIGHT USE IT FOR
* alphabetic	Changes number into corresponding lowercase letters	aa	Catalogs
* Alphabetic	Changes number into corresponding uppercase letters	AA	Catalogs
* Arabic	Arabic	27	Most applications
* cardtext	Cardinal text	Twenty-seven	Insertion into text, especially for numbers below 20
* dollartext	Cardinal text with fraction	Twenty-seven and 00/100	Check, purchase orders

Table 21.4 (Continued)

Numeric Formats
Controlled by the * Switch

THIS SWITCH	CREATES THIS	LOOKS LIKE THIS	YOU MIGHT USE IT FOR
* hex	Hexadecimal	1B	Computing applications
* ordinal	Ordinal	27th	Dates
* Roman	Roman numerals	XXVII	Publications

As usual, the switch is placed after other field instructions:

```
{ =joesales * .05 \* dollartext }
```

Painting a Numeric Picture

You use the * switches to control the kind of text into which your numbers are transformed. But what if you're perfectly happy with plain old Arabic numbers (1, 2, 3...), but want to control how they appear?

For this, Word offers a different switch: \#. You use this switch to paint a *numeric picture* of how you want your numbers to appear. A numeric picture is simply a generic model of how you want to format your numbers. For example, you're using fields to set up a list of numbers. If you use Word's default format, they'll look like this:

```
327.8
15.96
29
18.223
```

Sloppy. You want them to look like this:

```
327.800
 15.960
 29.000
 18.223
```

You can combine the \# switch with two kinds of placeholders, # and 0, to create a numeric picture of how your numbers should appear. To get the cleaned-up list, use the following switch with each field:

```
\# ###.000
```

Quotation marks are optional unless you're combining the number with text. The # symbol tells Word: If there's no number in that location, insert a blank space. The 0 symbol tells Word: If there's no number in this location, insert a 0.

A numeric picture using # or 0 placeholders rounds off a fractional number that requires more digits than you allowed. For example, the field code { =1/4 } by default displays the result 0.25.

NOTE. *Word's default is to round off to hundredths.*

But if you add a switch like this:

```
{ -1/4 \# #.# }
```

Word rounds off the last digit, like the following:
0.3

The # placeholders to the right of the decimal point also tell Word to round off any additional digits without a corresponding # symbol. # and 0 are probably the elements used most often. Not surprisingly, Word provides several others as well, all listed in Table 21.5.

NOTE. *Several prefabricated # and 0 variants are available through the =expression Field Type box in the Insert Field dialog box.*

Table 21.5

Characters You Can Use in Numeric Pictures

THIS CHARACTER	DOES THIS	SAMPLE USAGE	SAMPLE FIELD RESULT
#	Substitutes a blank space where no number is present. Rounds off extra fractional digits.	{ =1/4\# #.# }	0.3
0	Substitutes a zero where no number is present	{ 1/4\# 00.000)	00.250
$	Places a dollar sign in your field result	{ 5/2\# $#.00 }	$2.50
+	Places a plus or minus sign in front of any field result not equal to zero	{ 1/4\# +#.## }	+.25
-	Places a minus sign in front of negative numbers	{ 1/4\# -#.## }	-.25
.	Inserts a decimal point	{ 1/4\# #.# }	0.3
,	Inserts a comma separator	{ 8500/2\# #,0 } (note: also use at least one 0 or #)	4,250

Table 21.5 (Continued)

Characters You Can Use in Numeric Pictures

THIS CHARACTER	DOES THIS	SAMPLE USAGE	SAMPLE FIELD RESULT
;	Enables you to specify more than one option for displaying numbers, depending on whether the numbers are positive, negative, or zero	{ revenue-expenses \# $###.00; ($###.00); 0 }	$250.00 ($250.00) or 0
x	If placed on the left, truncates digits to its left. If placed on the right, truncates digits to its right.	{ 4875\# #x## }	75
"text"	Includes text in the numeric picture. Place the entire numeric picture in double quotation marks, and the text in single quotation marks	{ = "####'lira'" }	3472 lira

Date and Time Formatting

As with numbers, you can format dates and times in many different ways. Usually, the quickest way to format date and time is to create your field with **In**sert, Fi**el**d; the Field Options dialog boxes have most of the formats you need. However, it doesn't hurt to know what's going on if you need a specialty format.

The date-time switch is \@. Similar to what you've already seen with numbers, \@ creates a date-time picture—a model of how your dates and times should look. This date-time picture is usable with the following fields:

Date
Time
Created
Printdate
Savedate

You can use the characters in Table 21.6 and Table 21.7 in date-time pictures. Note that in contrast to numeric formatting, the number of times a character is repeated can change its meaning substantially—as can its case.

You can add separators, such as the following:

: - /

Table 21.6

Characters You Can Use in Date Formatting

THIS CHARACTER	PRESENTS THIS	SAMPLE USAGE	SAMPLE FIELD RESULT
M	Month in numeric format, 1-12 (M must be capitalized)	{ DATE \@ "M" }	7
MM	Month in numeric format, adding a zero to months that have only one digit	{ DATE \@ "MM" }	07
MMM	Month as 3-letter abbreviation	{ DATE \@ "MMM" }	Jul
MMMM	Month, spelled out	{ DATE \@ "MMMM" }	July
d (upper or lowercase)	Day of month in numeric format, 1-31	{ DATE \@ "d" }	6
dd	Day of month in numeric format, 01-31	{ DATE \@ "dd" }	06
ddd	Day of week as 3-letter abbreviation	{ DATE \@ "ddd" }	Thu
dddd	Day of week, spelled out	{ DATE \@ "dddd" }	Thursday
y	Year (last two digits)	{ DATE \@ "y" }	97
yy	Year (all four digits)	{ DATE \@ "yy" }	1997

Table 21.7

Characters You Can Use in Time Formatting

THIS CHARACTER	PRESENTS THIS	SAMPLE USAGE	SAMPLE FIELD RESULT
h	Hour, based on a 12-hour clock running from 1 to 12	{ TIME \! "h" }	8
hh	Hour, based on a 12-hour clock running from 01 to 12	{ TIME \! "hh" }	08
H	Hour, based on a 24-hour clock running from 0-23	{ TIME \! "H" }	17
HH	Hour, based on a 24-hour clock running from 00-23	{ TIME \! "HH" }	06

Table 21.7 (Continued)

Characters You Can Use
in Time Formatting

THIS CHARACTER	PRESENTS THIS	SAMPLE USAGE	SAMPLE FIELD RESULT
m	Minute running from 0-59 (use lowercase m only)	{ TIME \! "m" }	3
mm	Minute, running from 00-59 (use lowercase mm only)	{ TIME \! "mm" }	03
AM/PM	Morning/afternoon data in the format AM or PM	{ TIME \! "h:mm AM/PM" }	9:30AM
am/pm	Morning/afternoon data in the format am or pm	{ TIME \! "h:mm am/pm" }	9:30am
A/P	Morning/afternoon data in the format A or P	{ TIME \! "h:mm A/P" }	9:30A
a/p	Morning/afternoon data in the format a or p	{ TIME \! "h:mm a/p" }	9:30a

wherever you want. For example:

```
M-d-yy   3-8-56
MM/dd/yyyy03/08/1956
```

Notice that to avoid a conflict, M is always capitalized for Month; m is always lowercase for minute.

You can also add text to a date-time picture by enclosing the text in apostrophes within the field instruction:

```
{ TIME \@ "'This had better be done by' MMMM-d H:mm" }
```

Finally, you can add character formatting to the time or date by adding it to the field characters that represent it. For example, to underline just the month:

```
{ TIME \@ "'This had better be done by' MMMM-d H:mm" }
```

■ Nesting Fields

If you want the result of one field to affect what another field does, nest one field inside another. This might sound abstract, but it is immensely useful. The logistics are the easy part.

Create a field; press Ctrl+F9.

Edit the field as much as possible. Then place the insertion point where you want the nested field to appear.

Press Ctrl+F9 to insert a new field within your existing field. A sample (and simple) nested field appears below:

```
{IF {DATE \@ "d-MMM"}="25-Dec" "Merry Christmas" "Ho, ho, ho... Not today!"}
```

In this example, the If field checks the date returned by the Date field. If the date and format match 25-Dec, Word reports: Merry Christmas. If not, it reports: Ho, ho, ho... Not today!

Here's an example of how you can use nested fields to ask a user for an article name and then place that article name in Summary Info and anywhere else in the document. Start by inserting a Set field, which sets a bookmark on the text that follows it. Call the bookmark Articlename:

```
{ SET ARTICLENAME }
```

Normally, the bookmark is followed by text. However, in this case, you need a Fillin field that asks the user to key in text:

```
{ SET ARTICLENAME { FILLIN "What is the article title?" } }
```

Next, create another nested field that uses Articlename as the document title, and also puts it in Summary Info. If you want the title to appear in your document footer, place this field there:

```
{ TITLE { REF articlename } }
```

With this nested-field technique, you can ask a user for any information and automatically place that information anywhere in the document.

■ Which Fields Do You Need

You'll almost certainly never use all 70+ Word fields. The trick is to recognize which fields might help the most with the documents you create. Table 21.8 offers a starter list.

Table 21.8

Which Fields Should You
Be Interested In?

IF YOU CREATE...	THESE FIELDS MIGHT HELP YOU...
Articles	Author, Date, Edittime, Noteref, Numwords, Ref, Revnum, Seq, Subject, Time, Title
Books/Documentation	Noteref, Index, Pageref, RD, Ref, Seq, Styleref, TC, Title, Toc, XE
Brochures/ Newsletters	Includepicture, Includetext, Link, Quote, Revnum, Symbol
Contracts	Autonumlgl, Createdate, Date, Include, Link, Pageref, Print-date, Revnum, Seq, TA, TOA
Financial Reports	DDE, DDEAuto, Embed, =Expression
Forms	Ask, Date, Fillin, Gotobutton, Time, Formtext, Formcheck-box, Formdropdown
Letters	Autotext, Createdate, Lastsavedby, Username, Userinitials
Print-merged form letters	Ask, Data, Database, Fillin, If, Mergefield, Mergerec, Mergeseq, Next, Nextif, Skipif
Web Pages	Hyperlink

In this chapter, you've learned about fields, Word's powerful technique for automatically updating and tracking text and other elements in your document. In Chapter 22, you'll go beyond automating you document to customizing Word itself, so that it works the way you do—and always gives you easy access to the tools you need.

- *Starting Word Automatically*
- *Starting Word with a Particular Task*
- *Taking Stock of Word's Customization Features*
- *Customizing the Toolbars*
- *Adding Your Own Toolbar*
- *Renaming or Deleting a Custom Toolbar*
- *Restoring Toolbars to Their Original Settings*

- *Customizing the Menus*
- *Resetting Menus You've Changed*
- *Adding Your Own Menus*
- *Adding Keyboard Shortcuts*
- *Adding Keyboard Shortcuts to Commands on Existing Menus or Buttons*
- *Using Add-In Programs*
- *Hiding Parts of the Interface*
- *Working with a Blank Screen*
- *Changing Word Options*
- *Changing View Options*
- *Changing General Options*
- *Changing Editing Options*

22

Customization: Make Word Work Exactly as You Want

Y OU MIGHT NEED TO BE CONVINCED TO READ THIS CHAPTER AND take it seriously. Until recently, most programs have been immutable objects. You did things their way. And if you didn't, you risked disaster. By now, you've all learned that lesson in the same way cats learn not to jump on hot stoves: You've been burned. So you figure that Word can do just about anything as it is. Wouldn't it be easier for me to learn how Word does it than to figure out how to make Word do it my way?

Not anymore. First of all, Word 97 makes customization easy. And it's also easier to restore Word's default settings if you don't like your changes. So the risks are nil. Second, you can use customization to turn nearly any task you perform into a one-step process accessible from a toolbar, a menu, or the keyboard.

You've already learned how templates, macros, styles, AutoText, and other Word features can cut the amount of time required to perform specific tasks—often by 90 percent or more. In a sense, customization completes this process, because it enables you to bring your shortcuts to the surface, where you can get at them right away. The following are a few examples:

Suppose that you often have to alphabetize lists. Put the Sort A-Z button on your Standard toolbar, and suddenly it's a one-button command. (A Sort A-Z button is already available. You just have to put it where you can see it.)

Or suppose that you often insert index entries. That's currently a several-step process, even in Word 97. But you could record a macro that selects your current word to be indexed, opens the appropriate dialog box, and marks the entry. If you then assign that macro to a button on your toolbar, indexing, too, becomes a one-button process.

Or suppose that you're a salesperson. Your Normal (NORMAL.DOT) template could include a toolbar that provides buttons to create or open each of the documents you use most (see Figure 22.1). You could add buttons that start the print envelope routine you use to direct mail to clients, or the file-sorting routine that helps you to sort through the various memos you have sent to clients.

Figure 22.1

You can create a custom toolbar to speed up everyday tasks.

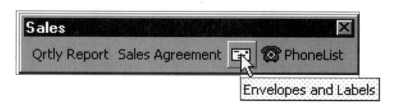

Or suppose that you're in charge of your organization's personnel policies. You could customize everyone's copy of Word to add a menu containing your forms and (read-only) personnel manual. A user might then see what's shown in Figure 22.2. The custom company menu can provide direct and immediate access to the information your employees need the most regarding personnel policies, requisitions, and benefits.

Customization offers a lot of potential, after you get past the notion that Word is not to be messed with. This chapter starts with a few basic techniques for automating the way Word runs when you load it in the morning.

Figure 22.2

Custom menus provide
easy access to
frequently used
templates, documents,
and commands.

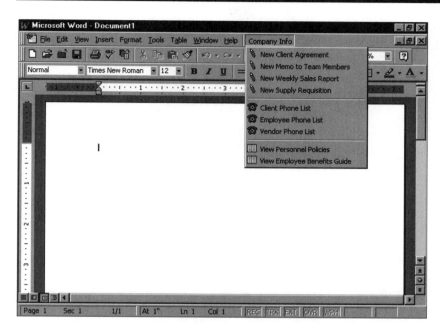

Then you go on to the heart of the chapter: customizing the way Word presents itself to you so that you can get more done, more quickly.

Finally, you learn about some options for making Word a more comfortable place to be. Chances are, you'll be spending a lot of time there—you might as well get comfortable.

■ Starting Word Automatically

If Word is your primary application, you might want to start it automatically every time you turn on your computer. Here's how:

1. Click on Start on the Taskbar and position the mouse pointer over Settings.

2. Choose Taskbar. The Taskbar Properties dialog box opens.

3. Click on the Start Menu Programs tab (see Figure 22.3).

4. Click on Add. The Create Shortcut window opens (see Figure 22.4).

5. Click Browse to find your Word program file. The Browse window opens (see Figure 22.5). It's similar to the File, Open dialog box you've worked with before. Winword, the file that starts Microsoft Word, is probably in your Microsoft Office or Winword folder. (Try C:\PROGRAM FILES\ MICROSOFT OFFICE\OFFICE.)

Figure 22.3

Use the Taskbar
Properties dialog box
to customize the
Start menu.

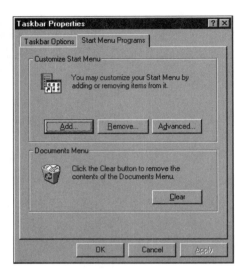

Figure 22.4

The Create Shortcut
dialog box is used to
specify a program name
when creating a shortcut
on the Start menu.

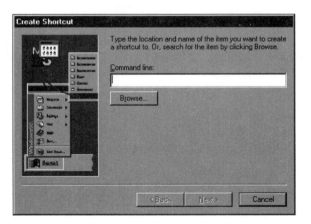

6. When you find Winword, click on it, and choose Open. You're returned to the Create Shortcut window.

7. Click Next to display the Select Program Folder dialog box (see Figure 22.6).

8. Select the StartUp folder, and then click Next.

9. Type Microsoft Word in the Select a Title for the Program dialog box, and then click Finish.

10. Click on OK to close the Taskbar Properties dialog box.

Figure 22.5

Use the Browse dialog box to find Winword, the file that starts Microsoft Word.

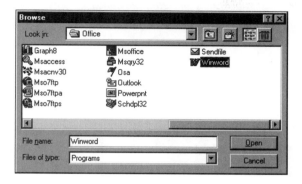

Figure 22.6

Use the Select Program Folder dialog box to tell Windows 95 where in the Start menu system to add Word.

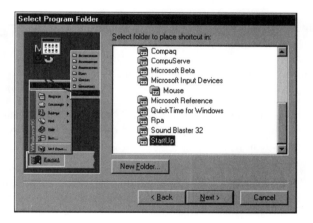

The next time you turn on your computer, Windows 95 will take care of starting Microsoft Word automatically!

■ Starting Word with a Particular Task

Now take it a step further. Suppose that you use Word almost exclusively to write sales letters. You've created a template for sales letters that includes substantial boilerplate text, along with AutoText entries that you can use to fill out the letter with specifics.

Now record a macro that opens your sales letter template, and name the macro AutoExec. If you use this special macro name, whenever you run Word it automatically creates a new sales letter document. (This feature is covered in more detail in Chapter 11, "Macros.")

NOTE. *If you looked under the hood, you'd find that AutoExec is actually a short macro. Just substitute your template name for Saleslet.dot in the following:*

```
Sub AutoExec()

Documents.Add Template:= _

        "C:\Program Files\Microsoft Office\Templates\Saleslet.dot" _
        , NewTemplate:=False
End Sub
```

Another idea for AutoExec is to open automatically the last document you worked on. Just record a macro that selects 1 from the **F**ile menu, as in

```
Sub AutoExec
RecentFiles (1).Open
End Sub
```

■ Taking Stock of Word's Customization Features

Now changing any Word toolbar, menu, or keyboard shortcut is easy. You can even add your own menus and toolbars.
What can you put in them?

- Any of the hundreds of Word buttons already assigned to specific tasks. (Many already appear on one or another of Word's toolbars, but quite a few don't.)

- Any Visual Basic for Applications command corresponding to any individual task Word can perform. These commands include every Word menu item and most Word formatting options.

- Any macro you've recorded, or written in Visual Basic for Applications.

- Any font available on your computer. (In other words, you can create a toolbar entry that reformats text using the font you specify.)

- Any AutoText entry you've created. (So that your custom toolbar entries or menu selections can add specific boilerplate text.)

- Any style you've created or any built-in Word style.

You can add customized menus, toolbars and keyboard shortcuts to the Normal template—in which case all documents will have access to these shortcuts unless you specify otherwise. Or you can customize a specific template. Thus, you can create different working environments for different situations.

Suppose that three people share a computer. Joe has poor eyesight; Joe's template automatically displays enlarged toolbar buttons and text magnified to 150 percent. Diane is the part-time office manager; Diane's template includes toolbar buttons for sending e-mail, creating purchase orders, and compiling quarterly reports on office activity. Kevin is a salesperson who's on the road most of the time; Kevin's template duplicates the customized template in his notebook PC.

NOTE. *On his notebook PC, Kevin can automatically load new documents based on the Kevin template by recording an AutoNew macro that does this job. The AutoNew macro runs each time Kevin starts a new file using this template. That makes things easier to manage, because he'll be using the same template (Kevin) on both the notebook and the desktop PC.*

■ Customizing the Toolbars

You can dock a toolbar along any of the four sides of the screen or you can drag it to the middle of the screen so that it "floats" in its own window. Floating toolbars can be reshaped by dragging any of their borders, as shown in Figure 22.7. You can control many other aspects of toolbars as well. In this section, you learn how to change the way the buttons appear on-screen; how to control which buttons appear on which toolbar; and how to add commands, macros, and other options to toolbars.

Figure 22.7

You can change the shape of a floating toolbar by dragging its borders.

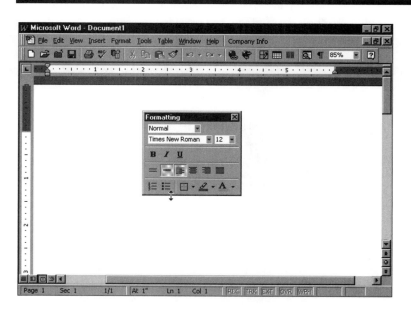

To control how toolbars are displayed on the screen, choose Toolbars, Customize. The dialog box shown in Figure 22.8 appears.

Figure 22.8

Use the Customize dialog box to specify which toolbars to display and control the appearance of the toolbar buttons.

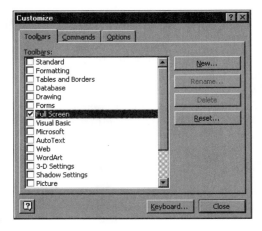

By default, the Standard and Formatting toolbars are displayed, so a checkmark appears next to their names in the Customize dialog box. Word sometimes displays other toolbars automatically, depending on the tasks you perform. If you insert a picture and then open it for editing, for example, Word displays the Drawing toolbar at the bottom of the screen.

You can open or close any toolbar here by checking or unchecking its box. To control the appearance of the buttons, click the Options tab at the top of the Customize dialog box (see Figure 22.9).

Figure 22.9

Control the appearance of toolbar buttons on the Options tab of the Customize dialog box.

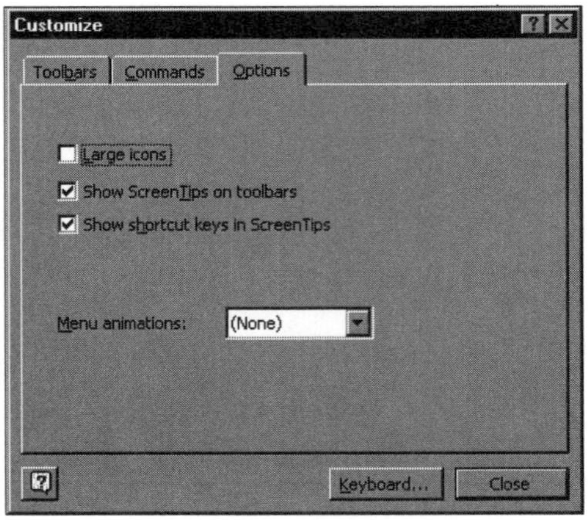

Large Icons. When this option is checked, all of the buttons on all your toolbars are enlarged. Large icons are most helpful when you're working at higher screen resolutions, such as 1024 x 768. Some buttons on some toolbars might not be visible at lower screen resolutions.

Show ScreenTips on toolbars. This option is turned on by default. When the mouse pointer hovers over a button in a Word toolbar, a brief description appears below the button. These descriptions are called ScreenTips. If you prefer not to see ScreenTips, clear the Show ScreenTips on toolbars check box.

Show shortcut keys in ScreenTips. If you like ScreenTips, you can make them even more useful by telling Word to display the equivalent keyboard shortcuts along with the description (see Figure 22.10). Enable the Show shortcut keys in ScreenTips checkbox. Displaying keyboard shortcuts is a good way to learn the keyboard shortcuts you're most likely to use.

Figure 22.10

Word can include equivalent keyboard shortcuts in ScreenTips.

NOTE. *If all you want to do is open or close a toolbar, right-click any toolbar to display the shortcut menu. Check or uncheck the toolbar you want to display or hide. This method opens only toolbars available from where you're working.*

Customizing Preformatted Toolbar Buttons

You can add, change, or delete buttons on any of Word's toolbars. To change the buttons on a toolbar, choose View, Toolbars, and then choose Customize. Click the Commands tab at the top of the dialog box to see lists of categories and commands, as shown in Figure 22.11.

The commands are organized into categories that correspond to Word's menus and context-specific toolbars. If you are familiar with the location of commands in the menu system, you'll have no trouble finding them in the Customize dialog box.

But Word still has a few surprises for you. Many of the commands that can be added to toolbars have no equivalent on any menu or on any built-in toolbar. In other words, you have plenty of new one-button choices you can't get at any other way.

The sample custom toolbar in Figure 22.12 and the descriptions in the following table show a few examples of features that have preassigned buttons not found on any toolbar. If you use these features extensively, you might want to place their buttons on your own custom toolbar—or replace buttons on the Standard toolbar that you don't use much.

Figure 22.11

Use the Commands tab of the Customize dialog box to add commands to toolbars.

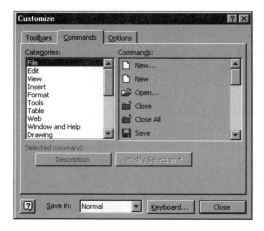

Figure 22.12

This sample toolbar contains buttons not found on any other Word toolbar.

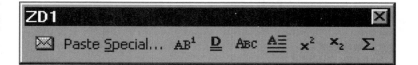

Feature	Category
Mail Recipient	File
Paste Special	Edit
Footnote	Insert
Double Underline	Format
Small Caps	Format
Drop Cap	Format
Superscript	Format
Subscript	Format
AutoSum	Table

The next sample toolbar shown in Figure 22.13 (and described in the table that follows the figure) contains features that do appear on toolbars but aren't typically displayed by default:

Feature	Category
Date	Insert
Time	Insert
Page Number	Insert
Envelopes and Labels	Tools
Update Field	Tools
Shrink One Page	Tools
Sort Ascending	Table
Sort Descending	Table

Figure 22.13

These buttons can be found on context-specific toolbars.

To add a button to an existing toolbar, follow these steps:

1. If the toolbar is not already displayed, choose View, Toolbars, and then click its checkbox. Or, if you want to work with a context-specific toolbar, open the document (or the part of the document) that displays the toolbar. (You can view the Header and Footer toolbar, for example, only by choosing View, Header and Footer.)

2. Choose Tools, Customize, and then click the Commands tab; or if you're already in the Customize dialog box, click the Commands tab.

3. Select the desired category from the list on the left side of the dialog box.

4. Scroll through the command list on the right side of the dialog box. When you find the command you want, drag it to the toolbar. When you release the mouse, the new button will appear on the toolbar.

5. Close the Customize dialog box.

NOTE. *If you want to modify a toolbar that is only available when you use a particular template, start by creating or opening a document based on that template, then follow the above steps.*

Modifying the Appearance of a Toolbar Button

You can change the appearance of any toolbar button. You can, for example, change the image used on the button, include or exclude text, edit the image itself, as shown in Figure 22.14, or change the button's name. If you're really ambitious, you can even manufacture a new button—one pixel (dot) at a time. Why would you want to go to all this trouble, you ask?

Imagine that you want to include a button on the standard toolbar that displays the Templates dialog box. (Did you notice that there are two "New" commands listed under the file category in the Customize dialog box? The one followed by ellipses opens the Templates dialog box.) The image for the New... button is the same as the one used on the button that creates a new, blank document based on the Normal template. To differentiate between the two, you could draw the letter "T" (for template) on the button.

To edit the image on a button, follow these steps:

1. Choose Tools, Customize and then click on the Commands tab at the top of the dialog box.

2. Select the button on the toolbar and then click the Modify Selection button.

3. Choose Edit Button Image to display the Button Editor dialog box shown in Figure 22.14.

Figure 22.14

Use the Button Editor dialog box to change the image on a toolbar button.

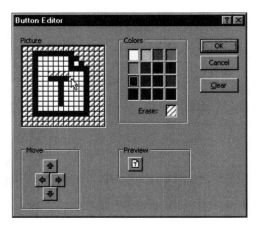

4. To use a color in your picture, click on the color in the Colors box, and then click on the individual pixels you want to color. If you click a pixel a second time, it reverts to the background color.

As you change pixels, the button image changes; you can see your changes in the Preview box.

5. To change the position of the button image slightly, use the Move buttons. (You can't move the edge of an image beyond the boundaries of the button.)

6. When you are finished, click OK to close the Button Editor dialog box, and then click close in the Customize dialog box.

Importing a Button Image

Unless you're an artist blessed with patience, you might find that creating your own button image from scratch with the Button Editor is difficult. You do have an alternative: you can import an image from a clip art library or graphics program.

Unfortunately, relatively few clip art images, including Word's, were designed to be clear at 1/4 inch-square. But if you want to try to import art, follow these steps:

1. Open the application containing the artwork.

2. Copy the artwork you want into the Clipboard. If you have a choice, copy it as a bitmap.

3. Switch back to Word.

4. Make sure that the toolbar button you want to change is visible.

5. Choose **T**ools, **C**ustomize.

6. With the dialog box open, right-click on the button you want to change. The Button shortcut menu opens, as shown in Figure 22.15.

7. Choose Paste Button Image.

Figure 22.15

You can paste an image onto a toolbar button.

Editing Existing Button Images

One possible solution to the clip art problem is to import from another source and then edit the imported art in the Button Editor. What you want, ultimately, is an image with strong outlines and not much internal detail except for shading.

To edit an image, paste it onto a button. Then, with the Customize dialog box still open, right-click to reopen the Button shortcut menu, and choose Edit Button Image.

You can use Edit Button Image, Paste Button Image, and the rest of the Button shortcut menu only when the Customize dialog box is open. The same story goes for moving buttons between toolbars with the mouse and some other features covered later.

Widening Boxes

Several of the items you can place in toolbars are boxes, not buttons—such as the style list, font list, and zoom box. You can change the width of these boxes. If you use long style names, for example, you might lengthen the style box. Otherwise, you might shrink the style box or font list box to accommodate another button.

Choose Tools, Customize. Click on the box you want to modify and point to its right edge. Your mouse pointer changes to the sizing arrow (the same one you may have seen if you changed the width of table cells). Drag the right edge of the box to narrow or widen it.

Moving and Copying Buttons among Toolbars

You also can move or copy buttons among toolbars.

To move a toolbar icon, choose Tools, Customize, and drag the button from its current location to its new location. To copy a toolbar icon, follow the same procedure, but hold down the Ctrl key while you drag the button.

Adding a Menu to a Toolbar

Huh? Add a menu to a toolbar? Okay. Imagine that you want to gain as much screen real estate as possible for your document. You are familiar with keyboard shortcuts for many of the tasks you perform, so you'd like to have just one toolbar that is limited to the commands for which there are no keyboard equivalents. Or say you'd like to have your macros available on a toolbar, but you have so many macros that they won't all fit on one toolbar if they're displayed as buttons.

To add any of Word's built-in menus to a toolbar, follow the steps below:

1. Choose Tools, Customize, and then click on the Commands tab at the top of the dialog box.

2. Select Built-In Menus from the category list.

3. Drag the desired menu from the Commands list to the toolbar. It will appear as a drop-down list button on the toolbar.

4. Close the Customize dialog box.

To add a custom menu to a toolbar (as shown in Figure 22.16), follow the steps below:

1. Display the Commands tab of the Customize dialog box.

2. Select New Menu in the Categories list.

3. Drag the New Menu command to the toolbar.

4. Click the Modify Selection button.

5. Drag across "New Menu" in the Name box and type the appropriate name for the new menu, and then press Enter.

6. Click the new menu button to display the empty menu.

7. Drag a command to the new menu.

8. If necessary, use the Modify Selection options to change the appearance of the commands on the new menu.

9. Close the Customize dialog box.

Figure 22.16

Word lets you add a custom menu to any toolbar.

Removing a Toolbar Button

Let's face it, there are buttons on the Standard and Formatting toolbars that you never use. If you want to make room for other commands that you use more frequently, you can remove the unused buttons. Simply display the Customize dialog box, drag the unwanted button off of the toolbar, and then close the Customize dialog box. That's all there is to it!

Giving Your Toolbar Buttons Breathing Room

You might have noticed that most Word toolbars group their related buttons, using a separator line between the groupings. This design makes the toolbars easier to understand and use. You can add a group separator between any two toolbar buttons.

Suppose, for example, that you have the four buttons shown in Figure 22.16, above. Now assume that you want to visually separate the third button from the first two buttons:

1. Display the Customize dialog box.

2. Right-click the third button, and choose Begin a Group from the short-cut menu. Word places a group separator line between the second and third buttons, as shown in Figure 22.17.

3. Close the Customize dialog box.

Figure 22.17

Use Separators to make it easier to work with the buttons on a toolbar.

Separator line

■ Adding Your Own Toolbar

Because the Standard and Formatting toolbars already have no vacancies, you might consider building your own custom toolbar. Then you can fill it with the supplemental buttons you use most and still leave the Standard and Formatting toolbars alone. This way, your documentation, including this book and Word's Help, will still be accurate when discussing the buttons available on the Standard and Formatting toolbars.

To create a new custom toolbar, follow these steps:

1. Choose Tools, Customize, and then click the Toolbars tab.

2. Click New to display New Toolbar dialog box shown in Figure 22.18. Type a new name for the toolbar in the **T**oolbar Name box.

3. Choose whether you want the toolbar available to all documents (the Normal template) or to a specific open template. (The template must be open before you can choose it.)

4. Click OK. A new, empty toolbar appears.

Figure 22.18

Use the New Toolbar
dialog box to name your
new toolbar.

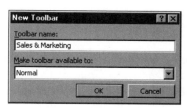

You now can drag new toolbar items into the empty toolbar as you've already learned. When you finish, close the Customize dialog box. Then decide where to place the toolbar. You can either float it over the document area or dock it on any of the four sides of the screen.

■ Renaming or Deleting a Custom Toolbar

After you create a custom toolbar, it appears in the **T**oolbars tab of the Customize dialog box, so you can easily display, hide, modify, or delete the toolbar.

NOTE. *An even easier way to display or hide Word's most commonly used toolbars is with the toolbar shortcut menu. Right-click any buttonless area of a toolbar, and the shortcut menu opens. Then just check or uncheck the toolbar you want to show or hide.*

You can change your custom toolbar the same way you change any other toolbar: by opening the Customize dialog box and moving buttons in or out.

To rename an existing toolbar, select it in the Toolbars tab of the Customize dialog box, click Rename to display the Rename Toolbar dialog box shown in Figure 22.19, type the new name, and then click OK.

Figure 22.19

Type a new name
in the Rename
Toolbar dialog box

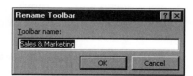

If you know that you don't need a custom toolbar anymore, you can delete it. (But you might simply want to hide it instead. You never know.) To delete a toolbar, follow these steps:

1. Choose **T**ools, Customize, and then click the Toolbars tab, if necessary.

2. Select the toolbar by clicking on its name.

3. Click Delete. (You can't delete a built-in Word toolbar.)

4. Click OK to confirm.

5. Close the Customize dialog box.

NOTE. *After you delete a custom toolbar, it's just about gone. You can't reset it like you can a built-in toolbar. Even Undo can't bring it back. Your only option is to close the document without saving changes to the template. You lose all your other changes, too, but at least you still have the custom toolbar.*

◼ Restoring Toolbars to Their Original Settings

You might find that you're not satisfied with the toolbar changes you've made—or maybe you simply don't need them any more. To change a built-in toolbar back to its original settings, follow these steps:

1. Choose Tools, Customize.

2. Select the toolbar to be reset.

3. Click the Reset button.

4. Close the Customize dialog box.

NOTE. *Many context-sensitive toolbars, such as Headers and Footers, don't appear on the View toolbars list unless you display them first.*

◼ Customizing the Menus

You have just as much control over menus as you do over toolbars. You can add or delete items and even create new custom menus. To customize a menu, first choose Tools, Customize, and then click the Commands tab. Deja vu?

If you've customized your toolbars, the procedures for changing your menus will feel very familiar. You can add the same categories of items to menus as you can to toolbars, including menu commands, macros, AutoText entries, and styles.

As you saw when you were modifying your toolbars, the organization of the commands in the Customize dialog box basically correspond to Word's own menu structure. And, as you noticed when working with toolbars, many of the available commands don't actually appear on any of Word's built-in menus.

Adding a Command to an Existing Menu

To add a command to an existing menu, follow these steps:

1. Display the menu to be modified.

2. Select a category from the **C**ategories list.

3. Drag the desired command to the menu, positioning it where you want it to appear.

4. Close the Customize dialog box.

Adding a Keyboard Shortcut to a Menu Item

You've probably noticed that many of the Word menu items have shortcut keys associated with them. If no shortcut key is already associated with your new item, use the following steps to add one:

1. Click the Keyboard button in the Customize dialog box to display the Customize Keyboard dialog box shown in Figure 22.20. Press the combination of keys to be used as the shortcut.

Figure 22.20

Use the Customize Keyboard dialog box to assign a keyboard shortcut to a menu item.

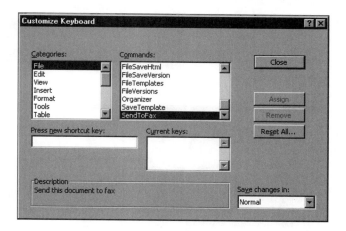

2. Check below the Press new shortcut key box to see if the combination has already been assigned to another command. If so, use the backspace key to remove the keyboard shortcut and try again with a different key combination.

3. Click the Assign button.

4. Close the Customize Keyboard dialog box.

5. Close the Customize dialog box.

Changing the Name of a Menu Item

Imagine that you added the New command that creates a blank document based on the Normal template (that's the New command that doesn't have the ellipses following it) to the File menu. You now have two commands called New. For the uninitiated, it might be a little difficult to tell what each of the New commands will do. You could change the name of the New command that you just added to "Blank Document" to clarify things. To change a menu item's name, use the following steps:

1. Choose Tools, Customize, and then click the Commands tab.

2. Display the menu and click the item whose name should be changed.

3. Click the Modify Selection Button.

4. Select the text in the Name box and type the new name for the menu, as shown in Figure 22.21.

5. If you want to add a mnemonic character (an underlined letter that can be used to execute the command from the keyboard) to the menu item's name, type an ampersand (&) before the character. Be careful not to use a letter that is already assigned to another item in the same menu.

6. Close the Customize dialog box.

Figure 22.21

Use the Name box to give a new name to the menu item.

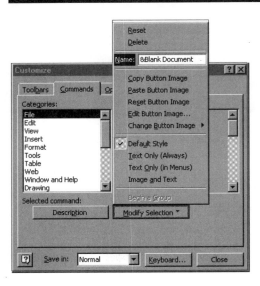

NOTE. *If you want to use "&" as a character in a menu name, type && in the menu name. The doubling of the character tells Word that you meant the character to appear in the menu name, not to cause the next character in the name to be underlined.*

Notice that Word commands and macros, which normally require a one-word title, can have a menu name of more than one word.

Adding a Separator

If you're adding several similar items to a menu—for example, several fonts—you might want to separate them from the rest of the menu. To add a *separator*, a line that Word provides for this purpose, follow the instructions below:

1. Display the Commands tab of the Customize dialog box.

2. Display the menu to be modified and select the menu item above which the group separator should be placed.

3. Click the Modify Selection button.

4. Choose Begin a Group.

5. Close the Customize dialog box.

Removing a Command

You can remove a command by displaying the Customize dialog box, selecting the command from its menu, and then dragging it off of the menu. But Word provides a nifty keyboard shortcut. Follow these steps:

1. Press Ctrl+Alt+minus sign. The insertion point becomes a thick horizontal line.

2. Choose the menu item you want to delete. Instead of performing the action specified by the menu item, Word deletes the menu item.

To move a menu item from one menu to another, delete the item from the first menu and add it to the other.

■ Resetting Menus You've Changed

As with toolbars, Word "remembers" its original menu settings in case you need them again. To reset all your built-in menus, eliminating any changes you've made, follow these steps:

1. Choose <u>T</u>ools, <u>C</u>ustomize.

2. Right click the menu's name in the menu bar.

3. Choose Reset from the shortcut menu.

4. Close the Customize dialog box.

■ Adding Your Own Menus

You also can add an entirely new Word menu. Earlier in this chapter, for example, you read about a suggested special Company menu that loads forms and (read-only) procedure manuals. You can create menus for many other applications. For example:

- Indexing and tables of contents, figures, and authorities could use a menu of their own. (Right now, they're all buried deep in the **I**nsert, Inde**x** and Tables menu selection.)

- If you have several commonly used AutoText entries or macros, you can create a new AutoText menu and a customized macro menu.

   To add a new menu, follow these steps:

1. Choose Tools, Customize.

2. Select New Menu from the bottom of the Categories list.

3. Specify whether you want to save the changes in the Normal global template or in another template that's already open.

4. Drag the New Menu command to the menu bar.

5. Click the Modify Selection button and type the name of the new menu in the Name text box. Place an **&** symbol before the letter you want as your mnemonic character.

6. Display the new menu and add commands.

7. Close the Customize dialog box.

■ Adding Keyboard Shortcuts

Out of the box, Word comes with more than 250 keyboard shortcuts. Many tasks have more than one keyboard shortcut. What more could you want?

Well, you might be switching to Word from another word processor. Maybe you're used to its keyboard commands, and you find yourself constantly pressing the wrong keys in Word. You can redefine some of the more annoying commands so that they work the way you've come to expect.

And, notwithstanding all the built-in shortcuts, many aspects of Word have few or no keyboard shortcuts at all. Three good examples are drawing, tables, and forms. If you use these features regularly, you might want to assign them keyboard shortcuts.

■ Adding Keyboard Shortcuts to Commands on Existing Menus or Buttons

To assign a new keyboard shortcut to a task that's already on a button or menu, follow these steps:

1. Press Alt+Ctrl+plus sign. (Use the + on the numeric keypad.)
   Your mouse pointer changes to the command symbol.

2. Click on the toolbar button, or choose the menu item you want to give a keyboard shortcut. (If you're using a toolbar button, make sure that the toolbar is displayed first.)

3. The Customize Keyboard dialog box appears, showing the command you've chosen in the Commands box. A description of the task appears in the Description box.

4. The Insertion point is already located in the Press New Shortcut Key box. Press the key or combination you want to associate with this task. Your keystroke or combination of keystrokes appears in the box.

   If the shortcut key you indicate is already associated with a task, that task appears in the Currently Assigned To area. You can [backspace] to remove the proposed shortcut key combination and try again with another combination.

5. Click the Assign button. The new key combination appears in the Current Keys box.

Adding Keyboard Shortcuts to Other Commands

Many of the commands built into Word don't have menu or toolbar equivalents. And neither do macros, fonts, AutoText entries, or styles, unless you've added them yourself. You can provide or change keyboard shortcuts for these, too.

You also can use the following technique to simplify the convoluted finger-stretches required to type characters such as ñ.

To create or change a keyboard shortcut for one of these elements, follow these steps:

1. Choose Tools, Customize.

2. Click the Keyboard button. The Keyboard dialog box appears—this time, containing all possible commands for which you can create a keyboard shortcut.

3. Narrow your search for the command you want by choosing a category from the **C**ategories list.

This list is the same one you worked with when you customized toolbars and menus, with one addition: Common Symbols.

Common Symbols includes Word's default keyboard shortcuts for many foreign language characters and a few other special characters, such as ellipses, trademark and copyright symbols, and curly quotation marks.

4. Select a command or other element—Macr**o**s, F**o**nts, Aut**o**Text, St**y**les, or C**o**mmon Symbols, depending on your choice in step 3.

5. As in the earlier example, move the mouse pointer to Press new shortcut key box, and press the key or combination you want to associate with this task. You see your keystrokes in the box; if you've chosen a combination that's already assigned, Word notifies you in the Currently Assigned To area.

6. To reassign this key combination, choose Assign. To assign another combination, backspace to erase the combination in Press new shortcut key and try again.

7. Close the Customize Keyboard dialog box, and then close the Customize dialog box.

Removing or Resetting Key Combinations

You can tell Word to remove a specific key combination or to reset all key combinations to what they were when you installed the software. (Resetting also eliminates other key combinations you might have assigned earlier to new macros.) Follow these steps:

1. Choose Tools, Customize.

2. Click the keyboard button.

3. To remove a specific keyboard combination, select the command to which it is assigned, and then click **R**emove.

4. To reset all key combinations, click Reset All. The dialog box shown in Figure 22.22 appears.

5. Choose **Y**es to reset.

Figure 22.22

Click Yes to reset all keyboard shortcuts, including those assigned to macros and styles.

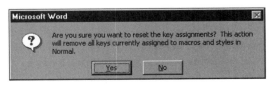

■ Using Add-In Programs

For years, several small companies made a living marketing *add-ons* to Word. These programs have generally been specialized macros or document templates that simplify special tasks.

Now, Word also supports *add-ins*. These are programs that load into Word and become part of it. (If you're involved in desktop publishing, you might be familiar with this concept. You can supplement Quark XPress with third-party programs called Quark Xtensions, and Aldus PageMaker now has the equivalent Aldus Additions.)

Superficially, they're similar to macros, but add-ins run faster. Like macros, add-ins can be added to toolbar commands, assigned menu selections, and given keyboard shortcuts.

And, according to Microsoft, you often can adapt add-ins from existing code written in the popular computer language C. Thus some pretty sophisticated add-in programs could be around the corner.

To load an add-in program, follow these steps:

1. Choose Tools, Templates and Add-Ins to display the dialog box shown in Figure 22.23.

Figure 22.23

Use the Templates and Add-Ins dialog box to make an add-in program available.

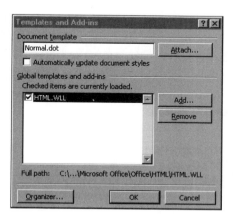

2. Select the checkbox for the add-in you want from the **G**lobal templates and add-ins box.

3. If you don't see the add-in in the list, click **A**dd, select it from the appropriate folder, and then click OK.

4. Click OK.

To remove an add-in program, follow the preceding steps 1 and 2, removing the check mark from the add-in's checkbox. To remove it from the list of available add-ins, click the Remove button.

Add-ins written for Word 6 or Word 7 will need to be updated for Word 97.

■ Hiding Parts of the Interface

You've learned how to add toolbars to the interface. But what if you find the Word interface cluttered as it is? Answer: You can delete some or all of it.

You've already seen that you can hide toolbars by right-clicking the Toolbar and unchecking the toolbars you want to hide in the shortcut menu. And you know that you can hide the ruler by choosing Ruler from the View menu and unchecking that option.

You can hide the status bar, the horizontal scroll bar, or the vertical scroll bar by following these steps:

1. Choose Tools, Options.

2. If necessary, click the View tab.

3. In the Window group at the bottom of the dialog box, uncheck the screen element you want to hide.

4. Click OK.

■ Working with a Blank Screen

The ultimate interface is none at all, and Word will oblige. Choose Full Screen from the View menu. Everything goes away except your text and the Full Screen toolbar, shown in Figure 22.24.

Click on the Full Screen button to return to your previous interface. If you can't find the Full Screen toolbar, press Esc to return Word to its normal interface.

Any appropriate shortcut menus are still available when you're working in full screen mode.

TIP. *You can eliminate even more screen clutter by hiding the Windows 95 taskbar. Right-click the Taskbar, choose Properties, enable the Auto hide checkbox, and then click OK. The Taskbar will slide down out of view. When you next need to work with it, move the mouse pointer to the bottom of your screen and the Taskbar will slide up, ready to serve you!*

Figure 22.24

The Full Screen command lets you focus on your document instead of the Word interface.

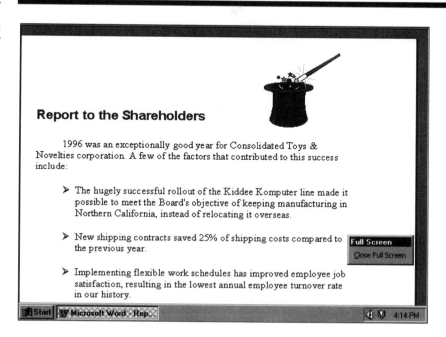

■ Changing Word Options

In this chapter and throughout the book, you've learned about many aspects of Word that you can adjust in Options dialog box. Some of these changes fall into the category of personalizing Word, so they are covered here.

Some of these options also make Word run a little bit faster.

■ Changing View Options

You've already visited the View tab of the Options dialog box (accessed via Tools, Options, View) twice in this chapter. (The dialog box is shown in Figure 22.25.)

Remember that the options on the View tab will change depending on whether you are working in Normal, Page Layout, or Online Layout View.

As mentioned previously, using the draft font option, at least while you're doing routine editing, can speed up Word on a slow system.

Another kick in the pants for a sluggish system is **P**icture Placeholders. This option tells Word not to waste energy displaying graphics all the time—just show a blank box where they're located.

Figure 22.25

The View tab of the
Options dialog box

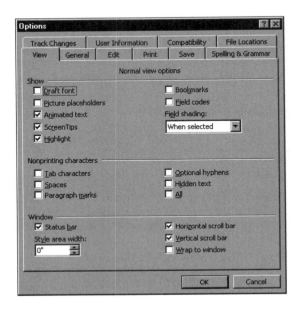

The third item worth covering here doesn't speed up your computer, but it could make your life much more convenient. It's called Wrap to Window.

Suppose, for example, that you use wide margins or you like to magnify your document above 100 percent (perhaps to preserve your eyesight). Often, then, not all your text fits on-screen at once. You find yourself moving from left to right as if you were watching a Ping-Pong match. *Annoying.*

You could change your margins—but that affects many aspects of your document, and you have to remember to change them back. Or you could choose the Page Width option in the Zoom Control list box. But that defeats the purpose of enlarging your text. Neither of these is an ideal solution.

Check Wrap to Window, however, and your text fits within your screen; all your pagination remains as it should be; and your text remains as large as you want.

If you use Wrap to Window regularly, you might find that you no longer need your horizontal scroll bar.

■ Changing General Options

Next you need to know about a few general options for personalizing your system that haven't been covered elsewhere in the book. Look at the

General tab, which you access by choosing Tools, Options, and then General (see Figure 22.26).

Background Repagination, normally set to on, automatically repaginates your document while you work. To pick up a little speed, you can turn it off while you work in Normal or Outline view. Word still repaginates when you go into Print Preview or Page Layout view, when you print, or when you ask for a word count.

Provide feedback with sound, also normally set to on, is fairly straightforward: when you make a mistake, Word beeps. If you hate to be beeped at, uncheck it.

Recently Used File List tells Word how many of the files you've closed lately should be listed in the File menu. The list is provided so that you can conveniently restart where you left off. Typically, it's four. You can choose any number from zero to nine.

As mentioned before, you can tell Word to display its ruler and dialog-box measurements not in inches but in centimeters, points, or picas. Select your new measuring system from the Measurement Units list box.

Finally, Macro virus protection is an important option. Some folks in this world need a life, and that's the kindest thing anyone can say about people who intentionally create and distribute viruses. At least Word will warn you if you open a document that might contain macro viruses. It will prompt you anytime you open a document that contains customized macros, toolbars, menus, and shortcuts. You then have the option of opening the document with or without the macros.

■ Changing Editing Options

Let's look at one more page of the Options dialog box in this chapter: Edit (see Figure 22.27).

The first option, checked by default, is Typing replaces selection. When you select text, that text disappears as soon as you start typing over it. Most people find that a useful shortcut. Some people—maybe you're one of them—find that it deletes text they intended to preserve. If you prefer, uncheck it.

Similarly, Drag-and-drop text editing enables you to select text and drag it to a new location. Some people find themselves inadvertently dragging text they didn't intend to move. You can turn off the feature here if you choose.

The next option, When selecting, automatically select entire word, just might drive you crazy if you frequently need to select a portion of a word or a word without the following space. You can turn it off if you prefer.

The next two options—Use the INS key for paste, and Overtype Mde—are off by default.

Figure 22.26

The Edit tab of the
Options dialog box

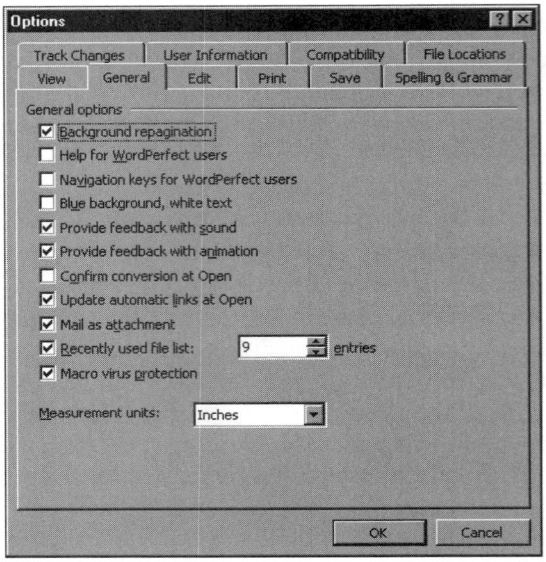

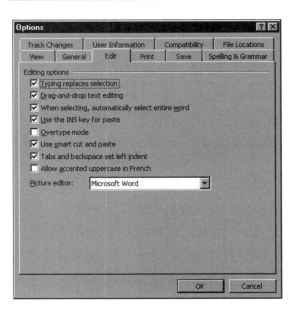

Figure 22.27

The Edit tab of the
Option dialog box

Use the INS key for paste allows you to use the Insert key to paste text or graphics, as is the case with some other word processors (including earlier versions of Word). With this feature on, pressing Insert no longer switches you to Overtype mode. Also, INS rather than Ctrl+V is listed as the shortcut for Paste on the Edit menu (though both shortcuts work).

Choosing Overtype mode tells Word to type over existing text, replacing it instead of moving it to the right. (You also can enter Overtype mode temporarily by pressing Insert, unless you've enabled the Use the INS key for paste option.)

The next Word feature, Use smart cut and paste, is turned on by default. With this option, if you cut a word from one location and paste the word into another location, Word makes sure that one space—no more, no less—falls between the pasted word and the words before and after it. You might not even notice that the feature is on; you might just find yourself doing less cleanup. If, however, you find the feature disconcerting, you can turn it off.

The Tabs and backspace set left indent option, which is turned on by default, allows you to increase a paragraph's indent level by pressing Tab, and decrease it by pressing [Backspace].

Allow accented uppercase in French is specifically targeted for text you format as French (by using Format, Language). It is turned on by default. The option enables Word's Format, Change Case feature and its French proofing tools (if you have them) to suggest adding accents to uppercase letters when appropriate.

Finally, the Picture editor option lets you choose the program that should be used for editing pictures. For example, if most of the pictures you work with are photographs, you might consider using Microsoft Photo Editor as your default picture editor.

In this chapter you learned how to customize Word so that it works the way you do. You learned how to create and modify toolbars, menus, and keyboard shortcuts. You also learned how to reset some of Word's default settings. Now go ye and customize!

- *Using Excel Data in Word*
- *Using PowerPoint with Word*
- *Using Outlook with Word*
- *Using Binders to Combine Multiple Documents*
- *Using the Microsoft Office Shortcut Bar*
- *Looking Up References with Microsoft Bookshelf Basics*

- *Using the Microsoft Photo Editor*
- *Using MS Organization Chart 2.0*

Microsoft Office: Leverage the Power of Those "Other" Programs

LIKE THE NEW KID ON THE BLOCK WHO NEEDS A GENTLE PUSH from his mother before discovering all the wonders of his new neighborhood, maybe you need a little persuasion before venturing into the topics covered in this chapter. After all, you ask, why complicate things if I can accomplish most of what I want to do from within Word? Well, why use the spin cycle on your washing machine when you can wring out all those wet clothes by hand?

The point is that while Word is very flexible and can do all kinds of wonderful things, other programs are often better at performing certain kinds of tasks. Consider mail merges, for example. You know that you can use Word to create the data document that will be merged with your form letter. But Word is no match for a relational database like Access when it comes to managing large amounts of data. Furthermore, if the data you want to use for your merge already exists in a database, why should you type it all over again?

All of the programs in the Microsoft Office suite are tightly integrated so you can use the best features of each to accomplish your tasks. And Word is pretty smart when it comes to working with information that was created with another Office product. In fact, the folks at Microsoft have made it almost child's play to take advantage of all of this power.

■ Using Excel Data in Word

Whether you're building a house or building a document, your motto ought to be "Use the best tools for the job." Excel is far superior to Word when it comes to crunching numbers and creating charts. It's even better at maintaining lists of information. Then there are things that Word flat out can't do, like make maps, for example.

After you massage your data in Excel, you can plug it right into your Word document, either by copying it via the Windows Clipboard or by importing an entire file. You can even maintain a link to the original information so that if it changes in the source document, the change will be reflected in your Word document.

Inserting a New Excel Worksheet into a Word Document

This technique allows you to create an Excel worksheet directly in your Word document. The procedure is reminiscent of creating a Word table, but you'll have all of Excel's tools available to you, even though you're actually in a Word document. Here's how to do it:

1. Place the insertion point where you want the Excel worksheet to appear.

2. Click the Insert Microsoft Excel Worksheet button and drag in the grid to create the desired number of columns and rows (see Figure 23.1). A worksheet area is created in your document and the Word toolbars and menus are replaced by Excel toolbars and menus (see Figure 23.2).

3. Type and format the information in the worksheet area.

4. Click outside of the worksheet area when you are finished to restore Word's menus and toolbars.

Figure 23.1

Use the Insert Excel
Worksheet button to
create a worksheet area
in the Word document

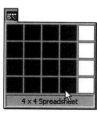

Figure 23.2

An Excel worksheet is
inserted in the Word
document and Excel's
toolbars are displayed.

Excel's Standard Toolbar

**Excel's Formatting
Toolbar**

Excel's Formula Bar

Excel Worksheet Area

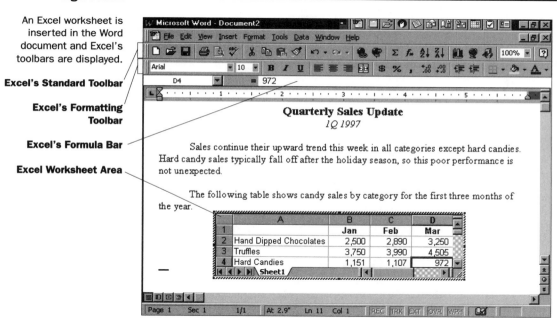

You can still modify the worksheet area even after Word's toolbars and
menus have been restored. To edit the worksheet, simply double-click within
the worksheet area. Excel's toolbars and menus will reappear.

Importing Excel Objects

If you already have an existing worksheet or chart in Excel that suits your
purposes, you don't have to recreate the information in Word. You can either
copy and paste the information or import it. Then you'll have to decide
whether to create a linked or embedded object.

Linked worksheets and charts are displayed in your Word document, but
the data is actually maintained in a separate Excel workbook (the source). If

changes are made to the source workbook, those changes will be reflected in the Word document. Since the data does not physically reside in the Word document, the size of the Word file can be kept smaller.

Embedded worksheets and charts are stored directly in the Word document. When you embed a worksheet in your Word document, the entire workbook is actually embedded, even though you can only see one worksheet at a time.

Follow the steps below to include an Excel worksheet as a linked object:

1. Start Excel and open the desired Excel worksheet.

2. Select the information in the Excel worksheet and then choose Edit, Copy.

3. Switch to Word and place the insertion point where you want the Excel worksheet to appear in your Word document.

4. Choose Edit, Paste Special (see Figure 23.3)

Figure 23.3

The Paste Special dialog box

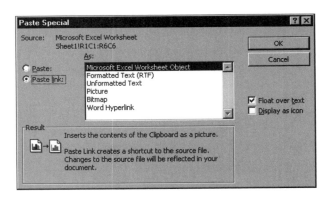

NOTE. *If you choose Paste instead of Paste Special, the Excel data will be pasted into your document as a Word table. Changes to the Excel source file will not be reflected in the Word document.*

5. Select Microsoft Excel Worksheet Object in the As list.

6. Click the Paste link option button.

7. Click OK.

NOTE. *The Float over text option places the worksheet object in the drawing layer, which means it can float independently in front of or behind the text in your document. The Display as icon option inserts the worksheet as an icon that must be double-clicked to be displayed.*

If you need to modify the information in the Excel worksheet object, double-click on the worksheet area. You will be switched to Excel (it will be loaded into memory if it is not already running). Make your changes in Excel and save and close the workbook. When you return to Word, the linked worksheet will reflect the changes you made in Excel.

Use the following steps to embed an Excel worksheet object:

1. Start Excel and open the desired Excel worksheet.

2. Select the information in the Excel worksheet and then choose Edit, Copy.

3. Switch to Word and place the insertion point where you want the Excel worksheet to appear in your Word document.

4. Choose Edit, Paste Special.

5. Select Microsoft Excel Worksheet Object in the As list.

6. Click OK.

Remember that when you embed a worksheet object, the entire workbook is actually inserted. So, if you need to display a different worksheet from the same workbook, double-click the worksheet area in the Word document, click the desired sheet tab (see Figure 23.4), and then click outside of the worksheet area.

If you prefer to do things the hard way, there is another way you can import Excel data into your Word document.

1. Choose Insert, Object.

2. Click the Create from File tab at the top of the Object dialog box (see Figure 23.5).

3. Type the name and location of the file or use the browse button to locate the file.

4. Enable or clear the Link to file, Float over text, and Display as icon checkboxes, as appropriate.

5. Click OK.

6. If the correct worksheet is not displayed, double-click the Excel object, then click the desired worksheet tab.

7. If necessary, resize the Excel object and, if the object is a worksheet, use the horizontal and vertical scroll bars to display just the information you want.

8. Click outside of the Excel object to finish the operation.

Figure 23.4

Use the worksheet tabs to display a different worksheet in the embedded Excel object.

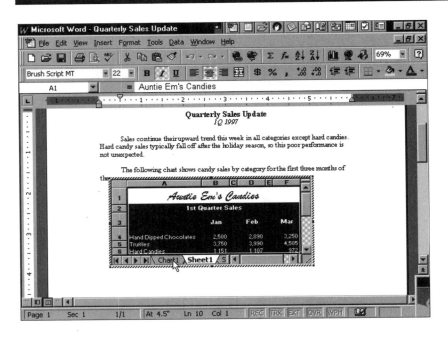

Figure 23.5

Use the Object dialog box to import an Excel file.

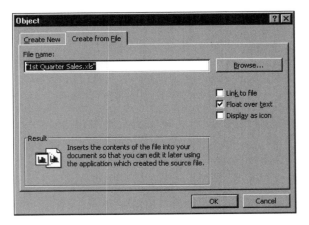

Mail Merge Using Excel Data and Microsoft Query

You learned the fundamentals of merging in Chapter 16, including how to use an external data source, such as an Excel file. So why am I bothering you with this topic again? Well, this time around you'll get a chance to see how Microsoft Query can help you to get just the records you need for your merge.

Word does a fairly good job of filtering records for you, but you are limited to using only six criteria statements. When you need the "big guns," you can use Microsoft Query instead of Word to filter records.

1. Start by creating your main document for the merge, including any non-variable text and formatting instructions.

2. Save your main document and then choose Tools, Mail Merge to display the Mail Merge Helper dialog box.

3. Click the Create button, choose form letters, and click the Active Window button to tell Word to use the main document you created earlier as the basis of the merge.

4. Click the Get Data button, and then choose Open Data Source.

5. Click the MS Query button.

6. Select Excel Files (not sharable) in the Databases tab of the Choose Data Source dialog box (shown in Figure 23.6), and then click OK.

Figure 23.6

Selecting the data
source type

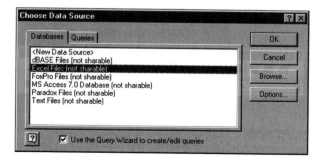

7. Select the Excel file in the Database Name list shown in Figure 23.7 (you may have to double-click the folders in the middle of the dialog box to browse for the file), and then click OK.

8. When you click on the file you want, the Query Wizard shown in Figure 23.8 will appear. If you want to use all of the fields in the Excel file for your query, click the file name in the Available tables and columns list.

9. If you want to select individual fields to be used in the query, click the expand button to the left of the file name (it has a plus sign on it), select a field name, and then click the button displaying the greater than symbol.

10. Repeat step 9 until all of the desired field names have been moved to the Columns in your query box, as Figure 23.8 shows, then click Next.

Figure 23.7

Use the Select Workbook dialog box to identify the file to be queried.

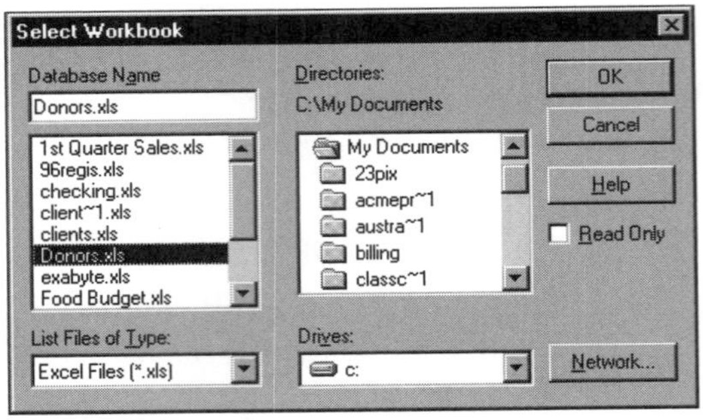

Figure 23.8

In the Query Wizard, when you choose all of the fields of a document for a query, the + to the left of the file name turns to a –, indicating the document has been expanded, and the fields appear in the columns for your query.

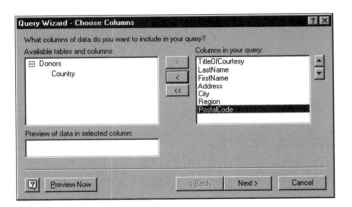

11. Select the field name to be used for criteria. Then display the first drop-down list and select an operator (such as "equals"); display the second drop-down list and select the value that the field name should be compared to (such as "Dr.").

12. If you need to add another criteria statement, repeat step 11, selecting a different field name. (Don't be alarmed, your first criteria information will seem to disappear, but MS Query's memory is as good as an elephant's.)

13. Click Next.

14. Establish a sort order using the drop-down lists to select field names, and then click Next.

15. Make sure Return Data to Microsoft Word is selected, and then click Finish.

16. When Word reports that it found no merge fields in your main document, click the Edit Main Document button.

17. Insert the merge fields as you learned to do in Chapter 16 and save the changes to the main document.

18. Click the Merge to New Document button.

Exporting Access Reports to Word

You learned about using an Access table or query as the data source for merges in Chapter 16, so we won't go over old territory again. Rather, we'll look at how Word can play host to Access reports.

Why, you ask? Well, let's imagine that you don't know very much about Access. Once you get the structure of the report created using the Access Report Wizard, you might find it easier to format it and make it look attractive in Word. Or maybe you are going to work with the report on a computer that doesn't have Access installed on it.

When you use the Publish It with MS Word feature on the OfficeLinks menu, Access formats the report in Rich Text Format (*.rtf), saves a copy of the file in the Access directory, and sends the output to Word. You can then use Word's formatting features to modify the report, save the changes, and print the report. Here's how:

1. In Access, select the report and click the Preview button.

2. Click the right side of the OfficeLinks button on the Print Preview toolbar to display the list of options shown in Figure 23.9.

3. Click Publish It with MS Word.

4. Make any necessary changes to the document.

5. Choose File, Save As, specify a location for the file, change the Save as type setting to Word document, and click Save. (Word will retain the name of the report as the name for the new document. You can change the suggested file name if you want.)

6. Print the report and close it.

Inserting Data from Another Type of Database

Earlier in this chapter and in Chapter 16, you learned how a Word mail merge can retrieve data directly from Excel and Microsoft Access. But you also might want to retrieve data from another database application—and not just for mail merges. Word offers a solution: the Insert Database button on the Database toolbar.

Figure 23.9

The options for printing a report

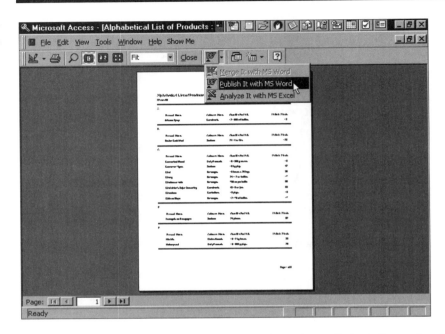

The most basic database retrieval simply gathers all the information in a database file and inserts it into a Word table, at which point you can edit it. To accomplish that, do the following:

1. Display the Database toolbar by right-clicking any visible toolbar and then clicking Database on the shortcut menu.

2. Click the Insert Database button on the Database toolbar (see Figure 23.10).

Figure 23.10

The Insert Database button on the Database toolbar

3. Click the Get Data button. The Open Data Source dialog box appears (see Figure 23.11).

4. Select the type of database file you want to open from the Files of type list box. Word's available choices are listed in Table 23.1. If your file doesn't show up here, select All Files.

Figure 23.11

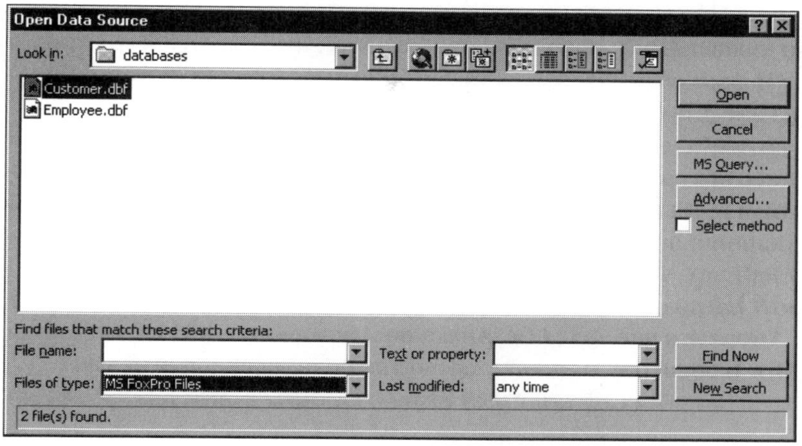

Use the Open Data
Source dialog box to
select the database file.

Table 23.1

Types of Database Files
Word Can Open
without Assistance

TYPE OF FILE	EXTENSION
Word documents	(*.doc)
Rich Text format	(*.rtf)
Text files	(*.txt)
Microsoft Access databases	(*.mdb)
Microsoft Excel worksheets	(*.xls)
Microsoft Query files	(*.qry)
dBASE files	(*.dbf)
Microsoft FoxPro files	(*.dbf)
Paradox files	(*.db)

NOTE. *Word can successfully retrieve data from Microsoft Access, FoxPro, Paradox, and dBASE because it comes with ODBC drivers for these products.*

NOTE. *If you have another type of database, find out if that database product supports ODBC. If not, you can still use that database's data by exporting it to a file format Word can understand, such as comma- or tab-delimited files.*

5. Select the file you want. You might need to change folders or drives, or use Find File.

6. Click Open.

7. Select the appropriate ODBC driver in the Confirm Data Source dialog box (as shown in Figure 23.12). If the ODBC driver you want to use is not listed, click the Show all checkbox.

Figure 23.12

Use the Confirm Data Source dialog box to select the ODBC driver.

8. Click OK.

9. If you want all fields and all records inserted into your document, click Insert Data.

Establishing Criteria to Control the Record Subset

If you want a little more control over which fields and which records are inserted into your Word document, use steps 1 through 7 above, and then continue with these steps:

1. If you want to select only records and fields that meet your criteria, click the Query Options button.

2. To use Word's features to select the records, click No when Word asks if you want to use Microsoft Query.

3. Click the Filter Records tab of the Query Options dialog box (shown in Figure 23.13) to set the criteria that return just the records you want. First, drop down the Field list in the first row and select the appropriate field for the comparison. Then drop down the Comparison list to select an operator, such as "Greater than" or "Not equal to." In the Compare to text box, type the value Word should use to select the records you want.

4. Click OK.

5. Use the Sort tab of the Query Options dialog box (shown in Figure 23.14) to establish a particular sort order. Click the Field drop-down list to select the field that will be used for the first sort key. Click either the Ascending or Descending option button. If necessary, you can add two more sort keys by using the Then by sections of the dialog box.

Figure 23.13

Use the Query Options dialog box to set criteria.

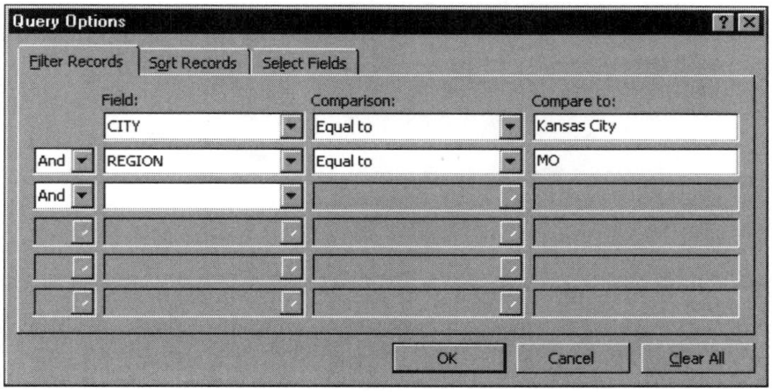

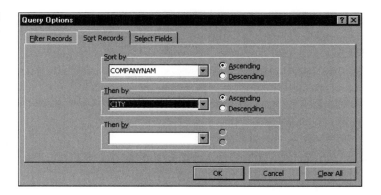

Figure 23.14

You can establish a sort order for the records that will be placed in your document.

6. Click the Select Fields tab of the Query Options dialog box (shown in Figure 23.15) to tell Word which fields of information it should copy to your document. Click on any unneeded field name in the Selected fields list, and then click Remove. If you want only a limited number of fields returned to your Word document, start by clicking within the Selected Fields list and then click Remove all. Next, click the name of the first field to be included in the Fields in data source list, and then click select. Repeat this last step until all of the required fields have been selected. If you do not want the field names included in your Word document as column headings, clear the Include field names check box.

Figure 23.15

Select which fields of
information should
be returned to your
Word document.

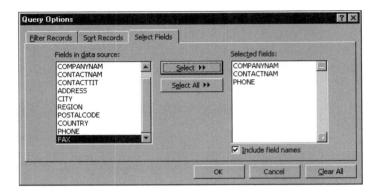

7. Click OK.

8. If you want Word to format your data table, click Table AutoFormat to
   display the dialog box shown in Figure 23.16. Select the desired format
   from the Formats list, and click OK.

Figure 23.16

Use the Table AutoFormat
dialog box to change
the appearance of
the data table.

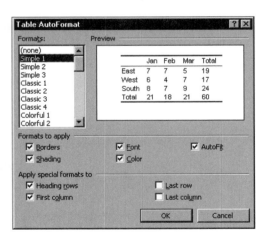

9. Click Insert Data, choose whether you want to insert all records that
   match your criteria or a particular range in the Insert Data dialog box,
   and then click OK.

   If you need more power than Word offers to retrieve the correct subset
of records (perhaps, heaven forbid, you need to use more than six criteria
statements to filter the records properly), use Microsoft Query. Start by

using steps 1 through 7 in the first set of instructions in this section of the chapter, then continue with these steps:

1. If you want to select only records and fields that meet your criteria, click Query Options.

2. Click Yes when Word asks if you want to Use MS Query.

3. Click Show/Hide Criteria on the Microsoft Query toolbar to display the Criteria pane (see Figure 23.17).

Figure 23.17

Use the Microsoft Query window to establish criteria.

Field List Box

Criteria Statements

Inforrmation that will be copied to Word

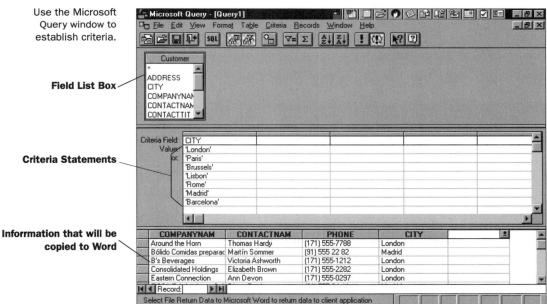

4. From the Field List box, drag to the Criteria Field row of the Criteria frame the names of the fields that will be used to limit the records returned to Word.

5. Type values that match the records you want in the "Value" and "or" cells below the corresponding field name(s).

6. Click in any column you do not want to copy to Word and choose Record, Remove Column from the menu bar.

7. From the menu bar, choose File, Return Data to Microsoft Word.

8. Click the Insert Data button.

9. If you want to insert all of the records, click OK in the Insert Data dialog box. If you want to restrict the records even further, type the starting and ending numbers of the records to be included. If you want to insert the data as fields so that Word will be updated whenever the records in the source database change, enable the Insert as field checkbox.

10. Click OK.

Merging with Other Databases

Word still can use data from other database programs even if they don't have this luxurious level of interactivity. Word can recognize text files exported from your database program as tab-delimited or comma-delimited text files.

NOTE. *A delimiter is a character that separates one field or record from another.*

Occasionally, you might have to perform some cleanup. Your goal, of course, is to come up with something as close to a Word database table as possible.

You might find some simple problem that you can fix with a global Replace command, which allows Word to recognize your database and open it relatively cleanly. (Remember, Word's Replace feature can search for and replace tabs, paragraph marks, and many other special characters.)

■ Using PowerPoint with Word

If you use Microsoft PowerPoint 97 to make presentations, you might want to create the text for your presentation in Word—where you have access to Word's extensive editing capabilities—and then move it into PowerPoint to format it as a presentation. Fortunately, PowerPoint and Word are designed to work together.

Start by creating your presentation using Word's built-in heading styles. It's easiest to do this in Outline view, using the Promote and Demote buttons on the Outline toolbar to apply the appropriate heading styles. Every topic formatted with the Heading 1 style will become a new slide. Any topic formatted with the Heading 2 style will become bulleted text, subordinate to the Heading 1 text. Once you've finished your outline, save it as a Word document just for safekeeping—you never know...

The ability to export your outline directly to PowerPoint is now built into Word 97. As shown in Figure 23.18, simply choose File, Send To, PowerPoint. Voila, your outlined text appears in PowerPoint!

NOTE. *PowerPoint imports only paragraphs formatted with a heading style such as Heading 1, Heading 2, or Heading 3. Other text in your Word document is ignored.*

Figure 23.18

You can now export an
outline created in Word
directly to PowerPoint
as a presentation.

Now all that's left to do is to apply a design scheme and save your slides
as a PowerPoint presentation. Here's how:

1. Choose Format, Apply Design.

2. Select the design you want from the Name list in the dialog box that
   appears (see Figure 23.19). Notice that the preview area changes when
   you click on a different design name.

Figure 23.19

Use the Apply Design
dialog box to apply a
predefined design
scheme to your slides.

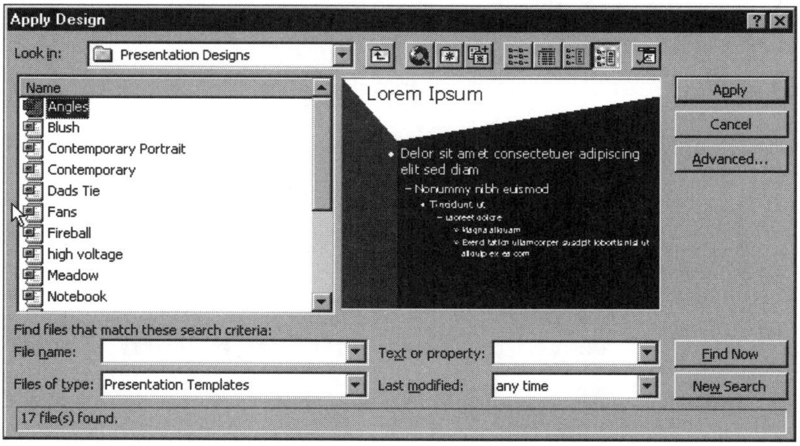

3. Click the Apply button.

4. Choose View, Slide Sorter to get an overview of your presentation as shown in Figure 23.20.

Figure 23.20

The new PowerPoint presentation in Slide Sorter view

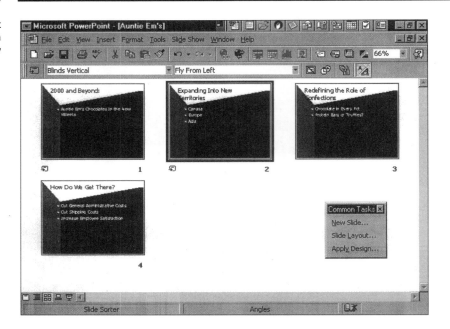

5. If you will be using a computer to deliver your presentation, you can add transitions and effects from the drop-down list boxes on the Slide Sorter toolbar.

6. Choose File, Save As, specify a location for the presentation, type a name in the File name box, and then click Save.

Exporting PowerPoint Files to Word

The Word/PowerPoint relationship is a two-way street: you can choose File, Send To, Microsoft Word to export slides as an .RTF file containing heading styles and display the file in Word for editing.

■ Using Outlook with Word

As you learned in Chapter 16, Outlook is your desktop information manager. You can use it to keep track of your appointments, contacts, e-mail messages, and tasks. Outlook can keep track of the files you use, and it can also track the history of any activity on a timeline. In Chapter 16, you learned about using the Outlook address book as a data source for mail merges. Now we'll look at using Outlook in Word to track our files.

To start Outlook, click the Start button on the Windows 95 Taskbar, and then select Microsoft Outlook from the Programs menu. Outlook loads and initially presents you with your Inbox so you can check your e-mail messages.

The left frame of the Outlook window contains icons that change the view of the right frame of the window. For example, if you click the Contacts icon, you'll see the names and addresses of any contacts you've added to Outlook. If there are more icons than room to display, you can use the small arrow buttons at the top and bottom of the left pane to scroll the icons into view. The buttons Outlook, Mail, and Other change the group of icons visible in the left pane of the window.

Opening Word Files from Within Outlook

You can open any Office document from within Outlook. Start by clicking the Other button. You should see the My Computer icon and the My Documents and Favorites folders. When you double-click these icons, the display to the right changes.

When you find the file you want to open, double-click on its name. If the file was created with an Office program, the program and file will load automatically.

The Outlook Journal can keep track of your Word documents by the date and time they are created or modified. If you don't see your Word files listed when you click the Journal icon, you may have to change your options. Do it like this:

1. Choose Tools, Options.

2. Click the Journal tab in the Options dialog box.

3. Enable the checkbox next to Microsoft Word in the Also record files from section of the dialog box (see Figure 23.21).

Figure 23.21

Enable the Microsoft Word checkbox so the Outlook Journal will keep track of your documents.

4. Click OK.

To open a file listed in the Outlook Journal, simply double-click the file.

■ Using Binders to Combine Multiple Documents

Occasionally, you might have related documents from the various Office programs that you would like to work with together. If you came by Microsoft Word as part of Microsoft Office, you have access to Microsoft Binder, a program that enables you to assemble multiple files from different Office programs and work with them from a single location. You can even integrate the page numbering among documents in the same binder, even if they were created using different Office programs.

You can use Binder to pull together existing files, create new files and place them in empty binders, or use one of four built-in binders that already include Word, Excel, and PowerPoint templates.

To create a new report binder, click New Office Document on the Microsoft Office toolbar. Click the Binders tab, select the Report template, and then click OK.

Report binders include Word templates for cover letters, executive summaries, and analyses; an Excel template for supporting data; and a PowerPoint slide show template.

To start from a blank binder, click the Start button on the Taskbar, then choose the Microsoft Binder command on the Programs menu.

Working with Binders

After you open a binder, the files in that binder appear as icons along the left-hand side of your screen (see Figure 23.22). To open a file, double-click on its icon; the file opens in whatever application it requires, with all the application's capabilities. You might not immediately notice the change, because the title bar still says Microsoft Office Binder—and because Microsoft Office applications share all but one menu, as well as many of the same toolbar buttons. (This is an example of what Microsoft means by document-centric computing—documents become more prominent than the applications that display them.)

If you want to dedicate the entire screen to the document you're working on, click on the Show/Hide Left Pane button (it's located to the left of the File menu and looks like a vertical bar with left and right arrows).

Managing Your Binder

When you work on a Word document in a Binder, Binder commands appear in the File menu. However, most of the other menus contain Word commands, and Word's Standard and Formatting toolbars are also available.

A new menu also appears, called Section (see Figure 23.23). A set of File commands that enable you to manage the binder as a whole replaces your

Figure 23.22

In a binder you can open
and work on documents
created in any of the
Office applications.

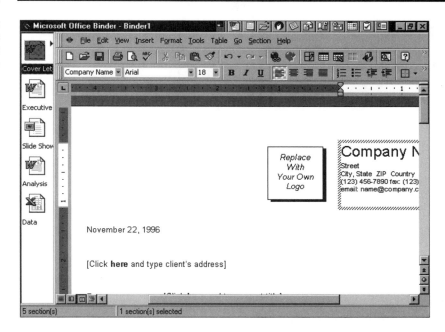

normal File commands. The Section commands enable you to manage, add, and remove binder sections and control some elements of individual sections formerly controlled from the File menu. The Section menu, for example, provides commands for managing a section's Page Setup, for Printing a section, and for viewing Section Properties. From within the Binder, each section looks and behaves like a separate document file, even though they are *not* separate files—they're all part of one Binder file, stored with an .OBD extension.

Adding New Blank Binder Sections

To add a new blank section to an existing binder, choose Add from the Section menu to open the Add Section dialog box. Choose a template for the type of document you want to be created, and click OK. The new file is created with a generic name, such as Section 1. To rename the file, click in its file name, and after the rectangle appears, enter the new file name.

Incorporating an Existing File in a Binder

To include an existing file in an Office binder, choose Add from File from the Section menu to open the Add From File dialog box. It responds just like the File Open dialog box: locate the file you want to include and choose A<u>d</u>d. When you add a file to your binder, you create a duplicate copy of it. Changes

Figure 23.23

The Binder Section menu

you make in the copy within the Binder aren't reflected in the original copy, nor are changes you make in the original copy reflected in the Binder.

Rearranging Files in a Binder

To rearrange the files in a binder, drag them to the locations you prefer, or choose Rearrange from the Section menu. Select the section you want to move and use the Move Up and Move Down buttons to relocate the section (see Figure 23.24).

Figure 23.24

You can use the Rearrange Sections dialog box to organize the documents in your binder.

Viewing a Section from Outside the Binder

You occasionally might want to view a document from inside Word itself rather than from inside Microsoft Binder. For example, you can't run Word's Print Preview command from inside a Binder. To open a section inside Word itself, display the section, and then choose View Outside from the Section menu.

Keep in mind that the section still isn't a separate file. You can, however, create a separate file that contains the section. If you already are viewing the file from outside the Binder, choose Save Copy As from the File menu. (As you might already have noticed, when you view a section from outside the Binder, the File menu changes yet again.)

Save Copy As essentially acts the same as Word's Save As command, creating a separate copy of the file that exists only outside the Binder. After you use Save Copy As, however, the original section remains open, so the changes you make in your current session are stored in the Binder, not in the new duplicate file. When you use Save Copy As, changes you make in the Binder section aren't reflected in the duplicate file, or vice versa. If, however, you later update the duplicate file, you can always remove the original section from the Binder and insert the revised copy.

To simply update the Binder file that includes the section you're editing, choose Update from the File menu, the equivalent of the File, Save command. In fact, the keyboard shortcut Ctrl+S updates a binder section just as it normally would save a file.

After you finish working outside the Binder, you can return to the Binder by choosing Close & Return to from the File menu.

■ Using the Microsoft Office Shortcut Bar

If you purchase Word with Microsoft Office, another bonus you get is the Microsoft Office Shortcut Bar (OSB). If you've installed it, the OSB gives you a quick way to create or open documents, open other programs, or perform tasks built into Microsoft Outlook, such as making an appointment. If the OSB is not visible, click the Start button on the Windows 95 Taskbar, and choose Microsoft Office Shortcut Bar from the StartUp submenu of the Programs menu. The Office Shortcut Bar is anchored at the top right side of the screen, as shown in Figure 23.25.

NOTE. *If you don't want to use the Office Shortcut Bar, you can add program icons to one of your existing Word toolbars, using the Tools, Customize features discussed in Chapter 22. You also can write macros that open specific files or new files based on specific templates and then attach those macros to toolbar buttons.*

Figure 23.25

The Office Shortcut Bar
gives you a quick way
to perform tasks.

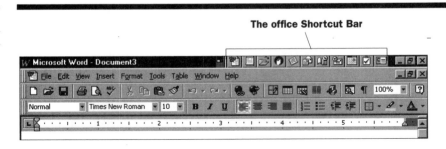

Choosing an Office Shortcut Bar

You can choose among several predefined shortcut toolbars:

- *Office.* Shows the icons for the Office programs.

- *Desktop.* Shows all the program icons that currently appear on your Windows desktop. You can use Desktop as an alternative to minimizing Word and viewing the desktop.

- *QuickShelf.* Includes icons for displaying reference works that are part of the Bookshelf Basics collection.

- *Favorites.* Displays the shortcuts to the files and folders you store in the Favorites folder—generally, the files you use most often.

- *msn.* Shows the Microsoft Network startup icon and any Microsoft Network shortcuts added to your Windows 95 desktop.

- *Programs.* Displays Microsoft Office programs; major components of Windows 95, such as Windows Explorer, Microsoft Exchange, The Microsoft Network, and an MS-DOS prompt; and other programs available from the desktop.

- *Accessories.* Shows Windows 95 accessory programs, such as Paint and WordPad.

To select an OSB toolbar, click the colored square icon on the left side of the OSB toolbar and choose Customize. Click the Toolbars tab, enable the checkbox for the toolbar you want to use (see Figure 23.26), and then click OK.

Moving an Office Shortcut Bar

You can drag the Office Shortcut Bar anywhere you want: click on the area just below the colored square icon on the left side of the toolbar and drag. Some users like to keep the shortcut bar along the right edge of the screen, to the right of the scroll bars, as shown in Figure 23.27. If you have a large monitor, you might even let it float in an otherwise empty space. The Word window resizes automatically to accommodate the shortcut bar on the top, bottom, or side of the screen.

Figure 23.26

The Office Shortcut Bar can be customized.

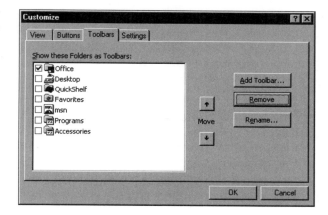

Figure 23.27

You have choices as to where to dock the Office Shortcut Bar.

The Office Shortcut Bar docked on the right side of the screen —

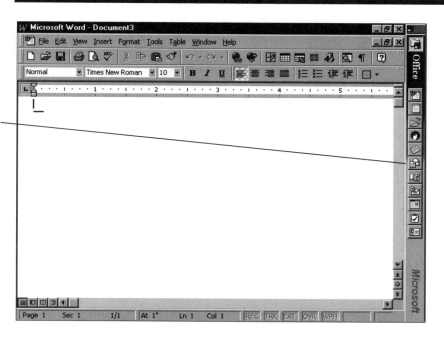

Customizing the Office Shortcut Bar

You can customize any OSB toolbar by right-clicking on the Office Shortcut Bar menu button at the left edge of the Microsoft Office Shortcut Bar and choosing Customize from the menu. The Customize dialog box appears; it contains the following four tabs:

- *View.* Allows you to customize the color and appearance of the toolbar itself, whether it uses small or large buttons, and several other aspects of toolbar behavior. For example, you can choose to Animate Toolbars and use Sound whenever you click a button. If you have the OSB toolbar displayed along the sides or bottom of the screen, the Auto Hide between uses option makes the toolbar slide out of view when it's not being used.

- *Buttons.* Lets you check or clear boxes to display or hide buttons for each program or file available on an open toolbar. (You can't check or clear boxes in a toolbar you haven't displayed.) You also can add buttons for additional programs or folders by clicking on Add File or Add Folder. Finally, you can move toolbar buttons within a toolbar by using the up- and down-arrow Move buttons.

- *Toolbars.* Enables you to specify which toolbars to display and to create new toolbars. After you display a toolbar here, you can use the other tabs to customize it. Creating new toolbars is especially useful if you use an eclectic group of programs and files—not simply the ones Microsoft sells!

- *Settings.* Controls where Office stores templates for individual users and for your workgroup.

    To create a new toolbar, follow these steps:

1. Choose Customize from the OSB menu. The Customize tabbed dialog box appears.

2. Click the Toolbars tab.

3. Choose Add Toolbar to open the Add Toolbar dialog box (see Figure 23.28).

4. Click Create a new, blank Toolbar called:, and enter the name of the toolbar.

5. Choose OK.

6. The next step is to populate your new toolbar with buttons. Choose the Buttons tab, and choose Add File. Locate the program or file icon you want to add and choose Add.

7. Repeat step 5 for each program or file icon you want to add.

8. Choose OK.

Figure 23.28

The Add Toolbar
dialog box

Using the Office Shortcut Bar to Install or Remove Word Program Components

Somewhere along the line, you might need to install or remove a component of Word. You might, for example, begin to receive files in an unusual format that requires you to use an import filter you never needed before. This requires you to run the Office Setup program again. If you installed the Microsoft Office Shortcut Bar and the Office Setup program when you installed Office, finding and running Office Setup is much easier.

Simply choose Add/Remove Office Programs from the Office Shortcut Bar menu. If you have installed several Microsoft programs, you're prompted for which one you want to install or uninstall. Choose the program; if you want to install new components to Word, choose Microsoft Office. The Office setup program runs; from there you can specify which Word, Excel, PowerPoint, or other Office components you want to add or remove.

■ Looking Up References with Microsoft Bookshelf Basics

If you don't need a dictionary or thesaurus, you're a better man than I, Gunga Din. Lucky for us, Microsoft Bookshelf Basics, which includes a set of reference materials, is bundled with Microsoft Office. Included are a dictionary, thesaurus, and gathering of quotations. Also included are previews of an encyclopedia and almanac, among other things. To start the program, click its icon in the Office Shortcut Bar—then wait patiently because it takes a while to load.

To filter the information, click the All Books button on the left side of the screen below the menu bar, and then select the book you want—the dictionary, for example.

You can type the word or reference that you're looking for or you can scroll through the Contents or Gallery lists. When you see the reference you need, click on it and it will be displayed on the right side of the window (see Figure 23.29).

Figure 23.29

Displaying a definition in the dictionary

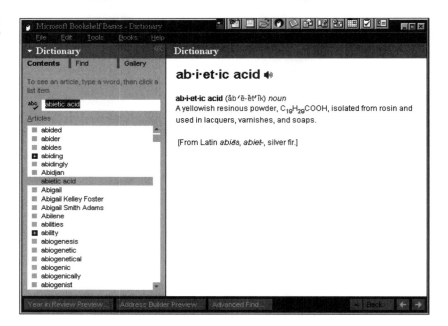

■ Using the Microsoft Photo Editor

A picture is worth a thousand words, so they say. If you want to include a picture in your Word document, Microsoft Photo Editor is just the ticket. Here's how to do it:

1. Choose Insert, Object.

2. Select Microsoft Photo Editor 3.0 Photo (or Scan) in the Object type list.

3. Select Open an Existing Picture in the new dialog box, and then click OK.

4. Select the file containing the photograph to be inserted, and then click OK. (If you don't have a scanned photograph of your own, you can use one of the photos included on the Office CD under Clipart\Photos.)

5. Drag the sizing handles to change the dimensions of the photo, if necessary.

6. Use the tools on the Picture toolbar to adjust the contrast brightness and other image attributes.

7. To crop the photo, click the Crop button, then drag one of the sizing handles surrounding the photo (see Figure 23.30).

Figure 23.30

Inserting a photo in your Word document

8. When you're finished, save and print your masterpiece, Ansel Adams!

■ Using MS Organization Chart 2.0

Have you ever tried to create an organization chart by drawing boxes and lines? It's an exercise in sheer frustration, to say the least. Now that MS Organization Chart comes bundled with Microsoft Office, though, it's a simple task. Follow these steps to insert an organization chart in your Word document:

1. Choose Insert, Object.

2. Select MS Organization Chart 2.0 in the Object type list.

3. Click OK.

4. Drag across the placeholders in the boxes and type the names and titles of the individuals who should be included in the organization chart.

5. To add another box, choose the button that describes the relationship of the individual being added to the chart.

6. Click on the side of the box that matches the relationship of the box being added—the bottom for a subordinate, for example. (See Figure 23.31.)

Figure 23.31

Creating an organization chart

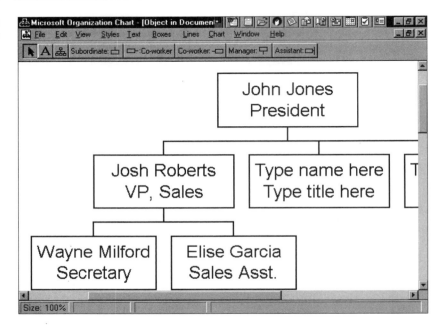

7. To remove a box, select it and press Delete.

8. Use the Styles, Text, Boxes, Lines, and Chart menus to change the appearance of the chart.

9. When you are finished adding and removing boxes and formatting the chart, choose File, Exit and Return to <Document>.

You've earned the key to the neighborhood in this chapter. You started by learning about importing Excel, Access, and other database information into Word. You went on to importing and exporting to and from PowerPoint, working with Binders and customizing the Office Shortcut Bar. As if that weren't enough you learned about managing your files in Outlook, looking up references in Microsoft Bookshelf Basics, and, last, but certainly not least, you learned to insert Microsoft Photo Editor and MS Organization Chart objects into your Word documents. That was a lot of territory and I wouldn't be surprised if your hair is standing on end—or if you needed a nap! But whatever your current state of mind, don't wait for your mom to push you out the door—get out there and play!

- *Using the Office Resource Kit*
- *Planning Your Word and Office Installation*
- *Installing and Using Word on a Network*
- *Using Office 97 Policy Templates*
- *Setting Registry Options on a Single Computer*
- *Using Workgroup Templates*
- *Working with Colleagues Using Word 6 or Word 95*

24

Managing Word: Making Word the Good Corporate Citizen

Today, most business pcs run in a networked environment—and someone has to be in charge of making sure Word runs properly in such an environment. Managing Word begins with planning and installing it across the network, but it doesn't end there.

If you're in charge of managing Word, you'll have a variety of issues to be aware of, including:

- Where shared document files and templates will be stored

- How to manage environments that are split between users of Word 97 and older versions

- How to control the way users use Word, consistent with your corporate policies

- How you can use Word's customized setup features to provide centralized access to important business information

In this chapter, we'll discuss each of these issues and introduce tools Microsoft provides—both on the Office 97 CD and as part of the Office 97 Resource Kit—to make it easier to manage Word and Office.

■ Using the Office Resource Kit

If you're responsible for managing Word in your department or company, get a copy of the Office 97 Resource Kit. It's available for downloading at no charge at Microsoft's Web site (currently stored at www.microsoft.com/organizations/corpeval). It can also be purchased in printed form at most bookstores. The Office 97 Resource Kit contains comprehensive technical information about using and programming Word. It also has a variety of important management tools, including sample system policies you can use to control the way your users work with Word and Office.

■ Planning Your Word and Office Installation

Depending on the size of your organization, rolling out a new version of Word can be a sizable undertaking. You may need to plan the following steps:

1. Understand Word 97's features well enough to make at least tentative decisions about how you'll install it.

2. Make sure your systems running Windows 95 or Windows NT are prepared for Office 97. For example, if you want to use Office's collaboration features, make sure Microsoft Exchange or another compatible electronic mail system is already installed on your client systems and network.

3. Consider whether you'll need to upgrade any custom software, templates, or macros that were designed for earlier versions of Word and Office. For example, custom software that uses 16-bit DLLs, which worked perfectly with Word 6, must be updated to work with the 32-bit Office 97

locally or across the network. Not surprisingly, Run from CD tends to deliver worse performance, especially in a networked environment. However, it may be an option if hard disk space is tight on both your network and client systems.

Since you're installing across a network, you have a fourth option: *Run from Network Server.* This is similar to Run from CD, in that critical Office files are copied to an individual user's hard disk, but most files are kept centrally on the server and retrieved as needed. Run from Network Server is typically significantly faster than Run from CD, however, because server hard drives are typically optimized for performance, whereas CD-ROMs are typically much slower than standard hard drives.

Choosing Media to Install From

You can install Word and Office from floppy disk; from the Office CD-ROM; or from your network server. If you install from floppy disk or CD-ROM, you need to be physically present at each computer where you're installing Word or Office. If you install from a network server, you can install on many machines from a central location—but your network connection will have to be available constantly during the installation process.

Determining the Role Users Will Play in the Installation Process

You have three options in installing Word and Office. The first is to allow users to run Setup themselves, from floppy disk, CD-ROM, or from your network server.

If you allow users to install from a network server, you must first prepare for, and then run, an *administrative setup* on your server. After you've done this, users can install Word or Office from your network server with no involvement on your part. Actually running the administrative setup is relatively easy: you insert the Office or Word CD-ROM (or the first floppy disk), choose Run from the Start menu, and enter the drive name you're using, followed by

```
setup /a
```

This loads the administrative installation program. From there, you simply make choices, much like the choices you're presented with in a standalone installation. Among those you'll need to make are to specify a name and a path for two folders: the folder where you'll store the main Office application files and the folder where you'll store shared Microsoft applications such as Microsoft Graph. Collectively, these two folders are known as the *administrative installation point.*

Preparing your server requires a little more effort. Before running administrative setup, you'll need to:

- Make sure you have at least 500 MB disk space free and that you're running Windows 95 or Windows NT 3.51 or a later version.

- Make sure any existing Office-related folders are empty.

- Give yourself read, write, delete, and create permissions to all the folders and disks you'll work with.

- Log off all users, and while you're running the administrative install, prevent network user access to the folders you're working with.

- Disable any virus protection software you're running.

Before or after the administrative install, you'll also have to give users read-only access to your administrative installation point (the folders on your server containing Word and Office installation files).

Customizing How Word or Office Installs

You can customize the way your employees install Word or Office by developing a setup script that provides new default settings. Once you've created and enabled such a script, you can either allow users to make changes to your new defaults or require them to install the defaults just as you customized them.

To customize Word's installation script, run the Network Installation Wizard (niw.exe), which is included on the CD-ROM that accompanies the Microsoft Office 97 Resource Kit. This program guides you through the delicate process of editing two files that Setup depends on throughout the installation process. One is an .STF file that specifies which files are to be installed, in which order, and which registry entries are to be created. The other is an .INF file that contains extensive details about all Office files, and is checked by the .STF file during installation.

You can customize a wide range of settings using the Network Installation Wizard, including which features are installed and which folders will be used for files, templates, and workgroup templates. (Workgroup templates are covered in more detail later in this chapter.)

It's worth mentioning that the Network Installation Wizard can do more than simply specify which existing Word or Office files to install and where to place them. You can also use it to install additional files you've created, such as templates that contain customized menus, toolbars, AutoText entries, and macros; or custom dictionaries you want to make available to all users.

Once you've created the settings you want, store your customized .STF and .INF files along with the Setup program on your server. Rename your original .STF file to save it as a backup (don't rename any .INF files). Then, give your modified .STF file the name Office looks for by default: Off97std.stf for Office Standard installations, or Off97pro.stf for Office Professional installations. Once you've done all this, your customized setup script will run automatically whenever a user installs Word or Office from the server.

Choosing How to Run a Customized Setup Script

Now that you have a customized setup script, you can use it in one of two ways. Your users can run setup normally, by double-clicking the Setup icon in the folder where you've placed it. Your custom settings now appear as Word's or Office's default settings, but users can change them. Alternatively, you can tell users to install Word or Office using a command line such as

```
setup.exe /q1
```

In this example, the **q1** parameter tells Setup to proceed without further user intervention, automatically installing the software based on the customized settings you've created. This is called a *batch installation.*

Installing With No User Involvement

You can go one step further: you can perform a "push" install, which runs automatically on a user's computer with no intervention, whether they like it or not. To do this, include the appropriate customized Setup command line in the user's system logon script. Your setup script, whether customized or generic, will automatically run the next time the user logs on.

■ Using Office 97 Policy Templates

Even after you install Word and Office 97, you can control the way users access a wide variety of Word features and behaviors. The mechanism through which you control system policies is the System Policy Editor (poledit.exe), a tool provided with the Windows 95 Resource Kit or the Windows NT Workstation Resource Kit. Using the System Policy Editor, you can customize policy files that apply to all users, to groups of users, to specific computers, or to specific users on specific computers. Whenever a user logs onto the network with his or her identification, the relevant system policy files for that user are downloaded and the settings in the local user's registry file are edited to reflect it.

For system policies to work on Windows NT networks, Client for Microsoft Networks must be the client workstation's primary network logon client and a domain must be defined. For system policies to work on NetWare networks, Microsoft Client for NetWare Networks must be the primary network logon client, and a preferred server must be specified for that client workstation.

Microsoft provides a sample policy template for Word and Office 97 as part of the Office 97 Resource Kit. It's called Office97.adm. To use its settings as provided, or to adapt those settings to your own needs, run the System Policy Editor (see Figure 24.1). Choose Policy Template from the Options menu to specify the template you want to use (see Figure 24.2); then open the Office97.adm file.

Figure 24.1

System Policy Editor

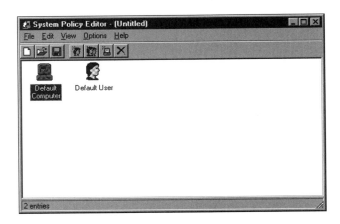

Figure 24.2

Choosing a policy template to base your policy file upon

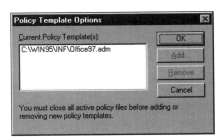

Think of policy templates the way you think of Word templates: you open a new file based on a template, make the changes you want, and then save that file. Once you've specified the policy template you want to use, choose File, New Policy, and then choose Edit, Properties for the specific computer, user, or group you want to create policies for (see Figure 24.3).

To see the options available to you, click Word 8.0 and then choose a category of options. You'll see a series of items, each with one of three settings. Checked means the policy is in effect whenever a user logs onto the network.

Figure 24.3

The Default User
Properties dialog box,
displaying overall
categories
of customizable
Word properties

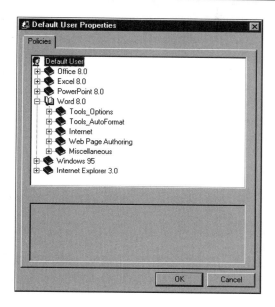

Cleared means the policy is not in effect. Grayed means the user's configuration settings will be left alone whenever he or she logs on.

Using the Office97.adm policy template, you can change five categories of policies:

- *Tools_Options settings* that correspond to settings in the Tools, Options dialog box.

- *Tools_AutoFormat settings*, in particular, the way AutoCorrect behaves when it encounters a plain-text document while Word is being used as an e-mail editor.

- *Internet settings*, in particular where Word and Internet Explorer will connect to when users choose Help, Microsoft on the Web (or whether the option will even be available). Also included in this setting is whether users can connect to Microsoft or to a site on your intranet to download updated file converters.

- *Web Page Authoring settings*, especially where Word will look for clipart, bullets, and other multimedia resources.

- *Miscellaneous settings*, such as Word's default time and date settings, and whether editing time will be included in the File, Document Properties, Statistics box.

When you're finished customizing your policy template, save it as config.pol; all policy files use the extension .POL.

■ Setting Registry Options on a Single Computer

There are many settings built into Word that cannot be edited from the Office97.adm policy template but can be changed locally through the user's registry. The Support8.dot template includes a macro, RegOptions, which can control these settings.

First, make sure that the template Support8.dot has been installed. If it hasn't, copy it from the \Office\Macros folder on the Office CD-ROM. Next, use Tools, Templates and Add-ins to load Support8.dot as a global template, making its macros available. Select Tools, Macro, Macros to display the list of macros; choose RegOptions and click Run. The Set Registry Options dialog box opens (see Figure 24.4).

Figure 24.4

The Set Registry
Options dialog box

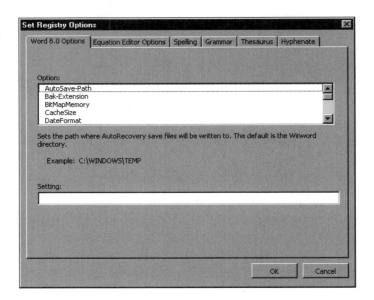

Here, you can make local changes in a wide variety of settings, including the paths where files are stored, the dictionaries used by Word's proofing features, the behavior of the Equation Editor, and a number of other settings that can improve performance in specialized situations. For example, you can change the setting BitMapMemory to increase the size of the Word bitmap cache, which can increase the performance of Word documents that are graphics-heavy. Using Word's cache setting, you can also increase the size of the cache Word sets aside beyond the default 64K, potentially improving the performance of file I/O and other Word operations.

■ Using Workgroup Templates

Word allows you to specify a location on your network where all workgroup templates can be shared. Specifying a workgroup template location enables you to centralize templates that are relevant to your entire workgroup or department, so they're all easily accessible and so they can all be updated at once. You might use a workgroup template location for:

- Templates that add menu items or specific toolbars to users' copies of Word

- Form templates that allow users to fill out requests for vacation time, pension plan changes, and the like

- Templates that create proposals, reports, or other regularly used information

By default, no location for workgroup templates is specified. If you wish, you can establish or change the location of workgroup templates from individual workstations. Choose Tools, Options, File Locations (see Figure 24.5). Choose Workgroup templates, and click Modify; then select a new location from the Modify Location dialog box and click OK.

Figure 24.5

Setting a location for Workgroup templates

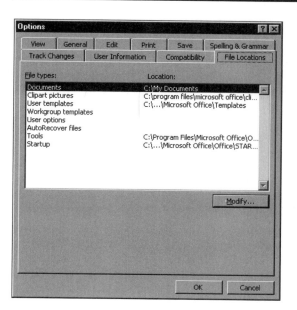

If you have many workstations to manage, however, you may prefer to specify workgroup templates centrally. You can do so by setting a location for workgroup templates as part of your custom setup script, or afterwards as part of a system policy file.

■ Working with Colleagues Using Word 6 or Word 95

It's unlikely that everyone in your organization, or everyone you share documents with, will upgrade to Word 97 at the same time. How can you continue to work smoothly in mixed Word 6/Word 95/Word 97 environments? You have two options.

First, you can save Word 97 files back to the Word 6/Word 95 format. You can do this informally by asking people to save files manually to the Word 6/Word 95 format. You can also use Tools, Options, Save's "Save Word files as" option to set each system's default Save format to Word 6/95. Or you can use the System Policy Editor to establish Word 6/Word 95 as the default setting that File, Save will use whenever files are saved. In either case, Word actually saves the files as Rich Text Format (.RTF) files with .DOC extensions. Users won't notice the difference unless they're using software that can recognize .DOC files but not .RTF files.

The advantages of saving Word 97 files in Word 6/Word 95 format are straightforward: anyone who uses Word 6 or Word 95 will be able to open the files you save this way. The disadvantages are equally straightforward: if you use features that only exist in Word 97, such as text boxes, hyperlinks or VBA macros, those elements will disappear from documents saved in Word 6/Word 95 format.

Your alternative, also imperfect, is to distribute the Word 97 file converter contained on the Office 97 CD-ROM, and have all users of Word 6 or Word 95 install it. Now, users of Word 6 can open Word 97 files—but they still can't save to the Word 97 format. (A work-around is to open Word 97 files and save them immediately under a new name.)

Converting Many Files Between Formats at Once

In managing the transition to Word 97, you may wish to convert a large number of files at once. For example, if you're upgrading to Word 97 from WordPerfect 5.1 for DOS, you may have a large number of WordPerfect documents. Instead of having users convert them one at a time, you might wish to convert them all at once.

Conversely, you might at some point have a large number of Word documents that you want to export—perhaps to HTML format for use on an intranet or on the World Wide Web. Word comes with a tool designed for exactly these situations: the Conversion Wizard. This file, Convert8.dot, can be found in the \Office\Macros folder of the Office 97 CD-ROM. Double-click on Convert8.dot to run the Conversion Wizard, as shown in Figure 24.6.

Click Next to display your options for converting files to or from Word. Then select the batch conversion you want to perform. (Depending on the

Figure 24.6

The Conversion Wizard's
options for converting
files to or from Word

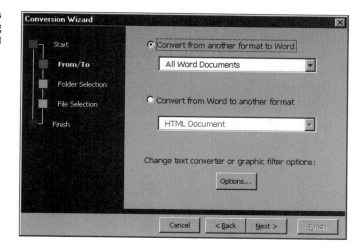

conversion you've chosen, you may be able to control certain aspects of how
Word performs the conversion. To see the available choices, click Options.)
When you've finished selecting a conversion and any relevant options, click
Next. The Conversion Wizard asks you to select source and destination fold-
ers for the files you're converting (see Figure 24.7). Click Browse to select
specific folders other than C:\.

Figure 24.7

Selecting source and
destination folders for
files to be converted

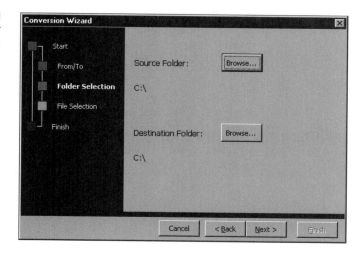

Once you've chosen source and destination folders, click Next to display the File Selection window, where you can select from a list of files to be converted (Figure 24.8). Click Next, then click Finish, and the Conversion Wizard will convert all your files.

Figure 24.8

Selecting specific files to be converted

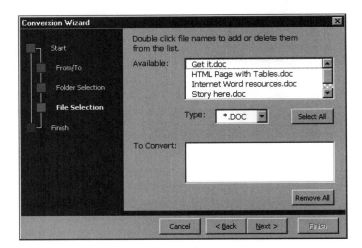

In this chapter, you've reviewed some of the special issues you'll need to be aware of in managing Word in a networked, business environment, and you've learned about some of the resources available to help you do so. Next, you'll move on to Word 97's piece de resistance: the Visual Basic for Applications programming language that allows you to build on Word and Office, creating a platform for virtually any custom application your organization may need.

- *Recording a Macro*

- *Recording Your Macro*

- *Running Macros*

- *Troubleshooting Macros*

- *Running Word Commands from the Macro List*

- *Creating Macros That Run Automatically*

- *Finding Good Tasks to Record*

- *Moving Macros Among Templates*

- *Using Macros That Come with Word*

25

Recording Basic Macros: You Can Do Plenty Without Coding

IN THIS CHAPTER, YOU'LL SEE HOW FAR YOU CAN GET WITH MACROS without doing any Visual Basic for Applications programming. Then, in the following chapter, you'll see how much further you'll get once you *do* learn the fundamentals of Visual Basic for Applications.

With a macro you can assemble a set of procedures and run it automatically with a single command. You might have special character formats or paragraph formats, for example, that you'd like to set with a keystroke rather than from a dialog box. You can assign keyboard shortcuts to these macro procedures, so you can make these formatting changes more quickly than you could using dialog boxes.

Think about recording a macro the next time you have to use the five steps normally required to transpose two wrongly typed letters in a word, or start working on a page that has to be formatted in two columns, or display Print Preview in full-screen mode so that you can see more of your document, or add a footer that contains a title already in your document. Virtually anything you do is often worth recording and automating.

A macro can contain many steps and accomplish a remarkable amount of work. I'll give you a personal example. I write catalog copy; much of the same copy is also used for other purposes. I create the copy in the format of a Word table, so once I've done the writing, I can use Word's Mail Merge feature to generate any type of copy I want. Once I've run Mail Merge, I run a macro that cleans up the copy by running several consecutive Find & Replaces that get rid of extra spaces, flags missing data, and the like. The result: I've automated 90% of the non-thinking work that goes with generating my catalog copy. And I didn't have to write a program to do it; I simply recorded the steps.

Now, once I have that macro, I can use Visual Basic for Applications to give myself much more control over how it works, build intelligence into it so it can decide when to make certain kinds of changes, and make it do even more. With Visual Basic for Applications, it's possible to write macros that will streamline or automate virtually anything Word can do. And if I were developing this macro for others to use, I could also use Visual Basic for Applications to display dialog boxes, present choices, and provide help to guide users in working with my macro.

As we've mentioned, the following chapter will introduce you to the power of Visual Basic for Applications. But first, in this chapter, you'll learn all the ways macros can save you time even if you never write a single line of code. You'll learn how to record a macro, use the macro toolbar, decide what to record, and assign a keyboard shortcut to your macro. You'll also learn how to run a macro you've recorded and how to create macros that run automatically.

NOTE. *Word 97 is the culmination of Microsoft's long-term commitment to move to a standard macro language for all Office applications. It replaces WordBasic, Word's former programming language. In addition to Word 97, Excel 97, Access 97, and PowerPoint 97 all support Visual Basic for Applications.*

■ Recording a Macro

You can create a macro by *recording* it. The process you go through is no different from using your VCR; in fact, in creating a macro, you work with controls that resemble VCR controls. Word's built-in *macro recorder* translates your keystrokes and mouse actions into Visual Basic for Applications macro commands. You merely type and click as you ordinarily would to accomplish the task. The macro recorder does the rest, and you have usable macros immediately.

Planning to Record a Macro

Macro recording, like most other tasks, benefits from advance planning. Before recording a macro, make sure that:

- Your document is in the same condition it will be in when you actually use the macro. For example, if you're recording a macro that transposes letters, make sure that your insertion point is already just before or after those letters. If you're planning to search and replace hidden text, make sure the text is always visible in your document, by first recording a command to make it visible.

- You've thought about ways to avoid any messages Word might display. If your macro closes a document, when it runs, Word will interrupt you with a message to save the document. (The solution: record saving the file immediately before you record closing it.)

- Your macro doesn't depend on the presence of text or other elements that only appear in your current document. You'll want to use the macro in many documents.

- You've planned in advance the keyboard shortcuts you'll need to know. Word can't record mouse movements, such as those you might use to move through a document or select text. But keyboard equivalents like Ctrl+Home (go to the beginning of the document) or Shift+Control+RightArrow (select the next word) work just fine. Here's a good opportunity to finally learn some of those pesky shortcuts!

- You record Edit, Find and Edit, Replace commands using the Search All option (not just Search Down or Search Up).

■ Recording Your Macro

Once you've thought through your macro and positioned your insertion point appropriately, choose Tools, Record New Macro. The Record Macro dialog box opens (see Figure 25.1).

Figure 25.1

The Record Macro
dialog box

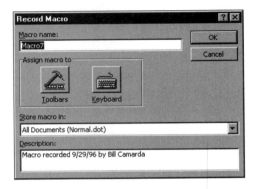

Before proceeding, you have a few decisions to make. First, name the macro. Macro names can't include spaces. Names must begin with letters of the alphabet, although numbers can be included afterward. Mixed uppercase and lowercase are not only okay, they're pretty much required to make your macro names comprehensible, as in this built-in Word command macro:

```
DrawBringInFrontOfText
```

Next, decide where to store your macro. By default, Word stores new macros in the Normal.dot template. However, you can choose another open template, and in Word 97, you can also choose to store a macro in your current document. Here's how to choose:

- If you're planning to use the macro in a wide variety of situations, store it in Normal.dot.

- If you're only planning to use the macro in specialized situations that are associated with a specific template, store it in that template. (For example, if you have a template that you only use to generate invoices for one specific client, and you write a macro that calculates your invoice based on discount pricing that only this client qualifies for, you'll probably want to store the macro with the client's invoice template.)

- If you're planning to distribute your document to others who may not have access to your templates, store the macro in your document.

Fortunately, Word's Organizer makes it easy to move macros among templates, so this decision isn't irrevocable.

Next, type a description of the macro in the **D**escription box. Be specific. Don't skip this step. You'll find it indispensable later when you try to remember what the macro does. (If you plan to assign a keyboard shortcut to the macro so it can be run more easily, you might describe the keyboard shortcut here, as well.)

Choosing Whether to Assign a Macro to a Toolbar or Keyboard Shortcut

Next, decide whether to assign the macro to a toolbar or a keyboard shortcut. You don't have to assign it to either one; you can always run the macro from the list of macros Word can display. But if you plan to use the macro often, using a keyboard shortcut or toolbar usually makes more sense. How to choose which to use?

- If you use an existing toolbar, such as the Standard or Formatting toolbar, adding new buttons may not leave room for the existing ones, unless you delete some you rarely use. That's especially the case if your buttons need to include text that describes the macro, rather than an icon. And the more standard toolbar buttons you remove, the more you may confuse users working from the manual. There's one big advantage, however: the buttons will always be visible to users.

- You might choose to create a new toolbar specifically for your most-used macros; then you can display that toolbar whenever you expect to use the macros. However, your screen will get more cluttered; some folks don't like to see any more toolbar buttons than are absolutely necessary.

- Keyboard shortcuts are extremely quick and effective, and don't take up space on your desktop. But you'll have to make sure you document them immediately: Word still doesn't offer an easy way to view the keyboard shortcut associated with a specific macro. (That's why we suggested documenting the keyboard shortcut in your Description box.)

Next, we'll briefly show you how to assign a macro to either a keyboard shortcut or a toolbar. Some of the techniques we'll show you are covered in more detail in Chapter 22, "Customization."

Assigning a Macro to a Keyboard Shortcut

To assign a macro to a keyboard shortcut, open Tools, Macro, Record New Macro, and assign the macro a name and a location, as discussed earlier. Next, click the Keyboard button. The Customize Keyboard dialog box appears, as shown in Figure 25.2.

Figure 25.2

The Customize
Keyboard dialog box

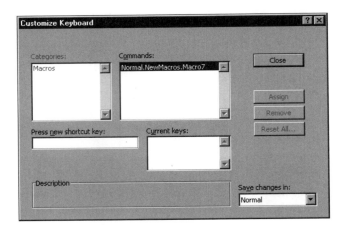

Press the new shortcut key combination exactly as you plan to use it when you run the macro later. If the command is already associated with a Word shortcut, Word will display what the current shortcut is; you can try a different shortcut or override the existing one. Once you've selected the shortcut you want, click Close; Word will display the Macro Recording toolbar and you can begin running the macro.

TIP. *Word doesn't have any preassigned keyboard shortcuts that combine the Alt key with a letter.*

Assigning a Macro to a Toolbar

First, a warning: Assigning macros to a toolbar may be the single most non-intuitive procedure I've run into in Word 97. (But then, that's what we're here for.) To assign a macro to a keyboard shortcut, open Tools, Macro, Record New Macro, and assign the macro a name and a location, as we discussed earlier. Next, click the Toolbar button. The Customize dialog box opens (see Figure 25.3).

Look around Word; is the toolbar where you want to add this macro already open? If so, great. If not, click the Toolbars tab, and check the box associated with that toolbar. (If you want to create an entirely new Toolbar, click New, and follow the instructions in Chapter 22.) Once you've done so, click the Commands tab, and highlight the name of the macro you're recording. (Notice that Word 97's Visual Basic for Applications presents the name a little differently than WordBasic did. If you've just named your new macro FindReplaceExtraSpaces, and stored it in the Normal.dot template, Word displays the name as Normal.NewMacros.FindReplaceExtraSpaces. Now drag

Figure 25.3

The Customize dialog
box, showing the
Commands tab

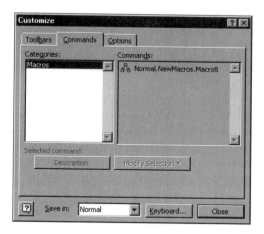

the highlighted macro to the toolbar where you want it, and drop it in the location where you want it. Word will display the entire name of the macro in the toolbar, as shown in Figure 25.4.

Figure 25.4

Macro names,
surrounded by svelte
icons, tend to look
unwieldy in toolbars.

Well, it's pretty cumbersome to have a toolbar with 12 buttons with slick icons, plus one new button labeled NORMAL.NEWMACROS.FIND-REPLACEEXTRASPACES. So you'll probably want to rename the macro on the toolbar, or assign it a button. Right-click on the macro name as it appears on the toolbar; a shortcut menu appears, as shown in Figure 25.5. In the Name box, edit a new name for this toolbar button. Or else, choose Change Button Image, pick one of Word's built-in buttons, and then check the Default Style box. Now, only the button will appear.

There's a lot more you can do to customize how your macro will appear on a toolbar; see Chapter 22 for that. For now, let's move on, since we still haven't actually recorded anything! Click Close, and Word displays the Macro Recording (Stop Recording) toolbar.

Figure 25.5

The shortcut menu you can use to change the name of your macro on a toolbar

Recording the Steps You Want to Perform

With the Stop Recording toolbar open (see Figure 25.6), perform the steps you want Word to record. When you're finished, press the Stop Recording button (the square button). The Stop Recording toolbar disappears, and Word stores the contents of the macro.

Figure 25.6

The Stop Recording macro toolbar

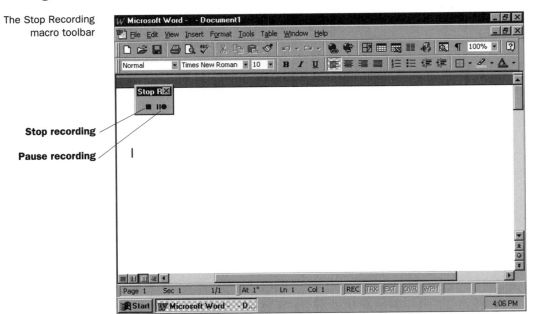

At times, you might want to pause recording for a moment, and perform some steps that Word doesn't record. For example, you might want Word to search and replace a complex chunk of text; instead of opening Find & Replace and entering the text manually (which could be susceptible to errors), you might want to copy the text from the document. But you don't want to record the copying process. To temporarily stop recording without ending the macro, click the Pause Recording button.

Recording an Example Macro

Now that you've learned the basics, let's walk through an example. You'll record a macro that will help you proofread your documents. Although grammar checkers are pretty good and getting better, they may not find every incomplete sentence in a document. Most grammar checkers miss incomplete sentences caused when long introductory phrases have been split off as sentences by accident, as in the following:

```
Although grammar checkers are good and getting better all the time. They have
difficulty finding every sentence fragment in a document.
```

Or...

```
Sitting in the park on a sunny Saturday afternoon and feeding the pigeons
popcorn. I felt my mind wandering back to the question of how to finish the
quarterly report.
```

This sample macro moves you from period to period through the document. It helps you find incomplete sentences by focusing on the punctuation mark that creates them. Reading to the left and right of each period to make sure that a full sentence lies on either side enables you to trap them every time. To record the macro, follow these steps:

1. Choose Tools, Macro, Record New Macro.

2. Type a name in the Macro Name dialog box. We'll call it PeriodCheck.

3. In the Store Macro in box, choose where you want to store this macro.

4. Write a description of the macro. (For purposes of this example, we'll skip creating a keyboard shortcut or a toolbar button.)

5. Click OK. The Stop Recording toolbar appears, and the mouse pointer now displays a running audiocassette tape.

6. Choose Edit, Find, and insert the period in the Find what box. Make sure Search is set to All.

7. Click Find Next.

8. Click the Stop button on the Stop Recording toolbar.

Now, each time you run the macro, it moves to the next period. A macro like this lends itself to a keyboard shortcut, of course, so you can run the macro repeatedly, one time after another. Or you might extend the macro with Visual Basic for Applications, so that it automatically pauses after every period and then, when the user is ready to move on, continues to the next, stopping at the end of the document.

■ Running Macros

To run a macro that you haven't assigned to a toolbar, menu, or keyboard shortcut, follow these steps:

1. Select **T**ools, **M**acro, Macros.

2. Select the Macro from the **M**acro Name list. By default, **M**acro Name lists all macros built into every open template and document. If that list is unmanageably long, you may want to view the macros in a specific template.

3. Choose **R**un.

■ Troubleshooting Macros

Occasionally, instead of running to completion, a recorded macro will stop and display an error message. First check again to make sure you followed all the planning steps discussed in the "Planning to Record Your Macro" section.

If you can't record a macro, check to make sure that you aren't working in a read-only document. If you are, the words [Read-Only] will appear in the title bar.

■ Running Word Commands from the Macro List

One large group of macros is not displayed in the All Active Templates list: the more than 500 macros that correspond to Word's built-in commands, many of which aren't on toolbars or menus. Many of the names of these commands are organized by Word menu or toolbar category. For example, File-CloseAll is a File-related command that doesn't appear on the File menu.

To run these Word commands, choose Word Commands from the Macros in box. Then select the macro and run it. You can also create new macros that consist of one or more of these Word commands and assign keyboard shortcuts to make them more accessible.

■ Creating Macros That Run Automatically

What if you want to run a macro automatically every time you load Word? For example, let's say you've recorded a macro that opens the document numbered 1 on your file list—the last document on which you worked. If you could make that macro run automatically whenever you start Word, you could have Word automatically reopen whatever file you were working on last.

Or suppose you want to run a macro every time you create a new document? For example, you can record a macro that displays fill-in fields. The user types the requested information, and that information automatically becomes part of the document. Or what if you want to make sure that your Word settings revert to the way they were when you first started Word, eliminating any special settings you temporarily added during a session?

You can make a macro do any of these things if you name it with one of the five special names Word recognizes (see Table 25.1).

Table 25.1

Macros That Run
Automatically

MACRO NAME	WHEN IT RUNS...
AutoExec	When you start Word
AutoNew	When you create a new file
AutoOpen	When you open an existing file
AutoClose	When you close a file
AutoExit	When you exit Word

AutoExec and AutoExit always reside in NORMAL.DOT. You can place the others either in NORMAL.DOT or another document template. The advantage of using a document template is that you can choose to have your AutoNew, AutoOpen, or AutoClose macros run only on a specific kind of document.

You can override AutoExec macros by adding the /m switch to the command line that Windows uses when you run Word. To specify running a specific macro, add the /m switch and the macro name. Word will run the macro you specify instead of the Autoexec macro.

■ Finding Good Tasks to Record

As you work, keep an eye out for tasks you perform repeatedly. The tasks are different for everyone, but the following list provides some ideas:

- Formatting, such as Small Caps, and combinations, such as Bold Underline, that don't have toolbar shortcuts

- Closing all open files (create a macro that chooses the FileCloseAll command from the **T**ools, **M**acro, Word Commands list)

- Saving a file to a floppy disk

- Changing between two connected printers

- Inserting AutoText entries with a single keyboard combination (create a macro that types the AutoText name and presses F3)

- Displaying the Drawing toolbar and opening the dialog box to choose a picture

- Applying a specific Table AutoFormat

- Compiling an index or table of contents with custom attributes

- Inserting a specific header or footer, perhaps containing bookmark fields that add information from elsewhere in the document

- Displaying hidden text

■ Moving Macros Among Templates

As mentioned earlier, macros in Word 97 can live in either templates or documents. If you want a macro to be available to a class of documents that doesn't use a specific document template, copy the macro. You use the Organizer to copy macros, as you learned in Chapter 8. Briefly, follow these steps:

1. Choose Tools, Macro, Macros.

2. Choose Or**g**anizer. The Organizer dialog box appears (see Figure 25.7).

3. Choose the macro you want to copy. (You might have to close the existing template and open another template containing your macro.)

4. Choose where you want to copy the macro.

5. Close Organizer when you finish.

Figure 25.7

The Macro tab of the
Organizer dialog box,
from where you can copy
macros among
documents and templates

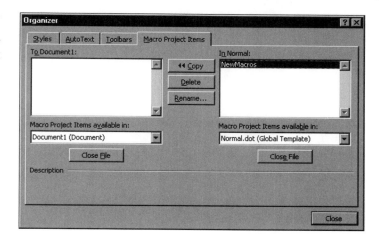

■ Using Macros That Come with Word

Word comes with seven files full of macros: Converter Options,
Docmgmt8.Dot, Layout8.Dot, Legal Tools.Dot, Support8.Dot, Tables8.Dot,
and Window8.Dot. When you install the macro files, they're contained in the
Winword\Macros folder. The macro files are not available until you make
them available, and you can do this in a couple of ways.

Using the Organizer, you can move some or all of the macro files to
NORMAL.DOT, making them available to all documents, or move them to
a specific document template, so they're available to documents created with
that template. You also can copy one or more of these macro files to the
WINWORD\STARTUP folder, where they load as global templates along
with NORMAL.DOT whenever you run Word.

When you load a template this way, all its macros are available to all
your documents. More macro code has to sit in memory, however. This is a
bit like making Word carry extra suitcases around. It can slow things down.

In this chapter, you've learned how much you can do with Word's macro
feature even if you never write a single line of code.

In Chapter 26, you'll start using Visual Basic for Applications to write
new macros—or enhance the ones you've recorded. And then you'll *really*
discover the meaning of power!

- *What Is VBA?*
- *Modifying a Simple Recorded Macro*
- *Understanding VBA's New Editing Environment*
- *Fundamental VBA Programming Concepts*

26

Word and VBA

IN THIS CHAPTER, YOU'LL LEARN HOW ADVANCED WORD USERS work behind the scenes to change the way Word behaves. When you use Word, your tools are not limited to Word's menus and toolbars. If Word does not support a feature you want, you can actually add that feature to Word's repertoire.

Starting with Office 97, Microsoft Word includes Visual Basic for Applications, usually shortened to just VBA. Previous Word users who worked with WordBasic (Word's older programming tool that VBA replaced in Office 97) will be somewhat familiar with VBA, although VBA's style capabilities go far beyond WordBasic's.

Be warned that modifying Word's behavior with VBA and adding functionality such as advanced VBA automation routines are not trivial tasks. VBA takes some time to master. You will learn here what's involved so you then can decide if VBA programming is in your future.

■ What Is VBA?

Throughout this book, you've learned how Word helps you prepare effective and attention-getting documents. Although Word does not make you a better writer, Word does help you produce better documents, and Word's IntelliSense features speed the writing process. Until now, all of your attention has been focused on the end-result that your readers will see: the finished document.

Visual Basic for Applications has very little to do with the actual document. VBA's primary goal is to help you in the document-creation process. VBA works under the hood to add automation that macros alone are not powerful enough to tackle. VBA lets you integrate Word and other Office 97 products together in ways that go beyond the standard cross-application links.

VBA is not just for Word and the other Office 97 products. Several non-Microsoft companies have announced plans to add the VBA language to their products. Companies such as Attachmate, Intergraph, Symantec, and Texas Instruments, among other large companies in the PC industry, believe enough in VBA solutions to incorporate VBA into their products. Therefore, when you learn VBA for Word, you also learn VBA for the other Office 97 products as well as for several other major PC software products on the market. As VBA becomes used more and more, companies that do not yet support VBA should follow with a VBA interface.

VBA Adds Power to Word

Consider the power you have when, with VBA, you can actually change the behavior of a menu option so that the Spelling and Grammar checkers check the spelling and grammar only of text you have not underlined, centered, and boldfaced! Such a complex spell check could bypass any formatted titles and headlines you put in your documents but would check the rest of the regular text. Modifying the behavior of menu options is just one of the many ways you can use VBA to control Word sessions.

Not only can you change the current menu commands, but you can also make up your own. Add a new menu bar option named Goto that contains these options: Lunch and Home. When you select one or the other (or both), Word could monitor the internal clock and beep when it's time to leave work.

Suppose you work at a medical center and you design a document that asks for—with a series of dialog box controls—personal medical history information so you can print a comprehensive medical report for patient files. Instead of typing each patient's information inside a master document, you can more easily, quickly, and accurately use VBA dialog boxes to gather the information so that your VBA instructions can consolidate the information and print the report.

A VBA Programming Overview

The bottom line is that when you write a VBA routine, you give VBA a set of instructions that Word will follow. This set of instructions has many names:

- Module
- Procedure
- Program
- Code
- Routine

Word speaks the language of VBA which, sadly, is not exactly the same language we humans speak. Visual Basic for Applications is a set of specific commands and built-in macro-like procedures. You must learn these commands before you can write any VBA code. Although the commands are often familiar words (such as If and For), some VBA commands can be cryptic, such as this line from a VBA program:

```
Case Is > 8 And Number < 11
```

VBA programs might consist of one line or several hundred lines, depending on your requirements. Once you write the VBA program, you'll store the program in a disk file. Word does not automatically perform the instructions in a VBA program until you execute or run the VBA program. As with macros, you can run a VBA program from a menu command, a toolbar button, a shortcut keystroke, or you can execute the program by the name under which you stored the program on the disk.

When you write a VBA program, you have truly moved from an applications user to a full-fledged computer programmer, but you take on all the responsibilities that power totes along. Programs rarely work correctly the first time (or even the fifth or sixth!). Programming requires that you constantly test and review your code for mistakes. Program mistakes are called *bugs* by computer professionals. Programmers call getting rid of the bugs *debugging* and sometimes debugging is difficult; although you know there's a bug somewhere in your VBA code, that bug might be hard to find.

As stated earlier, VBA works behind the scenes and does not directly appear with your document's text. VBA works on document text manipulating words and phrases as your VBA program directs, but you must store the VBA program's text somewhere other than in the document window. Therefore, to write VBA programs, you must master yet another text-editing environment called the VBA editor. Figure 26.1 shows a sample Word session with an open VBA editor window. As you can see, you will create VBA programs in a window that is separate from Word's editing window. The editing window looks fairly complicated, but as with most Office 97 products, you can customize the window to make the window easier to work with. The editor receives your VBA commands and Word honors the instructions inside the editor when you execute the program.

Figure 26.1

Writing a VBA program requires the use of the program editor.

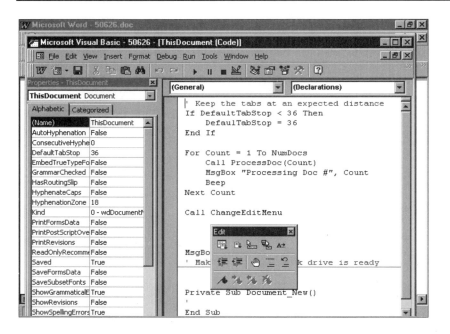

Throughout the rest of this chapter you will learn more about VBA concepts and learn the specifics of some of the VBA language and how to use the VBA editor. Although this chapter only gives you a high-level VBA overview, computer programming will be far less mysterious than perhaps it is now by the time you complete this chapter.

Why Replace WordBasic?

Advanced Word users might wonder why, now that they've mastered WordBasic, they must convert their thinking to Visual Basic for Applications. Although Visual Basic for Applications is similar to WordBasic, major differences do exist and WordBasic programmers will have to change to VBA if they want to automate their Word tasks past the power that macros alone can provide.

NOTE. *This chapter does not assume you already know WordBasic. Nevertheless, many current Word users have worked some in WordBasic and this section explains what's now in store if you've already taken the time to learn WordBasic.*

Before describing some of the fundamental differences between the two languages, you should understand why Microsoft chose to replace WordBasic with VBA. As the next section explains, all of the Office 97 products include VBA, whereas WordBasic existed solely for Microsoft Word. Therefore, you would have to learn the WordBasic programming language even if you already knew other Basic programming language dialects.

Basic programming language dialects have been around since the 1960s. Originally named BASIC (note the uppercase letters), Dartmouth College professors developed the language for students who needed a simpler language from the more rigid programming languages of the day. The name BASIC was an acronym for Beginner's All-Purpose Symbolic Instruction Code. Through the years, software developers have made major changes to BASIC, but the language still retains many of its original keywords (commands and built-in supplied routines) and the original BASIC's simple nature. Microsoft has been the major reason the language survived the language shakeout of the early 1980s. When others thought BASIC's life was over, Microsoft's developers breathed new life into BASIC when they designed Visual Basic, the parent of VBA.

WordBasic and VBA: A Comparison

This section briefly describes specific differences between WordBasic and VBA. If you are unfamiliar with WordBasic, this section will seem fairly advanced. By reading this section's language comparison, however advanced it may appear, you'll more quickly master VBA concepts. Later sections will discuss these concepts in more detail.

The WordBasic language consists of a set of data items, commands, and built-in routines (called functions). You would combine these data items, commands, and routines into a programmed set of instructions. For example, you might write a series of three WordBasic code lines that change the selected text to underlined, boldfaced, italicized, text like this:

```
Underline 1
Bold 1
Italic 1
```

Instructions such as these are not linked to any particular Word element. Although VBA also follows a programmed instruction format, one approaches the VBA language from the modern-day object-oriented programming (often called OOP) perspective. Instead of concentrating so much on a series of commands, as you would do with a WordBasic program, you concentrate on VBA objects. Objects are the primary data elements in your Word document.

OOP-based programming focuses on data and not on commands. When you learn VBA, you will learn a lot about Word's available objects and what you can do with those objects. Here is a partial list of some of Word's objects:

```
Application
Dictionaries
Document
MailingLabel
Selection
SynonymInfo
```

When you want to work with an object, such as make a change to an object's formatting, you'll need to learn which properties that object supports. A property describes an attribute (such as whether the object is selected or underlined). Many property values are either True or False; if a Word object is underlined, its Underline property will be True and if that object is not underlined, the object's Underline property will be False. Other property values can take on one of several attributes such as a color code value that represents a particular color.

In VBA, you can turn on the selected text's properties to make the selected text underlined, boldfaced, and italicized with these instructions:

```
Selection.Font.Underline = True
Selection.Font.Bold = True
Selection.Font.Italic = True
```

The equal sign performs an assignment and assigns the property value on the right to the property (the selected text's font) on the left. You will learn more about such assignments later in the section named "Data and Variables."

NOTE. *Most VBA programs consist of far more than three lines.*

TIP. *Search Word's online help for the topic entitled, "Visual Basic Equivalents for WordBasic Commands." As Figure 26.2 shows, the online help provides a statement-by-statement comparison between the two languages that will prove invaluable to those who already know WordBasic.*

Figure 26.2

Word's online help
moves you from
WordBasic to VBA.

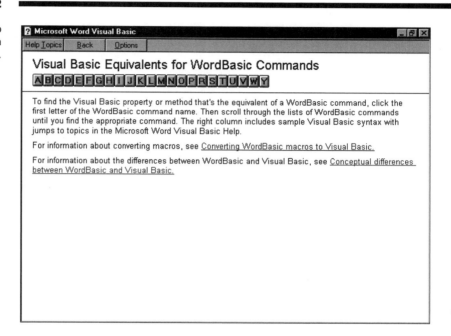

As you are beginning to see, the end-result of WordBasic and VBA programs is often the same for both languages but the approach each uses is different. Whereas much of a WordBasic program consists of commands, much of an equivalent VBA program consists of property assignments.

The VBA language does support active commands, similar to WordBasic's commands. When you must apply a command to a specific object, however (as opposed to controlling the program's flow), you'll usually use a method. The VBA objects each support a unique set of methods which are commands you apply only to those objects and not to all data in general.

Perhaps the most tedious part of learning VBA is not learning how to program but learning all the available Word objects along with their unique sets of properties and methods. Fortunately, you will not have to memorize all the properties and methods that go with all the objects. Most of the time, you'll work with only a small subset of the objects, properties, and methods and the more common ones—such as the underlining, italicizing, and boldfacing properties you saw here—will be obvious and available when you need them.

TIP. *If you are not sure what a property or method is called, you can search the online help. If you still cannot locate exactly what you're searching for, record a simple keystroke macro that works with the object you want to work with. View the macro's code (using the techniques you will learn in the next section) and the chances are great that you'll see the property or method you need to apply to the object in your VBA program.*

The actions you want to perform on Word objects almost always translate into properties and methods. As you saw earlier in this section, the name of the current text selection text's object is Selection, its italic property is named Italic, and so on. If you request help for the object with which you want to work, the online help displays hyperlinks to properties and methods defined for that object. Figure 26.3 shows the Property window that appears when you click on the Selection object's Property hyperlink.

Figure 26.3

Hyperlinks can display
lists of properties
and methods for
all VBA objects.

**Click here to display the
Properties window**

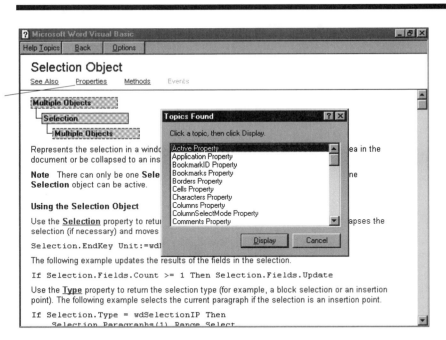

Word automatically converts your old WordBasic modules to equivalent VBA modules. You'll learn more about Word's conversion later in a section entitled, "VBA Support for Existing WordBasic Macros."

One Language for All Office Applications

In one respect, VBA acts like a global macro language across all the Office 97 applications. When you learn VBA for Word, you also know VBA for Access, Excel, and PowerPoint. In addition, VBA is completely compatible with Visual Basic 5, a Windows programming language not directly tied to the Office 97 applications. If you learn VBA, you'll then be able to write your own programs with Visual Basic 5 that can perform any computer work you need done such as balancing your checkbook or playing games.

Although macros automate common keyboard-based tasks and can perform routine and generic edits and groups of commands, a macro cannot process data as well as a programming language such as VBA can. VBA programs can analyze multiple documents, make intelligent changes and edits, print selected items based on criteria, merge information between applications, and interact with the user by displaying dialog boxes and receiving the values the user enters into the dialog box.

Word's VBA procedures can communicate with Excel's VBA procedures as well as all the rest of the Office 97 suite of products. You can tie VBA code into Visual Basic 5 programs also. In addition, you can even interact with the Internet by utilizing advanced Web browser controls and utilities.

TIP. *Once you master VBA, you will not only be able to add advanced automation to Word, but you will be able to add Word automation to other applications as well! For example, if you write a Visual Basic 5 program that needs to use spell-checking, you will be able to borrow (through VBA code) Word's spell-checking objects so you don't have to write one line of spell-checking code except for the trivial code that pulls Word's spell-checking objects into your application. Such object use is called automation.*

VBA does not replace macro programming. You will still use macros. As a matter of fact, you'll often begin a VBA program by first creating a macro that performs a similar (but simpler) operation. You then can modify and add to the macro's code with the VBA editor.

VBA Support for Existing WordBasic Macros

If you've written macros in Word 6 or Word 95, Office 97's Word will convert your macros to Word's new format and everything should work as you expect. Word converts your old macros to VBA program modules. If the macro contains WordBasic code, Word converts the WordBasic code to equivalent VBA code.

When you open a Word 6 or Word 95 template, create a new document based on the older template, or attach the template to a document, Word converts the macros in the template to VBA modules.

TIP. *Be sure to save the converted template so that Word will not have to convert the template once again the next time you open the template.*

WARNING! *Macros can contain viruses that affect your system. Word helps protect you from macro-based viruses. Figure 26.4 shows the dialog box that Word displays when you open a document that contains a macro. Click Enable Macros if you trust the document's source. If you are unsure about a document, click Disable Macros and look at the macro code before enabling the macros the next time you open the document. If you want to know more about possible virus infection through macros, click the Tell Me More button. If you always open documents from reliable sources, click the dialog box's checkbox option so Word does not display the dialog box in the future.*

Figure 26.4

Word can protect you from possible macro viruses.

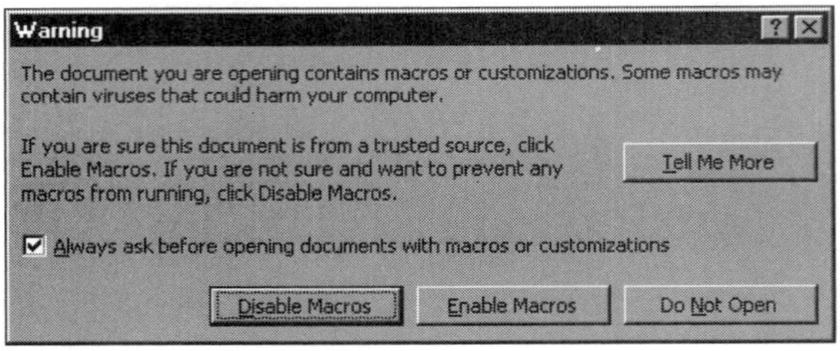

■ Modifying a Simple Recorded Macro

Word's macro editing tools makes editing your recorded macros simple. To get you started thinking in VBA terms, the next two sections describe how you can edit macro code. You'll learn more about VBA's macro editor throughout the rest of this chapter, but these sections will get you started.

Where Are Macros Stored?

With the inclusion of VBA, Word does not distinguish as clearly between macros and VBA code as previous versions of Word did with macros and WordBasic. Although previous versions did treat macro code as if it was a program you entered (instead of recording a list of your keystrokes, the most common macro-generating method), the distinction was not as clear as the VBA-based Word that comes with Office 97.

To work with a macro's VBA code, you need to understand that you access the macro only from within the VBA editor. Use the Macros option on the Tools menu bar to view and edit the macro's code. When you select the macro to edit (as explained in the next section), VBA automatically opens the editing window and displays the macro.

Macros are stored in Word modules. Remember that module is another name for program; module better suits the nature of VBA macros that are generally smaller routines than stand-alone programs that you might create with Visual Basic. The module code stays with its Word template but you'll always edit the module in the VBA editing window.

NOTE. *As you can see, the distinction between macros and VBA code is blurry. Basically, the only difference is the way you create them. You create macros from the keyboard (as you learned in the previous chapter) and those macros become small VBA modules. Instead of creating the initial module via the macro-style method of recording keystrokes, you can create a VBA program from scratch from within the VBA editing window.*

Learning from Your Recorded Macros

If you were comfortable writing and editing macros in Word 6 or Word 95, you will learn VBA quickly by studying the code contained in the converted macros.

To see the macro code, select Tools, Macro, Macro (the shortcut key is Alt-F8). All the converted macro names end with .MAIN so the entry named NumListFirst.MAIN refers to the macro named NumListFirst. Figure 26.5 shows the Macro dialog box with some newly converted macros.

Figure 26.5

Macros converted to VBA module code

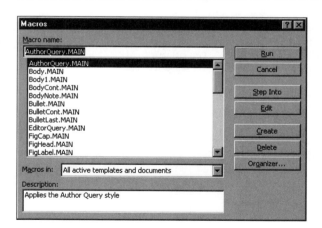

Highlight the macro and click the Edit command button to view the macro's converted code inside the VBA editing window.

Implementation Differences

Although macros and VBA code now use the same VBA language, the macro recorder often includes extra and unneeded material in the macro's module that you do not need. These extras often come in the form of redundant modifiers which describe an object in more detail than is necessary for the task at hand. If you use recorded keystroke macro modules within larger VBA modules (you can nest code modules and execute each one as needed), you might want to streamline the code by removing some of the unnecessary clutter. In doing so you will make the entire module more readable and more maintainable later.

In addition to redundancy, macros often refer to specific objects, such as a named bookmark within the macro's original document. The VBA code attempts to keep references more general so the program code still might work even if the document's attributes change.

NOTE. *Program maintenance costs programming departments much more in time and labor and machine costs than writing the program to begin with. A program gets written only once but programmers must constantly update the code to meet the needs of a changing business environment. Therefore, once a program is written for one specific purpose, people will have to modify (maintain) the program throughout the program's life so that the program stays current. The more you document your programs and the clearer your code is (as well as the code you borrow from recorded macros), the quicker someone will be able to find what needs changing and change the program. Therefore, clear code is worth a lot and you should strive to write and maintain clear, concise, well-documented code. VBA code is, by its OOP nature, clearer than WordBasic.*

Although this chapter is only intended to give you an overview of VBA's programming requirements, keep these guidelines in mind as you work with macros and integrate recorded macros into larger VBA modules:

- If a macro refers to a specific named bookmark or file name, write VBA testing code that checks to see if that bookmark or file name exists before performing the macro on that object. If you do not check for the existence of a named object, VBA will issue a nasty error message in the middle of the user's Word editing session if the object no longer exists. (The error will not shut down Word; the user's document will still be intact, but your reputation will not be.)

- Macros often use a specific reference to the selected object (labeled with the keyword Selection). To make the macro's code more general purpose, you should convert the Selection reference to a Range object. A Range object is simply a VBA definition of the currently selected object in the document, whether that object is a character, word, sentence, paragraph, or the entire document.

- Use VBA's With...End With command set to eliminate modifier redundancy. Whereas a macro's generated code might refer to the same object in 20 successive lines of code, you can eliminate every reference by pulling out the name into the With...End With statement.

Recorded macros are notorious for recording every option inside a dialog box selection even if you only need to set one or a few options. For example, Listing 26.1 contains a recorded macro where the user selected a word and then changed the word to all capital letters (using the Selection object's AllCaps property). Nether you nor your program needs to know all the other dialog box entries at the time the user closed the dialog box but the recorded macro saved every dialog box anyway. Listing 26.2 contains the same code after the programmer chiseled away at the excess and redundant qualifying properties and left only the AllCaps property setting in the module (the opening and closing code, called the wrapper lines, still must appear at the top and bottom of the code to keep the macro a valid VBA module). As you can see, you can include only as much information with a With...End command set as your current needs require.

Listing 26.1

Recorded macros record
far too much dialog
box information.

```
Sub MyFirstMacro()
'
' MyFirstMacro Macro
' Macro recorded 10/16/97 by Judy Lark
'
    Selection.MoveUp Unit:=wdLine, Count:=1
    Selection.MoveRight Unit:=wdCharacter, Count:=4, Extend:=wdExtend
    With Selection.Font
        .Name = "Courier New"
        .Size = 12
        .Bold = False
        .Italic = False
        .Underline = wdUnderlineNone
        .StrikeThrough = False
        .DoubleStrikeThrough = False
        .Outline = False
        .Emboss = False
        .Shadow = False
        .Hidden = False
        .SmallCaps = False
        .AllCaps = True
        .ColorIndex = wdAuto
        .Engrave = False
        .Superscript = False
        .Subscript = False
        .Spacing = 0
        .Scaling = 100
        .Position = 0
        .Kerning = 0
```

Listing 26.1 (Continued)

Recorded macros record far too much dialog box information.

```
            .Animation = wdAnimationNone
        End With
End Sub
```

Listing 26.2

You can shrink dialog box code to eliminate redundant macro code that you will find.

```
Sub MyFirstMacro()
'
' MyFirstMacro Macro
' Macro recorded 10/16/97 by Judy Lark
'
    Selection.MoveUp Unit:=wdLine, Count:=1
    Selection.MoveRight Unit:=wdCharacter, Count:=4, Extend:=wdExtend
    With Selection.Font
    .AllCaps = True
    End With
End Sub
```

WARNING! *I warned you earlier that VBA code can look cryptic! Concentrate on the fundamental and conceptual differences between VBA and recorded macro code for now.*

■ Understanding VBA's New Editing Environment

Remember that you'll be creating VBA program code, whether you create a macro by recording keystrokes, converting a previous Word version's macros to VBA, or creating VBA routines from scratch. All your VBA work will appear inside the VBA editor so you must understand how to use the VBA editor to program Word effectively.

WARNING! *The VBA editor contains several windows and new sets of commands, scroll bars, and scrolling lists. Don't expect to master the editor right away. Most of the time, you'll use only a fraction of the editor's features. Typically, your VBA work will not demand a lot from the VBA editor.*

The Visual Basic for Applications Editor

To start the VBA editor, select Tools, Macros, Visual Basic Editor from Word's menu bar. Figure 26.6 shows the VBA editor and labels each of the VBA windows.

NOTE. *Programmers use the terms editor and editing window interchangeably.*

Table 26.1 describes the editor's most common and useful windows and elements that you see in Figure 26.6:

Figure 26.6

The Visual Basic for Applications editing window

Menu bar

Tool bar

Properties window

Editing window

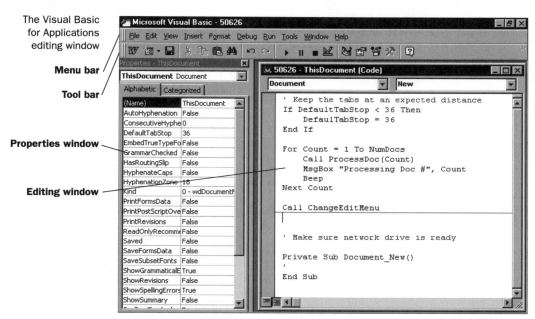

Table 26.1

Useful VBA editor elements

ELEMENT	DESCRIPTION
Menu bar	A Word-like menu bar with options that let you open, save, print, test, modify, and execute the VBA programs you write.
Toolbar	Contains a list of tools that give you one button push to common commands and menu tasks. The next section explains each of the toolbar's buttons.
Properties window	Supplies you with a list of all the properties you can assign to various objects within your program.
Code window	Gives you a place in which you can enter and edit your VBA code. The code never appears inside the document on which the VBA program is running but rather inside the VBA editor's code window. When you change the list of instructions in the code window, you change the VBA program itself. If your VBA program needs debugging, you will perform the debugging here in the code window.
Status bar	Constantly updates to issue warnings and messages that relate to your editing session.

As with virtually all windows, you can move, resize, open, and close the editor's windows as you need to. Due to the fact that the VBA editor's screen gets cluttered in a hurry, you will often take advantage of the editor's ability to hide and minimize many of its various windows. During a debugging session, for example, you could have as many as six or seven windows on your screen, not including Word's document window that resides elsewhere (to which you can switch to with Alt-Tab).

WARNING! *You'll run across several other VBA windows as you learn more about the environment. For example, VBA contains windows that help you find bugs in complicated VBA code.*

Although the VBA editor is powerful enough to warrant its own book, here are a few guidelines to get you started within the editor.

Most of your VBA work will occur inside the code window. You might want to increase the size of the code window to give you more room in which to work. The VBA code window is similar to a word processor in that you can insert, delete, cut, and paste. The most notable absence is the automatic word wrap feature. Each instruction in your VBA module must end with the Enter keypress because paragraphs do not exist in a VBA program.

The code window supports color-coded syntax highlighting. Although the name might sound foreboding, color-coded syntax highlighting automatically colors different parts of your program so you'll know at a glance whether you are viewing a command, object, or program remark. Just as a spoken language has different parts of speech, a programming language does also. The color-coding of the language syntax (syntax refers to a language's spelling and grammar) many times gives you instant feedback that you've typed something incorrectly. (You can turn off the color-coded syntax highlighting from within the Tools, Options dialog boxes.)

The Properties window contains a list of document properties that are currently in effect. You can modify the properties as you wish by clicking on their value and selecting or entering a new value. Your program can also change document properties but those changes do not occur until your program runs. The code window's instructions are stored instructions, just as a recorded macro's instructions are stored, and those instructions do not execute until the program is triggered via a menu option, toolbar button, keystroke, timer, or other user event that you've designated to run the program.

As you work within the editor entering and editing code, VBA keeps a sharp watch for any problems you might cause. Not only will the color-coding sometimes aid your debugging search (when a command that you type stays the same color as an object, you know right away that you misspelled the command) but the editor contains a pre-execution debugger that warns you of serious syntax errors by displaying a dialog box such as the one in Figure 26.7. You can get additional help with the error by clicking Help or you can click OK and correct the offender.

Figure 26.7

VBA lets you know if
you've made an error.

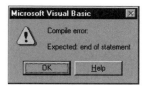

The constant error dialog boxes can be extremely helpful or they can be a headache. In some instances, you might be planning a program by scattering a few commands and remarks here and there to organize your thoughts and outline the code. If you don't type the code exactly as VBA expects (VBA does not tolerate ambiguity), the constant error dialog boxes will get in your way. Once VBA issues a dialog box for an error, when you click OK to close the dialog box you don't have to fix the error right away; VBA will not bother you with that same error a second time unless you make the mistake elsewhere. Nevertheless, during such brainstorming programming sessions, consider turning off the automatic syntax checking option at the top of the Tools, Options dialog box shown in Figure 26.8.

Figure 26.8

You can control the
automatic syntax
checking.

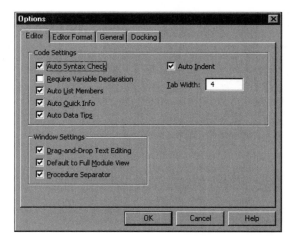

The Visual Basic Toolbar

As with the other Office 97 products, you'll come to rely on the VBA editor's toolbar to perform may of your common tasks. When you first open the editor, you'll see the Standard toolbar shown in Figure 26.9.

Figure 26.9

The Standard toolbar contains useful buttons.

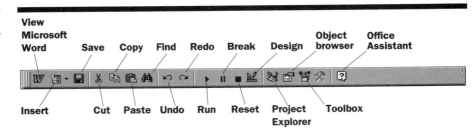

The Standard toolbar contains the most useful and common buttons that you will need as a VBA programmer. Table 26.2 describes the Standard toolbar buttons.

Table 26.2

The Standard toolbar buttons

STANDARD TOOLBAR BUTTON	DESCRIPTION
View Microsoft Word	Switches from the VBA editing window to your document window. You can press Alt-Tab to switch back to the editor.
Insert	Inserts a new user form (a user form is a window or dialog box you want to display in the document), module (a secondary program you want to use in conjunction with the editor's current code), a class module (a special kind of module that defines new objects), and an additional procedure that you want to add to the current program.
Save	Saves the code to the disk.
Cut, Copy, Paste, Find	Provides the equivalent Word clipboard and search functions.
Undo, Redo	Corrects any mistakes you make during the editing session.
Run	Executes the program currently displayed in the editor.
Break	Halts the executing program so you can examine the memory or the program's effect on the current document contents.
Reset	Returns the halted program to its pre-executed state by clearing all program memory locations.
Design Mode	Turns on the design view so you can modify the design of a dialog box or form.
Project Explorer	Displays Figure 26.10's Project Explorer window from which you can see a hierarchical list of the current project (the collection of all the code, user forms, and objects).
Properties window	Displays the Properties window showing all the properties of any selected object.

Table 26.2 (Continued)

The Standard toolbar buttons

STANDARD TOOLBAR BUTTON	DESCRIPTION
Object Browser	Displays Figure 26.11's Object Browser window from where you can analyze every available object (over 500 of them exist in Word alone) and its properties and methods.
Toolbox	Displays the Toolbox window that contains all the tools such as command buttons and non-Word Office 97 objects into your VBA code. The next section entitled, "The Visual Basic Control Toolbox," describes the toolbox's tools.
Office Assistant	Displays the Office Assistant online help from within the VBA editor.

Figure 26.10

The Project window gives you one-stop access to the entire VBA application.

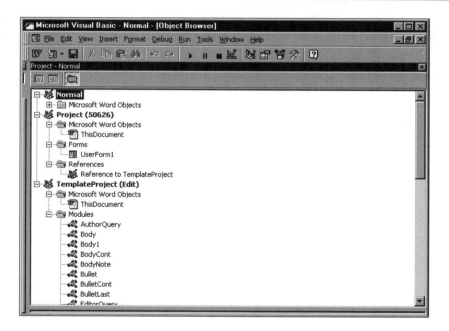

By supporting the project concept, VBA lets you edit multiple modules at once. You can also import and export project modules from and to other application sources. The Project window lets you manage all those products from a central location. Despite this power, you will often work with only a single module inside a project unless you create large-scale automation applications with VBA.

Figure 26.11

The Object Browser
window lists every
available object.

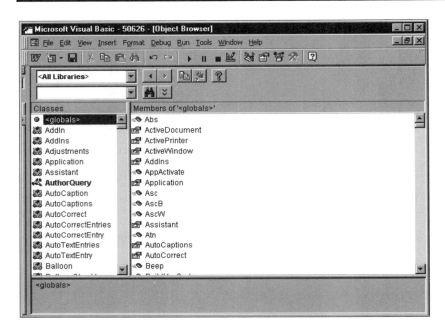

In addition to using the Office Assistant for help within the editor, your VBA programs can manipulate the Office Assistant so that whoever uses your program will see an animated Office Assistant behaving in the way you programmed the assistant to behave. For example, you might want to write a VBA program that presents several new help topics that describe a dialog box the user will see and fill in. Instead of using pop-up message boxes or adding your own online help, you can program the Office Assistant to describe the dialog box for the user.

Besides the Standard toolbar, you can also display the other helpful toolbars described in Table 26.3. Display or hide the toolbars by selecting View, Toolbars and choosing the appropriate toolbar.

Table 26.3

Other VBA editor toolbars

TOOLBAR NAME	DESCRIPTION
Debug	Provides commands you'll need while debugging your VBA code.
Edit	Gives you helpful tools that come in handy during advanced editing sessions.
UserForm	Displays the toolbar that contains numerous commands for working on user forms such as dialog boxes.

TIP. *Each of VBA's toolbars are dockable, meaning you can drag the toolbar to any screen location you want or dock the toolbars to their usual position beneath the menu bar. As Figure 26.12 shows, you can display all the toolbars at once although if you hide the ones you don't currently need, you will gain screen real estate that you can use for the program editor.*

Figure 26.12

All four toolbars can rest on the VBA screen at once.

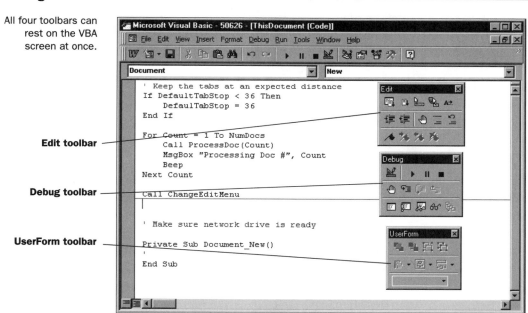

The Visual Basic Control Toolbox

As you work with VBA and begin developing applications that support Word behind the scenes and that contain advanced user forms such as dialog boxes, you'll need a toolbox of the tools that you can place on the forms. VBA's tools generally consist of controls such as command buttons, drop-down listboxes, and labels. Therefore, when you need a label, you will only have to drag a label from the toolbox window (shown in Figure 26.13) and place the tool on the form.

Although the goal of this chapter is not to teach you how to build dialog boxes (complete books on dialog box creation and design could be written), you should take a few moments to familiarize yourself with the toolbox tools. By learning about the tools, you will understand more about the pieces of dialog boxes.

Figure 26.13

The toolbox window offers tools for you to use.

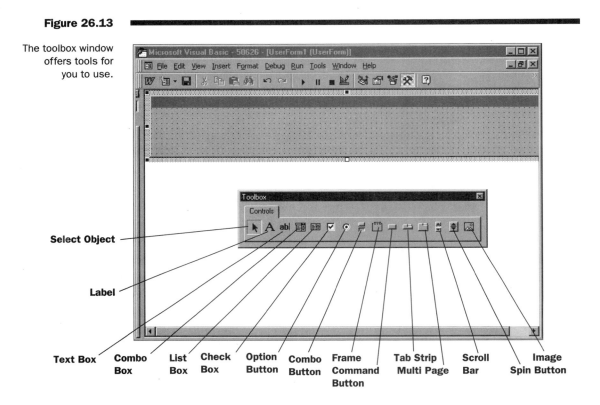

WARNING! *You cannot dock the Toolbox window to the toolbar. The Toolbox window always floats on top of the VBA screen as a detached window. You can move and resize the Toolbox window.*

Table 26.4 describes the toolbar buttons and explains the kinds of tools held there. Most of the tools become objects that have properties and methods just as the Word objects do. For example, the Label tool produces labels on your form that has font, color, and size properties that describe the label and uniquely separates one form label from other label objects on the form.

As you gain programming skills you will learn about ActiveX controls and might want to use them in your VBA code. VBA lets you insert ActiveX tools into your VBA Toolbox window. An ActiveX control is a cross-language control that you can use in the VBA toolbox after you insert the ActiveX control into the Toolbox window. Previous versions of Visual Basic supported a control named VBX or Visual Basic Controls and VBA supports those controls as well. Once you add a control to the Toolbox (with the Tools, Additional Controls option), you work with that control just as you work with the other controls that come with VBA.

Table 26.4

The Toolbox tools provide useful controls for dialog boxes on your VBA program forms.

TOOLBOX TOOL NAME	DESCRIPTION
Select Objects	Lets you click on form objects, such as labels and other tools, to select the object for copying, cutting, or editing. You can hold the Ctrl key while clicking on objects to select more than one object at once. (The Select Objects control is the only Toolbox window control that does not appear on the final user form.)
Label	Sends non-editable text to the form for titles and descriptions.
Text Box	Produces a boxed editing area in which your users can enter data such as names, addresses, and dollar amounts.
Combo Box	A combination list box and text box control that lets the user select values from the list or enter new values. You must initialize the initial combo box values from within your VBA module and those values do not appear on the user form until the code executes.
List Box	Provides a list of values from which the user can select. As with the combo box control, you must initialize the list box at runtime.
Check Box	Provides options that the user can click to select one or more true (if checked) or false (if unchecked) conditions.
Option Button	Provides options that the user can click to select one and only one true or false condition. Only one option button can be selected at one time. VBA will automatically deselect the currently selected option at runtime when the user selects a different option button.
Toggle Button	Gives the user an on or off condition that changes when the user clicks the toggle button. For example, you might specify a toggle button to turn on the calculation of tax but the user can click the toggle button to change to a tax-free sale.
Frame	Collects, holds, and displays groups of other controls. If you want to provide two or more sets of option buttons on a single form, VBA lets you do so as long as each appears in its own frame.
Command Button	Gives the user a button to select choices and trigger actions.
Tab Strip	Defines multiple dialog box pages (often called property sheets) for an area of the form.
Multi Page	Defines multiple dialog box screens as a single group.
Scroll Bar	Inserts either a horizontal or vertical scroll bar on your user form. The scroll bar's property values determine its orientation and scrolling distance.

Table 26.4 (Continued)

The Toolbox tools provide useful controls for dialog boxes on your VBA program forms.

TOOLBOX TOOL NAME	DESCRIPTION
Spin Button	Lets the user click an up or down arrow to increase or decrease a particular value (such as a text box that might hold a color or hue value that the user can control by clicking the spin button's arrows).
Image	Displays a graphic image on the form. Your VBA module's code can change the displayed image when the program executes.

NOTE. *You will hear a lot about ActiveX in the future as products begin to support it. A company can supply an ActiveX control that does about anything, including mimic worksheets, draw advanced 3-D graphics, and access database information. Once you insert that ActiveX control into your Toolbox window, VBA displays the ActiveX control along with the standard Toolbox window controls. Drag whatever control you want to use into your application's user form.*

Visual Basic Design Mode

The design mode is the opposite of run mode. When you create and edit a program—along with its user forms such as dialog boxes—you do so from the design mode. When you (or a user) eventually triggers the execution of the code, the program enters the run mode. During the design mode, you do the following:

- Write and edit VBA code

- Design and name the data holders (the controls and variables that you will learn about later in this chapter)

- Create the user forms

- Assign initial property values to the program's controls

- Specify the order of procedure execution if your code module contains multiple procedures

- Specify the object methods that the code will use when the program executes

During run mode, Word follows the code's instructions, displays the user forms, and returns to the document when the program ends. Some properties can only be changed or assigned during runtime. In addition, the user's responses to the program's execution often directs the order of execution and determines the property values of certain controls.

NOTE. *When you create a form, the form might appear inside grid lines, with sizing handles around the selected controls, and with some controls not yet initialized as you see in Figure 26.14's UserForm window.*

Figure 26.14

In design mode, the form appears on a grid.

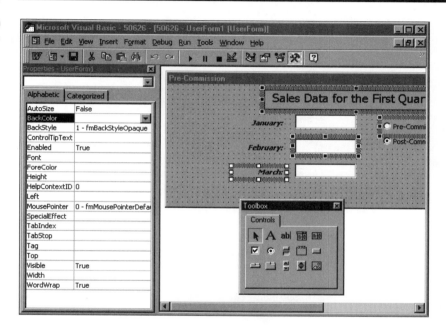

■ Fundamental VBA Programming Concepts

The following sections introduce you to specific VBA language commands and supplied routines. In addition to the object properties and methods, you must have a way of controlling the runtime code sequence and you must be able to repeat a section of code automatically when the program needs repetition.

Much of a VBA module consists of data definitions. You will have to assign property values and define temporary storage areas for intermediate values that you don't want to send to controls right away. Although you cannot become a programming expert in only a few overview pages of the VBA language, you will have a good grasp of the skill set you'll require as a VBA programmer by the time you finish the rest of this chapter.

VBA Statement Syntax

VBA's language syntax determines the kind of instruction you are issuing in the code. Before you can understand how to control a program, you must understand how to define and initialize data values.

Although learning VBA is not as difficult as learning a foreign language, one of your most common errors, especially when you first begin VBA programming, will result from a syntax error. VBA refuses to execute your program instructions until you eliminate all the program's syntax errors. Once you eliminate the syntax errors, VBA will execute the instructions. During the execution, you may still see program bugs. Runtime bugs occur when you've told VBA to do the wrong thing (such as print negative check amounts) or something that's impossible (such as divide by zero).

TIP. *The AutoStatement Builder helps reduce the number of syntax errors by displaying the format of VBA statements after you begin typing the first few characters. Just as Word's AutoText entries complete text that you begin typing, VBA's AutoStatement Builder kicks in, as shown in Figure 26.15, when you begin typing VBA statements and built-in routines. The AutoStatement Builder displays a pop-up syntax description of the command so you don't have to memorize long lists of exact statement and built-in routine formats.*

Figure 26.15

The AutoStatement Builder displays pop-up help when you begin typing VBA commands.

The AutoStatement Builder's help

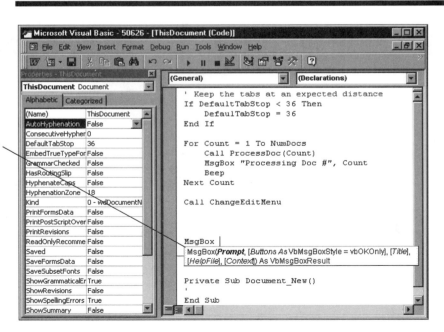

Data and Variables

Although controls hold data (their property values), you must be able to define data holding areas, called variables, that store intermediate program data that you are calculating before assigning that data to an object's property. Variables can hold all kinds of VBA data and you'll often assign variables to property values. You can also assign a property value to a variable for storage of the property value. For example, you can store, in variables, a true or false value that indicates which of the form's option buttons the user selected last, or a value such as an age value entered by the user in a dialog box that you displayed previously in the program.

WARNING! *Variables are active (hold data) only at runtime and they lose their values as soon as your program ends. Unlike data on your disk, the data in variables goes away when the variable's visibility (such as the program termination) ends. Some like to think of variables as working storage areas where you can store intermediate and temporary values during a program's execution.*

To store data in variables, you must learn VBA's data types. Table 26.5 describes each data type. Their distinction is important because you often cannot mix data types; for example, you could not want to store words in a variable defined to hold only numbers.

Table 26.5

VBA's data types

DATA TYPE NAME	DESCRIPTION
Boolean	Two possible values: True or False.
Currency	Money values with two decimal places. Formats the data according to your Windows international settings.
Date	Dates from January 1, 0100 to December 31, 9999.
Double	Extremely large or extremely small decimal values from approximately -1 followed by 308 decimal places to +1 followed by 308 decimal places.
Integer	Whole numbers (numbers without decimals) from -32,768 to +32,767.
Long	Extremely large or extremely small whole numbers.
Object	Any Word (or other application's) VBA object.
Single	Decimal values from approximately -3 followed by 38 decimal places to +3 followed by 38 decimal places.
String	From 1 to approximately 64,000 characters, including alphabetic, numeric, and special characters.
Variant	A generic data type that can take on any of the other type forms.

The data type you use depends on the data your program must work with. For example, you would use a string data type to hold names and addresses and you would use an integer data type to hold people's ages.

WARNING! *Although you can use a long integer data type to store an age value, doing so would waste memory and make your program less efficient. Therefore, when you have the opportunity to choose a data type, pick the smallest data type (integer, long, single, or double) that will represent the data values that you need represented.*

When your program deals with constants (values that do not change) you will not usually have to worry about the constant's data type. For example, if you multiply a value by 10, you will just type the 10 in your program and not worry about its data type. However, if you work with control properties, objects, and the named storage areas called variables, you will have to stay aware and use correct and consistent data types.

NOTE. *Often, but not always, you can mix data types. For example, you could add a long integer data value to a regular integer or multiple a single decimal value by a long or regular integer. You must, however, be sure that you store the result somewhere that holds the largest data type in the calculation or overflow might occur and you could lose data.*

The most important thing to learn about a new programming language is its data types and variable declarations. When you declare a variable, you inform VBA that you will need the variable and you assign a name and data type to the variable. Once you declare the variable, VBA makes it available for you to use throughout the rest of the module.

WARNING! *Depending on where you declare variables and the nature of your code, variables are not always available to your entire program after you declare the variables. You will learn more about variable scope (the range of the code that can recognize a declared variable) as you learn more about VBA. For now, concentrate on variable declarations and data types.*

Typically, VBA programmers use the Dim statement to declare variables. The following code declares three variables of three different data types:

```
Dim sName As String
Dim iAge As Integer
Dim fSize As Single
```

The variable name follows the Dim command. Notice that each variable name here begins with a letter indicating the variable's data type. Although you don't have to add the data type prefix character, doing so helps reduce confusion later in the program and you are then less likely to assign incorrect data types to the variables. The data type must follow the As keyword. (A keyword is a predefined command or routine.)

You can name a variable anything you wish as long as you follow these rules:

1. Names must begin with an alphabetic character.

2. Names can contain a mixture of letters and numbers. (You can mix uppercase and lowercase letters.)

3. Names cannot be a keyword.

4. You cannot give two different variables the same name.

NOTE. *When you learn more about data scope (which describes the life span of variables in a program), you'll learn that you can break rule number 4 in certain situations.*

Variable names can contain some special characters, such as the underscore, but you'll be better off using only letters and numbers if you don't want to inadvertently use a special character that VBA does not allow.

Once you declare variables, you can assign values in the variables with the assignment statement. The following statements assign values to the previous variables:

```
sName = "Judy Murdoch"      ' Remember the quotes
iAge = 37                   ' Tell the truth!
fSize = 6.533               ' What is this?
```

To assign a value to a variable, separate the variable from its value with an equal sign as done here. As you can see, you must enclose string constants in quotation marks. Notice the text to the right of the three statements that begin with the apostrophe. Each assignment statement has a remark following it. Remarks are optional and do not affect the program's execution at all. Scatter remarks throughout your code for notes that describe the program to the programmer (who may be you or someone else) who may need to maintain the program. A program without remarks is often difficult to follow.

In addition to constants, you can assign variables to variables as well. The following statement assigns three variables to three other variables (assume that all variables are already declared and that the variables on the right of the equal signs are initialized to values):

```
iVar1 = iOldValue1      ' Assigns 3 variables to 3 variables
iVar2 = iOleValue2
iVar3 = iOldValue4
```

Table 26.6 lists common math operators that you can use in variable assignments that require expressions.

Table 26.6

Common VBA math operators.

OPERATOR	MEANING
+	Addition
-	Subtraction
*	Multiplication
/	Division

Here are some example assignment statements that contain mathematical expressions:

```
sNetSales = sGrossSales - sTaxes
cBonusFactor = cPay * .13
iCount = iCount + 1   ' Adds one to the variable
dAvg = (dVal1 + dVal2 + dVal3 + dVal4) / 4.0
```

VBA uses a standard math hierarchy to evaluate expressions that contain multiple operators. VBA always performs multiplication and division in the left-to-right order that they appear in expressions. If addition or subtraction also appears, VBA finishes all multiplication and division before the addition and subtraction. You can override this default calculation order with parentheses as done on the last line in the previous code. Without the parentheses that force the addition calculation first, VBA would first divide dVal4 by 4.0 before adding any of the other results and this calculation order would not compute a true average.

WARNING! *If you declare a variable to be of type Object, you must precede the assignment statement with the Set keyword. Set only assigns values to object variables. You don't use Set if you assign properties directly to objects but only to variables you declare as objects.*

The assignment statement works for object properties as well as for variables. For example, you might create a user form named cashierForm (you can assign names to forms in the Properties window after you create the form). To add, with VBA code, a title to the form that will appear in the form's title bar, assign the form a caption like this:

```
cashierForm.Caption = "At The Register".
```

Caption is not a variable and neither is cashierForm. Caption is a property of the form you've named cashierForm and the new title will appear in the form's title bar as soon as the statement assigns the title during the run mode.

NOTE. *We've only scratched the surface! Now that you know about data and assignments, you are better prepared to understand the VBA programs you see and you can begin to write your own. I hope this introduction demonstrates that programming is not difficult.*

Control Structures

Your programs often make decisions based on data. For example, you might use a Word document for your company's corporate sales tax reports. The corporate sales tax is one of two values depending on whether or not your corporate client was a government agency or a private company. In other words, you can write VBA code that computes either one value or another value and prints the correct value at the bottom of the report.

Before learning the specifics of such a report, you need to master the conditional operators. Whereas the math operators manipulate and return numeric values, the conditional operators manipulate any kind of data and return Boolean results based on comparisons. Table 26.7 describes the conditional operators.

Table 26.7

VBA's conditional
operators

OPERATOR	EXAMPLE	DESCRIPTION
=	cTotal = cMax	Tests for equality
<	iAge < iLimit	Tests for less than
>	dTax > dIncome	Tests for greater than
<=	iCount <= 100	Tests for less than or equal to
>=	lBonus >= lFactor	Tests for greater than
<>	Selection.Text <> "Stop"	Tests for not equal to (inequality)

NOTE. *As with the math operators, you can use constants, variables, and object properties on either side of a conditional operator.*

Several VBA statements use conditional operators, but the one most common is the If statement. Here is the general format of If:

```
If conditional comparison Then
     One or more VBA statements
End If
```

Suppose you want to buzz the computer's speaker every time the daily receipts surpass $1,000. The Beep VBA statement sounds the speaker. The following code will beep if and only if the daily receipts (stored in a variable named cDailyReceipts) are more than $1,000:

```
If (cDailyReceipts > 1000.00) Then
     Beep    ' Ring the PC's speaker
End If
```

Nothing happens if the receipts are not yet $1,000. The If conditionally executes statements depending on the value of the conditional comparison. As you can see, the program makes a decision to execute a statement based on the contents of variables at runtime.

As many statements as you need can go between the If and the End If statements. The following code calculates net pay only if the record is taxable:

```
If (bTaxable = True) Then    ' Compute only if taxable
     cTaxes = sTaxRate * cGrossPay   ' 1st, compute taxes
     cMed = .03 * cGrossPay          ' 2nd, compute medical
     cNetPay = cGrossPay - cTaxes - cMed
End If
```

TIP. *As your programming skills improve, you will begin to notice shortcuts that make your VBA code more efficient. If, in the previous If statement, bTaxable is a Boolean variable—which it is—a Boolean variable can only hold one of two values, True or False. Therefore, you don't need to test for the equality to True; instead, you could rewrite the first line of the If statement like this:*

```
If (bTaxable) Then    ' An efficient If
```

Often, programmers use an optional addition to If called the Else block. Here is the format of the If-Else statement:

```
If conditional comparison Then
     One or more VBA statements
Else
     One or more VBA statements
End If
```

VBA executes the code between If and Else only if the conditional comparison equates to True. If the conditional comparison equates to False, VBA executes the statements between the Else and the End If. The following code expands on code you saw earlier:

```
If (cDailyReceipts > 1000.00) Then
     Beep    ' Ring the PC's speaker
Else
     lblWarning.Caption = "Get your sales up!"
End If
```

If the daily receipts are not yet $1,000 at the time of this code's execution, a label on the form named lblWarning displays the caption assigned to it in the Else portion.

One of the problems of attempting to review VBA at such a high level is that you cannot always see the big picture of how VBA code interacts with a Word document. Remember that the lead-in to this section described a Word sales tax report that prints the result of a sales tax based on a government or private section status. To prepare such a report, you would follow these general steps:

1. Create the Word document.

2. Insert a field that will hold that sales tax at the bottom of the report.

3. Name the field fldSalesTax.

4. Open the VBA editor and create a VBA module.

In the module, you'll write code that looks something like the following If statement.

```
If (iCorpStatus = 1) Then    ' Government entity
    fldSalesTax = sGovTaxRate * cSales
Else                         ' Private entity
    fldSalesTax = sPrivateTaxRate * cSales
End If
```

When the code executes, the sales tax will reflect the status of the corporate entity being computed.

TIP. *You can embed If statements within If statements, but if you need to perform a series of If-based decisions you might want to learn VBA's Select Case statement. Check the online help reference for details on Select Case.*

WARNING! *The previous list is an overview only. The code still needs some work, most notably the code needs to reside inside a procedure as you will learn about in the next section.*

Subroutines and Functions

As you now know, modules are the complete code-holders that go with Word documents and hold the VBA code you write. To organize your VBA code, you will break the code into procedures which are groups of VBA instructions that relate to do a job. VBA support two kinds of procedures: Function procedures and Sub procedures.

A Function procedure takes data that you optionally send to the function called arguments, performs work with the arguments that usually involve calculations, and returns a result based on the work done. Therefore, variables and controls are often assigned Function procedures just like you can assign routine data to variables and controls. The following statement assigns the variable named cGrandTotal the result returned from the function calcTotals:

```
cGrandTotal = calcTotals(cSales, cBonus, sRate)
```

The parentheses after the function name contain the arguments sent to the function that the code inside the function can work on. Whereas the other assignments you've seen in this chapter assign data directly to controls and variables, this statement actually pauses and runs all the code inside the function named calcTotals a chance to execute and return a result. The returned result goes ino cGrandTotal.

A Function procedure is distinguished by the opening and closing code that surrounds the procedure. Here is the format of all Function procedures:

```
Function procedureName(argument1, argument2, ...)
     One or more VBA statements go here
     procedureName = aValue
End Function
```

The following Function procedure returns the average of its arguments:

```
Function CalcAvg(A1 As Single, A2 As Single, A3 As Single) As Double
' Compute and return the 3-argument average
     CalcAvg (A1 + A2 + A3) / 3.0      ' Returns average
End Function
```

Notice that the Function procedure declares each incoming argument's data type. The As Double following the argument list declares the Function procedure's return data type. You must declare all incoming argument data types as well as the return data type when writing Function procedures or your code will not run.

Sub procedures are similar to Function procedures in that they are sections of related code but Sub procedures do not return values and are somewhat simpler to implement. Often, you'll write Sub procedures to organize your module's code into manageable units. Also, if you must execute the same series of statements from several places in your module, you can place that group of statements in a Sub procedure and then call the Sub procedure from wherever in the code you need the procedure's result. For example, if you print your company's name and address from several places in a module, consider putting the printing statements in a Sub procedure; when you get to a place in the module where you need to print the company's name and address, call the Sub procedure instead of duplicating the same code in more than one place in the module.

Here is the general format of a Sub procedure:

```
Sub procedureName(argument1, argument2, ...)
    One or more VBA statements go here
End Sub
```

No returning assignment is necessary because Sub procedures do not return values. The following Sub procedure computes the area of a circle given the passed radius argument and assigns area to a document field named fldArea:

```
Sub SubComputeArea(Radius As Single)
    Dim Area As Double' Declare local variable
    Area = (3.14159 * Radus * Radius    ' Area of circle
    fldArea = Area                      ' Display in field
End Sub
```

To execute a Sub procedure, use the Call statement from wherever in the module you need the Sub procedure's code like this:

```
Call SubComputeArea(25.0)    ' Calls Sub procedure
```

Flow Control

Unless you specify otherwise, VBA executes your instructions one at a time, from the first instruction in a procedure to the last. As you know, the If statement forces VBA to make a decision, and some statements may not execute depending on the results of the If's conditional result.

The procedures you learned about in the previous section also change the normal program flow; when VBA must execute a procedure, the current instruction that calls the procedure is put on hold until the procedure terminates.

Depending on your application, you may need to repeat certain sections of your VBA code. For example, you may need to ask the user for multiple values before you can properly fill out field values in a Word document. In addition, if you display a dialog box on the document and the user does not enter a required value, you'll need to repeat the code that displays the dialog box until the user enters the expected information.

NOTE. *Code that repeats is called a loop.*

VBA uses the following statements to repeat sections of a program:

For-Next: Executes VBA instructions a certain number of times depending on a beginning, increment, and ending value that you supply.

Do: The Do looping statement actually occurs in four forms: Do-While condition, Do While-condition, Do-Until condition, and Do Until-condition. The differences lie in where VBA checks for the conditional comparison and whether VBA loops while the comparison is True or until the comparison is

True. Although so many forms of the Do statement can be confusing, you can write any loop needed using any form of the Do statement. The choice of which Do loop that programmers use is a matter of personal preferences most of the time.

For-Each: Lets you perform various calculations and processes on a collection of objects. VBA lets you group two or more objects into a single collection. Once you define the collection, you can write one set of statements and apply them to each object in the collection instead of having to apply the statements to each object individually.

■ Appendix

■ What's on the CD

Sometimes there's just no substitute for watching someone walk through a procedure to show you how it's done. That's why the *Windows Sources Microsoft Word 97 for Windows SuperGuide* contains more than 40 movies demonstrating many of Word's most interesting features. With this exclusive CD-ROM, you can watch—*and listen*—as the book's author walks you through Word features like:

- Connecting to the Web

- Mail merge

- Inserting a table of contents

- Compiling an index

- Inserting cross-references

- Recording a macro

- And much more

The movies on this CD-ROM are all *executable files:* that means that all you need to do is double-click on them, and they'll run. Some were recorded with Lotus ScreenCam; others with Microsoft Camcorder, the screen recording utility that's bundled with Microsoft Office. (In general, movies were recorded with Lotus ScreenCam unless we found system conflicts between ScreenCam and the late beta version of Microsoft Word 97 we were running.)

Whether the movies were recorded in ScreenCam or Camcorder, we utilized the programs' respective features for building files that can play by themselves, so you do not need to own ScreenCam or Camcorder to run these movies. However, you should be aware that Microsoft Camcorder files may require 16MB of RAM to run properly, while Lotus ScreenCam movies generally have lower memory requirements. (Of course, you'll also need a sound card and speakers or headphones to hear the narration on any of these movies.)

Lotus ScreenCam and Microsoft Camcorder are similar in many ways; in this Appendix, we'll tell you what you need to know about working with each one. You'll find the movies stored within a Movies folder on the CD-ROM in folders that correspond with the chapters where similar topics are covered in the book. The following Table shows you *what's* on the CD-ROM, and *where* it's located.

Table 1.A

Movies on the
*Windows Sources
Word 97 for Windows
SuperGuide* CD-ROM

FOLDER	FILENAME	TOPIC	HOW RECORDED?
Chap03	alphatiz.exe	Alphabetizing a List of Names	Lotus ScreenCam
Chap03	autfortb.exe	Automatically Formatting a Table	Lotus ScreenCam
Chap03	calculat.exe	Doing Calculations in Word	Microsoft Camcorder
Chap03	drawtabl.exe	Drawing a Table	Lotus ScreenCam
Chap05	autocorr.exe	Creating a New AutoCorrect Entry	Microsoft Camcorder
Chap06	browsobj.exe	Using Word's New Select Browse Object Feature	Lotus ScreenCam
Chap06	documap.exe	Using Word's New Document Map Feature	Lotus ScreenCam
Chap06	replfrmt.exe	Searching For and Replacing Formatting	Microsoft Camcorder
Chap06	replpara.exe	Searching For and Replacing Extra Paragraph Marks	Microsoft Camcorder
Chap06	view2doc.exe	Viewing Two Parts of a Document at Once	Lotus ScreenCam
Chap07	autfordc.exe	Automatically Formatting Your Document	Lotus ScreenCam
Chap07	prevstyl.exe	Previewing How Your Document Would Look With Different Styles	Microsoft Camcorder
Chap08	letwizrd.exe	Using Word's New Letter Wizard	Microsoft Camcorder
Chap08	newtempl.exe	Attaching a New Template to Your Document	Lotus ScreenCam
Chap09	autosumm.exe	Automatically Summarizing Your Document	Lotus ScreenCam
Chap10	outlnumb.exe	Automatically Adding Outline Numbers To Your Document	Lotus ScreenCam
Chap11	index1.exe	Creating an Index (Part 1: Inserting an Index Entry)	Microsoft Camcorder
Chap11	index2.exe	Creating an Index (Part 2: Compiling the Index)	Microsoft Camcorder

Table 1.A (Continued)

Movies on the
*Windows Sources
Word 97 for Windows
SuperGuide* CD-ROM

FOLDER	FILENAME	TOPIC	HOW RECORDED?
Chap11	tablcont.exe	Creating Tables of Contents	Lotus ScreenCam
Chap12	crossref.exe	Inserting a Cross-Reference	Microsoft Camcorder
Chap13	hyplnk1.exe	Using Hyperlinks (Part 1: Inserting and Following a Hyperlink)	Microsoft Camcorder
Chap13	hyplnk2.exe	Using Hyperlinks (Part 2: Creating Automatic Hyperlinks)	Microsoft Camcorder
Chap13	mastdoc1.exe	Using Master Documents (Part 1: Creating and Inserting Subdocuments)	Microsoft Camcorder
Chap13	mastdoc2.exe	Using Master Documents (Part 2: Working With a Master Document)	Microsoft Camcorder
Chap14	webconnc.exe	Connecting to the Web from Word	Microsoft Camcorder
Chap15	comment.exe	Making Comments on a Document	Lotus ScreenCam
Chap15	comp2ver.exe	Comparing Two Versions of a Document	Microsoft Camcorder
Chap15	trackchg.exe	Tracking Changes in Your Document	Microsoft Camcorder
Chap16	mmerge1.exe	Using Mail Merge (Part 1: Creating a Main Document)	Microsoft Camcorder
Chap16	mmerge2.exe	Using Mail Merge (Part 2: Creating a Data Document)	Microsoft Camcorder
Chap16	mmerge3.exe	Using Mail Merge (Part 3: Inserting Merge Fields)	Microsoft Camcorder
Chap16	mmerge4.exe	Using Mail Merge (Part 4: Running the Mail Merge)	Microsoft Camcorder
Chap17	autocapt.exe	Creating Captions Automatically	Lotus ScreenCam
Chap17	columns.exe	Creating a Document With Two Columns	Lotus ScreenCam
Chap17	textbox1.exe	Using Text Boxes (Part 1: Inserting a Text Box)	Lotus ScreenCam

Table 1.A (Continued)

Movies on the
*Windows Sources
Word 97 for Windows
SuperGuide* CD-ROM

FOLDER	FILENAME	TOPIC	HOW RECORDED?
Chap17	textbox2.exe	Using Text Boxes (Part 2: Inserting an Autoshape)	Lotus ScreenCam
Chap17	textbox3.exe	Using Text Boxes (Part 3: Linking Text Boxes)	Microsoft Camcorder
Chap17	wordart.exe	Using WordArt	Microsoft Camcorder
Chap20	forms.exe	Creating Forms	Microsoft Camcorder
Chap22	newmenu.exe	Adding a New Menu to Word	Lotus ScreenCam
Chap22	newtool.exe	Adding a New Toolbar to Word	Lotus ScreenCam
Chap25	macrorec.exe	Recording a Macro	Microsoft Camcorder

■ Running the Movies from the CD-ROM

As we've mentioned, you can run a movie from the CD-ROM by double-clicking on its icon. However, since the movie files are large, you may get better performance if you first copy them to your hard drive—assuming you have the space. The movie files total approximately 45 megabytes.

When you run a Lotus ScreenCam movie, a control panel appears in front of the movie, which you can use to pause, rewind, fast forward, play, or control the volume of your movie (see Figure A.1). When you run the standalone Camcorder movies provided on this disk, you can press Esc to stop a movie in progress.

We hope you'll find these movies valuable—and many thanks for purchasing the *Windows Sources Microsoft Word 97 for Windows SuperGuide*!

Figure A.1

Lotus ScreenCam
player controls

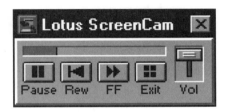

■ Index

■ **END-USER LICENSE AGREEMENT**

READ THIS AGREEMENT CAREFULLY BEFORE BUYING THIS BOOK. BY BUYING THE BOOK AND USING THE PROGRAM LISTINGS, CD-ROM, AND PROGRAMS REFERRED TO BELOW, YOU ACCEPT THE TERMS OF THIS AGREEMENT.

The program listings included in this book and the programs included on the CD-ROM contained in the package on the opposite page ("CD-ROM") are proprietary products of Macmillan Computer Publishing USA and/or third party suppliers ("Suppliers"). The program listings and programs are hereinafter collectively referred to as the "Programs." Macmillan Computer Publishing USA and the Suppliers retain ownership of the CD-ROM and copyright to the Programs, as their respective interests may appear. The Programs and the copy of the CD-ROM provided are licensed (not sold) to you under the conditions set forth herein.

License. You may use the CD-ROM on any compatible computer, provided that the CD-ROM is used on only one computer and by one user at a time.

Restrictions. You may not commercially distribute the CD-ROM or the Programs or otherwise reproduce, publish, or distribute or otherwise use the CD-ROM or the Programs in any manner that may infringe any copyright or other proprietary right of Macmillan Computer Publishing USA, the Suppliers, or any other party or assign, sublicense, or otherwise transfer the CD-ROM or this agreement to any other party unless such party agrees to accept the terms and conditions of this agreement. This license and your right to use the CD-ROM and the Programs automatically terminates if you fail to comply with any provision of this agreement.

U.S. GOVERNMENT RESTRICTED RIGHTS. The CD-ROM and the programs are provided with **RESTRICTED RIGHTS**. Use, duplication, or disclosure by the Government is subject to restrictions as set forth in subparagraph (c)(1)(ii) of the Rights in Technical Data and Computer Software Clause at DFARS (48 CFR 252.277-7013). The Proprietor of the compilation of the Programs and the CD-ROM is Macmillan Computer Publishing USA, 5903 Christie Avenue, Emeryville, CA 94608.

Limited Warranty. Macmillan Computer Publishing USA warrants the physical CD-ROM to be free of defects in materials and workmanship under normal use for a period of 30 days from the purchase date. If Macmillan Computer Publishing USA receives written notification within the warranty period of defects in materials or workmanship in the physical CD-ROM, and such notification is determined by Macmillan Computer Publishing USA to be correct, Macmillan Computer Publishing USA will, at its option, replace the defective CD-ROM or refund a prorata portion of the purchase price of the book. **THESE ARE YOUR SOLE REMEDIES FOR ANY BREACH OF WARRANTY.**

EXCEPT AS SPECIFICALLY PROVIDED ABOVE, THE CD-ROM AND THE PROGRAMS ARE PROVIDED "AS IS" WITHOUT ANY WARRANTY OF ANY KIND. NEITHER MACMILLAN COMPUTER PUBLISHING USA NOR THE SUPPLIERS MAKE ANY WARRANTY OF ANY KIND AS TO THE ACCURACY OR COMPLETENESS OF THE CD-ROM OR THE PROGRAMS OR THE RESULTS TO BE OBTAINED FROM USING THE CD-ROM OR THE PROGRAMS AND NEITHER MACMILLAN COMPUTER PUBLISHING USA NOR THE SUPPLIERS SHALL BE RESPONSIBLE FOR ANY CLAIMS ATTRIBUTABLE TO ERRORS, OMISSIONS, OR OTHER INACCURACIES IN THE CD-ROM OR THE PROGRAMS. THE ENTIRE RISK AS TO THE RESULTS AND PERFORMANCE OF THE CD-ROM AND THE PROGRAMS IS ASSUMED BY THE USER. FURTHER, NEITHER MACMILLAN COMPUTER PUBLISHING USA NOR THE SUPPLIERS MAKE ANY REPRESENTATIONS OR WARRANTIES, EITHER EXPRESS OR IMPLIED, WITH RESPECT TO THE CD-ROM OR THE PROGRAMS, INCLUDING BUT NOT LIMITED TO, THE QUALITY, PERFORMANCE, MERCHANTABILITY, OR FITNESS FOR A PARTICULAR PURPOSE OF THE CD-ROM OR THE PROGRAMS. IN NO EVENT SHALL MACMILLAN COMPUTER PUBLISHING USA OR THE SUPPLIERS BE LIABLE FOR DIRECT, INDIRECT, SPECIAL, INCIDENTAL, OR CONSEQUENTIAL DAMAGES ARISING OUT THE USE OF OR INABILITY TO USE THE CD-ROM OR THE PROGRAMS OR FOR ANY LOSS OR DAMAGE OF ANY NATURE CAUSED TO ANY PERSON OR PROPERTY AS A RESULT OF THE USE OF THE CD-ROM OR THE PROGRAMS, EVEN IF MACMILLAN COMPUTER PUBLISHING USA OR THE SUPPLIERS HAVE BEEN SPECIFICALLY ADVISED OF THE POSSIBILITY OF SUCH DAMAGES. NEITHER MACMILLAN COMPUTER PUBLISHING USA NOR THE SUPPLIERS ARE RESPONSIBLE FOR ANY COSTS INCLUDING, BUT NOT LIMITED TO, THOSE INCURRED AS A RESULT OF LOST PROFITS OR REVENUE, LOSS OF USE OF THE CD-ROM OR THE PROGRAMS, LOSS OF DATA, THE COSTS OF RECOVERING SOFTWARE OR DATA, OR THIRD-PARTY CLAIMS. IN NO EVENT WILL MACMILLAN COMPUTER PUBLISHING USA'S OR THE SUPPLIERS' LIABILITY FOR ANY DAMAGES TO YOU OR ANY OTHER PARTY EVER EXCEED THE PRICE OF THIS BOOK. NO SALES PERSON OR OTHER REPRESENTATIVE OF ANY PARTY INVOLVED IN THE DISTRIBUTION OF THE CD-ROM IS AUTHORIZED TO MAKE ANY MODIFICATIONS OR ADDITIONS TO THIS LIMITED WARRANTY.

MACMILLAN COMPUTER PUBLISHING USA'S LICENSOR(S) MAKES NO WARRANTIES, EXPRESS OR IMPLIED, INCLUDING WITHOUT LIMITATION THE IMPLIED WARRANTIES OF MERCHANTABILITY AND FITNESS FOR A PARTICULAR PURPOSE, REGARDING THE SOFTWARE. MACMILLAN COMPUTER PUBLISHING USA'S LICENSOR(S) DOES NOT WARRANT, GUARANTEE OR MAKE ANY REPRESENTATIONS REGARDING THE USE OR THE RESULTS OF THE USE OF THE SOFTWARE IN TERMS OF ITS CORRECTNESS, ACCURACY, RELIABILITY, CURRENTNESS OR OTHERWISE. THE ENTIRE RISK AS TO THE RESULTS AND PERFORMANCE OF THE SOFTWARE IS ASSUMED BY YOU. THE EXCLUSION OF IMPLIED WARRANTIES IS NOT PERMITTED BY SOME JURISDICTIONS. THE ABOVE EXCLUSION MAY NOT APPLY TO YOU.

IN NO EVENT WILL MACMILLAN COMPUTER PUBLISHING USA'S LICENSOR(S), AND THEIR DIRECTORS, OFFICERS, EMPLOYEES OR AGENTS (COLLECTIVELY MACMILLAN COMPUTER PUBLISHING USA'S LICENSOR) BE LIABLE TO YOU FOR ANY CONSEQUENTIAL, INCIDENTAL OR INDIRECT DAMAGES (INCLUDING DAMAGES FOR LOSS OF BUSINESS PROFITS, BUSINESS INTERRUPTION, LOSS OF BUSINESS INFORMATION, AND THE LIKE) ARISING OUT OF THE USE OR INABILITY TO USE THE SOFTWARE EVEN IF MACMILLAN COMPUTER PUBLISHING USA'S LICENSOR HAS BEEN ADVISED OF THE POSSIBILITY OF SUCH DAMAGES. BECAUSE SOME JURISDICTIONS DO NOT ALLOW THE EXCLUSION OR LIMITATION OF LIABILITY FOR CONSEQUENTIAL OR INCIDENTAL DAMAGES, THE ABOVE LIMITATIONS MAY NOT APPLY TO YOU.

Some states do not allow the exclusion or limitation of implied warranties or limitation of liability for incidental or consequential damages, so the above limitation or exclusion may not apply to you.

General. Macmillan Computer Publishing USA and the Suppliers retain all rights not expressly granted. Nothing in this license constitutes a waiver of the rights of Macmillan Computer Publishing USA or the Suppliers under the U.S. Copyright Act or any other Federal or State Law, international treaty, or foreign law.